Strategic Management

A METHODOLOGICAL APPROACH

FOURTH EDITION

Alan J. Rowe
School of Business Administration
University of Southern California

Richard 0. Mason
Edwin L. Cox School of Business
Southern Methodist University

Karl E. Dickel
The Boston Consulting Group
Stockholm, Sweden

Richard B. Mann
University of Pittsburgh
Johnstown, Pennsylvania

Robert J. Mockler
Saint John's University
New York, New York

STRATEGIC MANAGEMENT

A METHODOLOGICAL APPROACH

FORTH EDITION

This book previously published by:
Addison-Wesley Publishing Company

We want to express our utmost appreciation to our families, friends, and colleagues, for their patience, support, and understanding of the many hours spent on completing this book.

Library of **Congress Cataloging-in-Publication Data**
Strategic management: a methodological approach / Alan J. Rowe...
[et al.].-4th ed.
p. cm.
Includes bibliographical references and index. ISBN 0-20158638-X
1. Strategic planning-United States.
2. Management-United States   I. Rowe, Alan J.
HD30.28.R677 1993
658.4'012dc2O

93-6599
CIP

12345678910-D0-959493

PREFACE

A new standard of performance is being applied to strategic managers, who must cope with an increasingly turbulent environment. No longer is strategy simply the analysis of alternatives, or determining what marketing approaches will beat out competitors. Rather, strategic management needs to parallel the approach that has been taken when applying total quality management (TQM). Our emphasis in this revision extends the TQM approach to considering total "value" management. Performance measures such as return on investment, earnings growth, and market share must be augmented to include such other measures as flexibility, responsiveness, adaptability, and social responsibility. To achieve these objectives, organizations need to utilize shorter development cycles, prepare designs that take manufacturing considerations into account, ensure zero defects, introduce concurrent design and manufacturing, develop shorter delivery cycles, and become more customer-oriented. Thus "managing value" casts what corporate strategy must achieve in a new light.

Today's organizations will need to have leaner staffs, to empower their employees by sharing decisions, to obtain commitment and innovation from employees, and to evolve a culture that promotes the ability to be adaptive and responsive. They also need leaders who have the vision required to shape meaningful strategies and deploy them throughout the organization. Is this asking too much of management? Perhaps, but what is the alternative? A faltering, ineffective management that will not survive the onslaught of competition and of ever-present corporate raiders. Accordingly, we dedicate the fourth edition of *Strategic Management* to helping managers and aspiring managers succeed in the 1990s. The tools provided here will help them understand all aspects of the environment and the organization so that they can formulate achievable and effective strategic plans.

Because organizations are dynamic—they have different cultures and values, are in different phases of their life cycles, employ multiple management styles, and have changing portfolios of products—there are few pat answers to the questions that arise. Herein lies the crux of strategic thinking. Managers must think beyond current conditions and arrive at courses of action that respond effectively to problems. A sound strategic analysis provides the factual basis on which to formulate strategic alternatives and helps managers evaluate the consequences of a given strategy.

The perspective we have taken is that in a capstone course in business such as this, the material covered should stand on its own. Although considerable reference is made to material addressed in courses leading up to the strategic management course, the body of knowledge that has evolved over the past 10 to 15 years provides a solid foundation for strategic management. Many of the methods used at this level are distinct from those applied in other courses. For example, early courses in strategy relied primarily on the integration of prior knowledge. In our approach to the field of strategy, however, we have also included research findings and specific methods applied by major consulting organizations such as the Boston Consulting Group.

CHANGES IN THE CURRENT EDITION

In preparing the fourth edition of this book, we have paid special attention to the helpful suggestions made by the reviewers and by the many users of the previous three editions. We have also updated material in every chapter and have added new material and new chapters.

The changes include expanded material on topics such as organizational restructuring, competitor analysis, cost de-averaging, and the use of information technology to gain a competitive advantage. There is more emphasis on the management aspects of strategy, on industry analysis as part of environmental analysis, on leadership, and on the change process. We have expanded the material on global strategy, strategic alliances, and the impact of Europe ECC. New topics include time-based competition versus cost-based competition, total quality management, value-based strategies, concurrent design and manufacture, and the application of expert systems as a strategic support tool. In addition, we have expanded coverage of generic competitive strategies, sustainable competitive advantage, and strategic computer applications. Our new thrust retains the unique attributes that distinguish this text from the others in the field. But we have streamlined the text material by emphasizing critical methodologies and have placed supporting methodologies in appendices at the end of several chapters.

We have restructured the sequence of the chapters in the book to focus more clearly on the *process* of formulating strategy. Each chapter focuses on a step in the process of determining which strategy leads to the desired goals specified by the organization. Thus each chapter starts with an indication of where in the process the material fits and how it contributes to formulating an effective strategy. Each of these chapters helps meet the overall objective of formulating a strategy that contributes to a sustainable market penetration and profitability. The methods employed are used to help analyze the requirements that ultimately lead to "total value management."

In addition to the strategic process model that can be associated with each chapter, at the beginning of each chapter we show the four dominant factors that impinge on the organization and create the need for change. Strategic techniques help managers determine what changes are needed and how to evaluate possible alternatives. The four-force model looks at the problem from a systems perspective and makes it easier to get a complete picture of a given situation. The forces that managers should consider when formulating strategy are

1. The *external environment*, including competitor analysis, stakeholder analysis, global and government considerations, and industry studies.
2. *Allocation of resources*, including financial planning, analysis of investment capital expenditures, and R&D.
3. *Organizational culture and leadership*, organization life cycle, organizational change, and the acceptance of change.
4. The *internal environment*, including performance evaluation, implementation, technology, and competitive advantage.

CASES IN THIS EDITION

The choice of the cases we have included for analysis in this book was based on the following criteria:

1. Students often need information from other sources to prepare their case analyses. We chose cases for which this supplemental information is readily available.
2. All cases either have been updated or are no more than 1 or 2 years old.
3. Cases cover the broad spectrum of businesses and include service as well as manufacturing companies.
4. Where appropriate, we chose well-known companies.

We have continued to emphasize the executive memo as a means of summarizing a case analysis. We feel preparing such a memo sharpens understanding by forcing the analyst to be concise and to emphasize critical issues. Furthermore, many executives insist on summaries of studies that are done, so skill and practice in preparing the executive memo are valuable in their own right.

The methods discussed in the book can be viewed as a means of imposing order on a complex set of relationships. These methods and approaches, however, do not provide final answers; they offer guidelines and enhance understanding. Without analysis, managers would be forced to rely on intuition and experience alone as the basis for making strategic decisions.

PRIMARY OBJECTIVES OF THE BOOK

Our goal in preparing this text has been to provide a sound foundation to formulating strategy, analyzing cases, and implementing strategy. By applying one's understanding of future trends, one can see how to sustain a competitive advantage. To this end, we have sought to

1. Offer students an opportunity to exercise the analytical and conceptual skills that case analysis requires.

2. Give them experience in using methods that are currently applied by major organizations and consulting groups.
3. Provide conceptual frameworks (such as strategic thinking and total value management) that act as overall guides in strategy formulation.
4. Introduce new concepts (such as leadership style and expert systems) that help stretch the individual's imagination and broaden his or her perspective on strategic issues.
5. Facilitate more effective decision making by developing strategies based on sound analysis rather than guesswork.
6. Provide a basis for understanding both the economic and the organizational implications of strategic decision making.
7. Provide a basis for integrating prior business knowledge into a systematic and methodological approach to strategy formulation.

With these objectives in mind, we feel confident that those who use this text will find that they not only have developed useful skills but also have achieved a better understanding of business functioning and the role of strategy in sustaining a competitive advantage.

STRATEGY SUPPORT TOOLS

To facilitate the application of the various strategic methods covered in this book, we have shown worksheets for the methods used in the book. In addition, there is available from Addison-Wesley a supplemental text on strategic models that provides computer support for a number of methods covered in the book. A special student edition of fisCAL, a computer program that covers the various financial analyses employed in strategy formulation, is also available. We have made no attempt to include spreadsheets such as Lotus, Quattro-Pro, or Excel because of the wide availability of such programs. In many cases, however, instructors may want to use a computer simulation as part of their teaching approach.

ACKNOWLEDGMENTS

First and foremost, we want to thank the many teachers, students, and business managers whose ideas and suggestions we have incorporated in this text. The dedication, patience, and understanding of our families and colleagues are what makes such work a meaningful endeavor. Equally vital have been our secretaries, whose conscientiousness and skill made this book possible.

The colleagues who were generous in providing comments, reviews, support, direction, and much-needed encouragement, but who are in no way responsible for the results, include Jack Alcalay, John Basch, Arvind Bhambri, Doug Basil, Warren Bennis, Phil Birnbaum, Israel Borovits, James Boulgarides, John Carlson, John Clarkeson, Pat Connor, Dorothy Dologite, John Fleming, Gary Fisher, Alan Goodman, Larry Greene, Larry Greiner, Carl Hamilton, Tom Hout, Rudyard

Istuan, William Kelly, Matt Klempa, Thomas Lewis, John Jaeger, Dewey Johnson, Peter Lorange, Craig Lundberg, Mike McGrath, Ian Mitroff, Bill Paisley, Alan Patz, Bill Paulin, Ray Price, Heinrich Rutt, Marcus Schwaninger, Hans Seifert, V. J. Seshan, Mel Shader, Arthur Sharplin, Herold Sherman, Richard Snyder, Ivan Somers, George Stalk, Jr., George Steiner, Bill Strassen, and George Walker. We are especially grateful to the following reviewers whose insights have helped to make *Strategic Management* an even stronger instructional tool: Kim B. Boal, Texas Tech University; Gary Dessler, Florida International University; Roy H. Gordan, Hofstra University; Charles Gowen, University of Northern Illinois; Dewey Johnson, California State University, Fresno; Richard Kolasheski, University of Maryland; Leland Lahr, Lawrence Tech University; Eugene H. Melan, Marist College; Michael Merenda, University of New Hampshire; Rebecca Morris, University of Nebraska, Omaha; Daniel Slate, University of New Mexico; Wayne Smeltz, Rider College; James Thurman, George Washington University; and Arieh Ullman, State University of New York, Binghamton. The authors of the cases deserve special thanks for their contribution to making the book a valuable educational vehicle. We also wish to thank our students, who diligently studied the material and provided invaluable feedback, and our secretarial staff, Johna Miller and Janet Andrews, for their steadfast help.

Thanks, too, to the Addison-Wesley staff and freelancers, who have helped this book come to fruition: Mac Mendelsohn, Beth Toland, Kim Kramer, Kathy Diamond, Connie Day, and Nancy Benjamin.

Los Angeles, California	A. J. R.
Dallas, Texas	R. O. M.
Stockholm, Sweden	K. E. D.
Johnstown, Pennsylvania	R. B. M.
New York, New York	R. J. M.

CONTENTS

CHAPTER EIGHT

Financial Planning and Competitive-Cost Analysis 340

CHAPTER NINE

Entrepreneurship, Mergers and Acquisitions, Restructuring, and the Service Sector 416

CHAPTER TEN

The Leadership Factor in Strategy and Implementing Strategic Change 458

CHAPTER ELEVEN

Information Technology and Future Directions in Strategy 529

CASES

LIST OF WORKSHEETS

CHAPTER ONE

A Framework for Strategic Management

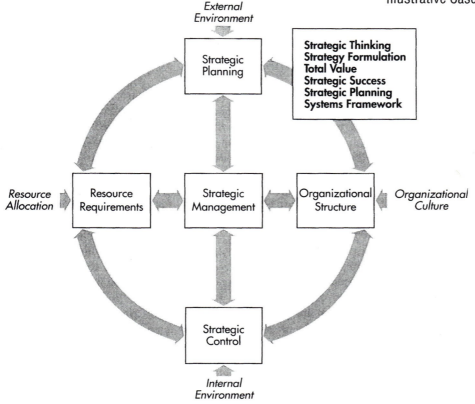

Chapter 1 A Framework for Strategic Management	**Chapter 2** Strategic Analysis	**Chapter 3** Strategic Visioning, Goals, Ethics, and Social Responsibility	**Chapter 4** The Competitive Environment	**Chapter 5** Capability-based Strategy	**Chapter 6** Market Dynamics and Sustainable Competitive Advantage
How to approach strategic management	*Application of strategic analysis*	*Understanding vision, values, ethics*	*Coping with competitive forces, stakeholders*	*Assessing company capability, timeliness, quality*	*Determining trends, gap analysis, and market dynamics*

Chapter 7 Strategy in a Global Environment	**Chapter 8** Financial Planning and Competitive- Cost Analysis	**Chapter 9** Entrepreneurship, Mergers and Acquisitions, Restructuring, and the Service Sector	**Chapter 10** Leadership Factor in Strategy and Implementing Strategic Change	**Chapter 11** Information Technology and Future Directions in Strategy
Assessing global trade, foreign markets, monetary exchange	*Preparing a financial plan and competitive-cost analysis*	*Importance of small business, entrepreneurs, restructuring*	*Strategy implementation, leadership, culture*	*Information technology, trends, new management*

INTRODUCTION

Why are some companies successful while others struggle just to stay afloat? Is the answer better products, better marketing, more efficient production, better quality, timely delivery? Is it a productive organization with a supportive culture and effective leadership? Or is it some combination of the way the organization operates and the quality of its management? Questions such as these demand answers if a company is to be successful in today's increasingly competitive and turbulent environment. The answers are many, but they all focus on one basic requirement. *In order to succeed, a company must offer value to its customers.* That is, it must provide *total value.* Value represents the customer's perception of what is delivered, at what price, and with what features that serve their real needs. Pages 7 and 8 describe value and total value in greater detail. *Strategic management* is the process by which organizations determine what value is needed and how to add that value. It is a means for ensuring that organizations can cope effectively with the myriad of demands placed on them from within and without. This book aims to provide an understanding of the strategic management process and of methods that can be used to formulate appropriate strategies. These tools can help companies achieve and sustain a competitive advantage.

As an illustration of why companies require effective strategic management, consider the issue of *Business Week* dated June 24, 1991. In it, the following stories appeared.

1. Clorox, which was once part of Procter & Gamble, is now battling P&G over a detergent–bleach combination product. The result is that Clorox has taken the new detergent–bleach combination off the market. But in the process, P&G has lost some of *its* market share for core bleach products.
2. Motorola, the company known for cracking the Japanese market, had a difficult time selling chips to IBM. After many years, Motorola decided to allow other companies to produce its high-performance microprocessors while it concentrated on producing the reduced-instruction-set-chip (RISC). Motorola is working with IBM to design a low-cost version of the chip to power both IBM and Apple work stations.
3. On the other side of the Pacific, Nippon Electric in Japan is working with American Telephone and Telegraph, along with Sun Microsystems Inc. and MIPS Computer Systems Inc., to produce the RISC chips that will be the heart of future work stations and advanced personal computers.
4. Across the Atlantic, Ford of Europe is working at breakneck speed to be ready for the opening of borders in 1992. Ford will launch an image-building "blitz" across Europe and will speed up the introduction of new models. It will cost Ford $11 billion to improve its technology, introduce new models, and upgrade dealers.
5. Goodyear's miracle man Stanley Gault will attempt to pull Goodyear out of its slump. It is estimated that it will cost $11 billion to remake the ailing tire-maker—and this during a devastating slump in auto sales.
6. Faced with a $400 million loss, USAir has had to close many of its facilities, ground aircraft, and furlough 7,000 employees. It has also had to defer orders for 28 Boeing jets and cut back on its expansion plans for Cleveland and Baltimore. CEO Seth Schofield faces the challenge of discovering exactly where USAir fits.
7. The recent plunge in real estate values has propelled the banking industry toward disaster. Office vacancies are the highest they have been in years, property values have fallen, and bad loans have been increasing at an alarming rate. By taking an aggressive approach to identifying bad real estate loans and building adequate reserves, banks now appear to be on the mend and expect their loan portfolios to stabilize by the end of the year.
8. In an attempt to introduce more pro-family policies, du Pont has appointed Faith Wohl as "in house conscience." Her job is to help employees balance family concerns with their careers. She has done this by setting up day care centers and promoting generous leaves on the occasion of the birth or adoption of a child or the sickness of a relative.

STRATEGIC THINKING

Strategic management is essential for dealing with the continuous stream of changes that flood all organizations. Managers need to cope with pressures of rapid change in order to achieve organizational goals effectively. Thus "strategic thinking" is an on-going process in which significant events are dealt with in a comprehensive manner. For example, Michael Porter (1987) describes strategic thinking as being intimately linked with implementation. He states, "There are no substitutes for strategic thinking. Improving quality is meaningless without knowing what kind of quality is relevant in competitive terms. Nurturing corporate culture is useless unless the culture is aligned with the company's approach to competing. Entrepreneurship, unguided by a strategic perspective, is much more likely to fail than succeed. And, contrary to popular opinion, even Japanese companies use strategic thinking. The successful ones are strong believers in planning and avid students of their industries and competitors."

In their article "The Anatomy of Strategic Thinking," J. Roger Morrison and James G. Lee (1989) describe strategic thinking in the following cogent terms: "The successful strategic thinker is guided by a clear business concept based on a thorough understanding of the economics of [the] business and of the success factors in [the] industry."

It is superior strategic thinking, not sophisticated planning systems, that underlies most successful competitive strategies. Effective strategic thinking focuses on achieving competitive advantage by gaining and holding the initiative. Good strategic thinking also implies an understanding of how situations will change over time. Business strategy, like military strategy, is a matter of maneuvering for superior position and anticipating how competitors will respond and with what degree of success. Successful strategists aim always to keep one step ahead of the competition. They plan their moves well in advance and have contingency plans for the most likely outcomes.

The research of James Brian Quinn (1980) indicates that strategic decisions often are made without the benefit of formal strategic planning, even where there is wide acceptance of planning in the organization. This implies a reliance on strategic thinking as a substitute for formal planning. Larry Greiner (1987) also found little evidence to support the contention that major changes in the direction of an organization are based on normative assumptions that result from the strategic planning process. Greiner found that successful strategic change relies on the core values of an organization rather than acceptance based on formal planning.

No matter how they are arrived at, strategic decisions affect the very survival of an organization, and consequently, they require some form of strategic thinking. The president of A&E Plastipak, Bernard Denburg, stressed this when he said, "Strategic thinking is the continuous process of managing strategy consistent with strategic goals and cultural values of the organization." Strategic thinking, then, starts with the strategy formulation process and moves beyond merely doing an analysis of data. As Porter, Greiner, and others have pointed out, a strategy must also be managed. Strategy formulation involves knowing the competitive environment and knowing how to allocate resources, how to restructure organizations, and how to implement plans. It also involves managing the strategy formulation process. To do this, executives must be leaders with vision who are also aware of the behavioral factors that influence performance and the cultures that support the core values and mission of the organization.

Examples of environmental forces with which managers have had to cope include

- The stock crisis of 1987 and its impact on raising equity capital
- The recession of the early 1990s and its effect on consumer spending
- Continued Japanese dominance of traditional U.S. markets
- The rapid increase in breakthroughs in technology, especially in electronics and biogenetics
- The establishment of whole new industries in telemarketing and biotechnology
- Intensified global competition and changes resulting from the European Economic Community
- Changing values of employees, customers, and other stakeholders
- Iraq's invasion of Kuwait in 1991 and its potential effect on oil prices
- Formation of a commonwealth in what was formerly the Soviet Union and the resulting trade considerations
- Reunification of East and West Germany, leading to changes in the unified Germany's competitive position
- The projected return of Hong Kong to China in 1997 and the potential for changes in trade restrictions

All these events have affected how well various organizations can compete. Such volatility in the external environment makes strategic management and strategic thinking a necessity.

STRATEGY FORMULATION

This book presents a number of methods that can help managers analyze requirements and formulate a strategy that will achieve a competitive advantage. For example, many organizations have found that to be competitive, they must provide customers with QVST: quality, value, service, and timeliness. Obviously, there are variations on the theme. McDonald's, for example, uses QVSC—quality, value, service, and cleanliness—as its guiding principles. Nonetheless, the basic approach still applies. Customers increasingly expect products or service that perform as specified; they expect the best possible value at a reasonable cost; they demand the service needed to maintain products and assurance that the products will perform as specified. In our frenetic, competitive world, an appreciation of the importance of time often spells the difference between winning competitors and companies who "also ran." For example, Ford is planning to spend billions to upgrade its ability to introduce new models more quickly. In the service industry, timeliness is often the difference between getting a client or an order and losing out.

Strategic managers faced with many complex factors must utilize strategic thinking. In today's rapidly changing environment, it is no longer sufficient to prepare a strategic plan once a year or even once a quarter. Strategic managers need to monitor conditions continuously and must be willing to modify strategic decisions whenever the need arises. They have to understand the consequences of actions that are proposed and to weigh the merits of a new strategic thrust. Given the complexity of coping with many problems, managers need to use aids to decision making that can ensure that they have taken all the relevant facts into and dealt with them appropriately. The methods presented in this book can assist managers in their quest to be adequately prepared and can ensure that they will not make a decision that is obviously wrong. Such tools help strategic managers use all the relevant intelligence available when making strategic decisions.

A number of cases are used throughout this text to show how to formulate strategies and how to define the requirements of carrying out a strategy. The first illustrative case describes how American Hospital Supply Corporation succeeded in becoming one of the largest distributors of medical supplies. But, because they did not focus on maintaining a "sustainable competitive advantage," they were acquired by Baxter Tavenol. Nonetheless, the steps AHSC took to achieve its initial competitive position illustrate how a focus on "total value" can contribute to achieving a competitive advantage.

The second illustrative case examines the problems that Polaroid had when the company introduced "Polavision" without doing an appropriate strategic analysis. Juxtaposing these two cases shows how taking the right strategic actions led to a strong competitive position for one company and how lacking a formal strategy and adopting a take-it-or-leave-it attitude with customers led to dismal performance in the other.

Using the concept of total value management, we will examine how organizations develop and utilize their value concepts to meet changing customer demands. Peters and Waterman (1982), in their monumental book *In Search of Excellence,* provided a useful framework for examining how the basic values and beliefs of an organization affect strategic performance. We will look at some of their findings later in this chapter.

A basic premise of business is the need to create value for all stakeholders—but especially for customers. With this in mind, we attempt in this book to show how strategy contributes to the success of a business and point out where and how value needs to be added during the strategic planning process. Figure 1.1 offers a succinct roadmap that covers the major topics and tools used in the text.

STRATEGIC ANALYSIS

Decision-making tools are primarily used to help managers formulate strategic alternatives and to reduce uncertainty. However, such methods are only part of what is needed. To adequately formulate strategy, decision makers need to consider links among the key elements of strategy. Figure 1.1 shows some of the important topics that are covered in each chapter of this book and relates these topics to the chapter sequence. There is no convenient way to cover the linkage between key elements and chapter sequence; therefore, material will be used wherever appropriate, whether its appearance is shown in the chapter title or not.

WHAT IS VALUE?

The term *value* as used here refers to the contribution that management can make to the organization, the products, and the stakeholders, including the customers. A busi-

FIGURE 1.1 | **Strategy Process Model**

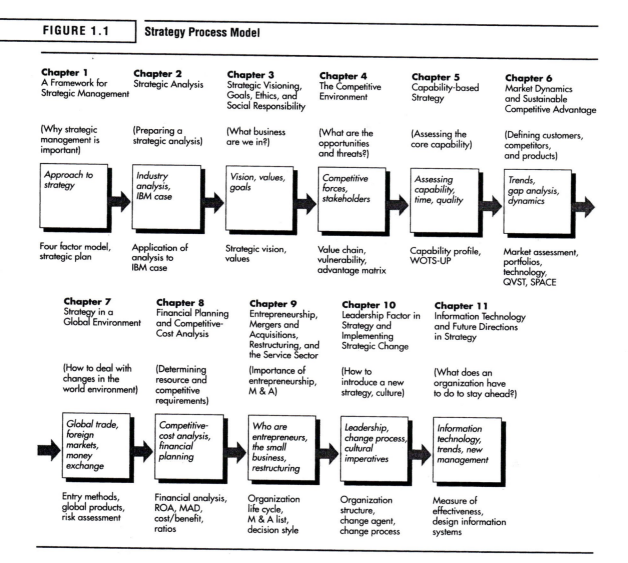

ness can succeed only when its products or services are perceived as having value. Thus, a key element in the determination of value is acceptance by the customer. Value is dependent on the vision of leaders, on the performance of the work force, on the imagination of the engineers, and on the support of all the functions in the organization and the suppliers outside the organization. The value of products or services can have the following qualities, which we have divided into four general categories.

    I. Customer considerations
        a. Customers perceive value in the product.
        b. Price is attractive relative to that perceived value.

    c. Products are reliable and consistent in their performance.

    d. The product is aesthetically pleasing.

    e. Products help customers be more efficient.

II. Capabilities

    a. Products conform to standards or specifications.

    b. Products are durable and perform satisfactorily throughout the warranty periods.

    c. Products are safe and meet all environmental requirements.

    d. Products are easy to use and to understand.

    e. Products have unusual capabilities.

III. Service

    a. Products can be readily serviced at a reasonable cost.

    b. Service of products is timely and convenient.

    c. Products are easily adjusted and easy to maintain.

    d. Products can be upgraded when required.

    e. Products are easily transported or moved when required.

IV. Competitive considerations

    a. Products are highly differentiated and have desirable features.

    b. Products are superior, or at least equivalent, to those of competitors.

    c. Products are readily available.

    d. Quality is built into the basic design of the product.

    e. Products have superior warranties.

This list may seem long and exhaustive, but we could undoubtedly cite many more considerations. It is obvious that adding value to products or services involves more than incorporating uniqueness of design, price, location, and the like. Value is the end that is sought both by the organization and by customers. Achieving value is a total effort that requires careful coordination and planning. Strategic management can contribute to adding value and thereby ensure a competitive advantage.

TOTAL VALUE

"Strategy isn't beating the competition; it's serving customers' real needs" (Ohmae, 1988). When one recognizes that customers have changing expectations, it becomes obvious that the way to beat competitors is to deal directly with what the customer wants. Ohmae points out that the smartest strategy in war is to avoid the battle. There is no better proof of the validity of this statement than the price wars that ensue when strategy deteriorates into cost competition alone. The current battle in the PC computer field also illustrates that price wars simply erode the profits of all the suppliers of a product and rarely lead to a sustainable competitive advantage for anyone. Similarly, price clubs find that they cannot meet customers' need for service. In a provocative article entitled "Roaches Outlive Elephants," Drucker (1991) suggests that some of the largest corporations are in trouble and may not survive the current business environment. He places General Motors and IBM in this category.

Size alone is no longer enough to sustain current organizations; witness the linking of IBM with Apple and with Siemens in Europe. Flexibility and time to delivery may yield greater competitiveness than what used to be considered economies of scale, because economies alone no longer suffice.

According to Forker (1991), meeting customer needs is only a starting point. She insists that surpassing customer expectations should be the goal of every organization. Anticipate customer needs and then supply them in a "value added" mode to ensure that you keep a competitive edge. Bergsma (1989) maintains that there is a new standard of performance expected of top management: the management of value. He cites Deming, who considered quality of design, conformance, and performance as essential for meeting customer expectations. Managers increasingly will be called on to ensure that the organization focuses on the creation of value. But how does management make certain that the greatest value is achieved from the assets under their control? Thorbeck (1991) suggests that the best way to compete in the marketplace is to invigorate workers and focus on special skills. He points out that whereas unhealthy organizations lack coherence, healthy organizations are coherent and their personalities, capabilities, and attitudes help achieve desired goals. He describes a company where the factory was only an hour away from headquarters but no CEO had visited it in over four years. Building a cohesive team requires interaction and leadership. Involvement on the part of management is crucial to achieving an organizational culture that focuses on creating value and thereby competitiveness. This has been demonstrated by Levi Strauss, where CEO Robert Haas recognized that the company's major asset was the aspirations of its people (Howard, 1990). Haas employs company values to define what people are responsible for, and then he uses these responsibilities to shape performance and training. The result? A remarkably flexible and innovative company that has been one of the fastest growing in the apparel industry. At the same time, Levi Strauss has sustained its commitment to dealing with social issues.

Value marketing builds on the concept that quality, service, and pricing are the key to survival (Power et al., 1991). Value implies that the company is meeting customer needs and demands; however, that high quality does not mean higher prices. Value marketing ensures the customer that the product will perform as advertised and that customers will get even more than they expect. Guarantees reinforce consumer confidence and help build relationships based on the facts pertaining to the product. Finally, Power recommends that unrealistic prices be avoided, especially where a product does not justify the price. This, however, does not preclude specialty stores such as Tiffany Jewelers from charging higher prices, because the price incorporates prestige and special service. For example, one might wonder whether spending $175,000 for a Rolls-Royce reflects the pursuit of value or prestige.

The 1990s have been described as the era of the "quality imperative." This era was ushered in by highly competitive Japanese products and fostered by W. Edwards Deming and J. M. Juran, who are both pioneers in the field of statistical quality control (Port, 1991). A global revolution in marketing is clearly under way; every facet of the business is affected, and products and services will continue to improve. Port and Carey (1991) have cited a number of interesting statistics comparing the United States with Canada, Germany, and Japan on the attributes shown in the accompanying table. These data are based on 500 companies in the automotive, banking, computer, and health care industries. Although the United States is still a formidable competitor, it is obvious that in most categories, Japan leads the pack. In a comparison between U.S. companies and Japanese companies related to engineering and design, it was clear that the Japanese were much more responsive than were U.S. companies to the quality imperative. Japanese companies invest significantly more money in initial screening, evaluation, and planning. The result is that their average operating revenues are 42%, compared with the U.S. figure of 22%. Income from operations is 29% for the Japanese compared with 18% for the best American companies. These data depict the tangible benefits that can be derived from applying the quality/value approach.

	U.S.	Japan	Germany	Canada
Customer satisfaction reported	37%	41%	22%	43%
Competitiveness factors	29%	32%	6%	26%
Use of the time-based approach	21%	55%	7%	19%
Amount of process simplification utilized	12%	47%	6%	19%
Performance evaluation used	54%	59%	54%	51%

As the foregoing comparison shows, product design can contribute significantly to both quality and profitability. Hauser and Clausing (1988) have developed an approach that provides a conceptual map allowing for interfunctional planning and communications. The conceptual map groups the things customers want into bundles of attributes reflecting customer concerns. The preferences are weighted to reflect their relative importance and then related to competitive advantage. Engineering changes of the product are evaluated by team members. Thus the conceptual map shows how engineering decisions affect customer perceptions. Both of these are then related to process and production planning to yield the final desired quality. The authors of this approach call it "quality function deployment." Using it, Japanese auto makers completed 90% of their changes in an average of 17 months and had approximately half as many changes as the American automotive companies, who were much later in completing their design changes. Most of the design changes in American companies came between 1 and 3 months before final production, and many had a fair number of changes 3 months after completion.

Using an approach called "smart design" for the Mercury Sable, Ford was able to outsell General Motors (Nussbaum et al., 1988). Their approach to design blended form, function, quality, and style. In order to support this approach, companies such as IBM are using computer programs to analyze and simplify all the parts that go into their products. Another source of quality and value is the more intelligent use of time. A time-based competitive advantage can be achieved where flexible manufacturing with rapid response systems helps firms to expand the variety of products available in a shorter period than competitors (Stalk, 1988). To illustrate how the time-based approach works, consider that the United States produced 10 million automobile suspension components in 1987, compared to 3.5 million for the Japanese. But the United States required 242 employees to do so, the Japanese only 57. Not only were U.S. costs higher ($100 per part for the United States versus $49 for the Japanese), but the United States had only 11 varieties of finished parts whereas the Japanese had 38. It is obvious that when it is properly applied, the time-based approach significantly affects strategies. It will be an important factor to consider in the '90s.

Northern Telecom recognized that moving in the direction of a time-based strategy would mean rethinking almost every aspect of the business and would disrupt most of the company's current systems and practices. Here again, however, moving faster led to significant improvements. Over a five-year period, manufacturing intervals were reduced 75% to 80%, inventory was reduced approximately 30% over a 5-year period, and overhead was reduced approximately 30%. At the same time, customer satisfaction improved 25%. One of the major advantages of a time-based approach is knowing where costs occurred. Northern Telecom's new P&L statement showed that many costs were previously lumped into overhead. Now, with a flexible and knowledgeable workforce, company managers have adopted a "pay-for-skill" program. Northern Telecom considers improving delivery a never-ending process. When it reaches its 5-year milestone, it will reassess its strategy. If required, planners expect to modify their objectives. "There's no time to stand still in a time-based environment" (Merrills, 1989).

The well-known camping equipment company, Coleman of Wichita, Kansas, found that sales were grinding to a halt. By switching to a faster and more flexible approach, it made significant improvements in growth and is now considered a formidable competitor (Dumaine, 1991). Two years ago Coleman offered 20 models of ice coolers that could be had in three colors. With its new flexible approach, it now has 140 models in 12 colors—and was at the same time able to cut inventory costs by $10 million, reduce scrap by 60%, and increase productivity by 30%. Achieving flexibility required more than changes in equipment; it also required the cooperation of the union and workers. However, Coleman felt that if people were not deeply involved in understanding the business, they would not be able to perform well. The company's prior approach to design never allowed any mistakes, and meeting this standard required so many approvals that very little could be done. Now product development teams can make their own decisions without further approvals, a system that has resulted in significantly increased profits. As another example, Intel has found that the only way it can compete in the fast-changing chip market is to produce new designs in half the time it used to take and thus lock out competitors (Hof, 1992). However, even more rapid delivery may not be enough to stem Intel's losses. For example, Intel's 486 chip has a relative speed of 19, compared with IBM's RISC chip, which clocks in at 89—almost 5 times faster.

Most approaches to adding value have focused on improvements internal to the organization. Value marketing and total quality management illustrate the importance of dealing with the customer. Thus the customer is acknowledged as the key to achieving competitive advantage. (We have come full circle: for many years, the saying "The customer is king" stressed that the market's acceptance of products was the bottom line.) Flexible manufacturing, speedier delivery, and a greater emphasis on quality, service, pricing, and value have contributed to meeting customer expectations. An additional factor has now been added that can extend the ability of firms to increase value and better meet customer demand in order to beat the competition. Forging "strategic alliances" or "value-adding partnerships" helps to extend the firm's value-adding capability beyond the firm itself by combining the best of two or more organizations. There are many examples of strategic partnering. Ford and Mazda have built a strong team (Treece et al., 1992). Developing a new model car can easily cost over $2 billion. By using a strategic tie-in, the two companies can share these costs to the benefit of both, even where there appears to be obvious competition. Both organizations remain independent and continue their own research and development, but they work as partners on projects they feel will contribute to their mutual benefit. For example, Mazda wanted to develop a sporty utility vehicle and buy it from Ford. Ford was willing to provide a modified version of the Explorer, because this gave them the opportunity to manufacture pickups for Mazda.

One challenge facing computer chip makers may require strategic partnering to succeed. It is estimated that by the year 2000, electronic components will be etched on silicon chips that will require circuits to be less than 0.2 microns (millionths of an inch) in size (Pitta, 1992). Sematech, the consortium of U.S. chip makers, is using partnering to improve chip-making techniques. Nearly perfect cleanliness will be required to manufacture these new electronic devices. Motorola has already spent $650 million to build a Class I factory. Japanese chip makers have indicated that they would be willing to invest whatever is needed to produce the most advanced chips. Without strategic partnering, the United States might be left out in the cold.

A similar concern was noted by Johnston and Lawrence (1988). They consider partnering an alternative to vertical integration for small companies that do not have enough capital to acquire another company. The approach they advocate is for a group of independent companies to work together closely in providing goods and services along the entire value chain. For example, the McKesson Corporation, a $6.67 billion drug and health care distributor, relied on value-adding partnerships to compete with large drugstore chains. What McKesson did was to offer small, independent drugstore operators the advantages of the computer system it had developed (which no small drugstore could afford to develop on its own). By doing this, McKesson formed strong and lasting relationships with the firms in the value chain that were responsible for the final distribution of its products.

Partnering can build a viable infrastructure based on a stakeholder analysis to identify where the interdependencies exist. Value and ways to achieve it have become the key underlying elements in meeting customer needs.

STRATEGIC SUCCESS AND ORGANIZATIONAL VALUES

In 1982 Thomas Peters and Robert Waterman published *In Search of Excellence*, in which they summarized the results of years of study and consulting experience addressing the question "What lessons can we learn from the best-run companies in the United States?" Peters and Waterman came up with eight recurring attributes of excellence among the companies they studied. These attributes were based on operating values: beliefs strongly held and acted on by the executives involved.

Continuing our examination of "total value management," we will consider how organizations develop their value concepts. The factors researched by Peters and Waterman provide a useful framework for exploring the basic values and beliefs of an organization and their effect on strategic performance.

1. *A bias for action.* Excellent companies want to get things done. They "do it, try it, fix it," as the adage goes. They don't sit around waiting for good things to happen to them. Merrill Lynch acted on this value when it introduced "cash management" programs for its customers. Merrill Lynch put the service into effect before it knew what features customers would want and how best to operate the service internally. Then the company monitored performance and kept "fixing" it until the operation ran smoothly, beating others to the marketplace and achieving a competitive advantage.

   AHSC did much the same thing with its automated purchasing system. Early in the implementation of its strategy, the company made a commitment to developing a new computer telecommunications network that would provide full catalog and ordering services for its customers.

2. *Closeness to the customer.* Excellent companies are customer-oriented. They are deeply concerned with product quality and service, and they listen closely to their users' wants and needs. These companies realize that a customer buys not only a product but also utility. Utility is achieved when a product or service works as it's supposed to, when it lasts, when the customer knows how to use it, and when it's easy to use and achieves the desired results.

   IBM has been very successful at selling utility, largely because its founder, Thomas Watson, believed that one should offer "not machines for rent, but machine services." For Watson, services included timely advice and counsel on how to use the machines in the customer's place of business, as well as prompt repair and maintenance to ensure that the machines worked properly.

3. *Autonomy and entrepreneurship.* Excellent companies encourage innovation from within. In order to do this, these companies give their subunits or divisions considerable autonomy and foster an entrepreneurial spirit among their personnel. To ensure success, they often associate this value with another that "allows" individuals to make a reasonable number of mistakes.

   A chief feature of entrepreneurship within a large organization is almost always the emergence of a "champion": a person who believes strongly in an idea and who is willing to take risks for it. The successful champion finds a network of support people throughout the organization.

ILLUSTRATIVE CASE: AHSC

Our first illustrative case describes how American Hospital Supply Corporation achieved strategic success. Founded in the early 1920s, American Hospital Supply Corporation (AHSC) enjoyed modest success for the first 50 years of its existence. Just a few products, such as intravenous solutions, syringes, surgical gloves, and suction tubing, constituted its total product offering. In the late 1970s, executives took stock of what they believed to be a deteriorating situation. The company was not growing as fast as its president, Foster G. McGraw, and his associates thought it should. Inventories were accumulating rapidly. Profits were stagnant. They wondered what they could do to turn the company around. One thing they realized was that they had very little useful information about their customers' preferences and needs. They did not know why customers bought medical supplies from AHSC or from AHSC's competitors. Furthermore, they did not fully comprehend the forces that shaped the demand for their products and influenced their customers' purchasing decisions. As a first step to get a handle on its problem, AHSC undertook a comprehensive survey of the purchasing agents in hospitals, laboratories, and clinics throughout the United States. Hospital purchasing agents were considered the primary customers, because they were the ones who ordered AHSC's products.

When the results of the survey were in, the executives were rather surprised. The purchasing agents reported that they experienced great difficulty in placing orders for medical supplies. The agents were confused because there were so many different suppliers, and they were dissatisfied because sources of supply frequently were not dependable. There was also a morass of paperwork to deal with, and it was often a week or longer before they received the supplies ordered. Their hospitals' accounts payable were in disarray because of partial shipments, discounts, and complicated billings. Bookkeeping costs were mounting. It was nearly impossible to keep track of inventory. Consequently, each hospital generally carried

75–90 days of inventory for each item to ensure availability of supplies.

AHSC's executives viewed this chaotic situation as an opportunity because no single distributor met the hospitals' needs. AHSC decided to embark on a "full-line" product-distribution strategy. This meant adding a significant number of new products to the existing product line and developing a new distribution system. The company set the key objective of its strategy as follows: to place "at the purchaser's fingertips" the capacity to order all of the hospital's supplies directly from AHSC. It then set out to find the means to achieve this objective.

The essence of AHSC's strategy was to create a competitive advantage by developing the most reliable and responsive distribution system possible. AHSC placed a computer terminal in each hospital purchasing agent's office and linked it, via a nationwide network, to the central office. Purchasing agents immediately liked the system because it relieved them of a substantial burden.

AHSC's strategy proved successful. More and more purchasing agents ordered goods from AHSC, and they did so even if another vendor offered a particular item at a lower cost. By 1985, competitive bidding in the medical supplies market had virtually ceased. Customers became ever more dependent on AHSC, and business flourished.

Customer service was the key to AHSC's strategy. The driving force of that strategy was an efficient distribution system. Major strategic decisions about acquisitions, mergers, divestitures, and repositioning all revolved around this crucial resource. AHSC created a system to solve its strategic problem. It specified measures of performance for the system, including fast, easy ordering for the customer and 24-hour delivery. Finally, it committed the company's resources to achieving these strategic goals.

In order to diversify, managers at AHSC concentrated on a planned merger with Hospital Corporation of America. However, a rival firm, Baxter Travenol Laboratories, Inc. (now Baxter International), was making plans to acquire

AHSC, CONTINUED

AHSC. Baxter Travenol, itself a major manufacturer of hospital supplies, offered AHSC $50 per share. AHSC resisted Baxter's $50-a-share bid, and HCA attempted to stop Baxter by canceling a $100-million contract to buy intravenous solutions from Baxter and threatening to cancel nearly $1 billion in other purchase agreements. After several weeks, AHSC's resistance and HCA's threats failed, and Baxter Travenol acquired AHSC with a final bid of $51 per share (or $3.8 billion). The merger of AHSC, with $1.8 billion in sales, and Baxter Travenol, with $3.4 billion in sales (1984 figures), created the largest health care company in the United States.

Why was acquisition of AHSC a good strategy for Baxter Travenol? For one thing, the two companies were in the same business, which allowed Baxter to expand without diversifying. Another benefit of the merger was economies of scale. Baxter Travenol's acquisition of AHSC increased its sales volume, which enabled it to produce and distribute more products at less cost and thereby create more profit. Baxter's net income increased from $29 million in 1984 to $138 million in 1985, the year of the merger. By 1986 Baxter's sales totaled $5.6 billion, up from $3.5 billion in 1984. Net income jumped to $271 million in 1987, and based on first-quarter statistics, projected net income for 1988 was $364 million.

Finally, Baxter Travenol benefited from AHSC's strengths, particularly its computerized order and distribution system, called ASAP (Harvard Business School Case, 1985). Baxter expanded the ASAP system, which allows customers to order supplies directly through a central computer by means of a telephone-linked terminal. The system was tailored to individual customer needs, enabling hospitals, laboratories, and other customers to order products in predetermined groupings. It also provided price information, order confirmation, and a procedure for payment.

Shortly after it merged with AHSC, Baxter Travenol began to consolidate its operations to cut costs. After it swallowed American Hospital Supply, Baxter's size was tripled. Baxter's current posture is to trim down acquisitions, because they are not always the answer to achieving either profitable growth or a sustainable competitive advantage. Vernon R. Loucks, Jr. has restructured Baxter three times since 1986 by shedding plants, workers, and businesses. Loucks expected that these measures would be a means to respond to the constant pressure for cost control in health care (Siler, 1990). It was estimated that restructuring would save $275 million by 1993 on sales of $7.4 billion in 1989. In part, the problem stemmed from the struggle to absorb the 1985 hostile takeover of AHSC. Loucks expected to eliminate 6,000 jobs, but the number that it was possible to cut back proved far smaller. A vicious price war with Abbott Laboratories broke out shortly after the AHSC takeover devastated Baxter's profits. At the same time, hospitals began negotiating as a group and were able to obtain lower prices from suppliers. Following this was the loss to Abbott of a major contract with Voluntary Hospitals of America. As if all this were not bad enough, in Chicago a federal grand jury was hearing evidence to determine whether Baxter, the world's largest hospital supply corporation, was in violation of a federal anti-boycott law by pledging to Arab League officials not to do business with Israel (Siler et al., 1991). Baxter was eager to sever relations with Israel because of a lucrative joint venture with Nestlé in the $2 billion clinical nutrition market. And in addition to the anti-boycott case, Baxter was accused of paying physicians who make referrals. Medicare prohibits this kind of kickback.

Tracing the path of once-successful AHSC through to its takeover by Baxter illustrates that acquisitions call for continuous changes in strategy to contend with fierce competition and the unpredictable behavior of customers. Any unethical behavior that Baxter engaged in may also have contributed to its problems.

The 3M Corporation fosters internal autonomy and entrepreneurship through venture teams. A venture team at 3M consists of a small group of volunteers who represent various disciplines within the company—research and development, manufacturing, marketing, sales, and finance—and who, under appropriate leadership, make a full-time commitment to developing a new product. The members of the team are well motivated because each participates in the economic success of the product. Masking tape, 3M's first major product, is the result of just such an entrepreneurial approach, as is its famous Scotch tape. Most of 3M's current product line was generated by this system of venture teams.

4. *Productivity through people.* Excellent companies draw on the talent of their employees, seeing them as contributors of ideas, not just as a source of physical labor. In other words, they accord them respect. Many approaches encourage productivity through people: management by objectives (MBO), quality control circles, distributed decision making, and flat, interactive organizational structures are examples. Successful organizations tend to motivate employees by ensuring that

   - Each person's job is reasonably demanding. (Sheer endurance does not count.)
   - There is some variety and occasionally some novelty in each job.
   - Each employee can learn and grow on the job.
   - Each employee has an area of decision making that can be considered his or her own.
   - Each employee gets social support and recognition.
   - Employees can identify their jobs and the firm's products as part of their social life.
   - Each job leads to some sort of desirable future goal for each employee.

   During the 1970s and early 1980s, Hewlett-Packard (HP) built its personnel strategy around these ideas. From its inception, HP had never been a hire-and-fire company. During the 1970 recession, HP did not lay people off. Instead everyone was asked to work 10% fewer hours and take a 10% cut in pay. HP involved its employees in most corporate decisions and gave them considerable freedom and autonomy. This even included free use of electrical and mechanical laboratory equipment for personal projects. The value of respecting employees and encouraging them to stand out has been responsible for much innovation at Hewlett-Packard.

5. *Hands-on, value-driven executives.* One of the remarkable characteristics of a successful company is that its executives tend to "get their hands dirty" and participate periodically in some of the minute details of the business. These executives usually like hands-on, face-to-face engagements. They occasionally make sales calls on potential customers or operate a new piece of production machinery. These actions communicate their values to co-workers and customers and keep them in touch with the realities of doing business.

   Peters and Waterman identified three characteristics of successful executives. (a) They have values they believe should guide the business: striving to be best, the importance of details, belief in people as individuals, the company as an extended family, the importance of profits, and the need for superior quality and service. (b) They know how to articulate and communicate these values to others. (They often choose slogans or almost ritualistic activities to do so.) (c) They use special indicators to monitor the company's progress. These indicators are in keeping with the company's values and do not alienate employees.

Author Tom Peters cited Willard J. Marriott, Sr., as a case in point. The founder of Marriott Hotels always believed strongly in quality, service, and cleanliness. He would read every customer complaint that his hotels received—a time-consuming task as his chain of hotels grew. But it kept him close to the business, and his dedication communicated to others the importance of the values he stood for.

All successful strategies are based on values like these. Furthermore, most successful companies develop measures of performance, or score cards, that tell them how well they are doing with respect to goals and values. (In Chapter 3 we will consider how values are determined, goals and objectives set, and measures of performance developed.) Values are derived from the deep-seated beliefs of a company's executives, and the companies that achieve excellence live by these values.

6. *Stick to knitting.* Excellent companies maintain a focus, even if they undertake a wide variety of activities and compete in many different markets. Unifying it all are an underlying theme and a definite sense of direction.

Too much diversification tends to diffuse a firm's focus. Richard Rumelt (1974, pp. 114–115) discovered this in his study of approximately 200 of the largest corporations in the United States. Rumelt found that companies that diversified into *related* businesses (especially when the related business involved a particular skill or resource that the company had perfected in its dominant business) outperformed companies that became conglomerates or acquired unrelated businesses. On the average, the related businesses had higher profits, higher rates of growth, and higher price-earnings ratios.

Rumelt's findings suggest guidelines for developing strategies. First, the successful company innovates and acquires other firms but does not venture far from its core skills and resources or from its executives' realm of experience. That is, the company "sticks to its knitting." Second, Rumelt's research revealed that product-division firms show average growth rates in earnings per share substantially larger than rates of firms without separate product divisions. This finding indicates the benefits of autonomy and entrepreneurship within an organization. It also shows why having product divisions yields so many benefits.

Ling-Tempco-Vought (LTV), the conglomerate brain child of flamboyant Jimmy Ling, is an example of a firm that diversified beyond its ability to focus. LTV lost track of its corporate strengths. It became involved in steel, meats, and high technology but found no common denominator with which to manage them. When LTV's Jones and Laughlin Steel holding suffered financial setbacks, the entire LTV structure nearly collapsed.

3M, on the other hand, identified its principal strength and strategic advantage—its coating and bonding technology—and forged a successful strategy based on this superior technological capability.

AHSC did much the same thing: it defined the medical-supplies field as its core capability and decided that excellence in distribution would be its driving force. Every acquisition and new venture fit into a carefully laid out product-line strategy. AHSC then focused on its three most distinctive competencies—telecommunications, computer-based order entry, and 24-hour delivery—in that order.

7. *Simple form, lean staff.* Excellent companies avoid excessive bureaucracy and red tape. A company experiences crises as it moves from the initiation or entrepreneurial phase of the cycle to the bureaucratic phase, then to the divisional, product group, and matrix phases.

One way to cope with each crisis is to incorporate more overhead. This means adding reports and forms, new managers and staff, and possibly luxuries if the company is profitable. This method of coping with crisis has led to the popularization of Parkinson's Law (work expands to fill the time available). The result is that the company becomes sluggish, and its profits tend to decline.

In the early 1980s, Schlumberger (pronounced "shlum-bare-zhay"), a little-known oil equipment and exploration information firm, was the world leader in making physical measurements of rocks, oil, and gas in newly drilled oil wells. It was one of the world's most profitable firms, and it practiced the "lean and mean" value. At the close of 1981, it had a total stock market value (price per share times number of shares in the market) of over $16 billion. This ranked it fourth, behind AT&T, IBM, and Exxon. Schlumberger employed approximately 75,000 people worldwide but ran its two major headquarters in New York and Paris with a total of 197 people, including its chairman and chief executive officer, Jean Riboud. Ken Auletta, in a *New Yorker* profile entitled "A Certain Poetry" (1983, p. 46), described Riboud's approach to form, staff, and surroundings as follows:

Riboud's office has a single telephone with just two lines, and no private bathroom; there are white blinds on the windows, and a simple beige sisal carpet on the floor. His desk is a long, rectangular teak table with chrome legs; on it are a few memoranda but no "in" or "out" boxes and no books. His personal New York Staff consists of one secretary, Lucille Northrup, to whom he rarely dictates; memoranda and paperwork are frowned upon at Schlumberger, and when Riboud wants to send out a memorandum, he first writes it in long hand.

8. *Simultaneous loose–tight properties.* Finally, excellent companies find ways to be flexible, decentralized, and entrepreneurial while maintaining the ability to be inflexible, centralized, and controlled when necessary. These companies develop a corporate culture with a clear set of values, habits, and procedures— a "way of going." The individual who works with and promotes these core values is supported, rewarded, and given a great deal of freedom, whereas the individual who goes against these core values is disciplined, castigated, or chastised. If the violation is severe enough, the individual is fired.

McDonald's, under the leadership of the late Ray Kroc, mastered the balance between freedom and control. For instance, small groups within the company were given the freedom to experiment with ideas such as McDonald's breakfast menu, which, by 1985, accounted for about 40% of the company's total business. To this day, McDonald's operates with a very loose structure. Most major decisions are made in informal daily meetings of the home-office executives. The store managers and franchisees are given a great deal of autonomy.

Members of McDonald's top management team spend great amounts of time in the field inspecting operations and observing employees. In management's eyes, there are no greater offenses than serving stale or undercooked french fries, not being pleasant and courteous to the customer, leaving wrappings and paper cups strewn around the restaurant and parking lot, or serving food that doesn't meet McDonald's standards. These violations are dealt with rapidly and decisively. The perpetrators are warned, disciplined, and if need be, fired. Quality, service, cleanliness, and value (QSCV) are central to McDonald's strategy and firmly integrated into its culture.

These eight operating values have served as principles of management for some of America's most successful companies. The strategies of many successful companies are based on one or more of them. AHSC followed all eight to some extent.

In *A Passion for Excellence* (Peters and Austin, 1985), Tom Peters reemphasized the importance of several of the eight attributes contributing to success, particularly the hard-to-measure qualities embedded in attributes 2 through 5:

- Closeness to the customer (customer service)
- Autonomy and entrepreneurship (motivation and innovation)
- Productivity through people (quality)
- Hands-on, value-driven executives (leadership style)

Peters and Austin went on to say that the real success secret of well-run companies is their style of leadership, particularly a style that boosts productivity by empowering employees to be both motivated and innovative.

There are, of course, other values that might guide a successful company's strategy. A company could, for example, simply strive for technological superiority, following the adage that if you build a better mousetrap, the world will flock to your door. The essential point, however, is that *all strategies are based on values.* The first—and sometimes also the last—task of strategic managers is to determine what values will guide the organization.

MAINTAINING AND RENEWING SUCCESSFUL STRATEGIES

Success and excellence are temporary phenomena. Once achieved, they must be pursued continuously or they will erode. Strategic management involves constant monitoring of the methods and assumptions that underlie it.

In 1984, two years after Peters and Waterman published *In Search of Excellence,* *Business Week* ran an article called "Who's Excellent Now?" The article reported that some of the firms cited in the book as excellent companies had slipped from the top. At least 14 of the 43 excellent companies that Peters and Waterman identified were no longer considered among the nation's best. Hewlett-Packard no longer passed the test; neither did Atari, Delta Airlines, Disney, Kodak, or Texas Instruments. Why did these excellent companies falter? Was it because they abandoned attributes and values that made them successful? Were they victims of unexpected environmental forces? Or did they fail to recognize, in time, that they needed to formulate new strategies for changing conditions? The answers varied. Atari, for example, violated seven of the eight operating values identified by Peters and Waterman. Delta, at that time, was unprepared to deal with an external force—deregulation of the airline industry. As Robert Waterman wrote in response to the *Business Week* article, "Nobody said that excellence was forever" (Waterman, 1984).

STRATEGIC FAILURES

Perhaps the most striking example of the impermanence of excellence can be found in the U.S. automobile industry of the 1970s. From the 1930s until the early 1970s, the largest of the U.S. automobile manufacturers dominated the world market. Times changed, but the U.S. automobile industry did not.

In a talk entitled "The Failure of Success" (O'Toole, 1985, p. 55), Professor James O'Toole of the University of Southern California attributed the U.S. automobile companies' downfall to their failure to reexamine and challenge ten basic assumptions that had served them well for 40 years but were no longer appropriate. He recounted the obsolete assumptions of General Motors, Ford, Chrysler, and other U.S. companies, to which he gave the collective name "Monolithic Motors." Their obsolete assumptions follow.

1. *Monolithic Motors is in the business of making money, not cars.* This assumption focused managers' attention on finances and cash management and diverted it from their customers' changing wants and needs and from shifts in the marketplace.
2. *Success comes not from technological leadership, but from having the resources to quickly adopt innovations successfully introduced by others.* This failure to manage technology strategically permitted the Japanese manufacturers first to gain technological parity and then to surpass the American automobile manufacturers' technological advantage.
3. *Cars are primarily status symbols. Styling is therefore more important than quality to buyers who are, after all, "trading up" every other year.* Changes in economic conditions and in individual values changed this once-salient assumption. In the 1970s, many customers began to want utility, economy, and longevity more than status; several foreign-manufactured automobiles satisfied these desires better than U.S. models.
4. *The American car market is isolated from the rest of the world. Foreign competitors will never gain more than 15% of the domestic market.* Today the

United States is part of a global economy brought about by increased transportation, communication, and commerce. In a global society and economy, no one country can isolate itself effectively.

5. *Energy will always be cheap and abundant.* OPEC in the early 1970s ended the validity of this assumption.

6. *Workers do not have an important impact on productivity or product quality.* The prevalence of Henry Ford's great contribution, the mass-production assembly line, may have reached its limits. As the Lordstown plant's worker rebellion and other, similar events indicated, workers have a great deal of influence on production, quality, and quantity. Working together with the aims of the company in mind, they can enhance performance. Working apart and against the company, they can destroy performance. Interestingly enough, the more automated the plant (the more robotics it employs), the more important worker cooperation becomes.

7. *The consumer movement does not represent the concerns of a significant portion of the American public.* Ralph Nader's book *Unsafe at Any Speed* changed this assumption. Subsequent problems with product liability and financing reinforced the need for a change in thinking.

8. *The government is the enemy. It must be fought tooth and nail every inch of the way.* This assumption became a management cop-out for the U.S. automobile industry: an excuse for not addressing some real concerns about safety, pollution, and performance. By making the assumption universal, the automobile industry failed to address some legitimate issues and incurred substantial legal costs.

9. *Strict, centralized financial controls are the secret to good administration.* Like so many strategic assumptions, this is a half-truth that outlived its usefulness. When Alfred Sloan brought financial controls to General Motors in the 1920s, he brought order to chaos. But by the 1970s, the controls had become masters rather than servants. The result was that innovation, creativity, and long-range thinking were stifled.

10. *Managers should be developed from the inside.* Too much inbreeding in the U.S. automobile industry resulted in too little vision and much complacent thinking.

The failure of the U.S. automobile firms to monitor and challenge these ten assumptions—in short, their failure to think strategically and to change their strategies—permitted the Japanese and others to capture U.S. markets and prosper in them.

The automobile manufacturers have not been alone in basing strategies on incorrect assumptions. Robert F. Hartley summarized several such failures in a book entitled *Management Mistakes* (1983). Hartley's main conclusion after studying errors in strategic management was the same as O'Toole's. Success does not guarantee continued success; indeed, it can lead to failure.

In his book *Running American Business*, Robert Lamb (1987) looked at other reasons why some companies do not succeed. Lamb investigated failures in the executive suite and concluded that many chief executive officers are risk-averse and caught up in short-term thinking and that boards of directors are little more than rubber stamps. Lamb believes that executives give technology very low priority and are overly concerned about being members of the "phantom club" of chief executive officers (CEOs).

STRATEGIC RENEWAL

How can companies adapt their strategies to take advantage of changing conditions? Owens-Illinois, long a successful manufacturer specializing in glass containers, faced the classic dilemma of how to achieve growth in a declining industry. The solution was to refocus the company's business to include industries spurred on by population growth, particularly the growth of the elderly population. In 1984, under the leadership of chairman Robert Lanigan, Owens-Illinois began to refocus by manufacturing plastic containers and diversifying. The company phased out of glass-container manufacturing and invested $600 million to modernize production and increase output of its remaining product line. In addition, Owens-Illinois acquired a mortgage company—Alliance Mortgage—and began to invest in nursing homes. The change in strategy contributed to the profitability of Owens-Illinois.

The changes at Owens-Illinois exemplified corporate renewal through new strategies based on the recognition of new opportunities. Robert Waterman's book *The Renewal Factor* (1987) identified eight factors that companies should use in their corporate renewal efforts. Like the eight attributes he and Peters identified in *In Search of Excellence*, the eight renewal factors emphasize operating values and attitudes. Waterman's new directives follow.

1. *Informed opportunism.* Keep abreast of the latest information to maintain strategic advantage and flexibility.
2. *Direction and empowerment.* Identify what needs to be done and allow subordinates the freedom to find ways of doing it.
3. *Friendly facts and congenial controls.* Use financial controls as checks and balances but give managers the freedom to be creative.
4. *A different mirror.* Recognize that ideas can come from every source, including customers, competitors, and employees.
5. *Teamwork, trust, politics, and power.* Accept relentless fighting as a consequence of power politics while stressing teamwork and trust in getting the job done.
6. *Stability in motion.* Respond to changing forces with the recognition that some consistency must be maintained and norms retained; allow rules to be broken when necessary.
7. *Attitudes and attention.* Realize that attention is more effective than exhortation at getting things done and that symbolic behavior makes the words come true.
8. *Causes and commitment.* Maintain an awareness of the grand cause so that it permeates all action.

PREPARING AND COMMUNICATING A STRATEGIC PLAN

Strategic plans evolve from careful analysis of a firm's competitive advantage, threats posed by competitors, environmental forces, customer demands, and ways of measuring how well company goals are being met. The final plan should help executives make policy and operational decisions according to corporate guidelines, but it should not stifle creativity or prevent executives from dealing effectively with contingencies and changing conditions. The strategic plan also serves as the vehicle for communicating proposed strategy to individuals in the organization who are responsible for its implementation as well as soliciting input from those individuals.

A strategic plan can have the following components:

1. A definition of the desired future scope of the company, including a statement of identity. "What business is the company in or should it be in and what kind of company is it or should it be?" (Andrews, 1971, p. 28).
2. A description of the competitive advantage of the company, including its distinctive competence in relation to its competitors and the market niche it intends to occupy.
3. A statement of the purpose, mission, goals, and objectives of the company and the measures used to evaluate performance.
4. A statement of how to allocate resources needed to implement and execute the plan.

STRATEGIC PLANNING AT OMICON INDUSTRIES, INC.

Let us examine in detail the dynamics of strategic analysis at a major international corporation, Omicon Industries, Inc.

Omicon is a highly diversified company with $3 billion in sales and 24,000 employees. The company's core areas of expertise include processing paper and pulp, developing specialized chemical systems for paper and pulp factories, producing chemicals for forestry and agriculture, manufacturing heavy transport equipment, and engineering marine technologies. Omicon also develops, manufactures, and markets a wide variety of medical products and pharmaceuticals, serving doctors, nurses' committees, and hospitals. The 35 diversified business units are organized into the following four divisions:

- Engineering and distribution
- Pharmaceuticals
- Health care
- Consumer goods

Omicon's current return on investment of 11% is lagging behind that of its competitors.

To begin the analysis of the data, Omicon summarized the strategies of its business units by focusing on the economics and competitive nature of each business unit. Thus the process integrated information and creative insights from managers of each unit. It also involved these managers in the analysis, which usually leads to a more realistic action plan that the line managers understand and are committed to pursuing. The strategic planning helped higher-level managers to develop corporate strategy and more effectively allocate resources.

Omicon's strategic planning covered the following for each business unit:

1. Business definition: main thrust of the business, most important business activities.
2. Key success factors: manageable variables that can help Omicon gain competitive advantage in the industry.
3. Environmental assumptions: the market and competitive environment in which the strategy is to be pursued; major assumptions about the market; customers' purchasing criteria; technology; costs; and competitors' actions, which may represent opportunities or threats.
4. Omicon's competitive position: an assessment of Omicon's key success factors compared to key success factors of the major competitors.
5. Performance objectives: assessment of profits that can be made by improving competitive position and taking advantage of opportunities.
6. Action plan: major actions that need to be taken to maintain and improve competitive position and take advantage of opportunities.
7. The fit with corporate goals: an assessment of each business unit's compatibility with corporate goals and of the potential for improved fit.

Figure 1.2 shows how these seven components of strategy are related. Strategy, in this exhibit, is represented by the performance objectives. The arrows in Figure 1.2 show how the different components serve as a "reality test" for the entire strategic analysis. For example, component 3, environmental assumptions, is a key reality test for component 4, Omicon's competitive position, and component 5, performance objectives. An awareness of interactions among the seven components helps strategic planners to test the logic and assumptions of each one.

BUSINESS DEFINITION

The first objective in business definition was to distinguish each business unit at Omicon from the next. This was done by finding the point at which their key success factors started to differ significantly. Omicon defined its business units as having distinct products and/or services, target customer groups, and geographic regions in which they operated.

The business unit was further defined by specific customer needs and the manner in which they were satisfied. Figure 1.3 shows how key questions asked in defining each business led to key questions about other strategic components.

KEY SUCCESS FACTORS

The key success factors defined areas of possible competitive advantage. Why would a customer buy a product or be willing to pay more for it? How might a competitor succeed in persuading a customer to do both? In answering these questions, Omicon identified the most important key success factors and limited them to factors that could be acted on by competitors in the same business.

In Omicon's case, the most important key success factors were (1) increasing the product's value to the customer and (2) promoting cost-effectiveness. An

FIGURE 1.2 | **Seven Components of Strategy Formulation**

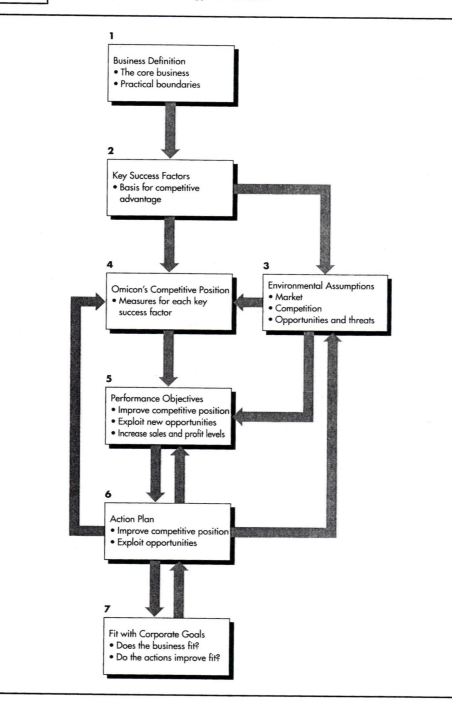

FIGURE 1.3	Key Questions Asked in the Analysis of Strategic Components One, Two, Three, and Six

Business Definition	Key Factors	Environmental Trends	Competitive Position	Opportunities
What are we selling?	Which competitors do we respect most?	Has the market been growing or declining? Will this trend continue?	Is the main competitor equal to us in all success factors or gaining?	Where are the weakest points in our competitive position?
How?	What do they do that we don't?	Are there any substitute products?	Is the main competitor losing money?	How quickly can we change things?
To whom?	What are the most important elements of cost?	Have there been any mergers or acquisitions?	Does the main competitor have a sustainable competitive advantage?	What do we have to do to succeed?
	Do customers want the cheapest product?	What is the position of imports?		
	What is a success factor and what is necessary to stay in business?	Does technology have much influence on costs?		
	Are the success factors the same for all businesses?			

assessment of customers' purchasing criteria was used to determine a product's value to the customer. Results were broken down into three categories of value:

- *Value of the product itself.* This value was a function of price, general performance, reliability, and up-to-date technology. These variables were applied to compare the value of Omicon's products to the value of competitors' products.
- *Value of customer service.* This value was a function of efficient communication of customers' service requests and promptness of service.
- *Value of start-up time.* This value was a function of how soon the customer could have a functioning product or equipment in place. It depended on manufacturing capacity, installation efficiency, and the effectiveness with which the customer was introduced to technological features or new system design.

Key success factors affecting cost-effectiveness included:

- Economies of scale in manufacturing or marketing
- Costs of raw materials and labor
- Productivity
- Manufacturing approaches
- Design, technology, engineering, or patents
- Location relative to the market

- Government subsidies or regulations
- Other considerations unique to the product

An alternative approach to the key success factors was developed by Kenichi Ohmae (1982). He evaluates a business strategy by using four categories:

1. Compete wisely.
   a. Old existing strategy—key factors for success
   b. New creative strategy—aggressive initiatives
2. Avoid head-on competition.
   a. Old existing strategy—relative superiority
   b. New creative strategy—strategic degrees of freedom

Ohmae then describes how to strengthen a company's competitive position.

1a. Focus resources in areas where the company can improve its competitive advantage.
1b. Challenge the accepted assumptions by using aggressive initiatives.
2a. Exploit relative superiority rather than competing across the board.
2b. Search for areas untouched by competitors and vigorously exploit these.

Ohmae summarizes his approach as "avoid doing the same thing, on the same battlegrounds, as competition."

ENVIRONMENTAL ASSUMPTIONS

The environmental assumptions made by Omicon integrated diverse information about the external business environment. These environmental assumptions were based on information about

- The market (size, growth, profitability, market shares of major competitors)
- Customers' purchasing behavior
- Technology
- Competitors
- Government regulations, politics, and so on

This information enabled Omicon to identify opportunities and threats.

COMPETITIVE POSITION

The determination of competitive position was based on the list of key success factors. Its purpose was to measure Omicon's market position for each factor relative to that of major competitors. Figure 1.4 shows Omicon's competitive advantages and disadvantages for three divisions. For example, a cost-effective advantage could be based on besting competitors with respect to economies of scale, productivity, product design, or efficiency of manufacturing.

Another important theme was innovation and new business opportunities. The strategy must not only maintain and improve competitive position but also continually upgrade Omicon's ability to innovate. Omicon could improve its competitive

FIGURE 1.4	Analysis of Competitive Position

| Division | Competitive Position | Projected Profit Growth (1989) | |
		Dollars (millions)	Percentage
Distribution division	Competitive disadvantage Control cost or provide full service? Have stock turnover or carry a full range?	$ 3.3	112%
Pharmaceutical division	Radical change in historic R&D focus Competitive position in raw materials Reduction of a key project Reduced investment plans	2.9	86
Health care division	Competitive disadvantage Need to focus geographically Cost reduction opportunities	0.8	118
Total		$ 7.0	105%

position by recognizing its sources of disadvantage and correcting them. For example, Omicon could increase its sales efforts to make the market aware of a product's advantage. Omicon could also improve its competitive position by recognizing entirely new sources of advantage, or *advantage innovation.* An advantage innovation might be a new manufacturing approach producing the same value at lower cost. Another form of innovation would be to identify an entirely new form of customer value. Such *value innovation* would represent new business opportunities. This difficult form of innovation involves predicting how the market, customer purchasing criteria, technology, and costs will evolve and how these developments might interact to provide new opportunities for increased value. Value innovation would also promote a spirit of entrepreneurship.

PERFORMANCE OBJECTIVES

Performance objectives emerged from assessments of competitive position and environmental assumptions. These objectives were designed to improve Omicon's competitive position, exploit new opportunities, and increase sales and profits as measured by

- Income level
- Change in income (percentage)
- Net income
- Return on sales (percentage)
- Operating cash flow
- Total assets
- Return on assets (percentage)
- Market share (percentage)

THE ACTION PLAN

The action plan was designed to achieve the performance goals. This plan included the specific actions required, capital investment proposals, and strategic expense (budget) proposals.

One important budget consideration for Omicon was to properly allocate funds in order to maintain its well-established competitive position. Capital investments and the strategic budget also had to be sufficient to achieve the strategies that would ensure continued strategic advantage.

FIT WITH CORPORATE GOALS

The next step in Omicon's strategic planning was to assist operating management in translating the corporate goals into a specific set of performance objectives for the individual businesses. This process was carried out in the context of the company's major purpose and goals, which are to build a balanced and growing portfolio of profitable and growth-oriented businesses based on

- Use of high-quality human resources
- Superior product design and engineering
- Delivery of value and service to the customer
- Focused international activities
- Lowest costs consistent with desired quality

By keeping corporate goals in mind, strategic planners could direct the company's resources into business units that had the highest chances of success. Planners were also able to allocate resources in directions consistent with corporate goals. Figure 1.5 shows where Omicon used corporate goals to guide the strategic-planning process.

One basic question that Omicon asked was "Can the business units create value through product engineering?" Although one of Omicon's corporate goals is to create value through design and engineering, Omicon had to consider costs. The company also had to ask, "Which business units have the best chance of success?" Omicon has a large number of business units. For each, the chance of success is obviously higher if it receives the time and attention of top management and budgetary resources. Businesses that were strong and closely related to corporate goals were likely to enjoy greater allocations of time and resources. Weak businesses less compatible with corporate goals and businesses without great sales potential were likely to be allocated less time and fewer resources. Figure 1.6 shows how Omicon based its final action plan on an assessment of its strengths and weaknesses.

A SYSTEMS FRAMEWORK FOR STRATEGIC MANAGEMENT

Unlike general management, which is primarily concerned with internal operations, strategic management is equally concerned with the external and the internal environment. A key objective of strategic management is to match the organization's

FIGURE 1.5	Role of Corporate Goals in Strategy Questions Asked at Omicon

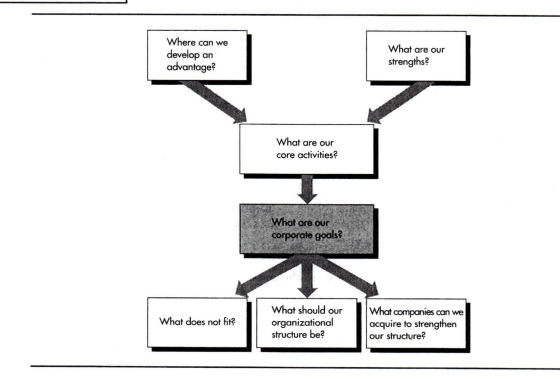

FIGURE 1.6	Action Plan Based on Omicon's Strengths and Weaknesses

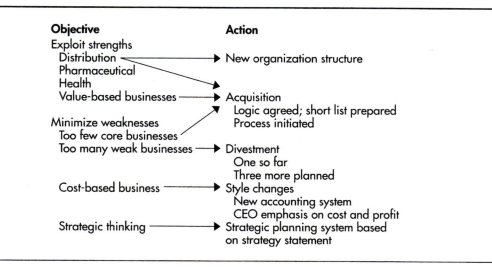

internal capability with the external opportunities and threats in order to formulate strategies that will achieve basic goals and maintain organizational values. Strategic management also enables the organization to adapt profitably to the vagaries of an unpredictable environment.

Any system of strategic management involves the five imperatives that C. West Churchman suggested in *The Systems Approach* (1968).

1. Identify the business's fundamental values and the goals and objectives that arise from them.
2. Assess the business's environment—forces outside the business itself that may be opportunities or threats.
3. Assess the business's resources and capabilities—those things within the control of the business, such as people, machinery, facilities, contracts, image, and goodwill—that can be allocated to achieve goals and objectives.
4. Identify or form the organization's components: (a) internal units that receive allocated resources and carry out the business's work and (b) an organizational structure that includes the units themselves and the relationships of authority, responsibility, and communication that they have with one another.
5. Develop the management and decision-making structure: the process used to allocate the business's resources to its components so as to realize goals and sustain values within the constraints of the environment.

THE STRATEGIC FOUR-FACTOR MODEL

The strategic four-factor model shown in Figure 1.7 illustrates a systems framework for strategic management. At the center of the model is embedded Churchman's first imperative: to identify the organization's values. Without knowledge of its values, an organization cannot develop its mission, goals, and objectives. Churchman's remaining four imperatives can be found within the four boxes in the circle. These imperatives are part of strategic planning, organizational structure, strategic control, and resource requirements. Outside the boxes are the forces and constraints that affect the four factors. The entire model shows how the organization's strategy must balance the demands imposed by external and internal forces, suit the overall functioning of the organization, and use resources in a manner that meets goals and satisfies values.

The arrows in Figure 1.7 show important interdependencies among the four factors of strategic management. Each of these factors links strategic management to the realities of the organization's internal or external environment, and each factor affects the other three directly or indirectly.

Strategic management, at the hub of the four-factor model, is the process of managing all four factors to achieve a strategy. The function of strategic management is to align the internal operation of the organization, including the allocation of human, physical, and financial resources, to achieve optimal interactions with the external environment. Strategic management is based on the organization's operational values—its fundamental beliefs about how the business should be conducted. The process of strategic management incorporates into strategies the types

---

| **FIGURE 1.7** | **Strategic Four-Factor Model** |

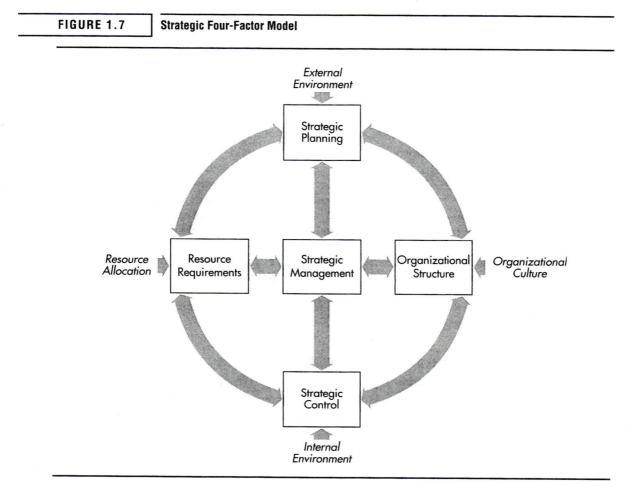

of values identified by Peters and Waterman (1982), Peters and Austin (1985), and Waterman (1987).

Strategic planning is the key link between strategic management and the organization's external environment. It is the one factor that requires a careful analysis of the external environment. Having identified external threats and opportunities, strategic planners analyze available resources and organizational strengths and weaknesses. The next step is to formulate alternative strategies that take advantage of external opportunities and internal strengths. Selected alternatives are then made into plans of action that have specific resource and organizational (structural and operational) requirements.

Resource requirements link strategic management to the organization's resources, including finances, facilities and equipment, land, access to information, goodwill, and personnel. Strategic planners have to determine resource requirements and their means of acquisition and allocation. In formulating strategic alternatives, planners must ask, "Can this strategy succeed, given the organization's available resources?" Various methods of analysis are used to assess resources and, if the strategy is feasible, to plan their allocation.

Organizational structure links strategic management to organizational realities. In formulating strategic alternatives, planners consider whether the organizational structure is suited to implementation of the strategy. Does the strategy fit the goals, objectives, labor pool, and operational procedures of the organization's units? Do the units have appropriate communication systems and procedures to monitor and control performance? Sometimes, as in the case of AHSC in the early 1980s, the organizational structure is changed to suit the strategy. Strategic planners must also determine whether the company's "unofficial" power structure, its culture, and the decision-making style of its managers will help or hinder implementation of a strategy. The style of leadership, operational values, and vision of top executives may be the most important factors determining whether an organization can succeed at implementation. Therefore, strategic planners must consider whether a strategy suits the leadership style of the organization's managers.

Strategic control is related to the implementation of a strategy. This factor links strategic management to the organization's internal environment because it involves evaluating how well the organization is implementing the strategy. Strategic control has two components, one internal and one external. The internal component involves monitoring resource allocation and organizational operations and suggesting changes needed to implement the strategy better. The external component involves measuring the strategy's success. Among the measures used are units sold, market share, gross sales, and profits. In a service-oriented business, the data might include customer evaluations of its service, such as the guest-comment cards read by Willard Marriott, Sr. Data related to specific performance goals may be as complex as the information analyzed by computerized management-by-objectives (MBO) systems. Strategic control is an ongoing process used to adapt implementation in response to (1) data about how well the strategy is doing and (2) changes in the internal or external environment.

In every chapter of this book, the strategic four-factor model and the strategy process model at the beginning of each chapter will be used to guide the reader through the phases involved in formulating an effective strategy for sustaining a competitive advantage.

ILLUSTRATIVE CASE: POLAROID

Our second illustrative case shows how a company in trouble can turn itself around with a careful strategic plan. In his article "Polaroid Struggles to Get Back in Focus," Peter W. Bernstein (1980) describes the stark evidence of trouble. In a warehouse near Cambridge, Massachusetts, where the company had its headquarters, piles of unsold Polavision sets were stored, testimony to the failure of Polaroid's highly touted instant-movie-camera system. Stockrooms from Santa Ana, California, to Paramus, New Jersey, overflowed with cartons of instant cameras and film. In Andover, Massachusetts, a vacant building that was once destined to house a film-assembly plant capable of producing millions of boxes of instant film stood empty, and then the building was sold. South of Boston, in Freetown, a building that was converted into a chemical factory went unused. After extensive layoffs, there were far fewer workers on the assembly lines of the camera production plants in Norwood than there had been in previous years.

A company in crisis, Polaroid paid heavily for past mistakes. Its miscalculation on Polavision was costly, and the company took a $68.5 million write-down, effectively reducing the inventory value of the sets to nothing. In addition, Polaroid misread the market for instant movie cameras; demand fell off just as the company was gearing up to produce more of them.

What went wrong at Polaroid? Why was top management unable to succeed at diversification? Was it a failure of leadership, or were the company's problems more deeply rooted? What could CEO William McCune have done? What information would he have needed to decide on a course of action? What sources of information could he have drawn on?

Polaroid's marketing of Polavision was at least as faulty as the technology. Consumers had been cool to home movies for a long time. Instead of coming to grips with Polavision's inherent marketing disadvantages, Polaroid chose to ignore them. Its strategy was simply to distribute this new product as broadly as it had the SX-70 five years earlier. But the public did not know what to make of the product, and Polaroid failed to devise a way for sales clerks to demonstrate its capabilities in a convincing and inviting way.

In the long run, how Polaroid solves its problems will depend on who is running the company. Edwin Land believed in developing the technology first, then selling consumers on its merits. "My motto," said Land, "is very personal and may not fit anyone else or any other company. It is: Don't do anything that someone else can do. Don't undertake a project unless it is manifestly important and nearly impossible. If it is manifestly important," Land continued, "then you don't have to worry about its significance. Since it's nearly impossible, you know that no one else is likely to be doing it, so if you do succeed, you will have created a whole new domain for yourself" (Chakrevarty, 1987). That was precisely what Edwin Land did with the Polaroid Corporation from his founding of the company in 1937 to his resignation as CEO in 1980. His motto proved successful until the late 1970s, when Land's blindness to the realities of the market led to severely declining sales.

In 1985 I. MacAllister Booth succeeded McCune as president and CEO, and McCune was made chairman of the board. Booth continued many of the policies that were in place in the early '80s. Booth paid off Polaroid's $130 million long-term debt and financed all growth out of cash flow. He assumed an accessible, open, managerial style, encouraging new ideas and inventions. He continued the change in marketing strategy by insisting that marketing was the key to increasing sales and therefore had to be more sophisticated. Accordingly, Booth used consumer research to develop the Spectra camera—the one that people really wanted.

In the style of Edwin Land, Polaroid has continued to invest in research and development, keeping a keen eye on marketability. In May of 1988, Polaroid revealed new technology that

POLAROID, CONTINUED

produces high-resolution black-and-white photographs from video images. The company also demonstrated a computer printer that produces color-photo images from television screens or computer screens. Although the payback for this type of long-range research is far in the future, Polaroid has worked toward financially firm ground today in order to invest in tomorrow. Polaroid has a strong brand identification, little long-term debt, and a stable film business. Management has combined Edwin Land's belief in undertaking nearly impossible projects of manifest importance with the profitability of well-researched markets. (In strategic terminology, Land subscribed to a highly differentiated strategy that provided a unique capability and a sustainable competitive advantage.)

The strategic planning of the '80s seems to be paying off for Polaroid. Shoring up its profitability for the '90s, Polaroid won the largest patent infringement case in history against Kodak. After a 15-year legal battle, Polaroid forced Kodak to withdraw all its instant photography products (Weber, 1991). Yet in spite of its $925 million award from Kodak, shareholders are expressing dismay at the stock selling for $32 per share in 1992 compared with an offer of $45 per share in 1989 from Disney's Shamrock Holdings, Inc. (Alster, 1992). MacAllister Booth will have to look for other areas in which to expand beyond instant photography. The stockholders are not happy with the flat earnings that would make new-product development possible. To address these concerns, Booth is focusing on electronic scanners and cameras for Citicorp's photo credit cards. In the long run he hopes to move into the "imaging" business for medical equipment, slides, computer graphics, and digitized photos for computer storage. The Helios medical imaging system promises $100 million in sales in 1994. But even after 12 years of research on electronic image sensors, Polaroid still does not have a strategy for successfully introducing the product.

SUMMARY

A number of basic concepts were introduced in this first chapter. Strategic management is based on "thinking strategically," a continuous process that involves the interaction of every major strategic decision that is made. The AHSC case showed the vital link between strategic analysis and the key elements of strategy. A methodological approach to strategy formulation is considered important because it enables planners to avoid inconsistency, misallocation of resources, hazy focus, and the rigidity of blindly following policy. A methodological approach does not preclude creativity; rather, it ensures that appropriate data are employed in the formulation of a strategy that creates value.

A systems framework helps tie together the elements of strategy and identifies the four key forces impinging on the firm. The concept of "total value management" was described as the counterpart to "total quality management." The importance of an appropriate strategic focus, in terms of organizational values, was illustrated. We also saw how strategic failures often result from inappropriate strategy formulation or focus. An actual strategic plan followed at Omicon, a major international company, demonstrating the use of a methodological approach in preparing a strategic plan.

REFERENCES AND SUGGESTIONS FOR FURTHER READING

A troubled Polaroid is tearing down the house that Land built. 1985. *Business Week,* April 29, p. 51.

Alster, Norm. 1992. Double exposure. *Forbes,* September 14, pp. 408–410.

American Hospital Supply Corporation, *1987 Annual Report.*

American Hospital Supply. 1985. Let your customers work for you. *Executive Technology,* November, p. 47.

Auletta, Ken. 1983. A certain poetry. *The New Yorker,* June 6.

Barney, Jay B. 1986. Organization culture: Can it be a source of sustainable competitive advantage? *Academy of Management Review,* no. 11, pp. 656–665.

Bergsman, Ennius E. 1989. Managing value: The new corporate strategy. *The McKinsey Quarterly,* Winter, pp. 57–72.

Bernstein, Peter W. 1980. Polaroid struggles to get back into focus. *Fortune,* April 7.

Boston Consulting Group. 1991. Strategic platforms. *BCG Conference for Chief Executives,* Paris, January.

Chakrevarty, Subrata N. 1987. The vindication of Edwin Land. *Forbes,* May 4, p. 83.

Churchman, C. West. 1968. The systems approach. New York: Delacorte Press.

Clausing, Don and John R. Hauser. 1988. The house of quality. *Harvard Business Review,* May–June, pp. 63–73.

Drucker, Peter F. 1973. *Management: Tasks, responsibilities, practices.* New York: Harper & Row.

Dumaine, Brian. 1991. Earning more by moving faster. *Fortune,* October 7, pp. 89–90, 94.

Forker, Laura B. 1991. Quality: American, Japanese and Soviet perspectives. *Academy of Management Executive,* 5, no. 4, pp. 63–74.

Forrester, Jay W. 1961. *Industrial dynamics.* Cambridge, Mass.: M.I.T. Press.

G.E. keeps those ideas coming. 1991. *Fortune,* August 12.

Grant, Robert M. 1991. The resource-based theory of competitive advantage: Implications for strategy formulation. *California Management Review,* Spring.

Grover, Ronald and Keith H. Hammonds. 1988. Maybe I'll raid you—and maybe I won't. *Business Week,* September 5, p. 25.

Hamel, Gary, Yves Doz, and C. K. Prahalad. 1989. Collaborate with your competitors and win. *Harvard Business Review,* January–February, pp. 133–139.

Hammonds, Keith H. and Gail DeGeorge. 1991. Where did they go wrong? *Business Week,* October 25, p. 34.

Hamson, Ned. 1988. Visions of excellence and quality. *Forbes,* April 4, pp. 94–103.

Hartley, Robert F. 1983. *Management mistakes.* Columbus, Ohio: Grid Publishing.

Hauser, John R. and Don Clausing. 1988. The house of quality. *The Harvard Business Review,* May–June.

Heltzer, B. 1987. How Polaroid flashed back. *Fortune.* February 16, p. 72.

Hof, Robert D. 1992. Inside Intel: It's moving at double-time to head off competitors. *Business Week,* June 1, pp. 86–94.

Howard, Robert. 1990. Values make the company: An interview with Robert Haas. *Harvard Business Review,* September–October, pp. 133–144.

Hunsicker, F. Quincy. 1980. The malaise of strategic planning. *Management Review,* March.

Imai, Masaaki. 1989. *Kaizen, the key to Japan's competitive success.* New York: Random House.

Is Polaroid playing to a market that just isn't there? 1986. *Business Week,* April 7, p. 82.

Johnston, Russell and Paul R. Lawrence. 1988. Beyond vertical integration—The rise of the value-adding partnership. *Harvard Business Review,* July–August, pp. 94–101.

Jones, Dorothy E. 1985. Baxter Travenol calls it quits—and others may follow. *Business Week,* February 11, p. 42.

Katz, Robert L. 1970. *Management of the total enterprise.* Englewood Cliffs, N.J.: Prentice-Hall.

Lamb, Robert. 1987. *Running American business.* New York: Basic Books.

Merrills, Roy. 1989. How Northern Telecom competes on time. *Harvard Business Review,* July–August, pp. 108–114.

Nussbaum, Bruce, Otis Port, Rich Brandt, Teresa Carson, Karen Wolman, and Jonathan Kapstein. 1988. Smart design. Quality is new style. *Business Week,* April 11, pp. 102–117. In the same issue, see Paul Angiolillo, Ease and economy in the lab, p. 104; Katherine M. Hafner, Whimsy goes mainstream, p. 105; Katherine M. Hafner, Taking ideas from plant to plant, p. 106; and Joan Hamilton, Gray expectations: A new force in design, p. 108.

O'Toole, James. 1985. *Vanguard management.* Garden City, N.Y.: Doubleday.

Ohmae, Kenichi. 1988. Getting back to strategy. *Harvard Business Review,* November–December, pp. 149–156.

Ohmae, Kenichi. 1982. *The mind of the strategist.* New York: McGraw-Hill.

Pepsi keeps on going after number 1. 1991. *Fortune,* March 11.

Peters, Thomas J. and Nancy Austin. 1985. *A passion for excellence.* New York: Random House.

Peters, Thomas J. and Robert H. Waterman. 1982. *In search of excellence.* New York: Random House.

Pitta, Julie. 1992. Cleanliness is next to competitiveness. *Forbes*, February 17, p. 134.

Polaroid can't get its future in focus, 1983. *Business Week*, April 4.

Polaroid sharpens its focus on the marketplace, 1986. *Business Week*, February 13, p. 132.

Polaroid vs. Kodak: The decisive round, 1986. *Business Week*, January 13, p. 37.

Polaroid's Spectra may be losing its flash, 1987. *Business Week*, June 29, p. 31.

Popplewell, Barry and Alan Wildsmith. 1990. How to gain company-wide commitment to total quality. Gower Publishing Group.

Port, Otis. 1991. Dueling pioneers. *Business Week*, Quality Issue, p. 17.

Port, Otis and John Carey. 1991. The quality imperative. *Business Week*, Quality Issue, pp. 7–17. In the same issue, see Otis Port and John Carey, Quality: A field with roots that go back to the farm, p. 15.

Power, Christopher, Walecia Konrad, Alice Z. Cuneo, and James B. Treece. 1991. Value marketing. *Business Week*, November 11, pp. 132–140. In the same issue, see Christopher Power, Card wars: My value is bigger than your value, p. 138, and Christopher Power, Sears catches the value bug, p. 140.

Prahalad, C. K. and Gary Hamel. 1990. The core competence of the corporation. *Harvard Business Review*, May–June, pp. 79–91.

Quinn, James Brian. 1980. *Strategies for change. Logical incrementalism*. Homewood, Ill.: Irwin.

Rose, Frank. 1991. Now quality means service too. *Fortune*, April 22, pp. 97–110.

Rumelt, Richard P. 1974. *Strategy, structure and economic performance*. Cambridge, Mass.: Harvard Business School.

Rummler, Geary A. and Alan P. Brache. 1990. *Improving performance. How to manage the white space on the organization chart*. San Francisco: Oxford Press.

Schein, Lawrence. 1990. The road to total quality. *The Conference Board Bulletin*.

Siler, Julia Flynn. 1990. Will another round of surgery help Baxter? *Business Week*, April 30, p. 92.

Siler, Julia Flynn, David Greising, and Tim Smart. 1991. The case against Baxter International. *Business Week*, October 7, pp. 106–115.

Skousen, Mark. 1991. Roaches outlive elephants. *Forbes*, August 19, pp. 72–74.

Snow, Charles C. and Lawrence G. Hrebiniak. 1980. Strategy, distinctive competence, and organization performance. *Administrative Science Quarterly* 25, pp. 317–336.

Stalk, George, Jr. 1988. Time—The next source of competitive advantage. *Harvard Business Review*, July–August, pp. 41–51.

Stalk, George, Jr. and Thomas M. Hout. 1990. *Competing against time*. New York: The Free Press.

Stata, Ray. 1989. Organization learning—The key to management innovation. *Sloan Management Review* 36, Spring, p. 63.

Stevenson, Howard H. 1976. Defining corporate strengths and weaknesses. *Sloan Management Review*, Spring, pp. 51–68.

Sullivan, L. P. 1986. Quality function deployment. *Quality Progress*, June.

Teitelbaum, Richard S. 1992. Topps Co.: Timeliness is everything. *Fortune*, April 20, p. 120.

The Polaroid promise, 1987. *Forbes*, February 9, p. 8.

Thomas, Phillip R. 1990. *Competitiveness through total cycle time*. New York: McGraw-Hill.

Thomas, Rich. 1990. Spiraling out of control. *Newsweek*, September, pp. 47–48.

Thorbeck, John. 1991. The turnaround value of values. *Harvard Business Review*, January–February, pp. 52–62.

Treece, James B., Karen Lowry Miller, and Richard A. Melcher. 1992. Surprise! Ford and Mazda have built a strong team. Here's how. *Business Week*, February 10, pp. 102–107. In the same issue, see Karen Lowry Miller and James B. Treece, GM and Isuzu a waste of synergy, p. 107.

Waterman, Robert H. 1987. *The renewal factor*. New York: Bantam Books.

Waterman, Robert H. 1984. Who said excellence was forever? *Business Week*, November 26, p. 9.

Weber, Jonathan. 1991. Kodak settles Polaroid case for $925 million. *Los Angeles Times*, July 16, p. D3.

Who's excellent now? 1984. *Business Week*, November 5, pp. 76–78.

Wilke, John. 1988. Are sharks circling Polaroid? *Boston Globe*, June 7, p. 43.

Willoughby, Jack. 1985. Excellence isn't enough. *Forbes*, June 17, pp. 104–105.

CHAPTER TWO

Strategic Analysis

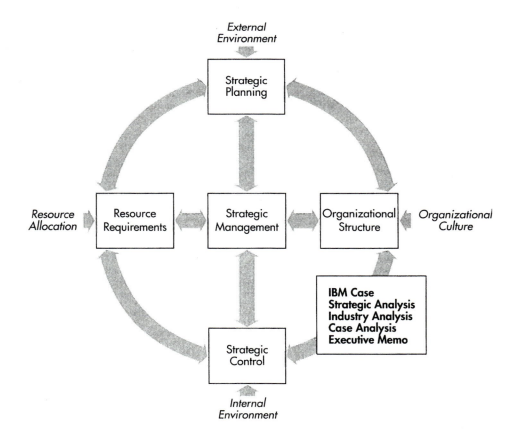

Chapter 1 A Framework for Strategic Management	**Chapter 2** Strategic Analysis	**Chapter 3** Strategic Visioning, Goals, Ethics, and Social Responsibility	**Chapter 4** The Competitive Environment	**Chapter 5** Capability-based Strategy	**Chapter 6** Market Dynamics and Sustainable Competitive Advantage
How to approach strategic management	Application of strategic analysis	Understanding vision, values, ethics	Coping with competitive forces, stakeholders	Assessing company capability, timeliness, quality	Determining trends, gap analysis, and market dynamics

Chapter 7 Strategy in a Global Environment	**Chapter 8** Financial Planning and Competitive-Cost Analysis	**Chapter 9** Entrepreneurship, Mergers and Acquisitions, Restructuring, and the Service Sector	**Chapter 10** Leadership Factor in Strategy and Implementing Strategic Change	**Chapter 11** Information Technology and Future Directions in Strategy
Assessing global trade, foreign markets, monetary exchange	Preparing a financial plan and competitive-cost analysis	Importance of small business, entrepreneurs, restructuring	Strategy implementation, leadership, culture	Information technology, trends, new management

INTRODUCTION

What business is a company in? Where should it be one, five, or ten years from now? How can it get there? We noted in Chapter 1 that part of the answer to these questions can be found in the values of the organization and of the executives who lead it. Today's business environment is characterized by rapidly advancing technology, keen competition within a world economy, increased government intervention, and vocal, informed stockholders. A major challenge facing executives is knowing how to introduce strategic change. To deal with this challenge an executive needs vision, creativity, flexibility, and entrepreneurship—in short, strategic thinking.

Although it is true that strategic management requires creativity, a framework for developing and executing strategy is also vital. Companies with multiple strategic thrusts, and especially companies that are multinational in scope, can no longer be managed by intuition. It is rare to find a major corporation anywhere in the world that does not have some form of systematic planning. The executive needs ways and means to deal with complex operations and to empower the organization to carry out a strategic plan.

What are the key elements of a strategic plan, and what must be done to ensure its success?

The strategic plan often starts with the gleam in the founder's eye—a vision of what might be achieved. Sometimes a formal document is prepared to encourage investment by venture capitalists. More typically, the chief executive officer's (CEO's) guiding principles clear the way through the maze of problems confronted during start-up. Once the company has a marketable product, process, or service, the difficulties that arise are typically operational. The strategy of a startup company is simple: survive and grow so as to achieve a position of stability. From that position, the company may be acquired, merge with other companies, or aggressively pursue its own growth. After a company has reached a stable point, formal strategic planning becomes essential.

For the larger or more mature organization, strategic planning is necessary for continued growth and profits. All organizations—like all products, industries, technologies, communities, and even nations—experience periods of growth and intervals of decline that may be followed by revitalization. Management itself goes through cycles as new members are brought in, mergers or acquisitions occur, or competitors take away market share. These inevitable changes demand strategic planning.

The problem with formal strategic-planning systems is that they tend to become ends in themselves as they are institutionalized within the firm. When too much effort is focused on meticulously developing "optimal" strategies rather than on challenging the assumptions on which these strategies are based, the mechanics of preparing the plan quickly overshadow the substance of a strategy. In a sense, the company is paralyzed by its own strategic-planning process. A rigid strategic plan can lead to misdirection, inefficiency, and waste by superimposing artificial guidelines and rules that prevent managers from making needed changes.

The illustrative case that follows is reprinted from a 1991 issue of *Fortune* magazine. It deals with John Akers's attempt to reinvent IBM and, by restructuring the organization, make it more competitive. A contrasting example was described in Chapter 1, where we saw the American Hospital Supply Corporation follow all the right strategies, but it became complacent and did not aggressively pursue a growth plan, and this error led to the company's acquisition by Baxter Travenol. These two cases illustrate that strategy is an ongoing process. When implemented properly it leads to success, whereas improper implementation spells poor performance or decline.

A number of updates for the IBM case are shown on pages 65 and 67. The latest change occurred in March of 1993. IBM's board announced that Louis Gerstner, Jr., an outsider, would be the next chairman and CEO. At an interview after the announcement, Gerstner commented, "The first thing I want to know is what is IBM's strategy and how does it relate to the competitive environment and customer needs." He went on to say, "Over the next few months, we will look at every single business with a no-holds-barred approach" (Scheier, 1993). Gerstner has a reputation for restructuring businesses and believes strongly in decentralization. As an outsider, he will take a fresh look at the problems confronting IBM. Based on his past experience, Gerstner believes in setting overall direction but allowing the division heads to formulate their own strategy. His principal view is that, like GE, IBM should be in those businesses where they are number one or two in terms of market share. John Akers was not able to turn IBM around—will Gerstner be able to do the job?

ILLUSTRATIVE CASE: CAN JOHN AKERS SAVE IBM?

To understand fully just what a disaster IBM has been, and just how blind its own management was to the depth of its problems, step back to a moment in late 1986. IBM was more than a year past a boom period and struggling. Revenue growth was miserable, earnings growth was nonexistent, and IBM's stock, then $125 a share, had lost nearly $24 billion in market value from a peak of $99 billion just seven months earlier. In an interview with *Fortune*, Chairman John F. Akers nonetheless exhibited gritty confidence: Four or five years from now, he asserted, people will look back and see that the company's performance has been superlative.

It is now 4½ years later. The stock was recently just below $100, which means another $18 billion in market capitalization has been shredded into megabits. IBM's total revenues have dragged, rising over the past five years at an average annual rate of only 6.6% against 13.4% for the data-processing industry as a whole. In unhappy concert, the company's worldwide market share has dropped from 30% to 21%. Each percentage point lost represents $3 billion in annual sales.

IBM's profits, though still the biggest of any company's in the world, have been roughed up as well. In 1990 the company made $6 billion on $69 billion in revenues and, mindful of four sour years just passed, bravely classed that as a "good" year. But the $6 billion was an embarrassing 10% less than IBM made in 1984 on only $46 billion of revenue. Then, IBM had a star return on shareholders' equity: 24.9%. For 1990 the figure was a mediocre 14.1%. Then, IBM perennially headed *Fortune*'s list of the most-admired U.S. corporations. In the most recent list, it was No. 32.

So far, 1991 has produced two shocks— IBM's last-minute disclosures in both the first and second quarters that it would earn much less than security analysts were estimating. The litany of continuing bad news has been only partly recession related: Price wars in the computer industry have grabbed the news and held it.

Unless IBM snaps back strongly in the last half, it will make less this year in regular profits (that is, not counting a special charge taken in the first quarter for retiree health benefits) than it did a decade ago, when it earned $3.3 billion. In short, this onetime symbol of corporate might—this national asset, by everybody's description—has had a serious industrial accident.

How did IBM get into this unprecedented trouble? Can John Akers pick up the pieces? Sitting in his Armonk, New York, office, his jacket off, Akers addressed those questions in a wide-ranging, more than an hour long interview with *Fortune*, his first with the press since the storm of 1991 broke. In his comments, Akers displayed a mixture of deep disappointment, resolve, and, in brief moments, a jarring insouciance. Asked just what went wrong—just why his forecast of superlativeness was so far off the mark—he replied with a stunner: "I don't think anything went wrong." Then why, one might reasonably ask, did he tell his managers in May that IBM was "in crisis," a characterization made in private and quickly leaked to the press? And, if IBM stock has lost $42 billion in value since 1986, just how far would it have fallen if something really had gone wrong?

Akers subsequently made clear that he meant only to emphasize that IBM is caught up in an industry moving so fast and changing so much that nobody in it can adjust quickly enough. But he conceded that no outside force was responsible for IBM's loss of market share. That could be laid, he said, first to the fact that IBM is so heavily in hardware—from which it gets 60% of its revenues—rather than software and services, the faster-growing parts of the industry. "And No. 2," he said forthrightly, "we didn't execute as well as we should have."

In fact the Big Blue machine crumpled in both products and marketing and left the company, in the words of a midlevel executive, "fighting for its life." The prognosis is uncertain, though clearly it includes good news and bad. After a total remake, the product line is now

CAN JOHN AKERS SAVE IBM?, CONTINUED

much improved; Akers even calls it "sparkling." But marketing is still flawed, and that failing raises a momentous question as to how successfully IBM will perform even after the economy picks up again.

Unsure of the answer himself, Akers has a strategy for both now and then. Girding for the worst, though he expects better than that, he is pushing to cut IBM's expenses to where the company can tolerate revenue growth that barely crawls. Trying to remix the business, he is striving for growth in software, services, and what's called OEM—original equipment manufacturing, meaning production by IBM of its hardware for resale under another company's name. At the same time, in what amounts to a declaration of war on IBM's competitors, he says, "We're going to ship our spiffy product, and we're going to price it to maintain or gain market share."

In an industry already gone kamikaze on prices, that strategy may produce some not-so-spiffy profits. But Akers plainly has his back up about market share. He indicated as much repeatedly in the now-famous remarks he made to his managers in May. The leaked notes of his talk reveal Akers as angry, frustrated, and particularly aghast at the failure of his marketing strategies. Much of his optimism in 1986 sprang from his ongoing drive to increase the size of IBM's sales force and thereby get the company into closer touch with its customers. The U.S. marketing force grew 25%, from 20,000 people to 25,000. But for all this effort, U.S. revenues rose less than 7% over four years, from $25.4 billion to $27.1 billion. "Where's my return for the extra 5,000 people?" Akers demanded, in tones that caused the notetaker to escalate to capital letters, "Where's the beef? What the hell are you doing for *me*?"

That "me" resonates for special reasons. This is a man keenly aware that his time as boss is speeding by fast. No, that does not mean he is about to get fired or, as one particular rumor has it, that Ross Perot will be called in to replace him. IBM's directors appear to be solidly behind Akers. Says one of them, Thomas S. Murphy, chairman of Capital Cities/ABC: "John is doing all the right things. The situation is just incredibly difficult."

Because IBM executives are required to retire at 60, Akers, now 56, must step down by January 1995. He will then have been in office ten years. Unless matters improve drastically, the Akers era is going to be remembered, fairly or unfairly, as the period in which IBM dissipated its greatness. For this man with a lifetime of accomplishment behind him—as a Navy flier, as a standout IBM salesman, as a junior executive slated early for glory—that would be a bitter outcome. He told *Fortune* as much in 1986: "There have only been six chief executives of IBM. I hope that when my tour is over, people will look back and say, 'He deserved to be among them.'"

The scorecard at tour's end, as now, will be complex. In justice to Akers, appraisals of his tenure should take into account the complicity of his immediate predecessors as CEO, Frank T. Cary and John R. Opel, who handed him a fat, overconfident company. Any reckoning must also acknowledge, as Akers intimates, the chaos of today's computer industry. At its top are a few large, vertically integrated, globally spread companies, still very much headed by IBM. Its revenues are five times those of either Hewlett-Packard or Digital Equipment, the next-biggest U.S. companies, and more than twice those of the foreign leader, Fujitsu (*Fortune*, June 1). One size down is the latecomer crowd—such specialty companies as Apple, Compaq, and Sun Microsystems. All told, the computer and office products segment of the Fortune 500 includes 22 companies today, up from 15 ten years ago.

Layered further below is the industry's seething substructure, which by IBM's count includes a mammoth 50,000 competitors. Most of these are niche players. Many are startups, apt to be driving compulsively for revenues so they can cash in by selling out. In companies of all sizes, corporate alliances are so common that it's

CAN JOHN AKERS SAVE IBM?, CONTINUED

tough to keep straight who's competing, collaborating, or both. "We've all learned how to drink coffee together at ten and beat each other's brains out at two," Akers said in June, his envoys fresh from a strudelfest with archrival Apple at which they talked possible deals.

In between those kaffeeklatsches, the industry drums out technological advances with bewildering speed, constantly improving price–performance ratios. Price wars have turned the market increasingly into a spectacle of commodity economics. Allen J. Krowe, a former IBM executive who is now a senior vice president at Texaco, shakes his head in wonderment: "The industry has more Ph.D.s per square foot than any other. Yet its pricing calls to mind soybeans and sowbellies."

Amid this tumult, a revenue-hungry IBM is ever more flexible about how it conducts business. Credit Akers for that. Yet in a generally disaggregated world, IBM is still an asset-heavy, people-laden, bureaucracy-ridden aggregate. Another starkly important fact: Fortress IBM has patently lost its moat—its historical ability to get the business just because it is IBM, that nice, safe, fuzzy-blanket choice. Publications, including this one, have been saying for many years that the moat was drying up. Now the proof of the drought is there for all to see in IBM's deteriorated, and perhaps still deteriorating, financial results. IBM's executives themselves do not deny that the moat is gone.

But that does not mean they call the castle lost. President Jack D. Kuehler, 58, says everything is on the table to be reevaluated. "No company is going to survive in tomorrow's global marketplace by virtue of its history," he explains. Wouldn't past IBM managements have said the same? Sounding very much like a man recently deprived of a moat, he replies, "Ten years ago, I wouldn't have said it."

"Survive" is a serious word—but at least for the moment we are not talking survival with a capital S. Instead, IBM equates survival with a certain financial standard of living, a kind of

compromise between the high style it once took for granted and the mediocrity it has lately been reduced to. Seven years ago, top management was confidently predicting that return on equity would continue to average above 20%. Today the goal is down to 18%. That rate, say IBM executives, will allow the company, after paying dividends, to meet all its capital needs and keep pace with an industry whose revenues it expects to grow annually at 7% to 10%. That range is an obvious comedown from the average of 13.4% recorded between 1985 and 1990. Growth came in lower as those years passed, to 5% in 1989 and 10% in 1990, and IBM has downsized its expectations accordingly.

It has also wrenched its annual growth in costs—what Akers calls "the expense machine"—down to under 10% and is clawing for 6%. From its top employment of 405,500 in 1985, the company has cut back 31,700 and has special offers on the table right now that could bring the total trimmed to 50,000. Among the departures this year are the 4,000 employees of the division making keyboards, typewriters, printers, and supplies, 90% of which was sold in March for $1.5 billion to the leveraged-buyout firm of Clayton & Dubilier. Inside IBM, many people opposed that move. But these products earned poorly, in large part because they got scant attention from IBM's computer-minded sales force. So Akers stepped up to the hard decision to sell.

When a division like that departs, the overhead that was allocated to it stays around. Severing thousands of employees also costs money. But Frank A. Metz Jr., senior vice president for finance, reckons that IBM has now built tremendous amounts of operating leverage into the business—that is, it has pared expenses to the point where a major portion of every incremental revenue dollar will come straight to the bottom line. That's fine if there happen to be any incremental dollars, which there certainly haven't been in the first half of 1991. "Shame on us," admits Metz. "We haven't demonstrated we can

CAN JOHN AKERS SAVE IBM?, CONTINUED

take advantage of the operating leverage that's there."

Nor has the company demonstrated that it spends investment dollars wisely. IBM's ability to do that matters enormously because its outlays are so huge. The puzzle for outsiders, who mainly see only the macro results, is to figure out whether the company is getting much for its vast efforts. Here the evidence is not reassuring. One miss, at least so far: IBM's purchase over the past five years of $6 billion of its own stock, at prices averaging $119 a share.

The much larger investment dollars at issue are those going into capital projects and research, development, and engineering. Last year outlays of this sort ran to a full $14.5 billion: capital expenditures of $6.1 billion, investment in software of $1.9 billion, and $6.5 billion for R&D and engineering. Over the past decade the total for these three kinds of expenditure was an immense $101 billion—about four times what the Reagan and Bush Administrations have spent on Star Wars.

Since IBM's return on equity has skidded, a presumptive case can be made that this wad, or major parts of it, has been ill spent. But the case is not provable. There is no way of determining, first, what the returns would have been had the money not been spent nor, second, how returns may benefit in the future because it was. One thing is certain, though: A delayed return—a bird in the bush—does not have the value of a revenue-generating bird in the hand.

The greatest perplexities about IBM's investments concern its huge spending on semiconductors. IBM is the largest manufacturer of chips in the world, though it produces only for itself, not for outside sale. The company searches unceasingly for technological breakthroughs. At its East Fishkill, New York, plant, it has recently sunk undisclosed but clearly colossal sums into an experimental manufacturing technology known as X-ray lithography, which may or may not prove out. In this process, a specially engineered cyclotron spins out the X-rays that engrave the

chips. There is only one other machine with similar capabilities in the U.S., owned by the government. In the semiconductor stronghold of Japan, Metz notes, there are 13 such cyclotrons. So IBM is extraordinarily proud of its machine.

But do these chip investments make economic sense? Jack Kuehler, who rose to the president's job through the technology side of the business, strongly defends the outlays as essential if IBM is to stay on the leading edge of chip technology and have recurring opportunities to be first in the market with "the best box." Buying chips from outsiders, he says, requires that these suppliers be clued in to IBM's product plans—an information handoff the company would prefer to avoid.

All this would sound more persuasive were it not that IBM buys chips by the carload from outside vendors for its low-end products all the time—as it is doing, for example, with its brand-new laptop computer, which uses an Intel microprocessor. On the other hand, IBM made a "best box" kind of announcement in June, when it said it was beginning production of new 16-megabit chips that it expects to have installed in its mainframe computers by next spring. That should give IBM a lead of perhaps six months—but no more than that—over several Japanese and South Korean companies that are also developing this next-generation technology.

An IBM announcement like that gladdens Akers's heart. True, he acknowledges the enormous cost of supporting IBM's semiconductor establishment. The tariff, in fact, has induced him to sign up both Siemens and Motorola as partners in bearing parts of the load. He also says that IBM's R&D budget is under a lot of pressure these days: "If you were to wander around our laboratories, you would find people waving their arms, saying, 'My God, what's going on around here?' I think that's healthy."

Even so, he argues that it is a huge plus for IBM to be the master of its own destiny in chip manufacture. He says he does not want to depend on the technology of his competitors,

CAN JOHN AKERS SAVE IBM?, CONTINUED

who are mainly Japanese. His thinking brings to mind the old Cold War days of massive deterrence. Just as skeptics sometimes questioned the merits of that military doctrine, so investors today sometimes scratch their heads about IBM's do-it-yourself approach. Lewis A. Sanders is president of Sanford C. Bernstein & Co., a money manager that is a huge, war-weary, and yet still optimistic holder of IBM stock. He once questioned the strategic advantages of IBM's approach as perhaps too nebulous, but now inclines to the company's view. In any case, those who choose to buy IBM stock should recognize that they are casting their lot with a company determined to carry the U.S. flag in chip technology.

Former IBM executive Allen Krowe seems to believe that some tough thinking about investments is a key to IBM's recovery. Asked what scenario might lift the company once again to a high return on equity, he focuses first on the thought that IBM needs to be "very prudent and very demanding" in the way R&D and engineering funds are spent to be sure each dollar provides a potential return. That indeed sounds like a reasonable top priority.

A related question about IBM's investments has to do with the company's delays and miscues in getting products to market. The new laptop, a major example, is the successor to two past failures. Also in the queue of much-delayed projects is OfficeVision, a software system that would help computer users network their machines. Then there are workstations—sophisticated, desktop computers for technical use. In this sector, such competitors as Sun and Digital Equipment leaped off to a lead while IBM just sort of hung around. Only last year did IBM finally come out with its own hot ticket, the RISC System/6000.

RISC, the prevailing technology for workstations today, stands for reduced instruction-set computing. Its history helps explain why IBM has struck out in revenue growth. The RISC semiconductor was an IBM baby, born in its Yorktown Heights, New York, lab in 1974. But internal arguments over how, and even whether, the chip should be used kept IBM fiddling while Sun and other companies decisively powered ahead. IBM finally put a RISC workstation on the market in 1985, but it was technologically a half-step behind the competition, says Kuehler, and did poorly. Andrew Heller, an IBM executive who had long led the development of workstations, later resigned with a blast at IBM's slow-moving culture: "Technology is like fish. The longer it stays on the shelf, the less desirable it becomes."

By the time IBM got its good product, the RS/6000, to market in 1990, the industry's annual sales of workstations were up to $7.5 billion and growing 40% a year. Playing a respectable game of catch-up, IBM snagged 7% of the 1990 total. But Sun got more than four times that much.

Says Kuehler of the workstation experience: "We just didn't really thoughtfully define the opportunity and make it happen in an efficient manner." Do insiders say IBM blew it? "Oh, yes. Oh, yes." But he notes that the RISC technology and the workstation market came along at a time when IBM wasn't listening much to its customers about the products they needed, something it is working to do in the Akers era. So Kuehler hopes that if IBM were to produce another RISC-like baby today, it would do a better job of bringing it up.

The RS/6000 is at least a solid component of what IBM has recently been describing as "the strongest lineup of products and services in our history." There is a certain pitifulness to the claim, given that this vaunted collection is producing so little in revenues and profits. But many outsiders agree with the company's contention—among them Naomi Seligman, co-director of the Research Board, whose 40 members are the management information chiefs at such huge computer buyers as American Airlines, State Farm, and Du Pont. Because of the potentates she represents, Seligman gets inside looks at what the major computer chefs have cooking. Four years

CAN JOHN AKERS SAVE IBM?, CONTINUED

ago, when *Fortune* interviewed her for an IBM article, she was not impressed with the company's product line. Today she thinks IBM has finally muscled a good array into place and also has important technologies in the wings.

Kuehler says that IBM's efforts to speed the development of products has it working simultaneously on three different generations of mainframes. IBM's more recent offerings include the first generation of those mainframes, called ES/9000, introduced last September, and a midrange or minicomputer, the AS/400. This machine got to the market later than it was needed, in 1988, but last year accounted for no less than $14 billion, or one-fifth, of IBM's revenues. About two-thirds of that business came from Europe, which has a big population of smallish businesses that have a particular need for minis.

The wobbler in IBM's wares is its personal computers, which sell in a soybean-and-sowbelly, price-driven market. They lack distinctive qualities that might allow them to command the premium prices IBM keeps trying to get. The company's interest in securing certain of Apple's technologies reflects its continuing search for an edge. Behind the scenes, also, Kuehler has focused IBM's formidable technological prowess on this underachiever by directing the heads of some key IBM labs around the country to make quarterly visits to Boca Raton, IBM's PC hub. Like smoke-eaters converging on the oil well fires in Kuwait, IBM specialists are flying in from the kingdoms of disk drives, AS/400s, mainframes, and basic research. Kuehler asks them all one question: "What is your contribution to the personal computer line?"

The extraordinary attention focused on the PC reflects, first, IBM's wish to hold its ground in every corner of the industry and, second, its awareness that a lot of the world sees a future in which little boxes, packed with cheap chips supplying evergrowing amounts of computing power, largely supplant the big, high-margin boxes that are IBM's pride. Long-held doubts about the viability of the mainframe business pushed James H. Gipson of Pacific Financial

Research, a well-regarded money manager, into writing a 1989 letter to his clients headed "Why We Don't Own IBM." Similar misgivings even seem to have invaded the households of key IBMers. Nicholas Donofrio, 45, recently told his daughter, Nicole, that he was moving from head of IBM's workstations division to head of mainframes. Said Nicole: "Dad, that seems like going from a quarter horse to a dinosaur."

Donofrio says he'd substitute Clydesdales for dinosaurs, but the statistics back up Nicole. According to estimates compiled by Gartner & Co., the industry's mainframe revenues grew at an annual rate of 8.9% from 1985 through 1990, against 21% for the desktop category that includes PCs and garden-variety workstations. What does the future hold for mainframes? An obvious downward pull is the ever-expanding ability of small computers to handle large, sophisticated jobs once considered big-box property, such as payrolls. Another is the fact that much of the computer industry's output goes to the service sector of the economy, where banks, insurance companies, and airlines, for example, are all feeling a pinch on the bottom line. Stephen S. Roach, senior economist at Morgan Stanley, estimates that about 85% of the installed base of computers belongs to service companies. Many of them, he thinks, have unused mainframe capacity.

The countervailing arguments include, not surprisingly, IBM's own view that the proliferation of desktop machines will create a continuing need for mainframes to serve up data and manage corporate networks. IBM wins some support from James Fischer of Andersen Consulting, which gets much of its $1.9 billion in revenues from advising corporations on their computer systems. Says Fischer: "As long as you have corporations controlled centrally, you're going to have a computing structure that is also centralized. And that is one of the forces that will not let the mainframe die."

Emphatic backing for these positions appeared recently in "The Future of the Mainframe Industry," a lengthy report by two

CAN JOHN AKERS SAVE IBM?, CONTINUED

Bernstein analysts, Philip Rueppel and Don Young (who has since gone to Shearson Lehman). Tracking the demand for mainframe computing power over the past five years, the analysts concluded that installed mainframe MIPS—millions of instructions per second, a measure of computing capacity—had grown vigorously, at an annual average rate of 39%. But that led to only a 5% rate of growth in mainframe units for two reasons: First, users added much of the power by upgrading the innards of existing computers rather than by buying new hardware. Second, responding to the growing reliability of their machines, users simply kept them on the job longer, slowing the retirements of MIPS from 15% of the installed base in 1985 to about 5% in 1990. Leaning on a survey they made of 50 big buyers of computers, the analysts predict that demand for mainframe MIPS will grow at perhaps a 33% annual rate over the next few years and that the decline in the retirement rate will stop. The result, they conclude, will be annual growth in IBM's mainframe revenues of around 9.5% through 1995, vs. 8.1% in the five years just past. Making a host of other assumptions—remember that this intelligence emanates from a firm that has long been bullish about IBM stock—the analysts estimated 1995 earnings for IBM at $11.6 billion, close to twice the figure for the "good" year of 1990.

They like that report at IBM. Unfortunately, the accuracy of neither its forecast about mainframes nor any other is provable until the results are in. One restrained conclusion about IBM's product line: It is better than it was a few years ago, still needs work, and is unquestionably getting it.

FOR WALL STREET, ONE SURPRISE AFTER ANOTHER

Speaking to a meeting of CEOs in May, John Akers began by recalling his days as an IBM salesman: "If we were behind on quota, we would come into the office on Saturday morning to get some sales help from our managers. Well, on this Saturday morning I'm behind on quota, and I'm hoping one or more of you people in the room might be able to help me out." The audience roared, knowing full well what he meant: On March 19, a bare 12 days from the end of IBM's first quarter, the company had shocked the investment world by telling security analysts that earnings for the period were going to be about half Wall Street's estimates.

Three months later IBM did it again. On June 20, Big Blue said even the most bearish analysts were wrong: Second-quarter earnings would be off at least 80%. Corporate America takes it as gospel that large companies don't have earnings surprises of this kind. Ask other big-company CEOs about the IBM shockers and they just roll their eyes. So how to explain these bombs?

The story goes back to the third quarter of 1989, when IBM had another surprise shortfall—this one arising mainly from manufacturing problems with a new line of disk drives. Soon, a new director of investor relations, James Clippard, moved to the firing line as IBM stock fluctuated its way through 1990. Short sales of the stock were large. Then came the last quarter, traditionally strong for IBM, but this time a true rouser: $2.5 billion in earnings, or 40% of the year's total. Analysts got the good word on January 17 in a conference call. Reflecting IBM's pent-up frustration, Clippard let go a zinger: "This earnings release is dedicated to the shorts and pessimists on IBM."

Akers said in his May remarks to managers that he knew as early as November that first-quarter results would trail 1990's. IBM says now that it kept trying to "tamp down" analysts' estimates. Nobody paid much heed. Recession or no, war or no, the Street had seen the fourth quarter and had heard Clippard.

Along about the 15th working day of each month, IBM's management information system delivers to Armonk headquarters a quarterly forecast based on orders data from the company's marketing units. Business in January and

CAN JOHN AKERS SAVE IBM?, CONTINUED

February was poor, but the February forecast indicated that IBM could still have a decent, typically "back-loaded" quarter bolstered by strong sales in March. Nothing was certain, though: IBM customers can cancel an order at any time right up to the shipping date. Says analyst Don Young of Shearson Lehman: "IBM has a softer definition of 'order' than most computer companies do."

Sure enough, when it got to be "white-knuckle time"—what IBM salesmen call the waning days of a quarter—the business wasn't there. Orders had buckled all over the world. Akers has singled out business in Japan as "disastrous." The horrendous news was worsened by an adverse shift in currency rates—a rise in the dollar that made March sales in Germany and Japan less valuable when translated into dollars.

Once burned, twice shy, so after March 19 analysts handled the IBM hot potato nervously. The company said second-quarter business wasn't good, but didn't elaborate much. One veteran computer analyst, Barry Bosak of Smith Barney, visited Armonk in early June and gained so little knowledge he was embarrassed to put the trip on his expense account.

Probably IBM stayed mum because it knew white-knuckle time might again produce a shock. And so it did: When the June tidings arrived, there was no alternative to another conference call to analysts. The best news in it: In the third quarter IBM would begin shipping the high-end models of its new mainframe line on schedule.

A postscript: In between Earnings Surprises One and Two, a shareholder in Chicago sued IBM for failing to disclose the bad first-quarter prospects in a timely fashion. The lawsuit asks damages for all investors who bought IBM stock after November 30, 1990, and still held it on April 12, when the company officially released its earnings. IBM says the suit lacks merit.

By contrast, IBM's marketing skills don't seem any better than they did a few years ago and definitely trail those of the frontier days described by Thomas J. Watson Jr. in his 1990 book *Father, Son, and Co.*, written with *Fortune* editor Peter Petre. Said Tom Jr. of IBM's success in computers: "Technology turned out to be less important than sales and distribution methods. Starting with Univac [Remington Rand's first computer, in 1951], we consistently outsold people who had better technology because we knew how to put the story before the customer, how to install the machines successfully, and how to hang on to customers once we had them."

Oh, to have all that today! John Akers recognized the absence of those historical strengths around five years ago, when IBM's world began to disintegrate. His strategy then was to move those thousands of employees—the "redeploys," in IBM's lexicon—into the field, where they were going to help the company get closer to customers. Later on, as it became apparent in Armonk that the strategy wasn't delivering revenue growth, the U.S. marketing effort was reorganized several more times.

One customer who knows the consequences all too well is Thomas Pirelli, head of Enterprise Systems, a suburban Chicago company that sells specialized software to hospitals for computerized purchasing. Pirelli says the local IBM office was shaken up three different times in 1988 and early 1989. Three different sets of IBM managers called him, asking to drop by and explain how they were now doing things differently. "They wanted a day," says Pirelli. "By the third one, I was only giving an hour. And in those three sessions, they never asked about our needs. They don't listen. All they do is talk and show you the charts they've brought along."

In the confusion, Pirelli says, one IBM newcomer even had to ask how much business Pirelli did with the company. The answer then was about $2 million a year. "But since he plainly didn't know," says Pirelli, "I just made up a figure of $20 million. That got his attention—until he realized it wasn't true. I told him, 'We use an IBM computer for that kind of data. You ought

CAN JOHN AKERS SAVE IBM?, CONTINUED

to try it.' I'm not exaggerating about all of this. It was a parody!" Pirelli says that about 90% of the PCs in the hospitals he deals with used to be IBM's, but he estimates that these customers are buying only about one-third of their new ones from the company.

Can Pirelli's experience be explained by the fact he is a small-business man, a class of customer that IBM has never starred with? It appears not, since complaints from large customers also abound. The Research Board's Naomi Seligman says that most of the organization's members are "fed up with the mediocrity of IBM's marketing." These buyers, she says, complain that too many people were put on their accounts, that the "knowledge base" of the IBM sales force is poor, and that Big Blue is still not providing solutions their companies need to network their computers and get full value from their investments. "It's too bad," says Seligman. "The customers can't get what they want from small computer companies—they just aren't set up to provide solutions—and the customers are short of staff to do the job inside. IBM would have a real edge if it had the skills and particularly if it could find the right ways to motivate its employees."

In meetings, says Seligman, her organization's members discuss the kind of IBM salesman they would like—"and the model is always Al Johnson." Allen M. Johnson, 55, manager of the Bloomington, Illinois, office for 18 years, has only one customer, State Farm Insurance. In collaboration, State Farm and IBM have developed four generations of a sophisticated computer system for the insurer's 17,500 agents. The two companies are also working now with a California start-up, Go Corp., to test keyboardless hand-held computers on which the user—a State Farm claims adjuster, say—can write with a stylus.

Norman L. Vincent, head of data processing at State Farm, says he cannot say enough good things about Johnson: "From what I hear from other buyers, many IBM account execs just try to keep their noses clean for three years so they can get promoted. They say, 'If my customer wants something IBM doesn't want to give, I'm not going to the mat for it.' Well, Al is just the opposite. He'll go anywhere in IBM to get what State Farm needs. He'll run into some guy who says, 'My budget won't allow that,' and Al will ask, 'Okay, who controls your budget, and where do I find him?'"

In the late 1970s, Vincent recalls, Johnson's zeal got him into trouble. Johnson was then organizationally part of IBM's dataprocessing division, which sold the company's "big iron"— mainframes. But State Farm, trying to devise a computer system for its agents, needed small machines that were sold by another division. Johnson set about lining up the small stuff for State Farm. He says some "big-iron bigots" came after him, urging that he be fired.

Having survived, and having won nation-wide repute for serving his customer well, Johnson rates a question: Has the IBM management ever asked him to teach other marketing people in the company how to do their job better? Answer: "No." That suggests a lack of judgment up the line. Indeed, the biggest indictment of Akers's management would seem to be that he has failed to fix IBM's marketing problems. He came from the world of sales. Surely he should have managed to whip it into shape.

He is still trying. Under way is yet one more revamping of U.S. marketing, which today is under the direction of George H. Conrades, 52, often mentioned as a prospect to succeed Akers. The new plan changes the way people are rewarded. Formerly, IBM's branch managers and sales reps were on a quota system that paid them best if they sold high-margin products, such as mainframes. That doesn't necessarily leave you pushing what's best for your customer.

So the new plan pays these folks according to what they produce in revenues—any kind of revenues. And top management is sounding tough about demanding results. In his much

CAN JOHN AKERS SAVE IBM?, CONTINUED

quoted May remarks, Akers said, "The fact that we're losing share makes me goddamn mad. I used to think my job as a rep was at risk if I lost a sale. Tell them theirs is at risk if they lose."

At management levels above the branches, a different incentive system now applies to 64 new geographical territories, organized into seven areas. The managers of all these units are paid primarily on profits and secondarily on the returns they achieve on assets under their control, mainly accounts receivable. That doesn't mean IBM has a receivables problem: Financial executive Metz says few companies have less of one. Instead, the standard is part of Armonk's drive to get management at all levels to focus on return on assets and cash flow. Says Metz: "This is a signal to middle management and the rest of the organization that these things are not just something Akers and Metz give speeches about, but are really, really something important."

This message might be coming through more clearly were there not considerable bitterness in IBM's ranks about the performance of management itself and, most particularly, about compensation at the top. Last year, counting his cash take and restricted stock grants (but not options, which would add another layer of pay), Akers earned $4.6 million, which is not all that extraordinary for the CEO of the biggest corporate earner in the world. But the $4.6 million was no less than a 138% raise over 1989. The four executives just below Akers also got increases over 100%. Unfortunately, the news of this largess hit the street just as the company was disclosing its bleak first-quarter earnings.

It did not look good—and never will. IBM's rationale for the raises was spelled out recently by Walton E. Burdick, senior vice president for personnel. The explanation harks back to 1989, when top management was docked slightly in pay because a $2.4 billion write-off knocked earnings down more than 30%, to $3.8 billion. Coming along next, the earnings of $6 billion in the "good" year of 1990 had a certain sheen to

them, and Burdick says that's why big pay raises were justified.

The trouble is that IBM's employees have been asked to buy this argument at a time when they are feeling stepped-up pressures to deliver sustained performance. Technically, IBM's hallowed principle of "full employment"—no layoffs—is still in place. Firings, though, are permitted. In IBMspeak these are called MIS, for "management initiated separations," and, by any name, Akers and crew want to see more of them. Says Burdick: "We are escalating standards of performance. We are raising the bar."

The words may seem discordant, given management's own lack of kick. But some employees—not to mention the shareholders—will deeply welcome the overdue tightening of standards and any resulting move toward streamlining. Despite Aker's vigorous efforts to decentralize and drive decision-making authority further down into the company, IBM's bureaucracy still lives and thrives. Almost everyone who deals with the company comes away with a numbing sense of how slowly it moves, how many people must weigh in on a decision, how the competing interests of one camp in the company must be balanced against those of other camps. Donald Coggiola, senior vice president of Policy Management Systems, a software developer and a business partner of IBM's, recently made a remark quoted in the *Wall Street Journal* that is likely to enter the lore about IBM. He described the company approval process as "giant pools of peanut butter we have to swim through."

The Japanese have a saying that it is hard for a large man to fully exercise his wits. The suspicion must persist that IBM is still oppressively rotund—a sumo wrestler, so to speak, trying to grapple with a whole gymnasium full of agile, clever, lesser weights. As the big fellow's designated manager for the next 3½ years, Akers faces a job that surely must be counted among the most difficult ever dealt an executive.

CAN JOHN AKERS SAVE IBM?, CONTINUED

Akers credits IBM with being able to adjust to shifting conditions, and history bears him out. IBM missed out early on minicomputers—and adjusted. It stumbled getting into PCs—and adjusted. His point, of course, is that this time too the company will make the requisite course corrections and ultimately prevail. The opposing argument is that those comebacks occurred in the days when the doubts about mainframes were small and the moat was wide. IBM could then make money with one hand and play catch-up with the other. Today, as IBM's results for 1991 show, it takes both hands—and both feet—just to stay in the game

Given the severity of that challenge and IBM's gymful of troubles, it is ironic that some knowledgeable outsiders still give the company high grades for depth of management, one of IBM's historical virtues. Says a critic of the company who is a fan in this respect: "IBM has ten people at the top who could run any other computer company." That may be true. But they certainly haven't yet proved they can run IBM.

Source: Carol J. Loomis, "Can John Akers Save IBM?" *Fortune,* ©1991 The Time Inc. Magazine Company. All rights reserved.

BACKGROUND FOR THE IBM STRATEGIC ANALYSIS

To illustrate how to analyze a company, we will first examine IBM's recent history and then analyze the foregoing illustrative case. The title, "Can John Akers Save IBM?" is provocative because IBM is such a well-known company. Following our discussion here, we will illustrate how to apply approaches that are covered in this book. As Figure 1.1 shows, strategic analysis begins with looking at the business itself and proceeds to examine the industry and the general economic and social environment in which the company operates. This external environment defines the context in which strategy needs to be formulated.

Starting with an examination of the business itself, we find that IBM dominated the computer field for many years, holding the largest market share in the sale of mainframe computers. Early competitors such as GE and RCA dropped by the wayside because they did not have the commitment or the competitive capability to withstand the IBM onslaught. In a bold attempt to ensure that the mainframe continues to be an important element of the computer industry, IBM is incorporating it as a key element of networking (Verity, 1989).

Can John Akers reinvent the IBM of the past? A look at some of the historic developments suggests that if properly managed, it can once again become a dominant force in the computer industry, which is itself being transformed into a telecommunications and computerized video industry. With the laser as a technological force behind many of the changes taking place, vast adjustments are needed to keep pace in the industry. Companies such as Dell Computer with only 1,900 employees can sell PCs cheaper than IBM, which has $69 billion in sales (Flannigan, 1991). To counter this threat, IBM will test selling its PCs by mail order

(Carroll, 1992b) and is planning to sell in Europe a PC clone made by an Asian firm (Carroll, 1992a). Over the years IBM has made significant contributions to developments in computers and software. As early as 1952, IBM introduced the 701 computer for scientific calculations. In 1958 it came out with the 7000 series, and in 1964 it introduced the system 360 computers. It continued to innovate in computer design in 1985, introducing the 3090 mainframe computer and the RISC computer (Lewis et al., 1988).

What happened at IBM to make one of America's most admired companies lose its luster? In 1988 IBM fell from America's most admired company to number 23 (Schultz, 1988). In 1992 IBM plunged to 118th on the list of most admired companies (Ballen, 1992). The criteria used by *Fortune* to assess a company's reputation included:

1. Quality of management
2. Financial soundness
3. Quality of products or services
4. Ability to attract, develop, and retain talented people
5. Use of corporate assets
6. Value as a long-term investment
7. Ability to innovate
8. Community and environmental responsibility

Fortune polled corporate directors, senior executives, and analysts, and 82% cited quality of management as the paramount factor (Ballen, 1992). What does this imply for IBM's future?

ANALYZING THE INDUSTRY

The next step in the strategic analysis is to examine the industry and the general economic and social system of which that industry is a part. An industry analysis includes an environmental scan to determine what forces external to the organization have a direct impact on its competitive position and what competitive actions need to be taken to achieve a sustainable competitive advantage. An industry analysis also helps determine what competitors are doing, what threats and opportunities exist, and whether the company should enter, remain in, or exit from an industry.

Determining in which industry a company fits can be a difficult task, because many companies are in several industries. It is often appropriate to begin an industry analysis by considering the "core" competency of the business that is its major source of income or by considering a specific strategic business unit (SBU). One can examine the standard industrial classification code; however, any conclusions based solely on the SIC code can be misleading if no additional information is used (such as what products are dominant in a given industry, what markets are served, and what percentage of the company's total sales are derived in a given industry classification). Nonetheless, the SIC code is a useful reference point because all companies are confronted with these same limitations. Where possible, industries are grouped by location, size, profitability, growth, or other factors that contribute to the direct or indirect competitive environment.

After an industry has been classified, it is useful to explore the strategic groups in that industry. This analysis includes those companies that compete in a given industry and how they affect the subject company's competitive ability. For example, although Apple might not be thought of as a competitor to IBM, Apple has taken away market share in the personal computer market and is a formidable force in that segment of the computer industry. Strategic groups can be found for most segments within an industry. Porter (1980), for example, looks at strategic groups as those companies that contribute to rivalry in an industry because of price, quality, product differentiation, overall size, market share, or willingness to take risks. The ease with which it is possible to enter or leave a group depends on the structure of the industry, which includes barriers to entry, maturity of the industry, cost structure, technology, product differentiation, and mobility of the company.

Having identified the group in which a company competes, one can draw a group map to show the member companies' relative size, importance, ability to compete, resources, and similar factors that contribute to rivalry among firms. An industry group map is shown in Figure 2.1.

Within a group, such as for mid-range computers, the relative percentage can be shown for each company in that group. The following are the relative percentages of the market for each of the dominant players (InfoCorp, 1993).

Company	Percentage
IBM	24
HP	17
DEC	13
NCR	8
Other	38

Using a similar approach for each of the groups, one can determine which companies are the major competitors within an industry and within a group. Developing an effective strategy depends on knowing who the competitors are and how strong they are. The industry group map can help planners determine how best to compete in a given arena.

Industry forces strongly influence what strategies are viable and whether the industry has growth potential or profit potential. Some of the major questions Porter (1980) believes are important to consider when examining an industry follow.

1. Is the industry fragmented, concentrated, mature, or declining? The personal computer industry is highly fragmented, whereas the automotive industry is highly concentrated. Steel has been both a mature and a declining industry.
2. How strong are competitors, what are their weaknesses, and how willing are they to compete vigorously? Philip Morris had considerable financial strength, but for many years it lacked technical know-how in industries such as wine making and eventually divested itself of its wine holdings.
3. How important is technology and how readily available is it? Does the industry have the infrastructure to sustain its differentiation against substitute

---

| FIGURE 2.1 | Industry Group Map |

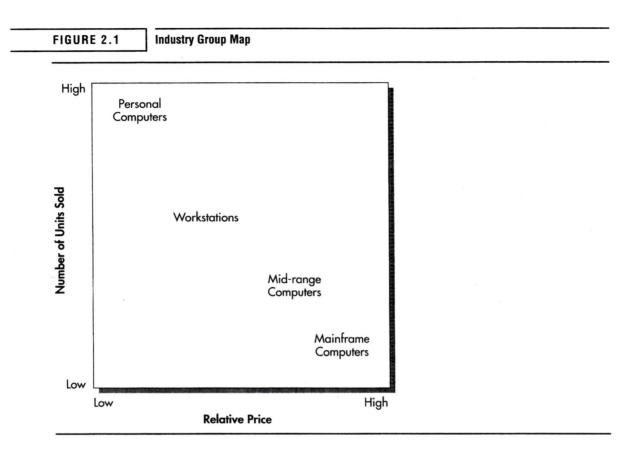

---

technologies? The electronics industry, which includes IBM, has suffered both from the need for new technology and from the proliferation of substitute products, especially computer clones.

4. What are the resources required to function effectively in the industry? Is it capital-intensive? Is there an adequate supply of skilled labor or technical and managerial personnel? Is the industry attractive to the financial community? Junk bonds have played havoc with banks, insurance companies, and stock brokerage houses because people relied on value that did not exist.

5. What are the long- and short-term trends in the industry? Are significant demographic changes taking place? Are suppliers and distributors reliable, and is their use cost-effective? What is the impact of global competition on the industry? The recession of 1991 and 1992 has had a direct impact on companies that make consumer products and has also affected those that depend indirectly on consumer spending. Global competition is increasingly becoming a fact of life that almost every industry must confront in order to survive.

6. What are the potential regulatory effects, especially in terms of pollution, labor, and restrictions on plant location or operation? Are significant laws

pending that would affect the industry? Is the industry subject to litigation, such as in health care or product liability?

7. What are customer expectations and needs? Do customers have significant power, are changes in buying practices under way, are customers subject to brand switching, and how price-elastic is the demand for the industry's products? Customers increasingly expect quality, service, timeliness, and performance, all of which contribute to what we call a product's value.

8. What are the channels for distribution of the products? Are needed services readily available? Is timing critical for delivery, and must inventory be kept on hand? What level of advertising and promotion is normal for the industry? Joint ventures, strategic alliances, and industry consortiums are becoming important ways to compete in today's turbulent environment.

9. Is the industry cyclic or seasonal in nature, or is demand predictable? Is there considerable uncertainty regarding the future of the industry (such as surrounds atomic energy, for example)? Is extensive R&D needed to maintain a technological edge? Motorola has shown that by spending large sums of money on R&D, it could reduce defects to the point where it was able to crack the Japanese market.

10. How is value added to products produced by the industry? Can cost be contained? Are mergers and acquisitions a problem? How vulnerable are companies in the industry to such takeovers as have occurred in the airline and cable industries?

IBM is still dominant in the mainframe segment of the computer industry, from which it derives 49.8% of its gross profits (Hammonds, 1991). Although the battle for mainframe customers has gotten really nasty, IBM still holds 69.7% of the U.S. market. Once the key computer company in Japan, IBM has dropped from number one to number two and most recently to number three, behind Fujitsu and NEC (Drefuss, 1988). IBM hopes that by making equipment for rival Mitsubishi it can recapture second place in Japan.

U.S. competitors such as DEC are striving to beat IBM in the mid-sized computer market. DEC is relying on an open system architecture to restore profits and market share (McWilliams, 1991). In order to compete in this market, IBM recently announced that it will offer a cheaper minicomputer, dropping the cost from $16,000 to $12,000 (*L.A. Times*, 1991). Using a "sizzling" RISC (reduced instruction-set computer) system, IBM hopes to position itself competitively in the workstation segment (Reinhardt & Smith, 1990).

IBM has had a major triumph with its AS/400, even though most companies had given up the mini-computer as dead (Verity, 1992a). IBM defied conventional wisdom and was able to build a $14 billion business. This success shows that IBM has the potential to remake itself. This theme is elaborated in the book *The Silverlake Project* (Bauer et al., 1992), which describes the transformation that took place in Rochester, Minnesota, over 1,000 miles from IBM headquarters in Armonk, New York. As the authors point out, IBM had become a product-driven company, as opposed to a customer-driven company. It had overlooked customer needs. But in the AS/400 venture, IBM vowed to change this. Against all odds—the project was completed in 2 years, involved 37 sites on 3 continents, used RISC technology, and entailed 10 million parts and 2,500 applications programs—the Silverlake Project succeeded. It did so by adhering to 10 basic principles:

1. Appoint a leader with the vision to release people's creative energies.
2. Pick the right people and give them a clearly defined mission.
3. Empower these people and trust them to use their own judgment.
4. Utilize work teams that criss-cross the organization.
5. Choose an appropriate market segment in which to position the product.
6. Gather data, and analyze it using a model of the markets and the business.
7. Allocate resources based on priorities, using tradeoffs.
8. Do things right the first time and break time constraints by using concurrent processes.
9. Recognize that the customer is your partner and tap into external expertise.
10. Meet and continuously exceed your customer's expectations.

Will all this be enough to offset competitors such as DEC and Sun who are targeting high-powered workstations that are beginning to look more like powerful minicomputers (Weber, 1991)? Other competitors include Apple, which has the dominant market share in the personal computer segment and AT&T, which recently purchased Teradata to tap into the database computer arena. These companies continue to nibble away at IBM's market share and profits (Moffat, 1991). Over the 10-year period from 1982 to 1991 the largest growth was in the personal computer segment, which rose from approximately $2 billion to $32 billion while the mainframe computers went from approximately $11 billion in 1982 to an estimated $20 billion in 1991 (Verity and Lewis, 1987).

The hardware portion of the computer industry is primarily an oligopoly of a few dominant companies. Segments such as the personal computer arena are highly fragmented because of the clones that have copied IBM's open architecture of the personal computer. Another important aspect of the computer industry is the software (computer programs) that makes the hardware useful. IBM has relied on companies such as Microsoft to supply programs that help it to be more competitive. IBM's own efforts in the software segment have been less than successful. In 1987 IBM promised to develop software that would link all its computers, but 30,000 programmers later, it still exhibits "software gridlock" in this one segment (Schwartz, 1991). Problems such as these and false starts on investments put an end to one of the most embarrassing chapters in IBM's history. IBM had hoped, for example, that its investment in Rolm would launch it into the rapidly growing telecommunications industry, but this effort failed because "people who understood the market best were not asked" (Hof and Keller, 1989).

ANALYZING INTERNAL PROBLEMS

By shifting our analysis from the competitive forces in the industry to the internal problems confronting IBM, we obtain additional information that we need for analyzing the case and formulating a recommended strategy to improve the situation. In its 1991 annual report, IBM noted significant improvements over 1989 operations because of "management's strategy to transform the company by increasing emphasis on quality and customer solutions, improving competitiveness of IBM's products and services, and achieving greater efficiencies from cost and expense management and strategic restructuring." The results included a 10.1% increase in revenue to $69 billion and net earnings of $6 billion, compared to $3.8 billion in 1989. However, *Business Week's* 1992 ranking of the top 1,000 companies showed that IBM lost $564 million in 1991.

Although there are many vocal critics, and IBM is far from being out of the woods, it is making progress toward improvement. By examining what led to the current situation, a strategic manager can determine what (if any) changes in strategy are needed to maintain and enhance a company's competitive position and profitability. IBM is under siege at every part of its vast empire as it tries to maintain its competitive position. It is a formidable competitor, but it no longer looks invincible. From a high of 46% of the personal computer segment, it now has only 23%, its mainframe share dropped from 80% in 1983 to 69% in 1991, and its stock price declined from a high of $168 in 1987 to $103 in mid-1991 (McCarroll, 1991). By the end of 1992, the stock had plummeted to $52. And this despite a major restructuring of its $69 billion revenue (Weber, 1991).

John Akers is taking some revolutionary steps to try to correct what he considers a crisis situation. "The fact that we're losing shares makes me goddamn mad. . . . The tension level is not high enough . . . the business is in crisis" (Byrne et al., 1991). Byrne reports that outsiders have criticized Akers for not accepting responsibility and for being reluctant to change the old way of doing things. Elsewhere, IBM has been accused of jettisoning paternalism in order to become more competitive (Evan I. Schwartz, 1991).

CORE COMPETENCIES

As we indicated at the outset, a case analysis should consider the environmental forces impinging on the organization, regulatory considerations (such as the 1980 antitrust suit brought against IBM), industry analysis, competitor analysis, customer analysis, and internal analysis.

At this point, we will examine the core competencies of IBM and what future options are open in its effort to formulate a sustainable competitive strategy. Prahalad and Hamel (1990) look at the roots of competitiveness by recognizing the need to rethink the corporation to determine where and how to develop organizational capability that can create products that customers need even though they may not be aware of them. For example, from 1980 to 1988 Cannon grew by 264% and Honda by 200%. Comparing this record with those of companies such as Xerox, Chrysler, and IBM makes it obvious that considerable potential exists for U.S. companies. In the short run, competitiveness depends on the company's ability to build an organization that can produce products at a lower cost, in a more timely manner, with value added in new products that were not previously anticipated. This was accomplished in the Silverlake Project that produced the AS/400. A core competency is not developed by spending more money on R&D; rather, it is an outgrowth of distinct advantages in the products produced. Furthermore, a core competency should be difficult for competitors to imitate. Skills have to be embedded in the organization and cannot be obtained from outside. Although it is appropriate for a firm to acquire portions of its products from other sources or to develop strategic alliances, the core competencies need to be protected. Prahalad and Hamel (1990) introduce a "competency map" that helps to identify the product areas in which a company can excel. This map shows where the competencies exist in the organization and what skills contribute to differentiated products. General Electric restricted its core competency to those product areas wherein it could be number one or two in the world. Using the competency map, a company can develop a "strategic architecture" that can be used to guide the deployment of assets in a way that builds the competitive structure of the company and helps to define in what products and in what areas it can compete most effectively.

It is not necessary to spend an excessive amount on R&D in order to exploit a core competency. The organization simply needs to identify its core competency and to allocate resources to develop a differential advantage. This competitiveness stems from the ability to produce at a lower cost, and more rapidly, than others. The source of competitive advantage is the ability to focus skills to produce competencies, which helps empower employees and enhances the company's ability to adapt rapidly to changing opportunities.

Taking this perspective, where do we find IBM's core competencies? The company seems to be focusing on the following areas (Verity et al., 1991):

1. Personal computers and workstations: $14 billion
2. Memory storage products: $10.8 billion
3. Software: $10.6 billion
4. Maintenance: $8 billion
5. Printers: $2 billion
6. Systems integration: $2 billion
7. Facilities management: $0.5 billion
8. Semiconductors: not sold outside in 1991

It has been suggested that the new IBM would resemble a holding company more than an integrated manufacturer. The restructuring has resulted in over 50,000 employees departing IBM for various reasons. The strategy of a cost-conscious IBM would sound the death knell for IBM's no-layoff practice. It would also pit the PC and workstation group against the mainframe group. The issue of redistribution of expenses, advertising, and corporate office costs is still unresolved (Loomis, 1991). IBM is fighting hard in Europe against the Japanese in a winner-take-all battle. To do this, IBM is cementing ties with former rivals (Levine and Schares, 1991). It has teamed up with Siemens to develop a high-capacity, 64-megabyte chip in 1995. (Today the 1-megabyte chip is fairly standard.) IBM is selling everything from chips to subsystems to European rivals and has become a major source of venture capital for small European companies, investing more than $100 million in 200 software and service firms. It has also linked up with Bull and with Italy's Olivetti. For an investment of $100 million, Bull will sell IBM a 5.7% stake in its equity; Bull, in turn, will base future computers on IBM's RS/6000 microprocessor (Levine, 1992).

While IBM looks to a brighter future, it reported a $2.8 billion loss for the first time in its 80-year history. IBM claims this was due to a sluggish economy and to the costs associated with reducing its workforce by tens of thousands (Moffat, 1992). This loss was incurred in spite of IBM's selling 11 of its $22.8 million System/9000 machines to Sears. Along with this news came the announcement that the RS/6000, which the company is hoping to sell to Bull in Europe, will have to be put on hold because of a faulty chip design (Hamilton, 1991).

With the PC now ten years old, IBM faces an uncertain future in this profitable segment of its business. There are some 60 million PCs in the United States today. To bolster its position in the '90s, IBM teamed up with Apple and will engineer a chip that will run both companies' programs. This design incorporates a major new method of writing software called OOP (object-oriented programming). The risks in developing such a product are high, but Apple is betting its whole company on it (Schlender, 1991). The estimate of PC sales worldwide is $93 billion, with U.S. sales estimated at $37.1 billion.

Multimedia computing is now here and will undoubtedly expand in the future. Laser disks are available that can hold encyclopedias, voice, video, text, drawings, dial-in videos, and data services of all kinds. Software will become increasingly easy to use and will extend into the realm of expert systems and "artificial intelligence" (Depke and Brandt, 1991). IBM envisions a growth in processing using its systems network architecture (SNA). IBM also will continue to support its large installed base of 3745 voice band processors (Horwitt, 1992). It has said it will provide support for the beleaguered semiconductor industry. This is a radical departure from IBM's policy of avoiding any interaction with competitors. In another move, it backed the purchase of Perkin-Elmer Co. to prevent Nikon Corp. from taking over the vital technology of sophisticated semiconductor manufacturing equipment (Lazzareschi, 1990). Thus, we see IBM changing in structure and behavior and even forging strategic alliances that previously were not done.

What should IBM do, given its situation in July of 1991, and what can we expect to follow? Six experts who were asked this question offered the following advice (Byrne et al., 1991).

1. Irving Shapiro, former director of IBM: It should continue to provide strong support for R&D so that it can remain competitive with the Japanese.
2. Kenneth Iverson, CEO of Nucor: Akers should create an environment where the focus is on costs and efficiency.
3. Rosabeth Moss Kantor, editor of the *Harvard Business Review*: Akers needs to communicate clearly to the organization what kind of company he expects it to be. He should also strongly indicate what is rewarded and what is valued. He should identify the "local heroes" who contribute to the long-term service thrust. Finally, he must examine the problems of bureaucracy, provide a statement of values, and articulate his vision for the company.
4. Thomas Peters, management consultant: It should not hesitate to break the company up into five pieces. Loosen up the atmosphere and reduce the top-heavy structure. It should try not to be heavy-handed and arrogant.
5. Amory Houghton, former IBM director: Shake the place up and loosen the horsepower and science that is already available.
6. Jeffrey Sonnenfeld, director of leadership studies at Emory University: Akers should avoid finger pointing and deal with the broad management issues. He

needs to take charge, explain his plan for correcting the situation, and accept responsibility for what has happened to date.

Each of these comments tends to focus on the main problem confronting IBM, the need to reinvigorate the management and the organization. IBM has abundant talent, outstanding technology and manufacturing capability, strong image and market position, and excellent potential. The critical issue is how to utilize these valuable resources to restore the luster to what was once the most admired company in the United States. All this can be accomplished, according to Schrage (1991), who suggests that IBM should adopt the approaches used by such enormously successful and innovative companies as Japan's Sumitomo and Mitsubishi. The question now confronting IBM is how to restructure so that the values and culture bind everyone together and encourage the release of highly innovative—though perhaps now dormant—forces.

ANALYZING THE IBM CASE

What went wrong at IBM? Why was top management unable to succeed? Was it a failure of leadership, or were the company's problems more deeply rooted? What could CEO John Akers have done? What information would he have needed to decide on a different course of action? What sources of information could he have used?

Asking these kinds of questions is generally a good way to begin a case analysis, the basic method used for many years to study strategic management and planning. Case analysis begins with pertinent facts about an organization and ends with possible solutions to problems that those facts reveal. This approach enables the strategic manager to become immersed in the complex, ill-structured, and sometimes chaotic circumstances in which organizations operate. Case analysis brings order to the statement of strategic problems and provides information that is useful in the development of strategic solutions.

Performing a case analysis gives students an opportunity to work as a team. While working on a strategic problem, members of the team hone their own communication and leadership skills and gain insight into group decision-making processes.

To be useful, the ideas developed must be stated clearly and buttressed by supporting arguments. A common failing in the preparation of written cases is the lack of a formal structure. All too often, excellent points are buried in excess verbiage.

Another important consideration is how best to prepare the case analysis. It is usually helpful to scan the case quickly in order to obtain a general impression of the key ideas and issues. This overview is followed by a more careful examination of the material and by the identification of relevant facts. The methodology covered in this book will be especially helpful in isolating and organizing the important facts from the mass of material presented.

SAMPLE CASE ANALYSIS FORMAT

A case analysis should follow a clear format to facilitate presenting ideas in a logical, consistent sequence. The sample format shown in Figure 2.2 readily fits a variety of strategic problems. The following example demonstrates how this framework can be applied.

Statement of the Problem

This statement identifies the main problem to be examined in the analysis. It is important to avoid such pitfalls as confusing symptoms with problems, making premature evaluations, taking information at face value, and applying old stereotypes to new problems. The problem has to be stated explicitly, and its short-term aspects distinguished from its long-term concerns. The statement should also include any assumptions to be made in the analysis. The following example illustrates a statement of the problem IBM was facing in 1991.

Example Statement of the Problem: IBM

IBM is confronted with a crisis of confidence and is facing continued loss of market share in both the mainframe and PC computer lines. The huge write-off of $5.4 billion has contributed to the lowering of IBM's credit rating by Moody's. Voluntary departures have resulted in the elimination of over 100,000 jobs worldwide since 1985, which has led to severe morale problems, with several key executives having defected. The economic decline in the United States and in Europe has contributed to the downturn in sales and to the losses incurred. Although management appears frustrated by the downturn, it is not clear that the changes that have come about were anticipated. Akers seems to be responding in a crisis mode rather than confronting the situation in a strategic manner with a carefully developed plan of action. He has tried to "reinvent" IBM but has not delegated enough authority to the new divisions for them to compete effectively.

Analysis of the Data

The first step is to identify important data to use in analyzing the case. Relevant data might include information about environmental issues, current economic conditions in the industry, market share, competitive strategy, customer reaction, available funding, profit, government regulations and their impact, product problems, productive capacity, work performance, and managerial style.

Managers can use a number of different methods to analyze these kinds of data and solve strategic problems, but they often rely on past experience or a cursory analysis of limited amounts of information. For example, managers who have had relevant experience with similar problems or are aware of research or other data may apply creative problem solving and estimate the risk of different outcomes. This informal approach does not, however, ensure that they will find appropriate solutions to complex problems. Rather than "winging it," managers

FIGURE 2.2	Sample Format for Case Analysis*

Topic	Methodology	Topic	Methodology
Statement of the Problem (What's going on?)		*Formulation and Evaluation of Alternatives (What can be done? Which alternatives are feasible, compatible, consistent?)*	
Company background	Situation audit		
Recent problems	Company capability profile	Status quo	Multiattribute analysis
Industry history	Strategic 4 factors	Concentration	Pareto law
Analysis of Data (What information do I need? Where can I find it?)		Horizontal integration	Heuristics
Industry analysis (What patterns and trends are important?)		Vertical integration	
		Diversification	
Growth	WOTS-UP analysis	Joint ventures	
Market structure	Environmental scan	Restructuring	
Competition	Growth-vector analysis	Divestiture	
Product analysis (Do our products have a competitive edge?)		Liquidation	
		Innovation	
Market share	Competitive portfolio	Others	
Pricing	PIMS analysis	*Recommendations (Are the recommendations specific?)*	
Promotion	Experience curve		
R&D	Product life cycle	Alternative(s)	
Distribution	SPACE analysis	Reasons for recommendations	
Key success factors	Critical success factors	Possible competitor reactions	
Financial analysis (Financial performance? Projections?)		Impact on the company	
		Implementation (Can recommendations be implemented, and how?)	
Profitability	Dupont formula		
Liquidity	Strategic funds programming	Resource allocations	
Leverage		Costs, returns	
Activity	Sustainable growth	Feasibility	
Growth requirements	Baseline projections	Budgets, timetables	
	Financial ratios	Management commitment	
Management and organization (What kind of organization is this?)			
Top-management strategy	Hierarchy of objectives		
	Key result objectives		
Values and mission	Decision styles		
Goals and objectives	Organization life cycle		
	Organization structure		

*Note: Terms used in this table will be explained in later chapters.

should augment their creative thinking with a systematic approach that does not overlook important factors that could affect the success of a strategic plan.

Formulation and Evaluation of Alternatives

Generally, several alternative strategies should be suggested. The following are some examples of such alternatives.

- Maintain the status quo.
- Broaden the product line.
- Expand into new areas through acquisition.
- Restructure the organization.
- Expand the firm's global alliances.

The next step is to evaluate the feasibility of each alternative. This involves examining the company's available resources or adding new information that supports one or another point of view. The preceding alternative strategies might be evaluated as follows:

- If IBM does nothing, its current problems will only increase.
- As a hedge against market maturation and competition, IBM should expand into other areas that would draw on either technology or marketing strategies similar to those now in use. Examples might include telecommunications and multimedia and wide area networks.
- IBM has the financial capability to make acquisitions, but the potential problems may outweigh the benefits.
- Restructuring the organization would be difficult but may be needed.
- Global alliances demand careful definition and analysis. For example, early expansion in Japan was initially successful but then encountered considerable local competition.

Recommendation of a Strategy

The choice of what strategy to recommend should be justified. For example, a "good" strategy that the company cannot implement is not acceptable. Some possible recommendations that IBM could choose are

- Expand into other lines of business where technology or marketing strategies similar to those used for current products could be employed.
- Restructure the organization into separate business units such as Johnson & Johnson has done.
- Prepare a management training program that emphasizes an entrepreneurial culture.
- Expand global alliances into Eastern Europe and Russia.

Implementation: Statement of the Plan of Action

The strategy that is chosen must be feasible and must also include a plan for carrying it out. The plan of action is often a series of steps needed to ensure that desired objectives are achieved. The following items illustrate what one might expect in a plan of action for the strategies shown above.

- Establish clearly defined criteria for accepting or rejecting new products
- Develop potential new products that IBM would find desirable and assess them using the criteria established.
- Examine the strategic fit of potential new products.
- Determine the resource requirements of new products.
- Examine the industry growth potential and the strength of competitors.

- Prepare a list of possible acquisition candidates.
- Exercise the necessary due diligence when considering an acquisition.
- Determine the strategic advantages of acquisitions and the resources needed for them.
- Examine alternative organization structures to determine which would best fit IBM's culture.
- Determine whether downsizing is needed, given IBM's recent losses.
- Establish a study team to explore how best to carry out any possible restructuring.
- Provide adequate communication and involvement to ensure acceptance of a reorganization.
- Examine IBM's policy of not outsourcing and its implications for restructuring.
- Expand the existing executive training to ensure that leadership, empowerment, teamwork, creativity, and an open culture are achieved.
- Provide for greater freedom of operation of individual units.
- Prepare a plan to find potential global partners.
- Explore the advantages and disadvantages of additional global strategic alliances.
- Determine whether forming alliances in Eastern Europe is desirable.
- Set a timetable to pursue the various options being explored.
- Assign responsibility for carrying out the various steps in the action plan.

PRESENTATION OF FINDINGS

Before a plan of action can be implemented, it must be communicated and accepted. Acceptance involves understanding and a sense of ownership to ensure that individuals are willing to commit themselves to undertaking a new strategy. In part, the material in Chapter 10 on organizational change deals with this issue. Empowerment and teamwork are two very powerful approaches that are being used increasingly to gain acceptance of a strategic plan.

When presenting a recommended strategy to top management or the board of directors, it is often advisable to summarize the material in an executive memo. This allows the executive to determine whether he or she is willing to pursue the matter further.

The executive memo serves two purposes:

1. It is a concise way of summarizing the findings and recommendations of the case analysis. Its one-page format forces the writer to address the issues clearly and succinctly.
2. It emphasizes that the case analysis is only a basis for arriving at viable strategic alternatives. The final choice involves a number of considerations, not the least of which is active involvement of the CEO.

A sample executive memo for IBM is shown in Figure 2.3. An effective executive memo presents

- Critical issues. What are the key problems, assumptions, and the like, and why? What are the expected results?
- Justification. Which methods of analysis were used, what data were considered, and how are they related to the proposed strategy?
- Action plan. What specific steps, resources, and timing are needed to carry out the recommended strategy?

Another purpose of the executive memo is to involve the CEO and other top managers in choosing and implementing strategies. Ideally, the CEO should enter the arena early in the process and set objectives, challenge assumptions, clarify options, and generally orchestrate the diverse elements that are needed to get a strategy formulated and implemented. In reality, top-management involvement in the strategic-planning process often amounts to little more than the allocation of corporate resources to implement proposals prepared by subordinates. This is unfortunate, because the effectiveness of implementation is often directly related to the level and visibility of the CEO's support.

FIGURE 2.3	**Sample Executive Memo**

To: John F. Akers
From: Alan Rowe, et al.
Re: The IBM business crises
Date: December 18, 1992

CRITICAL ISSUES

For the first time, IBM has reported $2.8 billion in losses, decreased market share both in PCs and mainframes, has had over 100,000 in staff reductions, has reported write-offs of $5.4 billion in 1992 which are expected to rise to $6.0 billion, and has been confronted by increasing competition, especially in the PC segment of the market. Morale is slipping with the defection of key personnel.

RECOMMENDED STRATEGY

Considering that the market is mature, fragmented, and price-sensitive, IBM needs to take forceful measures to counter the adverse forces that have caused serious problems. A number of alternatives were reviewed. Those that IBM should consider include

1. Expand telecommunications, multimedia, networks, and further development of the company's RISC chips.
2. Acquire companies that round out required technical competence in the foregoing areas. Expand the marketing of clones by subsidiaries, using mail order or telemarketing.
3. Restructure the organization into independent strategic business units to provide flexibility and the greater entrepreneurial spirit that fostered development of the original PC and the system AS 400 computer.

(continued)

FIGURE 2.3	Sample Executive Memo (continued)

4. Obtain training support to smooth the organizational transition and to help foster a more open, less bureaucratic structure. Emphasize creativity, entrepreneurial spirit, and teamwork.
5. Expand strategic alliances both in the United States and abroad. Position the company to operate in a European common market and to exploit opportunities in such developing areas as Eastern Europe and Southeast Asia.
6. Provide superior service to users, and consider entering the "outsourcing" business. Timeliness, quality, value, and pricing need to be brought into line with competition.
7. Reduce the emphasis on the mainframe segment, and focus on the AS/6000 and related machines.

JUSTIFICATION

Using a number of analytical methods (including industry analysis, competitor analysis, technology analysis, financial analysis, and others), IBM can readily evaluate the merits of the proposed strategy. Worksheets covering stakeholders, core competency, product portfolio, and the like provide support to the other methods of analysis.

ACTION PLAN

The actual steps needed to carry out the strategy, including the timing and expected results, are crucial to ensuring a positive outcome. This phase is often associated with strategy implementation, which therefore also includes considerations related to organizational change. Some of the actions required for the foregoing strategic plan would include preparing a budget to allocate resources, preparing and communicating a new organization chart along with product and/or customer responsibility, determining the level of R&D needed to expand into new products, appointing a marketing team to re-examine all products and determine the potential areas for global expansion or alliances, preparing a training program reflecting the managers' assessment of which needs must be satisfied first, and developing an appropriate basis for evaluating and rewarding performance.

SUPPORTING MATERIAL

Append any worksheets, analysis, and supporting documents, and refer to them in the justification section.

UPDATE ON THE CASE

The following events have occurred subsequent to those described in the case presented at the beginning of the chapter.

1. A new SLC chip microprocessor for the IBM PC computers was introduced (Fitzgerald, 1992).
2. C. Michael Armstrong, chairman of IBM World Trade and the heir apparent to Akers, jumped ship to become chairman and CEO of Hughes Aircraft Co. (Margolis, 1992). He followed Ed Lucente, president of IBM World Trade, who left to join Northern Telecom.

3. To increase the sale of the PC, IBM has decided to sell clones in Europe that were made by an Asian firm (Carroll, 1992a) and to try selling PCs by mail order (Carroll, 1992b).

4. IBM has been courting Time Warner to develop a strategic alliance for transmitting video. The venture would rely heavily on technology development by IBM for "interactive" video using current cable TV systems.

5. Lucie Fjeldstad was appointed manager of IBM's multimedia business. Her formula for success is to
   - Bring in executives from outside the computer industry, which runs counter to IBM's culture.
   - Manage the multimedia business independent of IBM.
   - Offer incentives to ensure strong profit.
   - Exit from businesses that are not essential to IBM's future.

6. James Cannavino, who is in charge of IBM's personal computers and workstations, refuses to conform to Big Blue's bureaucracy. He has so far stopped the PC hemorrhage, and he is attempting to satisfy customer needs (Verity, 1992).

7. Considering strategic alliances or investments in other companies, IBM has
   - Talked electronic media with MCA, Disney, Lucas, and Speilberg.
   - Proposed using networking to deliver Time Warner movies into homes.
   - Considered equity positions in Sapiens, Northgate, Parallan, Group Bull, and Auspex.

8. IBM has announced that it may spin off its Personal Systems Division into a wholly owned subsidiary (Perratore, 1992).

9. With less than 12% of the PC market in Europe, IBM has disclosed that it would take 17,500 of its workers out of a contract with the I. G. Metall union (Templeman and Hollifield, 1992).

10. To oppose PC clones, IBM has decided to build its own clone called Value Point. This follows a drop in its PC market share from 21% in March 1992 to 16% in August (Arnst, 1992).

11. The electronics industry is facing "deconstructing" as a result of changes in the importance of the mainframe (Levine and Hof, 1992). Competitors will now become more responsive to customer needs by being smaller, leaner, and faster.

12. In its continued consolidation, IBM announced in December 1992 that 25,000 additional jobs would be cut. IBM has eliminated 100,000 jobs to date, using voluntary departures (Zonana and Weber, 1992).

13. Akers may have signaled his heir apparent by elevating five executives to the position of senior vice president. But analysts say that this may be misleading (Verity, 1992b).

14. In a surprise move, Akers rehires two of IBM's previous top executives, Paul Rizzo and Kaspar Cassani. Both men will act as advisors to John Akers (Associated Press, 1992).

15. Breaking with the past, IBM is expected to advertise the street prices of the new PS/ValuePoint line of personal computers. The message is that IBM intends to meet mail-order PC competitors head on (Perratore, 1992).

16. Nominated as the product of the year for 1992, IBM's "color notebook" shows that IBM can meet competition when it puts its technology to work (Seymour, 1993).

Giant firms such as GM and IBM need a new vision. They must either change or die, because worldwide, customers have a surplus of products to choose from and at declining prices (Flanigan, 1992).

It is clear from the actions being taken by IBM that it really does intend to "reinvent" itself. This will undoubtedly be accomplished by the breaking up of IBM reported in *Fortune* (Kilpatrick, 1992). The new company will have thirteen major "baby blues." These are divided into the following eight operating divisions and the following four marketing services:

Operating Divisions	Revenues in Billions	Product/Service
Enterprise Systems	$22.0	Mainframes
Adstar	$11.9	Storage devices
Personal Systems	$11.5	PCs, workstations
Application Systems	$11.4	Minicomputers
Programming Systems	$2.8	Software
Pennant Systems	$2.1	Printers
Application Solutions	$2.2	Software services
Technology Products	NA	Chips, circuits
Networking Systems	NA	Mainframe networks
Marketing Services		
Europe, Middle East	$26.1	IBM products
North America	$24.4	IBM products
Asia Pacific	$9.3	IBM products
Latin America	$5.0	IBM products

This breakup will give more autonomy to the separate businesses. However, IBM intends to retain a single sales force. In addition to the breakup, IBM is feverishly forming partnerships with other major computer companies. Time will tell whether this new strategy will pay off.

S UMMARY

This chapter discusses the important considerations that analysts must take into account before formulating a strategic plan. The chapter revolves around a case analysis addressing recent problems of the IBM Corporation. It also shows how to prepare an executive memo that summarizes a strategic analysis and the recommendations that follow.

REFERENCES AND SUGGESTIONS FOR FURTHER READING

Alster, Norm. 1991. IBM as holding company. Wonderful leverage. *Forbes*, December 23, pp. 117–120.

Arnst, Catherine. 1992. COMPAQ. *Business Week*, November 2, pp. 146–152.

Ballen, Kate. 1992. America's most admired corporations. *Fortune*, February 10, pp. 40–72.

Bauer, Roy A., Emilio Collar, and Victor Tang. 1992. *The Silverlake Project*. New York: Oxford University Press.

Byrne, John A., Deidre A. Depke, Stephanie Anderson Forest, Jonathan B. Levine, Robert Neff, and John W. Verity. 1991. IBM: What's wrong? What's next? *Business Week*, June 17, pp. 27–34. In the same issue, see Evan I. Schwartz, Hot dogs, roller coasters, and complaints, pp. 28–29; Keith H. Hammonds, Why big companies are so tough to change, pp. 30–31; and Judith Dobrzynski, What should Akers do next? Six gurus weigh in, p. 33.

Byrne, John A. 1992. IBM's heirs apparent? *Business Week*, December 14, p. 38.

Carroll, Paul. 1992a. IBM to see PC clone made by Asian firm. *Wall Street Journal*, March 11, p. B1.

Carroll, Paul. 1992b. IBM will test selling its PCs by mail order. *Wall Street Journal*, June 29, p. B1 and B5.

Coy, Peter. 1992. IBM needs a new network—but not too new. *Business Week*, April 20, pp. 95–96.

Depke, Deidre A. and Richard Brandt. 1991. PCs: What the future holds. *Business Week*, August 12, pp. 58–64.

Dreyfuss, Joel. 1988. IBM's vexing slide in Japan. *Fortune*, March 28, pp. 73–77.

Dvorak, John. 1992a. Inside track. *PC Magazine*, February 25, p. 95.

Dvorak, John. 1992b. Will IBM dump the mainframe? *PC Magazine*, June 15, p. 93.

Fitzgerald, Michael. 1992. IBM PC future rides on system advancements, SLC chip. *Computer World*, February 24, p. 1.

Flanigan, James. 1992. GM and IBM face that vision thing. *Los Angeles Times*, October 25, pp. D1 and D7.

Flanigan, James. 1991. What's behind IBM's contortion act? *Los Angeles Times*, December 11, pp. D1 and D12.

The Global 500. 1991. *Fortune*, July 29, pp. 245–246 and 265–266.

Hamilton, Rosemary. 1992. IBM tries casual approach to development. *Computer World*, February 24, p. 1.

Hamilton, Rosemary. 1991. IBM wins one, fumbles another. *Computer World*, September 23, pp. 1 and 10–11.

Hof, Robert D. and John J. Keller. 1989. Behind the scenes at the fall of Rolm. *Business Week*, July 10, pp. 82–84.

Horwitt, Elisabeth. 1992. IBM sees peer-to-peer future for processor. *Computer World*, February 10, p. 55.

InfoCorp. 1992. IBM, HP lead mid-range charge. *PC Week*, January 4, p. 21.

IBM 1990 Annual Report. 1991. Management discussion, pp. 38–42.

IBM offers cheaper minicomputer. 1991. *Los Angeles Times*, September 5, p. D3.

IBM rehires retired top executives. 1992. *Los Angeles Times*, December 22, p. D5.

IBM seeks alliance with Time Warner. 1992. *Los Angeles Times*, May 30, pp. D1 and D4.

Kirkpatrick, David. 1992. Breaking up IBM. *Fortune*, July 27, pp. 44–58.

Lazzareschi, Carla. 1991. IBM will build mainframes for rival Mitsubishi. *Los Angeles Times*, November, pp. D1 and D3.

Lazzareschi, Carla. 1990. Competitiveness. *Los Angeles Times*, April 1, pp. D1 and D8.

Levine, Jonathan B. 1992. Look who's helping defend fortress Europe. *Business Week*, February 17, p. 131.

Levine, Jonathan B. and Gail E. Schares. 1991. IBM Europe starts swinging back. *Business Week*, May 6, pp. 52–53.

Lewis, Geoff, Anne R. Field, John J. Keller, and John W. Verity. 1988. Big changes at Big Blue. *Business Week*, February 15, pp. 92–98. In the same issue, see John W. Verity and Geoff Lewis, The reorganization man's idea of fun, p. 95, and Peter W. Bernstein, How IBM cut 16,200 employees—without an ax, p. 98.

Loomis, Carol J. 1991. IBM's Akers turns revolutionary. *Fortune*, December 30, pp. 9–10.

Margolis, Nell. 1992. Armstrong jumps IBM ship. *Computer World*, February 24, p. 4.

McCarroll, Thomas. 1991. The humbling of a computer colossus. *Time*, May 20, pp. 42–44.

McWilliams, Gary. 1991. Open systems may be DEC's open sesame. *Business Week*, June 24, pp. 101–103. In this same issue, see Gary McWilliams, The big engine that hasn't, p. 102.

Moffat, Susan. 1992. IBM reports first loss—$2.8 billion. *The Times*, January 18, pp. A1 and A16.

Moffat, Susan. 1991. AT&T buying Teradata to tap into database computer arena. *Los Angeles Times*, December 3, pp. D1 and D5.

Moody's lowers stellar credit rating of IBM. 1992. *Los Angeles Times*, March 5, p. D2.

Perratore, Ed. 1992a. IBM may spin off personal systems division. *Byte*, October, p. 42.

Perratore, Ed. 1992b. New systems . . . new IBM? *Byte*, November, p. 50.

Porter, Michael E. 1980. *Competitive strategy.* New York: The Free Press.

Prahalad, C. K. and Gary Hamel. 1990. The core competence of the corporation. *Harvard Business Review,* May–June, pp. 79–91.

Redfern, Andy. 1992. European portable workstation project launched. *Byte,* October, p. 42.

Reinhardt, Andy and Ben Smith. 1990. Sizzling RISC systems from IBM. *Byte,* April, pp. 124–128.

Scheier, Robert L. 1993. Outsider will lead the new charge at IBM. *PC Week,* March 29, pp. 1 and 16.

Schine, Eric. 1991. Mike Armstrong's leap of faith. *Business Week,* March 9, pp. 66–67.

Schlender, Brenton R. 1991. Happy birthday PC. *Fortune,* August 26, pp. 40–48.

Schrage, Michael. 1991. IBM should use Japan's formula. *Los Angeles Times,* November 28, pp. D1 and D4.

Schultz, Ellen. 1988. America's most admired corporations. *Fortune,* January 18, pp. 32–52.

Schwartz, Evan. 1992. The Lucie show: Shaking up a stodgy IBM. *Business Week,* April 6, pp. 64–65.

Schwartz, Evan I. 1991. 30,000 programmers later, software gridlock. *Business Week,* July 15, pp. 134–135.

Schwartz, John. 1991. The blues at Big Blue. *Newsweek,* December 16, pp. 44–46.

Schwartz, John. 1990. Big Blue's new assault. *Newsweek,* September 17, p. 50.

Seymour, Jim. 1993. The product of the year: IBM's color notebook. *PC Week,* January 4, p. 97.

Templeman, John and Ann Hollifield. 1992. IBM drops a bomb on labor. *Business Week,* July 13, 1992, p. 45.

Van Dyk, Jere. 1992. Partners in opportunity. *Beyond Computing,* Premier Issue, pp. 33–37.

Verity, John W. 1992a. IBM's major triumph in minis. *Business Week,* March 16, p. 111.

Verity, John W. 1992b. Room at the top. *Business Week,* March 18, pp. 27–29.

Verity, John W. 1992c. Surprise! The new IBM really looks new. *Business Week,* May 18, pp. 124–126.

Verity, John W. 1989. A bold move in mainframes. *Business Week,* May 29, pp. 72–78. In the same issue, see Diedre A. Depke, The software that ties it all together, pp. 74–75; Gary Weiss, On the street, Big Blue is big blah, p. 76; and John W. Verity, Why IBM is cramping its biggest customers' style, p. 78.

Verity, John W. and Geoff Lewis. 1987. Computers: The new look. *Business Week,* November 30, pp. 112–123. In the same issue, see Geoff Lewis, PCs that can roar almost as loud as the giant, p. 118, and John W. Verity, Mainframes aren't ready for the mothballs yet, p. 121.

Verity, John W., Thane Peterson, Deidre A. Depke, and Evan I. Schwartz. 1991. The new IBM. Is it new enough? *Business Week,* December 16, pp. 112–118. In the same issue, see Deidre A. Depke, Any complacent IBMers left?, p. 115; Deidre A. Depke, Why even the Japanese are worried about IBM, p. 116; and John Carey and Peter Coy, The research is first class. If only development was too, p. 118.

Weber, Jonathan. 1991a. Traders wary of IBM pledges; stock off again. *Los Angeles Times,* December 10, pp. D1 and D6.

Weber, Jonathan. 1991b. Sun Microsystems aims at new market segment. *Los Angeles Times,* April 13, pp. D1 and D10.

Weber, Joseph. 1992. A big company that works. *Business Week,* May 4, pp. 124–132.

Zonana, Victor F. and Jonathan Weber. 1992. IBM will slash 25,000 jobs in restructuring. *Los Angeles Times,* December 16, p. A1.

APPENDIX A

Sample of Sources of Information for an Industry Analysis

1. *Business Week*
2. The Securities and Exchange Commission's 10K Reports
3. *Business Conditions Digest*
4. *U.S. Industrial Outlook*
5. *Conference Board, Business Outlook*
6. *U.S. Industrial Directory*
7. *Industry Week,* "Trends and Forecasts"
8. *Business Week,* "Survey of Corporate Performance"
9. *Forbes,* "Annual Report on American Industry"
10. *New York Times Index*

CHAPTER THREE

Strategic Visioning, Goals, Ethics, and Social Responsibility

External Environment

Strategic Planning

Strategic Vision
Grand Strategy
Assumptions and Beliefs
Values
Corporate Culture
Social Responsibility
Ethics and Strategy

Resource Allocation

Resource Requirements

Strategic Management

Organizational Structure

Organizational Culture

Strategic Control

Internal Environment

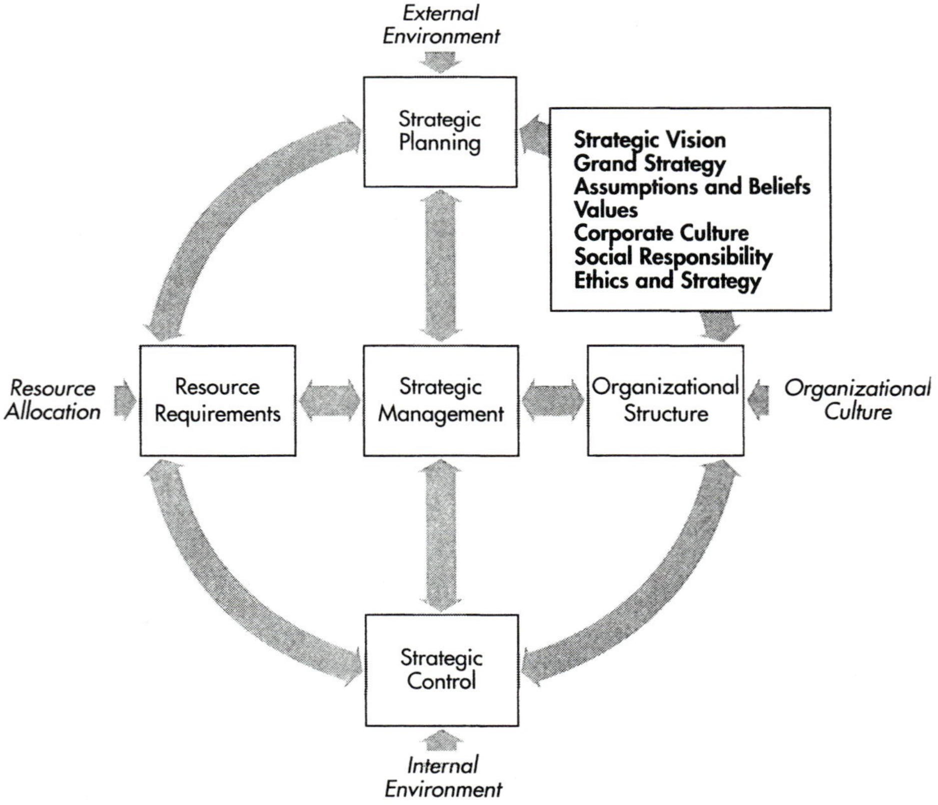

Chapter 1 A Framework for Strategic Management	**Chapter 2** Strategic Analysis	**Chapter 3** Strategic Visioning, Goals, Ethics, and Social Responsibility	**Chapter 4** The Competitive Environment	**Chapter 5** Capability-based Strategy	**Chapter 6** Market Dynamics and Sustainable Competitive Advantage
How to approach strategic management	*Application of strategic analysis*	*Understanding vision, values, ethics*	*Coping with competitive forces, stakeholders*	*Assessing company capability, timeliness, quality*	*Determining trends, gap analysis, and market dynamics*

Chapter 7 Strategy in a Global Environment	**Chapter 8** Financial Planning and Competitive-Cost Analysis	**Chapter 9** Entrepreneurship, Mergers and Acquisitions, Restructuring, and the Service Sector	**Chapter 10** Leadership Factor in Strategy and Implementing Strategic Change	**Chapter 11** Information Technology and Future Directions in Strategy
Assessing global trade, foreign markets, monetary exchange	*Preparing a financial plan and competitive-cost analysis*	*Importance of small business, entrepreneurs, restructuring*	*Strategy implementation, leadership, culture*	*Information technology, trends, new management*

INTRODUCTION

As the saying goes, "If you don't know where you're going, any road will take you there." A strategy, in a comparable sense, is just a means to achieve an objective or goal. Therefore, before a strategy can be proposed or implemented, the organization has to develop a clear idea of where it is going, and why. How is this accomplished? It usually begins with a *vision* of where the organization intends to be at some future date. The vision might call for continuation of a present strategy or for the development of a new strategy that would require radical organizational changes.

Choosing a goal and finding a strategy that leads there are fairly straightforward tasks. Complications enter in, however, because it is necessary to take into consideration the interests of stakeholders, of the organization, and of its employees.

In this chapter, we first discuss the strategic visioning process. Organizational variables that are difficult to measure objectively—values, beliefs, assumptions, and culture—are examined, and the role they play in the formulation of a strategic vision is explained. The role of specific strategies, goals, and objectives is discussed, together with values that are used to develop effective strategic visions. Values also affect how companies live up to their social responsibility and whether they pursue ethical behavior. The chapter explains how the social responsibility matrix and the ethics audit are used to evaluate a company's social posture.

THE CONCEPT OF STRATEGIC VISION

In his book *On Becoming a Leader* (1989), Warren Bennis describes the fundamental role that visioning plays in strategic leadership. To gain the support of stakeholders, executives need a challenging vision that translates what is essentially an act of the imagination into terms that describe possible future courses of action for the organization. Vision is the spark that is needed before the remaining steps are taken to achieve a successful strategy. To give the vision meaning, communication is vital. Executives must establish trust, to demonstrate their commitment to the vision, and act with confidence and positive self-regard in carrying it out.

Three principal factors materially influence how a strategic vision is created: the assumptions and beliefs of executives and leaders, their values, and the values reflected in the culture of the organization. Once a strategic vision is conceived, it is given substance and direction by three other managerial considerations: grand strategy, goals, and objectives. The relationships among these and other strategic-management concepts are shown in Figure 3.1.

ONE CHAIRMAN'S VISION: USAA

General Robert McDermott, the chairman of USAA (a major U.S. insurance company in San Antonio), had a vision for the company when he took it over in the late 1960s (Magnet, 1992). This company was originally organized to sell automobile insurance to military officers, but McDermott saw opportunities to expand the firm's product line and to offer the insurance to officers' dependents and relatives as well. At the same time, he focused on the need to provide high-quality, exemplary service to customers, especially in claims processing. As a result, USAA's phenomenal growth during the last two decades made the company one of the largest general insurance companies in the world.

Recently "Mac D," as he is usually called, sponsored a "Vision 2000" planning program to position USAA for its future. The company believes that its customer base could grow by at least 64% to 2.3 million clients by the year 2000. The median age of its primary customers is projected to increase to about 53, and that of their ex-dependents to about 37. The proportion of its customers who are permanently retired will probably increase by 12% to about 28% of its customer base. Meanwhile, USAA believes that its net worth will increase by about 20% or more. These represent significant changes in the business and require fresh thinking about the company and its mission. Vision 2000 was designed to provide this new insight and a new sense of direction.

The vision that emerged from the planning sessions includes several key concepts. First, the mission of the firm has been changed from providing insurance policies primarily in three categories: security (insurance products), asset management (banking and investment services), and quality of life (discount purchasing plans and loans.) To make the new vision viable it is necessary to focus on customers as individuals. This is a key element of USAA's vision that is "event-oriented services." Each active or potential customer of USAA is a member of what is called the life events program. Thirty-three pivotal events are considered, such as a

FIGURE 3.1   Strategic Vision

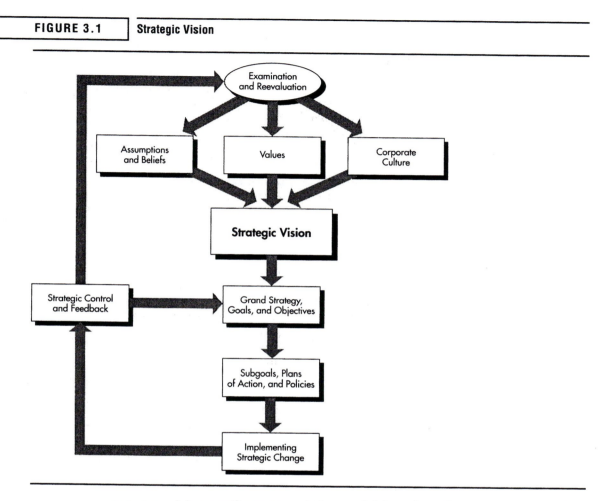

person receiving a military commission, a child reaching driving age, a household move, a vacation, a retirement, or the death of a loved one. Each event triggers a need for one or more of USAA's products and services. The company is positioning itself to respond to any life event in the simplest and most effective manner in order to convince members that they lose something of value if they go to a competitor. Carrying out this program has required an expansion and redirection of the company's information technology services. McDermott's approach is straightforward: "We should be able to satisfy a customer's needs with a single phone call. When a customer calls us for one reason, we should be able to make an assessment of what other services we might be able to provide (the life events concept aids in doing this) while the customer is still on the phone."

USAA's Vision 2000 is representative of what a good strategic vision should be. It is simple but not simplistic. It is specific, market- and customer-oriented, and focused on a problem or an opportunity rather than on how to carry out a program.

(The "how to do it" comes later.) Throughout USAA, General McDermott has also displayed the effective leadership that Bennis described. He initiated the effort to create a new vision, and now that Vision 2000 has been created, he is actively communicating it to all parties involved. He has made or supported the organizational changes and the investments in technology needed to achieve the vision. Using this approach, the company has remained on target in achieving its vision for the year 2000.

To be effective, a vision need not be so comprehensive as McDermott's. George David, the CEO of Otis Elevator, sums up his vision for the company in two basic ideas: "The only good elevator is an unnoticed one. Our objective is to go unnoticed" and "I want any salesperson in the company to be able to order an elevator with a single phone call." Ralph Lettieri, executive vice president of Benjamin Moore Paints, cast his vision as follows: "I wanted the customer to be able to walk into a home decoration center with a sample of color and walk out again with paint that exactly matched that sample." Another vision—one that resulted in major changes in the mutual fund industry—was stated simply by Ned Johnson, chairman of Fidelity Investments, who said "It might prove advantageous if we could give customers prices for our mutual funds on an hourly basis." Fidelity acted on the idea. Customers liked it, and Fidelity's competitors were forced to respond with comparable service.

One of the more famous and perhaps the most comprehensive visions in business history was that of David Sarnoff, who envisioned a new future for America and for the company that eventually became RCA. It demonstrates just how dramatically a strategic vision can affect an organization. In early 1914, as Sarnoff was sailing out of New York harbor, he listened to one of the first experimental radio programs of phonograph music that was being broadcast from the American Marconi station in New York's Wanamaker Building. He was enthralled by the experience and by the possibilities it suggested. Upon returning to New York, Sarnoff began to formulate his vision, which he summarized in a memorandum dated September 30, 1915, and addressed to Edward J. Nally, then vice president and general manager of the Marconi Wireless Telegraph Company of America (a predecessor of RCA). Called the "Radio Music Box" memo, it represents one of the rare cases in which a strategic vision was written and preserved for subsequent public review. Excerpts from Sarnoff's memo follow.

> I have in mind a plan of development which would make a radio a "household utility" in the same sense as the piano or phonograph. The idea is to bring music into the house by wireless.
>
> While this has been tried in the past by wires, it has been a failure because wires do not lend themselves to this scheme. With radio, however, it would seem to be entirely feasible. For example, a radiotelephone transmitter having a range of, say, 25 to 50 miles can be installed at a fixed point where instrumental or vocal music or both are produced. The problem of transmitting music has already been solved in principle, and therefore all the receivers attuned to the transmitting wavelength should be capable of receiving such music. The receivers can be designed in the form of a simple "Radio Music Box" and arranged for several different wavelengths which should be changeable with the throwing of a single switch or pressing of a single button.
>
> The "Radio Music Box" can be supplied with amplifying tubes and a loudspeaking telephone, all of which can be neatly mounted in one box. The box can be placed in the

parlor or living room, the switch set accordingly, and the transmitted music received. There should be no difficulty in receiving music perfectly when transmitted within a radius of 25 to 50 miles. Within such a radius, there reside hundreds of thousands of families; and as all can simultaneously receive from a single transmitter, there would be no question of obtaining sufficiently loud signals to make the performance enjoyable. The power of the transmitter can be made 5 kilowatts, if necessary, to cover even a short radius of 25 to 50 miles, thereby giving extra-loud signals in the home if desired. The development of a small loop antenna to go with each "Radio Music Box" would likewise solve the antenna problem (Sarnoff, 1968, pp. 31–34).

Later in the memo, Sarnoff predicted that sales of the Radio Music Box would reach "a gross business of about $75 million." RCA's actual sales of radios from 1922 to 1924 were $83.5 million. By the end of radio's "golden age" (1934–1941), over 830 AM stations were established, broadcasting about 270 hours of commercial network programming per week to radios in some 29,300,000 households (81.5% of the nation's households) and 8,750,000 cars (29.6% of the automobiles registered). In 1941, radio sets in households and automobiles represented an installed base worth about $1.5 billion. Annual industry income was in excess of $216 million, and annual radio advertising income was nearly $250 million (Sterling and Kittross, 1978).

The scientific knowledge that made radio possible was developed by people such as Michael Faraday, James Clerk Maxwell, and Henrich Hertz. Guglielmo Marconi, John Fleming, Lee de Forest, and Edwin Armstrong all produced innovations that helped convert the science into a workable technology. Both Marconi and de Forest started companies to commercialize their ideas. It was David Sarnoff, however, and his steadfast pursuit of the Radio Music Box vision, that made radio a large-scale, nationwide business that permeated nearly every aspect of American life. After a short period of experimentation during the 1920s, radio took off as a commercial enterprise. By the mid-1930s, Sarnoff's vision was realized. Radio is still a big business, even in today's era of television.

Other great entrepreneurs have realized their strategic visions in much the same way as Sarnoff. At a time when most office equipment was sold by "drummers," Thomas Watson, Sr. envisioned a company from which executives would purchase information solutions from professional businessmen who were backed by a strong service force. His vision became IBM. Ray Kroc believed that the concepts and assembly-line efficiencies pioneered by Henry Ford could be applied to popular foods, such as hamburgers, french fries, and milk shakes. His vision became McDonald's. Walt Disney dreamed that people would enjoy going to an amusement park dressed up as a fantasy world. His vision became Disneyland. Almost all successful companies begin with a strategic vision that is realized by means of effective strategies, plans, and policies.

A VISION OF REVAMPING: GE

Strategic visions often involve changing an established organization. Jack Welch, chairman and CEO of General Electric (GE), pioneered the revamping of that company. Long before most chief executives knew what corporate restructuring was, he was doing it. In 1981, after becoming GE's eighth—and, at 45, its youngest—chairman, he quickly eliminated thousands of jobs, removed entire echelons from the management hierarchy, and shifted assets from mature manufacturing businesses into fast-growing, high-technology, and service operations. In the five years between 1981 and 1986, GE sold 190 companies for a total of $5.5 billion and bought 70 companies for a total of $10 billion.

Welch's vision of a new, more competitive GE was based on two simple premises:

1. It is impossible to be outstanding in every field.
2. Laggard businesses tie up capital and management talent without earning a commensurate return. Individually they may be satisfactory, but overall they have a negative effect.

Based on these two premises, he divided the company into three groupings, which he sketched as shown in Figure 3.2. Within the three circles, Welch listed businesses with similar patterns of success:

- The traditional, core business, with 46% of profits
- High-technology businesses (31% of profits)
- Services (23% of profits)

FIGURE 3.2 | **The Shape of the New GE**

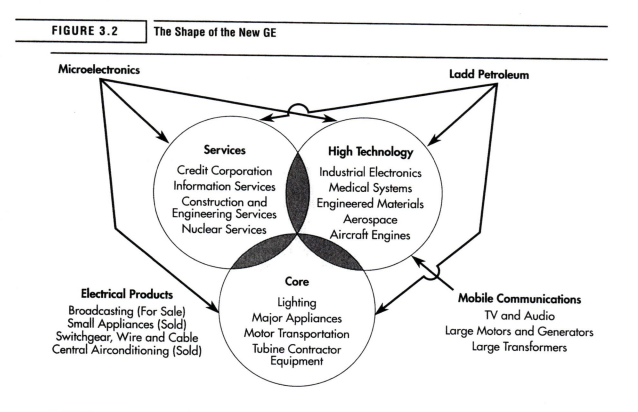

Welch placed GE's remaining businesses outside the circles. Some were profitable; others were not. These "outside" businesses received word that they had to become the "top players" in their industries or they would be sold or closed. Two of the outsiders, Microelectronics and Ladd Petroleum, had links to all three core business groupings and thus were spared from this dictum.

Welch's simple drawing became a vision, or guiding principle, that was communicated readily throughout the organization. Welch's actions aroused considerable controversy. From 1981 to the start of 1988, he eliminated over 100,000 jobs (one in four) and increased revenues from $27 billion (in 1982) to $40.4 billion (in 1987). Operating profits increased from $3 billion in 1982 to $5 billion in 1987, and the price of GE's stock rose more than threefold.

Jack Welch's vision made GE more competitive. GE has become less bureaucratic and has pushed authority down to the operating divisions. Welch nurtured a new breed of manager who could thrive on turmoil and push for even stronger performance. At GE Medical Systems, the new management types are described as "win-aholics" (*Business Week,* 1987).

As the examples described illustrate, the vision of the CEO is extremely important. A successful strategic vision is an idea about a desirable future state that can gain broad consensus and support throughout the organization. A vision should be able to motivate employees and mobilize resources. This ability often makes the difference between a vision that leads to excellence and one that leads to mediocrity.

DEVELOPING A STRATEGIC VISION

Developing a strategic vision relies on being creative and intuitive. The methods described in this book can facilitate the thinking and analysis necessary for development of a new strategic vision, but they cannot make the final creative leap. That is the role of the strategist.

A *strategic vision* can be described as the concept for a new and desirable future reality that can be communicated throughout the organization. The organization's response should be to marshal its resources to achieve the vision. To accomplish these ends, a vision needs to be:

1. Simple, clear, and easily understood by most of the people. The key element of a strong vision is that it translates complex problems into understandable choices.
2. Distant enough in time to allow for dramatic changes, but close enough to gain commitment from the organization. The vision must be realistic, credible, and able to withstand hypothetical, cause-and-effect examination. The vision must also create a sense of urgency.
3. Able to focus the organization with respect to scope and time. The vision should focus the organization on the right things, particularly the things it does best.
4. Frequently articulated by top management to gain a solid consensus that the vision is desirable and achievable. The CEO must personify the vision and live by it. The vision must challenge the entire organization. Presentation of the vision is a very important step.

How can systematic analysis aid in the development of the vision? This question requires that existing and proposed businesses and products be assessed with respect to their potential. Assessment of potential involves two more questions:

1. Can this business/product be made more valuable to the customer? (Increasing a business's or product's value to the customer and the customer's recognition of it is known as *leveraging customer value*.)
2. Can this business/product maintain or increase its competitive cost advantage through *system innovation?*

These two questions form the basis for the *corporate development matrix* shown in Figure 3.3. To use this matrix, strategic planners categorize each business/product with respect to its potential for increasing in value to the customer (left axis) and its potential competitive cost advantage (bottom axis). Depending on its position in the matrix, a business/product is assigned high or low priority within the organization.

The "losers"—businesses/products with little potential for leveraged customer value or competitive cost advantage—should be sold or closed. Businesses/products listed in quadrants I ("watch and wait") and III ("unstable cash bonanza") need to be analyzed further. Those in quadrant I tend to be businesses/products that can,

---

FIGURE 3.3 | **Corporate Development Matrix**

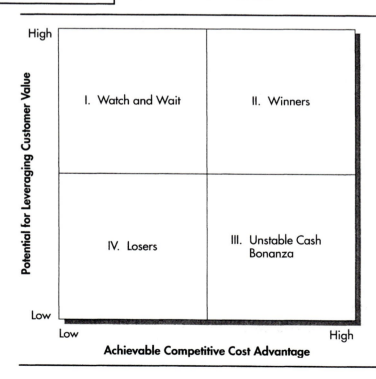

Potential for Leveraging Customer Value

High

I. Watch and Wait

II. Winners

IV. Losers

III. Unstable Cash Bonanza

Low

Low

High

Achievable Competitive Cost Advantage

through specialization, carve out a profitable niche but that, because of the competitive situation, cannot establish a sustainable cost advantage. An example of a quadrant I business is GE's TV and audio business (see Figure 3.3). This business is driven by changes in consumer tastes and spending patterns and is under constant threat of price cutting by offshore suppliers. To retain a competitive advantage, GE must stay ahead of its competitors with respect to technology, customer service, new-product development, and so forth. But to stay ahead, top management must allocate time and resources in amounts disproportionate to TV and audio's contribution to the corporate portfolio. Thus GE's top management had to watch and wait for signals that helped them resolve TV and audio's status. Ultimately, GE sold its consumer electronics business to Thompson S.A. of France in exchange for Thompson's medical equipment business (*Fortune*, 1987).

The businesses listed in quadrant III typically manufacture products with high competitive cost advantage but little potential for further leveraging of customer value. While temporarily stable and very profitable, these products typically are vulnerable to severe margin and/or substitution pressures as the market matures. GE's turbine business is a classic example. Although GE holds a clear technological and market lead in this business, low-cost suppliers from the Far East are starting to erode this position. Only a significant technological breakthrough might increase the customer value of GE's turbine enough to offset this trend.

Only the "winner" businesses/products of quadrant II have the potential for continued value leveraging *and* competitive cost advantages that can be achieved through system innovation.

Jack Welch utilized the logic that underlies the corporate development matrix when he shaped his vision of the "new GE." And Table 3.1 shows how well GE was able to achieve that vision. With the exception of factory automation, it was either

TABLE 3.1	GE Business Ranking, 1989	

	United States	World
Aircraft engines	first	first
Broadcasting (NBC)	first	NA
Circuit breakers	first	first
Defense electronics	second	second
Electric motors	first	first
Engineering plastics	first	first
Factory automation	second	third
Industrial/power systems	first	first
Lighting	first	second
Locomotives	first	first
Major appliances	first	second
Medical diagnostic imaging	first	first

first or second in the businesses that remained after the restructuring (Carlson, 1991). Jack Welch transformed the GE bureaucracy into a formidable competitor built on a vision of core capability. He took a sleeping giant and built it into a $60 billion company with profits of $3 billion in 1992 (Smart, 1992). Fortunately, Welch knew how to "grow" a business. He took the $40-million-a-year plastics division and turned it into a $5-billion business. His entrepreneurial spirit also moved the medical technology unit and the financial division into highly profitable status. When asked about the upheaval he created and the layoffs, his response was that his only regret was that he might have been too cautious in making changes.

GRAND STRATEGY, GOALS, AND OBJECTIVES

Grand strategy is concerned with achieving the vision of the organization. A long-term, five-to-fifteen-year focus on the external environment is needed to develop a grand strategy effectively. A grand strategy is not formulated, put on the shelf, and dusted off every five years. Rather, the grand strategy is a firm's integrated approach to achieving a vision while responding to a constantly shifting external environment.

As indicated in the strategic four-factor model shown at the beginning of each chapter, formulation of a grand strategy (top of the model) involves a multidimensional approach that balances the external and internal considerations. A preliminary formulation of grand strategy takes into account the external and internal environment and must be analyzed for consistency and appropriateness in light of restraints imposed by the factors shown on the horizontal axis of the four-factor model (financial resources and organizational considerations).

The importance of considering financial resources and the organization's structure and culture can be seen from RCA's experience in the mainframe computer business. RCA in the 1960s chose to enter the business of manufacturing and distributing mainframe computers in direct competition with IBM, the industry giant, and several other major firms, such as Burroughs, Sperry Rand, and Control Data. RCA was strong in technical areas of electronics. For the most part RCA was reasonably successful in analyzing and evaluating the elements of the vertical axis of the strategic four-factor model. However, RCA did not do well in evaluating financial and organizational resources. IBM's financial staying power considerably outlasted RCA's. Most important, however, was IBM's ability to provide customer services that RCA could not develop quickly. This lack of responsiveness contributed to the ultimate failure of RCA's venture into computers.

Very much like the vision upon which it is based, a grand strategy reflects the values, interests, and personality of the CEO or founder. For example, the technical and cultural interests of Armand Hammer led Occidental Petroleum to pursue a strategy of developing business relations with the Soviet Union. The grand strategy of Mary Kay cosmetics reflects the personal style and marketing approach of its founder, Mary Kay. In a bureaucratic organization, however, a grand strategy is typically forged through bargaining, coalitions, and power plays among stockholders, top managers, and other stakeholders.

The grand strategy is a framework within which independent *substrategies* are developed. Substrategies generally are developed and implemented at the division or business-unit level and are likely to be concerned with resources (divestment of assets, sources of funds, capital allocation, asset management) or functions (production, marketing, distribution, research and development). At the division and unit levels of the organization, function and product/marketing substrategies tend to dominate. Most of the methodologies presented in this book are tools used to work through grand strategies to substrategies.

An *organizational goal* is a specific outcome that the organization seeks to attain or maintain. Organizational goals are chosen to implement the grand strategy or a substrategy or to align the organization more closely with its values and mission. One example of an organizational goal is to increase market share. Each goal is broken down into *objectives*—measurable accomplishments to be implemented within a specific period of time. An objective for the goal of increasing market share might be to increase it by 5% within six months to one year. The goals and objectives of substrategies are based on the same principle: the goals are aimed at implementing the substrategy, and the objectives are aimed at attaining the goal.

ASSUMPTIONS AND BELIEFS

Assumptions and beliefs about possible future outcomes are a key underpinning of vision and strategy. Data provide valuable input, but beliefs and value judgments inevitably color their interpretation. Managers have no choice but to make assumptions, because they cannot know the future. Assumptions carry risks and have consequences. For example, the stock market crash of October 1987 was predicted by some, but most investors blithely assumed that the bull market would last forever. This assumption had serious consequences. For some individuals and companies, the crash was merely a paper loss that would take effect only if the securities were sold. Some investors in this group assumed that the market would rebound. They figured that if they did not sell their securities, there would be no out-of-pocket losses. (In general, such investors were right.) The point is that any investment or managerial decision is based on assumptions.

Assumptions are made by strategic planners and by top managers who must determine the desirability of alternative strategies. Some managers are risk takers who envision a bright future with a strong growth market and limited competition. Others, who have the same set of facts, see a bleak future and favor conservative strategies. Who is right? Only the outcome, or consequences, will tell.

Unfortunately, strategic planners seldom identify specific consequences that could ensue from the strategic alternatives they are proposing. By ignoring possible consequences, these strategic planners invite disaster. The remedy is prevention. Strategic planners should carefully assess the assumptions, beliefs, and consequences—the ABCs of strategic management—of each strategic alternative they plan to propose. This assessment involves

1. Identifying every assumption associated with the strategy
2. Gauging the strength with which each assumption is felt
3. Specifying every possible consequence (good and bad) of each assumption

The ABCs are an important consideration in case analysis, particularly the first phase of case analysis, formulating a statement of the problem. Invalid assumptions and beliefs can be the cause of an organization's strategic problems.

What are beliefs, and how do they influence choices of strategy? In their book *In Search of Excellence,* Peters and Waterman (1982, p. 285) identified seven dominant beliefs held by executives in successful companies:

1. A belief in being the "best"
2. A belief in the importance of the details of execution; the nuts and bolts of doing the job well
3. A belief in the importance of treating people as individuals
4. A belief in superior quality and service
5. A belief that most members of the organization should be innovators, and its corollary, that the organization should be willing to support failure
6. A belief that informality enhances communication
7. Belief in and recognition of the importance of economic growth and profits

In each of the successful companies Peters and Waterman observed, the managers found a way to focus on these beliefs and get others at all levels in the organization, down to the lowest position, to share them.

Strategies are based in part on shared beliefs about the nature of the firm's environment. The validity and strength of these beliefs significantly affect the success of the organization. Beliefs also influence the way managers respond to situations. For example, managers who believe strongly in organizational stability are likely to reject strategies that would require organizational upheaval, no matter how much data is presented to support the potential for success. Many a merger has been rejected because of managers' belief in stability.

Beliefs that have led to success in the past tend to be reinforced and perpetuated by the organization. Success creates a powerful incentive to do more of what has worked, to do it more efficiently, to do it better, and to train the next generation of managers to do the same. Organizations reinforce successful behavior and build information systems, incentive plans, and organizational structures around beliefs that have worked in the past. For example, if an organization believes itself to be a specialist supplier, it adheres to a strategy of maximizing gross margin and price realization. If, on the other hand, the organization believes that it is selling a commodity, it stresses output, efficiency, and low costs.

Unfortunately, belief-driven mechanisms continue to push the organization in the same direction for some time, even after competitive conditions have significantly changed. The very same system that previously ensured success for the organization can become its worst enemy. U.S. car manufacturers, for example, took about 10 years to change their assumption-based beliefs about the realities of global competition. Early warning signals, such as a slow but persistent increase in the imports' market share, were certainly not ignored, but the domestic suppliers seemed unwilling or unable to take any action to stem the rising tide of imports. The U.S. manufacturers were too committed to their ingrained beliefs to recognize that these beliefs were based on eroding assumptions.

What this and countless other examples show is that change rarely results from proposing a strategy that is not consistent with (1) shared beliefs about what makes the business successful or (2) established organizational structures and methods of operating. Real change has to begin with changes in beliefs; new strategies and actions can then follow those changes.

Zakon (1985) devised a *beliefs audit,* which can be used to (1) test the validity of a set of beliefs against current realities and guard a strategy against possible threats, if appropriate, and (2) build a new set of beliefs appropriate for environmental changes that have occurred (or are foreseeable) so as to initiate new strategies.

Ideally, the beliefs audit should be continuous and ongoing so that it can detect early warning signals and emerging patterns. For practical purposes, however, a structured and managed group effort at critical junctures in the company's development is adequate. The beliefs audit involves careful articulation of the basic beliefs and belief-driven strategies and actions that characterize the firm. The beliefs can be elicited from the organization's employees, suppliers, and customers; inferred from the organization's actions; or determined from tests of the control system that show how beliefs motivate behavior. Most of the questioning can be informal, free-flow, and ad hoc, but it may be augmented by responses to questionnaires, particularly if large groups of stakeholders are involved.

The following set of questions should be asked during the beliefs audit:

1. What has made our business successful?
   a. Why do we make a profit?
   b. What do our customers particularly value (and pay for) in our products?
2. Will we still have today's advantages five years from now?
   a. What will happen if all competitors continue to operate as they do today?
   b. Will changes in the external environment change our business value to customers? If so, why and how?
   c. Which advantages will we be able to defend? Which will we be unable to defend?
3. How could we transform the means of gaining competitive advantage in this business?
   a. Could we change the entire system of delivering goods and/or services to customers (faster, better, more cheaply, more reliably)?
   b. Can new segments or subsegments be created?
   c. Can new advantages be gained through acquisitions or mergers?
4. How can we lead our organization in such a way as to exploit advantages in the future?
   a. Are our organizational structure and information systems still compatible with the market demands?
   b. Do our incentive systems still recognize the specific needs of each of our businesses?

    c. Are responsibility and authority properly balanced in the organization?

    d. Does our organization block rather than foster innovation?

    e. Can/should we improve communication within the organization?

Answers to these questions should be based on as much data and analysis as possible.

Early warning signals that beliefs may need to be changed can come from the following sources:

1. The marketplace
   a. Major accounts lost or gained
   b. Recent swings in overall volume
   c. Changes in price premiums paid for different products
   d. Changes in price–volume relationships
   e. Emerging substitute products
2. Distribution channels
   a. Change in distributors' margin or viability of the channel
   b. Change in the range of products sold by distributors
3. Competitors
   a. Counterintuitive behavior of a competitor
   b. New competitors emerging
   c. An established competitor suddenly gaining market share
4. The organization itself
   a. Unusual defection of key managers
   b. Systems not capable of answering relevant questions
   c. Misleading or erroneous information
   d. Management fumbles despite a seemingly adequate decision process
   e. Declining morale

Initial review and interpretation of the data should be confined to the top-management group, because the process can be a fairly painful and disruptive examination of the organization. Why alarm people in the organization when it may turn out that the company's beliefs and strategy are basically correct and need only minor adjustments? More often than not, the CEO's intuition about the validity of the organization's beliefs is what counts. If the organization is indeed no longer congruent with its environment, the beliefs audit can help top managers to develop a new vision for the organization.

VALUES

THE HIERARCHY OF VALUES

Corporate strategy, according to Christensen, Andrews, and Bower, is the "pattern of decision in a company that (1) shapes and reveals its objectives, purposes or goals, (2) produces the principal policies and plans for achieving these goals, and (3) defines the business the company intends to be in and the kind of economic and human organization it intends to be" (1978, p. 125).

Values are the general, abstract ideas that guide thinking; objectives are the well-defined, precisely stated, measurable targets to be achieved within a specified period of time. A business in high technology, for example, may be characterized by the value of discovering scientific truths before its competitors do. It may formulate a mission: to excel in research and development in electronics. This mission may lead to a goal: to become the number-one scientific firm in the industry. And this goal may lead to an objective: to obtain four new patents in electronics during the year 1993. In organizations, values fan out into mission, mission fans out into goals, and goals fan out into objectives. Corporate culture and beliefs determine how the values, mission, goals, and objectives are communicated to others and brought into being.

The grand strategy of an organization is generally based on satisfying this hierarchy. In this sense, vision and values set the stage for strategic management.

ORGANIZATIONAL VALUES

Values are abstract ideas that guide thinking and action. *Organizational values* are closely tied to the fundamental, underlying beliefs managers have about the business and about people. These values influence managers' choices of mission, goals, and objectives for the firm. In short, values dictate strategy.

Although they are often abstract, vague, and difficult to define, values are revealed by the actions people take, what people think, and how they allocate their time, energy, and skills. Willard Marriott, Sr., for example, valued the delivery of high-quality service at the Marriott Hotels. He is reported to have read every customer-complaint card, and he devoted large amounts of time, energy, and talent to ensuring that his high standards of quality were met. Quality was his first priority and, in his mind, the most critical factor for success. He devoted more time and energy to ensuring quality than he did to any other aspect of his business.

Milton Rokeach, a sociologist who has studied human values and their effect on public attitudes, defines values rather precisely:

> To say that a person has a value is to say that there is an enduring prescriptive or proscriptive belief that a specific mode of behavior or end-state of existence is preferred to an opposite mode of behavior or end-state. This belief transcends attitudes toward objects and toward situations; it is a standard that guides and determines action, attitudes toward objects and situations, ideology, presentations of self to others, and attempts to influence others. (Rokeach, 1973, p. 5)

The management theorist Chester Barnard considered the development and communication of appropriate operational values to be the highest calling of the executive. In The Functions of the Executive (1979), he summarized three key executive functions as "first, to provide the system of communications; second, to promote the securing of essential efforts; and third, to formulate and define purpose." Barnard's experience as an executive at the New Jersey Bell Telephone Company, and the extensive studies he made of other managers, led him to conclude that these three functions were essential to successful management. In Chapter 1, we saw how managers of America's most successful companies adhered to Barnard's prescription. They formulated clear operating values and communicated them effectively to all members of the organization, making sure to monitor activities and follow up persistently (Peters and Waterman, 1982). With effective leadership, then, values become infectious. They affect people's habits of thinking; their ways of relating to one another; the technology they employ; and the policies, rules, procedures, and job descriptions they work by.

PERSONAL VALUES

In 1928 the German philosopher Eduard Spranger identified six categories of people based on their dominant *personal values*. The six categories follow.

- *The theoretical person.* Truth is the dominant interest of the theoretical person. This person's interests are empirical, critical, or rational, leading to such occupations as intellectual, scientist, or philosopher. The chief aim of the theoretical person is to order and systemize knowledge.
- *The economic person.* Wealth (plenty) and efficiency (productivity) are the dominant interests of the economic person. This person wishes to create utility, is quite practical, and conforms well to the prevailing stereotype of the average American businessperson.
- *The aesthetic person.* Beauty and harmony are the dominant interests of the aesthetic person. Each individual situation is judged from the standpoint of its grace, symmetry, or fitness. For this person, the intrinsic value of each of life's events must be realized and enjoyed for its own sake.
- *The social person.* Love, cooperation, and humanism are the dominant interests of the social person. The social person prizes other people as, in Immanual Kant's words, "ends-in-themselves." In return, this person is kind, sympathetic, and unselfish and is likely to find theoretical and economic persons "cold and inhuman."
- *The political person.* Power is the dominant interest of the political person. The political person wishes to bring other people and resources together in order to achieve some personal goal. Leaders in any field generally possess this value in greater-than-average amounts. For some, this value is uppermost, driving them to seek personal power, influence, and recognition.
- *The religious person.* Unity is the dominant interest of the religious person. This person looks beyond human experience to comprehend the cosmos as a whole or delve deeply into the specific, infinitesimal aspects of experience to discover its limits. At either extreme, the religious person embraces the mystical and must rely on faith and belief.

Two researchers, William Guth and Renato Tagiuri, at the time professors at the Harvard Graduate School of Business, used Spranger's six-fold classification to demonstrate that "personal values are important determinants in the choice of strategy" (Guth and Tagiuri, 1965). Using a questionnaire developed by Allport, Vernon, and Lindzey, they found that U.S. executives attending Harvard's Advanced Management Program one year had the following average value profile:

economic, 19%; theoretical, 18%; political, 19%; religious, 16%; aesthetic, 15%; and social, 14%. The executive's average value profile differed from the average profiles of other professionals. Ministers, for example, prioritized their values as religious, social, aesthetic, political, theoretical, and economic—almost the reverse of the executives' priorities.

Guth and Tagiuri cited the case of National Duplicating Products Corporation, a small manufacturer of office equipment whose president's values were chiefly (1) social and (2) aesthetic. The company's strategy was consistent with these values: it produced very high-quality products with aesthetic appeal; emphasized product differentiation, not price competition; had an independent-agent form of sales organization; and promoted the security, welfare, and happiness of the employees.

The authors compared National Duplicating Products with Acoustic Research, Inc., a manufacturer of high-fidelity loudspeaker systems. The values of Acoustic's top executives tended to be (1) theoretical and (2) social. Consistent with these values, Acoustic's strategy stressed "truth and honesty" in relationships with suppliers, dealers, employees, other stakeholders, and the public. In order to carry out its strategy, Acoustic developed the concept of a "minimum acceptable level of profitability" and concentrated on developing high-quality products at the lowest possible price. This often meant that Acoustic's dealers received lower margins than their competitors were offering.

At both National Duplicating and Acoustic Research, the personal values categorized by Spranger guided corporate strategy. Spranger's six values are broad, abstract, timeless ideas that identify a person's strongest concerns. These values differ from the eight operating values of Peters and Waterman. Operating values identify preferred means rather than ends. Therefore, operating values (such as a bias for action, closeness to the customer, autonomy, and entrepreneurship) can be used to satisfy Spranger's more basic values. For example, an operating value such as "closeness to the customer" can satisfy aesthetic values through the production of attractive products and can satisfy social values through joint problem solving and cooperation.

Spranger's six values are applicable to every strategic situation. Some companies examine each strategic option to find out to what extent it incorporates each of Spranger's six values. Two of Spranger's values—the economic and theoretical values—are often regarded as rational. Economic analysis and the scientific method can be used systematically to achieve them. The other four values are sometimes called nonrational; they cannot be readily measured or applied systematically. For this reason, Churchman (1968) referred to them as "enemies" of the systems approach to strategic management. Though they may be "enemies" of systematic and logical thinking, the aesthetic, social, political, and religious values are always present in organizational life, and strategic managers should consider them.

SOCIETAL VALUES

Strategic managers must look beyond organizational and personal values to identify the values that are operative in society. *Societal values* are an important part of the organization's external environment—the environment in which it conducts its business.

The great social anthropologist Pitirim Sorokin argued in an extensive four-volume work (1937–1941) that society's values reflect its dominant socioeconomic pattern. In an agrarian society, the primary values are aimed at survival and security. People desire food, clothing, shelter, and protection from threats to their lives. As an agrarian society progresses and becomes able to produce a surplus of these basic needs, people are able to form cities and develop industries. These socioeconomic changes are accompanied by changes in values. The new values of industrial societies Sorokin called "sensate." Sensate values are the values of materialism. People want jobs, money, productivity, a higher standard of living, radios, television sets, automobiles, and vacation homes. In short, they want to participate in industry and the production process, increase their wealth, and enjoy material success.

As an industrial society achieves material success, it moves on to still another set of values. Sorokin labeled these new values "ideational." Alvin Toffler called them the third wave (1980). The post-industrial society is one where production shifts from tangible goods to services and information (a shift that took place in the United States somewhere around 1975). The new values come to center on the ability to express oneself in work and play. Maslow (1968) termed it "self-actualization." In highly developed, affluent societies, individuals strive for autonomy and control over their activities, enjoyment of the natural pleasures of life (a value that, if carried to its extreme, is referred to as hedonism), and becoming "at one with nature." Finally, despite a strong strain of individualism, ideational values include a desire for community and rewarding relationships with others.

A number of organizations have chosen to base strategies on current societal values. Volvo of Sweden, for example, incorporated ideational values into the redesign of its production procedures. Volvo did away with assembly line production and began having teams build cars from start to finish. This and other changes gave Volvo's workers more autonomy, freedom of expression, and sense of community. American firms such as Lincoln Electric, Donnelly Mirrors, Harwood Manufacturing, Harman International Industries, Hewlett-Packard, Dana Corporation, Delta Airlines, and Levi Strauss also have incorporated ideational values into their strategies.

IMPLICATIONS FOR STRATEGIC MANAGEMENT

Values, then, are fundamental to strategic management for a number of reasons. Values that are used to guide the business need to be appropriate for the time, place, and conditions in which the business operates. It is not a case of applying good or bad values (values are simply values), but rather of applying *appropriate* values. Some values, for example, are contrary to the laws of the society in which the company is to operate—a serious problem in international business. Other inappropriate values lead to the offering of products and services that customers are unwilling to pay for. In most situations, more than one set of values can be used to create a successful business. But whatever the values are, the success of the business depends on their appropriateness to the situation in which they are employed. In other words, the success of a strategy depends on the values that underlie it.

To be effective and operative, values must be embodied in the firm's *culture*—its atmosphere, norms, and attitudes about how business should be conducted. Perhaps the most important function of leaders is to ensure that organizational values become part of the firm's culture. Thomas Watson, Sr. understood this process very well. Among his values was to have customers perceive the company (IBM), and not individual salesmen, as providers of information systems and guarantors of high-quality service. One way he accomplished this was to impose a rigid dress code for the salesmen. Dressed in the IBM "uniform" (dark suit, white shirt, conservative tie, and well-polished shoes), the salesmen "disappeared" as individuals and became representatives of IBM.

One especially effective method of institutionalizing values within an organization's culture was developed at *The New Yorker* magazine. To appeal to its elite and sophisticated readers, the magazine set out to become known for superior writing, clear expression, and the absence of misprints and errors. At *The New Yorker,* extreme care is taken with the quality of every issue. Fact checkers retrace writers' steps, look up sources, and contact informants. The legal office examines every article for potential cases of libel. Editors and proofreaders comb every sentence for incorrect English usage and typographical errors. All of these procedures ensure that the magazine's values are part of its daily activities and culture.

The New Yorker reinforces its values by printing, as column fillers, humorous bloopers and examples of careless writing from other publications. Some are preceded by headings such as "How's That Again?" and "Letters We Never Finished Reading." Others are followed by sharp quips that highlight confusion created by the author's writing or the printer's errors. This practice serves a very useful purpose: it keeps the magazine's standards of excellence continuously in the minds of its employees, writers, and readers.

CORPORATE CULTURE

Corporate culture is the result of many factors. Among the most obvious are the type of business the organization is in, its products, its customers, its size and location, its competitive position, its financial and human resources, its formal structure, its methods of operating, and its facilities. Even more important, however, are the intangible factors: assumptions, beliefs, values, and the unwritten, often unspoken, and frequently unconscious norms and rules of the game that are *really* operating in the firm. Norms often reflect the values of the CEO or the founder of the firm.

Strategic managers ignore corporate culture at their peril because, to be implemented successfully, strategy must be consistent with the culture. New strategies almost always require changes in corporate culture. Strategic failures are often attributed to the inability of a firm to change its culture in ways that would make the new strategy work. There is often a gap between the existing culture and the appropriate culture for strategic success. Because culture consists largely of personal and social relationships and work tasks, such gaps are often defined as involving too much or too little of the following:

- Innovation in tasks and in task definition
- Support for task performance
- Attention to social and interpersonal relationships
- Personal freedom given to individuals

Studies show that the well-run businesses of the world have distinctive cultures that promote the creation, implementation, and maintenance of successful strategies (Schwartz and Davis, 1981). Because an organization's culture is crucial to the success of its strategy, part of strategic planning is to assess the culture and determine whether it would promote or defeat a proposed strategy. If it would defeat the strategy, can the culture be changed? Kilmann, Saxton, and Serpa (1985) suggested asking five basic questions about an organization's culture in order to assess its capacity for change.

1. What is the impact of culture on the organization's ability to carry out its activities and plans? The answer depends on the direction, pervasiveness, and strength of the culture. A *positive* culture supports the organization's mission and helps achieve its strategies. A *negative* culture, on the other hand, causes people to behave in ways that run counter to the expressed mission and strategies of the organization. A *pervasive* culture is widespread and shared by most of the organization's employees. *Strength* is the amount of pressure the culture exerts on employees, regardless of direction. A positive culture that is also pervasive and strong helps an organization carry out its activities and plans. "It points behavior in the right direction, is widely shared among the members of work groups, and puts strong pressure on group members to follow the established cultural guidelines" (p. 4). A negative culture that is strong and pervasive points people in the wrong direction and makes it hard to implement new strategies, policies, or plans.

2. How deep-seated is the culture? Kilmann, Saxton, and Serpa suggested three levels of depth: behavioral norms, hidden assumptions, and human nature. "Behavioral norms are just below the surface of experience . . . [and] describe the behaviors and attitudes that the members of a group or organization pressure one another to follow" (p. 5). "Wear only dark business suits to work" is such a norm. Hidden assumptions are the unstated beliefs people have about the organization's stakeholders—its suppliers, customers, competitors, allies, and regulators. (More will be said about stakeholders in the next chapter.) At the deepest level is human nature: employees' wants and needs, personal values, and the intellectual abilities they bring to the job. Cultures that penetrate all three are thus deep-seated and are the most difficult to change.

3. How many cultures does the organization have? Few organizations have just one culture, although some very successful corporations, such as IBM, General Electric, General Motors, and Texas Instruments, have an overarching, common culture. Different divisions of a company tend, however, to have different cultures, each with a direction, pervasiveness, strength, and depth of its own. The finance staff tends to have a much different culture than, say, the marketing group. Scientists in research and development view the world and the

company differently from managers and executives. Any successful change must deal with all the variations of corporate culture. Mergers and acquisitions often present very difficult problems of fusion—sometimes of diametrically opposed cultures.

4. How changeable is the culture? This answer depends on the answers to the three preceding questions. The direction, pervasiveness, strength, depth, and number of cultures present determine how readily an organization's culture or cluster of cultures can be changed. Another factor is the degree and type of cultural reinforcement offered by the organization's leaders. Executives can use rites, ceremonies, and reward systems to reinforce the current culture or to promote a new one. This leads to the last question.

5. Can culture alone be changed? The answer is generally no, because culture is made up of the assumptions, beliefs, and values of an organization's people and the tasks and activities they perform. What, then, must be changed to change corporate culture? Organizational structure, reward systems, work procedures, knowledge and skills, attitudes—all may have to be done if a new strategy is to succeed (see, for example, Kilmann, 1984, and Schein, 1985). In Chapter 10, we will describe methods for assessing an organization's culture and evaluating its ability to change.

CORPORATE SOCIAL RESPONSIBILITY

"America's top CEOs maintain that integrating the urban underclass into the national economy isn't just right—it's essential to everyone's prosperity" (Kirkland, 1992). This is the heart of the issue of corporate social responsibility. It is not a matter, as some would say, of being a do-gooder or ignoring the economic realities of the marketplace, and it is not solely an issue of what is right for business. It is nothing less than a matter of the survival of our economic system. Examples of socially responsible organizations illustrate that being a good "corporate citizen" is also good business. Baldor Electric CEO, Boreham, recognizes that restructuring that results in layoffs often means the loss of experienced and loyal workers who may be difficult to replace. Companies take this no-layoff approach in order to build a good company and sustain morale (Faltermayer, 1992). Joseph Vittoria, CEO of Avis, just says no to layoffs even when profits are down. Delta Airlines, in spite of a loss of $343 million, has not laid off a permanent employee in 35 years. Lincoln Electric believes in reducing the work week rather than losing experienced workers, and Nucor has been working four-day weeks for an extended period of time. While GM closes plants, Ford has refused to use dismissals and maintains that an experienced workforce helps ensure quality (Faltermayer, 1992).

The continuing downturn in business has, of course, led some companies to cut ethical corners in order to sustain profits. Yet James Burke, CEO of Johnson & Johnson, evaluated ten companies (J&J, Coca-Cola, Gerber Products, IBM, John

Deere, Kodak, 3M, Xerox, J.C. Penney, and Pitney Bowes) and showed that they grew an average of 11.3% from 1950 to 1990 while the Dow Jones industrial average increased only 6.2% for this same period. Each of the companies mentioned by Burke was considered an example of a responsible organization, and their growth records suggest a positive payoff (Labich, 1992). On the other hand, Steiner and Steiner (1991) reported on a study extending from 1972 to 1985 that showed that one could *not* conclude that socially responsible organizations have improved economic performance. They go on to specify what they consider a reasonable approach to social responsibility.

1. Each business must take into account the situation in which it finds itself in meeting stakeholder expectations.
2. Business is an economic entity and cannot jeopardize its profitability meeting social needs.
3. Business should recognize that in the long run, the general social good benefits everyone.
4. The social responsibility expected of a business is directly related to its social power to influence outcomes.
5. Social responsibility is related to the size of the company and to the industry it is in.
6. A business should tackle only those social problems in which it has competence.
7. Business must assume its share of the social burden and be willing to absorb reasonable social costs.

Though not prescriptive in an absolute sense, these seven guidelines provide a basis for reviewing each company's social responsibility posture. It is also possible to examine social responsibility by using Figure 3.4. This matrix helps explain both the basis for social choice (whether discretionary or legal) and how the company chooses to react to pressing social issues (proactive or reactive). Thus, for example, many companies respond on the basis of economics or beliefs because they only "react" to legal requirements such as mandated pollution control. Others are more "proactive" and choose to behave in an ethical or moral manner, as Johnson & Johnson did at the time of the Tylenol scare. More and more companies are expected to shift to this latter mode of social responsibility.

Historically, the term *responsibility* was used to describe moral actions. People were considered answerable for their actions and, accordingly, just recipients of the rewards, praise, blame, or punishment that flowed from their actions. Three central attributes of responsibility came from this idea:

1. *Obligation.* The notion that there are some actions a person can and must perform.
2. *Liability.* The notion that the neglect of a person's obligations is punishable. Legal liability makes a person bound to make good any loss or damage that occurs in a transaction.
3. *Incentive.* The notion that the fulfilling of a person's obligations should lead to rewards.

| FIGURE 3.4 | Social Responsibility of Business |

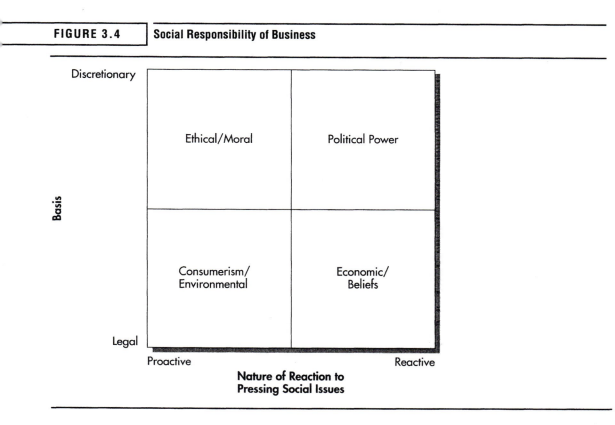

Underlying these attributes of responsibility is a fundamental psychological theory: motives cause human behavior. Motives can be conditioned by rewards and punishments, and they should be conditioned in such a way as to ensure that the resulting behavior is good, moral, or ethical.

This notion of responsibility was firmly held until the invention of the corporation as a legal entity. With the advent of the corporation, a single fictitious legal "person" was created who authorized a group of people to act as a single unit. This raised a new question: Do corporations have responsibilities just as people do?

In *The Wealth of Nations*, Adam Smith responded to this question and argued that corporations do have responsibilities. The profit motive and a well-functioning market, he argued, ensured that corporate behavior was socially good. The marketplace did this by regulating rewards and punishments via the profit mechanism and the free decisions of well-meaning customers. As a result, corporations that survived were socially responsible. The system guaranteed that only those firms that satisfied consumer needs would survive.

As late as 1919, this was the dominant legal view as well. In a classic case, *Dodge vs. Ford Motor Company* (S. Ct. Mich. 1919: 204 Mich. 459), the court opined:

> There should be no confusion (of which there is evidence) of the duties which Mr. Ford conceives that he and the stockholders owe to the general public and the duties which in law he and his co-directors owe to protesting, minority stockholders. A business corporation is organized and carried on primarily for the profit of the stockholders.

As corporations became more successful and more powerful, however, this view began to be challenged. Sylvia and Benjamin Selekman, in their book *Power and Morality in a Business Society* (New York, 1956), mounted their challenge as follows:

> The crisis which has led to the concern about social responsibility is much more complex. It stems from nothing less than the age-old problem of power—with its dangers as well as its beneficent aspects. Not until businessmen recognize that they are the administrators of power systems can they face realistically the task of how to discharge morally the power they wield.

Today there can be no doubt that modern society expects more of business than it once did. Ironically, as the Selekmans suggest, it is the very success of our economic system that has led to these expectations and has resulted in increased social demands being placed on corporations. And these demands extend far beyond the basic economic responsibilities of business. According to Davis (1973, p. 321), "Social responsibility has become a hallmark of a mature, global civilization," but the debate continues.

Along with these increasing pressures on the corporation from the public and from the state have come a steady erosion of institutional autonomy and, not surprisingly, a general decline in confidence in leadership. As Bennis (1977, pp. 36–37) puts it,

> What seems to have happened is this: the environmental encroachments and turbulence, the steady beat of litigation, the fragmentation of constituencies along with their new-found eloquence and power, multiple advocacy, win–lose adversarial conflicts between internal and external forces—all of this—had led to a situation where our leaders are paralyzed, or at least "keeping their heads below the grass," as Lyndon Johnson once put it. To grow and stay healthy an institution must strike a proper balance between openness to the environment and protection from too much permeability.

As corporations have come under increasing pressure on such issues as environmental protection, equal opportunity, and product safety, many have addressed these issues in their annual reports. Abbott and Monsen (1979), for example, found that the number of firms voluntarily reporting social responsibility disclosures increased from a little over 50% in 1971 to more than 85% in 1975. Society now demands that a modicum of corporate social responsibility take precedence over profit maximization. Moreover, it does not appear that this social involvement has been dysfunctional for the firm's stockholders. Socially responsible firms tend to perform as well as or better than those that are not.

This chapter is structured to help strategic managers assess the ethical and socially responsible dimensions of strategy. In the long run, an unethical or irresponsible strategy is as damaging to a firm as is an uneconomical strategy. This is because a corporation cannot survive without establishing the social legitimacy of its claim on social resources. In his book *Management: Tasks, Responsibilities, Practices* (1973), Peter Drucker describes succinctly the mutual relationship between strategy and legitimacy.

> The first job of management is, therefore, to identify and to anticipate impacts—coldly and realistically. The question is not, "Is what we do right?" It is "Do we do what society and the customer pay us for?" And if an activity is not integral to the institution's purpose and mission, it is to be considered as a social misfit and as undesirable.

Thus strategy becomes part of the social contract between an organization and its stakeholders. It is legitimate to the extent that it satisfies the functions and expectations for which these stakeholders allocate its resources. How can an organization's social legitimacy be determined? The methods described in the next three sections of this book were designed to help the strategic manager answer this question.

The first method, the *corporate social performance matrix* (CSPM), helps the manager evaluate the impact of a strategy on each of the firm's stakeholders with regard to pressing social issues influencing the firm. The result is a map of the critical issues and a scaling of the relative importance of each issue to the success of the strategy. (See Figure 3.5.) The CSPM also suggests which stakeholder demands may create liabilities and obligations for the firm.

The *ethical audit of strategy*, which we examine after an in-depth discussion of the relationship between ethics and strategy, penetrates deeper into the social legitimacy of a strategy. Drawing on basic ethical theory, it requires that a specific set of ethical issues be examined and discussed. The strategy is evaluated in terms of whether it violates or promotes a basic human right, produces good or harm to people, or is just or unjust in its assumptions about the distribution of organizational wealth.

Finally, a method that has been used successfully for role-playing in corporations and classrooms is presented. It is based on the writings of C. West Churchman, who has devoted his life to the pursuit of logic, systems analysis, and rational thinking as

---

FIGURE 3.5 | **Corporate Social Performance Matrix**

	Stakeholders						
Pressing social issues	A	B	C	D	E	F	...
1							
2							
3							
4							
5							
⋮							

a means by which the human intellect can solve social problems. His inquiry reveals the limitations of rational analysis as well. He calls these limitations "enemies" and identifies four key ones: politics, morality, aesthetics, and religion. The *enemies check* offers a creative way to go beyond the constraints of the CSPM and the ethical audit and to explore the full range of forces that may shape strategy.

CORPORATE SOCIAL PERFORMANCE MATRIX

BACKGROUND

There have been several attempts to operationalize the concept of corporate social responsibility, most notably Carroll's (1979) three-dimensional conceptual model of corporate performance and Halal's (1977) return-on-resources model of corporate performance. We will examine the former in detail.

Carroll defines *corporate social responsibility* as the entire range of obligations business has to society. These obligations must include economic, legal, ethical, and discretionary categories of business performance. It is often argued that businesses have traditionally emphasized their economic and legal responsibilities, whereas now there is also a growing response to ethical and discretionary aspects of social responsibility. However, these four categories are not mutually exclusive, and the boundaries between them are difficult, if not impossible, to define. Also, these terms are not value-free, and they will be interpreted differently by different people. Management, for example, may view a certain decision as discretionary, while another group of stakeholders may see it strictly as an economic response.

No corporate social posture will be value-free, and this is what makes corporate social responsiveness such a difficult undertaking. Halal (1977, p. 25) states that a firm can only attempt to unite "the diverse interests of various social groups to form a workable coalition engaged in creating value for distribution among members of the coalition." It is obvious that beyond a certain level of economic activity, the social issues at stake may become conflicting (an example is profitability versus pollution control) and that *tradeoffs* must be made by management. These tradeoffs involve both economic and ethical decisions that will not necessarily satisfy the needs of every stakeholder.

METHODOLOGY

The *corporate social performance matrix* (CSPM) is a tool that helps the strategic manager make these socioeconomic decisions. This method, which evaluates the total social performance of the organization on the basis of how well it is dealing with pressing social issues and satisfying stakeholder needs, is based on a simple model:

(organizational performance on an issue) × (importance weight of the issue)
= (evaluation on the issue).

FIGURE 3.6	A Checklist of Pressing Social Issues

1. **Economics**
   a. Profitability
   b. Market penetration
   c. Customer loyalty, goodwill
   d. Financial stability

2. **Environment**
   a. Pollution control
   b. Repair of environment
   c. Recycling of waste material

3. **Discrimination**
   a. Minority employment
   b. Employment of women
   c. Equal opportunities
   d. Minority business partners

4. **Personnel**
   a. Occupational health and safety
   b. Salary level
   c. Training; education
   d. Counseling

5. **Products**
   a. Safety
   b. Quality
   c. Product improvement

6. **Community Involvement**
   a. Community activities
   b. Public health
   c. Education; arts

7. **Others**

Adding the resultant scores for all issues gives a measure of the corporate social performance for the organization as a whole.

This method should be extended, however, because the evaluation of performance on an issue is very much dependent on the point of view of the stakeholder involved. A thorough assessment requires the formulation of a stakeholder/issue matrix (see Figure 3.5). This matrix is used to evaluate the organization's performance with regard to each key stakeholder and for each pressing social issue.

To use this method, the strategic manager first identifies the pressing social issues facing the organization. Figure 3.6 can be used as a checklist for this task. Next the manager evaluates the organization's current performance for each stakeholder and each issue, using a scale of 0 to 9. A zero is assigned if there is no issue that is relevant for that stakeholder. A 9 is assigned if the performance needs significant improvement.

After completing these entries, the strategic manager has a more comprehensive picture of how the company meets the different social demands made by its stakeholders. Furthermore, weights can be assigned to reflect the importance of the different issues. Suggested weights are as follows: very important = 4; important = 3; moderately important = 2; marginally important = 1. When the values are summed across the rows and then multiplied by the "importance weights" of the different issues, this table provides an indication of what the company needs to address. The strategic manager can find out how the different stakeholders can benefit from the firm's performance. Finally, the combined total of *all* the evaluations on the different issues gives an overall indication of how well the company is addressing the social issues it faces. An application of this method is shown in Worksheet 3.1.

| **WORKSHEET 3.1** | **Corporate Social Performance Matrix** |

Case ___Polaroid___

Date ___1990___

Name ___John Doe___

Stakeholders

Pressing social issues	Importance weights	1 Stockholders	2 Customers	3 Management	4 Employees	5 Government	6 Local communities	7 Suppliers	8	Row total	Performance evaluation
1. Economic	4	2	3	1	1	0	1	0		8	32
2. Environment	3	1	1	1	0	1	1	0		5	15
3. Discrimination	2	0	0	2	1	1	1	1		6	12
4. Personnel	2	2	0	2	3	1	2	0		10	20
5. Products	3	1	4	3	2	3	1	2		16	48
6. Community involvement	1	0	0	1	0	1	2	0		4	4
7. Other											
Stakeholder evaluation		6	8	12	7	5	3	3		Total	111

(Performance ratings span stakeholder columns 1–8)

Discussion

Excellent performance in product safety and quality. Somewhat weak economic performance paired with low responsiveness to personnel and community needs (layoffs, shutdowns). Currently, the company rates rather low in terms of its responsiveness to social issues. Customers and management seem to benefit from the company's current performance, whereas shareholders, employees, and local communities presently gain little benefit from the company. Much of the company's below-average performance, however, is due to its current economic problems and should improve as these problems are solved. The company seems to be strongest in the treatment of environmental and product issues.

ETHICS AND STRATEGY

Two additional factors affecting the choice of a strategy are (1) the ethical norms of the society in which the firm does business and (2) the ethical principles of its leaders. Professor Mark Pastin, who is director of the Center for Private and Public Ethics at Arizona State University, believes that there is a strong link between ethics and strategy. Pastin argues that ethical thinking and strategic thinking are inseparable. Furthermore, ethical thinking teaches the executive some important lessons about strategic thinking because it opens up new pathways of analysis, often with surprising results. For one thing, ethical analysis alerts managers to social and political problems (and opportunities) that they might otherwise have ignored.

Ethics is also inseparable from the values that guide executives in the setting of organizational purposes, goals, and objectives. Ethics poses two key questions that need to be answered when formulating strategy:

1. Are the values that underlie the strategy defensible?
2. Are the effects of the strategy on the firm's stakeholders moral?

Answering these questions involves bringing to the surface the value assumptions that underlie the strategy and relating them to the various stakeholders. Next these assumptions must be examined from an ethical point of view. This evaluation requires ethical criteria drawn from the analyst's background on ethical thinking.

ETHICS IN PRACTICE

The strategic decisions managers make reveal the basic values and ethical principles to which they subscribe (Andrews, 1989). The size of most companies makes direct influence or control by management exceedingly difficult. Company policy can easily be ignored because of the communication problems posed by distance and by the many layers of management. As more companies decentralize and globalize, the possibility of corruption and misconduct expand. The CEO often helps to avoid these problems by making appropriate moral judgments, as in the case of the Tylenol recall. But leaders can also exert a bad influence: witness the S&L scandals and cheating on reports to the government by some aerospace companies. Ultimately, then, the executive is the one responsible for building a culture wherein trust, confidence, and honesty are rewarded. Quick action against offenders helps convince everyone that lapses in ethical conduct will not be tolerated.

Unfortunately, executives often exert pressure to compromise on ethical behavior (Richard, 1991). A survey done at Central Michigan University revealed that financial executives felt pressured to compromise on regulatory or legal requirements. In a number of cases, people were either "eased out" or terminated for refusing to act unethically. The majority of the respondents chose to do something about the situation (55%), compared with 18% who said they would do nothing and 27% who simply avoided the situation.

In a study of ethical codes of conduct at companies in the Fortune 500, Pelfrey and Peacock (1991) found some signs of improvement. For example, approximately half of the companies surveyed claimed they had a formal code of conduct. The survey revealed that 69% of the responding firms instruct their employees to contact legal counsel if they become aware of misconduct. Even so, in a number of incidents (such as the Watergate scandal and the explosion of one of the space shuttles), the "whistle blowers" suffered because of their willingness to speak up.

To help encourage ethical behavior, a number of companies are introducing training programs that foster an ethical culture by showing how it creates a competitive advantage (Harrington, 1991). Codes of ethics by themselves do not create a culture where ethical conduct is expected. To ensure that strategic decision makers will take ethical considerations into account, companies increasingly are turning to ethics training. However, to be successful, these programs must make it clear just how ethical behavior contributes to attaining a strategic advantage. Some executives complain that these programs have been a dismal failure, in part because participants sense that management is not sincere in its desire to support an ethical corporate culture. Ultimately, ethical behavior becomes meaningful when executives strongly support its incorporation into corporate culture and when there is clear evidence that ethics is an integral part of strategic decisions.

RIGHTS AND THE CATEGORICAL IMPERATIVE

In a school of thought that philosophers call "deontological ethics," there are said to exist rights and duties that should not be compromised under any circumstances. Thomas Jefferson referred to these as "inalienable rights" when he wrote the Declaration of Independence. It is the philosopher Immanual Kant, however, who is generally credited with the fullest development of the idea of rights. In *Foundations of the Metaphysics of Morals* (1787) he argues that society should strive to become a "kingdom of ends" in which all persons are treated as ends in themselves—never as only a means to achieve someone else's ends. The key to achieving this is in finding moral laws that are applied equally to everybody and from which no exceptions should be made (Kant thought "Thou shall not kill" was such a rule). This line of reasoning gives rise to rights—things a person has an inviolable and justifiable claim to—and to duties—obligations an individual cannot ignore.

An ethical strategy must adhere to the duties imposed on a firm by law or by custom. Furthermore, any strategy that would violate one or more stakeholder's rights is unethical. The following are some rights to be considered in strategic thinking (*Source:* Cavanagh, Moberg, and Velasquez, 1981, pp. 365–366).

1. *Right to life.* Acts taken under the strategy should not endanger the life of any stakeholder or subject a stakeholder unduly to injury.
2. *Right to property.* Acts taken under the strategy should not violate any stakeholder's claim to ownership of material possessions or "property."
3. *Right to free consent.* Stakeholders have a right to be treated by the firm only as they knowingly and freely consent to be treated.
4. *Right to privacy.* Stakeholders have the right to a private life and to choose what they share with others in intimate relationships.

5. *Right to freedom of conscience.* Stakeholders have the right to refrain from carrying out any order that violates the moral or religious norms to which they adhere.
6. *Right to free speech.* Stakeholders have the right to criticize conscientiously and truthfully the morality of actions taken by others so long as their criticism does not violate the others' rights.
7. *Right to due process.* Stakeholders have the right to a fair and impartial hearing whenever they believe that their rights have been violated.

Policies with respect to employees, consumers, and communities can be evaluated by means of the criteria suggested by these rights and others.

JUSTICE

The ideas of justice and rights are related, justice being the more general concept. John Stuart Mill, for example, listed the violation of rights as one sense of "injustice." In the general sense, justice is *fairness*: Is each stakeholder being treated fairly? In a more specific sense, justice has to do with *each stakeholder getting what he or she deserves.* Students who participate in a class expect to be treated fairly and to be given the grade they deserve. The stakeholders who participate in a corporate strategy expect the same treatment. When they receive it, justice is served.

John Rawls, in *A Theory of Justice* (1971), proposed two principles by which a just society would live. His carefully worded work may be summarized and paraphrased as follows:

a. Each stakeholder is to have an equal right to the same basic liberties every other stakeholder has a right to.
b. Social and economic inequalities among stakeholders are to be arranged so that they are:
   1) To the greatest benefit to the least advantaged stakeholder.
   2) Attached to offices and positions open to all under conditions of fair equality of opportunity.

Cavanagh, Moberg, and Velasquez (1981, pp. 363–374) have summarized the concerns for justice in terms of three canons, which they append to the list of rights that we have just examined:

8. *Distributive rules.* Acts taken under the strategy should distribute benefits and burdens equitably among stakeholders and on the basis of criteria relevant to tasks and goals. The strategy should not result in a worsening of the position of the least advantaged stakeholder.
9. *Fair administration.* The rules and policies of the strategy should be clearly stated and consistently and impartially enforced.
10. *Compensation norms.* Stakeholders should not be held responsible for matters over which they have no control, and stakeholders should be compensated by the parties responsible for injustices done to them.

UTILITARIANISM

Jeremy Bentham, in his *Introduction to Principles of Morals and Legislation* (1948), argued that "Nature has placed mankind under the governance of two sovereign masters, *pain* and *pleasure*." Thus he proposed that a pain/pleasure calculus (not unlike cost/benefit analysis) be developed and applied to all decisions. The option with the greatest balance of pleasure over pain was to be preferred. This has come to be summarized as "the greatest good for the greatest number."

Utilitarianism suggests that in assessing a strategy, the firm should choose strategies that satisfy Bentham's criterion in terms of either the ends they seek or the means they employ. More precisely,

11. *Ethical ends.* The strategic outcome should result in the greatest good for the greatest number for the longest period of time.
12. *Ethical means.* The actions taken in implementing the strategy should constitute an efficient means for stakeholders to realize the greatest good for the greatest number.

ETHICAL AUDIT OF STRATEGY

The twelve principles just described constitute a checklist for evaluating a strategy from an ethical point of view. Each principle forces the manager to think about some aspect of a strategy that may have been overlooked. Sometimes these principles yield conflicting advice. For example, a strategy may involve endangering someone's life yet potentially provide great benefits to a large number of stakeholders. Based on these considerations, the manager must decide whether the strategy is ultimately ethical or not. Worksheet 3.2 provides a framework for arriving at such decisions.

It should be pointed out that some well-respected observers believe that this kind of ethical audit is unnecessary. Nor is it necessary, in their view, to undertake a separate corporate social responsibility review. They argue that the free market effectively does this. One of the strongest proponents of this view, University of Chicago economist Milton Friedman, summarizes his position in *Capitalism and Freedom* (1962, p. 133):

> There is one and only one social responsibility of business—to use its resources and engage in activities designed to increase its profits so long as it stays within the rules of the game, which is to say, engages in open and free competition, without deception or fraud.

He goes on to conclude that

> Few trends could so thoroughly undermine the very foundations of our free society as the acceptance by corporate officials of a social responsibility other than to make as much money for their stockholders as possible. This can be a fundamentally subversive doctrine.

You should decide for yourself on this. But try Worksheet 3.2 before you make up your mind.

WORSHEET 3.2	**Ethical Audit of Strategy**

Case _____

Date _____

Name _____

1. Impact on Right to Life

    Violates _____ Neutral _____ Promotes

2. Impact on Right to Property

    Violates _____ Neutral _____ Promotes

3. Impact on Right to Free Consent

    Violates _____ Neutral _____ Promotes

4. Impact on Right to Privacy

    Violates _____ Neutral _____ Promotes

5. Impact on Right to Freedom of Conscience

    Violates _____ Neutral _____ Promotes

6. Impact on Right to Free Speech

    Violates _____ Neutral _____ Promotes

7. Impact on Right to Due Process

    Violates _____ Neutral _____ Promotes

8. Impact on Distribution

    Just _____ Neutral _____ Unjust

9. Fairness of Administration

    Just _____ Neutral _____ Unjust

10. Norms of Compensation

    Just _____ Neutral _____ Unjust

11. Strategic Ends and Outcomes

    Great Good _____ Neutral _____ Great Harm

12. Strategic Means Employed

    Great Good _____ Neutral _____ Great Harm

THE ENEMIES CHECK

According to the philosopher G. W. F. Hegel, "Nothing great in the world has been accomplished without passion." It might also be said that many great intentions have been thwarted with passion. Criticisms of a business's products and policies, demands for new products and policies, and the changing attitudes of a business's managers, workers, customers, and clients all stem from people and their passions. *Any effective plan should mobilize the emotional force of the passion behind it and avoid those passions that might be directed against it.*

Unfortunately, most methods for formulating strategy are purely logical and rational. They depend on economic and technical analysis. Yet passions and the opportunities and threats they represent emerge from the nonrational—even the irrational—aspects of the environment. And they are generally neglected or ignored by rational analytical methods.

One example of the impact of passion on an organization comes from the Tennessee Valley Authority. The TVA was engaged in a major new dam building project when a group of impassioned environmentalists demanded that construction be stopped because the new dam endangered the only known habitat of a 3-inch fish called the snail-darter. As a consequence, a $120-million project was brought to a halt. Other examples include stockholders arguing that a firm should sell off its holdings in South Africa, citizens lashing themselves to trees so that lumbering companies cannot proceed with their work, protestors throwing themselves in front of trucks so that materials cannot be used to construct a nuclear power plant, strikes, sit-ins, and civil disobedience. These events are so well known that most executives and corporate planners use such terms as "show stoppers" and "wild cards" to describe them.

Is it possible to anticipate these rare, nonrational business forces? No surefire method is known. However, drawing on C. West Churchman's concept of the "enemies" of rationality, a simple, mind-expanding, brainstorming approach has been devised. In *The Systems Approach and Its Enemies* (1979), Churchman identifies four historical *enemies* of rational systems thinking: politics, morality, aesthetics, and religion. He argues that managers and planners should try to hear the "voices" of these enemies whenever they are developing a plan. It may be that one or more of these enemies will be responsible for the next show stopper. Each enemy, Churchman maintains, can have its own effect.

Politics affects a plan in that stakeholders, in the pursuit of their own interests—namely power, status, influence, and recognition—collect together to form a community around some aspect of that plan. That is, they form a *polis,* to use the Greek word.

Morality affects a plan in that stakeholders, as a part of their human spirit, possess a moral force. If some aspect of a plan impinges on that force, they respond with "that's wrong," "that's evil" or "that's right," "that's good."

Aesthetics affects a plan in that stakeholders respond to the beauty or ugliness of a plan, the "radiance" it gives off, its artistic form, or the tastefulness with which it is conducted. Considerations of form, symmetry, and harmony are part of the aesthetic dimension.

Religion affects a plan in that stakeholders react to it in terms of their orientation to unity in the universe and the creation of a satisfying and meaningful relationship with it. According to Churchman (1979, p. 173), the "religious approach to human affairs occurs *first* when we humans decide in terms of something we regard as superior, grander, more magnificent, than we feel ourselves to be" or "*second,* when we humans decide in terms of the small, minuscule, unique, which is not inferior to us, and is indeed superior because of its smallness." The Sierra Club's dedication to nature is an example of Churchman's first condition. E. F. Schumacher's passion for "small is beautiful" and "appropriate technology" is an example of the second condition. One company, Service Master, bases its mission on Christian values and sets as its goals "to honor God in all we do, to help people develop, to pursue excellence, to grow profitably," in that order.

The *enemies check* is a heuristic test to determine whether the nonrational forces of politics, morality, aesthetics, and religion are potentially working for or against the plan. It further aids in anticipating what form the wild card or show stopper might take. This method is based on the following thought-provoking questions:

1. Politics
   a. In what way might stakeholders be related to each other around a common issue such that they acquire power either to stop or to support the plan?
   b. Who are the agents likely to take action on this?
2. Morality
   a. What kinds of ethical issues, "wrongs" or "rights," does the plan raise?
   b. Who are the agents likely to take action on this?
3. Aesthetics
   a. What kinds of ugliness or beauty does the plan create?
   b. Who are the agents likely to take action on this?
4. Religion
   a. What basic beliefs about people and the universe are offended or supported by the plan?
   b. Who are the agents likely to take action on this?

The enemies check brings out threats to and support for a strategy that other methods usually fail to surface. Once an enemy of a strategy is identified, there are several actions one can take to deal with it:

- Confront, fight, or challenge it.
- Avoid it.
- Appease it.
- Surrender or concede to it.
- Convert it to a support.
- Love it.
- Incorporate it so completely that it becomes the plan.

Choosing one of these options for an identified enemy of the plan greatly enriches a strategy and improves its chances of success.

S UMMARY

Effective strategic management, particularly strategic planning, requires a thorough understanding of the organization itself. The vision of the organization's founder, CEO, or strategic-management team cannot be realized if it is not consistent with the assumptions and beliefs, values, and culture that prevail in the organization. One of the tasks of strategic planners is to assess these organizational qualities and, where inconsistencies are found, decide whether to change the vision or the organization.

Another task is to evaluate prevailing assumptions, beliefs, and values to determine whether they are helping or hurting the organization. Appropriate assumptions, beliefs, and values have two main characteristics: (1) they reflect internal and external realities, and (2) they help the organization to achieve its vision. Inappropriate assumptions, beliefs, and values have opposite effects and must be changed *before* top managers attempt to introduce a new vision.

Sometimes a strategic planning team works with the CEO and top managers to develop a new vision for the organization. If this is the case, knowledge about the organization's internal environment helps planners to develop an appropriate vision. The emerging vision also should meet two criteria for profitability: (1) It should involve businesses/products with the potential for leveraged customer value, and (2) it should involve businesses/products with the potential for increased competitive advantage through system innovation. These criteria are essential because they involve changes in customer perception and organizational operations, both of which can be achieved through effective management and should not require extensive capital outlays.

The strategic planning team helps the organization to devise a grand strategy to achieve the vision and then develops specific goals, objectives, and plans of action. Where the CEO and top managers have difficulty thinking through the strategy, goals, or objectives, these can be analyzed via the critical-success-factor method shown in Chapter 5.

The strategic manager must be concerned with the social legitimacy as well as the economic vitality of the firm's strategy. As new social issues—such as product safety, occupational health and safety, employment, equal opportunity, and pollution—have surfaced, they have become a matter of strategy. Not only do most corporations want to develop socially responsible and ethical strategies; they *must* do so as a matter of survival. Modern corporate leaders must be able to explain the organization's position and to defend it.

The three methods presented in this chapter assist the strategic manager in this process of establishing social legitimacy and defending it. The *corporate social performance matrix* identifies salient stakeholders and issues. The *ethical audit* evaluates a strategy on fundamental ethical issues. And the *enemies check* determines the robustness of a strategy in the face of nonrational claims against it.

The results of these three reviews are used for two purposes:

1. To shape a responsible and ethical strategy.
2. To prepare the arguments necessary to explain the social legitimacy of the strategy to all stakeholders, including stockholders, employees, government agencies, community leaders, public interest groups, and individual challengers.

R EFERENCES AND SUGGESTIONS FOR FURTHER READING

Abbott, Walter F. and Monsen, Joseph R. 1979. On the measurement of corporate social responsibility: Self-reported disclosures as a method of measuring corporate social involvement. *Academy of Management Journal* 22, no. 3.

Abegglen, James C. and George Stalk, Jr. 1985, *Kaisha, the Japanese corporation.* New York: Basic Books.

Andrews, Kenneth. 1989. Ethics in practice. *Harvard Business Review,* September–October, pp. 99–104.

Ansoff, H. Igor. 1972. The concept of strategic management. *Journal of Business Policy.* Summer.

Ansoff, H. Igor. 1965. *Corporate strategy.* New York: McGraw-Hill.

Barnard, Chester I. 1979. *The functions of the executive.* Cambridge, Mass.: Harvard University Press, p. 217.

Bauer, Raymond A. and Dan H. Fenn, Jr. 1972. *The corporate social audit.* New York: Russell Sage Foundation.

Bennis, Warren. 1989. *On becoming a leader.* Reading, Mass.: Addison-Wesley.

Bennis, Warren G. 1977. Where have all the leaders gone? *The McKinsey Quarterly,* Autumn.

Bentham, Jeremy. 1948. *Introduction to principles of morals and legislation.* New York: Hafner, Macmillan.

Carlson, W. Bernard. 1991. *Innovation as a social process.* New York: Cambridge University Press.

Carroll, Archie B. 1979. A three-dimensional conceptual model of corporate performance. *Academy of Management Review* 4, no. 4.

Cavanagh, Gerald F., Dennis J. Moberg, and Manuel Velasquez. 1981. The ethics of organizational politics. *Academy of Management Review* 3, no. 3, pp. 363–374.

Christensen, C. Roland, Kenneth R. Andrews, and Joseph L. Bower. 1978. *Business policy: Text and cases.* 4th ed. Homewood, Ill.: Irwin, pp. 247–259.

Churchman, C. West. 1979. *The systems approach and its enemies.* New York: Basic Books.

Churchman, C. West. 1968. *The systems approach.* New York: Delacorte Press.

Davis, Keith. 1973. The arguments for and against corporate social responsibility. *Academy of Management Journal* 16, no. 2.

Drucker, Peter F. 1973. *Management: Tasks, responsibilities, practices.* New York: Harper & Row.

Faltermayer, Edmund. 1992. Is this layoff necessary? *Fortune,* June 1, pp. 71–86.

Friedman, Milton. 1970. The social responsibility of business is to increase its profits. *New York Times Magazine,* September 13.

Friedman, Milton. 1962. *Capitalism and freedom.* Chicago: University of Chicago Press.

Garvin, D. A. 1983. Quality on the line. *Harvard Business Review* 6, no. 5. September–October, pp. 65–75.

General Electric—Going with the winners. 1984. *Forbes,* March 26, pp. 97–106.

Granger, Charles H. 1964. Hierarchy of objectives. *Harvard Business Review* 42, no. 3. May–June.

Guth, William D. and Renato Tagiuri. 1965. Personal values and corporate strategy. *Harvard Business Review* 43, no. 5, September–October.

Halal, William E. 1977. A return-on-resources model of corporate performance. *California Management Review* 19, no. 4.

Harrington, Susan. 1991. What corporate America is teaching about ethics. *Academy of Management Executive,* no. 1, pp. 21–30.

Hippel, Eric V. 1988. *The sources of innovation.* Oxford, England: Oxford University Press, p. 102.

Jack Welch: How good a manager? 1987. *Business Week,* December 14, p. 92.

Kilmann, Ralph H. 1984. *Beyond the quick fix: Managing the five tracks to organizational success.* San Francisco: Jossey-Bass.

Kilmann, Ralph H., Marry J. Saxton, and Roy Serpa. 1985. *Gaining control of the corporate culture.* San Francisco: Jossey-Bass.

Kirkland, Richard I., Jr. 1992. What we can do now. *Fortune,* June 1, pp. 41–48.

Labich, Kenneth. 1992. The new crisis in business ethics. *Fortune,* April 20, pp. 167–176.

Maslow, Abraham. 1969. *Toward a psychology of being.* 2nd ed. Princeton, N.J.: Van Nostrand.

Mott, P. E. 1972. *The characteristics of effective organizations.* New York: Harper & Row.

News/Trends: A Sweet Swap for GE and Thomson. 1987. *Fortune,* August 17, p. 8.

Pelfrey, Sandra, and Eileen Peacock. 1991. Ethical codes of conduct are improving. *Business Forum,* Spring, pp. 14–17.

Peters, Thomas J. and Robert H. Waterman, Jr. 1982. *In search of excellence: Lessons from America's best-run companies.* New York: Harper & Row.

Rawls, John. 1971. *A theory of justice.* Cambridge, Mass.: Harvard University.

Richard, Gary. 1991. Bosses pressure corporate financial executives to compromise ethics. *Program Manager,* July–August, pp. 34–41.

Rockart, John F. 1979. Chief executives define their own data needs. *Harvard Business Review* 57, no. 2. March–April.

Rokeach, Milton. 1973. *The nature of human values.* New York: The Free Press, p. 5.

Sarnoff, David. 1968. *Looking ahead.* New York: McGraw-Hill, pp. 31–34.

Schein, Edgar H. 1985. *Organizational culture and leadership: A dynamic view.* San Francisco: Jossey-Bass.

Schwartz, H. M. and S. M. Davis. 1981. Matching corporate culture and business strategy. *Organizational Dynamics,* Summer, pp. 30–48.

Selekman, Sylvia and Benjamin Selekman. 1956. *Power and morality in a business society.* New York: McGraw-Hill.

Smart, Tim. 1992. How Jack Welch brought GE to life. *Business Week,* October 26, pp. 13–15.

Sorokin, Pitirim. 1937–1941. *Social and cultural dynamics.* New York: American Book Company.

Spranger, Eduard. 1928. *Types of men.* Translated by P. Pigors. Halle, Germany: Niemeyer.

Steiner, George A. and John F. Steiner. 1991. *Business, government, and society.* New York: McGraw-Hill.

Sterling, Christopher H. and John M. Kittross. 1978. *Stay tuned: A concise history of American broadcasting,* appendix C. Belmont, Calif.: Wadsworth.

Toffler, Alvin. 1980. *The third wave.* New York: William Morrow.

Zakon, Alan J. 1985. The beliefs audit. *BCG Perspectives,* no. 282.

CHAPTER FOUR

The Competitive Environment

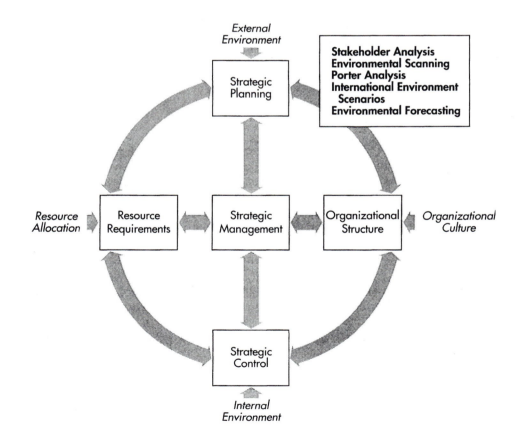

Chapter 1 A Framework for Strategic Management	**Chapter 2** Strategic Analysis	**Chapter 3** Strategic Visioning, Goals, Ethics, and Social Responsibility	**Chapter 4** The Competitive Environment	**Chapter 5** Capability-based Strategy	**Chapter 6** Market Dynamics and Sustainable Competitive Advantage
How to approach strategic management	*Application of strategic analysis*	*Understanding vision, values, ethics*	*Coping with competitive forces, stakeholders*	*Assessing company capability, timeliness, quality*	*Determining trends, gap analysis, and market dynamics*

Chapter 7 Strategy in a Global Environment	**Chapter 8** Financial Planning and Competitive- Cost Analysis	**Chapter 9** Entrepreneurship, Mergers and Acquisitions, Restructuring, and the Service Sector	**Chapter 10** Leadership Factor in Strategy and Implementing Strategic Change	**Chapter 11** Information Technology and Future Directions in Strategy
Assessing global trade, foreign markets, monetary exchange	*Preparing a financial plan and competitive- cost analysis*	*Importance of small business, entrepreneurs, restructuring*	*Strategy implementation, leadership, culture*	*Information technology, trends, new management*

INTRODUCTION

Organizations can be compared to ecological entities that have mutual relations with other entities in their environment. Like any ecosystem, an organization's environment holds opportunities and threats. Skillful strategic managers find in the firm's environment "market niches" that are particularly well suited to the products, services, and capabilities the organization has to offer. Failure to find a suitable niche leads the organization to encounter elements that can cause harm or even destruction. Successful strategic planning, therefore, requires a careful assessment of the external environment. Environmental assessment enables the organization to (1) find the best possible niche and (2) decide how it would respond to a range of environmental conditions that might occur in the future. Environmental assessment is a never-ending task for most firms because the environment is continuously changing.

Conducting an environmental assessment involves several different but interconnected layers see (Figure 4.1). In this chapter, we will discuss each of these layers.

As a start it is typically useful to conduct an environmental scan as a general overview. *Environmental scanning* is a method of identifying the economic, political, social, technological, competitive, and geographic factors that have an impact on the *firm* and then assessing their potential as opportunities or threats.

FIGURE 4.1	Levels of a Company's Economic Environment

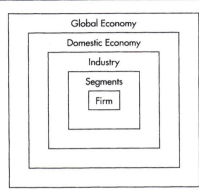

Source: Courtesy of The Boston Consulting Group, Inc. Reprinted with permission.

Strategic segmentation is essential in visualizing the competitive arena. The goal of strategic segmentation is to convert differences from competitors into a sustainable competitive advantage for the company. Understanding the different competitive environments and the forces driving an *industry* is essential in this process.

Stakeholder analysis covers the next level, that of the *domestic economy*. First, strategic managers identify the key stakeholders in the organization's business environment. Second, significant relationships among the stakeholders are charted to make a stakeholder map. The stakeholder map is a tool that strategic managers can use to identify the sources of environmental opportunities and threats and the ways they are transmitted to the organization. Third, managers identify and test assumptions about stakeholders, rank these assumptions, and determine which assumptions are most accurate and advantageous.

A discussion of the global economy follows. For most large companies today, global management is mandatory. It is also becoming increasingly important to medium-sized and smaller companies as countries around the world grow more closely linked culturally and economically. Entering foreign markets carries both significant opportunities and risks. Careful *assessment of the international environment* can be the basis for superior performance abroad.

Increasingly, companies are turning to environmental forecasting as a means of determining what strategies are needed to meet competitors' actions. Forecasting can be based on an analysis of such environmental data such as government or industry reports, industry trend analysis, competitor intelligence analysis, Delphi projections, or statistical analysis for predicting outcomes. Forecasting provides a basis for determining whether the courses of action under consideration will achieve the firm's goals and objectives.

An important forecasting approach that is fairly direct and has produced valuable results is scenario writing. This approach can utilize the expertise needed for a Delphi analysis or the knowledge of strategic planners who can project the likelihood of various outcomes. A number of approaches can be used to develop scenarios. These approaches, along with examples of how they are used, are discussed in this chapter.

ENVIRONMENTAL SCANNING

The external environment of an organization is defined by the set of forces with which that organization interacts. External forces include all kinds of stakeholders, economic trends, unforeseen events or crises, and various regulatory policies and laws. *Environmental scanning* is the first step in finding and analyzing external threats and opportunities. At this early stage in the strategic management process, managers need to identify all general events and trends that could be pertinent to the company's performance in the future.

Experience shows that environmental scanning is most productive when it consists of a brainstorming session by a group. Group sessions often result in a heightened awareness of reasons for strategic revisions or insights about future development. During the scanning session, managers try to identify environmental factors relevant to the following six key areas.

1. *Economics*: Factors related to the flow of money, goods and services, information, and energy
2. *Politics*: Factors related to the use or allocation of power among people, including dealings with local and foreign governments
3. *Social trends and demographics*: Factors that affect the way people live, including what they value
4. *Technology*: Factors related to the development of machines, tools, processes, materials, other equipment, and know-how
5. *Competition*: Factors that involve actions taken by current and potential competitors, market share, and concentration of competitors
6. *Geography*: Factors related to location, space, topography, climate, and natural resources

Scanning these six key areas reveals most of the environmental factors that need to be considered. Sometimes, however, managers find it useful to add another key area, such as the military, education, the law, medicine, or religion.

When all the relevant factors have been identified, managers can develop an environmental threat and opportunity profile (ETOP). The ETOP gives the first indication of potential external opportunities and threats. Depending on the impact and importance of each factor, managers can determine whether that factor may pose a threat to the firm, is neutral, or represents an opportunity. To assess its impact and importance, each factor is given a score. Scores for each factor's importance and impact are multiplied to obtain a combined score that is used to assess the organization's overall position with respect to its environment. An application of the ETOP to IBM's situation in 1992 is shown in Worksheet 4.1. Although the scores are only estimates, their relative weight (rather than their absolute value) indicates the firm's position.

WORKSHEET 4.1	Environmental Scanning

Case ___IBM___

Date ___1992___

Name ___Mary Jones___

Factors	Impact of Factor	Importance of Factor	Environmental Threat
Economic	7	8	56
Political	2	1	2
Social	1	2	2
Technological	8	9	72
Competitive	9	7	63
Geographic	2	5	10

Impact from 10 (strongly positive) to 1 (strongly negative).
Importance of factor ranked from 1 (unimportant) to 10 (very important).

Total ___205___

Comments:

Based on the analysis that was done in Chapter 2, IBM is in a fairly critical position because of external threats. A total score in excess of 60 signals that a company is "moderately vulnerable," and a score of 120 signals that a company is "vulnerable." IBM's score of 205 shows that it is facing serious economic, technological, and competitive threats.

Source: R. O. Mason, Copyright © 1984.

Environmental threats do not have to be accepted as givens. It is often possible to develop a strategy that will change them in a favorable way. In other words, the organization can choose to be proactive rather than reactive. If the threat is restrictive legislation, for example, the organization can either accept the restriction as inevitable or lobby the legislature in an effort to prevent its being enacted. This ability to anticipate and minimize the effect of threats explains why environmental scanning is an important early step for managers who are developing new strategies.

Let us pause a moment to note a technique that is widely used in analyzing factors related to one of the key areas in environmental scanning: the competition. Assessing the competition can be achieved by what is termed "benchmarking" (Main, 1992). Copying the smart practices of competitors is an approach used by Ford, Xerox, AT&T, Motorola, and many others to stay abreast of changes in the field. Main found that of 580 companies he surveyed, 31% regularly use benchmarking to compare their products and services with those of competitors. For example, IBM has done over 500 benchmark studies in the past two years. How is it done? The following guidelines provide a basis for assessing the state of the art:

1. Focus on a specific problem and define it carefully. Then find out what other leading companies are doing.
2. Use persons who are responsible for a change in your own firm to obtain information. They have a vested interest in finding and implementing solutions.
3. Be willing to share information with others.
4. Avoid sensitive issues such as pricing. Don't look for new-product information.
5. Recognize that the information you receive is confidential.

The use of benchmarking as an assessment tool is growing, and the American Productivity and Quality Center has established a Benchmarking Clearing House in Houston.

Strategic segmentation within an industry

Strategic managers must consider the full range of environments in which they might compete and the entire economic spectrum of a business activity, including suppliers, operations and production technology, distribution, marketing and sales, customer service, and so on. Only then can they identify strategic segments, or business activities, through which the company can

1. Establish an advantage relative to the competition
2. Defend this advantage over time
3. Enjoy secure and stable profitability

The key question in *strategic segmentation* is "In which parts of the industry can the company expect the highest long-term returns?" In other words, within which segments will it be possible for the company to

1. Develop a sustainable advantage relative to competitors in other, possibly adjacent, segments?
2. Deny competitors attractive returns on any investments required to enter the chosen segment?

The most important characteristic of a strategic segment is its defensibility. Proof that a segment exists is the barriers to competition that surround it. The higher these barriers, the higher the profit potential in that segment. Barriers can include

- Capital investment (such as the need for specialized equipment or a large-scale facility)
- Location (proximity to natural resources, for example, or transport-cost advantages for customers)
- Proprietary technological expertise and patents
- Established consumer franchise/trading relationships
- Tariffs and other trade barriers

Barriers can lead to a cost advantage, because of manufacturing, marketing, distribution, or a combination thereof.

As Figure 4.2 shows, strategic segmentation occurs at a more general level than market segmentation and involves decisions about production technology that entail long-term investment decisions. A *strategic segment* in the paper industry can be identified in terms of primary raw material (groundwood versus woodfree) and primary production process (uncoated versus coated). *Market segments* are identified by subdividing a strategic segment, such as artprint paper, on the basis of one or more product characteristics, such as quality, price, or weight.

Let's pursue a bit further the example of selecting a primary raw material for the production of paper. Woodfree papers, which are made from chemical pulps, require a completely different technology and production process from those made from groundwood. The decision to produce paper leads to considerable capital investments. Besides the paper machine, which can cost up to $500 million, coating equipment must be purchased. The choice of the strategic segment shown in Figure 4.2 can have a direct impact on which specific market segments will be served. Typically, a paper machine is built to produce a narrow range of paper weight. To switch to another range of weights requires that the firm rebuild existing equipment, incurring significantly higher capital costs. Coating can be done either by on-machine coaters, which are cheaper but produce lower-quality papers, or by off-machine coaters, which are more expensive but produce higher-quality papers. Therefore, the choice of machine (if that choice has already been made) determines which strategic segment the company should seek to compete in. These capital-investment decisions narrow down the number of market segments that are attractive for the company. For each market segment, further product differentiation can be pursued; for example, the company can choose to produce rolls or sheets and can choose to distribute the paper directly or through dealers.

Its choice of what product to offer also generally dictates in what region a paper company competes. Success in selling bulk papers, such as most groundwood grades,

---

FIGURE 4.2   Strategic Segments and Market Segments in the Paper Industry

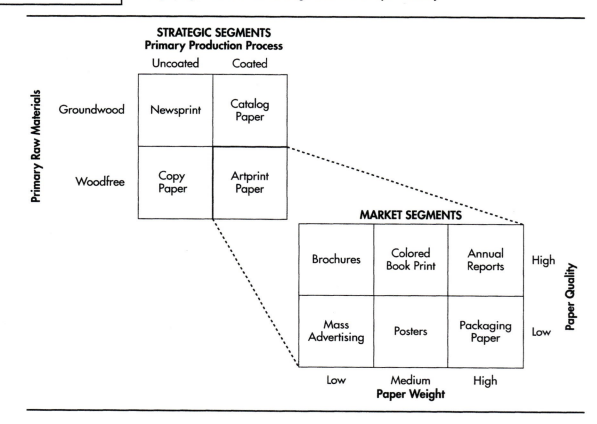

is heavily dependent on making the right choice of location on a worldwide basis, as well as on a favorable exchange rate. North American producers of newsprint, for example, enjoy a very favorable cost situation, especially when the value of the dollar is low relative to that of other currencies. During this time they can make substantial inroads into Europe and other parts of the world. Consequently, all the major paper producers of these grades of papers are pursuing global strategies. Other specialty papers tend to be more domestic or regional in nature. For example, writing papers are typically regional products, because they depend more on regional standards and distribution strength than on lowest production cost.

Initial profitability does not ensure that a company has defined a strategic segment correctly. Above-average profits in an area may or may not validate the existence of a strategic segment. Profits do not guarantee that the segment is defensible or that profitability can be maintained. Many companies have found that short-term concentration on areas with above-average profitability can lead to long-term organizational decline. One such example is the motorcycle industry in the United Kingdom and the United States. In the late 1960s, these countries were the major producers of large motorcycles. The Japanese at that time produced small motorcycles. At this stage, manufacturers in both the United States and the United Kingdom apparently decided that "super bikes" (bikes with engine capacity greater than 500 cc) were a valid strategic segment exclusive of smaller bikes. Therefore, they abandoned the "small-bike segment" to the Japanese. This assumption about market segmentation was wrong. There were, in fact, no real barriers separating the design, production, marketing, and distribution of large and small motorcycles. The Japanese were allowed to dominate the small-bike market and, while doing so, were able to build a considerable competitive advantage in *all* motorcycle categories. A similar phenomenon occurred in the machine tool industry when U.S. companies abandoned their markets for smaller, numerically controlled lathes and machining centers to the Japanese. As a result, the U.S. machine tool industry has been almost obliterated.

COMPETITIVE ENVIRONMENTS

In the 1970s, the Boston Consulting Group (BCG) developed the *advantage matrix,* a useful first screen for identifying strategic segments. In this matrix (Figure 4.3), four generic competitive environments are defined on the basis of (1) the potential size of the advantage that can be gained by a competitor and (2) the number of different means by which a competitor can establish leadership in the industry. For commodities, which have little potential for product differentiation, the basic segment boundary is the cost advantage to be gained by serving more than one market segment, or class of customers. For differentiated products, the segment boundary lies in the combination of features built into the product and their cost/price ratio. In identifying segments with the advantage matrix, managers also include all conditions of the transaction process, such as service, vendor reliability, and delivery schedules.

The competitive environments identified in the advantage matrix are described in the sections that follow. Figure 4.4 shows the typical patterns of return on assets in these four competitive environments.

Volume Businesses

In volume businesses (see Table 4.1), basic or inherent costs are the largest part of the cost structure, and economies of scale or experience reduce costs. Examples of volume businesses include television sets, mid-sized cars, newspapers, and fast-food

---

FIGURE 4.3	The Boston Consulting Group's Advantage Matrix

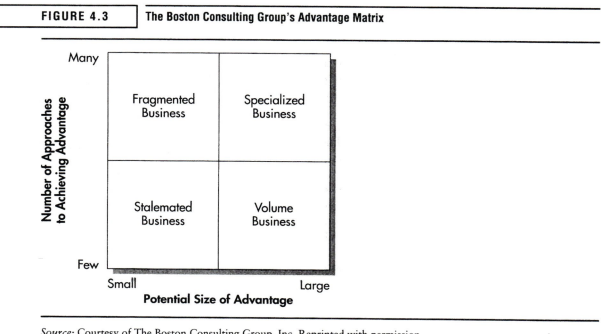

Source: Courtesy of The Boston Consulting Group, Inc. Reprinted with permission.

FIGURE 4.4	Patterns of Competitive Returns ROA=return on assets; S=segment; dots indicate different competitors

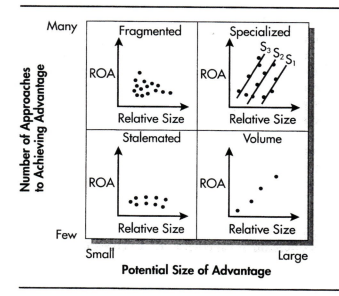

Source: Courtesy of The Boston Consulting Group, Inc. Reprinted with permission.

chains. A key strategy of a volume business is to be the cost and volume leader. Low costs and high sales volumes are two means of attaining competitive advantage. Followers survive only if the leader chooses to establish a price umbrella or if the business stalemates. Major threats to a volume leader are inadequate capacity for expansion relative to market growth (resulting in loss of market share), market maturation and differentiation, cost increases due to complexity, global competition, and technology stalemate.

TABLE 4.1	Competitive Environments Within the Machine Tool Industry

Competitive Environment	Examples of Products
Volume business	Small numerical control lathes, milling machines, machining centers
Stalemated business	Conventional lathes, drilling machines, sheet metal presses, mechanical forging presses
Specialized business	Multispindle lathes, single-spindle automatics, grinding machines, gear-cutting machines
Fragmented business	Vertical lathes, flexible manufacturing systems (FMSs), transfer lines

Stalemated Businesses

Stalemated businesses differ from volume businesses in that economies of scale do not have great cost benefits, often because technology and experience have stagnated throughout the industry and are widely shared among competitors. Examples of stalemated businesses include the steel, aluminum, shipbuilding, and paper industries. In these businesses, the cost advantages of high volume have shrunk, and establishment of a leadership position depends mostly on reducing factor costs, such as the costs of labor, energy, and capital. To reduce labor costs, many stalemated businesses move their manufacturing operations to newly industrialized countries, such as South Korea, Taiwan, or Brazil. Businesses that are sheltered by government subsidies can keep their domestic plants open, at least for a period of time.

Specialized Businesses

Specialized businesses are characterized by steep scale or experience effects in costs incurred by serving a specific market segment. They focus on a limited set of customers, or a "segment" of the market. Examples of specialized businesses include pharmaceuticals, cosmetics, book publishing, and luxury cars. By focusing on a selected part of the market, it may be possible to achieve significant price premiums, and a higher-than-normal price for a product. The main success factors for specialized businesses are market focus and segment leadership. Typically there are several highly profitable competitors, but each dominates a different market segment. Followers in each specific segment tend to be less profitable. Competitive battles are usually not head-on but rather tend to occur at strategic and market segment boundaries. It is also possible for a competitor to serve more than one market segment, which significantly lowers average costs. For a firm to do this, however, it must be possible to sell at different prices to each market segment, and the price in each segment must match value to the customer. One example is the entry of Japanese car manufacturers into the luxury car segment once dominated by Europeans.

Fragmented Businesses

The profitability of fragmented businesses is unrelated to size and strategic segmentation. Fragmented businesses are often regional businesses in which economies of scale are outweighed by the costs of complexity. Examples of such businesses include restaurants, engineering companies, handicrafts, and consulting firms. Competitive advantage can be sustained by innovation, operational efficiency, and market focus that is value-oriented. These factors are more important than relative competitive position in an industry that no one dominates.

Porter (1980) recommends a number of approaches for coping with fragmentation. First is to attempt an economic consolidation through franchising or mergers. He also advocates strategic segmentation that focuses on the customer, type of product, geographic location, or uniqueness of design. In addition, he recommends creating industry standards that make fragmented industries much more efficient because of their ability to reduce cost and to focus on value-added activities. Assumptions about the distribution of overhead and the allocation of new-product costs are covered in Chapter 8. Relying on a strategic discipline, a company can focus its efforts even within a highly fragmented industry.

COMPETITIVE FORCES

Strategic segmentation proceeds from identification of valid market segments and their competitive environments to a detailed analysis of the industry's competitive structure. Hence, moving outward in the levels of the economic environment shown in Figure 4.1, we find the next critical area that a strategic manager must assess: the industry in which the organization finds itself. One of the most comprehensive studies of the competitive environment in which a company operates was done by Porter (1980, 1985). His analysis will be covered in two parts. We will examine the impact of competition in an industry and some ways of dealing with industry evolution, fragmented industries, and strategic groups within an industry. Then we will present a means of assessing the attractiveness of a given industry. As is often the case, not all companies follow neat economic theory. Thus the guidelines described by Porter should be considered a useful overview, but they should be supplemented with other approaches. First we will examine the competitive forces in an industry using Porter's analysis. We will then use another approach called an "industry attractiveness analysis" to determine whether to enter or exit an industry.

PORTER'S ANALYSIS

According to Michael Porter, the key to competitive analysis is to identify the major competitive forces and assess their impact on the company's present and future market position (Figure 4.5). In particular, he singles out

1. Potential rate of growth in the industry
2. Threat of entry by new competitors
3. Intensity of rivalry among existing competitors
4. Pressure from substitute products
5. Dependence on complementary products and services
6. Bargaining power of buyers
7. Bargaining power of suppliers
8. Sophistication of technologies applied in the industry
9. Rate of innovation
10. Capability of management

These ten factors are discussed in the sections that follow. Analyzing them helps managers to formulate strategies that have a high likelihood of success, given the nature of the industry's competitive environment. Worksheet 4.2 evaluates each factor as it pertained to Polaroid's competitive situation in 1988.

| FIGURE 4.5 | Competitive Forces |

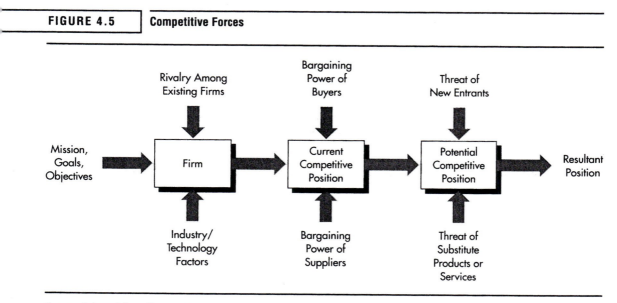

Source: Adapted from Porter, 1980.

| WORKSHEET 4.2 | Competitive Environment Analysis |

Case ___Polaroid_____

Date ___1988_____

Name ___John Doe_____

1. Potential rate of growth of industry (in real terms)

0–3% _____	9–12% _____	18–21% _____
3–6% _____	12–15% _____	>21% _____
6–9% _✓_	15–18% _____	

2. Ease of entry of new firms into industry

No barriers– ___ : ___ : ___ : ___ : ___ : ___ : _✓_ : ___ : ___ –Virtually impossible to enter
(patent protection)

3. Intensity of competition among firms

Extremely competitive– ___ : ___ : ___ : ___ : ___ : _✓_ : ___ : ___ : ___ –Almost no competition
(Kodak intense)

4. Degree of product substitutability

Many substitutes available– ___ : ___ : ___ : ___ : _✓_ : ___ : ___ : ___ : ___ –No substitutes available
(alternative photographic sources)

5. Degree of dependency on complementary or supporting products and services

Highly dependent– ___ : ___ : _✓_ : ___ : ___ : ___ : ___ : ___ : ___ –Virtually independent
(film processing, film suppliers)

6. Degree of bargaining power buyers and customers possess

Buyers dictate terms– ___ : ___ : ___ : ___ : ___ : ___ : ___ : _✓_ : ___ –Selling firms dictate terms
(few large, concentrated buyers)

7. Degree of bargaining power suppliers and vendors possess

Suppliers dictate terms– ___ : ___ : ___ : ___ : _✓_ : ___ : ___ : ___ : ___ –Purchasing firms dictate terms
(about average)

8. Degree of technological sophistication in industry

High-level technology– ___ : ___ : _✓_ : ___ : ___ : ___ : ___ : ___ : ___ –Very low-level technology
(R&D essential)

9. Rate of innovation in industry

Rapid innovation– ___ : ___ : _✓_ : ___ : ___ : ___ : ___ : ___ : ___ –Almost no innovation
(continual influx of new ideas)

10. General level of management capability

Many very capable managers– ___ : ___ : ___ : _✓_ : ___ : ___ : ___ : ___ : ___ –Very few capable managers
(probably average or slightly better)

Source: R. O. Mason, Copyright © 1984.

Potential Rate of Growth

Strategic managers must first assess the industry's growth potential, because this potential determines the nature of the game to be played. Industries with low growth rates (under 6% per annum) present few opportunities for new firms but enable established firms to maintain profitability if they can protect their position. Modest growth rates (6–12% per annum) present opportunities for aggressive firms. High growth rates (over 12%) present substantial opportunities, but they attract large numbers of new competitors and require that most competitors make substantial capital investments to keep pace.

Threats of Entry

Under what conditions will a new competitor enter a firm's strategic segment? What can the firm do about it? In general, a new competitor will not enter a strategic or market segment if the barriers to entry are high and a strong competitive reaction can be expected from existing firms. As mentioned earlier, one of the most important barriers to entry is capital requirements. The more money and resources needed to start up a new business (that is, the higher the "ante"), the less likely it is that a new competitor will want to enter. In clothing manufacturing, for example, there are few barriers for new-apparel makers, some of whom use undocumented workers in "sweat shops" to achieve a cost advantage. The manufacture of fine textile designer clothes, on the other hand, requires considerably more capital investment and know-how.

Another barrier is the ability of established companies to practice economies of scale. As a firm's volume increases and it gains more experience, its costs tend to decrease. And, of course, it takes a certain volume of sales to cover fixed costs and to begin to return a profit on each sale. These factors give established firms a distinct cost advantage over new competitors.

Barriers to entry can also consist of exclusive access to patents, information, or raw materials; a preferred location; or superior facilities. Product differentiation, such as unique automobile styling, serves as a barrier for a company's market segments. Product differentiation also tends to give the established firm the advantages of brand identification and customer loyalty. This advantage is often gained by means of advertising, good quality, and service.

For some types of customers, the switching costs (the costs of changing from one product to another) serve as protective barriers. For example, programs written for one computer frequently will not operate (without modification) on another manufacturer's computer. Reprogramming becomes a switching cost and serves as a barrier to entry for new firms entering the computer field.

Intensity of Rivalry

Many factors account for the intensity of rivalry among existing competitors in an industry. The first factor is the number of existing competitors. In general, the more competitors, the greater the rivalry. The second factor is similarity among competitors. The more nearly equivalent the competitors' size, skills, and market power, the greater the rivalry tends to be. The third factor is barriers to exit. If it is difficult for firms to leave the industry, they tend to see no options but to "fight it out" within the industry, thereby increasing the intensity of rivalry. Fourth, as industry growth stalemates or declines, the pressure on each firm to maintain its market share gets higher. Added to all of these factors is that magical ingredient, personal commitment to being number one. Some people and the companies they manage are simply more determined to succeed than others. In some cases, intense competitiveness results from a determination to enter and defend a strategic or market segment. In others, it is generated by the aggressive personality of the firm's leader.

In analyzing the intensity of competition, then, strategic managers should determine whether competitors are

- Numerous
- Similarly positioned in the industry
- Unable to leave the industry
- In an industry that is stalemated or declining
- Extremely committed to a strategy or to an aggressive leader

In general, the more intense the competition in an industry, the more difficult it is for new firms to enter and for existing firms to survive.

Pressure from Substitute Products

Sometimes an industry is "hit from its blind side." This happened in clothing manufacturing as synthetic fibers substituted for cotton fibers, detergents replaced soaps, and coin-operated dry-cleaning machines substituted for dry-cleaning services.

Product substitution follows a typical pattern. While the established firms concentrate on each other, another firm, usually by means of technological innovation, creates a product that can be substituted for the existing product. The new product has a different form but performs the same function. Competition by substitution had disastrous consequences for the AddressoGraph Multilith Corporation. At one time, this company monopolized the mechanized-addressing market. Today, however, computer-printed labels have all but eliminated the need for AddressoGraph machines, which imprint addresses using embossed metal plates.

To prevent being surprised by a substitute product, strategic managers must continuously assess the external environment. Environmental scanning, technological assessment, and stakeholder analysis are all suitable methods.

In general, the greater the pressure from substitute products, the less attractive the industry.

Dependence on Complementary Products and Services

Some products, such as candy bars, are consumed independently of other products. Others have either a correlated demand or a derived demand. *Correlated demand* for a product is due to the fact that customers prefer to consume certain products together, such as meat and potatoes or recreation and food. *Derived demand* for a product is due to the fact that the purchase of one product creates demand for another product. The sale of an automobile, for example, leads to a demand for accessories, an audio system, gasoline and oil, repair services, replacement parts, and tires. The sale of a computer and printer creates a demand for computer paper.

These products exhibit a degree of mutual dependence. People buy automobiles because they know repair services are available, and they buy repair services because they purchased an automobile.

A review of the complementary, correlated, and derived characteristics of demand for an industry's products enables strategic managers to assess the organization's dependence on the success or cooperation of companies in other industries. A high degree of dependence is a danger signal. If the firms in the other industry are successful, healthy, dependable, and reliable, then a derived-demand situation can be quite profitable. In this situation, however, the firm's destiny is controlled in part by the actions of the other firms. This is seldom a comfortable circumstance. Firms in the complementary industries must be monitored constantly. One strategy that is often used in these circumstances is to merge with or acquire a firm that produces the needed products. If the other firm's products are complementary, the acquisition or merger is called *horizontal integration*. If the acquired firm's products create a derived demand, it is called *forward vertical integration*.

Bargaining Power of Buyers

Candy bars are sold to millions of individual buyers. The purchaser does not negotiate the price or the terms of sale. Commercial aircraft, on the other hand, are sold to just a few large airlines, which have the power to negotiate many aspects of the terms of sale. Defense weapons are often sold to only one purchaser—the U.S. government. Therefore, the government has a great deal to say about the terms of sale. In industries with many sellers and few buyers, the sellers are at a disadvantage. Price competition tends to ensue. In industries with few buyers and few sellers, the bargaining powers of sellers and buyers are often about equal. In this situation, a seller's ability to negotiate and to "cut good deals" often determines its success.

A review of the relative bargaining power of the buyers of an industry's products enables strategic managers to gauge the firm's market power. In general, the greater the bargaining power of buyers, the less advantage the sellers have.

Bargaining Power of Suppliers

The flip side of an assessment of the relative bargaining power of buyers is an assessment of the relative bargaining power of suppliers. The firm's buyers influence prices and marketing costs. Its suppliers influence production costs. Suppliers tend to be powerful if there are just a few of them, there are few alternative sources of supply, their product is important for the firm's business, and they are not dependent on the firm's purchases to have a successful business.

A review of the conditions of supply in the firm's resource markets—the markets in which it purchases labor, raw materials, facilities, and other important factors of production—enables strategic managers to determine how much bargaining power its suppliers possess. In general, the greater the bargaining power of the supplier, the less advantage the firm has. A process called *backward vertical integration* is often used to acquire suppliers with which the firm has weak bargaining power.

Technological Sophistication of the Industry

Some industries, such as retailing, currently employ a relatively low level of technology. Others, such as oil field information and services, depend heavily on scientific research and high-level technology. A high-tech firm must invest heavily in research and development, must often locate itself near a university or other research organization, and must strive to protect its position through secrecy, patents, and copyrights. The low-tech firm, on the other hand, always faces the possibility of intense competition because of its lower barrier to entry. Therefore, opportunities and threats are present whether technology is high or low.

Strategies for success are quite different depending on whether high or low technology is employed. In general, established firms in high-tech industries must emphasize research and development and offer specialized services to be successful. Established firms in low-tech industries must emphasize product identification, marketing, competitive pricing, value, and quality, as well as providing general services.

Rate of Innovation

Some industries, such as the table salt industry, are placid, stable, and subject to little change. Others, such as those in the computer field, are characterized by continuous, dramatic innovation. Innovation depends on two things: new ideas and the willingness and ability to carry them out.

Technological change is often the primary stimulus for innovation. The other main stimulus for innovation is new ways of thinking about service. Thirty years ago, Ray Kroc's new idea about fast food service created McDonald's; Walt Disney's vision of a family-oriented park created Disneyland; and Colonel Sanders's idea that homemade southern-fried chicken should be available nationwide created Kentucky Fried Chicken. None of these three innovators relied heavily on technological development. Rather, they depended on new ideas about products, services, and markets. These ideas revolutionized the industries involved.

A technological assessment and an environmental scan for new ideas about products, services, and markets, together with an estimate of the willingness and capability of the industry to adopt innovations, enables strategic managers to determine the rate of innovation in the industry.

In general, if the rate of innovations in an industry is high, the firm must have a flexible organization and be heavily committed to R&D and strategic planning to succeed. If, on the other hand, the rate of innovation is low, the firm must focus on marketing, sales, and cost reduction.

Management Capability

All of the preceding factors are tempered by one final consideration: What is the quality of management in the industry? Are there many competent and capable managers, or are there just a few? How many top managers does the industry have, and how highly qualified is each one? The long-term resiliency of an industry depends on the number of outstanding managers and on the chain of succession. During the last two decades the overall quality of management slipped in the American automobile industry, allowing the Japanese to gain an important advantage. Ultimately, quality management depends on entrepreneurship, sound decision making, and the "fit" of the manager's style with the demands of the situation.

A review of the breadth and depth of good management enables strategic managers to determine the general level of management capability in the industry. In general, when there are many capable managers in an industry, it is difficult for one firm to gain an advantage over another. If there are very few capable managers, a firm with a few exceptional managers can often gain an advantage. Strategic managers must also look out for firms that, out of ignorance or incompetent management, make stupid moves that can affect the viability of the industry. An industry that is especially vulnerable on this dimension may not be a good choice to enter.

INDUSTRY ATTRACTIVENESS ANALYSIS

Using the information obtained by applying Porter's industry analysis, one can now utilize Worksheet 4.3 to determine how attractive an industry might be. For example, is there potential growth, or is it limited? How easy is it to switch brands? What is the profitability? And so on. Examining the 15 factors shown, one can look at the forces applicable to each of these factors and assign a score from 0 to 10 to reflect the degree of attractiveness that industry has for a given company. Where the industry requirements fit the core capability of an organization, the attractiveness score is highest. On the other hand, if the company is unable to meet the industry requirements, the attractiveness score is low. Thus, for example, a company that is able to cope with all 15 of the factors shown might "ideally" have a score of 150. There are very few such companies. The majority of companies are likely to fall in the range of 75 through 120. (If each of the scores were 5, then the total would be 75, whereas if each of the scores were 8, the total would be 120.) Where a score is lower than 75, the strategic manager whose firm was already in that industry would have to consider significant repositioning in the industry in order to continue to operate on a profitable basis. One such approach, segmentation, was described earlier.

Other factors that need to be considered in analyzing an industry include resource requirements, government intervention, and industry structure. The availability of resources often becomes a critical aspect of carrying out strategy. For example, if funds are not available, a company could be headed for bankruptcy. Thus one must determine capital-investment requirements along with how much working capital is needed to sustain the company. This may depend on the capital-intensity in a given industry. For example, many companies "outsource" their computer operations to reduce the investment required in equipment, facilities, and personnel. The analysis of strategic funds programming, covered in Chapter 8, shows the capital requirements for various strategic options. If key

WORKSHEET 4.3	Industry Attractiveness Analysis

Case _____

Date _____

Name _____

Factor	Force	Score
1. Growth potential:	Increasing or decreasing size	0 _____ 10
2. Market diversity:	Number of markets served	0 _____ 10
3. Profitability:	Increasing, steady, decreasing	0 _____ 10
4. Vulnerability:	Competitors, inflation	0 _____ 10
5. Concentration:	Number of dominant players	0 _____ 10
6. Product sales:	Cyclic, continuous	0 _____ 10
7. Specialization:	Focus, differentiation, uniqueness	0 _____ 10
8. Brand identification:	Ease of switching, substitution, value, quality	0 _____ 10
9. Distribution:	Channels, support required	0 _____ 10
10. Price policy:	Learning effect, elasticity, industry norms	0 _____ 10
11. Cost position:	Competitive, low cost, high cost	0 _____ 10
12. Service:	Timing, reliability, guarantees	0 _____ 10
13. Technology:	Leadership, uniqueness	0 _____ 10
14. Integration:	Vertical, horizontal, ease of control	0 _____ 10
15. Ease of entry and exit:	Barriers	0 _____ 10

personnel are lacking, the company may be unable to function effectively. If critical materials cannot be had at a competitive price, or if physical facilities and equipment are not available, the company may be unable to maintain a competitive position.

Government intervention may significantly affect the ability of a company to compete within an industry. Often local governments (such as the state of California) impose stringent ecological requirements that force companies to either spend huge sums of money to correct the situation or move out of the state. For example, Kaiser Steel in Fontana, California, had to shut down its steel mill there because it was deemed uneconomic to implement the pollution-control equipment needed to reduce the emission of smoke and harmful particles as much as the law required. Increasingly, requirements for health and pension benefits are imposing costs that can make an industry noncompetitive. A critical function of an organization is to assess changes in government requirements, social legislation, bankruptcy laws, and the like in order to ensure that it is in compliance and is able to compete effectively given the industry demands.

It is possible to assess the industry structure by using Porter's approach to determining the intensity of competition. One can also examine strategic group maps to identify the major competitors in an industry and reveal how they impact the organization's ability to compete effectively. In a sense, such a map is comparable to a stakeholders' assumption graph (see Figure 4.8) applied to companies within an industry. Defining the strategic group, however, requires a careful analysis of the important factors that determine inclusion in a group and their effect on strategic competitiveness. For example, the variables used for these maps include markets served versus cost position, price/quality versus market segment, technology versus market served, and so on. The position of a company in the group map can be shown along with a circle describing the extent of penetration. (These group maps, in this form, are analogous to the product portfolios described in Chapter 6.)

In addition to considering the foregoing factors, one must ascertain how the industry deals with the "four P's" that are related to marketing practices.

Product   What is the given product in the industry? Sometimes this is difficult to determine, especially in the field of electronics and high technology.

Prices   How are prices established in the industry? Are they related to cost or the learning curve? Are products in the industry price-elastic or -inelastic?

Promotion   An important consideration in gaining acceptance of products is the amount of funds spent on advertising and other promotional activities. Recent airline fare wars illustrate the importance of advertising in an attempt to gain new customers or increase utilization of air travel.

Place   Geography, distribution channels, infrastructure, and location all influence performance in an industry. Whether the firm uses direct sales, telemarketing, representatives, or other channels of distribution often determines where a company is located.

One final consideration in the analysis of an industry is examination of the industry life cycle. The majority of companies in an industry go through life cycles, and the cumulative effect leads to changes in industry size, profitability, and performance. As companies accumulate knowledge and their products and processes undergo innovation, industries tend to reach a saturation point. Thus, for example, the aircraft industry has reached the point in its life cycle where the technology is fairly well known, physical facilities are in place, and capital is also made available to sustain the companies within the industry. As a consequence, the rate of growth in that industry is limited by variables such as alternative modes of transportation, access to airport, and cost of gasoline. As is evidenced by McDonnell Douglas's seeking to sell a part interest in its company to the Taiwanese government, sustaining oneself in the aircraft industry is becoming increasingly difficult. At the present time, there are two dominant players, Boeing and the European Airbus.

While some industries merely reach a point of saturation or low growth potential, others enter a declining stage. Decline is often due to technological obsolescence, but it can also be caused by government regulation or consumer needs. If there is a decline in demand (as has recently been true in consumer durables), there are just too many competitors and too much capacity. When confronted with the problems of a declining industry, many companies may choose to exit. For example, the automotive industry has gone through a major restructuring, including the shut-down of a number of facilities. On another front, Avery International actually paid an Italian company two million dollars to take over its business because the cost of exiting imposed such severe financial demands when considering the cost of laying off workers. It was cheaper to pay someone to take the business than to shut it down.

Another perspective on analyzing an industry is illustrated in Table 4.2 (Kichen, 1992). This table summarizes key points, which are explored in greater depth in the article itself, about major industry segments such as aerospace, chemicals, and construction. For example, the comment following Aerospace and Defense is "They have to prepare for even more draconian cuts." While somewhat superficial, this table does provide an overall picture of both the state of the economy and the condition of selected industry segments. (It also refers the reader to the place in the article where each segment is discussed.)

STAKEHOLDER ANALYSIS

A *stakeholder* is anyone whose actions can affect an organization or who is affected by the organization's actions. Because of these mutual interactions, each stakeholder has a stake in what the organization does, and vice versa. Stakeholders are also the organization's claimants; that is, they depend on the organization for the realization of some of their goals. The organization, in turn, depends on stakeholders for the full realization of its mission. Because of this mutual dependency, each stakeholder is, in effect, an advocate for any strategy that furthers its goals.

TABLE 4.2	Annual Report on American Industry

Aerospace and Defense
"Preparing for even more draconian cuts"
   (Howard Banks, p. 96)

Business Services and Supplies
"Not much gain last year"
   (Reed Abelson, p. 98)

Capital Goods
"Are in good shape to rebound"
   (Brigid McMenamin, p. 102)

Chemicals
"Chemical exports increased"
   (Randall Lane, p. 108)

Computers and Communications
"Little more than commodities"
   (Julie Pitta, p. 112)

Construction
"Could be a construction industry turnaround in 1992"
   (Claire Poole, p. 116)

Consumer Durables
"Too many competitors, too much capacity"
   (Jerry Flint, p. 120)

Consumer Nondurables
"Americans weren't buying new houses, automobiles, or washing machines"
   (Amy Feldman, p. 126)

Electric Utilities
"Capacity shortages, no-growth"
   (Manjeet Kripalani, p. 130)

Energy
"1992 won't be so great"
   (William Barrett, p. 134)

Entertainment and Information
"Forced into cost-cutting"
   (Kathryn Harris, p. 140)

Financial Services
"Rescued by individual investors"
   (Matthew Schrifrin, p. 144)

Food Distributors
"Slow sales and a trend toward buying less expensive"
   (Toddi Gutner, p. 148)

Food, Drink, and Tobacco
"Profits keep rolling in for these companies"
   (Edward Giltenan, p. 152)

Forest Products and Packaging
"Packaging materials, paper, and lumber just finished a dismal year"
   (Linda Killian, p. 156)

Health
"Return on equity is still way above average"
   (Mary Beth Grover, p. 158)

Insurance
"Industry is struggling to restore its credibility"
   (Carolyn Geer, p. 162)

Metals
"Industry worked hard to prepare for the recession"
   (Vicki Contavespi, p. 166)

Retailing
"Latest 12-month earnings were down almost 6%"
   (Zina Sawaya, p. 168)

Transport
"Railroads enjoyed one of their better years in 1991"
   (Roula Khalaf, p. 172)

Travel
"In the 1990s they have a new, and painful, situation"
   (William Heuslein, p. 172)

Take, for example, a pharmaceutical company near Philadelphia that has just developed a new product. The question is whether this product, a drug, should be marketed as a prescription drug or one that can be sold over the counter. If it is sold as a prescription drug, the sales volume will be lower, so the price will be set higher. If it is sold over the counter, sales volume will be higher, and the price will be set lower. As the company's executives ponder this question, they realize that either answer will have substantial effects on strategies for the company's advertising, legal, marketing, sales, and distribution units. It soon becomes evident that to answer this important strategic question requires an understanding of the company's stakeholders and other aspects of the environment in which the company operates.

The success of the company's decision about the type and price of the new drug depends largely on actions taken by stakeholders in the pharmaceutical industry: competitors, government regulators, patients, physicians, pharmacists and other retailers, suppliers of the drug's raw materials, the parent firm of which this company is a subsidiary, and the company's managers, sales force, and stockholders. Success will also depend on inflation, world market conditions, and changing social and political trends in the external environment, especially those that affect major markets and suppliers.

MODELS OF STAKEHOLDER MANAGEMENT

The drug pricing problem is typical of many strategic-management problems. How can managers cope with the diverse priorities of many stakeholders? How can they structure strategic planning so as to consider the conflicting interests of many groups?

One of two models can be applied to this situation. The first is the *single-sovereign model* shown in Figure 4.6. In the single-sovereign model, the right and power to govern the organization are vested in a single ultimate authority—the chief executive officer (CEO). In the second model, the *steerer model,* the right and power to govern the organization are distributed among many individuals and groups, each of whom has a vital interest in the organization (Figure 4.7). The executive, as "steerer," attempts to achieve an equilibrium among the competing interests by forming coalitions and by creating synthetic and compromise solutions to organizational problems. The steerer's role is to guide the organization through the turbulent waters of diverse pressures and demands.

FIGURE 4.6	**Single-Sovereign Model**

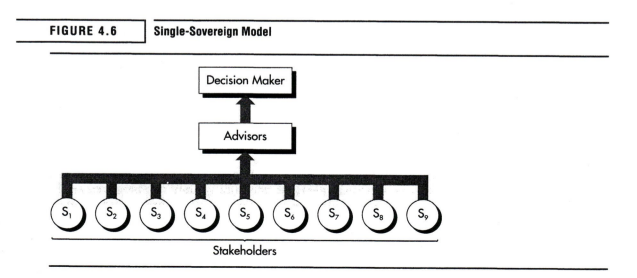

FIGURE 4.7	Steerer Model

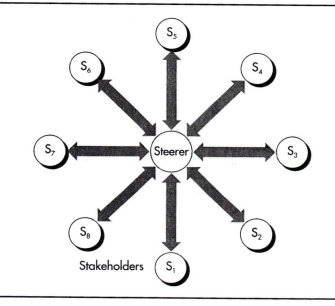

Applying the steerer model helped the drug company solve its drug-pricing problem. The company decided to sell a higher-priced, prescription drug. Company executives carefully weighed the interests and possible actions of the company's stakeholders and charted a course that was consistent with the interests and actions of the most important parties involved.

Key stakeholders for the drug company turned out to be in the external environment: federal regulators of drug sales, physicians, and third-party payers. The interests of the main stakeholders within the company canceled each other out. The marketing unit that sold to physicians favored marketing a high-priced, prescription drug to physicians. The unit that sold to retail stores favored marketing a low-priced, high-volume drug. Not surprisingly, each group favored the strategy that would send the most business its way.

The Food and Drug Administration (FDA) had the final say in whether the new drug would have to be sold by prescription. While the FDA was deciding, market research focused on the physicians. If the physicians were sensitive to the issues of price and accessibility of the drug, then the low-priced, over-the-counter strategy would be better. If, on the other hand, they were not sensitive to these issues, then the high-priced, prescription strategy would be best. When the FDA indicated that the drug could be classified either way, and when market research revealed that physicians were not very sensitive to the issue of price—the physicians stressed professionalism—it became clear that the high-priced, prescription strategy would work better. Other forces in the environment, especially the willingness of insurance companies to pay for prescribed medications, lent support to this strategy.

Most executives do not make strategic decisions on the basis of the steerer model, despite evidence that this model is most appropriate for running an enterprise today. Increasingly, diverse groups are making claims as stakeholders in organizations. Federal, state, and local governments are stakeholders by virtue of regulation and taxation. Employees, through unions and employee groups, are gaining rights and powers as stakeholders. Consumer advocates, community action groups, public interest groups, creditors, suppliers, and competitors all demand a voice in organizational decision making. Yet many of today's executives still cling to the single-sovereign model of management. Executives choose strategies in the isolation of the executive suite, shut off from knowledge of stakeholder claims and deprived of a full understanding of the forces stakeholders might bring to bear. Such decisions almost always lead to mistakes and unrest. Frequently, they create new pressures and strife with which the executive must deal in the future. Stakeholder analysis is designed to help managers devise strategies that avoid these pitfalls.

METHODS FOR STAKEHOLDER ANALYSIS

A stakeholder analysis is based on two premises. The first is that the current state of an organization is the result of the supporting and the resisting forces brought to bear on the organization by stakeholders. Thus the present status of the organization is, at best, a temporary balance of opposing forces. Some of these forces provide resources and support to the organization; others serve as barriers or constraints. The forces are generated by stakeholders in the course of pursuing their own interests, goals, and objectives.

The second premise is that the outcome of an organization's strategy is the collective result of all the forces brought to bear on it by its stakeholders during implementation of that strategy. The organization is always in a state of quasi-equilibrium as it attempts to balance the various stakeholder forces. Every time an organization acts and its stakeholders respond, a new temporary balance is achieved. The status and performance of an organization at a given point in the future depends on the equilibrium it achieves throughout the implementation period.

These two premises lead to an important conclusion: *The validity of a strategic plan always depends on the assumptions that are made about the organization's stakeholders and about the actions they will take during the planning and implementation period.* Therefore, strategic managers should perform a stakeholder analysis in order to

1. Identify stakeholders.
2. Map significant relationships among the stakeholders.
3. Examine the stakeholder map for opportunities and threats.
4. Identify, or bring to the surface, assumptions about stakeholders and the forces they exert on the organization.
5. Assess the relative importance and certainty of these assumptions.

Following the stakeholder analysis, strategic managers undertake activities that provide more information about stakeholder assumptions, guard against or neutralize threatening stakeholder forces, and facilitate and build on the supporting and driving stakeholder forces. Let's see what each of the steps in a stakeholder analysis entails.

Identifying Stakeholders

A stakeholder analysis begins with identification of as many relevant stakeholders as possible. The following checklist is a useful beginning. It should, however, be expanded, refined, and "customized" for the organization under study.

- Owners and stockholders
- Creditors
- Customers and clients
- Employees
- Labor unions
- Labor communities
- Local government
- State government
- Federal government
- Scientific labs
- University researchers and faculty
- Suppliers
- Competitors
- Corporate management
- Sources of new technology
- Public interest groups
- Persons in the media
- Persons in education
- Persons in the arts
- Religious groups
- Military personnel

The major stakeholders of most business enterprises can be listed under one of the following categories:

- Customers
- Suppliers
- Competitors
- Owners
- Regulators
- Employees
- Important interest groups

Preparing a Stakeholder Map

Having generated a list of stakeholders, strategic managers next prepare a *stakeholder map* by positioning the key stakeholders in a system, or network, that indicates primary relationships. The principle is the same as that used by ecologists to depict food chains within a natural environment. At first the map may look like a tangle of spaghetti, but upon examination, patterns of interdependence usually emerge. These patterns are portrayed on the revised map. Figure 4.8 is a stakeholder map that might be drawn for a pharmaceutical company.

Examining Stakeholder Maps for Opportunities and Threats

Figure 4.9 shows some of the important external and internal stakeholder relationships Polaroid's executives had to manage in 1980 (see Chapter 1). External stakeholders appear outside the box, internal stakeholders within it. Polaroid's main

---

FIGURE 4.8 | **Stakeholder Map for a Pharmaceutical Company**

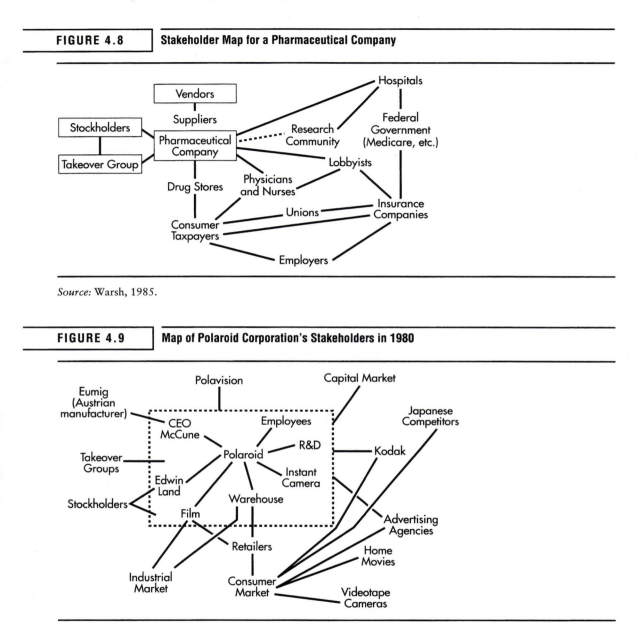

Source: Warsh, 1985.

FIGURE 4.9 | **Map of Polaroid Corporation's Stakeholders in 1980**

---

competitors are depicted at the upper right. Threatening substitute products, such as home movies and videotape cameras, are shown at the lower right. Polaroid's decision to segment its industrial and consumer markets is represented at the bottom. Other external forces being brought to bear include stockholders and takeover groups. The stockholders were putting pressure on the company to improve its profitability, while other investors viewed Polaroid's poor performance as a takeover opportunity. These pressures also concerned the primary supplier of Polavision, the Austrian manufacturing firm Eumig. Another important consideration was the effect that Polavision might have on Polaroid's film and instant camera businesses. Key internal stakeholders included Polaroid's founder, Edwin Land, and the (then) new CEO, William McCune. Polaroid's new strategy had to deal effectively with all of these relationships if it was to be successful and if it was to convince bankers to provide long-term loans.

Besides providing a "snapshot" of a company's current stakeholders, stakeholder maps can be used to identify trends based on past economic events and actions that were taken by various stakeholders. These maps are useful for tracking events as well as predicting the impact on future strategy.

Lessons from the Use of Stakeholder Maps   The central lesson to be learned from analysis of stakeholder maps is that actions taken by one stakeholder or group of stakeholders affect other stakeholders in the system. On the map, the affected stakeholders may be quite far removed from those who initiated the actions. The effects are propagated by means of economic, social, and political transactions among intervening stakeholders in the network. The technical term for significant changes in a stakeholder map is *structural change.*

Stakeholder maps for most organizations become more complex over time. As an organization grows, a variety of new stakeholders is added to the map. Some of the new stakeholders may be far removed geographically and culturally. The web of stakeholder relationships becomes more intricate, and the volume and diversity of transactions among stakeholders increase as time passes. Emery and Trist (1965) termed the web of relationships in a stakeholder map its "causal texture" and called the long-term trend toward increased complexity a movement toward a "turbulent environment."

The move toward increased complexity creates a need on the part of all stakeholders for (1) new responses that satisfy unmet needs, (2) faster responses, (3) more reliable responses, and (4) better ways of predicting the effects of chosen responses. These needs generate opportunities and threats for all the stakeholders involved in the system. Often, developing an effective response requires government action or cooperation.

Complexity also causes relationships among stakeholders to become more impersonal. Complexity, lack of personal relationships, and distance are among the reasons why stakeholder maps have become such valuable tools for strategic managers who are analyzing an organization's environment.

Strategic planners also use stakeholder maps to assess the effects of real or possible changes, such as

- New product technologies
- New process technologies
- Innovations in institutional relationships
- Changed demographics
- Deregulation by a government agency
- Regulation by a government agency
- Changes in the world economy
- Natural calamities

- Political crises
- Catastrophic accidents

Managers can assess each change by tracing its probable effects on the flow of materials, goods, services, money, information, and energy throughout the stakeholder map. In addition, planners consider where costs will accumulate, resources will be consumed, and revenues and benefits will be generated. Revenues and benefits are estimated for each stakeholder on the map to determine which part of the system is most likely to benefit from the change or to determine which part of the system is a beneficial niche.

Identifying (surfacing) and Testing Assumptions About Stakeholders   The success of any strategy depends on the validity of assumptions being made about the organization's internal and external stakeholders, particularly about how they are likely to respond as the strategy unfolds. Because the outcome of a strategy is the cumulative effect of actions taken by stakeholders during its implementation, strategic planners must identify and validate all of the assumptions being made about each stakeholder in the system. This process, called assumption surfacing and testing, involves

- *Assumption surfacing,* or identification of assumptions
- *Assumption rating,* or ranking of assumptions with respect to their importance and certainty
- *Assumption force-field analysis,* or determination of the net effects of assumptions that support a strategy and assumptions that do not support it

These three steps require information gained from all of the analytic methods described earlier, especially stakeholder identification and mapping.

Assumption Surfacing   Assumption surfacing is done to identify assumptions about how stakeholders will respond to a given strategy or to identify general assumptions about stakeholders. If the strategy has already been proposed, and the purpose of the analysis is to test the overall soundness of the strategy, then assumptions are surfaced by asking, "What are the most plausible assumptions the organization *must* make about each stakeholder for the strategy to be successful?" This is sometimes referred to as the "inverse optimal question." If no strategy has been proposed, and the purpose of the analysis is to uncover the most plausible set of assumptions upon which to base the new strategy, then assumptions are surfaced by asking, "What plausible assumptions can be made about each stakeholder?"

In either case, stakeholder assumptions can be classified into two categories:

1. Supporting or driving-force assumptions—those that indicate strategic opportunities and favorable conditions and are in keeping with organizational strengths.
2. Resisting or constraining-force assumptions—those that indicate threats, give rise to adverse and dangerous conditions, and take advantage of organizational weakness.

Worksheet 4.4 lists these two categories of assumptions for the Polaroid stakeholders of 1980.

WORKSHEET 4.4	Stakeholder Assumptions

Case __Polaroid__
Date __1980__
Name __John Doe__

Stakeholders	Major Assumptions	Assumption Rating	
		Importance	Certainty
	Supporting		
1. Major stockholder: Edwin Land	a. Will continue to conduct research on new inventions	6	4
	b. Will not interfere with McCune's running of Polaroid	7	5
	Resisting		
	a. His "looser association" will deprive Polaroid of his leadership	5	8
	b. Corporate resources will be diverted to his research activities	6	9
	Supporting		
2. CEO: William McCune	a. Has the experience and background to manage	8	4
	b. His "broader-based" teamwork style will be effective at Polaroid	7	8
	Resisting		
	a. He will be diverted by oboe playing, silversmithing, auto tinkering, and vacationing	5	6
	b. He is associated with the rising problems with Polavision	7	9
	Supporting		
3. Customers	a. Price: prefer to pay $700 for Polavision, versus $1,800 for videotape set	7	7
	b. Will respond to personalized promotions such as "Santa Claus" delivery	6	2
	Resisting		
	a. Cool to home movies	7	1
	b. Performance: prefer reusable videotape	7	3
	c. Features: prefer sound, clear visible picture, more than 2½ minutes, etc.	9	4
	Supporting		
4. Competitor: Eastman Kodak	a. Polaroid will continue to hold off Kodak in the instant-camera market	8	1
	Resisting		
	a. Have stronger marketing and financial resources	9	9
	b. Will push easy-to-use, less expensive 35-mm cameras	6	3
	Supporting		
5. Internal organization: R&D department	a. R&D will produce the "new marvel"	8	0
	Resisting		
	a. R&D expense will continue to be a drain on corporate cash	4	8
	Supporting		
6. Capital markets	a. Polaroid can borrow at reasonable rates since there is unused debt capacity because it has no long-term debt	2	9
	Resisting		
	a. Polaroid has a declining cash position because of high inventor costs and lower-than-expected revenues	4	9

Assumption Rating Assumptions about stakeholders vary with respect to the importance of these assumptions and the certainty with which they are held. Each assumption is rated on a scale of 0 through 9. For importance, the extreme values are as follows:

9 = very important assumption; one that has a most significant impact on the strategy and its outcome

0 = unimportant assumption; one that has very little impact on the strategy

For certainty, the extreme values are as follows:

9 = very certain assumption; one that is most likely to be true because either it is self-evident or there is substantial evidence to support its validity

0 = very uncertain assumption; one that has little or no supporting evidence, is questionable, and is likely to be invalid

These values are then graphed with the importance scale shown along the horizontal axis of the assumption-rating graph and the certainty scale shown on the vertical axis. An assumption-rating graph for the Polaroid case is shown in Figure 4.10.

FIGURE 4.10 | **Assumption-Rating Graph for Polaroid's Stakeholders in 1980**

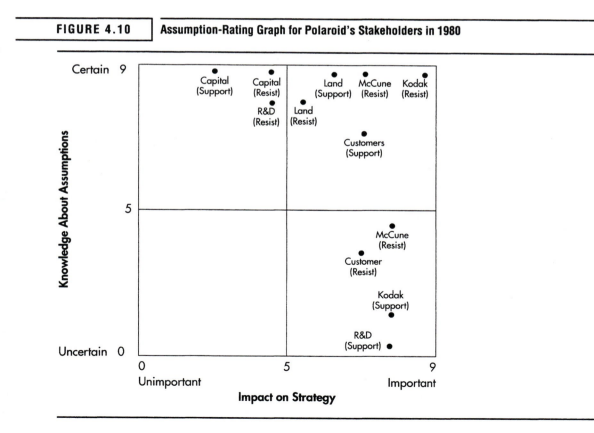

No manager is capable of dealing simultaneously with all the assumptions that underlie an organization's strategy. The assumption-rating graph helps by identifying the most critical assumptions. It also indicates how much is known about each assumption. Armed with this information, the manager can focus on those few assumptions that comprise supporting or limiting factors for the strategy. Certainty is a guide to the amount of knowledge the manager currently has about an assumption. Important but uncertain assumptions need to be investigated further. Importance is a guide to the amount of driving or resisting force an assumption exerts on the strategy. The importance rating is used in the assumption rating graph.

Referring to Figure 4.10, one can determine whether the stakeholders are supportive or will resist a proposed strategy. Stakeholders who are supportive and important will generally accept the proposed strategy, as shown in the upper right quadrant of Figure 4.11. Stakeholders in this quadrant who are expected to resist the strategy need to be convinced to change so that they are either neutral or accepting. The lower right quadrant covers both supporting and resisting stakeholders, because the level of their acceptance is uncertain. Their importance to the successful implementation of the strategy requires that management educate them to the benefits of accepting the strategy. The lower left quadrant covers those

FIGURE 4.11 | **Stakeholder Analysis Matrix**

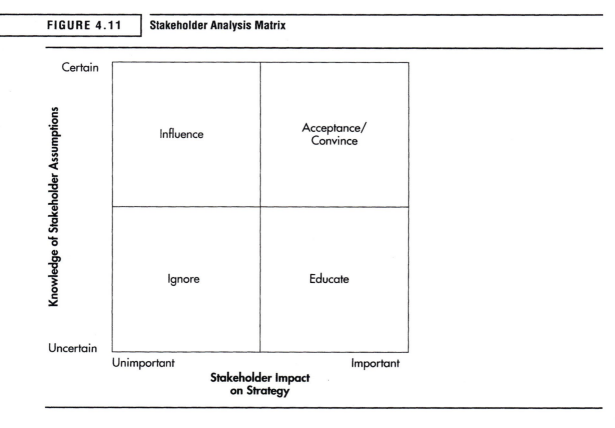

stakeholders whose acceptance is uncertain but who have a minimal impact on the outcome of the proposed strategy. This group can be ignored by management. Stakeholders in the upper left quadrant who are supportive can be ignored because their impact is unimportant. Stakeholders in this quadrant who are certain to resist the strategy need to be influenced by management in order to avoid possible interference with the strategy. Thus, we can see that the two right quadrants include the stakeholders who require the most attention. In some cases, the lower right quadrant is most important; in others, where there is strong opposition in the upper right quadrant, management must take remedial action to prevent interference with implementing the proposed strategy.

ASSESSING THE INTERNATIONAL ENVIRONMENT

Often strategic managers consider the external environment of the firm to be made up principally of those factors that are related to the national environment. However, as we will discuss more fully in Chapter 7, the global environment is becoming increasingly important. In some industries, it may be even more important than the national environment. Assessing the *international environment* is similar to assessing the domestic environment. An international assessment is more complex, however, because many more factors must be considered.

Doing business in a foreign country poses an entirely different set of problems than doing business in the United States. Distance, the difficulty of visiting foreign operations, and differences in language, culture, and political considerations are themselves barriers to entering a foreign market. Managers often have difficulty obtaining information about competitors and requirements for operating in the new environment. Personnel policies also differ; for example, in some countries the ethnic background of an individual may preclude his or her appointment to a managerial position. In Iran, Armenians are rarely appointed to key government posts. In France and Denmark, managers are often required to have an engineering degree or at least to have graduated from the right school or belong to the right professional society. In some countries, the government's permission must be obtained before an employee can be discharged. Sometimes, a huge severance payment must be made. To their chagrin, U.S. companies often find that employment policies that are domestically acceptable may not work abroad.

In conducting an environmental assessment of a foreign country, strategic managers seek to answer the following questions:

1. What is the market potential in the foreign country?
2. What are the market dynamics there with respect to competition, barriers to entry, resource requirements, and so on?
3. What risks are involved in entering this foreign market?
4. How can the firm best enter this foreign market?
5. What form of organizational structure and control would ensure the most effective operation?

REASONS FOR ENTERING FOREIGN MARKETS

A question that is frequently raised is why companies should be concerned with global strategies when there are ample opportunities at home. Vernon and Wells (1981) offered this answer: A firm should "go international" if there are profitable offensive or defensive functions it can perform in other countries. Among the possible objectives are (1) becoming a financial intermediary abroad, (2) becoming geographically diversified, (3) taking advantage of a technological lead, and (4) creating a market abroad. Let's look briefly at each of these objectives.

1. *Financial intermediary.* In this role, the multinational enterprise has access to foreign capital markets and can mitigate some of the problems of transferring funds from abroad where the dollar is devalued or there are differences in exchange rates.
2. *Geographic diversification.* The export of products to many nations increases the sales potential of the firm. By having a foreign subsidiary, the multinational firm may be able to overcome trade barriers, political considerations, transportation problems, or labor and material costs. Furthermore, a firm's presence in a foreign country can force its international competitors to protect that market, leaving the firm's home market more secure. Finally, geographic diversification enables the firm to make foreign investments that it can control.
3. *Technological lead.* In order to exploit a unique technological advantage that the firm may enjoy, it is often desirable to form a foreign subsidiary rather than to deal with the problems of exporting abroad. The larger market share obtained by successful penetration of foreign markets can also help cement the firm's lead at home.
4. *Foreign market.* Although it is possible to export or license products abroad, in many cases it is far better to create a foreign market that is under one's own control by expanding operations into one or more foreign countries.

As the world becomes smaller and distant countries more intertwined culturally and economically, people in business must reconsider assumptions about their markets. Domestic companies have significant opportunities to expand into foreign markets if they go about it in a manner compatible with the new cultures they enter. It is equally important to recognize that dangerous economic threats are mounting for firms that ignore foreign competition and fail to devise a strategy to deal with it.

Competing in international markets requires a different perspective than competing in domestic markets. How to enter a foreign market, how best to interact with customers, how to manage foreign joint ventures or subsidiaries effectively, and how to determine vulnerability and risk are examples of considerations pertinent to global competition.

International marketing operations cannot be undertaken by every business. For some, it may be a matter of survival to enter the global arena. For others, it may be a question of how to protect an existing domestic market from foreign competition. Few businesses, however, can afford to ignore the potential impact of foreign products or the growth potential that foreign markets offer.

The reason to go abroad is simple yet powerful: the world has become a single marketplace. National economics is being replaced by "globeconomics." Companies that ignore this fact find themselves in jeopardy. Today, over 70% of U.S.-made products face foreign competition.

Given these considerations, the question remains whether the entire business enterprise or just some part of it should become international. Rutenberg (1982) studied this problem and developed a checklist to help companies determine which aspects of the business should go international. His approach is based on three major considerations: (1) the current capabilities of the company's business units, (2) the nature of the external market, and (3) the potential costs and benefits of expansion. His list includes these questions:

1. What are the current capabilities of each business unit?
   a. Would it dilute management attention?
   b. Are products nontransferable?
   c. Are technology or marketing skills unique?
2. What are worldwide markets like?
   a. Do standards differ from those in the United States?
   b. Are most markets dominated by others?
   c. Is there market growth or potential?
   d. Are domestic markets threatened from abroad?
   e. Do tariffs or other restrictions exist abroad?
3. Can the business unit undertake expansion abroad?
   a. Is the unit already profitable and strong?
   b. Is technology unique, or is there a breakthrough?
   c. Does the unit have good domestic marketing skills?
   d. Does the unit have a strong market position in the United States?
   e. Is there real growth in demand for the products?
   f. Do the products have leadership positions in the United States?

Whereas Vernon and Wells's analysis helps the company establish objectives for international operations, Rutenberg's list is an aid to deciding which business units (that is, product lines and services) should be taken abroad.

RESEARCH ON FOREIGN MARKETS

Market potential is assessed by obtaining data about the foreign country and then determining the desirability of entering that country's market. Published sources of information regarding trade with foreign countries can be obtained from the consulates of those countries or from organizations that specialize in analyzing investment and trade in various countries around the world. Published sources are also listed in the Index to International Statistics, which can be found in large public and university libraries. Examples of such sources are

- *Business International:* One Dag Hammarskjold Plaza, New York, N.Y. 10017.
- *Eximbank Letter:* International Business Affairs Corp., Washington, D.C. 20571.
- *Foreign Exchange Review:* Manufacturers Hanover Trust Co., New York, N.Y. 10022.
- *Overseas Business Reports:* U.S. Department of Commerce, Washington, D.C.

Unfortunately, these sources of information seldom provide information on market potential or competitors' positions in the market. Obtaining the latter kind of information generally requires an in-country survey or information from foreign nationals or foreign organizations. The validity of the data may be subject to question because of the vested interests of such sources. Because of the uncertainty and sometimes the unreliability of information, organizations that are considering entering an international market may use either joint ventures or local agents to avoid the necessity of independent assessment and at the same time provide themselves with an opportunity to gain experience in a given country. In addition to gathering information, the company often has to work with legal counsel to be sure it does not violate specific laws, such as the Foreign Corrupt Practices Act.

Appendix A in Chapter 7 contains a list covering sources of information for international business. A description of the contents of each of the sources is included. Many institutions have direct access to these sources either through their library system or through computerized systems such as the National Trade Data Bank, which has over 30,000 entries covering a number of government agencies that deal with international trading.

ENVIRONMENTAL FORECASTING

The ability to forecast the future will become increasingly important in companies' efforts to plan appropriate strategies for a turbulent and complex world environment. The questions that strategic managers must consider are diverse: What will happen in the Middle East? Is a major world recession on the horizon? How will the break-up of what was formerly the Soviet Union affect the world economy? These and changing conditions of similar magnitude require a systematic response. Disappointed with using economics as the sole basis for forecasting (Linden, 1991), managers increasingly are looking for other ways to forecast the future meaningfully. Scenarios and the Delphi expert-opinion approach are two techniques that have been applied by the Center for Futures Research under the direction of Dr. Burt Manus. This organization formed the Club of 1000, which included a large panel of people actively engaged in understanding the future of the business environment. Using the data obtained from the Club of 1000, project director Selwyn Enzer covered areas with which business would be concerned. The topics covered included a forecast of when business might anticipate workable nuclear fusion, superbatteries, breakthrough pharmacy therapy, etc.

In their article "Manager's Guide to Forecasting," Georgoff and Murdick (1986) describe how managers at Compaq Computer Corporation chose the best combination of forecasting techniques to deal with difficult problems such as when IBM, Hewlett-Packard, and other companies would enter the portable computer market and how IBM's change in price would affect its potential profitability. They examined the problem of forecasting by taking into account the following considerations:

1. Time horizons—reasonable future period of time
2. Technical sophistication—expertise needed to forecast future events
3. Cost—the expense of updating forecasts
4. Data availability—currency, accuracy, and representativeness of data
5. Variability and consistency of data—relationships assumed among variables

Then they went on to examine four basic approaches that could be used for forecasting.

1. Judgment methods include the Delphi technique and scenario writing.
2. Data-oriented methods include market research, consumer surveys, and industrial and market surveys.
3. Time-series approaches include moving averages, exponential smoothing, and time-series extrapolation.
4. Casual models include correlation or regression models, leading-indicator forecasting, and econometric models.

The authors found that by combining forecasts, they were able to achieve results that were significantly more accurate than those yielded by any individual forecasting technique.

For many businesses, *quantitative forecasting* provides a basis on which current performance can be projected into future trends. Quantitative forecasting relies on the premise that the future can be predicted by identifying certain regularities in the past. This may be true in specific instances and for relatively short-term forecasting. For long-term forecasting, however, predictions based on past trends are not reliable. This is particularly true in times of instability, such as the months following the stock market crash of 1987. And it is becoming ever more true in the volatile global environment.

If managers cannot forecast critical events with certainty, then they need strategies to cope with uncertainty. Organizations today use sophisticated information and control systems to help them adapt to environmental changes. In addition, they make use of several *qualitative forecasting* techniques to overcome the shortcomings of quantitative approaches. Two key characteristics of qualitative techniques are that they (1) explicitly incorporate the subjective assessments of individuals or groups and (2) recognize that the decision makers have some influence on future developments.

One qualitative technique for predicting possible future events is the *Delphi method*. In this method, a panel of experts is queried repeatedly about possible developments in a particular area. In between rounds of inquiries, the experts review the responses of their fellow panelists. In most cases, the assessments converge very rapidly toward a set of assumptions that then becomes the basis for a prediction. The Delphi method is effective regardless of the forecast's planning horizon, but it is frequently very expensive.

Scenarios are often used in conjunction with the Delphi method. Scenarios are stories about the future that identify not only the likelihood of different new developments but also their impact and danger, as perceived by the individuals involved. This approach is discussed in detail in the next section.

In another qualitative forecasting technique, managers define future goals and objectives and then work backward to determine what assumptions are necessary to obtain the desired set of results. This method is not an attempt to forecast the performance of a particular strategy, but rather is an effort to predict the likelihood of its accomplishment, considering all the stakeholder and environmental assumptions necessary to make the strategy work.

SCENARIO WRITING

Scenarios have become increasingly powerful tools for developing strategic vision within organizations and for helping executives identify critical future paths. Peter Schwartz (1991), who has developed effective strategic-planning scenarios for a diverse set of organizations (including Royal Dutch/Shell, the White House, the EPA, Bell South, PG&E, Inland Steel, Volvo, Nissan, and London's International Stock Exchange) defines a scenario as: "a tool for ordering one's perceptions about alternative future environments in which one's decisions might be played out. Alternatively: a set of organized ways for us to dream effectively about our own future."

Two key characteristics of the scenario techniques are that they (1) explicitly incorporate the subjective assessments of individuals or groups and (2) recognize that the decision makers have some influence on future developments. A good scenario is based on facts and assumptions that have proved accurate in the past. Strategic planners then extrapolate the essence of these facts and assumptions to come up with alternative possible futures.

Some of the most useful information for strategic decision making comes from scenarios. Scenarios can be written or oral stories that describe the possibilities for a given set of conditions. They depict alternative futures and show how strategic decisions might lead to different outcomes. Scenarios help decision makers to "experience" the conditions imposed by these futures. They have the further advantage of providing a broad overview of the system and all its possibilities. Business scenarios can range from very simple depictions of future possibilities to highly sophisticated computer models.

One of the first companies to utilize scenarios in a significant way was Shell Oil. The article "Shell's 'Multiple Scenario Planning': A Realistic Alternative to the Crystal Ball" (1980) recounts how Shell's corporate planners described for their top management the bleak economic and political future for the 1980s. This forecast was based on an approach that forced managers continuously to question their assumptions about the future and to concentrate on qualitative arguments as a means of identifying significant and consistent patterns of economic and social development. In retrospect, one can see that this 1980 forecast was incredibly accurate. Shell does not try to forecast the future but rather examines reasonable potential happenings. Supplementing hard data with managers' opinions, Shell was one of the few companies that came through the 1973 energy crisis relatively unscathed: one of its scenarios predicted the possibility of a major disruption in energy supply.

Royal Dutch/Shell has continued to use scenarios as a planning technique that teaches managers how to think about unknown future possibilities. They separate what is predetermined from what is known or certain, and they separate what will happen from what cannot happen. The managers at Shell, based on the success of the 1973 scenarios, have come to accept this technique to cope with the necessity of constantly adapting and innovating in today's competitive environment (Wack, 1985). In a more recent article, Knowlton (1991) describes how Shell gets rich beating risk by utilizing scenarios. Over the years, Shell has developed a number of strategies to safeguard itself against unforeseen contingencies. With annual revenues of $107 billion in 1991, Shell is one of the world's largest industrial corporations. In addition to using scenarios, Shell also employs war gaming, which helps the company prepare for unexpected supply disruptions, accidents, or events such as the Gulf war. The two major scenarios on which they are working are called "Sustainable World" and "Global Mercantilism." These deal with major international economic disputes that can have environmental consequences. Regional conflicts in a destabilized world that has to deal with trade wars, recession, trading blocs, and similar uncertain events require the use of scenarios. Shell has clearly demonstrated the value of this approach by being one of the most profitable oil companies in spite of world turmoil.

Other industries have found that scenarios can be a useful tool in dealing with uncertain future environments. Southern California Edison introduced scenario planning. Mobasheri et al. (1989) described the need for scenario planning in order to have a meaningful resource plan. Based on a review of two decades of forecasting, the company was convinced that traditional techniques were inadequate. Top managers switched to writing scenarios wherein they could examine the implications of different conditions and the strategic responses required. The modern business environment is growing ever more chaotic, and understanding uncertainty and alternative actions has become a critical aspect of successful strategic planning.

Scenarios are used extensively by the Department of Defense to determine what military forces would be needed to deal with potential political and military conflicts. They are used in business to trace proposed strategies from their point of implementation through every outcome possible. A good scenario is based on facts and assumptions that have proved accurate in the past. Strategic planners then extrapolate the *essence* of these facts and assumptions to come up with versions of the future.

Scenarios help decision makers to "experience" the conditions imposed by these futures. They have the further advantage of providing a broad overview of the system and all its possibilities.

Most scenarios begin in the present. A series of assumptions is made about the present state of a system and about mechanisms likely to affect its future. The scenario spells out a future outcome for each alternative set of assumptions. All scenarios are intended to engage the imagination, stimulate discussion, and focus attention on critical strategic decisions. The following tasks are appropriate for almost all scenario writing.

1. Define the overall system, including its goals, environment, resources, decision points, and essential elements. This definition should specify subsystems and their relationships. A good system definition limits the scenario with respect to time, geographic extent, and number of stakeholders involved. It also identifies the rules and limits of the "game."
2. Specify the state of the system from which the scenario proceeds. This step involves choosing initial values for the system.
3. Develop a basic frame of reference. The frame of reference provides a context for the scenario. It includes, for example, the social, political, legal, economic, technological, and military milieus in which the scenario is embedded.
4. Define the objectives of each scenario and the policy issues it might address.
5. Choose a type of scenario, including starting points and methodology.
6. Collect data relevant to the strategic problem under consideration.
7. Specify the structural mechanisms through which the system changes. These will include cause-and-effect relationships among stakeholders, probable events, and points at which strategic choices have to be made. One general approach is to assume that the goal for the system is to achieve equilibrium among stakeholders and environmental forces and then to identify variables that affect the equilibrium one way or the other, review factors that may change the system, and explore the ways the system will react to restore its equilibrium.
8. Develop the scenario(s).

Let's look at several methods of developing a scenario.

1. *Premising method.* In the premising method, the frame of reference is stated as a series of premises from which a conclusion is projected. The premises might consist of current trends, which are projected into the future. These "naive" projections may be supplemented by "surprise-free" projections; such a projection has an outcome that is most likely to occur absent any unusual events such as earthquakes or strikes. Alternatively, "extreme" projections may be made by focusing on a few tendencies and exaggerating their evolution. Kahn and Bruce-Briggs (1972), for example, focused on incidents of terrorism and civil disobedience to project a future in which Americans lost faith in the democratic process and the country became ungovernable.
2. *Systems diagram method.* The systems diagram method was proposed by Ackoff (1974) as a way of discovering policy and strategy options. In this case, the frame of reference is a flow diagram of the system, such as an outline of a corporation's business, and the scenario suggests policy options for each component in the system. A scenario for a food processing company, for example, could involve expanding into other parts of the system in which it currently operates by entering the agricultural business, manufacturing food processing equipment, supplying wholesalers with equipment, acquiring wholesalers who are going into the retail business, or expanding into foreign markets.

3. *Critical site method.* The critical site method takes as its frame of reference the policy-making structure of the system. The scenario writer identifies key decision points at which stakeholders' interactions can change the system. The critical site might be a corporate board meeting, a congressional hearing, an election, a national convention, or some other point at which choices are made about courses of action. The scenario predicts how each stakeholder will act, what outcomes will emerge from the process, and how these outcomes will influence the future of the policy-making system as a whole.

4. *The newspaper headline method.* The scenario writer posits one or more hypothetical headlines for some future date, such as: "Hong Kong, March 20, 1998. The SHK Bank announced today that it has secured a 60% market share in all financial transactions moving between the West and Mainland China. This remarkable growth is because of a strategic plan launched 10 years earlier that . . ." or "Detroit, April 3, 1998. Monolithic Motors announced today that it is closing all of its facilities worldwide and is seeking protection under Chapter 11 of the U.S. Bankruptcy Code due to unprecedented losses. Strategic analysis say that this sad event is occurring because. . . ." The writer then develops a sequence of decisions and events through which the organization might plausibly move from its current situation to the one posited by the headlines.

5. *Logical possibilities method.* This method is used to supplement other methods. With it, the scenario writer generates alternative scenarios based on those already developed.

Cross-Impact Matrix

Scenarios are often developed with the assumption that events or outcomes are interdependent; that is, the occurrence of one event will make the occurrence of other events more or less likely. These relationships can be represented in a *cross-impact matrix* such as the one shown in Figure 4.12. This simple model considers eight possible events that could affect the future supply of energy. The second column contains the nominal probabilities, based on the opinions of experts, that the particular event will occur by 1999. Thus these experts believe there is an 80% chance that the United States will make expanded use of coal by the year 2000. The impact-on-events columns note the probability impact of each event given that another event does occur. For example, if the government should decide to ration the supply of gasoline, the probability that OPEC will collapse increases to 1.2 times 0.4, or 0.48. The two columns at the right show the probability impact that an occurrence of each event will affect two trends: the levels of production and of consumption of oil in the United States.

Computerized Scenario Generation

Because of the large number of possible events and trends, scenarios tracked using cross-impact matrices can become so complex that their analysis is not productive. In such cases an interactive computer simulation is used to develop different scenarios, all based on previous decisions and scenarios. The procedure is as shown in Figure 4.13. After repeating this process a number of times, the decision maker will

FIGURE 4.12	Cross-Impact Matrix

| Events | 1999 Probability | Cross Impact on Events (in table) | | | | | | | | Trend Impact | |
		1	2	3	4	5	6	7	8	U.S. Oil Production	U.S. Oil Consumption
1. OPEC collapses	0.4	—	0.9	0.9	0.9	0.9	1.5	0.5	—	—	1.05
2. Electricity from solar	0.5	1.1	—	0.8	0.9	0.8	1.2	0.9	—	0.99	0.95
3. Coal synthetics	0.7	1.1	0.9	—	0.9	—	1.05	0.9	—	0.99	0.95
4. Expanded use of coal	0.8	1.1	0.9	—	—	—	1.1	0.9	—	0.99	0.9
5. Oil shale/tar sands	0.6	1.1	0.9	—	0.9	—	1.05	0.9	—	0.99	0.95
6. Ban on fission	0.2	0.8	1.2	1.2	2	1.2	—	1.2	—	1.01	1.02
7. Gas rationing	0.55	1.2	1.2	2	1.2	2	0.8	—	—	1.02	0.9
8. U.S. offshore oil	0.2/year	1.05	0.98	0.98	0.98	0.98	1.05	0.9	—	1.1	1.01

Source: Used by permission of the Center for Futures Research, University of Southern California.

FIGURE 4.13	Use of Computer-Generated Scenarios

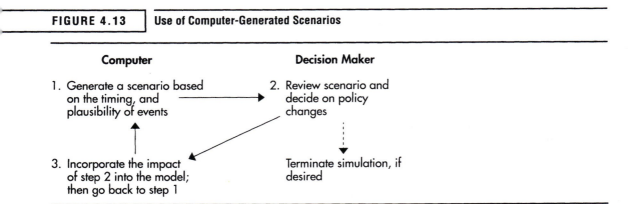

have run through several different projections. Their variety shows how different conditions affect corporate strategies. Computer simulations also permit the decision maker to test specific scenarios against changing conditions in the environment.

SCENARIO ASSESSMENT AND APPLICATION

To ensure that scenarios will be useful in strategy formulation, strategic planners check to see that the following criteria are met.

1. Scenarios should be internally consistent or they should demonstrate how progressive consistency in all dimensions of the system eventually results in a contradiction. A paradox, or internal contradiction, indicates that the system is

a candidate for a radical shift in its structure and thus presents new opportunities and threats. The point where this occurs is sometimes called a "dialectical point." One of the greatest contributions of scenario writing is that it provides a means for discovering potential dialectical points and, through the creativity of the scenario writer, for speculating about the possible outcomes.

2. A scenario should be credible. Either the outcome must be believable or the logic of the story must be so compelling that it cannot be dismissed out of hand.

Presented below are three scenarios based on projected 1990–2000 demographic and macroeconomic data. The purpose of these scenarios is to discover how population shifts and key economic conditions are likely to affect future demand for a company's personal computers and peripheral electronic communication devices.

1. *Most likely scenario.* There will be sufficient stability in personal disposable income during the 1990–2000 period. Monetary and fiscal policy, while not perfectly coordinated, will be carried out by the federal government in a cohesive fashion. The rate of inflation will remain low.

   The number of citizens in the 20–32 age group will decrease, the number in the 32–50 age group will increase, and the number in the 51–80 age group will increase significantly. Expenditures for consumer durable goods will remain generally strong, particularly for the first two age groups. Changing lifestyle trends will create demand for newer models, styles, and types of consumer goods, including electronics. Somewhat reduced demand will be experienced in the industrial Northeast and other depressed areas.

2. *Pessimistic scenario.* U.S. monetary and fiscal policy will be severely strained during most of this period. Declining productivity in the United States will remain unchecked. Several new attempts to bolster productivity and keep inflation low will be ineffective or minimally effective, at best.

   Consumer expenditures for durable goods and other noncash types of purchases will slow dramatically. All purchasing groups—families, singles, single-parent families, and so on—will lose real purchasing power. Expenditures for discretionary purchases of all types will have negative real growth during the 1990–2000 period.

   Further eruptions in the Mideast will raise oil prices again, producing a ripple effect in the economy. In general, manufacturers will not be able to pass these prices on to the consumer because of soft demand.

3. *Optimistic scenario.* New approaches to U.S. monetary and fiscal policy begun in the early 1980s and the consequent restructuring of U.S. industry will continue to drive robust growth between 1990 and 2000.

   Continued investment in R&D and capital expenditures will produce synergistic benefits throughout the economy. The resilient U.S. economy will contribute to a generally strong demand for all types of consumer goods. Demand for personal computers and home electronic communication devices will experience strong growth over the decade, as electronic classrooms and decentralized work patterns begin to emerge on a larger scale.

SUMMARY

One of the most important determinants of an organization's success is its external environment. Some companies have quite effective internal operations and yet fail because of unfavorable conditions in the environment. Others are able to generate good or even outstanding profits, despite a number of internal problems, simply because they happen to be in the right place at the right time.

To be successful and to maintain a competitive advantage, an organization must constantly monitor events, trends, and stakeholder demands in its economic, political, competitive, geographic, social, and technological environments.

A comprehensive environmental analysis includes

1. A detailed examination of the stakeholders and the underlying assumptions being made about them
2. An overall scan of the environment
3. Assessment of the organization's vulnerability to environmental threats
4. Methods of predicting how the environment might change in the future

A stakeholder analysis is the key to understanding an organization's environment. By identifying the key parties and mapping important relationships among them, the strategic manager is in a position to see how changes that affect stakeholders will affect the firm. Environmental scanning complements and reinforces the stakeholder analysis by identifying trends and events that affect every element of the organization's business system.

Powerful strategies are based on exploiting differences between a firm and its competitors. Each competitor tends to inhabit a strategic segment of its industry, a segment whose boundaries define the limits of the competitor's advantage and profitability. The segment boundaries shift as competitors respond to one another's actions and the changing demands of the market. Segment boundaries are the main arenas of competition within the industry. The key task of strategic segmentation consists of identifying industry segments that the company should seek to enter and dominate. In the automobile industry, for example, a strategic segment might consist of luxury cars or sports cars. The goal of strategic segmentation is to convert differences among competitors into a sustainable competitive advantage for the company.

Around the segment boundaries are four main categories of competitive environments, which are defined according to the characteristics of businesses found there. To determine which strategic segment is most appropriate and to formulate strategies for sustaining competitive advantage within it, the manager needs to know whether competition at the boundaries is dominated by high-volume, stalemated, specialized, or fragmented businesses. A company can, for example, more easily develop a sustainable competitive advantage in a high-volume or specialized business environment than in a stalemated or fragmented one.

Another task of the strategic manager is to identify competitive forces that bear on the strategic segment. Among the twelve competitive forces are potential rate of industry growth, intensity of rivalry for domination of the strategic segment, and the bargaining power of customers. Analysis of the major competitive forces helps the strategic manager to determine whether a proposed strategic segment is a suitable one to enter.

Once a strategic segment has been targeted for entry, the task is to formulate strategies for segment domination. A company or business unit can seek to gain a competitive advantage by lowering cost, adding value or uniqueness to the product or service, specializing in a product or service for a very narrow market, intensifying its competitive tactics, or engaging in gamesmanship—manipulations resulting in temporary advantage. The goal of this analysis is to discover which strategy best suits the products and capabilities of the company.

All of these strategies can be applied to domestic or international strategic segments. International strategies, however, are necessarily more complex. The company must decide whether its products and organizational structure are suited to foreign markets and, if so, must devise strategies that match the company's strengths with the socioeconomic, political, and market characteristics of each foreign market it seeks to enter. Generally, foreign markets should be entered slowly, after much research and strategic planning.

Environmental forecasting is increasingly being used to determine how external forces affect strategic options. Methods include industry trend analysis, competitor intelligence, Delphi projections, and statistical forecasts.

One of the emerging forecasting approaches is scenario writing. The advantage of this approach is that there is more involvement by management, which leads to greater acceptance of the actions needed to carry out the strategy that is chosen. The variety of approaches for writing scenarios offer great flexibility and ensure that most managers will find one with which they feel comfortable.

REFERENCES AND SUGGESTIONS FOR FURTHER READING

Ackoff, Russell L. 1974. *Redesigning the future.* New York: Wiley.

Allan, Gerald. 1976. *A note on the Boston Consulting Group concept of competitive analysis and corporate strategy.* Boston: Intercollegiate Case Clearing House, Case #9-175-175.

Amano, Matt M. and Erik Larson. 1983. A longitudinal study of Japanese business expansion in southern California. Corvallis: School of Business, Oregon State University, pp. 1–12.

Bloom, Paul and Philip Kotler. 1975. Strategies for high-market-share companies. *Harvard Business Review* 53, no. 6, November–December.

Boston Consulting Group. 1979. *Specialization.* Boston: Boston Consulting Group.

Boston Consulting Group. 1974. *Segmentation and strategy.* Boston: Boston Consulting Group.

Buzzell, Robert D., Bradley T. Buzzell, and Gale and Ralph G. M. Sultan. 1975. Market share: A key to profitability. *Harvard Business Review* 58, no. 1.

Coyne, Kevin P. 1986. The anatomy of sustainable competitive advantage. *The McKinsey Quarterly,* Spring, pp. 50–65.

The dangerous folly called Theory Z. 1982. *Fortune,* May.

Davidson, W. H. 1982. *Global strategic management.* New York: Wiley.

Demaree, Allan T. 1992. What now for the U.S. and Japan? *Fortune,* February 10, pp. 80–95.

Doz, Y. Y. and C. K. Prahalad. 1981. Headquarters influence and strategic control of MNC's. *Sloan Management Review,* Fall.

Dreyfuss, Joel. 1988. How to deal with Japan. *Fortune,* June 6, pp. 107–118.

Emery, F. E. and E. L. Trist. 1965. The causal texture of organizational environments. *Human Relations* 18, pp. 21–32.

Fahey, Liam and William King. 1977. Environmental scanning for corporate planning. *Business Horizons* 20, no. 4.

Garvin, David A. 1987. Competing on the eight dimensions of quality. *Harvard Business Review,* November–December, pp. 101–109.

Georgoff, David M. and Robert G. Murdick. 1986. Manager's guide to forecasting. *Harvard Business Review,* January–February, pp. 110–120.

Ghemawat, Pankaj. 1986. Sustainable advantage. *Harvard Business Review,* September–October, pp. 53–58.

Gluck, Frederick W. 1982. Meeting the challenge of global competition. *The McKinsey Quarterly,* Autumn.

Green, Robert T. and Trina L. Larsen. 1987. Only retaliation will open up Japan. *Harvard Business Review,* November–December, pp. 22–28.

Haner, F. T. 1980. *Global business strategies for the 1980s.* New York: Praeger.

Hedley, Barry. 1977. Strategy and the "business portfolio." *Long-Range Planning,* February.

Hofer, Charles and Dan Schendel. 1978. *Strategy formulation: Analytical concepts.* St. Paul: West.

Hout, T., M. E. Porter, and E. Rudden. 1982. How global companies win out. *Harvard Business Review,* September–October.

Hurd, Douglas A. 1977. *Vulnerability analysis in business planning.* SRI International Research Report no. 593.

Japanese managers tell how their system works. 1977. *Fortune,* November.

Johnson, Chalmers A. 1982. *MITI and the Japanese miracle.* Stanford, Calif.: Stanford University Press.

Johnson, Richard Tanner and William G. Ouchi. September–October, 1974. Made in America (under Japanese management). *Harvard Business Review.*

Kahn, Herman and B. Bruce-Briggs. 1972. *Things to come.* New York: Macmillan.

Kichen, Steve. 1992. Annual report on American industry. *Forbes,* January 6, pp. 94–176.

Killing, P. J. 1982. How to make a global joint venture work. *Harvard Business Review,* May–June.

Kirkland, Richard I., Jr. 1988. Entering a new age of boundless competition. *Fortune,* March 14, pp. 40–48.

Knowlton, Christopher. 1991. Shell gets rich by beating risk. *Fortune,* August 26, pp. 79–82.

Kupfer, Andrew. 1988. How to be a global manager. *Fortune,* March 14, pp. 52–58.

Levitt, T. 1983. The globalization of markets. *Harvard Business Review,* May–June, pp. 92–102.

Linden, Dana Wechsler. 1991. Dreary days in the dismal science. *Forbes,* January 21, pp. 68–71.

Luke, Timothy and Stephen K. White. 1985. Critical theory, the information revolution, and an ecological path to modernity. *Critical theory and public life,* ed. John Foster. Cambridge, Mass.: M.I.T. Press.

McLuhan, Marshal. 1964. *Understanding media: The extensions of man.* New York: McGraw-Hill.

Main, Jeremy. 1992. How to steal the best ideas around. *Fortune,* October 19, pp. 102–106.

Main, Jeremy. 1984. The trouble with managing Japanese-style. *Fortune,* April 2, pp. 50–56.

Mason, Richard O. and Ian I. Mitroff. 1981. *Challenging strategic planning assumptions.* New York: Wiley.

Meeks, Fleming. 1991. Throwing away the crystal ball. *Forbes,* July 22, p. 60.

Micallef, J. V. 1981. Assessing political risk. *Columbia Journal of World Business,* Summer.

Mobasheri, Fred, Lowell H. Orren, and Fereidoon P. Sioshansi. 1989. Scenario planning at Southern California Edison. *Interfaces* 19, no. 5, September–October, pp. 31–44.

Morrow, Lance. 1992. Japan in the mind of America. *Time,* February 10, pp. 16–22.

Oh, T. K. and M. D. Oh. 1982. Measuring the extent and effects of Japanese-style management. Paper presented at the Academy of International Business, Washington, D.C., October.

Ohmae, Kenichi. 1990. *The borderless world: Power and strategy in the interlinked economy.* New York: Harper Press.

Ohmae, Kenichi. 1985. *Triad power: The coming shape of global competition.* New York: The Free Press.

Ohmae, Kenichi. 1982. *The mind of the strategist.* New York: McGraw-Hill.

Outlook 1992, state of the union. *U.S. News & World Report,* December 30, 1991/January 6, 1992, pp. 37–66.

Porat, Marc Uri. 1977. *The information economy: Definitions and measurement.* United States Office of Technology Special Publication 77-121(1). Washington, D.C.: Department of Commerce, Office of Telecommunications.

Peters, Thomas J. and Robert H. Waterman, Jr. 1982. *In search of excellence: Lessons from America's best-run companies.* New York: Harper & Row.

Porter, Michael E. 1990. *Competitive advantage of nations.* New York: The Free Press.

Porter, Michael E., ed. 1986. *Competition in global industries.* Boston: Harvard Business School Press.

Porter, Michael E. 1985. *Competitive advantage.* New York: The Free Press.

Porter, Michael E. 1980. *Competitive strategy.* New York: The Free Press.

Quelch, John A. and Edward J. Hoff. 1986. Customizing global marketing. *Harvard Business Review,* May–June, pp. 59–68.

Reich, Robert B. 1991. *The work of nations: Preparing ourselves for 21st century capitalism.* New York: Knopf.

Ronstadt, Robert and Robert J. Kramer. 1982. Getting the most out of innovation abroad. *Harvard Business Review,* March–April, pp. 94–99.

Rothschild, William E. 1979. Competitor analysis: The missing link in strategy. *Management Review,* July.

Rowe, Alan J. et al. 1989. *Strategic management.* Reading, Mass.: Addison-Wesley, p. 175.

Rugman, Alan M., Donald J. Lecraw, and Laurence D. Booth. 1985. *International business firm and environment.* New York: McGraw-Hill.

Rutenberg, D. P. 1982. *Multinational management.* Boston: Little, Brown.

Schein, Edgar H. 1987. *The art of managing human resources.* New York: Oxford University Press.

Schonberger, Richard J. 1982. Production workers bear major quality responsibility in Japanese industry. *Industrial Engineering,* December, pp. 34–40.

Schwartz, Peter. 1991. *The art of the long view.* New York: Doubleday.

Shell's multiple scenario planning: A realistic alternative to the crystal ball. 1980. *World-Business Weekly,* April 7.

South, Stephen E. 1981. Competitive advantage: The cornerstone of strategic thinking. *The Journal of Business Strategy,* Spring.

Special report—Japan's troubled future. 1987. *Fortune,* March 30.

Stalk, George Jr. and Thomas M. Hout. 1990. *Competing against time: How time-based competition is reshaping global markets.* New York: The Free Press.

Steiner, George A. and John B. Miner. 1977. *Management policy and strategy: Text, reading and cases.* New York: Macmillan. Chs. 7 and 8.

Stevenson, H. 1976. Defining corporate strengths and weaknesses. *Sloan Management Review* 17, no. 3.

Stewart, Thomas A. 1991. Brain power: How intellectual capital is becoming America's most valuable asset. *Fortune,* June 3, pp. 44–60.

A survey of Japan. 1987. *The Economist,* December 5.

Tanner Johnson, R. and W. G. Ouchi. 1974. Made in America (under Japanese management). *Harvard Business Review,* September–October, pp. 61–69.

Therrien, Lois. 1989. The rival Japan respects. *Business Week,* November 13, pp. 108–118.

Utterback, James. 1979. Environmental analysis and forecasting in *Strategic management: A new view of business policy and planning,* ed. Charles Hofer and Dan Schendel. Boston: Little, Brown.

Van Mesdag, Martin. 1987. Winging it in foreign markets. *Harvard Business Review,* January–February, pp. 71–74.

Vernon, Raymond and Louis T. Wells, Jr. 1981. *Manager in the international economy.* Englewood Cliffs, N.J.: Prentice-Hall.

Wack, Pierre. 1985. Scenarios: Uncharted waters ahead. *Harvard Business Review,* September–October, pp. 73–89.

Warsh, David. 1984. *The idea of economic complexity.* New York: Viking Press.

World Bank. 1987. *World development report.* New York: Oxford University Press.

Zuboff, Shoshana. 1988. *In the age of the smart machine: The future of work and power.* New York: Basic Books.

APPENDIX A

Example of a Foreign Environment: Japan

As competition between the United States and Japan intensifies, it tends to mask the important fact that the two nations really need each other. In many ways they have strong ties and admire one another (Morrow, 1992). The results of a survey conducted to determine what Americans admire about Japan and what the Japanese think about America are given in Tables 4A.1 and 4A.2. Both countries have obviously found things they admire about the other that are more important than the differences that tend to be exploited. The basic issue confronting Japan and the United States is how to live with the apparent differences and still benefit from the mutual interdependency that exists. The most significant bone of contention between the two countries is the large trade deficit that the United States has had with Japan. This condition leads to the obvious question of what will happen now with trade between the U.S. and Japan (Denaree, 1992). Nonetheless, companies such as Schick razors have 69.5% of the market share in Japan, compared to only 30.3% in the U.S. Coca-Cola has 33% of the Japanese market, compared with 41% for the U.S. market. Other companies such as Toys-R-Us and Apple Computer are making significant inroads into the Japanese market. Laying the groundwork is a complex task, but it is clear that Japan offers an opportunity for growth for those companies that can match the quality and price of Japanese products.

A number of U.S. companies are focusing on meeting the requirements of a very demanding Japanese consumer. One company that Japan respects is Motorola, which emphasizes strong R&D, built-in quality, and zealous service (Therrien, 1989). For example, defects have been cut from approximately 3,000 per million to less than 200. This achievement, of course, required significant investment in R&D, along with a passion for quality. With its sales approaching $1 billion in Japan, Motorola has achieved a significant return on its investment.

FIGURE 4A.1	What Japan and the United States Admire in Each Other

	U.S. Admires About Japan	Japan Admires About U.S.
Form of government	23%	63%
World leadership	31%	84%
Scientific/Technological accomplishments	82%	78%
Freedom of expression	27%	89%
Variety of lifestyles	25%	86%
Industriousness	88%	27%
Educational institutions	71%	48%
Leisure time for workers	15%	88%
Respect for family life	75%	87%

FIGURE 4A.2	Comparison of Japanese's and Americans' Views of Each Other

	Americans' View of Japanese	Japanese's View of Americans
Friendly	59%	64%
Competitive	94%	50%
Devoted to fair play	35%	43%
Lazy	4%	21%
Hardworking	94%	15%
Prejudiced	53%	41%
Violent	19%	23%
Crafty	69%	13%
Poorly educated	12%	21%

GLOBAL MANAGEMENT IN THE 1990s

In an article about global management for the 1990s, *Fortune* interviewed a number of senior executives, soliciting their views on a global economy poised for expansion. New technologies, productivity, integration of world markets, political and economic coopera-tion, and global alliances have set the stage for an era of unprecedented growth. Companies are exploring new management strategies to deal with future opportunities. The following comments suggest how various leaders whose firms are important in the Japanese economy are preparing for a global business environment.

Thomas F. Jordan—Du Pont, Japan

"This is the most competitive market in the world. Customers are demanding, quality standards are excruciatingly precise, and the culture is sometimes difficult to penetrate. But if you make it, the profits can be very attractive, and you'll have established a significant global reputation for yourself. Furthermore, you can use Japan as a base for expanding business in the Asia–Pacific region."

Rainer H. Jahn—Mercedes-Benz, Japan

"Japan is a tough market. Japanese consumers are among the most demanding in the world."

William J. Weisz—Motorola

"Cracking the Japanese market wasn't easy. After some initial resistance, Motorola was able to establish a string of joint ventures in the 1970s with such Japanese companies as Toshiba and NTT to manufacture and market radio communications equipment and semi-conductors."

Hiroshi Saito—Nippon Steel

"We have always been concerned with the environment. Over the past twenty years, we invested about $3 billion in antipollution facilities, and from 1973 to 1990 we spent about $1.5 billion on energy conservation. We have also trained environmental engineers and provided environmental technology to others overseas."

Joichi Aoi—Toshiba

"The nature of global competition is changing. The technological and financial resources required to develop many of tomorrow's markets are beyond the resources of most big international firms, and this is leading to new corporate alliances. That, in turn, is accelerating the trend toward globalization among Japanese companies."

Tsutomu Kanai—Hitachi

"Today's high technologies tend to be integrated in many fields. Manufacturers are expected to offer software together with hardware and to provide complete systems as well as industrial products and components."

Koji Matsuno—Hitachi Metals

"The global business structure has been changing as well as our own. In the past, Japan tended to export to get itself out of trouble, but that is not possible today. Overseas markets demand investment, not exports. Protectionism is a serious concern, particularly from the newly industrialized countries. The entire global atmosphere is different and there is no single cure available."

Yoshio Tateisi—Omron

"We need to focus more closely on our own specialty technologies, shift to new growth areas, develop new technologies and generally improve the efficiency of our operations from the plant to corporate headquarters."

Tadahiro Sekimoto—NEC

"Technology, especially in the area of electronic miniaturization and artificial intelligence, is progressing so fast that the barriers between man and machine are rapidly disappearing."

Toichi Takenaka—Takenaka

"The companies that will survive are those that already have established the administrative structures and technologies to keep productivity high and costs low. Some relief can be sought in overseas markets, but the job of cost control must be done at home."

Susumu Yamaji—Japan Airlines

"JAL's concern with global warming is just one example of the company's commitment to behaving like a responsible member of the global society—a good corporate citizen."

JAPAN'S SOCIOECONOMIC AND TECHNOLOGICAL ENVIRONMENT

The Japanese economy has been undergoing a radical transformation. In 1983, Japan exported 12–13% of its gross national product (Britain exported 20%). Japan held 165,000 patents, compared to 62,098 held by the United States and 28,683 held by West Germany. Capital spending was almost identical to that by comparable industries in the United States, even though Japan is a smaller country.

In 1987, though still one of the strongest industrial countries in the world, Japan began to re-examine its position. Fear and uncertainty tempered the exuberance that existed in the past. Profits were down by 25% in 1986 and by 26% in 1987. Japanese steelmakers faced a loss of $2.2 billion and planned severe layoffs. Unemployment, while low by world standards, was the highest yet at 2.8%, and Japan's cost advantage had slipped compared to that of the United States and West Germany. With its industrial slowdown, an aging population, and more restless youth, Japan is facing difficult decisions ahead. Most of the country's raw materials have to be imported; virtually all of Japan's supply of crude oil comes from abroad. Technological progress has put Japan on a par with (and in certain areas even ahead of) the industrialized West, but the country's labor reserves are nearing exhaustion. Low wages combined with a high rate of inflation have produced a standard of living that fades in comparison with the country's degree of economic success. And, by all accounts, Japan endures the most polluted environment in the world.

Despite these problems, the country is forging ahead on most fronts. Japan spends approximately three times as much as the United States does on industrial research and 20% more on services. Probably the most significant change in Japan's grand strategy is a planned shift to an information economy. Sugiichiro Watari, past president of Toshiba Corporation, explained that Japanese companies are moving toward a new corporate strategy based on "integration, intelligence, and information" (*Fortune,* 1987). The economic aspects of the information society depend to a large extent on Japan's computer industry and factory automation. Japanese mainframes had achieved parity with those in the United States by 1980. Japan now leads the U.S. in the race to develop a supercomputer and is working on a fifth-generation computer language, while the United States still uses the fourth-generation language. Japan is also going all out in its development of artificial intelligence and for a long time has led the U.S. in the field of robotics. Because domestic demand is now leading the Japanese economy and should remain strong through the year 2000, both trade and current-account surpluses should remain enormous for years to come (*Economist,* 1987).

How has Japan's socioeconomic environment contributed to its success in the global marketplace? The following characteristics are embedded in Japanese business culture.

1. The importance of harmony in the national culture
2. Unquestioning acceptance of standards of performance
3. Loyalty on the part of employer and employee that often leads to lifetime employment in one firm
4. Slow performance evaluations and promotions
5. Careful decision making that gives the appearance of consensus
6. Ability to adapt readily to new conditions because of support by the government
7. High level of savings: about 20% of the GNP
8. Willingness to carry out all decisions
9. Importance of ritual, as typified by the tea ceremony
10. Emphasis on religion and philosophy
11. Ownership of up to 25% of a company by banks that provide financing to those companies at attractive rates, typically 5–7% interest
12. High value placed on technological development

The Role of Government in Japanese Business   Explanations of Japan's great economic power have focused on Japanese management techniques or on the cultural aspects of Japanese society that cannot be copied. Yet neither of these two factors seem to have been as critical as the collaboration between the Japanese government and private industry (Johnson, 1982). This collaboration results in a "state-guided market system" dedicated to rapid growth. According to Johnson, the United States is a "regulatory" state, in which the government merely sets the rules for conduct and attempts to provide a favorable business climate. Japan, on the other hand, is a "developmental" state, in which the government takes a leading role in determining strategies for national economic growth and controlling investment and technology accordingly.

Although the Japanese government has the power to exert considerable pressure on companies, the pressure is not in the form of regulations. Antitrust regulation, for example, barely exists. This made it possible for Japanese automobile companies to develop a common design for antipollution equipment, a collaborative action that would be illegal in the United States. The U.S. economy is regulated by politicians who are replaced every few years, whereas economic policy in Japan is strongly influenced by career technocrats at the Ministry of International Trade and Industry (MITI). As a result, the Japanese economy is planned on a long-term basis, which promotes continuity and growth. As is the case in many European countries, companies are typically owned by banks, not by individual shareholders. Bank ownership is made possible by a staggering savings rate that is approximately 20% of the GNP, compared to less than

5% in the United States. A number of economists believe that the propensity to save is, in the final analysis, responsible for Japan's phenomenal growth (see, for example, Bronfenbrenner, 1970).

Homogeneity and Social Conformity   Beneath the surface, Japan is still a deeply traditional and conformist society. Individualism, in the Western sense, is no more an ideal in contemporary Japan than it ever was. In fact, the Japanese word for individualism, *kojinshugi,* connotes selfishness rather than independence. Even such marginal expressions of nonconformism as the *zoko* ("tribe") phenomenon—youths wearing outlandish gear and dancing in the streets—is in keeping with the Japanese tendency to seek security within a group. While social criticism is not as unthinkable as in the past, it is not readily accepted.

Sooner or later, Japan will have to shift its orientation from impressive economic growth to genuine social welfare, a process that simply cannot come from the top. The need to face up to the ever-increasing gap between economic prosperity and social progress will put Japan's economy to a test more difficult than conquering export markets or producing products of ever-increasing quality.

Competition   The aggressiveness that Japanese companies display abroad is an extension of their competitiveness at home. Although Japan is critically dependent on exports to pay for its imports of raw materials, surprisingly few products are developed solely for the export market. On the contrary, many of the country's most competitive products abroad had to weather a tough domestic market first. In fact, the demanding Japanese consumer may well be responsible for the high quality of Japanese products. The Japanese demand for quality sometimes borders on perfectionism, and many of the Japanese cars exported to the United States would be unfit for the Japanese domestic market.

Most Japanese companies use an ethnocentric strategy for penetrating a foreign market. The Japanese domestic market serves as a perfect testing ground for the production and sale of high-volume, low-cost items. Once economies of scale and benefits of the experience curve are established, they are used to undercut competition in foreign markets and attain dominance in the low-price end of the market. After the market has been penetrated, the company can work its way into more complex and more profitable market segments. This scenario unfolded in the electronics and automobile industries. Today, Japanese companies are exporting many high-priced, top-of-the-line models. They began, in the 1970s, by exporting less expensive bottom-of-the-line models.

The Japanese are willing to diversify to gain a competitive edge. Yamaha Companies, for example, produce many different products. They started with pianos, then moved into propellers, motorcycles, woodwinds, snowmobiles, and now jet skis. Finally, Japanese competitiveness is fueled by determination. Aggressiveness on the part of Japanese top managers has made Japan into one of the strongest industrial powers the world has seen.

ORGANIZATIONAL CHARACTERISTICS OF JAPANESE COMPANIES

One of the most common misconceptions about Japanese companies is that they use a high degree of participative decision making and reach decisions only after long and laborious deliberations that involve employees at several layers of the corporation hierarchy and end in consensus. As Kenichi Ohmae (1982), a consultant with many of Japan's best-known companies, has pointed out, nothing could be further from the truth. Decentralized decision making is a characteristic of Japan's giant trading companies, but this organizational pattern exists more out of necessity than by design.

Consensus is not the means but rather the end result of the decision-making process in most Japanese corporations. What Americans mistakenly call consensus management may merely be a means of ensuring that all levels of management are informed and prepared to execute the decision once it is made. What really happens is the process of *nemawashi*, through which an unofficial understanding is reached before any official decision is announced. In U.S. companies, the closest thing to this kind of decision making is the common practice of leaking information, be it correct or incorrect, in order to test responses or prepare employees to accept an upcoming major decision. In any case, unofficial information comes from the top, not the bottom. The Japanese can more openly engage in this type of office politics because of (1) the greater willingness of Japanese subordinates to conform with whatever comes from the top, and (2) the fact that many jobs are secure for life. Thus what may appear to be management by consensus is really management by compliance.

Most Japanese companies are run by a single man or a small group that makes all the crucial decisions. In fact, Japanese companies are much more autocratic than most people believe. As Schein (1981) noted, autocratic systems can outproduce democratic systems, at least in the short run. And high productivity, even when achieved by autocratic methods, can build high morale.

In companies such as Matsushita, Sony, Honda, Yoshida, Yamaha, and Casio, the CEO is personally responsible for all liabilities in the company and thus is likely to make final decisions personally. Subordinates learn how to "play to" the chief executive's style.

A study reported by Amano and Larson (1983) revealed how restrictive life in the Japanese firm can be. For example,

- To be hired by a major firm, a candidate must have graduated from a top-ranked university.
- All key candidates are male.
- Preference is given to men with no prior employment.
- Non-Japanese workers, such as Koreans and Chinese, are excluded. Ancestry is traced to country of birth.
- Moderate and harmonious employees are sought.
- Promotion depends on degree of conformity, loyalty, and harmony. Individual freedom and private life are given up because of politics, factions, and indoctrination.
- The elite retire at age 55, and those who are incompetent are fired or reassigned to undesirable posts.

DECISION-MAKING STYLE OF JAPANESE MANAGERS

How closely can the effectiveness of a particular management style be related to the cultural, sociopolitical, and economic framework within which it is practiced? Critics of Japanese-style management often argue that superimposing the Japanese style on U.S. business would be difficult because of the obvious differences in culture between the two countries. Yet management style is not simply a matter of principle—it is also a matter of degree. To assume that there is only one right management style for any U.S. company is tantamount to ignoring the considerable variety that exists among companies.

Several Japanese companies that have opened manufacturing plants in the United States have proved that their management techniques can be transplanted successfully. Tanner and Ouchi (1974), reported on 20 Japanese companies operating in the United States, many of which were outperforming American companies in the same industries. Schonberger (1982) demonstrated how manufacturing concepts such as just-in-time (JIT) provisioning of manufacturing inventories or quality circles can be successfully adapted without a complete changeover to Japanese-style management. Thus while the Japanese system may admittedly be unacceptable as a whole, parts of it may be useful in developing more effective management of a particular U.S. company.

A study conducted in the early 1980s explored the views of American and Japanese employees of several Japanese-owned companies in Southern California (Oh, 1982). A series of open-ended interviews with American personnel directors and top Japanese managers revealed the following specific business practices.

1. *Decision making by consensus.* In no company was consensus actually used. Group input was solicited, and the issues brought up by the top management were discussed.
2. *Concern for employees.* Japanese top executives avowed concern for their employees as people. American personnel managers believed this concern to be no greater than that of executives in American firms.
3. *Job rotation.* No firms in the sample practiced job rotation.
4. *Evaluation and promotion.* Americans felt that they would not reach a top position because of Japanese control of their firms.
5. *Groupism.* Most companies did not practice groupism. It was found incompatible with American employees' values of individualism, independence, privacy, and professionalism.
6. *Job security.* In general, the companies tried to avoid layoffs but did not rule them out. All the firms sampled were willing to dismiss unsatisfactory employees.

From another perspective, the style of Japanese managers can be seen in their manner of thinking. Rowe (1989) drew the following conclusions after studying a group of Japanese managers and American managers in high-technology firms. The American manager is highly analytic, uses logic and careful analysis, and is concerned with short-term results. The Japanese manager, by contrast, is much more concerned with the future and harmonious relations with people. Saving face is a basic value.

Japan is perhaps the premier example of a foreign market that American companies are trying to enter, but Europe 1992 can also offer new opportunities. Though there has been some success, entering the Japanese market is largely problematic because of Japan's protectionist policies. For more than a decade, during which time the U.S. trade deficit has soared to new heights, Japan has promised to open its markets. The reason that Japan will not open up, according to Green and Larsen, is that the products we seek to export are precisely the ones that Japan is trying to protect (Green and Larsen, 1987). The answer, then, is for the United States to adopt a new trade policy that is retaliatory rather than protectionist and that requires carefully targeting Japanese markets. Japan protects its automobile and electronics industries through its Ministry of International Trade and Industry. The Ministry uses every means possible to prevent local businesses from importing products. Customs procedures, restrictive standards, unrealistic certification requirements, and discriminatory procurement policies all act as barriers to imports.

Protectionist policies focus on one product rather than on one country. Therefore, the United States has considered placing a tariff on all foreign car imports without singling out Japan. The U.S. could also nurture key competing industries through subsidies, low-cost loans, tax relief, R&D grants, and exclusion of imports. While these strategies seem like a radical departure from free trade, allowing free trade in one direction alone has had devastating effects on U.S. industries and the trade deficit.

CHAPTER FIVE

Capability-based Strategy

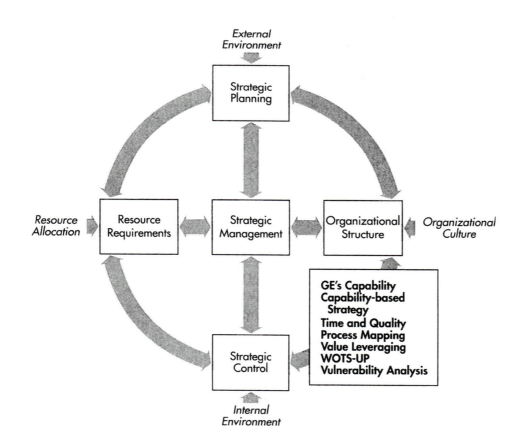

External Environment

Strategic Planning

Resource Allocation

Resource Requirements

Strategic Management

Organizational Structure

Organizational Culture

GE's Capability
Capability-based Strategy
Time and Quality
Process Mapping
Value Leveraging
WOTS-UP
Vulnerability Analysis

Strategic Control

Internal Environment

Chapter 1 A Framework for Strategic Management	**Chapter 2** Strategic Analysis	**Chapter 3** Strategic Visioning, Goals, Ethics, and Social Responsibility	**Chapter 4** The Competitive Environment	**Chapter 5** Capability-based Strategy	**Chapter 6** Market Dynamics and Sustainable Competitive Advantage
How to approach strategic management	*Application of strategic analysis*	*Understanding vision, values, ethics*	*Coping with competitive forces, stakeholders*	*Assessing company capability, timeliness, quality*	*Determining trends, gap analysis, and market dynamics*

Chapter 7 Strategy in a Global Environment	**Chapter 8** Financial Planning and Competitive- Cost Analysis	**Chapter 9** Entrepreneurship, Mergers and Acquisitions, Restructuring, and the Service Sector	**Chapter 10** Leadership Factor in Strategy and Implementing Strategic Change	**Chapter 11** Information Technology and Future Directions in Strategy
Assessing global trade, foreign markets, monetary exchange	*Preparing a financial plan and competitive-cost analysis*	*Importance of small business, entrepreneurs, restructuring*	*Strategy implementation, leadership, culture*	*Information technology, trends, new management*

INTRODUCTION

Successful strategies for the 1990s will rely more on capabilities, which are often difficult for competitors to detect and imitate. Strategies are becoming more "intelligent." Advantage will dwell within the processes and behaviors of the organization: in the responsiveness of its operations, in its management of new customer needs, in its organizational simplicity and flexibility, in the innovativeness of its people, and in its use and management of information technology. In short, responsiveness is becoming a key success factor.

Arthur Shorin, CEO of Topps Company, recognizes the importance of timeliness because he is in the baseball card business, wherein "hot items" can come and go in a matter of weeks. For example, in six weeks Topps produced the cards describing the Gulf war weaponry. By staying agile, Topps has managed to outpace all its rivals (Teitelbaum, 1992).

Capability-based strategies are founded on the notion that internal resources and core competencies derived from distinctive capabilities provide the "strategy platform" that underlies a firm's long-term profitability. Evaluation of these capabilities begins with a company capability profile, which examines the company's strengths and weaknesses in four key areas: managerial, marketing, financial, and technical. Then a WOTS-UP analysis is carried out to determine whether the company has the strengths necessary to deal with specific forces in the external environment. This analysis enables managers to identify (1) external threats and opportunities and (2) distinct competencies that can ward off the threats and compensate for weaknesses. The picture revealed by the WOTS-UP analysis helps to suggest which type of strategy, or strategic thrust, the firm should use to gain competitive advantage. This can be described diagrammatically as shown in Figure 5.1.

A new threat to traditional organizations is the emergence of capability-based competitors relying on total quality and time-based responsiveness. These competitors often develop completely new and different delivery mechanisms and organizations. In order to ensure that the core competencies reach the customer with maximum impact, they institutionalize time and quality as critical variables in their operations. They achieve a faster and better operation by examining the whole process rather than improving many individual phases. As a consequence, they gain substantial and lasting benefits.

The new rules of strategy are dictating a shift to competing on capabilities. Stalk, Evans, and Shulman (1992) have identified four principles that serve as guidelines to achieving capability-based competition.

1. Corporate strategy does not depend on products or markets but on business processes.
2. Key strategic processes are needed to consistently provide superior value to the customer.
3. Investment is made in capability, not functions or SBUs.
4. The CEO must champion the capability-based strategy.

Following up on this latter point, they claim that "a CEO's success in building capabilities will be the chief test of management skill in the 1990s."

FIGURE 5.1 | **Defining Core Competencies**

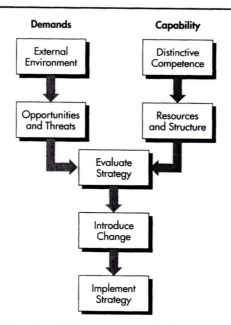

ILLUSTRATIVE CASE: GE'S NEW CAPABILITY-BASED STRATEGY

One firm that relies on capability-based strategy is General Electric, a company that has pioneered strategic planning and other management techniques and is in the process of revolutionizing U.S. management practices once again. This large, diversified company with a highly developed corporate management system is undergoing significant cultural change in order to become a more centrally managed firm. The key focus is on strengthening the firm's skills and resources in order to build a stronger foundation for its strategy.

The results of this effort are already showing. GE's new philosophy of running things more as a small business has boosted its productivity growth in the early 1990s to several times that of other large U.S. manufacturing firms. In 1990 the company's sales growth was $3.8 billion, more than the *total* sales of all but the largest U.S. companies, and with $4.4 billion in profits, it was second only to Exxon in earnings.

GE's new approach, which is bound to be emulated by many other companies in the 1990s, is based on speed, simplicity, and involvement of people at all levels in the organization. The three main management thrusts of this approach at GE are

1. *Work-out,* a way of getting employees involved in the decision-making process
2. *Best practices,* emulating the way other companies have sustained their competitive advantage
3. *Process mapping,* simplifying the way things are done, removing bottlenecks, and making the delivery system more effective

Work-out is essentially a forum where employees work on problems together in order to winnow unnecessary work out of their jobs. A group of 40 to 100 people from all ranks and functions within an organization gather for a three-day session. In many cases, some customers and suppliers are also invited to participate. The group members' main task is to develop as many practical solutions as possible to eliminate waste and to prune unnecessary tasks, meetings, paper-work, and approvals from their daily work. The manager typically opens the proceedings and then leaves.

The group breaks into five or six work-out teams that for a day and a half list their problems, look for possible solutions, and prepare presentations. On the third day the manager returns, together with other senior executives, to listen to the groups' findings. The rules are such that the executives can make only one of three responses to the workout teams' proposals: agree immediately, say no, or charter a new team that will define a particular issue in more detail by a given date. This third day of the work-out session can be a grueling experience for managers. They often have to listen to complaints that have been built up over a long period of time.

The *best-practices* step is basically to ask, "What is the secret of success of companies who over many years were able to maintain faster productivity growth than their competitors?" For this purpose a group of GE executives, together with an outside consultant, screened a large number of candidates. Of the 20–30 companies examined, about half required more thorough joint fact-finding before conclusions could be reached.

The results of these in-depth comparisons were surprisingly similar. Almost all of the best-practice companies (such as AMP, Chaparral Steel, Ford, Hewlett-Packard, Motorola, Xerox, and some Japanese companies) emphasized the management process rather than the specific functions. Instead of considering individual departments or tasks, they focused on optimizing cooperation along the entire value-adding chain, including suppliers, and on being faster than their competitors in new-product introduction and delivery. Unlike most other companies, GE had installed measurement systems that included indicators of the effectiveness of its processes, not just the outcomes.

The best-practices effort provided an empirical basis for changing the way things were managed and measured at GE. Now the company regularly shares new ideas with other leading

GE'S NEW CAPABILITY-BASED STRATEGY, CONTINUED

companies, and it stresses the superiority of continuous improvement to one-time measurements.

Process mapping offers a set of tools to bring issues systematically to the surface and provide benchmarks. All the relevant functions along the value-adding chain are used to make a flow chart of each and every step that goes into creating or making a product. Process mapping can be a very difficult task for management, because what really happens often differs substantially from the way it was planned or written down in a company manual.

When a process is mapped, the participants often have developed, for the first time, the capability to manage the entire operation in a holistic way. The results of this approach, which will be described later in this chapter in the section on time-based management, are often quite different from the outcomes of traditional management practices. The results that GE has achieved by applying this approach have led to drastic improvements in several of its operations.

Top management at GE realizes that it will be a long time—perhaps a decade—before this new philosophy fully takes hold at the company. As this new management approach and its successes at GE become better known, the company may well not only change its own corporate culture by the year 2000 but may also start a revolution in management thinking throughout U.S. business.

FORMULATING A CAPABILITY-BASED STRATEGY

Traditionally, strategy has been defined as the process of aligning the internal capability of an organization with the external demands of its environment, as shown in Figure 5.1. The process has focused on the changes in the environment that led to opportunities and threats to which the firm had to adjust. The internal process of alignment to these changes was often taken for granted. Yet a number of studies have shown that differences in profitability *within* industries are more important than such differences *between* industries; that is, some companies consistently thrive in difficult environments while others do not succeed even though their industry is very healthy.

Recently, as the example of GE shows, the capability-based strategy has become prominent as a means of developing new sources of competitive advantage. Capability-based strategies, sometimes referred to as the resource-based view of the firm, are determined by (a) those internal resources and capabilities that provide the platform for a firm's strategy and (b) those resources and capabilities that are the primary source of profit for the firm. A key management function is to identify what resource gaps need to be filled in order to maintain a competitive edge where these capabilities are required.

Several levels can be established in defining the firm's overall strategy platform (see Figure 5.2).

At the bottom of the pyramid are the basic *resources* a firm has compiled over time. They can be categorized as technical factors (patents, brand identity, manufacturing skills), competitive factors (economies of scale, market share), managerial factors (organizational culture, speed of response to changing conditions), and financial factors (access to capital, cost-competitiveness). Taken together, these

FIGURE 5.2 | **Strategy Platform**

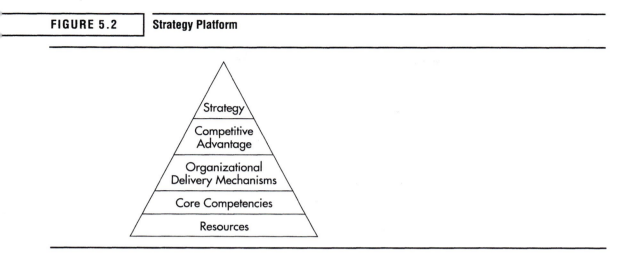

four factors establish the advantage base of the firm (Figure 5.3). We will examine the advantage base in detail in this chapter.

Core competencies, the second layer of the strategy platform, can be defined as the unique combination of the resources and experience of a particular firm. It takes time to build these core competencies, and they are difficult to imitate. Motorola, the maker of integrated circuits, mobile phones, automotive electronics, and other high-tech products, has succeeded in creating a flexible combination of its basic technologies together with generic management skills. This has allowed the company to be very competitive in a range of applications of its technologies and to stay ahead of its competition with innovative products. Other examples of firms that have succeeded in developing strong core competencies include Wal-Mart (fast-response systems in its distribution chain, combined with decentralized information flows), 3M (superior know-how in adhesive and coating technologies, combined with creative and fast new-product development), Honda (technical excellence in four-stroke engines, combined with flexible production), and Procter

FIGURE 5.3 | **Company Resource and Advantage Base**

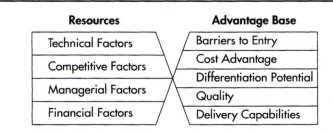

& Gamble (highly developed ability to understand market and customer trends, combined with strong management of international brands).

What seems to distinguish many of these successful firms is that they were able to combine strong technological skills or other know-how with a unique and fast way of (re)generating these skills and delivering them to the customer. Critical to sustaining these core competencies are their

1. *Durability*. Their lifespan is longer than individual product or technology life cycles, as are the lifespans of the resources used to generate them, including people.
2. *Intransparency*. It is difficult for competitors to imitate these competencies quickly.
3. *Immobility*. These capabilities and resources are difficult to transfer.

Successful firms have established effective mechanisms to safeguard and replenish these core competencies. At the same time, however, they are keenly aware that these core competencies will lose their strength if they are not constantly maintained and upgraded. Therefore, capability-based competitors realize that how they manage their processes is a critical component of their competitive edge. Excellence in delivering core competencies to the customer often requires organizational delivery mechanisms that are based on

1. *Speed of response*—the ability to preempt the competition with faster new-product introduction or a faster, more responsive service.
2. *Quality*—this increases customer satisfaction and allows the firm to win market share.
3. *Responsiveness to the customer*—the ability to better understand customer and competitive developments.
4. *Team organization*—the ability to be faster and more effective by breaking traditional functional departmentalization.
5. *Organizational learning*—the ability to learn through shared insights, models, knowledge, and experience and the ability to increase know-how and competencies within the firm.

PepsiCo is an interesting case in point. Besides its well-known cola brand, the company owns Frito-Lay, the highly profitable salty snack seller, as well as three restaurant chains: Pizza Hut, Taco Bell, and Kentucky Fried Chicken. PepsiCo has enjoyed some of the fastest growth in the food industry over the last ten years, and it is one of the most profitable companies in this industry. CEO Wayne Calloway jokingly identifies three main ingredients in PepsiCo's recipe for success: "Love change. Learn to dance. And leave J. Edgar Hoover behind." Learning to dance is Calloway's colloquialism for dealing with customers in radically new ways. PepsiCo's salespeople, for example, are making more daily sales contacts with customers than the representatives of any other company in the world. Leaving J. Edgar Hoover behind means managing those people in the "hands-off" way that the former FBI chief detested.

The most important element in PepsiCo's success is its passion for change. PepsiCo often revamps operations, marketing, or management even when things look fine, simply to keep a step ahead of the competition and retain its lead in its organizational delivery mechanism. Its main rule in making these changes is

"Simplify, simplify, simplify." Like other companies that compete on capabilities, PepsiCo concentrates on managing key delivery processes rather than on the measurement and refinement of goals. The emphasis is on delivering value to the customer, not on functional excellence.

The implications of a capability-based approach to strategy formulation are obvious. An analysis of the profit-generating potential of resources and capabilities shows that preservation and regeneration of these capabilities play a vital role in strategy development. The essence of strategy formulation, from this perspective, is to design a strategy that makes the most effective use of the firm's resources and core competencies and then to concentrate on developing the firm's mechanisms for effectively delivering these capabilities to its customers.

VALUE CHAIN ANALYSIS

Value chain analysis is derived from systems theory. Every entity on the stakeholder map (see page 138 in Chapter 4) is considered to be a system. Technically, each entity is a subsystem of the complex environment depicted by the stakeholder map. Each system receives inputs, performs transformation processes on them, and sends them as outputs to other systems on the map. These three activities are carried out via the *value chain.*

Input, transformation, and output involve the acquisition and consumption of resources—money, labor, materials, equipment, buildings, land, administration, and management.

How value chain activities are carried out determines costs and affects profits. A firm that seeks a cost leadership position reduces the amount of resources it consumes and the price it pays for them. Decisions governing each activity in the value chain determine the nature and quality of the output. A firm that seeks to gain an advantage through differentiation does so by performing its value chain activities, particularly transformation of the input, differently from or better than its competitors. Improving value chain functions is one of the best means of achieving competitive advantage.

Most organizations engage in hundreds—even thousands—of activities in the process of converting inputs to outputs. These activities can be classified generally as either primary or support activities that all businesses must undertake in some form. Figure 5.4 shows the primary and support activities of the value chain.

PRIMARY ACTIVITIES

According to Porter (1985), the primary activities are

1. *Inbound logistics.* Inbound logistics involve relationships with suppliers and include all the activities required to receive, store, and disseminate inputs. Materials handling, warehousing, inventory control, and vehicle scheduling are examples of these activities.
2. *Operations.* Operations are all the activities required to transform inputs into outputs (products and services). Machining, packaging, assembling, maintaining, and testing are examples of operations.

| FIGURE 5.4 | Activities Assessed by Means of Value Chain Analysis |

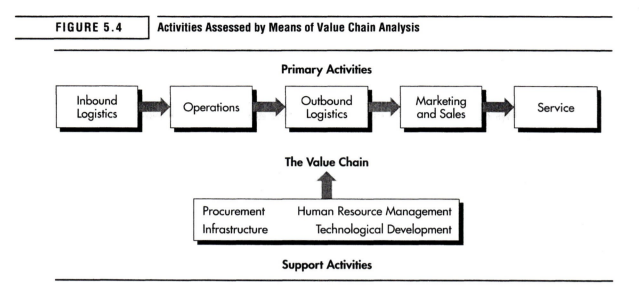

Primary Activities

The Value Chain

Support Activities

---

3. *Outbound logistics.* Outbound logistics include all the activities required to collect, store, and distribute the output. These activities focus primarily on the delivery of outputs to buyers. Warehousing, materials handling, delivery operations, shipping, order processing, and scheduling are examples of outbound logistics.

4. *Marketing and sales.* Marketing and sales activities inform buyers about products and services, induce buyers to purchase them, and facilitate their purchase. These activities focus primarily on the informational relationships established between the firm and its potential buyers. Pricing, selection of a distribution channel, channel management, advertising, promoting, selling, proposing, and quoting are examples of marketing and sales activities.

5. *Service.* Service includes all the activities required to keep the product or service working effectively for the buyer after it is sold and delivered. Training, consulting, installing, repairing, supplying parts, and fine tuning are examples of service.

Every firm performs all five primary activities to some degree and must ensure having a means for dealing with each. Which are emphasized, however, depends on the nature of the business. McDonald's and Disneyland, for example, have little need for proficiency in outbound logistics, but each must be very good at operations and at marketing and sales. Morton's Salt, on the other hand, must excel in outbound logistics in order to move its product into grocery stores efficiently. Computer and software firms increasingly must stress service in order to remain competitive.

Many of Polaroid's problems in the early 1980s derived from its operations (see the second illustrative case in Chapter 1). Polavision was an inferior product for which the company created too much production capacity and generated too large an inventory. Polaroid's marketing and sales activities were also deficient.

SUPPORT ACTIVITIES

Porter also identified four generic support activities. These are broad, systems management functions that support the primary activities and the firm as a whole. They are

1. *Procurement.* Procurement is the acquisition of inputs, or resources, for the firm. Although it is the designated function of the purchasing department, procurement is also carried out by every employee who purchases equipment, arranges for financing, gathers information, completes a real estate transaction, or acquires any but human resources for the firm.
2. *Human resource management.* Human resource management consists of all activities involved in recruiting, hiring, training, developing, compensating, and (if necessary) dismissing or laying off personnel. Human resource managers influence salary and wage levels and the overall cost of personnel. Through hiring and training programs, they promote levels of skill and motivation that affect the firm's overall performance.
3. *Technological development.* Technological development pertains to the equipment, hardware, software, procedures, and technical knowledge brought to bear in the firm's transformation of inputs into outputs. Its most important component is knowledge. Some forms of technological knowledge are scientific (chemical formulas). Other forms are more of an "art" (recipes used by restaurants). The use of computers and information systems also requires technological expertise. Technological development involves the identification, selection, adaptation, and (if necessary) creation of new technologies for use by the firm. Technology is embedded in the product itself and in the processes used to produce it. The function of technological development includes technology assessment to determine what new technologies a firm should consider adopting.
4. *Infrastructure.* Like cities, companies have infrastructures that serve their needs and tie their various parts together. In cities, the infrastructure includes roads, water lines, electrical lines, sewage systems, and government. In business organizations, the infrastructure consists of functions or departments, such as accounting, legal, finance, planning, public affairs, government relations, quality assurance, and general management. Though they are often referred to as "overhead," these functions are the glue that holds a firm together. If the infrastructure is working well, the firm can gain a substantial competitive advantage. If it is not working well, an otherwise effective firm can lose its competitive edge.

These four support activities permeate the entire organization. Therefore, strategic managers who are evaluating the support activities of a firm must look at how each activity is performed throughout the firm, *not* just by its designated unit. In fact, some of the most important support activities are not performed by the organizational unit that appears to be responsible for them. The hiring of senior executives, for example, is usually not done by the personnel department. The acquisition of major resources is usually not done by the purchasing department. Many important technological breakthroughs have come from "skunk works" where considerable freedom was accorded the managers, or other parts of the firm, not necessarily from the R&D unit. Every aspect of the firm needs to be examined to determine how support activities are conducted.

The success of many organizations depends on excellence in the execution of support activities. Consulting companies, such as the Boston Consulting Group and McKinsey and Co., sustain their competitive advantage by recruiting, training, and retaining high-quality personnel. The same is true of "big eight" accounting firms. The Corning Glass Works achieves competitive advantage through technological development. Its special processes for melting and molding glass into useful products have resulted in a long history of growth and profitability. Gallo Wineries has achieved a 15% cost advantage by growing and procuring grapes on a large scale. Federal Express has gained a competitive advantage in its industry by creating a comprehensive, computer-based infrastructure to keep track of each package from its point of origin to its final destination.

METHODOLOGY

The first step in performing a value chain analysis is to identify the key primary and support activities that the business conducts. A good way to start is to identify specific inbound-logistics activities. The manager uses the stakeholder map to determine the sources of incoming resources (inputs) and then asks, "What activities are necessary to obtain and handle these resources?" The next step is to identify activities needed to convert inputs to outputs. Then, using the stakeholder map, the manager identifies the destinations of the firm's outputs. The question here is, "What activities are necessary to move outputs from the firm to their final destinations?" The answer to this question defines outbound logistics. Marketing and sales activities and service activities are determined by focusing on each stakeholder who receives the firm's outputs. What activities are necessary to inform and persuade customers to buy the outputs, and what order-taking processes are necessary to complete sales? These constitute the marketing and sales activities. Finally, what activities are necessary to continue delivering value to the customer who has bought the product? What is required to maintain customer satisfaction? The answers define the service activities.

To identify the support activities—procurement, human resource management, technological development, and infrastructure—the manager reviews the primary activities and determines how each is helped by the support activities.

After the most important primary and support activities are identified, the manager assesses how each contributes to the company's competitive advantage. Does this activity give us a cost advantage? Does it help the firm differentiate its product from others in terms of quality or uniqueness? If the answers are yes, the manager asks, "Is this advantage sustainable over time?" Finally, the manager examines the sequence of activities in the firm's value chain for variations that decrease competitive advantage. The key question here is, "How does an error or deficiency in this activity affect an activity later?" The ability to correct or reduce key variations from competitive advantage determines whether the firm can implement a strategy successfully. Worksheet 5.1 is a value chain analysis that could have been done for Polaroid in 1988.

WORKSHEET 5.1	**Value Chain Analysis**

Case ___Polaroid/Polavision___
Date ___1988___
Name ___Dow Jones___

Primary Activities

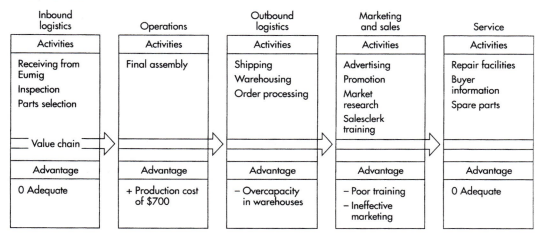

Inbound logistics	Operations	Outbound logistics	Marketing and sales	Service
Activities	**Activities**	**Activities**	**Activities**	**Activities**
Receiving from Eumig Inspection Parts selection	Final assembly	Shipping Warehousing Order processing	Advertising Promotion Market research Salesclerk training	Repair facilities Buyer information Spare parts
Value chain				
Advantage	**Advantage**	**Advantage**	**Advantage**	**Advantage**
0 Adequate	+ Production cost of $700	− Overcapacity in warehouses	− Poor training − Ineffective marketing	0 Adequate

Support Activities

Procurement	Advantage
Contract with Eumig Purchasing chemicals, parts, etc.	0 Adequate 0 Adequate

Human Resource Development	Advantage
Edwin Land Executive succession Organizational development	+ Still creative − Still confused − Morale is low

Technological Development	Advantage
General technological strength Polavision	+ Very strong, good R&D − Annoying bright light, grainy images, short time, no sound

Infrastructure	Advantage
Finance and accounting Systems Quality control General management	? No experience with debt 0 Adequate − Lacking in Polavision 0 Adequate

TIME AND QUALITY

Capability-based companies execute the value-adding chain faster and more effectively than their competitors. In general terms, a process can be defined as effective when it delivers a desired outcome at a predictable, dependable quality, at low cost, and in a fast, timely fashion. Not surprisingly, many large international Japanese competitors use the triad of quality, cost, and delivery as their main criteria for designing their internal operations. Successful Western companies have similarly embraced two main concepts that are interrelated: total quality management (TQM) and time-based management (TBM).

Quality and time are the bases of customer satisfaction. They are closely linked. Quality without responsiveness does not maximize customer satisfaction. At the same time, "doing things right the first time"—that is, having reliable procedures—is a prerequisite for being fast. In turn, productivity increases and cost comes down as time is compressed.

The Malcolm Baldrige Award, created in memory of the late U.S. Secretary of Commerce, was designed to capture these elements of competitive capability and to reward those U.S. companies that have increased their international competitiveness. The Baldrige Award has come in for a lot of criticism, but it serves the useful purpose of stimulating business to change managerial approaches. It also offers a basic framework for determining how well managers are achieving the goals of satisfied customers and employee involvement (Garvin, 1991). The Baldrige Award was named after the Malcolm Baldrige National Quality Improvement Act in 1987. The award covers three types of businesses: manufacturing, service, and small business. The criteria whereon the Baldrige Award is based, which were formulated by the National Institute of Standards and Technology, are given in Figure 5.5. These criteria are designed to cover the overall business perspective of a company, its quality capabilities, and its general business capabilities. Winners of the award have included Xerox, Motorola, Westinghouse, and the Cadillac Division of General Motors.

Sims, in an article entitled "Does the Baldrige Award Really Work?" (1992), covers the industry reaction to the award. The consensus seems to be that the criteria used in the award help identify needs but do not reveal how to achieve world excellence. Ultimately, the award can be viewed as a guide to investing in organizational transformation that produces overall, significant results.

Beyond staying at the minimum required level, capability-based competitors painstakingly develop mechanisms to keep themselves at the leading edge in terms of their core competencies. They realize that process excellence is essential to delivering these core competencies to the customer. Therefore, a growing number of companies are focusing on the two complementary concepts of total quality management (TQM) and time-based management (TBM). With these approaches, they manage substantial physical and cultural change and often achieve substantial competitive advantage.

TQM

To better understand the meaning of quality and TQM, it is useful to take a historical perspective on the progression of "quality thinking." Obviously, applying

FIGURE 5.5	Criteria for the Baldrige Award

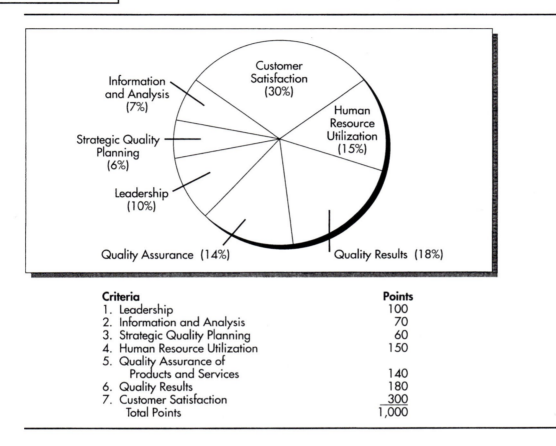

Criteria	Points
1. Leadership	100
2. Information and Analysis	70
3. Strategic Quality Planning	60
4. Human Resource Utilization	150
5. Quality Assurance of Products and Services	140
6. Quality Results	180
7. Customer Satisfaction	300
Total Points	1,000

quality as a strategic capability goes far beyond mere product quality. It permeates the entire system of creating, producing, selling, and servicing a product or service. A number of Americans have played a prominent role in the development of quality thinking, but much of the early efforts were made in Japan, and it took almost 40 years before U.S. companies started to wholeheartedly embrace these concepts. Here is a brief historical overview.

1948 In response to General MacArthur's request, Homer Sarasohn from M.I.T. and Charles Protzman from Western Electric designed a course to teach modern management techniques to the Japanese and help them become self-sufficient again, thereby reducing the need for U.S. economic aid. Over the coming years, they educated much of the elite of Japanese post-World War II industry. The result was that quality was measured using statistical process control (SPC).

1950   The Japanese Union of Scientists and Engineers (JUSE) invited W. Edwards Deming to come to Japan and introduce and teach his concepts. Deming introduced the concept of total quality control (TQC), which eliminated the need for final inspection by making quality the concern of *all* parts of the production process.

1954   Joseph M. Juran, a pioneer of statistical quality control (SQC) at Bell Telephone's Hawthorne Works, was invited by JUSE to evaluate its quality control processes. This resulted in quality control from an overall management perspective that evolved into quality improvement teams/quality circles (QCs).

1960   Philip B. Crosby, quality control vice president at ITT, began popularizing the concept of zero defects. He relied on four principles:

1. Quality is not an absolute measure but can be defined as conformance to requirements.
2. The approach to quality is prevention, not inspection.
3. The performance standard is zero defects.
4. The measurement of quality is the price of nonconformance (reworking, defects, warranty claims).

1966–1970s   Genichi Taguchi introduced his concept of design quality. Design quality is based on the notion of value to the customer. The outcome was the Taguchi method that was called quality function deployment (QFD).

Mid-1980s   Several U.S. companies (Ford, Xerox, Johnson & Johnson, Corning, Hoechst Celanese, Florida Power & Light, Westinghouse) began introducing continuous improvement programs. This is now known as total quality management (TQM).

1987   Congress established the Malcolm Baldrige award. The first winners were Globe Metallurgical, Westinghouse, and Motorola (1988) and Milliken, Xerox, and Florida Power & Light (1989).

What distinguishes TQM from earlier quality management approaches is that it provides a comprehensive framework for managing and improving all aspects of quality and that it involves all areas in a company in the process of achieving quality. This is well captured in the Total Quality Fitness Review diagram used at Westinghouse (Figure 5.6).

Total quality management (TQM) is used to improve activities in an integrated effort aimed at improving performance at every level of the organization. The company that uses TQM covers all the different phases of quality thinking, and it is constantly improving its customer responsiveness capabilities (Figure 5.7). Performance includes cross-functional goals of quality, cost, schedule, service, reliability, and customer relations. TQM integrates management efforts focused on continuous process improvement. These activities ultimately should increase customer satisfaction.

In TQM, an important element of timeliness is concurrent engineering, which integrates the design of a product with its manufacturing, operation, and support

FIGURE 5.6   Total Quality Fitness Review at Westinghouse

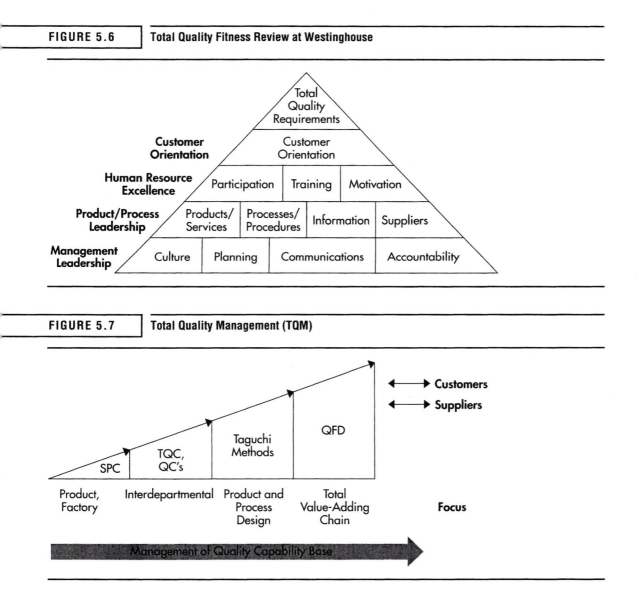

FIGURE 5.7   Total Quality Management (TQM)

processes. Concurrent engineering helps the company achieve low-cost development, production, operations, and support with the shortest schedule possible that maintains the quality of the products and services. Unlike a sequential development process, this approach requires the simultaneous development of all the processes in the entire system. Concurrent engineering teams are needed to ensure that all functional groups are integrated. To be successful, the development process must change what people do and when they do it.

TBM

Time-based management is a complementary approach to TQM. It is a powerful tool for completely revamping a company's processes and systems to achieve a capability edge over the competition.

Time-based Competitors

These companies are ones that change the rules of competition. Rather than looking at time savings purely as a source for improving productivity, they look at their entire value delivery system and ask, "What if we could provide our product in half the time our competitors take, or even less?" Successful time-based competitors have cut throughput times in half, then have halved them again, and in some cases have accomplished this feat a third time. As a result, their processes and organizations today often look radically different from those of their competitors. Consequently, they have built up a lead that it becomes increasingly difficult for their competitors to challenge.

Some of the companies that have embraced this philosophy are listed in Table 5.1. The companies on this list are from different industries. Some, such as Citicorp, are well established; others are fairly new, fast-growing companies such as Wal-Mart. What all of these companies have in common is an innovative approach to creating fast, responsive delivery processes that give them significant time advantages over their competitors. What these companies also have in common is that each is the leader, or is fast becoming the leader, in its industry.

| TABLE 5.1 | Time-based Competitors (Estimated Performance) |

Company	Business Advantage	Response Differences	Growth	Profit
Wal-Mart	Discount stores	80%	36 vs. 12%	19 vs. 9% ROCE[a]
Atlas Door	Industrial doors	66%	15 vs. 5%	10 vs. 2% ROS[b]
Ralph Wilson Plastics	Decorative laminates	75%	9 vs. 3%	40 vs. 10% RONA[c]
Thomasville	Furniture	70%	12 vs. 3%	21 vs. 11% ROA[d]
Citicorp	Mortgages	85%	100 vs. 3%	NA

[a] Return on capital employed
[b] Return on sales
[c] Return on net assets
[d] Return on assets

Source: Adapted with the permission of The Free Press, a Division of Macmillan, Inc., from *Competing Against Time: How Time-based Competition Is Reshaping Global Markets* by George Stalk, Jr. and Thomas M. Hout. Copyright © 1990 by The Free Press.

Citicorp, for example, uses the vast customer database from its credit card business to evaluate the credit risk of individuals quickly. This way it can approve mortgages in a few days—in some cases within minutes—compared to the weeks or months other lenders often need. Citicorp used to have a small market share in mortgage lending; today it is number one.

Wal-Mart replenishes the stock in its stores twice a week, on average, and for many products, it replenishes daily. Competitors such as K mart and Sears replenish their stock every two weeks. Compared to these competitors, Wal-Mart can maintain the same service levels with one-fourth the inventory investment, or offer its customers four times as much choice for the same inventory investment, or both. Wal-Mart is growing three times faster than the retail discount industry as a whole, and its return on investment has been consistently higher than average.

Ralph Wilson Plastics, a producer of decorative laminates, is another good example. The industry used to be almost completely dominated by Formica, the company whose name is often confused with the product. In the 1960s Ralph Wilson Plastics entered the business by offering ten-day delivery instead of the typical thirty-day delivery. Ralph Wilson Plastics' fast delivery appealed to the most time-sensitive market segments: the highly customized residential and the high-end commercial customers. Not fully aware of the value of fast delivery, Formica did not at first see this new competitor as a threat. Its market share was slipping, but the industry was still growing at a healthy rate. Ralph Wilson Plastics also used a unique process and machine set-up; Formica had difficulties in adopting this approach. As the growth in the industry slowed, Formica found itself much less able to sustain its price- and cost-competitiveness. Its sales and profitability fell while Ralph Wilson Plastics continued to grow, surpassing Formica as the industry leader in 1980.

How is it possible that companies with very similar backgrounds can differ vastly in delivery capability? The key differences of time-based competitors appear to be the following:

1. They view the entire system, including suppliers, distributors, and customers, rather than considering only individual functions.
2. They focus on reducing "non-value-adding" time rather than trying to make people or machines work harder or faster on value-adding activities.
3. They give the measurement of time and responsiveness the same priority as, if not higher priority than, the measurement of cost.

The idea of viewing operations as a system is not new; rather, it dates back to Jay Forrester's (1961) discussion of industrial dynamics in the 1960s. But only recently have large numbers of companies recognized the significance of this approach. A business can essentially be viewed as a series of interlinked operating cycles (Figure 5.8).

Time-based competitors put the customer first. Their view encompasses the entire time from customer order to delivery and payment. Customers are not interested in how their orders are put through the company, how many hierarchies are involved, when their orders are sequenced, and so on. They are concerned only about how fast, how new, or how unusual the product delivery is.

FIGURE 5.8 | Business—A Series of Interlinked Operating Cycles

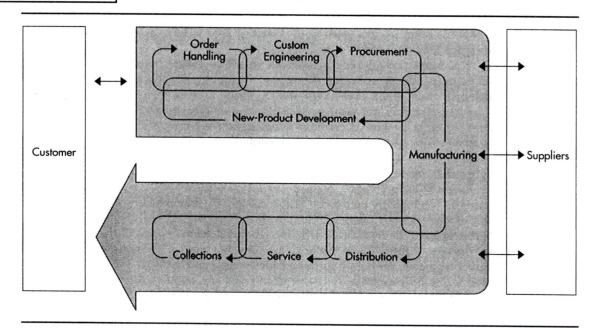

Wasted Time

Often bureaucracy grows as companies respond to changes by adding new functions or departments. As more departments are involved, additional time is consumed in hand-offs between departments and in checking and redoing work that was not completed correctly in other departments. Conversely, time is also wasted when individual functions are downsized at the expense of the overall operation. One car manufacturer, for example, reduced personnel in its order entry department to save several hundred thousand dollars. As a result, however, the quality of the code that was entered deteriorated. The entry of more errors into the system resulted in several million dollars of higher cost for rework on incorrectly ordered and manufactured parts.

The possibilities for eliminating wasted time in most traditional operating systems are great. Almost every traditional company adds value in only 5% or less of the elapsed time between order and delivery. The rest of the time, the product or service is waiting in queues to be processed or is being reworked. In most cases, the time spent in the white-collar part of the operations is significantly higher than in the blue-collar part. A car, for example, can be assembled in 20 hours. Yet, despite significant overcapacity in the industry, customers have to wait weeks or months for delivery.

Time-based competitors do not work harder, they work smarter. Instead of trying to reduce the value-adding time in the system with investments in ever more advanced machinery and information systems, they look at the tremendous amount of idle time and time spent "off the main sequence." Permanent coordination

meetings, redefinition of tasks, frequent hand-offs and sign-offs, sequential procedures, waiting time in front of capacity bottlenecks, and rework can all be sources
of significant waste and higher cost. Addressing these areas can often yield great
improvements without major investments.

Lost Time

A useful tool for displaying the lost time in the system is called *white-space analysis*
(Figure 5.9). By carefully following an order through the system, it is possible to measure the time during which this order was actually worked on (value-adding time)
and the time it had to wait in in-baskets and out-baskets, queues, or inventories or
when it had to be reworked (non-value-adding time). The company in Figure 5.9, a
maker of electronics with fairly modern production facilities, spent 89% of the time
in non-value-adding activities. Obviously, it was able to identify great potential for
time savings without having to look at the value-adding activities at all.

Rework is a particularly deceptive part of the white space, because it can
appear as a value-adding activity for an individual function, but for the system as a
whole it is unnecessary or duplicate work. Rework is clearly an expression of lack
of process quality, because things were not done right the first time. Therefore, a

FIGURE 5.9 | **White-Space Analysis**

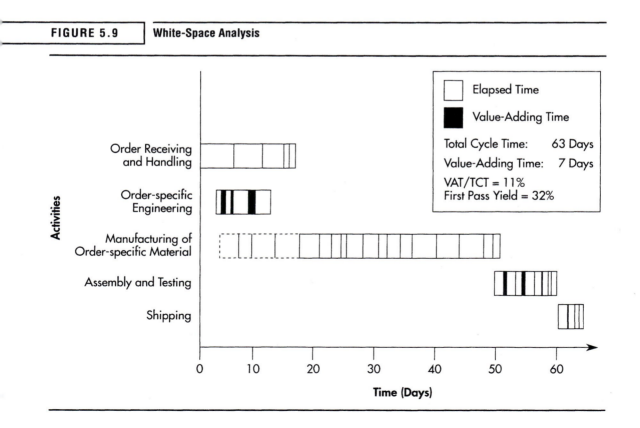

useful measure for process quality is *first pass yield,* the percentage of finished products that went through the system without requiring rework at any stage of the total process.

The first pass yield in most traditional, complex processes is extremely low. Suppose, for example, that an order has to pass through 20 stages with an average reject/rework rate of 5% at each stage. Statistically, the first pass yield is estimated at 36%. Thus 64% of the orders going through the system would require extra work in one form or another, which significantly adds to cost and time. To reach this same level of first pass yield in a process with 100 stages, the individual failure rate at every stage must not exceed 1%, on average. And in complex systems, such as car manufacturing, processes with several thousand stages are not uncommon.

A number of companies have begun to focus on this measure in their production processes, most notably in the electronics industry where extremely low failure rates are required. Some time-based competitors apply this measure of first pass yield throughout the entire company, which often reveals stunning levels of inefficiency, especially in the white-collar part of the operation.

The tracking of product teams is a key element in capability-based strategy. For example, Hewlett-Packard has over 50% of its sales from new products from the past three years, and over 50 products are in development (House and Price, 1991). Bill Hewlett said, "You can't manage what you can't measure." The measure his company uses is called a "return map," which captures both elapsed time and cumulative cost. By examining the relationship among development, manufacturing, and sales, H-P is able to track how well product teams are doing. This knowledge keeps management and the teams up to date.

Another important link in the delivery chain is the relationship with suppliers: time-based competitors establish partnerships with key suppliers and jointly reap the benefits. In this case, the white-space analysis can be extended to encompass the processes of the suppliers as well as the interfaces between buyer and supplier, including information exchange and the transport and storage of components.

Too many companies look only at the cost-savings and price-reduction potential; time-based competitors also take a careful look at the potential for realizing higher prices and then build the delivery performance needed. Fast, innovative product development often is the key to achieving such a position. Competitors with short cycle times can be first to incorporate changes in customer requirements into new products. The faster the pace of innovation, the more effectively the organization can use product variety to address specific market segments and increase overall market share. Through continuous learning from a rapid succession of product updates, the organization will out-compete slower competitors who wait for the great leap forward.

Product life cycles in many industries are getting shorter. Long development times can significantly cut into the time the company needs to earn a return on the initial R&D investment (Figure 5.10). The fast developer often spends less on the development of a product, introduces it earlier, reaches higher sales levels, achieves a faster payback, and attains higher overall profitability than its competitors. A case in point is the pharmaceutical industry, where some companies, such as Merck, consistently out-compete their rivals through fast product innovation.

FIGURE 5.10 | **Traditional vs. Time-based Product Developers**
(Dollar amounts in millions)

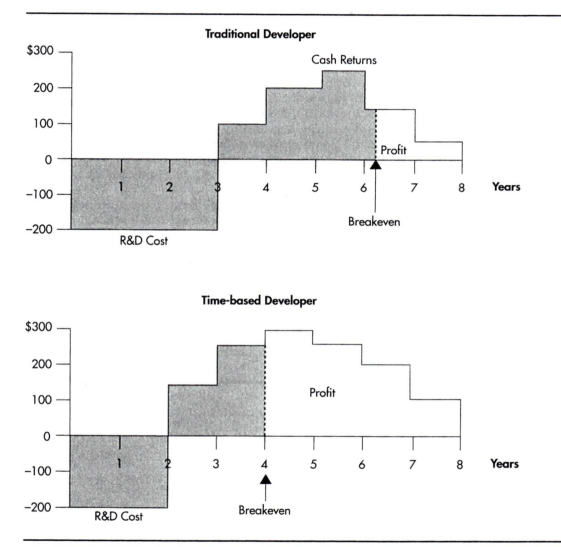

Process Mapping

The principal approach that time-based competitors use is mapping and measuring processes and then finding ways to simplify these processes. This can be done in repeated rounds of cycle-time reductions or, in other cases, through a completely different, innovative view of the business. Over a period of 15–20 years, Toyota went through repeated rounds of different approaches (Kanban, just-in-time,

quality circles) to give it a commanding productivity lead over Western car manufacturers. An example of applying a new perspective is Federal Express, whose
founder conceived a process for delivering mail that is markedly different from that
of the U.S. Postal Service.

While conceptually simple, *process mapping* is often not easy in practice. To
do it right, managers, employees, suppliers, and customers must work on the map
together to make sure that what the company thinks happens really does happen.
Typically, the actual maps of a process are substantially different from the designed
behavior, which often does not sufficiently consider informal channels, feedback
effects, exceptions, errors, rework, and other quality problems.

The main objective of mapping is to identify physical flows, stocks, and activities as well as information flows, decision points, and communication patterns.
Those doing the mapping therefore begin by asking those involved what happens
and the reasons behind what happens. In most cases, it is also helpful to track specific orders through the organization.

The display of this information can take on different forms, such as logistical
flow maps, decision point maps, and maps of locational and functional information interfaces and hand-offs. Figure 5.11 shows examples of these different types
of maps. After the process has been mapped and appropriate measures have been
applied, those involved can start considering how to improve the processes. Several
approaches to simplifying processes are available:

- Decentralize the organization so that it has fewer layers.
- Use process, not functional, organization form.
- Use parallel processing wherever possible.
- Use investments in areas that eliminate bottlenecks.

| FIGURE 5.11 | Three Examples of Process Maps |

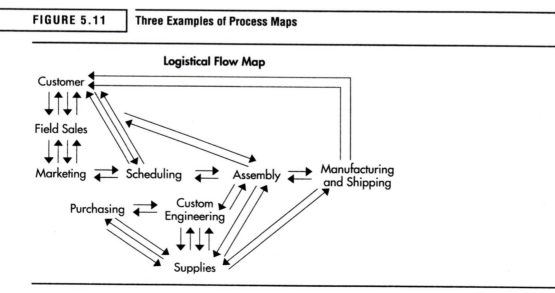

Logistical Flow Map

(continued)

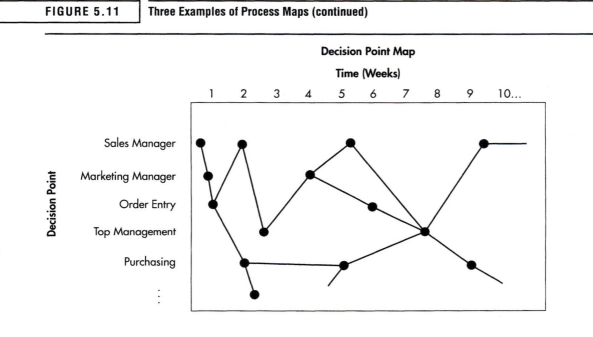

Decision Point Map

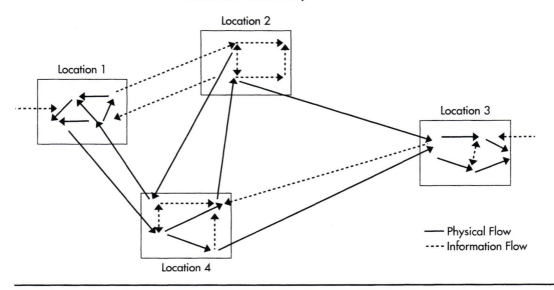

Locational Interface Map

Source: Courtesy of The Boston Consulting Group, Inc. Reprinted with permission.

- Produce smaller batch sizes.
- Synchronize procedures to balance work loads.
- Eliminate causes of rework at the source by not permitting incomplete work to be passed on.
- Apply flexible role definitions with a higher degree of integration.
- Implement standardization of the forms used and of work flows.

It is at this transition, from mapping and understanding the problems to making substantial physical and management changes, where good intentions often break down. Because of the sometimes radical changes needed to make the firm a more flexible, responsive organization, resistance builds up at several levels within the organization. Many companies are not able to go beyond the technocratic level of process redesign because of strong cultural barriers, such as resistance to change. Later in the book, we will discuss how to introduce the change process. Only those companies that are effective at bringing about change in the organizational culture and that exhibit strong leadership are able to achieve the flexibility needed for capability-based strategy.

VALUE LEVERAGING

Another approach that can be used to augment a capability-based strategy is to focus more directly on the customer. The leveraging of customer value, or *value leveraging,* begins with research designed to develop a thorough understanding of the customer's needs and problems. Various research tools are employed to gather information about customers: surveys, visit reports, analyses of competitive bids, panels, test marketing, and others. With the information it has gathered, the organization determines how it can serve customers better. Though this works well to satisfy customers' present needs, it seldom turns out to satisfy their future needs, perhaps because the information being analyzed is relevant only to the status quo. When it comes to innovations needed for the future, traditional suppliers to an industry often lag behind the market trends. Researchers at M.I.T. found, for example, that in the field of high technology it was the users (customers), not the manufacturers (suppliers), who developed the most new products (Hippel, 1988). These findings are shown in Table 5.2.

The key to value leveraging is for the organization to put itself "in the customer's shoes." This requires more than research and analysis of data; it requires imagination and vision. Coming up with innovations that will make the product more useful to the customer in the future is one means of value leveraging. Another is to increase the product's present value to the customer. This is accomplished by finding out how the customer thinks value can be increased or cost structure can be improved. The supplier may be concentrating on improving a product or service, whereas the customer may merely need help in using the product or service more efficiently. Thus rather than asking, "How can we make this product better?" the supplier should be asking, *"Can we increase the value of our product within the customer's system, and how?"* Answers to the second question often result in entirely different product/marketing approaches.

TABLE 5.2	Sources of Innovative Products First Tested in Practice

New Product	User (%)	Manufacturer (%)
Measuring instruments		
First instrument of its kind	100	0
Major functional improvements	82	18
Minor functional improvements	70	30
Processing equipment		
First equipment of its kind	100	0
Major functional improvements	63	21
Minor functional improvements	20	29

Source: Eric V. Hippel, *The Sources of Innovation* (New York: Oxford University Press, 1988), p. 15.

Federal Express is a company based on value leveraging and competitive cost advantage through system innovation. The idea of overnight mail shipment certainly must have occurred to many mail distribution firms, but they concluded that overnight delivery was not feasible or cost-effective, given the delivery systems then in use. To accomplish overnight delivery via the U.S. Postal Service, for example, with its thousands of distribution and sorting points and its many different modes of transportation, would have required a monumental effort. It would also have required substantial investment in faster modes of transportation at a time when transportation was already the major cost.

Fred Smith, the founder of Federal Express, developed his vision from an entirely different set of assumptions. He realized that the major cost of overnight delivery would be sorting and handling, not transportation. To reduce the costs of handling, he decided to try a new system. Instead of establishing many small distribution points, which would be difficult to coordinate, he decided to have all incoming mail sorted at one central hub, in Memphis. His idea works. Every evening, at around midnight, some 65 Federal Express planes converge in Memphis to disgorge about 600,000 envelopes and packages. The mail is quickly sorted on 45 miles of conveyor belts and loaded back into the planes by 4 A.M. When the planes arrive at their destinations, the mail is loaded into small delivery vans and rushed to recipients before noon.

Another innovative approach to value leveraging is exemplified by the Swedish furniture company IKEA. IKEA's vision has revolutionized the furniture industry in Europe, and the company has set out to do the same in the United States. IKEA noticed that a significant segment of the market was made up of young buyers who wanted inexpensive, modern-design furniture. To attract these buyers, traditional manufacturers had cut costs by reducing the amount of material used to make the furniture. This measure reduced appearance and quality as well. IKEA looked at ways to cut costs without sacrificing quality. It examined the entire value-adding chain, from production to final installation in the customer's home, and realized that the greatest savings could be gained by reducing assembly and delivery costs. Therefore, IKEA designed pieces that customers could transport in their own vehicles and easily assemble at home.

The common theme in these two examples of vision is that the companies involved looked for completely different ways to provide a service or a product rather than simply improving on existing approaches. Neither Federal Express nor IKEA is the low-price supplier in its market; that is, neither had to gain market share by offering lower prices. Rather, they leveraged customer value and were able to charge customers more.

Figure 5.12 shows how value leveraging and system innovation enabled Federal Express and IKEA to increase profits by raising prices and lowering costs.

SYSTEM INNOVATION

System innovation is vital in gaining a sustainable competitive cost advantage. Like IKEA, Toyota restructured its assembly and delivery system to create new value. Toyota's production system changed the rules of the game from cost-based

---

FIGURE 5.12 | **Effects of Value Leveraging and System Innovation on Costs, Price, and Profit Margin at Federal Express and IKEA**

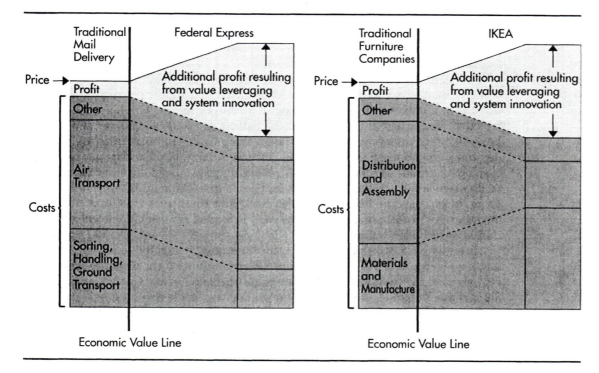

competition alone to cost-based competition plus time-based competition plus variety-based competition (Abegglen and Stalk, 1985). As shown in Table 5.3, this system allowed the Japanese manufacturers to produce cars at a faster rate and thus more cheaply than American manufacturers. Moreover, the Japanese learned to manufacture a more diverse line of products at virtually no cost penalty. The ability of the Japanese system—called the just-in-time (JIT) system—to respond rapidly to customers' demands for more variety is one of the major reasons that the system is now widely used.

Another system innovation that enabled the Japanese car manufacturers to gain a strong competitive advantage was their dedication to product quality. Initially, high quality was a requirement, because the distance between Japan and the United States meant that adequate service support could not be provided at acceptable costs. The Japanese were able to perfect a system that achieves higher quality and at the same time greater variety.

> Variety, at least in America, is often an enemy of quality. Reducing the number of design changes allows workers to devote more attention to each. . . . The Japanese, however, have achieved low failure rates even with relatively broad product lines and rapidly changing designs. . . . New designs account for nearly a third of all models offered each year, far more than in the U.S. (D. A. Garvin, 1983)

Poor product quality results in high after-sales costs. As a result of quality differences, U.S. manufacturers typically have significantly higher warranty costs than their Japanese counterparts. Garvin estimated the warranty costs of U.S. manufacturers to be about four times as high as those of the Japanese. Fortunately, though belatedly, many U.S. companies, such as Ford, have realized that "Quality is Job 1."

System innovation may depend somewhat on luck, but some organizations are consistently more successful at it than others. What are they doing right? These organizations have come to realize the hidden benefits of continuously demanding innovation from the system. One benefit of continuous innovation is that by the

| TABLE 5.3 | Impact of the Just-in-Time (JIT) Automobile Production System |

Factors Compared	U.S. Manufacturer	Japanese Manufacturer	Difference (%)
Cars	860	1,000	+16.3
Employment	2,150	1,000	−53.5
Employees per car	2.5	1.0	−60.0
Direct labor	1.25	.79	−36.8
Other labor, including salaried employees	1.25	.21	−83.2

Source: James C. Abegglen and George Stalk, Jr., 1985.

time the competition is able to understand and imitate it, the organization may already have moved on to something new. Another advantage is that people in the organization grow accustomed to change, which makes the firm more competitive.

The key to developing system innovation seems to be (1) sufficient vision to overcome functional specialization and look at the delivery system as a whole and (2) sufficient vision to consider quantum leaps, not just incremental improvements. To achieve significant results, strategic planners should consider the following three questions:

1. What kinds of changes in our delivery system would be valuable to our customers?
2. What would it mean to our customers if delivery cycle times could be cut in half, or if other performance criteria could be doubled?
3. What would a delivery system look like that could achieve these fundamental improvements?

If the organization is capable of making a quantum leap, the benefits of developing a new system of operation can be far-reaching. The more innovative the new vision, the greater its potential benefits to the organization.

Emerson Electric has consistently been profitable for the past 30 years (Knight, 1992). What accounts for this kind of performance, regardless of competition or business conditions? The answer is that Emerson focused on a strategy of being the best-cost producer (not the lowest-cost). Its success is attributable to the following six factors:

1. Commitment to total quality and satisfied customers.
2. Knowing the competition.
3. Competing on both process improvements and product design.
4. Involvement of employees and effective communications.
5. Continuous focus on cost reduction.
6. Supporting the strategy with the required capital expenditures.

Emerson implements these six factors by using careful planning and meaningful controls backed up with a value measurement chart that is used to assess value creation. Because operating managers are responsible for carrying out the planning, they have "ownership" of the decisions required to achieve performance.

ASSESSING COMPANY CAPABILITY

A key element in assessing its capability is knowing a company's strengths and weaknesses. Creating a capability profile can pinpoint strengths and weaknesses, and performing a WOTS-UP analysis can identify threats and opportunities as well.

THE CAPABILITY PROFILE

The *capability profile* is a means of assessing a company's managerial, competitive (or marketing), financial, and technical strengths and weaknesses. Worksheet 5.2 is a capability profile showing Polaroid's strengths and weaknesses in 1988. The

WORKSHEET 5.2 | **Company Capability Profile**

Case __Polaroid__
Date __1988__
Name __Mary Doe__

Managerial Factors	0%	Weak	Neutral (50%)	Strong	100%
1. Corporate Image, Social Responsibility					
2. Use of Strategic Plans and Strategic Analysis					
3. Environmental Assessment and Forecasting					
4. Speed of Response to Changing Conditions					
5. Flexibility of Organizational Structure					
6. Management Communication and Control					
7. Entrepreneurial Orientation					
8. Ability to Attract and Retain Highly Creative People					
9. Ability to Meet Changing Technology					
10. Ability to Handle Inflation					
11. Aggressiveness in Meeting Competition					
12. Other					

Competitive Factors	0%		50%		100%
1. Product Strength, Quality, Uniqueness					
2. Customer Loyalty and Satisfaction					
3. Market Share					
4. Low Selling and Distribution Costs					
5. Use of Experience Curve for Pricing					
6. Use of Life Cycle of Products and Replacement Cycle					
7. Investment in New-Product Development by R&D					
8. High Barriers to Entry into the Company's Markets					
9. Advantage Taken of Market Growth Potential					
10. Supplier Strength and Material Availability					
11. Customer Concentration					
12. Other					

| WORKSHEET 5.2 | Company Capability Profile (continued) |

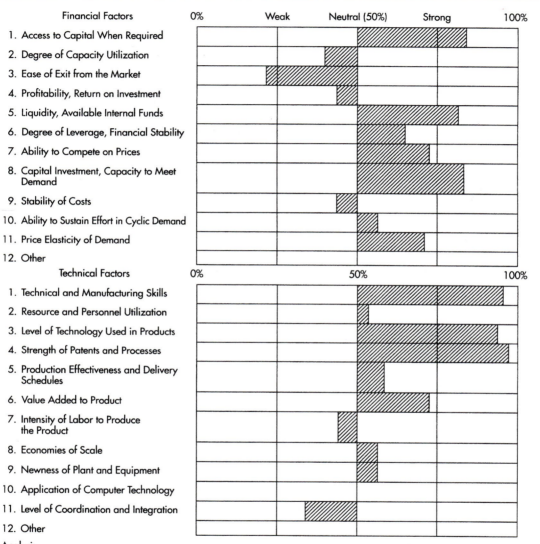

Financial Factors	0%	Weak	Neutral (50%)	Strong	100%
1. Access to Capital When Required					
2. Degree of Capacity Utilization					
3. Ease of Exit from the Market					
4. Profitability, Return on Investment					
5. Liquidity, Available Internal Funds					
6. Degree of Leverage, Financial Stability					
7. Ability to Compete on Prices					
8. Capital Investment, Capacity to Meet Demand					
9. Stability of Costs					
10. Ability to Sustain Effort in Cyclic Demand					
11. Price Elasticity of Demand					
12. Other					

Technical Factors	0%		50%		100%
1. Technical and Manufacturing Skills					
2. Resource and Personnel Utilization					
3. Level of Technology Used in Products					
4. Strength of Patents and Processes					
5. Production Effectiveness and Delivery Schedules					
6. Value Added to Product					
7. Intensity of Labor to Produce the Product					
8. Economies of Scale					
9. Newness of Plant and Equipment					
10. Application of Computer Technology					
11. Level of Coordination and Integration					
12. Other					

Analysis

Polaroid is quite strong in its competitive and technical capabilities. The company now has sufficient financial means to overcome its previous problems with Polavision. Management could be stronger in areas of forecasting, communication, and control. Expansion of market for the Spectra camera and video printouts should be undertaken.

graphic profile was created by drawing a bar opposite each factor that originated at the "neutral" center and extended into the "weak" or "strong" side of the graph.

The length of the bar drawn on the worksheet indicates the degree of strength or weakness for each factor. A blank line indicates that data are not available or are not applicable for the company being analyzed.

One can think of the bars as representing percentiles. "Neutral" signifies the 50th percentile. Therefore, strength can range from 50 to 100% and weakness from 0 to 50%.

A completed capability profile reveals "gaps" that need to be corrected and opportunities that should be pursued. It also helps managers to assess the relative position of the firm and decide whether aggressiveness or retrenchment is the proper strategic thrust.

WOTS-UP ANALYSIS

WOTS is an acronym for weaknesses, opportunities, threats, and strengths. (UP is simply added to make the term easy to remember.) As a companion methodology to environmental analyses and the capability profile, WOTS-UP analysis helps strategic managers to determine whether the organization is able to deal effectively with its environment. The more competent an organization is compared to its competitors, the more likely it is to gain market share and improve its profitability.

The issue of competency is central to three tasks of the strategic manager:

1. Identify the organization's distinctive competency. A distinctive competency is what the organization does particularly well. It includes the organization's unique resources and capabilities as well as its strengths and the ability to overcome weaknesses.
2. Find a niche in the organization's environment. A niche is a strategic and market segment to which the organization is well suited. Finding the correct niche enables the organization to take advantage of the opportunities that present themselves and avert threats from the environment and competitors.
3. Find the best match between the organization's distinctive competency and the available niches.

A WOTS-UP analysis helps find the best match between environmental trends (opportunities and threats) and internal capabilities. An *opportunity* is any favorable situation in the organization's environment. It is usually a trend or change of some kind or an overlooked need that increases demand for a product or service and permits the firm to enhance its position by supplying it. A *threat* is any unfavorable situation in the organization's environment that is potentially damaging to its strategy. The threat may be a barrier, a constraint, or anything external that might cause problems, damage, or injury. A *strength* is a resource or capacity the organization can use effectively to achieve its objectives. A *weakness* is a limitation, fault, or defect in the organization that will keep it from achieving its objectives. In general, an effective strategy is one that takes advantage of the organization's opportunities by employing its strengths and wards off threats by avoiding them or by correcting or compensating for weaknesses. The information in Figure 5.13 can be used to develop appropriate strategies.

A WOTS-UP analysis for Polaroid is shown in Worksheet 5.3. The first part of any WOTS-UP analysis is to collect a set of key facts about the organization and its environment. This database will include facts about the organization's markets, competition, financial resources, facilities, employees, inventories, marketing and distribution system, R&D, management, environmental setting (e.g., technological, political, social, and economic trends), history, and reputation.

The second part of a WOTS-UP analysis is to evaluate data to determine whether they constitute an opportunity, threat, strength, or weakness for the organization. Worksheet 5.3 shows how these evaluations are recorded.

WOTS-UP also can be used to analyze case studies in this text as follows:

1. Read the case rapidly for an overview.
2. Reread the case carefully, underlining key facts.
3. Evaluate each fact with respect to its potential as an opportunity, threat, strength, or weakness.

FIGURE 5.13 | **WOTS-UP Matrix**

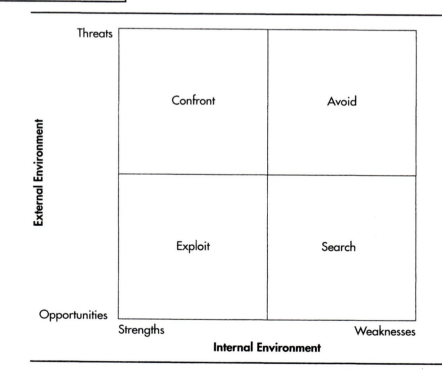

WORKSHEET 5.3	WOTS-UP Analysis

Case ___Polaroid___

Date ___1988___

Name ___John Doe___

Opportunities

Maintain market leadership	✓
New innovations; upgraded film	✓
Vertical integration	
Economy bouncing back	✓
Improved financial position	
New markets for the Spectra camera	
Diversification into new products including	
video printouts	

Threats

Technological problems continue	
Market saturation	
Strong competition from Kodak and	
35mm cameras	✓
Internal resistance to change	

Strengths

Market leadership in instant cameras	✓
Strong R&D and marketing departments	✓
Customers prefer Polaroid	✓
High-quality products	✓
High degree of self-sufficiency	
Paid off $130M in debt	

Weaknesses

Management changes	✓
Too much capacity	✓
Strategic management, forecasting	✓
Price of film	
Concentration on a few products	

(Check if critical.)

When a WOTS-UP analysis is prepared, it is helpful to have each individual involved perform the analysis separately. Then the results can be compared and discussed in the group.

It is important to note that any given fact may give rise to more than one evaluation. For example, the increasing numbers of women who are employed outside the home may pose both an opportunity and a threat for a direct-sales cosmetics company such as Avon Products. It is an opportunity because it means that women have less time to shop and may therefore prefer a direct-sales cosmetics service. It is a threat because it implies that these women may be harder to reach at home. An effective strategy will take into account both possibilities.

It is also important to recognize that opportunities can contain hidden threats and hidden opportunities. Therefore, it is helpful to ask, "How might this threat also be an opportunity?" and "Does this opportunity contain threats as well?" It is also useful to ask, "How might this strength turn out to be a weakness?" and "How does this weakness really represent a strength?" The answers to these questions may give managers new insights into choosing appropriate strategies.

VULNERABILITY ANALYSIS

Another means of assessing threats to a company is the use of a vulnerability analysis. Executives tend to emphasize the strengths and opportunities on which their company's strategy is based and to downplay or even neglect threats and weaknesses. Vulnerability analysis can assist in strategy formulation by having the manager play the devil's advocate—one who criticizes the strategy or plan. Vulnerability analysis begins with the following simple question: What supportive elements, if suddenly taken away, might seriously damage or even destroy the business?

These elements are the *underpinnings* upon which the organization depends for its continued existence. Hurd (1977) identified the following twelve categories of underpinnings:

1. Customer needs and wants served by the product or service
2. Resources and assets: people, capital, facilities, raw materials, technological know-how
3. Cost position relative to competition, by major cost components
4. Consumer base: its size, demographics, trends
5. Technologies required
6. Special skills, systems, procedures, organization
7. Corporate identity: logo, image, products, corporate culture, role models
8. Institutional barriers to competition: regulations, codes, patent laws, licensing
9. Social values, lifestyles, common norms, ideals
10. Sanctions, supports, and incentives to do business, particularly in such fields as medicine, nuclear materials, restaurants, securities, import–export
11. Customer goodwill: product safety, product quality, company reputation
12. Complementary products or services in the stakeholder system

Vulnerability analysis involves seven key steps:

1. Identify underpinnings.
2. State how removal of an underpinning would threaten the business.
3. State the most conservative consequences of each threat.
4. Rank the impact of worst consequences of each threat.
5. Estimate the probability that each threat will materialize.
6. Rank the company's ability to deal with each threat, should it materialize.
7. Determine whether the company's vulnerability to each threat is extreme or negligible.

Worksheet 5.4 shows a complete vulnerability assessment that was done for the IBM Corporation in 1991, a time when IBM needed to assess the impact that failure of its strategy might have on the company.

The first step, the identification of underpinnings, is carried out by a group of top managers. It is helpful if participants have diverse backgrounds and interests.

After the basic underpinnings have been brought to the surface in a brainstorming session, each member of the group phrases them in terms of threats to the business.

The third step is to establish the most conservative assessment of the consequences, or *down-side risk,* should a potential threat materialize.

Fourth, by imagining a worst-case scenario, managers get a feel for the potential impact of each threat, should it materialize. They can now rank impact on a scale of 0 to 10, where zero denotes no impact on the organization at all, and 10 means catastrophic consequences.

The fifth step in vulnerability analysis is to estimate the probability that a particular threat will materialize. Very serious threats often have a remote probability of occurring, which forces managers to clarify their willingness to assume certain business risks. At the least, a probability assessment forces managers to decide whether they need more information before they can make a decision. Assessing probabilities is difficult, particularly in situations having a high degree of uncertainty. Strategic planners should be aware that top managers tend to be optimistic in their assessments.

The sixth step is to formulate possible reactions, or plans for dealing with threats that materialize. Even if the probability estimate elicits a wait-and-see attitude, this step will result in some degree of preparedness. The firm's ability to react or retaliate can be ranked on a scale of 0 to 10, where zero means defenselessness and 10 means that the company can easily absorb the blow.

The seventh and final step of vulnerability analysis is to place the company's overall vulnerability to each threat in the context of a *vulnerability assessment graph* (Figure 5.14), a four-quadrant matrix whose axes consist of rankings of the threat's impact and of the company's ability to react. In the case for IBM, the dot indicates placement of underpinning 4 (customer base), which had an impact rating of 8 and a reaction rating of 8 (see Worksheet 5.4).

Against threats that fall into quadrant D of the chart, a company is almost defenseless. Any entry in this quadrant demands immediate attention by top managers. If possible, they should remove such threats by abandoning a particular plan, strategy, or business unit. In cases where this is not possible, managers must

| WORKSHEET 5.4 | Vulnerability Analysis |

Case ___IBM___

Date ___1991___

Name ___Doe___

Assumptions	Beliefs	Consequence	Impact 0–10	Probability 0–1	Capability 0–10	Vulnerability Assessment
1. Needs and wants served by product	Information processing	Compete with clones and others	9	.9	7	E
2. Resources and assets	Large and available	Current losses	9	.9	6	E
3. Cost position relative to competition	Recognized leader	Loss of position	6	.5	5	V
4. Customer base	World-wide	Difficult sales	8	.6	8	E
5. Technologies	Superior leader	Fallen behind	9	.6	9	E
6. Special skills	Sales and service	Cannot hold sales	8	.5	8	E
7. Corporate identity	Best managed company	Layoffs, restructure	5	.8	6	P
8. Institutional barriers to competition	Corporate accounts	Changing base	7	.6	8	E
9. Social values	Lifetime job, and care	Overhead expense	5	.3	8	P
10. Sanctions, supports, and incentives	Large sales of main frame	Declining market	8	.8	6	E
11. Customer goodwill	Proud of service	Changing expectations	5	.5	5	V
12. Complementary products or services	Software, mini-computers	Failed in software, AS 400	7	.8	6	E
13. Other						

FIGURE 5.14	Vulnerability Assessment Graph for IBM Corporation in 1991

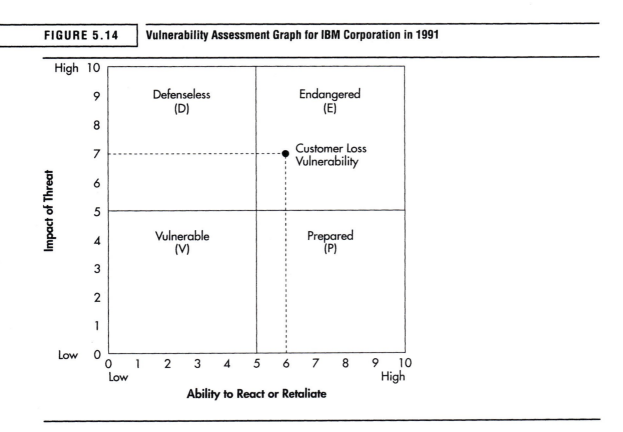

take immediate steps to upgrade the company's ability to react, thus moving the threat into quadrant E.

Threats in the second quadrant are still dangerous, but the company at least has sufficient capabilities to react or retaliate. For threats in this quadrant, managers should develop explicit contingency plans, particularly for those threats that are very likely to materialize.

Threats in quadrant P the company is prepared to deal with; therefore, very little monitoring of these possibilities is necessary.

The threats in quadrant V are light to moderate, and the company has very little to do if they materialize. Although explicit contingency plans do not need to be prepared, managers should at least try to monitor these threats for changes that indicate their escalation.

Figure 5.14 also shows how the vulnerability assessment graph can be used to evaluate a single threat, in this case the loss of underpinning 4, customer base (see Worksheet 5.4). Here, the loss of customer base falls into quadrant E, meaning that the company will be endangered by the loss of this underpinning. This graph can also be used to evaluate the overall vulnerability of the company. If IBM's impact and ability-to-react rankings were plotted for each underpinning listed in

Worksheet 5.4, eight of the underpinnings would fall in quadrant E, two in quadrant P, and two in quadrant V.

Vulnerability analyses, then, help managers to identify

- Underpinnings upon which the firm depends for its continued existence
- Forces that can destroy these basic underpinnings
- Factors that pose a threat and the strength of their potential impact
- The seriousness of the company's vulnerability to each threat
- The company's overall ability to compete effectively in its chosen industry

MEASURING ORGANIZATION PERFORMANCE

Whereas TQM and TBM assess *internal* or process performance, this section considers *overall* effectiveness and how it can be measured. Looking at a company's performance measurement system and seeing what is and what is not measured can be quite revealing. For example, it is interesting to observe that most U.S. companies have very intricate financial measurement systems in place, but only a few measure their processes in terms of timeliness or responsiveness. On the other hand, some selectivity in what is measured is essential. This section focuses on ways to measure the overall effectiveness of the organization. These measurements help the company's managers monitor the development of its key capabilities and core competencies.

STRATEGIC EFFECTIVENESS

Strategic effectiveness consists of overall organizational effectiveness rather than just unit, product, or operational effectiveness. Therefore, assessment of strategic effectiveness involves evaluating the organization's ability to meet all its goals, subject to environmental uncertainty and internal politics and constraints. Strategic effectiveness also measures the organization's sustainable competitive advantage.

The following general statements emerge from definitions of strategic effectiveness.

- It is multidimensional.
- It involves the systems the organization uses to get things done.
- It includes organizational change and adaptation.
- It includes efficiency and individual performance.
- It requires strategic management.

Strategic effectiveness, then, is concerned with the manner in which strategies are chosen and implemented. To ensure strategic effectiveness, a strategic manager must be able to

- Establish priorities and develop goals and objectives.
- Utilize resources and eliminate nonproductive time.
- Solve problems and determine risk.
- Make decisions based on valid data and assumptions.
- Communicate, listen to feelings, and build trust.
- Resolve conflicts and differences in values.

- Involve individuals in the organization and obtain commitment.
- Achieve results and develop bases for accomplishment.
- Develop workable plans within policy guidelines.
- Maximize the organization's potential to achieve the strategic plan.

INDICATORS OF PERFORMANCE

Because strategy is a comprehensive perspective on what an organization must do in order to achieve its goals, measures of performance must be broader than simply profit or growth. Consistent with this view of the need for a broad basis for measuring performance are (1) efficiency, (2) effectiveness, (3) equity, and (4) responsiveness. These four key indicators are useful measures of performance, because they are often central to statements of goals and objectives. The indicators are measured as follows:

1. *Efficiency is the ratio of outputs produced to resource inputs consumed.* Inputs are frequently measured in dollars or in labor hours. Measures of efficiency include:
   - Return on investment = profit/investment
   - Sales productivity = sales/total labor cost
   - Sales profitability = profit/sales
2. *Effectiveness is the degree to which a goal has been achieved.* Effectiveness is not always directly related to the resources consumed. Measures of effectiveness include the degree to which the following have been achieved:
   - Market share
   - Sales growth
   - Stakeholder expectations
3. *Equity is the fairness, impartiality, or equality with which an organization's stakeholders are treated.* Measures of equity are shown in Table 5.4. Equity might be achieved as appropriate through
   - Equal monetary payments to stakeholders
   - Equal disbursement of goods and services to stakeholders
   - Equal allocation of resources to stakeholders

TABLE 5.4	Measures of Equity

Stakeholder	Measure
Stockholders	Dividends
	Earnings per share
Customers	Price
	Quality
	Reliability
	Geographic areas served
	Income classes served
Community	Contributions
	Taxes paid
	Scholarships
	Employment

Equity is directly related to social responsibility because of concern for stakeholders, who include customers, competitors, and so on. With increasing concern about an organization's social responsibility, equity becomes an increasingly important measure of performance.

4. *Responsiveness is the extent to which the organization satisfies demands placed on it.* Responsiveness does not depend on the source of the demands or even on the cost of satisfying them. Measures of responsiveness include

- Average service time per customer
- Number of complaints satisfied
- Ability to react to organizational pressures
- Capacity to satisfy quality and operational requirements

Many successful strategies are based on responsiveness. American Hospital Supply Corporation, for example, established a 24-hour delivery time (see Chapter 1). Marriott Hotels seek to satisfy quickly every customer who lodges a complaint.

Other indicators of performance are tied directly to a firm's objectives (Drucker, 1973). Drucker suggested eight key areas in which objectives must be set and measures of performance reported: marketing, innovation, human organization, financial resources, physical resources, productivity, social responsibilities, and profit. Many organizations use these eight areas as a basis for measuring key results and for analysis of their performance. An alternate approach used by Ohmae was discussed in Chapter 1.

An approach called the balanced scorecard (Kaplan and Norton, 1992) has been proposed as a basis for tracking performance in an effort to achieve continuous improvement in operations. The scorecard includes

1. *Financial*: measures cash flow, income growth, return on equity, etc.
2. *Internal business*: measures technical capability, time-cost, yield, design productivity, meeting schedules, etc.
3. *Customer*: Measures sales of products, on-time delivery, suppliers' performance, cooperative partnerships, etc.
4. *Innovation and learning*: measures technology leadership, learning time, time to introduce new products, etc.

Other measures reported for internal operations include

1. Survey in which customers, employees, and suppliers rated company performance

2. Break-even time for new-product development

3. Reduction in process time from receipt of an order to delivery of a product

A key element of responsiveness to customer needs is flexibility of the organization. Comparing Japan and the United States makes it obvious why customers react more favorably to Japanese products. Table 5.5 shows these differences on two bases for flexibility: speed of innovation and meeting customer needs.

TABLE 5.5	Comparison of Flexibility Between the United States and Japan, Showing the Percent of Customers Whose Needs Have Been Met

1. Speed of Innovation	Japan	United States
Product features	82%	40%
High R&D content	80%	50%
Low price	78%	51%
Rapid change	81%	60%
Speed of product mix	78%	60%
Many new products	70%	52%
Advanced manufacturing	83%	66%

2. Meeting Customer Needs	Japan	United States
Handling orders	52%	77%
Supplier relations	72%	85%
Reliability of delivery	87%	98%
Distribution channels	36%	45%
Fast delivery	80%	88%
Durability	61%	68%
Flexible employees	75%	82%

Source: Thorton and Erdman, 1992.

CRITICAL SUCCESS FACTORS

John Rockart (1979) developed a three-step method for determining which factors contribute to meeting organizational goals. He had found that many executives tend to think in terms of what it takes to be successful rather than in terms of grand strategy, goals, and objectives. Therefore, Rockart developed a method that would help executives to derive a strategy, goals, and objectives from answers to the question "What does it take to be successful in this business?" Rockart termed the answers *critical success factors*. Once the critical success factors for the business are identified, executives can use them to develop strategies. The method can be applied by strategic planners within the company or by an outside management consultant or other advisor. The three steps in Rockart's method follow.

1. Generate success factors. In applying this approach in an organization, the strategic planner (advisor) meets with the organization's CEO and asks, *"What does it take to be successful in this business?"* The answers are recorded, as they are given, in a stream-of-consciousness fashion. A free flow of ideas is encouraged. The result is a preliminary list of critical success factors (CSFs).

2. Refine CSFs into goals and objectives. The advisor reviews the CSFs and evaluates and restates them in clearer and more precise language. Then the advisor asks, for each CSF, *"What should the organization's goals and objectives be with respect to this critical success factor?"* Once the list of CSFs is refined, the goals and objectives are stated for each one, the advisor meets again with the CEO. During this session, each CSF is discussed and restated. Unimportant factors are eliminated. If possible, the list is pared down to the seven to ten most critical factors.

3. Identify measures of performance. At this stage, the advisor reviews the organization's information system and other available sources of data to determine how to measure each CSF. The key question in this step is *"How will we know whether the organization has been successful with respect to this factor?"* The advisor constructs an indicator or measure that makes use of available data sources. In a third session with the CEO, the proposed measure of performance for each CSF is discussed and refined. If "hard" data are available, this process may be short and straightforward. If "soft" data must be used, however, the effort may be more time-consuming and will generally result in the identification of some indices, benchmarks, or milestones that can be used as indicators of how well the organization is doing in achieving its CSFs.

Rockart and his associates have applied the CSF method at several different organizations. Figure 5.15 is an example obtained from Microwave Associates.

Rockart's method can be used to identify and refine the CSFs named by top managers, not just by the CEO. Then the group discusses each CSF in turn and decides on its treatment. Sometimes subcommittees are appointed to consider a CSF and its performance measures in more depth. Finally, the top seven to ten CSFs are chosen.

FIGURE 5.15 | **Critical Success Factors and Their Measures of Performance**

Critical Success Factors	Measures
Financial image	Price/earnings ratio
Technological reputation	Quality/reliability
Market share	Change in market (each product) Growth
Risk	Years of experience Customer relationships
Profit	Profit margin
Company morale	Turnover, absenteeism
Performance	Budgeted/actual

Source: John F. Rockart, 1979, p. 89.

SUMMARY

Once a company has established a general direction, it can determine whether it has the capabilities to proceed. To do this, managers need to evaluate the company with respect to key determinants of performance, such as efficiency, productivity, equity, responsiveness, quality, and service. Armed with an understanding of the firm's capabilities and of the threats and opportunities in the external environment, managers are in a position to determine which strategic thrusts and alternatives best suit its mission, goals, and objectives. This process enables them to find the best "strategic fit"—that is, the strategic thrusts and alternatives that best match the company's capabilities with the demands of the external environment.

A number of methods can be used to achieve a good match. They include the company capability profile and WOTS-UP analysis. Vulnerability analysis also helps identify key threats and determine how prepared a company is to meet them. Beyond staying at the minimum required level, however, capability-based competitors develop mechanisms to keep them at the leading edge in terms of their core competencies. They realize that process excellence is essential to delivering these core competencies to the customer. Therefore, a growing number of companies are focusing on two complementary concepts: total quality management (TQM) and time-based management (TBM). Value leveraging is another approach that companies can use to enhance their core capability to meet customer demand. With these approaches managers can determine whether they are capable of achieving a substantial competitive advantage. CSF and performance measurement are the final steps.

REFERENCES AND SUGGESTIONS FOR FURTHER READING

Barney, Jay B. 1986. Organizational culture: Can it be a source of sustained competitive advantage? *Academy of Management Review*, 11, pp. 656–665.

Boston Consulting Group. 1991. Strategic platforms. *BCG Conference for Chief Executives. Summary of Discussions.* Paris, January.

Drucker, Peter F. 1973. *Management: Tasks, responsibilities, practices.* New York: Harper & Row.

Dumaine, Brian. 1992. Is big still good? *Fortune,* April 20, pp. 50–60.

Forrester, Jay W. 1961. *Industrial dynamics.* Cambridge, Mass.: M.I.T. Press.

Garvin, David. 1991. How the Baldrige award really works. *Harvard Business Review,* November–December, pp. 80–93.

Garvin, David A. 1988. *Managing quality: The strategic and competitive edge.* New York: The Free Press.

Garvin, David A. 1987. Competing on the eight dimensions of quality. *Harvard Business Review,* November–December, pp. 101–109.

GE keeps those ideas coming. 1991. *Fortune,* August 12.

Grant, Robert M. 1991. The resource-based theory of competitive advantage: Implications for strategy formulation. *California Management Review,* Spring.

Hamel, Gary, Yves Doz, and C. K. Prahalad. 1989. Collaborate with your competitors—and win. *Harvard Business Review,* January–February, pp. 133–139.

Hauser, John R. and Don Clausing. 1988. The house of quality. *Harvard Business Review,* May–June.

Imai, Masaaki. 1989. *Kaizen, the key to Japan's competitive success.* New York: Random House.

Kaplan, Robert S. and David Norton. 1992. The balanced scorecard—measures that drive performance. *Harvard Business Review,* January–February, pp. 71–79.

Knight, Charles F. 1992. Emerson Electric: Consistent profits, consistently. *Harvard Business Review,* January–February, pp. 57–70.

Pepsi keeps on going after no. 1. 1991. *Fortune,* March 11.

Popplewell, Barry and Alan Wildsmith. 1990. *How to gain company-wide commitment to total quality.* Aldershot, Hampshire: Gower Publishing Group.

Prahalad, C. K. and Gary Hamel. 1990. The core competencies of the corporation. *Harvard Business Review,* May–June, pp. 79–91.

Rummler, Geary A. and Alan P. Brache. 1990. *Improving performance: How to manage the white space on the organization chart.* San Francisco: Oxford Press.

Schein, Lawrence. 1990. The road to total quality. *The Conference Board Research Bulletin.*

Sims, Arden C. et al. 1992. Does the Baldrige Award really work? *Harvard Business Review* 70, January–February, pp. 126–140.

Snow, Charles C. and Lawrence G. Hrebiniak. 1980. Strategy, distinctive competence, and organization performance. *Administrative Science Quarterly,* 25, pp. 317–336.

Stalk, George, Jr. and Thomas M. Hout. 1990. *Competing against time.* New York: The Free Press.

Stalk, George, Philip Evans, and Lawrence E. Shulman. 1992. Competing on capabilities: The new rules of corporate strategy. *Harvard Business Review* 70, no. 2, March–April, pp. 57–70.

Stata, Ray. 1989. Organizational learning—the key to management innovation. *Sloan Management Review,* 63, Spring.

Steeples, Marion Mills. 1992. *The corporate guide to the Malcolm Baldrige National Quality Award.* Homewood, Ill.: ASQC Quality Press.

Stevenson, Howard H. 1976. Defining corporate strengths and weaknesses. *Sloan Management Review,* Spring, pp. 51–68.

Sullivan, L. P. 1986. Quality function deployment. *Quality Progress,* June.

Teitelbaum, Richard S. 1992. Timeliness is everything. *Fortune,* April 20, p. 120.

Thomas, Phillip R. 1990. *Competitiveness through total cycle time.* New York: McGraw-Hill.

Thorton, Emily and Andrew Erdman. 1992. Flexibility as a key in manufacturing strategy. *Fortune,* September 21, pp. 63–74.

CHAPTER SIX

Market Dynamics and Sustainable Competitive Advantage

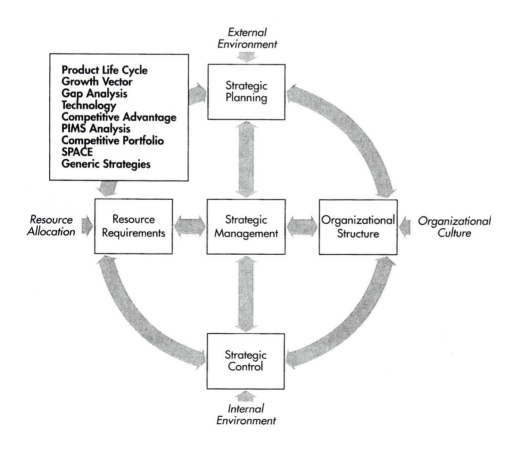

Chapter 1 A Framework for Strategic Management	**Chapter 2** Strategic Analysis	**Chapter 3** Strategic Visioning, Goals, Ethics, and Social Responsibility	**Chapter 4** The Competitive Environment	**Chapter 5** Capability-based Strategy	**Chapter 6** Market Dynamics and Sustainable Competitive Advantage
How to approach strategic management	*Application of strategic analysis*	*Understanding vision, values, ethics*	*Coping with competitive forces, stakeholders*	*Assessing company capability, timeliness, quality*	*Determining trends, gap analysis, and market dynamics*

Chapter 7 Strategy in a Global Environment	**Chapter 8** Financial Planning and Competitive- Cost Analysis	**Chapter 9** Entrepreneurship, Mergers and Acquisitions, Restructuring, and the Service Sector	**Chapter 10** Leadership Factor in Strategy and Implementing Strategic Change	**Chapter 11** Information Technology and Future Directions in Strategy
Assessing global trade, foreign markets, monetary exchange	*Preparing a financial plan and competitive-cost analysis*	*Importance of small business, entrepreneurs, restructuring*	*Strategy implementation, leadership, culture*	*Information technology, trends, new management*

Introduction

Every organization's success depends on how well it competes in its primary "field of battle," the marketplace. Strategies that enable the organization to influence or control the market, such as creating or expanding into new areas and gaining a dominant position before the competition has an opportunity to enter the field, improve the organization's position overall.

This chapter focuses on methods that help strategic managers understand the market environment in which their company operates. Several aspects of product/market behavior have important effects on the organization's strategic position and development. Particularly relevant are

1. The growth rate of market demand
2. Technological changes and substitutions
3. Product positioning and differentiation

Equally important is sustaining a competitive advantage once the firm has achieved it.

Understanding market dynamics allows managers to assess trends properly. The methods for assessing future market developments that are discussed include decision trees, product life cycle, growth vector analysis, gap analysis, and technology assessment.

Growth vector analysis is a method of examining the firm's product and market position and alternative directions for growth. An existing product in a new market poses opportunities and challenges different from those of a new product in an existing market. A systematic analysis of the market options can often reveal unexplored growth opportunities.

Gap analysis and an understanding of the *product life cycle* help strategic managers to anticipate structural changes in the market early enough to adapt the company's strategy advantageously. Changes in sales, profitability, and investment recovery occur as products move through the phases of the product life cycle. The life cycle concept helps managers identify potential performance gaps, analyze them, and develop plans to reduce or close them.

In the long run, businesses may survive or fail depending on how effectively they harness technological change. New technologies can alter the life cycle of a product or service and the cost and performance characteristics with which the product or service is delivered. In extreme cases, such as the replacement of mechanical office equipment by computers, a new technology can change the entire functional characteristics of a market. Therefore, strategic managers have to monitor and take advantage of technological developments. Methods explained in this chapter include *technology assessment* and the analysis of *technology substitution*.

To complete an assessment of product/market strategy, strategic managers can perform a *competitive portfolio analysis* and a *profit impact of market strategy (PIMS) analysis*. The *product portfolio analysis* enables managers to position each of the company's products based on its growth potential and cash-generation capacity. This analysis also ensures that interproduct effects will be taken into account in developing each product's marketing strategy.

Strategic position and action evaluation (SPACE) goes further and helps define the appropriate strategic posture for a firm based on a range of different input factors. Accordingly, it can form a basis for specifying the *generic competitive strategy* for a business.

The appendices to this chapter are designed to provide methodological support for understanding market dynamics. Appendix A describes how to carry out the product/market mapping activity that is typically used in market research. It covers a number of topics, such as multidimensional scaling, cluster analysis, discriminant analysis, and conjoint analysis. These methods are designed to provide a sound basis for understanding product dynamics and customer perception. Appendix B describes in detail how to conduct a technology assessment. Because of the increasing importance of technology in sustaining a competitive advantage, the methods described provide an important basis for evaluating a company's relative technological position and the rate of substitution of new technologies. These inputs are increasingly becoming critical in formulating competitive strategies.

Chapter 6 is built around a new illustrative case—the AMP case. This case, which is about a company in the electronic connector industry, will be used in this chapter and others to demonstrate the applicability of various methods to strategic management. AMP started making connectors 50 years ago and has reached over $3 billion in sales as a diversified manufacturer of electronic connectors. As the case illustrates, in today's highly competitive market, where technology is critical, strategic management is vital to achieving a sustainable competitive advantage.

ILLUSTRATIVE CASE: AMP CONNECTS ITS ONCE AND FUTURE GOALS

AMP Inc. is entering the '90s with the goal of doing as well as it did in the '70s.

That's a respectable goal. The 49-year-old electronic connector maker intends to return to 15% growth in an industry that's projected to grow by only 7% to 9% per year over the next five years.

As the largest connector maker in the United States with $2.8 billion in 1989 sales, Harrisburg, Pa.-based AMP is four to five times bigger than its nearest competitor, Molex Inc. Industry observers say AMP has reached that status by doing a lot of things right for a long time: a strict focus on its market, a global presence, commitment to quality, a conservative financial approach, and a 9% investment in research, development and engineering (RD&E). "They are the industry's technology leader," says connector industry consultant Ronald Bishop, a principal at Bishop and Associates, Wheaton, Ill. "They also ensure their customers get improved quality and on-time delivery—they will continue to be the market leader for the next decade."

But the connector industry is changing. Consolidation, price pressure, and shorter supplier lists have prompted AMP to change its strategy. The company has closed 36 U.S. plants, restructured its workforce and expanded overseas, says Harold A. McInnes, AMP chairman and chief executive. The company has also been cautiously diversifying into connector-related markets and systems, expanding sales through distribution, and making small acquisitions to fill out its product line. But to reach 15% growth, says Bishop, "AMP will have to become more of a systems manufacturer and make more acquisitions—both of companies and technologies." In June, AMP did just that, acquiring fiber optic manufacturer Kaptron Inc. for an undisclosed sum.

AMP currently holds 18% to 20% of the $17 billion to $18 billion connector market, which still leaves AMP plenty of room to grow. "We believe we are in the strongest position in our history," says McInnes. "We're optimistic that given a reasonable environment, we can return to our historic growth." AMP's 1989 sales increased only 5% over 1988's.

While different analysts estimate the current worldwide connector market anywhere between $14 billion and $25 billion depending on the connector-related products measured, AMP serves a market that includes connectors, terminals, splices, and packaging devices, according to AMP's head of investor relations, William Oakland.

AMP's greatest strength, industry watchers agree, is its consistent 9% investment in RD&E, which in 1989 amounted to $253 million—dollar- and percentage-wise the highest in the industry. Other strengths, according to connector industry consultant Kenneth Fleck of Fleck International Inc., Huntington Beach, Calif., include worldwide manufacturing with 70 locations in 26 countries, a direct sales force of more than 1,400 worldwide, superior application tooling and early customer involvement.

Fleck also mentions two managerial strengths: conservative financial practices and stable management. AMP's sales, general and administrative (SG&A) expenses are among the lowest in the industry: 18.1% of sales in 1989, and averaging for the past decade between 16.9% and 20.1%, compared with an industry range of 19.9% to 22.3%.

But there are some areas in which AMP hasn't been quite so strong. In the early 1980s, companies such as 3M Co., Thomas & Betts Corp., Augat Inc., Burndy Corp. and Robinson Nugent Inc. made inroads in the connector business at AMP's expense mainly by generating strong partnerships with electronics distributors, says Merrill Lynch Capital Markets' first vice president Jerry Labowitz. "AMP ignored the distributors until the early 1980s, and even then took a go-slow approach," he says. Even though AMP now runs a higher dollar volume through distributors, the current 10% volume compares with 30% for other connector makers.

Another weakness has been AMP's avoidance of the military market—part of a legacy

AMP CONNECTS ITS ONCE AND FUTURE GOALS, CONTINUED

from founder Uncas Whitaker who believed those markets were too entangled in red tape. But in 1988, in order to penetrate the military and commercial aerospace markets—the second-largest connector markets in the U.S. at around $1.3 billion—AMP acquired Matrix Science Corp., a maker of circular connectors, widely used in military and aerospace applications. Prior to its purchase of Matrix, AMP concentrated mainly on flat rectangular connectors.

AMP at a Glance

Fiscal Year	1989	1988
Sales ($ millions)	$2,797	$2,670
Net income ($ millions)	$281	$319
Net income/sales	10.0%	12.0%
Cost of sales/sales	65.0%	62.7%
R&D/sales	9.0%	8.9%
Marketing, G&A/sales	18.1%	17.5%
Number of employees	24,400	24,100
Sales per employee	$114,616	$110,774
Net income per employee	$11,513	$13,242
Capital expenditures/sales	9.0%	8.3%
Current ratio	1.98	2.06
Debt/equity ratio	0.17	0.15
Foreign sales/total sales	54.2%	54.2%

All figures for fiscal year ended December 31.
Source: Company reports.

INDUSTRY DYNAMICS

AMP has been adapting to industry changes in other ways. Faced with overcapacity since 1984, industry pricing pressure has been enormous. OEMs have been paring their supplier lists. Customers increasingly are calling for more highly engineered, quickly developed products delivered early or on time. The industry is also restructuring and consolidating. "We feel the trend of the strong getting stronger through consolidation will continue," says McInnes.

Customers are also looking for systems capability, and AMP is increasing its systems business. The AMP Cooperative Electronic Subcontractor (ACES) program—third-party cable and panel subassemblers—is part of that focus. According to AMP president and COO James E. Marley, the ACES program is an effort to serve OEMs better. "They service the end-customer," he says, "and AMP gives them higher volumes and better pricing."

Both cable and backplane assembly are higher-tech operations than AMP provides in-house. But some industry observers question whether ACES makes sense, pointing out that some ACES are distributors for other brands and there may

AMP CONNECTS ITS ONCE AND FUTURE GOALS, CONTINUED

be no brand loyalty for AMP. Some fear AMP could erode its own profit margins and create price disparity among some groups of sellers.

As products using connectors—PCs, desktops and laptops—get smaller, the degree of interconnection in them decreases. As Shearson Lehman Hutton analyst Stephen J. Balog points out: "The rise of the PC is a negative [for the connector industry]. There is less connector content in PCs—maybe 2% to 3%."

McInnes does not see this as a disadvantage. "As the stuff gets smaller, it also requires more integration. There are fewer connectors per system but more systems sold. And these systems have to be connected into LANs."

AMP has excelled in spotting such opportunities and pursuing them. In Europe, AMP has targeted a new generation of customer premise communications equipment incorporating ISDN standards and has created cross-connect product systems. AMP has sold this product to Siemens AG, N.V. Philips GL, Alcatel, STC, and LM Ericsson. AMP has 15 European subsidiaries.

DIVERSIFICATION STRATEGY

Overseas sales account for 54% of AMP's total sales. According to Labowitz, AMP's geographic breakdown by sales shows 46% for the U.S., 30% for Europe, and 19% for the Far East.

AMP has managed to maintain its strong hold also in the computer and office equipment and automotive markets. In the United States, major AMP customers are IBM, Compaq Computer Corp., and Digital Equipment Corp. AMP has also begun in recent years to offset any market weaknesses through acquisition and strategic partnering. In January, it announced a 50–50 joint venture with $9 billion Dutch company Akzo N.V. to develop and produce additive-process printed wiring boards, 3-D molded circuits, and related products.

In 1989, AMP also acquired Garry Screw Machine Corp. and Decolletage S.A. St.-Maurice,

producers of metal parts used in coaxial connectors, and Lytel, a maker of electro-optic devices.

AMP's product diversification, though, has been cautious. AMP has begun to emphasize value-added assemblies: backplanes, which are combinations of PCBs and connectors; and cable assemblies, combinations of cables and connectors. Labowitz notes that on the more highly engineered cable assemblies and backplanes, margins can be substantially higher than on connectors themselves.

AMP positions itself in high-growth markets through its balanced product line. Of the 684 connector product lines in the U.S., according to Fleck, about 49 of them are high-growth, and AMP is well-positioned in 41 of them. Much of AMP's strategic advantage comes from its leasing of application-tooling machines, which allow customers to rapidly cut and strip wire and terminate connection devices at the ends. AMP has supplied 54,000 application-tooling machines to customers, and Labowitz estimates two-thirds of AMP's sales are of machine-applied products. "AMP's application tooling is the industry standard and it helps lower customers' costs," Bishop says.

AMP's Worldwide Sales

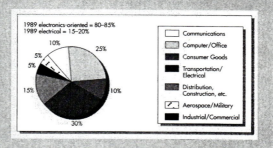

AMP has only recently begun to increase its sales through distribution; those sales now stand at nearly 10%, compared with less than 1% of total sales in 1979. But when AMP decided to sell through distribution, it did so with a vengeance. Says Steve Menefee, ex-vice president

AMP CONNECTS ITS ONCE AND FUTURE GOALS, CONTINUED

for sales and marketing with AMP distributor Hamilton/Avnet: "This company, in my opinion, acts and thinks like a semiconductor company. They're aggressive, cooperative, and a good listener. They've done many things to make their line look attractive to distribution."

From AMP's strategic standpoint, distribution broadened its customer base. "Ten years ago we looked at distribution," says McInnes. "We got involved in a casual way. Many components were moving through distribution and we knew some were coming out of direct sales and these were sales we were missing."

Chuck Poncher is president and CEO of Hawk Electronics Inc., Wheeling, Ill., a privately held specialty distributor that's carried AMP lines for eight years. "We've noticed changes in how AMP's been relating to distributors," says Poncher. "They've changed their price structure to benefit their distributors."

But could AMP's continued growth actually prove a hindrance? Bishop says AMP's size has made the company hard to do business with. "There were more procedures, red tape, and slow decision-making," he says. Bishop notes that AMP has been restructuring to push the decision-making down the line. "The people closer to the customer can serve him better," he says. "AMP's taking the slowness out of the machine."

Communication problems haven't gone unnoticed by AMP management. "In 1965 we first made the Fortune 500," says McInnes. "We've gotten bigger, and we've asked ourselves, 'How can we communicate around the world?'" As part of this effort AMP has created a "Planned Excellence" videotape for its employees, has formed international councils and has transferred employees between AMP's many regions.

FUTURE GROWTH

Observes analyst Labowitz: "The most important thing in the connector industry in the coming decade is that the U.S. will be the least exciting area for growth prospects. But connector makers have the most base in the U.S. If that's the case, AMP has to become inherently 'global'—in reality, they have to implement the things that have made them global so far. You have to communicate well—that's the challenge."

Marley says some of AMP's communication problems are being addressed, particularly overseas. "In order to participate in local markets you need a local team," he says. "In addition, a [global presence] enforces discipline: It suggests a product used in Japan can also be used in Europe. We've created a council to make sure we've addressed the nuances of every customer in every market."

Another challenge facing connector makers in a mature market is to know where the next opportunities will come from. Says McInnes: "We see growth in Europe with the economic community of 1992 along with potential of the Eastern Bloc. We should enjoy growth in the '90s in Asia and the Pacific." In the past five years, AMP has increased its overseas sales by 17.3%, says Bishop, compared with 2.6% sales growth in the U.S.

SMART BUILDINGS

Domestically, president Marley sees "smart" buildings and new technologies as areas of growth. There will be a need for rewiring of stores and buildings, and an area of major emphasis will be products and technologies that fit, he says. "Beyond that, there will be the impact of optical computers and superconductors."

But will these provide the environment necessary for 15% growth? Bishop foresees the emergence of new, smaller companies "niche-ing the heck out of AMP." He adds: "It's a conservative, well-managed company focused on engineering, but will have trouble maintaining its growth rate. As the industry matures, AMP is going to have competitors nipping at its heels. Where AMP will get beat up is where they can't turn a project around fast enough...."

Bishop also says the U.S. connector industry faces a very real Japanese threat, but AMP and

AMP CONNECTS ITS ONCE AND FUTURE GOALS, CONTINUED

Molex have excellent offshore manufacturing and are well-positioned to take advantage of the expanding marketplace. For instance, AMP's 10-year compound annual growth rate in the Far East was 15.6% and Molex's, 24.6%. The industry growth rate was 17.3%.

"As [Far East] transplants come to the U.S. and start procuring products locally, AMP and Molex will benefit from that business," notes analyst Labowitz. "But if they are serviced through a Japanese company, AMP will have to compete.

"AMP, along with Molex, are best positioned to be global companies—they have the ability and critical mass," Labowitz continues. "But to hold on to their business they have to effectively coordinate those things, and that's a real challenge to management."

Source: Reprinted from *Electronic Business*, September 3, 1990, © 1990 Reed Publishing USA.

Now that we are familiar with AMP's record and have heard what several industry analysts have to say about the company, let's give CEO Harold McInnes the floor. The following are excerpts from two speeches he delivered: the first in 1990 at the International Connector Symposium, and the second in 1992 at the Fleck International Connection Congress.

DECADE OF THE 1990s—THE GAME GETS TOUGHER*

Here's the likely scenario:

Financial. It will be much more difficult to obtain funds, debt or equity, because of government budget deficits, rising demand for capital throughout the world—particularly Eastern Europe—and the tightening of credit by banks in the U.S., Great Britain, Japan, and other countries. Venture capital will be harder to obtain and more costly. Governments obviously need to encourage more savings and investment and less consumption, but this is politically difficult. In many companies, internally generated cash flow will be insufficient to fully finance new product development, modernization, and expansion—and they will have to look for financial help, usually equity investments, from other companies.

Technology. Will require ever higher levels of expertise and resources, and must move from the laboratory to salable product at an ever faster rate. Many companies won't have the resources to do this effectively without help. A critical aspect for the U.S. is the development of a national policy on government involvement and funding in non-military technology areas. If the U.S. is to maintain its technology lead, the laissez faire, i.e., "no policy" approach of the 1980s must evolve into a more pragmatic, long-term, results-oriented partnership among government, industry, finance, and academia that faces the realities of how technology is being managed nationally in Western Europe, Japan, and several other countries.

Manufacturing. Following the lead of the Japanese, it is now being elevated to equal status with R&D, marketing, and finance after decades of second-class status. The need is now recognized for multi-discipline teams who design from conception for manufacturability and quality—and who use a simultaneous engineering approach. Excellent progress is being made throughout the world on improving productivity and quality—and MRP, JIT, CIM, TQC and many other systems will continue to be developed and implemented. Outsourcing will continue to increase. Manufacturing will continue to migrate to lower-cost areas. While U.S. manufacturing employment will continue to decline, the U.S. will retain a sufficient higher-technology manufacturing base to support and enhance the leading role it has in advanced technology. To gain economies of scale and reduce investment, companies will increasingly "rationalize" their facilities through tighter controls on a regional or worldwide basis where each facility has an assigned role in an integrated whole—instead of a collection of companies primarily serving their local markets.

Marketing. Must be increasingly done on a regional and/or global basis to be effective. Global sourcing will increase. Quality requirements will rise steadily until leading companies reach six sigma levels in the late 1990s. Requirements will continue to rise for on-time delivery to more precise delivery times, better service, and higher-level technology support. Supplier lists will steadily shrink as customers reduce to the few best in each product or service category. Partnering between customers and preferred suppliers will slowly but surely move from lip service to implementation. Standards—national, regional, global—will become increasingly important in both the development and marketing of products. The niche player will have to be very creative—unique patentable products, alliances, superior service—to survive.

Pricing. After steady erosion since the mid-1980s, pricing will firm up in the next year or two in many products because of higher capacity utilization levels, more partnering between customers and key suppliers, and better understanding of value and of the need for healthy margins to fund improvement and expansion.

What are some of the conclusions we can draw from this scenario?

Human Resources. Increasingly, the most critical factor in success will be the extent to which a company, or any organization, empowers, trains, and motivates its people. Leadership, communications, teams, and gain sharing must supplant authoritarianism, secrecy, and bureaucracy. The key to continuous improvement is to have all people, from CEO to the machine operator, understand and work toward common goals in a results-oriented, customer-oriented culture. Education must, and will, become much better—particularly in the U.S. where science and math have been neglected and 20% of adults are functional illiterates. But this will take years. Thus, short term the answer is much more and better on-the-job training because over three-fourths of the employees of the year 2000 are already on the payroll today. In leading companies, training will be a continuous, integral part of each person's job. At AMP we launched our plan for excellence earlier this year to provide a more comprehensive, longer-term approach to continuous improvement of quality, productivity and service. A cornerstone is a quantum leap ahead in training, and our training expenditures have doubled in the last few years and will keep rising. This is happening throughout the industrial world.

A Global—or at Least a Regional—Approach. Will be increasingly needed in all functions. But, as AMP and most multi-nationals are finding out, fully implementing a truly global approach requires an extremely strong commitment from top management and great attention to detail for many years to bring about the required change in attitudes, culture, and practices. Pronouncements and coordination aren't enough. It takes very deliberate changes in systems, transfers of people, adjustments in inter-company accounting, creation of rewards and penalties—so decisions are made on what is best for the entire company rather than the individual division or subsidiary. The ultimate goal is a "seamless" organization with no internal barriers.

Multi-nationals. Will become more dominant because they can effectively raise funds, transfer resources, gain economies of scale, make large investments, and match up globally with customers. Successful multi-nationals will be the markets and channels through which many smaller, more localized companies will do business.

Strategic Alliances. Will be essential to success for even the biggest and strongest companies. The external support system—suppliers, subcontractors, acquisitions, minority interests, joint ventures, venture capital investments, research consortiums, consultants—will be as critical as internal capabilities. They provide valuable leverage as companies increasingly concentrate their main resources on their own unique in-house core capabilities. Doing this successfully is a very real challenge to most managements because their experience is primarily internally oriented. Done poorly, it can drain away resources and unduly divert management attention.

Broader Role for Key Suppliers. The most successful suppliers will be those who take full advantage of the customer's growing need for conservation of resources, cost reduction, cycle time reduction, quality and productivity improvement—thus increasing proclivity by outsourcing, partnering, subcontracting, and strategic alliances. Expanding into value-added products, assemblies, and services requires more resources, greater expertise, new approaches. Only a small fraction of all suppliers will end up being formally approved and able to do all this effectively.

Indirect vs. Direct Costs. A steadily rising proportion of total costs will be indirect—benefits, communications, commuter systems, legal costs, insurance, product liability, training and development, environmental protection, waste disposal, RD&E, marketing. The gap may narrow on direct wage costs as wage rates continue to rise more rapidly in the newly industrialized nations, but the disparity in indirect costs among different countries will widen and make it increasingly difficult for companies in the more advanced countries to compete in low-technology manufacturing. Thus, managements throughout the world (but particularly in the advanced countries) will be under mounting pressure to limit or reduce benefits and shift more of this burden on workers and government, cut corners on environmental protection, skimp on RD&E, and take other actions for short-term relief from margin pressures. The challenge will be to effectively control these indirect costs while meeting rising legal and societal requirements and managing for superior long-term—not short-term—results.

Let me conclude with a challenge to the connector industry. We at AMP believe the next frontier in the connector industry is reliability—i.e., *the effective performance of the connection system over the entire life of the equipment in which it is used.* As electronic circuitry moves into further miniaturization and faster signal speeds, as electronic equipment is placed into new environments, as servicing becomes more difficult and expensive, and as the consequences of failures becomes greater—reliability must become the top issue in the 1990s.

*Reprinted with permission of AMP Incorporated.

THE GLOBAL BUSINESS ENVIRONMENT IN THE DECADE AHEAD

Most companies have a good foundation to build on in the 1990s. Some of the principles and goals you'll see progress on will include:

- Further use of employee teams.
- Continuous training of each employee as an integral part of that person's development.
- Gain sharing and incentive pay linked as directly as possible to individual, team, and unit performance at the team, unit, and company level.
- Extensive non-monetary recognition of accomplishments.
- Much greater sharing of information within the company.
- Career counseling for all employees.
- Open posting of all job openings.
- More transfer of employees between U.S. and international operations.
- Formal executive/professional development and human resources planning programs to identify and provide for future needs.
- More commitment by the company to employment security, and
- Much benchmarking with companies who are leaders in what they do.

The days of command and control are over—replaced by leadership and empowerment. Management must communicate, set an example, share responsibility and authority, enable people to do more, and reward good performance. The payoff for doing this well will be enormous.

Excerpts from AMP's 1991 Form 10-K and financial statements and annual financial ratios follow.

EXCERPTS: 10-K REPORT FOR YEAR ENDED DECEMBER 31, 1991

PART I.

Item 1. Business

The foldout and inside front cover, pages 1–25, and Notes 14 and 15 on page 35 of the Annual Report to security holders for the year ended December 31, 1991 are hereby incorporated by reference.

The business in which the Company is engaged is highly competitive. The Company believes it is the leading producer of electrical/electronic connection devices, and associated application tools and machines. Over 95% of its business is in this single business segment. Within this segment there is great variety: over 100,000 types and sizes are included in over 200 product families. These product families generally involve the same or very similar basic technology, materials, production processes, and marketing approaches. Over 60% of sales are of products provided in strip form on reels and applied by customers with special machines provided by the Company. Another 10% of sales are of products provided in single piece form and applied by customers with special AMP tools. The balance of sales is of pre-assembled devices, which do not require application tools or machines. Nearly 80% of sales are of products in just two Standard Industrial Classification 4-digit codes—Electronic Connectors and Current Carrying Wiring Devices. In all cases, the Company's products are subject to direct and indirect competition. Generally speaking, most of the Company's products involve technical competence in development and manufacture and are subject to active competition with products manufactured and sold by many other companies. The Company competes primarily through offering high-quality, technical products and associated application tooling with emphasis on product performance and service and only secondarily competes on a price basis. The Company has several thousand patents issued or pending, with no one patent considered significant. The number of competitors is estimated at over 1,200.

The Company feels it has adequate sources of supply and does not expect the cost and availability of materials to have a significant overall effect on its total current operations.

The Company's backlog of unfilled orders increased from $514,000,000 at year-end 1990 to $525,000,000 at year-end 1991, and has risen slightly so far in 1992. A majority of these orders were for delivery within the next ninety days, and substantially all were scheduled for delivery within 12 months.

The Company is not aware of any material claims against its assets. However, it is potentially liable for all or a portion of environmental clean-up costs at several National Priorities List sites. At one site, which is the subject of a Corrective Action Order under the Resource Conservation and Recovery Act, the Company has incurred costs of nearly $1 million since 1984 and anticipates incurring additional costs of $75,000–100,000 per year indefinitely. At another site, for which the Company shares potential liability with several other parties, the Company spent $144,000 in 1991 and will spend another $144,000 in 1992; a cost determination as to subsequent years' costs has not been made, but based on cost estimates related to other NPL sites, the Company's cost at this site should not exceed $4 million, to be incurred over six to eight years beginning in 1993 or later. The remaining sites are involved in preliminary investigative activities and neither liability nor total cost assessments have been made. However, the Company's future environmental compliance costs are not expected to have a material impact on the Company's financial results, liquidity or capital expenditures. Over the five-year period 1987–1991 the Company has spent several million dollars annually for remedial and preventative actions in protection of the environment.

The primary seasonal effect generally experienced by the Company is in the third quarter when there usually is a temporary leveling off or modest drop in the rate of new orders and shipments because of the softening of customer demand in certain markets such as appliances, automotive, and home entertainment goods arising from model year changeovers, plant vacations and closedowns, and other traditional seasonal practices. This seasonal effect is most evident in the Company's European operations. Also there is usually some seasonal strengthening in domestic sales and orders in the first quarter, although this strengthening was mild in 1992 because of recessionary effects.

Presently, there are no foreign exchange or currency restrictions in the various countries which would significantly affect the remittance of funds to AMP.

Highlights and Financial Data: AMP
(Dollar amounts in millions, except per share data)

Years Ended	1991	1990	1989	1988	1987	1986	1985	1984	1983	1982	1981
Net sales	$3,095.0	$3,043.6	$2,796.6	$2,669.7	$2,317.8	$1,933.1	$1,636.1	$1,812.8	$1,515.5	$1,243.4	$1,234.3
Income before income taxes	423.6	462.0	455.3	529.2	430.5	294.0	192.5	362.7	292.6	213.5	241.0
Income taxes	163.9	174.9	174.4	210.1	180.8	129.7	84.5	161.4	129.5	94.6	106.2
Net income	$ 259.7	$ 287.1	$ 280.9	$ 319.1	$ 249.7	$ 164.3	$ 108.0	$ 201.3	$ 163.1	$ 118.9	$ 134.8
Per share[1]	$ 2.45	$ 2.70	$ 2.63	$ 2.96	$ 2.31	$ 1.52	$ 1.00	$ 1.87	$ 1.52	$ 1.10	$ 1.25
Cash dividends per share[1,2]	$ 1.44	$ 1.36	$ 1.20	$ 1.00	85¢	74¢	72¢	64¢	53$^{1}/_{3}$¢	46$^{2}/_{3}$¢	40¢
Capital expenditures	$ 313.3	$ 338.4	$ 252.1	$ 220.3	$ 171.8	$ 151.7	$ 198.5	$ 255.7	$ 127.6	$ 121.9	$ 108.9

At December 31—

	1991	1990	1989	1988	1987	1986	1985	1984	1983	1982	1981
Working capital	$ 738.0	$ 665.2	$ 711.7	$ 700.9	$ 625.3	$ 475.5	$ 356.1	$ 389.4	$ 446.5	$ 415.6	$ 410.7
Property, plant and equipment, net	1,180.2	1,121.5	953.8	894.6	865.4	793.6	750.2	620.4	461.9	413.5	362.9
Shareholders' equity	1,913.0	1,792.8	1,625.4	1,521.3	1,348.6	1,134.9	996.9	923.2	800.9	714.5	660.5
Backlog	$ 525.0	$ 514.0	$ 489.0	$ 475.0	$ 384.0	$ 326.0	$ 307.0	$ 340.0	$ 374.0	$ 254.0	$ 253.0
Number of employees	25,000	24,700	24,400	24,100	22,000	21,800	22,800	24,500	21,300	19,750	19,650
Shares of stock outstanding[1](millions)	106.0	105.9	106.5	107.4	107.5	108.1	107.9	107.7	107.5	107.7	107.8

[1] Share data has been adjusted for the 3-for-1 stock split in 1984.
[2] On January 22, 1992 a regular quarterly dividend of 38¢ per share was declared—an indicated annual rate of $1.52 per share.

Consolidated Statements of Income (Unaudited): AMP
(Dollar amounts in thousands, except per share data)

	For the 3 Months Ended September 30	
	1992	1991
Net sales	$ 847,075	$ 736,318
Cost of sales	556,497	487,907
Gross income	290,578	248,411
Selling, general and administrative expenses	146,806	132,307
Income from operations	143,772	116,104
Interest expense	(6,826)	(9,761)
Other income (deductions), net	(8,019)	(4,605)
Income before income taxes	128,927	101,738
Income taxes	51,110	40,180
Net income	$ 77,817	$ 61,558
Per share—Net income	74¢	58¢
Cash dividends	38¢	36¢
Weighted average number of shares	105,188,969	105,850,212

	For the 9 Months Ended September 30	
	1992	1991
Net sales	$ 2,492,631	$ 2,304,350
Cost of sales	1,649,263	1,529,037
Gross income	843,368	775,313
Selling, general and administrative expenses	442,147	415,861
Income from operations	401,221	359,452
Interest expense	(22,982)	(31,407)
Other income (deductions), net	(15,595)	(9,627)
Income before income taxes	362,644	318,418
Income taxes	142,620	122,140
Net income	$ 220,024	$ 196,278
Per share—Net income	$ 2.08	$ 1.85
Cash dividends	$ 1.14	$ 1.08
Weighted average number of shares	105,634,132	105,900,503

Consolidated Balance Sheets (Condensed): AMP
(Dollar amounts in thousands)

	September 30, 1992*	December 31, 1991
Assets		
Current assets		
Cash and cash equivalents	$ 323,037	$ 370,829
Marketable securities	69,337	80,167
Receivables	630,876	589,212
Inventories—		
Finished goods and work in process	252,165	246,187
Purchased and manufactured parts	151,263	149,472
Raw materials	45,189	44,943
Total inventories	448,617	440,602
Other current assets	151,973	135,559
Total current assets	1,623,840	1,616,369
Property, plant and equipment	2,738,437	2,550,406
Less–accumulated depreciation	1,537,854	1,370,236
Property, plant and equipment, net	1,200,583	1,180,170
Investments and other assets	213,600	210,356
Total assets	$ 3,038,023	$ 3,006,895
Liabilities and Shareholders' Equity		
Current liabilities		
Short-term debt	$ 271,801	$ 336,660
Payables, trade and other	257,245	250,605
Accrued liabilities	305,521	301,142
Total current liabilities	834,567	888,407
Long-term debt	49,006	52,995
Other liabilities and deferred credits	184,814	152,450
Total liabilities	1,068,387	1,093,852
Shareholders' equity	1,969,636	1,913,043
Total liabilities and shareholders' equity	$ 3,038,023	$ 3,006,895

*Unaudited.

BUSINESS SEGMENTS

The Company's business is concentrated almost entirely in one product area—electrical and electronic connection, switching and programming devices—which are sold throughout many diverse markets. It is not possible, therefore, to divide AMP's business into meaningful industry segments.

However, the Company's operations are worldwide and can be grouped into several geographic segments. Operations outside the United States are conducted through wholly owned subsidiary companies that function within assigned, principally national, markets. The subsidiaries manufacture locally where required by market conditions and/or customer demands, and where permitted by economies of scale. Most are also self-financed. However, while they operate fairly autonomously, there are substantial intersegment and intrasegment sales.

Pertinent financial data by major geographic segments for 1990, 1989, and 1988 are:

(Dollars in thousands)	Sales to Unaffiliated Customers	Intersegment Sales	Total Sales	Pretax Income	Net Income	Total Assets
United States:						
1990	$1,237,237	$ 265,370	$1,502,607	$203,276	$133,249	$1,677,166
1989	1,281,864	234,705	1,616,569	186,953	124,511	1,574,894
1988	1,221,525	174,803	1,396,328	219,046	138,215	1,526,885
Europe:						
1990	$1,072,111	$ 19,828	$1,091,939	$165,535	$103,565	$ 755,881
1989	863,894	13,641	877,535	171,975	107,180	596,296
1988	809,785	14,971	824,756	193,403	113,938	505,477
Asia/Pacific:						
1990	$ 583,189	$ 20,067	$ 603,256	$ 74,671	$ 41,917	$ 567,772
1989	506,761	13,868	520,629	76,060	45,510	463,411
1988	514,138	10,876	525,014	95,492	47,597	457,560
Americas:						
1990	$ 151,052	$ 17,879	$ 168,931	$ 17,044	$ 7,692	$ 84,754
1989	144,117	15,227	159,344	23,866	11,263	81,398
1988	124,213	10,793	135,006	19,635	10,516	72,619
Eliminations:						
1990	$ —	$ (323,144)	$ (323,144)	$ 1,486	$ 689	$ (156,957)
1989	—	(277,441)	(277,441)	(3,567)	(7,557)	(186,240)
1988	—	(211,443)	(211,443)	1,647	8,857	(187,004)
Total:						
1990	$3,043,589	$ —	$3,043,589	$462,012	$287,112	$2,928,616
1989	2,796,636	—	2,796,636	455,287	280,907	2,529,759
1988	2,669,661	—	2,669,661	529,223	319,123	2,375,537

Transfers between geographic segments are generally priced at "large quantity customer prices less a discount" for items not requiring further manufacture and at "cost plus a percentage" for items subject to further processing.

Included in the assets of the United States segment are short-term investments at December 31: 1990—$405,946,000; 1989—$305,931,000 and 1988—$290,532,000; which generated interest income of approximately $18,371,000, $19,917,000, and $16,681,000, respectively.

Combined Balance Sheets: AMP Incorporated & Its Subsidiaries and Pamcor, Inc.
(Dollar amounts in thousands)

	December 31	
	1990	1989
Assets		
Current assets		
Cash and cash equivalents	$ 414,493	$ 309,164
Marketable securities	45,674	25,001
Receivables	557,484	520,028
Inventories	481,727	494,803
Deferred income taxes	69,565	56,144
Other current assets	49,468	32,098
Total current assets	1,618,411	1,437,238
Property, plant and equipment	2,803,328	1,927,541
Less—accumulated depreciation	1,181,784	973,786
Property, plant and equipment, net	1,121,544	953,755
Investments and other assets	181,661	138,766
Total assets	$2,928,616	$2,529,759
Liabilities and Shareholders' Equity		
Current liabilities		
Short-term debt	$ 378,636	$ 214,512
Payables, trade and other	244,655	224,924
Accrued payrolls and employee benefits	132,194	114,585
Accrued income taxes	151,384	129,765
Other accrued liabilities	46,341	41,711
Total current liabilities	953,210	725,497
Long-term debt	61,095	69,500
Deferred income taxes	79,840	71,609
Other liabilities	41,713	37,720
Total liabilities	1,135,858	904,326

(continued)

Combined Balance Sheets: AMP Incorporated & Its Subsidiaries and Pamcor, Inc. (continued)
(Dollar amounts in thousands)

	December 31	
	1990	1989
Shareholders' equity		
AMP Incorporated—		
Common stock, without par value—		
Authorized 350,000,000 shares,		
issued 112,320,000 shares	12,480	12,480
Pamcor, Inc.—		
Common stock, par value $1.00 per share—		
Authorized 64,000 shares, 20,000 shares	20	20
Other capital	77,746	77,156
Cumulative translation adjustments	114,108	67,911
Retained earnings	1,765,396	1,622,935
Treasury stock, at cost	(176,992)	(155,069)
Total shareholders' equity	1,792,758	1,625,433
Total liabilities and shareholders' equity	$2,928,616	$2,529,759

Combined Annual Income Statements: AMP Incorporated & Its Subsidiaries and Pamcor, Inc.
(Dollar amounts in thousands, except per share data)

	Years Ended December 31		
	1990	1989	1988
Net sales	$3,043,589	$2,796,636	$2,669,661
Cost of sales	2,012,394	1,816,821	1,672,718
Gross income	1,031,195	979,815	996,943
Selling, general and administrative expenses	543,437	505,191	467,045
Income from operations	487,758	474,674	529,898
Interest expense	(38,321)	(21,592)	(16,185)
Other income, net	12,575	2,255	15,510
Income before income taxes	462,012	455,287	529,223
Income taxes	174,900	174,380	210,100
Net income	$ 287,112	$ 280,907	$ 319,123
Net income per share	$ 2.70	$ 2.63	$ 2.96

Combined Statements of Cash Flows: AMP Incorporated & Its Subsidiaries and Pamcor, Inc.
(Dollar amounts in thousands)

	Years Ended December 31		
	1990	1989	1988
Cash and cash equivalents at January 1	$ 309,164	$ 247,788	$ 142,397
Operating activities			
Net income	287,112	290,907	319,123
Noncash adjustments—			
Depreciation and amortization	217,734	180,270	158,511
Deferred income taxes and investment tax credits	(5,765)	(15,720)	(22,120)
Increase to other liabilities	6,183	6,251	2,357
Other, net	17,881	7,879	20,116
Changes in operating assets and liabilities net of effects of acquisitions and disposition of businesses	55,780	(68,331)	49,728
Cash provided by operating activities	578,925	391,256	527,715
Investing activities			
Additions to property, plant and equipment	(338,389)	(252,122)	(220,257)
(Increase) decrease in marketable securities	(20,674)	58,843	(13,292)
(Acquisitions) disposition of businesses, less cash acquired, net	(3,466)	(13,971)	(25,725)
Other, net	(44,403)	(18,589)	(5,353)
Cash used for investing activities	(406,932)	(225,839)	(264,627)
Financing activities			
Changes in short-term debt	118,378	77,010	31,125
Proceeds from long-term debt	11,660	6,415	25,418
Repayments of long-term debt	(27,285)	(13,056)	(11,239)
Purchases of treasury stock	(26,037)	(44,881)	(92,596)
Dividends paid	(144,651)	(128,090)	(107,802)
Cash used for financing activities	(67,935)	(102,602)	(155,094)
Effect of exchange rate changes on cash	1,271	(1,439)	(2,603)
Cash and cash equivalents at December 31	$ 414,493	$ 309,164	$ 247,788
Changes in operating assets and liabilities			
Receivables	$ 6,465	$ (55,076)	$ (6,465)
Inventories	38,659	(15,048)	(55,923)

(continued)

Combined Statements of Cash Flows: AMP Incorporated & Its Subsidiaries and Pamcor, Inc. (continued)
(Dollar amounts in thousands)

	Years Ended December 31		
	1990	1989	1988
Other current assets	(14,184)	(346)	(2,249)
Payables, trade and other	(6,420)	9,654	50,642
Accrued payrolls and employee benefits	12,182	7,056	11,177
Other accrued liabilities	19,078	(14,571)	52,546
	$ 55,780	$ (68,331)	$ 49,728

Key Annual Financial Ratios: AMP

Fiscal Year Ended	December 31, 1990	December 31, 1989
Quick ratio	1.07	1.18
Current ratio	1.70	1.98
Net sales/cash	6.61	8.37
SG&A expense/sales	0.18	0.18
Receivables turnover	5.46	5.38
Receivables day sales	65.94	66.94
Inventory turnover	6.32	5.65
Inventory day sales	56.98	63.69
Net sales/Working capital	4.58	3.93
Net sales/Net plant and equipment	2.71	2.93
Net sales/Current assets	1.88	1.95
Net sales/Total assets	1.04	1.11
Net sales/Employees	123,222	114,616
Total liabilities/Total assets	0.39	0.36
Total liabilities/Invested capital	0.61	0.53
Total liabilities/Common equity	0.63	0.56
Times interest earned	13.06	22.09
Current debt/Equity	NA	NA
Long-term debt/Equity	0.03	0.04
Total debt/Equity	0.03	0.04
Total assets/Equity	1.63	1.56
Pretax income/Net sales	0.15	0.16
Pretax income/Total assets	0.16	0.18
Pretax income/Invested capital	0.25	0.27

(continued)

Key Annual Financial Ratios (continued)

Fiscal Year Ended	December 31, 1990	December 31, 1989
Pretax income/Common equity	0.26	0.28
Net income/Net sales	0.09	0.10
Net income/Total assets	0.10	0.11
Net income/Invested capital	0.15	0.17
Net income/Common equity	0.16	0.17

SUSTAINABLE COMPETITIVE ADVANTAGE

It is not necessarily difficult to achieve a competitive advantage by taking extraordinary steps. Sustaining it, however, is difficult. A *sustainable competitive advantage* has a reasonable lasting effect and helps the company to achieve its strategic goals. Three conditions of sustainable competitive advantage are

1. The customer consistently perceives a positive difference between the products or services offered by the company and those offered by its competitors. These differences include quality, uniqueness, value, or cost competitiveness.
2. The perceived difference results from the company's relatively greater capability.
3. The perceived difference persists for a reasonable period of time.

The positive difference is based on additional attributes, such as price, aesthetics, functionality, availability, visibility, and after-sales service. Positive differences in these areas help the company to establish a niche in the market.

Competitive advantage is durable only to the extent that it cannot be readily imitated. Four capability gaps have been identified that help to prevent imitation by competitors:

1. Business-system gaps such as good working conditions
2. Image gaps resulting from reputation, consumer awareness, and trust
3. Uniqueness gaps that limit competitors' actions, including patents, licenses, and regulations regarding consumer safety
4. Strategy gaps that reflect the organization's capacity for innovation, flexibility, and ability to adapt

To sustain its competitive advantage, the company must continue its expenditures for research and development, product improvement, performance enhancement, advertising, responsiveness to customer needs, delivery, and service. If a competitor can match these capabilities, the company may lose market share.

Ghemawat (1986) suggested that to sustain a competitive advantage, a company must focus on three areas: product innovation, new production processes, and marketing strategies besides pricing. In his view, sustainable competitive advantage depends on the company size in the targeted market, on superior access to resources or customers, and on restricted options of competitors.

An increasingly important factor in sustaining competitive advantage is maintenance of product quality. Garvin (1987) suggested eight absolute standards of product quality. They are, in order of customer preference,

1. *Performance.* The product must perform to specifications.
2. *Features.* Features in addition to basic performance can enhance the product's desirability.
3. *Reliability.* The product must perform consistently as specified.
4. *Conformance.* The product's design should meet established operating standards.
5. *Durability.* The product should function for a specified period of time, be repairable, and not become obsolete prematurely.
6. *Serviceability.* Product maintenance and repair should be provided with speed, courtesy, and competence. Maintenance and repair should not be difficult or complicated.
7. *Aesthetics.* The product should be a pleasing design, size, color, and so on.
8. *Perceived quality.* Reputation often is the basis of perceived quality.

Creating a sustainable competitive advantage requires a combination of different factors, the most important of which are shown in Figure 6.1. On the left side

---

FIGURE 6.1 | **Sources of Competitive Advantage**

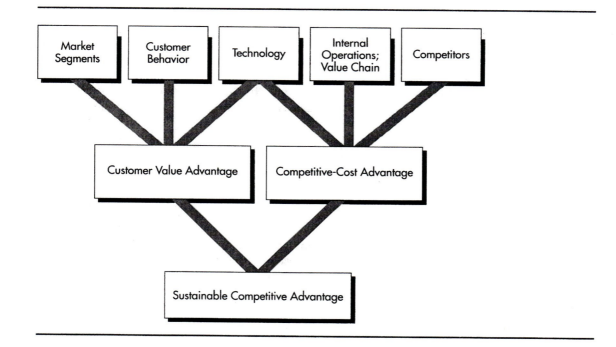

are customer-related areas in which a company can gain advantage, on the right side competitor-related areas. Technology affects both the potential for customer value advantage and that for competitive cost advantage.

Core competency can be created by finding new markets that are not currently there. Hamel and Prahalad (1991) describe how competitive battles were won in the 1980s by companies that used cost and quality advantages in known markets. In the 1990s, however, battles will be won by companies that use their imagination and create dramatically new markets for products that previously did not exist, such as speech-activated devices, multimedia computers, and genetically engineered medication.

Marketing strategy considers not only meeting competitive pressure but also identifying and serving real customer needs (Ohmae, 1988). In some instances, new products will generate a customer need, but in most cases, marketing means finding the need that matches readily available products. Ohmae describes the case of Yamaha, which had 40% of the global market for pianos but saw demand for them decreasing 10% per year. Recognizing that conventional pianos served a limited need, Yamaha added digital and optical technology to produce a modern "player piano." The results in sales have been explosive.

Consistent with our theme of total value, some of the ways of achieving a sustainable competitive advantage include

1. *Value*. The product is the best available for the price.
2. *Quality*. The product works well, looks good, and is very reliable.
3. *Service*. The customer can trust repairs that are timely and courteous.
4. *Price*. It is competitive but not the lowest.
5. *Distribution*. Able to meet demand at the lowest cost.
6. *Reputation*. Good image, name is known, location is convenient.
7. *Technology*. The product should be efficient and effective.
8. *Innovative*. Features are not available elsewhere.
9. *Functionality*. The product meets requirements as specified.
10. *Durability*. It doesn't break, can take abuse.
11. *Distinctive patent,* protection for unique features.
12. *Maintain relations* with suppliers, customers, networks.
13. *Flexible enough* to outpace competition—responsive to customer needs.
14. *Market focus*. Segmented, niche, or differentiated.
15. *Profitability*. Avoid price wars, discard obsolete products.

A company that recognizes the need to sustain its competitive advantage will choose ongoing strategies aimed at maintaining its market share and profitability. This requirement is not satisfied by preparation of a single strategic plan for the company as a whole or its SBUs but requires constant monitoring, updating, and focusing on actions that will sustain a competitive edge. Many companies that are now defunct did not recognize that the overriding "strategy" must be to stay ahead of the competition.

TREND ASSESSMENT

Strategic decisions deal with the future of the company. Therefore, understanding trends and exploiting them earlier than competitors can make for superior performance in an industry. Strategic managers must constantly assess market dynamics to determine which strategies are likely to be most advantageous for the company. Trend assessment is like playing a game of chess. Good players anticipate their opponents' moves and understand the second- and third-order effects of their actions. They also understand that future events are fraught with uncertainty and devise strategies to cope with that uncertainty.

DECISION-TREE ANALYSIS

The logical possibilities can be identified and the alternative outcomes can be assessed with the help of a diagram called a *decision tree* (Figure 6.2). The strategy

---

FIGURE 6.2 | **Basic Decision Tree**

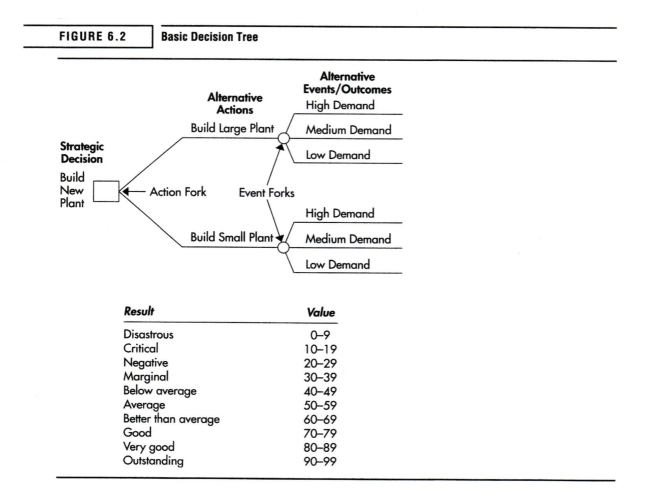

Result	Value
Disastrous	0–9
Critical	10–19
Negative	20–29
Marginal	30–39
Below average	40–49
Average	50–59
Better than average	60–69
Good	70–79
Very good	80–89
Outstanding	90–99

being considered is represented by a diagram whereon several branches show alternative courses of action. For example, if AMP needs to build a new plant to satisfy the demand for its products in a particular country over the next ten years, managers can use a decision tree to help them decide whether to build a large or a small plant. Any point at which they consider alternative actions is called an *action fork*.

Once the action branches have been drawn, managers have to consider how environmental conditions, or events, could affect the outcome of each action. Any point at which they consider events is termed an *event fork*. Event forks are represented by small circles. The events that the company wants to consider in Figure 6.2 are high, medium, and low demand for its product after the plant is built. These possibilities constitute the event/outcome branches. Other action forks, such as "expand/do not expand the small plant," or event forks, such as "competitive products enter/do not enter the market," can be added to this tree if they are germane to the problem.

Once the decision tree is complete, managers can use various criteria, such as profit margin or utility, to assess the outcomes of each action branch of the tree. Though monetary criteria are most frequently used, they exclude some relevant considerations. For example, trying to satisfy high demand with a small plant might be very profitable, but it could also result in considerable loss of sales and attract unwanted competition. Therefore, nonmonetary criteria should be used to measure the desirability of an outcome whenever appropriate.

If nonmonetary criteria are used, a scale of values can be applied to represent the desirability of outcomes (see the table in Figure 6.2). A value of 0 can, for example, be assigned to the worst possible outcome and a value of 100 to the best possible outcome. All the other possible outcomes are assigned some value in between. Experiencing high demand after a large plant has been built is the most desirable outcome. It would be assigned a value of 90 (Figure 6.3). Medium demand might be assigned a value of 50. Experiencing low demand with a large plant would be undesirable (negative) and hence would be assigned a value of 20. All other outcomes would be assigned values that lie between the two extremes.

After the decision tree has been structured and the value of each action/event branch has been defined, managers have to determine the probability that each event will occur. The AMP company, for example, might assume that there is a 40% chance of having high demand, a 35% chance of having medium demand, and only a 25% chance of having very low demand. The probabilities of all events on an action branch always add up to 100%.

Finally, managers have to decide which action to recommend. This involves computing the expected value of each action branch. *Expected value* is computed by multiplying the probability of occurrence (%) and the assigned value of each event/outcome and then totaling the results. Given the probability percentages and assigned values shown in Figure 6.3, the expected value of building a large plant would be computed as follows:

$$(.40 \times 90) + (.35 \times 50) + (.25 \times 20) = 58.5$$

As Figure 6.3 shows, the expected value of building the small plant is higher. Therefore, managers should recommend that the AMP company build the small plant.

FIGURE 6.3 | Decision Tree with Probabilities and Assigned Values

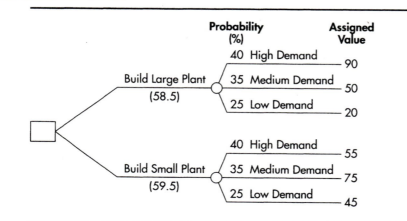

The riskiness of such a decision depends in part on the amount of information available about each possible event. If additional information can be obtained, even at additional cost, managers can come up with more accurate assigned values and probabilities of occurrence and thus arrive at a better decision. Suppose, for example, that the company had obtained additional information indicating that it should revise the probability estimates to 45% for high demand and 20% for low demand. Would the small plant still be the best alternative? It is always wise to verify a decision after gathering more information.

Because of the many variables impinging on a strategic decision and the degree of uncertainty associated with a long planning horizon, decision-tree analysis may be more valuable for defining a problem than for solving it. Decision trees are particularly useful for examining scenarios that contain many alternatives.

PRODUCT LIFE CYCLE

No strategic decision about marketing can be made without considering the phase of a product's or service's life cycle (Figure 6.4). What may be an appropriate strategy for one stage of a product's life cycle may be quite ill advised for another stage.

Most products have a life cycle of four stages: introduction, growth, maturity, and decline. The introduction stage is characterized by the creation of widespread awareness of the new product. Depending on the uniqueness of the product, the financial requirements of this phase can be extensive. In the second phase, growth, sales, and profits typically increase rapidly. As profits rise, competitors are attracted, and improved products or imitations enter the market. At this point, the product reaches maturity. Price competition intensifies, and growth in sales starts to

| FIGURE 6.4 | Characteristics of the Product Life Cycle |

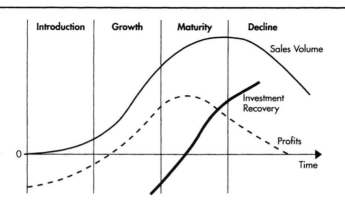

Characteristic	Introduction	Growth	Maturity	Decline
Concentration of competitors	High; few pioneers	Declining as more competition enters	Increasing after shakeout	High; few remaining harvesters
Product differentiation	Low, if any	Increasing; imitations and variations	High; increasing market segmentation	Decreasing as competitors leave market
Barriers to entry	High, if product can be protected	Decreasing; growing technology transfer	Increasing as capital intensity increases	High capital intensity, low returns
Barriers to exit	Low; little investment	Low, but increasing	High for large company	Decreasing; endgame
Price elasticity of demand	Inelastic, few customers	Increasingly elastic	Inelastic only in segments	Very elastic; bargaining power of buyers high
Ratio of fixed to variable cost	Generally low	Increasing	High	Decreasing
Economies of scale	Few, generally unimportant	Increasing capital intensity	High	High
Experience-curve effects	Large early gains	Very high; large production volume	Decreasing magnitude	Few
Vertical integration of competitors	Low	Increasing	High	High
Risk involved in business	Low	Increasing	Increasing	Declining exit barriers

decline, while profits reach their peak. In the decline phase, both sales and profits go down until the product is discontinued.

Investment in production capacity and market development takes place during the introduction and (in particular) growth phases. This investment often is not amortized until the product has entered the maturity phase. Companies can make the mistake of discontinuing products too early, before the products have fully contributed to investment recovery. The maximum contribution may well occur in the decline phase of the product life cycle.

Figure 6.5 lists several substrategies appropriate for each stage of the life cycle. In the initiation and growth phases of product life, operational controls should be relatively loose in order to facilitate expansion. At later phases, tighter control is needed to improve efficiency and reduce costs. The maturity phase represents a pivotal point in strategy formulation. During this phase, sales and market share decline rapidly. Consequently, to realize the product's potential to recover investment, operational procedures are formalized, and the responsibility for product strategy is gradually transferred from sales to finance. At the same time, new products must be introduced into the market if the company is to continue to increase its sales and income. The ability to maintain a stable growth rate depends on an "active" product policy.

Worksheet 6.1 shows sales and profit data for AMP indicating the products that are in the maturity phase of the product life cycle. As might be expected, profits have grown for the past few years and are now declining.

GROWTH VECTOR ANALYSIS

Growth vector analysis can be used to determine the position of each of the company's product lines and to identify all of the product/market options possible.

The two dimensions described are the company's product strategy and its market coverage. For companies with many different products, several product/market strategies will apply simultaneously. Different product and market strategies are shown in Figure 6.6. If, for example, a company focuses on a single product, it can build a strong distinctive competency that may enable it to dominate a particular market. AMP, for example, has concentrated on connectors and related tools and has become the leading supplier worldwide. Such a strategy can eventually, however, threaten profitability and growth as the market matures and becomes saturated. On the other hand, diversification into new and perhaps more profitable markets can be accompanied by unstable cash flows.

Worksheet 6.2 is an application of growth vector analysis to AMP. The company covers all product/market options. It has recently acquired several companies in related fields and is starting to expand its existing product range through value-adding services. The company seems well aware of the different market opportunities and takes well-planned and creative steps to exploit them.

GAP ANALYSIS

After strategic managers have isolated alternative growth strategies, they determine what the future sales potential of each alternative would be. This determination, which is based on a *gap analysis*, reveals (1) what the company can achieve, given its current performance, and (2) the sales it needs to have in 5 to 10 years, given its

FIGURE 6.5	Strategic Actions Appropriate for Different Phases of the Product Life Cycle

Product Strategy by Department	Life Cycle Phases			
	Introduction	Growth	Maturity	Decline
Marketing	Create widespread awareness; find acceptance	Concentrate on brand recognition; find niche; reduce price	Aggressively promote product, use defensive pricing	Phase out product
Production	Limit number of designs; develop standards	Add product variants; centralize production	Improve product and reduce costs	Prune product line
Finance	Plan for high net cash outflow and initial losses	Finance rapid expansion; still have net cash outflows but increasing profits	Redistribute increasing net cash inflows; declining profits	Liquidate unneeded equipment
Personnel	Staff and train new management	Add personnel in production, plan for overtime	Reduce workforce gradually; increase efficiency	Reallocate personnel
Research and development	Make engineering changes	Start developing successor product	Reduce costs; develop variants	Withdraw all R&D from product
Main focus of strategy	Engineering; market penetration	Sales; consumer loyalty	Production efficiency; successor product	Finance; maximum investment recovery

Source: Fox (1973, pp. 10–11).

FIGURE 6.6	Relative Advantage of Alternative Product/Market Strategies

Range of Product Strategies	Product Alternatives	Relative Advantages
	Present Product	Builds distinctive competence Economies of scale Clarity and unity of purpose Efficient utilization of resources
	Related Products	Broader product appeal Better use of sales force and distribution network Motivation from doing something new Flexibility to respond to changing market conditions
	New Products	Reduced competitive pressure Reduced risk of market saturation Smaller fluctuations in overall sales

Range of Market Strategies	Market Alternatives	Relative Advantages
	Present Market	Maximum market penetration Possible market leadership Expertise in specific market or market segment Market visibility
	Related Markets	Stable growth Stable cash flow requirements Increased plant utilization Extension of company's expertise and technology
	New Markets	Expansion of company's goodwill and reputation Reduced competitive pressure Diversification into more profitable markets Positive synergistic effects

WORKSHEET 6.1	Product Life Cycle

Case _____ AMP

Date _____ 1992

Name _____ John Doe

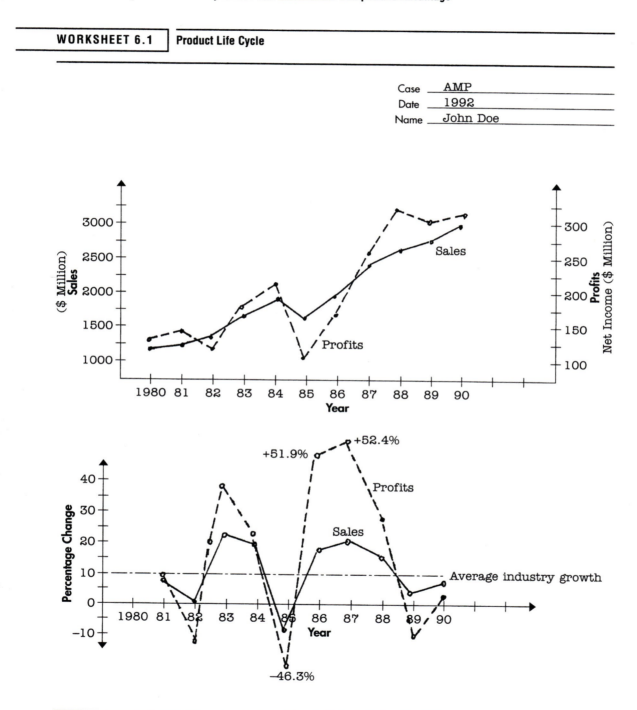

(continued)

WORKSHEET 6.1 | **Product Life Cycle (continued)**

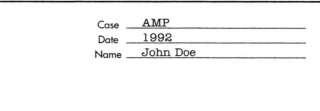

Case ___AMP___

Date ___1992___

Name ___John Doe___

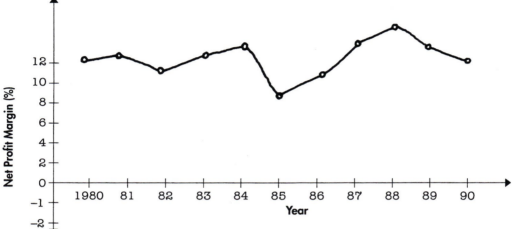

Analysis and Recommendations:

The chart of sales and profits indicates that AMP products have reached the maturity
stage of the product life cycle. Profits are very cyclical, and growth in sales is declining.
The second chart shows the strong decline in profit growth after 1987 and also indicates
that the growth in sales has fallen close to the industry average. The net profit margin
(third chart) has held very constant and solid. If these trends continue—that is, if AMP
does not adjust its strategy—the growth in sales can be expected to fall further in the
1990s. The two major strategy recommendations for this phase of the product life cycle
are to reduce the cost of the product and to look for potential successors of the current
products. Increased efficiency will result in AMP having an increase in net cash inflows,
which in turn can be used to introduce product variants. Control-oriented management
with standardized procedures should help to ensure maximum efficiency.

| WORKSHEET 6.2 | Growth Vector Analysis |

Case __AMP__
Date __1992__
Name __Mary Doe__

		Present products	Improved products	New products
Market Options	Existing market	Market penetration CONNECTORS, TERMINALS, SPLICES	Product variants; imitations PACKAGING DEVICES VALUE-ADDED ASSEMBLIES	Product line extension CIRCULAR CONNECTORS BACKPLANES
	Expanded market	Aggressive promotion COAXIAL CONNECTOR PARTS	Market segmentation, product differentiation ACES	Vertical diversification ADDITIVE PROCESS PRINTED WIRING BOARDS
	New market	Market development CABLE ASSEMBLIES	Market extension ELECTRO-OPTIC DEVICES	Conglomerate diversification FIBER OPTICS ISDN 3-D MOLDED CIRCUITS

Product Alternatives

Identify and evaluate the company's current strategic position and its strategic alternatives:

AMP is pursuing product growth based on its core competency in electronics and connectors. It has achieved carefully planned growth by considering all nine options shown in the growth vector analysis. Generally, products move from left to right (market penetration to variants or extensions) as the product life changes. This is referred to as new uses for products. This shift is done for each of the three market options shown on the left axis of the matrix.

growth strategy (Figure 6.7). To forecast the sales increases likely to result from implementation of alternative growth strategies, managers estimate the following three measures of market structure (Weber, 1977):

1. Industry market potential (IMP)
2. Relevant industry sales (RIS)
3. Real market share (RMS)

To estimate IMP, managers assume that (1) everyone who can reasonably be expected to use this product will do so, (2) the product is used as often as possible, and (3) whenever this is the case, the product is used to its fullest extent. Given these three assumptions, IMP represents the maximum unit sales possible for a particular product. The difference between this maximum and current sales represents growth opportunities for the company.

Relevant industry sales (RIS) equal the firm's current sales plus competitive gaps, while real market share (RMS) equals current sales divided by RIS (Figure 6.7).

Weber described how these four components contribute to a gap between a company's sales potential and its actual performance:

1. *Product-line gap.* Closing this gap entails completing a product line, either in width or in depth, by introducing improved or new products. AMP attempted to close a product-line gap by producing cassette-player–radio systems for cars.
2. *Distribution gap.* This gap can be reduced by expanding distribution with respect to coverage, intensity, and exposure.

| FIGURE 6.7 | Gap Analysis |

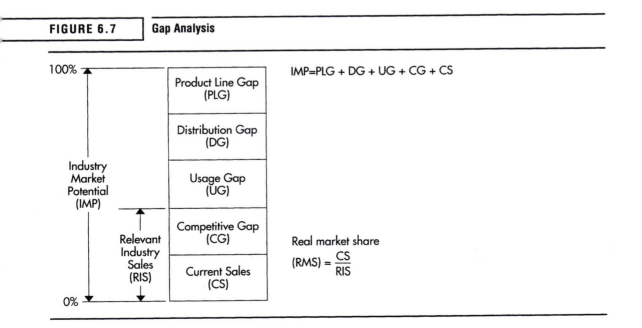

3. *Usage gap*. To close the usage gap, a firm must induce current nonusers to try the product and encourage current users to increase their usage.
4. *Competitive gap*. This gap can be closed by taking market share from direct competitors and those who sell substitute products.

Projected future sales or profit gaps can be closed by increasing the firm's total IMP, by increasing RIS while maintaining current RMS, or by improving RMS (Figure 6.8).

TECHNOLOGY ASSESSMENT

Technology often drives strategic planning. New products, new markets, new production processes, and new distribution systems usually originate from technological advances, which affect both productivity and profitability. Strategic managers have to monitor technological developments and manage their adoption by the company.

Different levels of technology have to be distinguished and managed appropriately (see Figure 6.9) and for this purpose the *technology pyramid* is useful. At the bottom of this pyramid are the *core technologies* of a company. These can be used in different product applications, and their development and protection are fundamental to the company's capability base. For example, optical technology is a core technology that is used in many of Canon's products from cameras to copy machines. Canon has unique and proprietary know-how in some of this technology, which enables it to offer products that often result in superior performance. A core technology for General Motors is its engine combustion technology, including electronics. This is why GM some years ago acquired Hughes and why it has recently taken a license on a new, revolutionary two-stroke engine in development. Production of computer chips is a core technology required for many applications.

FIGURE 6.8	Performance Gaps

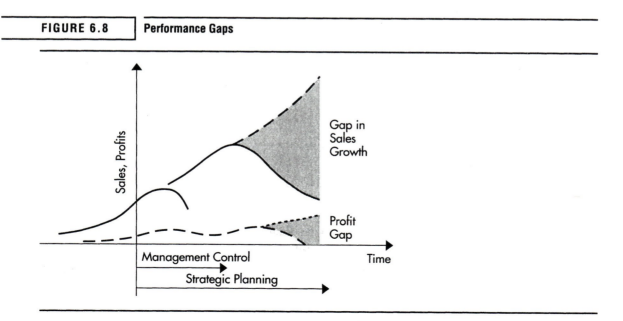

FIGURE 6.9	Technology Pyramid

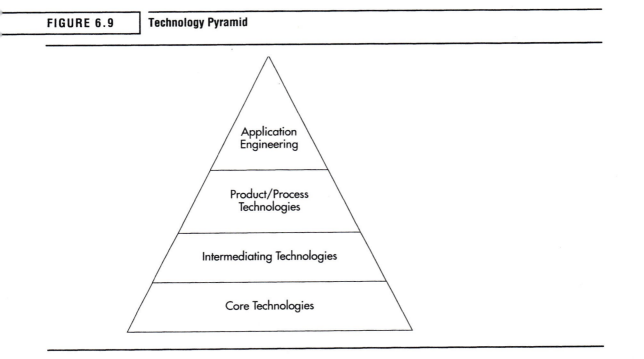

Not surprisingly, Japanese, North American, and European companies and consortiums are engaged in a fierce and expensive technology race.

The last example also shows that the maintenance and protection of core technologies today are often beyond the means of one company alone. Therefore, strategic managers must fully understand the significance and the financial requirements of different technologies, and they must often make tough choices about which technologies can and should be supported and which should not. Interestingly enough, Japanese companies often seem to be more focused on fewer core technologies than Western companies, and they spend more on these individual technologies. Instead, they rely more on partnerships and alliances where companies focus on developing different individual technologies but share the benefits in different final products. Western companies have a tendency to try to be competitive on many different technologies. As a result, they frequently either underspend on key development or are late with the newest generation.

Intermediating technologies are needed to arrive at complete final-product configurations. Canon, for example, needed technologies for making and cutting glass to maximize the impact of its core optical technology. In the case of combustion engines, there has been a growing trend toward four-valve technology, which makes for a cleaner burn and lower fuel consumption. To make this possible, new developments in metals and compounds, forging technology, and automotive electronics were needed. The strategic manager must be able to define

1. The "technology road map" that can deliver a core technology being developed. This entails understanding which intermediating technologies are needed and when they have to be available.
2. The necessary criteria for making the correct make-or-buy decision on these technologies. This requires an understanding of
   a. Whether to retain the technology know-how in-house or to rely on suppliers having the know-how.
   b. The potential for success of this technology.
   c. The cost associated with developing and marketing this technology.

The following technology check can be useful in doing the evaluation (see Figure 6.10). On one axis there is the success potential of technologies, which can be based on different inputs, such as market studies, growth estimates, or subjective evaluations. On the other axis is an evaluation of the company's own relative capability for this technology.

An interesting starting point is to take all ongoing R&D projects in a company and put them into this matrix. The circles shown in Figure 6.10 make up a portfolio that is not unlike those of many Western companies. The size of the circle indicates the relative numbers of dollars spent on projects A through K.

Concerning project A, for example, there is another company with a clear technology and time advantage. Rather than spending money on this R&D effort, management should ask whether it may be possible to outsource this technology or perhaps to acquire the other company, if necessary—similarly with projects G through K. They tie up valuable resources with questionable benefit. These resources could be redirected to give a much stronger push to projects B and C, which are vital to the company's future. Projects D, E, and F have a low success potential even though the company has a high technological capability in these areas. The recommendation is simply to maintain that capability and minimize the expenditure of resources for those projects.

Surprisingly enough, few companies do this technology check in a methodical and consistent fashion. Projects continue to be funded even though situations have changed. And yet, it is often this planned and deliberate technology portfolio choice that makes the difference between being first with new technologies and a follower.

Product and process technologies are what is delivered to the customer. A car, for example, consists of many different technologies. It is the combination of technologies and the focus on specific features that determines the cost/price relationship and differentiates the product. The link between these features and the perceived customer value is discussed in Appendix A, on product/market mapping. One important point to keep in mind is that the timing of core technologies and new products should typically *not* be linked. Companies often make the mistake of linking the success of a new product to the development of a completely new technology. The result often is a costly delay. Connor Peripherals, the maker of computer hard-disk drives, applies a different strategy. Every year this company redesigns about one-third of its product, incorporating the latest technologies available at this stage. Thus it can offer a newly designed product every year, and every third year it has come up with a new generation of drives. This has allowed the company to outpace its competitors both in terms of technology and in terms of sales and profit growth.

FIGURE 6.10 | **Technology Check**

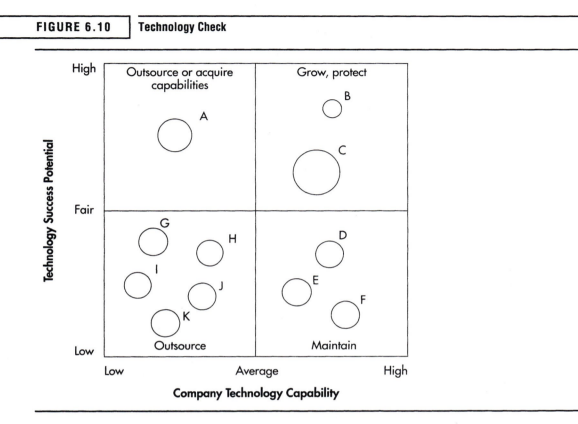

Finally, at the top of the technology pyramid is *application engineering*, which again should be clearly separated from product design. In today's world of "multiple choice," it is important to come up with customer-specific or segment-specific product variants, but it is also important to check the cost associated with this policy throughout the company, not just in the engineering department. Therefore, it is often wise to place application engineers closer to manufacturing and purchasing, rather than mixing them with R&D. Doing so limits costly product proliferation. It also involves suppliers as partners in the design process, thus speeding up design, reducing cost in the overall process, and enabling both to reap the benefits. Technological know-how and training within the company can be maintained through job rotation among the different technology and application areas.

When technology is used for competitive advantage, a low-cost strategy, used alone, is generally ineffective for achieving market dominance or rapid growth. This appears to contradict traditional arguments that favor economies of scale and first-mover advantages. Intel, for example, which moved into the 8-bit microprocessor field first, failed to maintain a dominant position despite economies of scale and first-mover status. Rather, it achieved market-share leadership by concentrating on customers' needs and on the actions required to sustain competitive advantage by providing superior customer service.

Does industry have to stay abreast of the very latest technology, or is familiarity with current technology sufficient to stay competitive? The answer depends on what competitors are doing, on what consumers demand, and on the ratio of the cost of switching technologies to the profit generated by the change. In many instances, new technologies become the driving force that creates demand. For example, 3-D printing could revolutionize product design and manufacturing (Allman, 1992). As another example, Sony engineers turn out an astounding average of four new products every day (Schlender, 1992). How does Sony do it? It hires generalists and turns them loose to work on advanced products. Its 9,000 engineers and scientists (out of 112,900 employees) work long hours to produce the advances that keep Sony out front. It spends $1.5 billion, about 5.7% of its revenues, on this effort. Closer to home, U.S. Surgical relies on its customers for new ideas that it can turn into products. Its salespeople visit operating rooms and doctors' offices to determine what is needed. In 1967 it was the first to bring out a "user-friendly" surgical stapler that revolutionized the closing of wounds. The result was a hundredfold increase in the company's stock value from 1987 through 1992.

To help maintain a competitive edge, the United States must have a viable technology policy. What is required in an era of global competitors is a policy that stimulates new ideas and products and that is flexible enough to meet urgent requirements. Sematech is one attempt at a collaborative approach in the electronics industry, but the United States may have to spend a significant amount to develop an infrastructure that emphasizes the ability to respond to competitors' advances and that can leapfrog their technology (Branscomb, 1992). Lewis Branscomb commented, "Whether it's tax cuts, collaboration, or hands off, U.S. technology policy needs a new twist." In today's global economy, he argues, what matters is not creating new technology but absorbing and applying innovations quickly. Instead of concentrating on the "supply" of new technologies, the U.S. government should stimulate "demand" for innovative ideas by encouraging collaborative research, investing in technological infrastructure, emphasizing the importance of precompetitive research, and helping companies improve their capacity to adapt innovations to specific business needs. Branscomb concludes that what we need is a "capability-enhancing technology policy." His proposal is to have the government support "generic technologies" that foster innovation across our industrial base. An example is congressional funding to upgrade a collection of over 2,000 computer networks that link university and research labs around the country and around the world.

PIMS ANALYSIS

In addition to a technology assessment, a company needs a means to assess the profit potential of its marketing strategy. The PIMS analysis provides a tool to make this type of assessment.

The *profit impact of market strategy* (PIMS) project was organized in early 1972 by the Marketing Science Institute at the Harvard Business School. A large database containing information on more than six hundred businesses was established and used to develop different PIMS profit models (Schoeffler, Buzzell, and Heany, 1974). These models were designed to answer the following questions:

- What factors influence profitability in a business, and how much influence does each one have?
- How does return on investment (ROI) change in response to changes in strategy and in market conditions?

The independent variables in the model were grouped under the following four major headings:

1. Competitive position of the business (relative market share, product quality, price, promotion, new-product development)
2. The business environment (growth in industry, rate of inflation, customers, replacement cycle)
3. Structure of the production process (capital intensity, degree of vertical integration, productivity)
4. Discretionary budget allocations (R&D budgets, marketing budgets).

The major findings of the study are summarized here.

- *Market share and relative market share.* Market share and relative market share (the company's market share divided by the combined shares of its three largest competitors) are strongly related to return on investment (ROI). Businesses with relatively large market shares tend to have above-average profits. The major determinants for the link between market share and profitability appear to be economies of scale, the effects of experience or learning, market power, and quality of management.
- *Product quality.* Leadership in a market appears to be based on unique competitive strategies and higher-quality products. This enables market leaders to sell at higher prices than businesses with smaller market shares.
- *Market growth.* Not surprisingly, market growth is positively correlated with ROI.
- *Vertical integration.* The degree of vertical integration of a business appears to have a positive effect on ROI later in the product life cycle. Early in the product life cycle, before experience and learning have reduced costs, the successful competitor concentrates on reducing manufacturing costs through gains in productivity. As the cost-reducing effects of experience take hold, ROI can be improved further by exploiting opportunities in the supply–production–distribution chain.
- *New-product activity, R&D sales ratio, and marketing sales ratio.* New-product activity and above-average ratios of R&D and marketing expenditures to sales play an increasing role in determining profitability in the later stages of the product life cycle. Businesses with weak market positions, however, may prefer

to seek new products without investing in R&D, simply by imitating successful products in the market. Furthermore, as market share increases, marketing expenditures may tend to become more effective; that is, marketing costs decline as a percentage of sales but without any noticeable decline in sales.

- *Investment intensity.* The higher the ratio of investment to sales (investment intensity), the lower the ROI tends to be. Businesses with high investments relative to sales are obviously not able to achieve sufficient profit margins. Investment in R&D tends to depress earnings sharply. High labor productivity appears to be vital to profitability when investment intensity is high.
- *Inventory levels.* High inventory levels damage profitability, particularly in businesses with few fixed assets.
- *Capacity utilization.* Adequate capacity utilization is very important for weaker businesses and for businesses with high capital intensity.

To perform a PIMS analysis, the strategic manager can use a checklist of variables, such as the one for AMP shown in Figure 6.11. After rating each variable in the checklist, the manager consults results of the PIMS study to determine which strategy will have the best chance of success.

COMPETITIVE PORTFOLIO ANALYSIS

Competitive portfolio analysis, which was developed by the Boston Consulting Group (BCG), is based on the close relationship between market share and cash generation. What distinguishes competitive portfolio analysis from PIMS is its focus on the specific role of each product in the overall strategy of the firm.

FIGURE 6.11 | **PIMS-based Evaluation of AMP's Professional Amplifiers**

Checklist		Ratings	
1. Market share	Low ____	Medium ____	High __✓__
2. Relative market share	Low ____	Medium ____	High __✓__
3. Product quality	Low ____	Medium ____	High __✓__
4. Market growth	Low ____	Medium __✓__	High ____
5. Vertical integration	Low __✓__	Medium ____	High ____
6. New-product activity	Low ____	Medium __✓__	High ____
7. R&D/sales ratio	Low ____	Medium ____	High __✓__
8. Marketing/sales ratio	Low ____	Medium ____	High __✓__
9. Productivity	Low ____	Medium ____	High __✓__
10. Capacity utilization	Low ____	Medium __✓__	High ____
11. Investment/sales ratio	Low ____	Medium __✓__	High ____
12. Inventory level	Low ____	Medium __✓__	High ____

Based on its cash flow characteristics and relative market share, each product can be positioned in a *product portfolio matrix* like the one in Figure 6.12. In the terminology used by the BCG, high-growth and high-market-share products are classified as "stars." These products usually have the highest profit margins, but they are also likely to require net cash outflows in order to maintain their market share. Eventually, stars become "cash cows" as growth slows and investment needs diminish in the maturity stage of the product life cycle.

"Question marks" are products with high growth potential but low market shares. They require large net cash outflows if market share is to be maintained or increased. If successful, these products become new stars, which will, in turn, become the cash cows of the future. If unsuccessful, they become "dogs," which are products with low market share and slow growth. Dogs generally remain in the product portfolio as long as they contribute some positive cash flow.

Each category represents a different stage in the product life cycle. Products start as question marks in the introductory phase, become stars as growth accelerates, develop into cash cows during the maturity phase, and finally become dogs as growth declines.

| **FIGURE 6.12** | **Product Portfolio Matrix** |

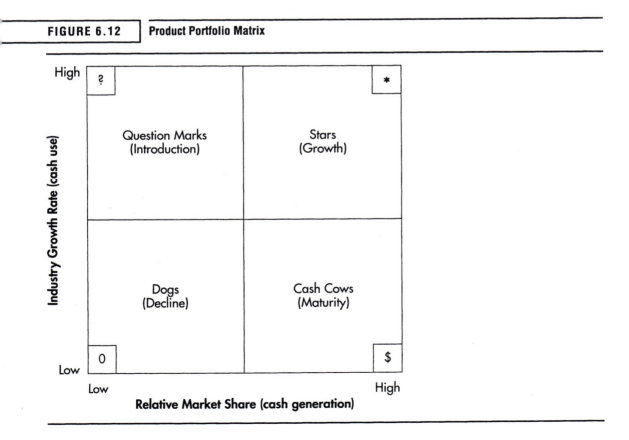

The product portfolio analysis can be used to allocate resources among products and to maximize long-run profits. The fundamental idea is to distribute cash generated by the cash cows to other products that will ensure future growth and profitability for the company. A financially balanced product portfolio contains products in each of the four categories. The different products also can be represented by different-sized circles that reflect their relative share of the company's sales. In this representation, a single, large cash cow might be balanced by several small stars and perhaps a few question marks and dogs.

Displaying each of a firm's products in a single matrix, such as the one in Figure 6.13, can help strategic managers to determine the products' competitive standing. To formulate an effective product/market strategy, it may also be necessary to develop product portfolio matrices for major competitors. Comparing the company's product portfolio with those of major competitors enables managers to avoid pitfalls. Attempting to increase a product's market share in a low-growth segment, for example, is very risky if the firm does not have a leadership position either in market share or in product strength.

Strategic managers can also use the product portfolio matrix to track the product life cycle through the four quadrants and adjust strategies as products move from one quadrant to another. As can be seen in Figure 6.13 successful product/market strategies bypass the decline/dog quadrant entirely. Products are eliminated from the portfolio or sold off when they evolve into this quadrant and cease to generate cash flow. Losses occur if a new product declines without passing through the growth/star and maturity/cash cow categories. The situation worsens if cash flow is directed from the growth/star quadrant to others. This sequence of

| **FIGURE 6.13** | **Normal Sequence of Product Strategies** |

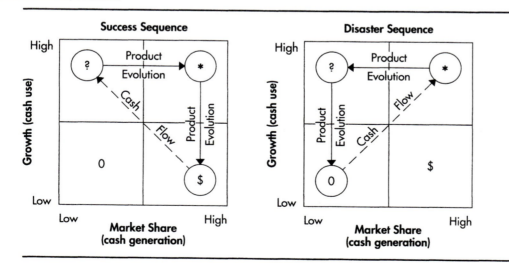

events, in which products do not evolve through the growth stage, keeps them from becoming cash cows. The result is seriously reduced profitability.

To develop a successful product/market strategy for each product, managers must first calculate its present market share relative to that of major competing products. The Boston Consulting Group has suggested that the market share of each product be compared to that of its single main competitor. Any product that has a relative market share greater than 1—that is, a product whose market share equals or exceeds that of its main competitor—is placed in the star/growth or maturity/cash cow category, depending on the market growth rate.

The BCG portfolio approach is used to evaluate products on the basis of their life-cycle phase and to ensure that products are optimally distributed among the four quadrants. If the product portfolio is unbalanced, the flow of products from question marks to stars to cash cows will cause cash flow difficulties. The portfolio analysis can also be used to evaluate business units within the organization. Like mature products, mature divisions can be spun off and new ones started to maintain a balance among the business units.

Strategic managers also use competitive portfolio analysis to establish product-development guidelines and targets, which are then finalized by top management. For example, management may set the cutoff point between low and high growth at 10% annually. Products exceeding this level receive funds for growth; other products are funded at a lower rate. The portfolio matrix for AMP is shown in Worksheet 6.3. The size of the circles is proportional to the sales volume for each product.

STRATEGIC POSITION AND ACTION EVALUATION (SPACE)

Strategic position and action evaluation (SPACE) is used to determine the appropriate strategic posture for a firm and each of its individual businesses. It is an extension of the two-dimensional portfolio methods, such as the BCG product portfolio.

Other methods include McKinsey's industry attractiveness/company strength matrix (Figure 6.14), General Electric's stoplight strategy, and the directional policy matrix (DPM) developed by the Shell Group (Figure 6.15). In each of these methods, one of the axes of the matrix measures the overall attractiveness of the industry in which the company operates, and the other axis represents the company's ability to compete in its market(s). The DPM, which uses market potential and company capability as its two dimensions, is perhaps more specific with respect to strategic implications.

The SPACE approach is an attempt to overcome some of the limitations inherent in the other methods. SPACE adds two key dimensions to the matrix (Figure 6.16). In a sense, the SPACE diagram can be viewed as a summary display of the findings of the PIMS study, because each dimension is viewed as a composite of several factors, which are evaluated separately. By including a large number of factors, the manager can examine a particular strategic alternative from several perspectives and will, therefore, be in a better position to select an appropriate strategy.

Financial strength and competitive advantage are the two major determinants of a company's strategic position, whereas industry strength and environmental stability characterize the strategic position of the entire industry. In the SPACE chart, these factors are rated on a scale of +6 to −6.

WORKSHEET 6.3	Product Portfolio Analysis

Case   AMP

Date   1992

Name   John Doe

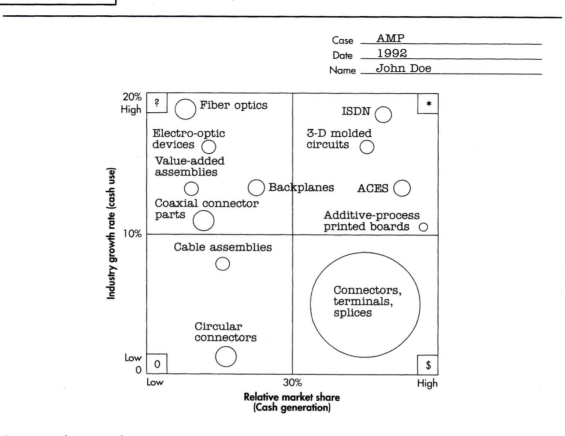

Comments and Recommendations:

AMP has started balancing its main business, connectors, which is becoming mature, by adding a range of new products and businesses. In some of these fields, such as ISDN connectors and 3-D molded circuits, AMP is an early technology leader. Fiber optics has high growth but is dominated by other companies already. AMP has to carefully define its niche, or area of specialization, if fiber optics is to avoid high cash outflows. Circular connectors, mainly for military applications, were added to round out the portfolio but have little growth potential. They should be managed for cash flow only.

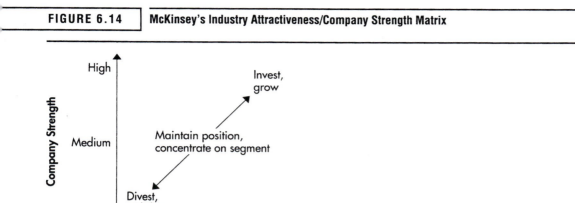

FIGURE 6.14 | McKinsey's Industry Attractiveness/Company Strength Matrix

FIGURE 6.15 | Directional Policy Matrix (DPM)

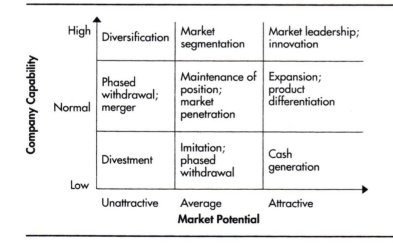

A company's financial strength is important when there are adverse economic conditions, such as rapid inflation or high interest rates. Equipped with a "cushion" to ease the pinch of difficult times, the financially strong company is in an excellent position to diversity into more attractive industries or to finance aggressive moves in its current industry at the expense of weaker competitors.

A company that enjoys advantages over its competitors in terms of market share, cost, or technology is usually able to maintain a higher profit margin as well.

FIGURE 6.16 | **SPACE Chart**

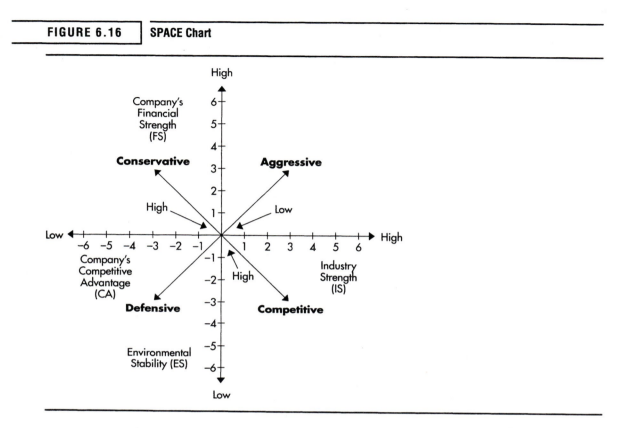

This competitive advantage can become critical in a declining market, where the marginally profitable firm finds it difficult to survive.

In an expanding market, an industry's financial and operating strength helps to maintain or increase the market's momentum, and even the marginal competitor can find a niche in such a situation. As the market's growth slows, however, the competitive climate in an industry deteriorates, and a firm finds it necessary to protect its competitive position. Therefore, industry strength can offset a company's competitive position.

Similarly, environmental stability can mitigate a firm's lack of financial strength. On the other hand, if a firm in a turbulent environment does not have a sound financial position, it finds survival very difficult.

For each strategic thrust in the SPACE chart, a number of factors are used. The strategic position and action evaluation (SPACE) includes the four input variables environmental stability, industry strength, competitive advantage, and financial strength to arrive at an aggressive, competitive, conservative, or defensive strategic posture for the firm. These postures in turn can be translated into generic competitive strategies, thus helping the manager define the appropriate strategic thrust for a business: overall cost leadership, differentiation, focus, or defensiveness.

1. Factors determining environmental stability (ES)
   Technological changes
   Rate of inflation
   Demand variability
   Price range of competing products
   Barriers to entry into market
   Competitive pressure/rivalry
   Price elasticity of demand
   Pressure from substitutes
2. Factors determining industry strength (IS)
   Growth potential
   Profit potential
   Financial stability
   Technological know-how
   Resource utilization
   Capital intensity
   Ease of entry into market
   Productivity; capacity utilization
   Manufacturers' bargaining power
3. Factors determining competitive advantage (CA)
   Market share
   Product quality
   Product life cycle
   Product replacement cycle
   Customer loyalty
   Competition's capacity utilization
   Technological know-how
   Vertical integration
   Speed of new-product introductions
4. Factors determining financial strength (FS)
   Return on investment
   Leverage
   Liquidity
   Capital required versus capital available
   Cash flow
   Ease of exit from market
   Risk involved in business
   Inventory turnover
   Use of economies of scale and experience

To apply this approach, a manager assigns appropriate numerical values to each of the factors. The averages determined for each group of factors are then plotted in the SPACE chart (Figure 6.16). By connecting the average values plotted on each axis, the manager obtains a four-sided polygon displaying the weight and direction of the particular assessment. It is important to recognize that the SPACE chart is a summary display and that each factor should also be analyzed individually. In particular, factors with very high or very low scores should receive special attention.

Another way of determining relative strategic position is to add the two scores on the axes opposite each other to obtain a directional vector that points to a specific location in the chart.

The basic strategic postures associated with the SPACE technique are illustrated and described in the following paragraphs and diagrams.

1. *Aggressive posture.* This posture is typical in an attractive industry with little environmental turbulence. The company enjoys a definite competitive advantage, which it can protect with financial strength. The critical factor is entry of new competition. Firms in this situation should take full advantage of opportunities, look for acquisition candidates in their own or related industries, increase market share, and concentrate resources on products that have a definite competitive edge.

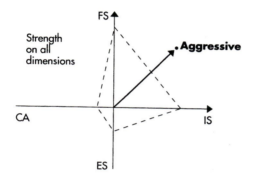

2. *Competitive posture.* This posture is typical in an attractive industry. The company enjoys a competitive advantage in a relatively unstable environment.

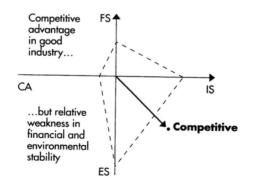

The critical factor is financial strength.Firms in this situation should acquire financial resources to increase marketing thrust, add to the sales force, extend or improve the product line, invest in productivity, reduce costs, protect competitive advantage in a declining market, and attempt to merge with a cash-rich company.

3. *Conservative posture.* This posture is typical in a stable market with low growth. Here the company focuses on financial stability. The critical factor is product competitiveness. Firms in this situation should prune the product line, reduce costs, focus on improving cash flow, protect competitive products,

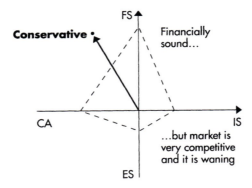

develop new products, and gain entry into more attractive markets.

4. *Defensive posture*. This posture is typical of an unattractive industry in which the company lacks a competitive product and financial strength. The critical factor is competitiveness. Firms in this situation should prepare to retreat from the market, discontinue marginally profitable products, reduce costs aggressively, cut capacity, and defer or minimize investments.

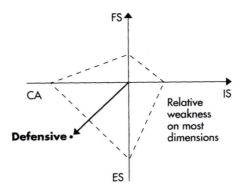

The four strategic thrusts identified by the SPACE method are very similar to the four strategic postures Miles and Snow (1978) discovered as a result of a historical analysis of hospitals and the textbook publishing, electronics, and food processing industries. In their study, they found the aggressive strategy to be the strategy of *prospectors*, who seek new product/market segments and employ broad planning approaches, decentralized controls, and extensive environmental scanning. Prospectors usually have some underutilized resources.

The defensive strategy is the strategy of *defenders*, who focus on a narrow product/market domain and guard it. Concentration, centralized control, and limited environmental scanning characterize this strategy. Defenders may, however, be rather cost-efficient; their products may be cash cows.

The conservative strategy is the strategy of *analyzers*. Endowed with financial strength but lacking a competitive advantage or industry potential, the company can pursue strategy that is based on careful analysis of the product/market opportunities and conservative development of them.

The competitive strategy is the strategy of *reactors*, who realize that the environment is unstable but the industry is strong. Unfortunately, they have neither the financial strength nor the competitive advantage to prosper in the face of environmental turbulence. This posture is generally an unstable strategic posture and frequently leads to failure.

Using Worksheets 6.4A, 6.4B, and 6.5 for AMP, we can determine which strategic alternative best fits under the conditions that the company faced in 1992. The diagram in Worksheet 6.5 shows that AMP should pursue an aggressive strategy because of its overall strong position.

SUPER SPACE

In order to enhance the use of SPACE, we have added two items: the relative importance of each factor (R) and the chance of sustaining the importance level of the factor (C). Multiplying these two items, we obtain a combined effect (E). The range of total value for E is approximately 0 to 50.

Total E Value	Expectancy
0–10	low
10–20	low/moderate
20–30	moderate
30–40	moderate/high
40–50	high
above	very high

The total E values indicate that the likelihood of maintaining a given factor is as shown above, whereas a basic SPACE analysis assumes they will continue at the current level in the future. Using Super SPACE yields the following results for AMP:

	Current	Sustainable
Company's financial strength	high	moderate
Competitive advantage	very high	moderate/high
Environmental stability	high	moderate
Industry strength	moderate	moderate/high

The advantage of Super SPACE is that it adds intelligence to the basic SPACE analysis. Thus strategic managers can assess their current position and determine whether additional effort must be invested in any of the factors in order to maintain the company's current competitive position in the future.

| WORKSHEET 6.4A | Strategic Position and Action Evaluation (SPACE) |

			Relative importance of factor	Chance of sustaining	Combined effect
Factors determining competitive advantage:			R	C	E
Market share	Small	0 1 2 3 4 5 ⑥ Large	3	.7	2.1
Product quality	Inferior	0 1 2 3 4 5 ⑥ Superior	8	.7	5.6
Product life cycle	Late	0 1 2 ③ 4 5 6 Early	5	.5	2.5
Product replacement cycle	Variable	0 1 2 3 ④ 5 6 Fixed	3	.3	.9
Customer loyalty	Low	0 1 2 3 4 ⑤ 6 High	7	.7	4.9
Competition's capacity utilization	Low	0 1 ② 3 4 5 6 High	5	.4	2.0
Technological know-how	Low	0 1 2 3 4 ⑤ 6 High	7	.8	5.6
Vertical integration	Low	0 1 2 ③ 4 5 6 High	3	.4	1.2
Other: Speed of new product introductions	Slow	0 1 2 3 ④ 5 6 Fast	8	.6	4.8

Average − 6 = −1.8   29.6

Critical factors:

AMP is benefiting substantially from its high market share and superior product quality.

Comments:

The company still enjoys strong competitive advantage because of quality and customer

loyalty. This advantage can be expected to diminish, however, because of improving

performance of competitive products and potential price aggressiveness of competitors

with low capacity.

Factors determining financial strength:			R	C	E
Return on investment	Low	0 1 2 3 4 ⑤ 6 High	5	.5	2.5
Leverage	Imbalanced	0 1 2 3 4 5 ⑥ Balanced	4	.6	2.4
Liquidity	Imbalanced	0 1 2 3 4 ⑤ 6 Solid	6	.4	2.4
Capital required versus capital available	High	0 1 2 3 4 ⑤ 6 Low	7	.3	2.1
Cash flow	Low	0 1 2 3 4 5 ⑥ High	9	.5	4.5
Ease of exit from market	Difficult	0 1 ② 3 4 5 6 Easy	5	.7	3.5
Risk involved in business	Much	0 1 2 3 4 ⑤ 6 Little	3	.6	1.8
Inventory turnover	Slow	0 1 2 3 ④ 5 6 Fast	4	.4	1.6
Economies of scale and experience	Low	0 1 2 3 4 ⑤ 6 High	7	.6	4.2

Average   4.8   25.0

Critical factors:

Excellent financials, but some risk diversification may be warranted.

Comments:

Financial position very strong.

WORKSHEET 6.4B | **Strategic Position and Action Evaluation (SPACE)**

Factors determining environmental stability:

				R	C	E
Technological changes	Many	0 1 2 3 ④ 5 6	Few	6	.6	3.6
Rate of inflation	High	0 1 2 3 4 ⑤ 6	Low	4	.3	1.2
Demand variability	Large	0 1 2 3 ④ 5 6	Small	7	.4	2.8
Price range of competing products	Wide	0 1 2 ③ 4 5 6	Narrow	3	.4	1.2
Barriers to entry into market	Few	0 1 2 ③ 4 5 6	Many	8	.3	2.4
Competitive pressure/rivalry	High	0 ① 2 3 4 5 6	Low	7	.6	4.2
Price elasticity of demand	Elastic	0 1 2 3 ④ 5 6	Inelastic	5	.3	1.5
Pressure from substitute products	High	0 1 2 3 4 ⑤ 6	Low	8	.8	6.4

Average − 6 = ___−2.4___

22.3

Critical factors:

Fairly stable environment; strong competition.

Comments:

Necessary to observe competitors and potential new entrants carefully.

Factors determining industry strength:

				R	C	E
Growth potential	Low	0 1 2 3 ④ 5 6	High	5	.5	2.5
Profit potential	Low	0 1 2 3 4 ⑤ 6	High	8	.6	4.8
Financial stability	Low	0 1 2 3 ④ 5 6	High	4	.6	2.4
Technological know-how	Simple	0 1 2 3 4 ⑤ 6	Complex	7	.8	5.6
Resource utilization	Inefficient	0 1 2 3 ④ 5 6	Efficient	5	.5	2.5
Capital intensity	Low	0 1 2 ③ 4 5 6	High	7	.4	2.8
Ease of entry into market	Easy	0 1 2 3 ④ 5 6	Difficult	5	.5	2.5
Productivity, capacity utilization	Low	0 1 2 ③ 4 5 6	High	6	.4	2.4
Other: Manufacturers' bargaining power	Low	0 1 ② 3 4 5 6	High	6	.5	3.0

Average ___3.8___

29.5

Critical factors:

Good growth and profit potential; strong rivalry has led to lower capacity utilization.

Comments:

Very attractive industry, but bargaining power both relative to buyers and suppliers is
low due to intense competitive rivalry.

WORKSHEET 6.5	Strategic Position and Action Evaluation (SPACE)

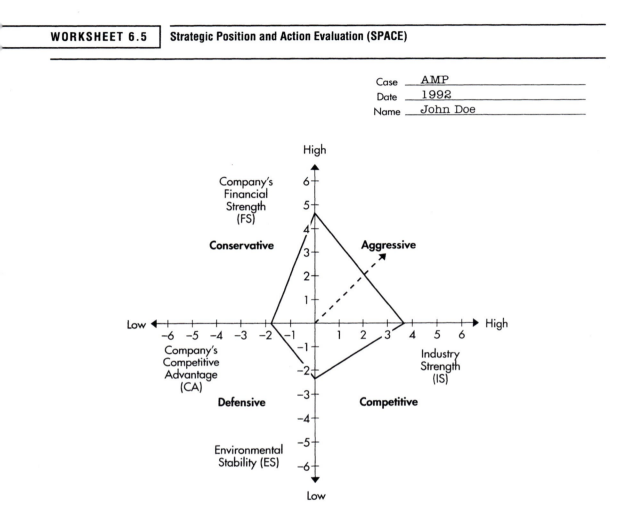

Case ___AMP___

Date ___1992___

Name ___John Doe___

Analysis and Recommendations:

AMP is generally in a very strong competitive position, which makes it possible to take a

fairly aggressive posture. Factors to watch out for are the potential future decline in

competitors' capacity utilization, which could trigger a price war. AMP has also begun

diversifying to reduce risk.

GENERIC COMPETITIVE STRATEGIES FOR STRATEGIC BUSINESS UNITS

Many companies plan their strategies on the basis of strategic business units (SBUs). The SBU is an organizational concept defined by the products offered to a market segment or strategic segment. It is used to determine the strategic action to be taken by the company in that segment and to evaluate the results. Some companies have only one SBU, in which case the SBU strategy is the same as that for the company as a whole. Others, such as General Electric, have many different SBUs. In this case the overall corporate strategy is related to the strategies of all the SBUs. Several authors have developed generalized concepts that can be used to describe the strategies being followed by SBUs or by a company as a whole. One of the most significant approaches to SBUs is Michael Porter's (1980).

Michael Porter has suggested three *generic competitive strategies* for dealing with the forces within an industry. A generic strategy is one that, when pursued, leads to a competitive advantage for the firm. The choice of generic strategies depends on the industry, the competitor analysis, and the capabilities of the firm. According to Porter, the company can base its strategy on

- Supplying its product or service more cost-effectively than competitors (overall cost leadership)
- Adding value to its product or service through differentiation (product differentiation)
- Narrowing its focus to a special product/market segment that it can monopolize (focus)

Successful implementation of these strategies typically results in the profit and market-share positions shown schematically in Figure 6.17. This figure also shows a fourth position that describes the condition in which many firms find themselves—stuck in the middle. This fourth position is not considered a generic strategy because it is a defensive position rather than one that leads to a competitive advantage.

1. *Overall cost leadership.* This strategy is based on the experience-curve concept: construction of large-scale facilities, tight control of production costs and overhead, vigorous pursuit of cost reductions associated with learning effects, and utilization of economies of scale for discretionary expenses such as R&D, promotion, and advertising. At a minimum, the prerequisites for successful execution of a cost-leadership strategy are access to sufficient financial resources, adequate process engineering skills, intense supervision of labor, and low-cost distribution capability.

2. *Product differentiation.* A product-differentiation strategy is intended to add value to a product or service and, accordingly, allows an increase in its price. To pursue such a strategy successfully, a company must be able to demonstrate the uniqueness of its product and justify the higher price. In general, this strategy requires strong marketing skills, superior product engineering and quality, and close coordination of the R&D, production, distribution, service, and marketing functions.

3. *Focus.* The first two generic strategies are aimed at an industry-wide market and, if successful, will result in above-average profits (Figure 6.17). To avoid getting caught in the middle, a company can isolate particular buyer groups,

---

| **FIGURE 6.17** | **Porter Curve: Profitability versus Market Share of the Four Generic Competitive Strategies** |

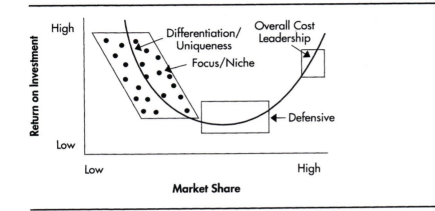

---

product lines, or geographic markets. By serving a narrower market segment, the firm can develop specific skills and reduce pressure from its industry-wide competitors. Firms that follow a focus strategy try, by definition, to monopolize a niche in the marketplace that may fall anywhere within the area on the left side of the Porter curve (see the area filled with dots in Figure 6.17). Their main competitive threat comes from other firms that are seeking the same focus.

The choice of generic strategy should be based on the firm's strengths and weaknesses vis-à-vis its competitors and on the number of strategic options available besides minimizing costs. Rarely is a firm as a whole suited for a combination of all three generic strategies. Figure 6.18 can be used as a guideline for selecting one of the three generic strategies based on the strengths and options of the strategic business unit (SBU). Each business unit can have its own generic strategy. For example, the light bulb division of GE would be considered cost-competitive, whereas the steam turbine division would more nearly fit the focus strategy.

Although not widely recognized as such, competition itself is a commonly used generic strategy. Aggressive competition is used to gain market share or high return on investment, and it always challenges the market position of established firms. Companies that engage in highly competitive marketing tactics may be new, in transition following restructuring, or in mature industries. They are constantly attempting to move into a cost-leadership position or a market niche. Competitive strategies typically involve fierce market-share battles, price wars, or other means of gaining customers from competitors. These actions are difficult to sustain and are not always successful, as the high failure rate of startup companies shows. In general, the competitive strategy is a defensive one that companies try to avoid because it seldom provides a sustainable competitive advantage. Furthermore, highly competitive moves invite retaliation and lead to price wars and other defensive measures. Restructuring has increasingly been used as a means of moving from a highly defensive position to a more competitive one.

| FIGURE 6.18 | Choice of Generic Strategy |

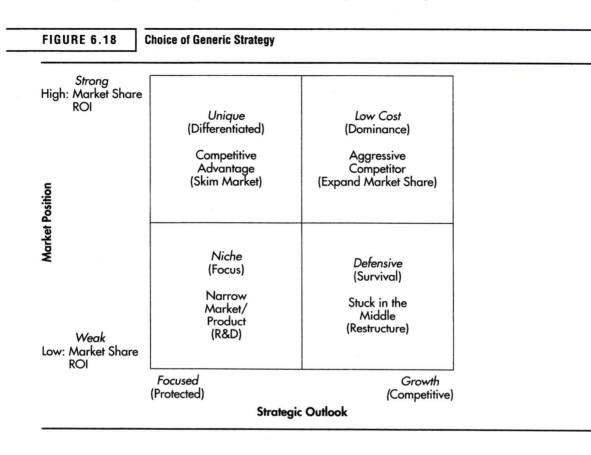

If market segmentation and product differentiation are not possible—that is, if no critical mass can be achieved by subdividing the marketplace or there are few ways to differentiate the product—a firm might try to become the cost leader if it is financially strong and if the market continues to grow until the experience curve can take effect. Competitors with weak positions in a mature industry do not have to withdraw from the marketplace if it is possible to harvest profits or use the SBU as a "cash cow," but these options generally are transitory.

If barriers to exit are low, one viable alternative is to liquidate the SBU. More often, the company faces a situation in which competitive advantage can be gained only at a competitor's expense. In this situation another generic competitive strategy—*gamesman-ship*—can be implemented at the business level. The effective strategic planner makes use of a variety of financial maneuvers to strengthen the company's position, stalemate the competition, and facilitate eventual exit from the marketplace (Figure 6.20).

The best strategy for the weak SBU is to focus its resources on a particular buyer group (market segment) that is reasonably large and can be defended. The strong competitor can use its resources to build and exploit differences in the cost structure associated with producing, distributing, and marketing the product.

An alternative way of using the Porter curve is to add "Iso-quants." These are lines of equal return on investment that are not dependent on market share (Figure 6.19). A number of companies are neither stuck in the middle nor are they precisely on the curve. Figure 6.17 showed regions around the curve, but the iso-quants show that the company could fit almost anywhere on the chart. The value of such a chart is to show typical regions of return for alternative market shares. This is especially important in the low-market-share range, where PIMS analysis typically shows poor returns. In addition, other methods of return (such as ROA, ROE, and ROS) are rapidly gaining favor over ROI for measuring return.

The four generic strategies can be related to the earlier SPACE approach. SPACE can be used to "measure" the strategic position of each of the firm's SBUs and to help managers determine an appropriate competitive strategy for it (Figure 6.20 and Table 6.1).

The purpose of the SPACE approach is to identify which strategy fits the firm, taking into account industry strength, environmental stability, competitive advantage, and financial strength. SPACE displays the "bottom line" of a strategic review, and a thorough analysis is necessary to assess the particular strategic moves. However, at least two features make SPACE a valuable tool for strategic

---

FIGURE 6.19 | **Use of Iso-quants with the Porter Curve**

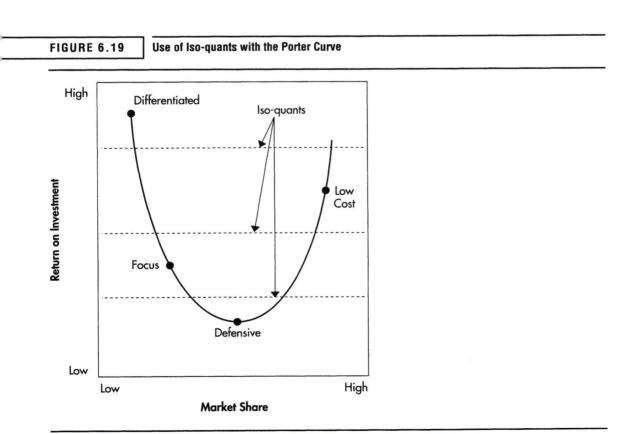

FIGURE 6.20	**Strategic Options and Generic Strategies** (FS = financial strength of the company; IS = industrial strength; ES = environmental stability; CA = competitive advantage of the company)

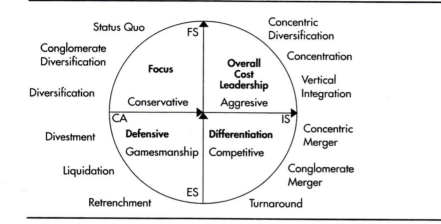

FIGURE 6.21	**Application of Strategic Position and Action Evaluation (SPACE)** **to Strategy Choices for Business Units**

Strategic Posture as Determined by SPACE	Appropriate Generic Strategy
Aggressive posture	Cost leadership through concentration, concentric diversification, or vertical integration
Competitive posture	Differentiation, such as through strong R&D effort funded by merger with cash-rich company
Conservative posture	Focus and selective diversification through acquisition of companies in other market segments
Gamesmanship posture	Defensive, particularly survival tactics, such as retrenchment, divestment, or liquidation

management. First, SPACE provides a comprehensive approach that gives managers at all levels of the organization a means for considering the many different factors relevant to proposing a particular strategy. Second, and perhaps more important, SPACE provides a systematic approach that can be used to communicate different assumptions about important strategy variables. That is, when managers carefully assess each of the factors in the SPACE method, they can more effectively examine alternatives and achieve consensus. It also helps management to recognize the significance of each of the factors needed to maintain a competitive strategic posture.

UMMARY

Two important responsibilities of strategic managers are (1) to understand how the organization's products or services are currently positioned in the market environment and (2) to determine how the organization can improve its position with existing or new products.

Knowledge about the status quo, with respect to the product and the market environment, enables strategic managers to identify the need for new product/market strategies. It is equally vital that the firm assess the trends that will affect the future of the company. In this chapter, we considered several tools available for this purpose. Decision-tree analysis helps managers identify alternative actions and their possible outcomes. Pinpointing existing products on the product life cycle also makes it easier to determine which strategies are appropriate. Growth vector analysis helps managers determine the most realistic and advantageous directions for growth, and gap analysis enables them to determine in advance where opportunities exist to pursue these new directions. Managers also have to consider whether new-product innovations or manufacturing technologies are needed to cut costs or boost sales. This requires continuous technology assessment.

PIMS analysis and competitive portfolio analysis help strategic managers to evaluate the financial consequences of product/market strategies. PIMS analysis enables managers to determine the impact on profitability of various strategies, based on models that have been developed from studies of hundreds of companies. Competitive portfolio analysis focuses on the cash flow that can be generated by a specific product/market strategy, such as having a balanced product portfolio or taking advantage of the experience curve.

In strategic position and action evaluation (SPACE), four input factors are used to arrive at different strategic postures for the firm: These postures identify generic competitive strategies and appropriate strategic thrusts for the business. Super SPACE adds importance of each factor and sustainability.

In this chapter, we also considered Michael Porter's three generic competitive strategies and how they are related to the SPACE approach.

REFERENCES AND SUGGESTIONS FOR FURTHER READING

Allan, Gerald and John Hammond. 1976. *The use of experience curves in competitive decision making.* Boston: Intercollegiate Case Clearing House, Case #9-175-174.

Allman, William. 1992. The ultimate widget: 3-D printing may revolutionize product design and manufacturing. *U.S. News and World Report*, July 20, pp. 55–56.

AMP Incorporated. 1991. *The Wall Street Transcript*, December 23, pp. 103, 763–765.

Barrett, Amy. 1990. Intimations of mortality. *Financial World*, September 18, pp. 30–33.

Birnbaum, Philip H. 1984. The choice of strategic alternatives under increasing regulation in high-technology companies. *Academy of Management Journal* 27, no. 3, pp. 489–510.

Birnbaum, Philip H. and Andrew R. Weiss. 1987. Competitive advantage and the basis for competition. Paper presented at the Seventh Annual International Conference of the Strategic Management Society, Boston, Mass.

Boston Consulting Group. 1974. Segmentation and strategy. BCG Perspective No. 156. Boston: Boston Consulting Group.

Specialization. BCG Perspective No. 240. Boston: Boston Consulting Group.

Branscomb, Lewis. 1992. Does America need a technology policy? *Harvard Business Review*, March–April, pp. 24–31.

Cardoza, R. N. and Y. Wind. 1985. Risk–return approach to product portfolio strategy. *Long-Range Planning* 18, no. 2, 77–85.

Cattin, P. and D. R. Wittink. 1982. Commercial use of conjoint analysis: A survey. *Journal of Marketing,* Summer, pp. 44–53.

Cohen, Warren. 1991. Spending on tomorrow today. *U.S. News and World Report*, July 22, pp. 45–46.

David, F. R. 1986. Evaluating alternative growth strategies—an analytical approach. *Long-Range Planning,* Spring.

Erdman, Andrew. 1992. AMP: Staying ahead of 800 competitors. *Fortune*, June 1, pp. 111–112.

Fox, Harold W. 1973. A framework for functional coordination. *Atlanta Economic Review* 23, no. 6.

Garvin, David. 1991. How the Baldrige award really works. *Harvard Business Review*, November–December, pp. 80–93.

Garvin, David A. 1987. Competing on the eight dimensions of quality. *Harvard Business Review*, November–December, pp. 101–110.

Ghemawat, Pankaj. 1985. Building strategy on the experience curve. *Harvard Business Review*, March, pp. 143–149.

Gould, J. M. 1983. Technology change and competition. *Journal of Business Strategy* 4, no. 2, pp. 66–71.

Green, Paul E. 1977. A new approach to market segmentation. *Business Horizons*, February, pp. 61–73.

Green, Paul E. and Frank Carmone. 1970. Multidimensional scaling and related techniques in market analysis. Cambridge, Mass.: Marketing Science Institute.

Green, Paul E. and V. Srinivasan. 1978. Conjoint analysis in consumer research: Issues and outlook. *Journal of Consumer Research*, September, pp. 103–123.

Hamel, Gary and C. K. Prahalad. 1991. Corporate imagination and expeditionary marketing. *Harvard Business Review*, July–August, pp. 81–92.

Hamermesh, Richard G. and Roderick E. White. 1984. Manage beyond portfolio analysis. *Harvard Business Review*, January, pp. 103–109.

Henderson, Bruce D. 1984. The application and misapplication of the experience curve. *Journal of Business Strategy* 4, no. 3, pp. 3–9.

Hofer, Charles. 1975. Toward a contingency theory of business strategy. *Academy of Management Journal* 18, no. 4.

Jorgensen, Barbara. 1990. AMP connects its once and future goals. *Electronic Business*, September 3, pp. 38–40.

Kehoe, William J. 1983. Strategic marketing planning: The PIMS model. *S.A.M. Advanced Management Journal*, Spring, pp. 45–50.

Kotler, Philip. 1972. *Marketing management*. Englewood Cliffs, N.J.: Prentice-Hall, Chapter 7.

Levitt, Theodore. 1965. Exploit the product life cycle. *Harvard Business Review* 43, no. 6.

McInnes, Harold. 1992. The AMP connection: Standard to strategy. National Center for Manufacturing Sciences, FOCUS, March.

Miles, Raymond E. and Charles C. Snow. 1978. *Organizational strategy: Structure and process*. New York: McGraw-Hill.

Ohmae, Kenichi. 1988. Getting back to strategy. *Harvard Business Review*, November–December, pp. 149–156.

Porter, Michael. 1985. *Competitive advantage*. New York: The Free Press.

Porter, Michael. 1980. *Competitive strategy*. New York: The Free Press.

Reese, Jennifer. 1992. Getting hot ideas from customers. *Fortune*, May 18, pp. 86–88.

Sarge, Dick. 1991. AMP is optimistic about global growth. *Sunday Patriot-News* (Harrisburg, Penna.), September 15, p. F-1, F-3.

Schiffman, Susan, et al. 1981. Introduction to multidimensional scaling. *Theory, Methods, and Applications*. Cambridge, Mass.: Academic Press.

Schlender, Brenton. 1992. How Sony keeps the magic going. *Fortune*, February 24, pp. 75–84.

Schoeffler, Sidney, Robert D. Buzzell, and Donald F. Heany. 1974. Impact of strategic planning on profit performance. *Harvard Business Review*, March–April.

Schuler, Joseph. 1991. 100,000 points of promise. *Pennsylvania Business and Technology*, Fourth Quarter.

Technology policy: Is America on the right track? 1992. *Harvard Business Review*, May–June, pp. 140–157.

The AMP connection: Standard to strategy. 1992. National Center for Manufacturing Sciences, *FOCUS*, March.

Urban, Glen L. and John R. Hauser. 1980. *Design and marketing of new products*. Englewood Cliffs, N.J.: Prentice-Hall.

Wasson, Chester. 1974. *Dynamic competitive strategy and product life cycles*. St. Charles, Ill.: Challenge Books.

Wasson, Chester. 1971. Product management. *Product life cycles and competitive marketing strategy*. St. Charles, Ill.: Challenge Books.

Weber, John A. 1977. Market structure profile and strategic growth opportunities. *California Management Review* 20, no. 1.

Willis, Clint. 1992. Cash in on U.S. companies that are hammering the Japanese. *Money*, April, pp. 69–72.

Wind, Y. and V. Mahajan. 1981. Designing product and business portfolios, *Harvard Business Review*, January–February, pp. 155–165.

Yelsey, A. A. 1984. Multiple image forecasting, *Planning Review*, pp. 27–29.

Zufryden, Fred S. 1988. Using conjoint analysis to predict trial and repeat-purchase patterns of new frequently purchased products. *Decision Sciences*, 19, pp. 55–71.

APPENDIX A

Product/Market Mapping

Product/market mapping and statistical analysis are typically used in market research. Strategic managers use the results of this mapping in making strategic decisions about how to differentiate products for sale to specific market segments.

Product/market mapping can help managers identify a product's key features or attributes in the eyes of its customers. With this input, managers can formulate successful product-differentiation and market-segmentation strategies.

The most commonly used product/market mapping techniques are

- Multidimensional scaling (MDS)
- Cluster analysis
- Factor analysis
- Adaptive perceptual mapping (APM)
- Discriminant analysis
- Conjoint analysis

We will look closely at the first and last of these. The choice of technique depends on the purpose of the analysis. Different techniques might be chosen, depending on

1. The focus of the analysis; whether information is available about physical/product features or psychological/demographic features
2. The depth of current knowledge about the market; whether information is needed to identify basic consumer choices or to fine-tune an existing market strategy

The data in Figures 6A.1 and 6A.2, developed by the Boston Consulting Group, constitute an index for the use of new digital telephone connectors in AMP's European market versus older analog standards. Between 1985 and 1990, the analog market grew from an index of 100 to 151, based on the continued addition of new telephone users. Digital connectors have slowly developed from 0.2% market share in 1985 to 7.4% in 1990.

Figure 6A.3 shows a forecast made using the S-curve computation. The substitution of digital devices for analog ones is projected to proceed rapidly and to lead to the quick demise of analog technology.

FIGURE 6A.1	Digital versus Analog Substitution Data for AMP

Index	Actual					
	1985	1986	1987	1988	1989	1990
Analog	100	112	123	132	143	151
Digital	0.2	0.5	1	2	5	12
Total	100.2	112.5	124	134	148	163
M (digital)	.2%	.4%	.8%	1.5%	3.4%	7.4%
	↓	↓	↓	↓	↓	↓
R	0.002	0.004	0.008	0.015	0.035	0.079

Index	Projected						
	1991	1992	1993	1994	1995	1996	1997
Analog	150.7	141.7	121.4	91.4	60.1	36.1	20.1
Digital	22.6	43.9	76.5	118.8	162.4	198.7	227.0
Total	173.3	185.6	197.9	210.2	222.5	234.8	247.1
M (digital)	13.0%	23.7%	38.7%	56.5%	73.0%	84.6%	91.9%
	↑	↑	↑	↑	↑	↑	↑
R	0.15	0.31	0.63	1.3	2.7	5.5	11.3

Note: M equals percentage of market share; R equals $M/(1 - M)$, which represents the rate of substitution, or the ratio of digital to analog technology.

FIGURE 6A.2	Digital versus Analog Substitution Graph

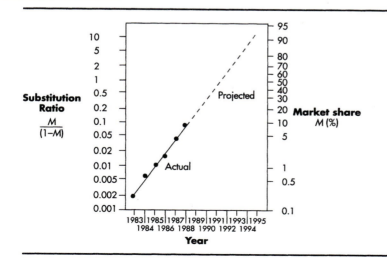

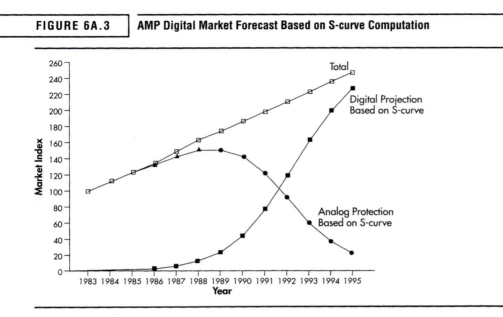

FIGURE 6A.3   AMP Digital Market Forecast Based on S-curve Computation

The matrix in Figure 6A.4 shows how each tool might be applied, given a focus and prior depth of knowledge about customer choices. Figure 6A.5 lists data input and output for each of the techniques. Because software for each of these techniques is available for personal computers, the user need only enter the data and interpret the results. The details of the technique are incorporated in the computer program. The articles and references at the end of the chapter provide sources of further information about how these tools can be applied. Strategic applications of two of them, multidimensional scaling and conjoint analysis, are described in the sections that follow.

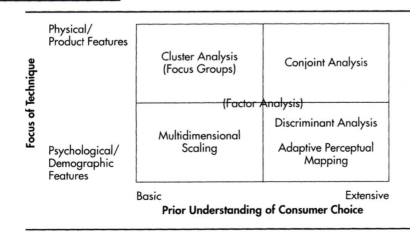

FIGURE 6A.4   Use of Product/Market Mapping Techniques

FIGURE 6A.5	Input and Output Data of Product/Market Mapping Techniques

Technique	Input	Output
Multidimensional scaling	Similarity rankings among products	Two-dimensional product map
Cluster analysis	Similarity ratings	Market groups or clusters with similar characteristics
Factor analysis	Attribute ratings	Factor loadings/collapsed dimensions
Adaptive perceptual mapping	Attribute ratings	Multidimensional product map
Discriminant analysis	Rating of consumers for different attributes	Group affiliation
Conjoint analysis	Product feature trade-offs	Feature share preference and market simulation

MULTIDIMENSIONAL SCALING

Multidimensional scaling helps strategic managers to evaluate similarities or dissimilarities between product attributes using indirect data provided by respondents. An indirect approach is used because, in many cases, the product attributes are not yet known or the respondents are unable or unwilling to represent their reasons for evaluation accurately. Computerized multidimensional scaling permits managers to identify product/market attributes based on simple input data, such as ratings on a scale of 0 to 10. On the scale, 0 means that the products are very similar with respect to an attribute, and 10 means that they are very dissimilar. The computer converts this information into a graphic representation in which the differences perceived by the respondents are seen as relative distances on the map. Figure 6A.6 shows such maps for automobiles and pain relievers. The task of the researchers is to add and describe dimensions, such as luxuriousness and sportiness for an automobile or gentleness and effectiveness for a pain reliever.

Figure 6A.7 illustrates the use of multidimensional scaling based on hard data, such as the airline distances between the major cities in the United States. The user enters the distances between pairs of cities, and the computer program is able to construct a map that positions all the cities relative to one another and in the right locations. This approach can be used to ascertain the relative position of products, services, or even a whole company based on differences ("distances") between pairs of objects. Researchers use these data to determine how "close" or similar each of these objects is to a competing product, service, or company. Multidimensional scaling is a proven strategic tool. It is invaluable for determining desirable product attributes and for positioning products relative to competing products.

Perceptual maps, such as the ones in Figure 6A.6 help strategic managers to identify (1) different customer or market segments, (2) product attributes that will appeal to specific segments, and (3) new-product opportunities. This knowledge guides product-development strategies and helps focus the efforts of the R&D, design, and marketing departments.

An MDS map of the car market, which is done yearly by the major car makers, helps them to identify weaknesses or "holes" in the product range that need to be closed. The map for 1970 (see Figure 6A.6) shows a void for cars with average luxuriousness and sportiness.

| FIGURE 6A.6 | MDS Maps of Consumer Perceptions of Automobiles and Pain Relievers |

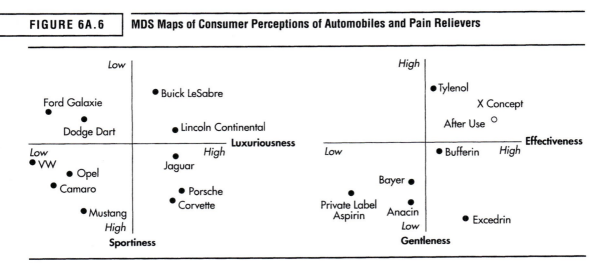

Source: Automobile map adapted from Greene and Carmone, 1970, p. 60; pain-reliever map adapted from Urban and Hauser, 1980, p. 221.

This gap was filled by Japanese manufacturers, who began to produce cars having the price and performance of a Volkswagen "bug" but more standard "luxury" features.

The map of the pain relievers (Figure 6A.6) was used to better position a new product in the market. After a careful market analysis, the pharmaceutical company planned to launch a new pain reliever (the **X** concept) that would approach Tylenol in gentleness but act faster and provide more pain relief. By collecting consumer ratings after the product was launched, the company discovered that its market position was not quite on target (after use **O**). The company then redesigned the product slightly to achieve the position targeted on the map.

CONJOINT ANALYSIS

Figure 6A.6 shows that perceptual mapping such as MDS typically focuses on psychological and demographic aspects of product positioning, not physical characteristics of the product. Once the desired position is identified, though, attention must be given to developing a product capable of achieving that position. Conjoint analysis is often used in this effort because it helps managers to

1. Quantify the relative value to the consumer of each individual feature of a product.
2. Identify feature-based segmentation patterns.
3. Assess the relative value of changing one or another product feature.
4. Predict consumer preference for new product features.
5. Predict relative market shares for existing or new products, and gauge the effect of feature and price changes on relative market shares.

FIGURE 6A.7 | Geographic Map Made from Hard Data; in This Case, Distances Between U.S. Cities

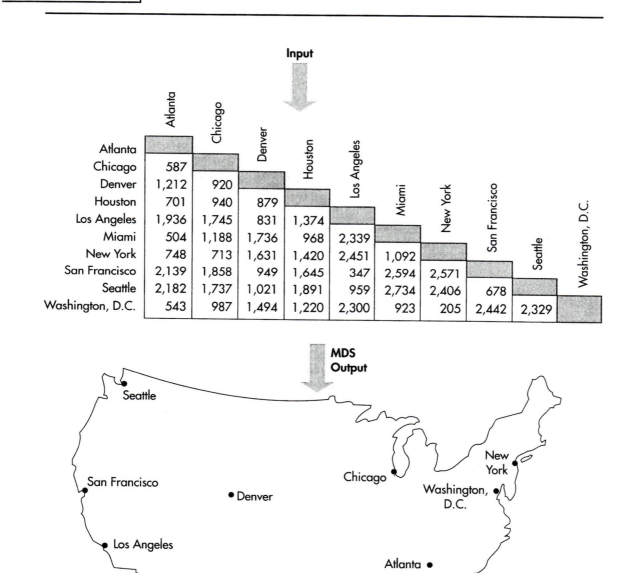

Input

	Atlanta	Chicago	Denver	Houston	Los Angeles	Miami	New York	San Francisco	Seattle	Washington, D.C.
Atlanta										
Chicago	587									
Denver	1,212	920								
Houston	701	940	879							
Los Angeles	1,936	1,745	831	1,374						
Miami	504	1,188	1,736	968	2,339					
New York	748	713	1,631	1,420	2,451	1,092				
San Francisco	2,139	1,858	949	1,645	347	2,594	2,571			
Seattle	2,182	1,737	1,021	1,891	959	2,734	2,406	678		
Washington, D.C.	543	987	1,494	1,220	2,300	923	205	2,442	2,329	

MDS Output

To conduct a conjoint analysis, managers must

1. Define the relevant attributes of the product.
2. Ask respondents (customers) to make a series of tradeoffs indicating their preference for one attribute from a pair of attributes.
3. Calculate respondents' preference scores for each attribute.
4. Simulate the effects of attribute changes.

Personal computer programs are available to perform tasks 2 through 4; the user defines the attributes (task 1) and then concentrates on analyzing the data. The following example illustrates an application of conjoint analysis.

A conjoint analysis that was performed to match products to market opportunities effectively explained the market dynamics seen in the personal computer industry. Late in 1983, a number of new personal computer (PC) models were prepared for market introduction in 1984, most notably the new Apple Macintosh and the IBM PC Junior. Conventional wisdom at the time was that the PC Junior would be a hit, because it was an IBM product, and that the Macintosh would be a flop like Lisa, an earlier Apple model with similar user-friendly features. At this point, a conjoint analysis of the PC market was conducted by the Boston Consulting Group (BCG). BCG surveyed more than 1,000 attendees at a Boston computer show. Only the responses of those who planned to buy a PC within a year were used.

The following product attributes were analyzed and a tradeoff prepared with respect to price, manufacturer's reputation, portability, data manipulation capability, database capacity, word processing capacity, and styling. For each attribute, variations were carefully chosen for their relevance to different products then available. Wherever possible, directly measurable attributes were used. For price, for example, three variations were set: $1,000, $2,000, and $3,000. Database-capacity (memory) variations were set as 256 K Bytes, 640 K Bytes, and 1 M Bytes. Other attributes, such as portability, required yes or no answers.

If asked which model would be ideal, people would, of course, say a 1 M Byte model for $1,000. In reality, this choice was not available. Therefore, for the conjoint analysis, respondents were asked to make tradeoff choices, such as:

Everything else being equal, which would you buy?

(a) A PC that has 1 M Byte of memory but costs $2,000.
(b) A PC that costs $1,000 but has only 640 K Bytes of memory.

The respondents ranked these tradeoffs, on a scale of 1 to 9, as shown in Figure 6A.8, where 1 means most desirable. This respondent to the price-versus-capacity question preferred answer (a) over answer (b); that is, he or she would prefer more computing power, even at a higher price. Only a further price increase would change this preference to a model with somewhat less power.

The combined responses were used to evaluate the relative importance of these attributes for segments as well as the total population (Figure 6A.9).

The next step was to enter the attributes of each of the products into the industry model in order to calculate the preference shares. The results showed how preference shares were likely to change when the Macintosh and PC Junior were introduced (Figure 6A.10). When the data on Macintosh were included in the model, with features based on press descriptions, it captured almost 50% of the first-choice votes. When data on the PC Junior were entered, on the other hand, they received no first-choice votes, and the market shares remained unchanged. At the time the model was tested, these results were counterintuitive. Yet in the spring of 1984, after the new computer models were launched, it became clear that the conjoint analysis had been quite accurate. The Apple

---

FIGURE 6A.8	Sample Response to Question in a Conjoint Analysis Survey

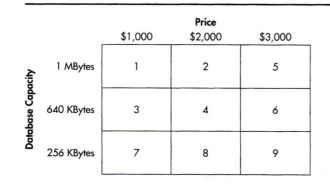

FIGURE 6A.9	Conjoint Analysis: Sequence of First Choices by Customers in Three Different Market Segments

Business	Education	Home
1. Database capacity	Word processing	Price
2. Word processing	Portability	Data manipulation
3. Manufacturer's reputation	Price	Styling
4. Data manipulation	Data manipulation	Word processing
5. Portability	Database capacity	Portability
6. Price	Styling	Database capacity
7. Styling	Manufacturer's reputation	Manufacturer's reputation

---

FIGURE 6A.10	Preference Shares of PCs, Based on Conjoint Analysis

	Share of Preferences (%)		
Product	Existing Models	Macintosh Introduced	PC Junior Introduced
IBM PC	46	30	30
Compaq	23	10	10
DEC Rainbow	19	9	9
Macintosh	—	47	47
PC Junior	—	—	0
Others	12	4	4
Total	100	100	100

Macintosh had an excellent start, whereas sales of the PC Junior quickly became an embarrassment for IBM.

IBM acted quickly to make changes in the PC Junior. Another conjoint analysis was used to predict the impact of alternative feature changes (Figure 6A.11). This analysis showed that dropping the price of the PC Junior, even by as much as 47%, would not solve IBM's problem. Increasing the memory of the PC Junior would significantly improve its market position but would seriously reduce preference for the more expensive IBM PC. If, on the other hand, the PC Junior were made portable, with no other changes, IBM would increase its total preference share from 25% (status quo) to 38% for both models.

As it turned out, IBM chose to increase the PC Junior's memory and not make it portable. Competitors started to take advantage of this situation and gained market share by adjusting their product policies and by offering portable models. IBM responded by introducing a portable version of the PC but never was able to duplicate its success in the desktop market. The PC Junior was finally abandoned in 1985.

This example shows the power of conjoint analysis as a method of simulating a product's reception in the market environment. Many companies have recognized this capability and regularly use conjoint analysis to test customer preferences for the attributes of a range of different products.

FIGURE 6A.11 | **Conjoint Simulation of Impact of PC Junior Feature Changes**

		Share of Preferences (%) IBM Options for PC Junior		
Product	Status Quo	Reduce Price from $1,900 to $1,000	Add Memory Without Price Decrease	Make Portable Without Price Decrease
IBM PC	25	23	7	23 } 38%
PC Junior	0	4	26	15
Compaq	20	19	16	14
DEC Rainbow	7	7	4	7
Macintosh	46	45	45	39
Others	2	2	2	2
Total	100	100	100	100

Note: Compaq had reacted to competitors' new products by reducing its price from $3,400 to $2,750 in order to regain market share.

Source: Courtesy of The Boston Consulting Group, Inc. Reprinted with permission.

APPENDIX B

Steps in Technology Assessment

Technology has two basic components: (1) a tangible component, in the form of machines, tools, and material, and (2) an intangible component, in the form of technological knowledge and expertise. Knowledge, especially scientific knowledge, is by far the most important component. It dictates what skills and techniques employees need to learn; the layout and design of industrial plants; the operating principles of machines; the choice of computer software; and the procedures, patents, and copyrights originating from laboratories. Technology is a strategic resource, whether it is developed within the company or acquired from external sources.

A technology assessment involves two phases: (1) an information-gathering phase, termed *technology scanning*, and (2) an information-analysis phase, termed *technology evaluation*.

Technology Scanning

To perform a technology scan, strategic managers

1. Subdivide the business as a whole into strategic business units (SBUs).
2. Determine the following for each SBU:
   a. Technology currently used by the company.
   b. Technology currently used by competitors.
   c. New technologies on the horizon. (This should include any technological development that might accomplish the same *function* for the business.)
   d. Source of the new technology and its effects on all stakeholders in the system, as traced on a stakeholder map (see Chapter 4).

Technology Evaluation

To perform a technology evaluation, strategic managers ask two fundamental questions about each of the technologies identified in the scan.

1. *How important is this technology to the success of the business?* Does it add value? Is it changing? Will it open up new markets?

2. *How strong is our current and future position with respect to this technology?* This is indicated by expenditure, history, patents, publications, R&D, personnel skills, and ability to adopt or adapt the new technology. In general, a company is either a leader (strong position) or a follower (weak position) in the use of technology.

The answers to these two questions can be plotted in a matrix (Figure 6B.1). Answers in quadrant A, the high/high quadrant, indicate a strong position—one that should be pursued aggressively in order to retain a competitive advantage. Answers in quadrant B, the high/low quadrant, indicate that the technology is important to the firm but it is not being used to its full advantage. The firm can choose to

1. Commit resources in order to improve the technology position and turn it into a competitive advantage (more R&D, equipment purchasing, hiring, education, and the like).
2. Move out of this area. Reinvest in other areas.
3. Adopt an *adequacy stance.* Commit enough resources to maintain a satisfactory defensive or follower position. Monitor developments and wait to take advantage of the next technological breakthrough.

Answers in quadrant C, the low/high quadrant, indicate that the firm has a strong position in an unimportant or perhaps obsolete technology. This often happens when new technologies have become available and competitors have taken advantage of them. In this case, the firm should make the best of what it has and move toward new technologies or diversify into other areas where its technology can be more useful.

Answers in quadrant D, the low/low quadrant, indicate that the firm has a poor position in an unimportant technology. The firm's involvement in this area should be thoroughly reconsidered. The technology might be phased out or used in new ways. Technology is not the force driving strategy in this case. Rather, marketing aspects of the product strategy are most important.

As we noted in the chapter, it is generally ineffective to apply a low-cost strategy alone in using technology for competitive advantage in achieving market dominance or rapid growth. Furthermore, technology alone cannot sustain competitive advantage. Though it is vital for

---

FIGURE 6B.1 | **Technology Evaluation Matrix**

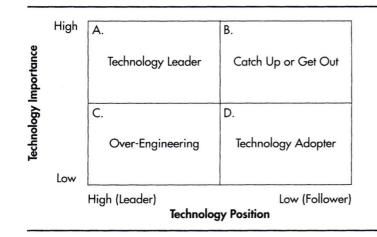

gaining advantage, especially during the introduction and growth stages of a product/industry life cycle, when a technology's relative importance to the industry is being determined, any technology must be backed up and supplemented by strategies that focus on marketing and customer service. One way to maintain competitive advantage from the maturity stage on is to focus on product changes that make the product easier and more advantageous for customers to use. This strategy might be useful for companies whose technological position falls in quadrant C or D of the technology evaluation matrix (Figure 6B.1).

TECHNOLOGY SUBSTITUTION

New technologies can radically change the demand for products that use an old technology. In addition, because many technological innovations do not come from the current technology leader, they tend to alter the competitive structure as well. The current technology leader is often put in a defensive position, from which it tries to ignore or thwart the growth of the new technological substitute. The leader slowly declines from quadrant A into quadrant C of the technology evaluation matrix, often without realizing it.

Why is it so difficult for the current leader to spot a new, superior technology? Mostly because the strategy is based on the old technology, which is still doing well and has achieved seemingly unassailable volume advantage. Take, for example, the slow adoption of reinforced fiberglass or plastics for the production of car bodies. Although these materials are potentially cheaper than steel, they are resisted because car manufacturers have made a significant investment in sheet metal presses and stamping machines. As these machines (which can cost up to $20 million and last up to 50 years) are taken out of the production process, the use of other materials for car bodies is slowly rising.

Technology substitution tends to succeed most easily if it enters or creates a new market segment. Because of high startup costs, plastic bathroom sinks were initially more expensive than the established ceramic ones. New extrusion technology, however, made it possible for designers to create more shapes and sizes. This enabled plastic sinks to penetrate the designer market and, eventually, to gain market share from ceramic sinks.

Plotted on a graph, technology substitution can be described as a gradual S-curve. Like an epidemic disease or other biological phenomenon, a new technology goes through an "incubation" period, during which it spreads relatively slowly, and then an "acute" stage, during which it spreads rapidly through an industry. The phenomenon of technological substitution proceeds by the following principles:

1. If a substitution has progressed even a few percent, it will proceed to completion.
2. The rate of substitution of new technology for old is proportional to the amount of the old remaining.

The process can be tracked by plotting the ratio of new to old technology:

$$R = M / (1 - M)$$

where R equals the rate of substitution and M equals the market share of the new technology. A characteristic of the S-curve is that R is 1.0 when M is 0.5 and becomes increasingly larger as M approaches 1.0. Plotted on semi-log graph paper, the substitution ratio R forms a straight line.

The substitution of front-wheel for rear-wheel-drive technology is plotted in Figure 6B.2. In 1960, less than 25% of the world's cars had front-wheel drive. Today, three times that number, or 75%, have front-wheel drive. Figure 6B.3 lists other examples of technology substitution, some of which occurred rather quickly.

Technology substitution data for the AMP case is shown in Figure 6A.1 (p. 274). First, the $M / (1 - M)$ ratios for the historical data are calculated and plotted on semi-log paper. As can be seen from Figure 6A.2, the resulting data points fall on a straight line that can be extended to project data points for future years. These points, which can be projected with simple linear regression or read directly from the graph, are then reconverted into market shares and a forecast for digital sales.

FIGURE 6B.2 | **Technology Substitution: Market Share (M) of Front-Wheel-Drive Cars, 1960–1986**

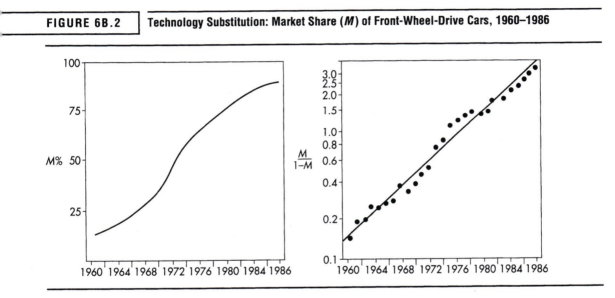

FIGURE 6B.3 | **Examples of Technology Substitution**

| | New Technology | |
New/Old Technologies	Year of First Application	Years Until 75% Market Share Reached
Power/manual auto steering	1962	20
Polyethylene/glass bottles	1963	18
Organic/inorganic insecticides	1946	17
Air conditioning/natural auto cooling	1968	15
Basic-oxygen/open-hearth steels	1968	10
Diesel/steam locomotives	1949	9
Color/black-and-white television	1972	8
Detergents/soaps	1951	8
Turbofan/turbojet aircraft engines	1961	5

CHAPTER SEVEN

Strategy in a Global Environment

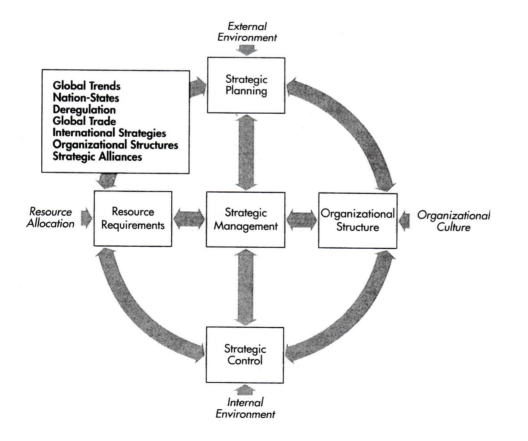

Chapter 1 A Framework for Strategic Management	**Chapter 2** Strategic Analysis	**Chapter 3** Strategic Visioning, Goals, Ethics, and Social Responsibility	**Chapter 4** The Competitive Environment	**Chapter 5** Capability-based Strategy	**Chapter 6** Market Dynamics and Sustainable Competitive Advantage
How to approach strategic management	*Application of strategic analysis*	*Understanding vision, values, ethics*	*Coping with competitive forces, stakeholders*	*Assessing company capability, timeliness, quality*	*Determining trends, gap analysis, and market dynamics*

Chapter 7 Strategy in a Global Environment	**Chapter 8** Financial Planning and Competitive- Cost Analysis	**Chapter 9** Entrepreneurship, Mergers and Acquisitions, Restructuring, and the Service Sector	**Chapter 10** Leadership Factor in Strategy and Implementing Strategic Change	**Chapter 11** Information Technology and Future Directions in Strategy
Assessing global trade, foreign markets, monetary exchange	*Preparing a financial plan and competitive-cost analysis*	*Importance of small business, entrepreneurs, restructuring*	*Strategy implementation, leadership, culture*	*Information technology, trends, new management*

INTRODUCTION

About midway between Hoteville and Bacavi Villages on the Third Mesa of the Hopi Indian Reservation, the Hopi Foundation has opened a not-for-profit solar electric enterprise. The enterprise will sell solar panels and systems to Hopis whose dwellings are sparsely scattered throughout the sun-baked, remote northern Arizona desert. Hitachi and other Japanese firms are the major source of technology and capital. Together with Arizona financial institutions, the Japanese are providing consumer financing for Hopi families. They are also supporting tests of solar hot-water heaters, which, when perfected, they intend to sell in Third World countries.

Just outside Denver, Colorado, a young real estate developer opened his one-person office. After striking a deal to buy a building from a local company, he found that his best financing opportunities came from German and Japanese banks, that the architect with the best design for remodeling was located in France, and that his first client would be a British firm with major operations in Singapore. (He later told his professors that because he planned to be a one-person small business, he did not devote much time to global studies while getting his business degree. He wishes he had.)

Indicative of some of the changes that organizations can expect in a global environment are trends such as China's renegade Guangdong province. This province has embraced an almost purely capitalistic economy that is growing faster than nearly any other in the world. It grew 27.2% in 1991 (Gibney, 1992). When visited by politicians from Beijing, local officials retorted, "What have you invested here? We pay for our railroads, our highways, and our power plants, and you have no right to tell us what to do."

When companies such as IBM, Toshiba, and Siemens decide to work together to develop computer components, the world really has changed (Weber, 1992). These three companies are expected to spend $1 billion in developing advanced semiconductors and advanced manufacturing processes. Schrage (1992) questions what's behind IBM's dutch-treat strategy. The answer seems to be that the next generation of advanced memory chips are needed to ensure global competitiveness and that the cost of development would be excessive for any one company alone. In another international venture, Fujitsu and Advanced Micro Devices have invested $700 million in sharing costs of development.

Asserting its clout in Europe, Germany is using its growing power to achieve what Helmut Kohl maintains that he wants, "a United States of Europe" (Templeman, 1992). As Germany flexes its economic muscle, the United States will have to accommodate to a changing market environment in Europe. Some individuals maintain that a strong Germany will actually enhance America's relations with Japan because Germany's markets are much more open to U.S. goods. Germany's new role in Europe made a major impact at the General Agreement on Tariffs and Trade (GATT). A new Western alliance may be forged, wherein Germany is firmly linked with the West.

These trends indicate that companies must change the way they conduct business if they are to remain competitive and profitable in the light of new consumer characteristics, such as

1. More particular and diversified lifestyles
2. An increased interest in fashion
3. Greater willingness to pay for intangible attributes in a product
4. Technology that saves time and is easy to use
5. A lack of interest in what country produced the product

In effect, we are becoming a truly borderless world where the successful corporation will be one that has a global outlook (Sera, 1992).

These few examples illustrate the global environment that affects enterprises of virtually all sizes and in virtually every industry. The task of strategic managers in today's business environment is to match and position their businesses in an increasingly complex, global environment. A business is like an ecological entity. It has mutual relations with other entities—called stakeholders—in its environment. A *stakeholder* is anyone whose actions can affect an organization or who is affected by the organization's actions. Successful strategic managers are able to identify the crucial stakeholders in their business's environment and to make realistic assumptions about them. These assumptions are used to develop business strategies. Increasingly, a firm's stakeholders are located at various and sometimes remote places all over the world.

Like any ecosystem, a business's environment holds opportunities and threats. Skillful strategic managers are able to find "market niches" in their firm's global environment that are particularly well suited to the products, services, and capabilities the organization offers. They are also able to develop organizational structures and arrangements that work effectively within the environment. Each of the four organizations described above was successful in doing this. Failure to find a suitable niche, however, can lead to damage or even destruction for an organization. For this reason, global environmental assessment is essential.

An organization's ability to cope with a changing environment is probably the most important determinant of its success or failure in a free-enterprise system. Changes in consumer tastes, political conditions, market structure, or technology cannot only affect individual companies but also make or break an entire industry.

Oil and automobiles provide a case in point. On October 16, 1973, delegates to the Organization of Petroleum Exporting Countries—five Arabs and an Iranian—met in Kuwait City and decided unilaterally to increase the price of oil to $5.11 per barrel. In September the price had been $2.90 per barrel; in December it reached $11.65. A panic set in as people everywhere in the world tried to reduce their dependence on petroleum. A few years later most American automakers were experiencing financial difficulties, and a few were on the brink of bankruptcy because they had failed to respond effectively to the price increases. They should have responded quickly by developing a line of more fuel-efficient cars. Foreign competitors looked upon the oil crisis as an opportunity. As a result, while Chrysler and American Motors were struggling for survival, Japanese manufacturers were thriving in the market by offering smaller, gas-efficient, low-maintenance automobiles. The lesson to be learned here is that failure to analyze the external environment for economic, political, competitive, geographic, social, and technological opportunities and threats can have a major disruptive impact on an organization.

A successful organization marshals its internal capabilities so as to interact profitably with its external environment. The many unknowns in the external environment introduce considerable uncertainty into strategic decision making. The concepts presented in this chapter are designed to help the strategic manager identify uncertainties in the external environment and plan how to deal with them. This chapter also presents an overall framework for global environmental analysis that includes a discussion of nine major trends that are affecting businesses of all types throughout the world. The basic concepts used to assess the global environment include the elements of competitive business strategies for global markets.

A FRAMEWORK FOR GLOBAL ENVIRONMENTAL ANALYSIS

Organizations do not exist in a vacuum. Rather, they are affected directly and indirectly by many stakeholders. Figure 7.1 is a graphical representation of an organization and its direct and indirect relationships with its stakeholders in a global environment. It is essential for an organization to understand who these stakeholders are, what their relationships are to the organization, and what assumptions the organization is making about them and their behavior. These assumptions should be tested for validity and appropriateness and should be reformulated as necessary. Classifying economic, political, social, technological, competitive, and geographic

---

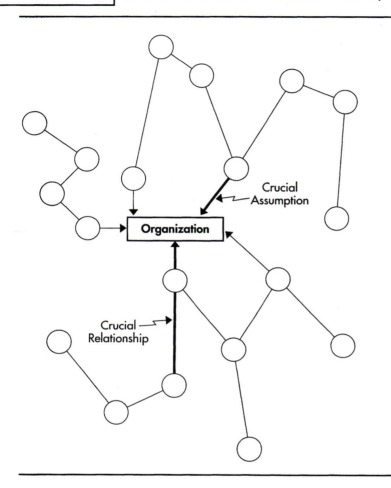

implications of these assumptions helps determine the nature of the relationships an organization has with its stakeholders and what impact their activities are likely to have on the organization. Tracing global trends (such as the trend toward global monetary superliquidity and increased use of information technology) and anticipating their effects on the organization's stakeholders further clarify the opportunities and threats the environment holds for the organization. Stakeholder maps, assumptions, and interpretations of those assumptions depict the critical uncertainties that an organization faces.

Some assumptions are pivotal and serve as the very underpinnings of the organization's policies, plans, and strategies. The organization is potentially vulnerable to changes and inaccuracies in these assumptions, so they must be examined carefully. The crucial stakeholders in an organization's environment also change over time, and today that change is rapid. Statistical forecasting and econometric modeling can be used to project some of these changes, as long as the fundamental relationships in the underlying stakeholder structure remain constant. Structural change in stakeholder environments, however, is common and frequent. Quantitative methods may not satisfactorily capture these major qualitative shifts. For this reason, qualitative environmental forecasting techniques are often used to describe and predict possible shifts in the web of relationships in the organization's stakeholder environment and to determine their probable effects on the organization.

A completed environmental assessment enables an organization (1) to find its best possible niche and (2) to decide how it might best respond to a range of future environmental conditions. Environmental assessment is a never-ending task for businesses, because their environments are constantly changing and they are continuously being affected by forces from abroad—and sometimes from the farthest reaches of the globe.

MAJOR GLOBAL TRENDS

Today's business exists in a global political economy. National, regional, and local economies no longer are independent structures or isolated entities. Instead, a worldwide framework of interactions exists both within and between national, regional, and local economies. This interdependence is the result of a long-term trend in the evolution of civilization, including the development of improved methods of transportation, communication, and information handling and the exploits of merchant adventurers beginning with the Phoenician sailors and continuing through the Roman speculators. The Venetian traders, the Hanseatic League, the Portuguese explorers, the Spanish conquistadors, the Dutch merchants, the British imperialists—all served to create a strong dependent relationship among peoples of the world.

World War II furthered global integration, because it made people more aware of opportunities and threats to which they were exposed from other parts of the globe. Advanced technologies were developed in communication and computation and in massive destruction. The dropping of atomic bombs at Hiroshima and Nagasaki alerted the world to the possibility of global destruction and to the need to control the proliferation of such weapons and avoid a nuclear catastrophe. Having learned the lessons taught by the impotent League of Nations and the ill-conceived Treaty of Versailles that followed World War I, world leaders sought to create more effective global institutions. The United Nations, the International Monetary Fund, the Organization for Economic Cooperation and Development (OECD), Comecon (the Eastern bloc's version of the Common Market, which was disbanded in 1991), and the World Bank are among the institutions formed to help nations and organizations deal with the new global political and economic environment. Working together, all these factors accelerated the creation of a truly global economy until, in 1978, Senator Hubert Humphrey could claim that "There isn't a nation in the world which controls even the value of its money, the central symbol of independence. Inflation, recession, and stagflation are global in nature."

Fortune's report on the world's largest 500 industrial corporations provides a useful starting point for examining global trends (Woods, 1992). Table 7.1 shows what countries have the greatest numbers of large companies and what is the largest company in each. Of the ten countries shown, the largest companies in four of them are automotive and two are in petroleum.

TABLE 7.1	Countries with the Most Fortune 500 Companies	
Country	**Companies on the List**	**Largest Company**
United States	157	General Motors
Japan	119	Toyota Motor
Britain	43	British Petroleum
Germany	33	Daimler-Benz
France	32	Elf Aquitaine
Sweden	14	Volvo
South Korea	13	Samsung Group
Switzerland	10	Nestlé
Australia	9	Broken Hill Propietary
Canada	9	Northern Telecom

Despite the number of its companies in the Fortune 500, the United States lags behind the rest of the world in fixed investments as a percentage of gross domestic product (Pennar, 1992). Table 7.2 shows these data for the major industrial nations.

TABLE 7.2	Percent of GDP Devoted to Fixed Investment
United States	15%
Britain	18%
France	20%
Germany	20%
Canada	22%
Japan	28%

Another perspective on global trends appears in Table 7.3 (Labate, 1992), where real domestic growth from 1987 projected through 1993 is shown for four major areas of the world. The forecast is for moderate growth for all four in 1993, as the world recovers from the 1991–1992 recession.

TABLE 7.3	Real Growth in GDP (in percent)						
Country	1987	1988	1989	1990	1991	1992	1993
Asia	12.0	9.5	6.0	7.0	8.5	7.0	6.8
Japan	4.0	6.5	4.8	5.5	4.5	2.5	3.4
Europe	2.7	4.0	3.5	3.0	0.8	1.5	3.0
United States	3.0	3.8	2.5	1.0	–1.0	2.5	3.0

ASSESSMENT OF THE GLOBAL ENVIRONMENT

Assessment of the global environment begins with a stakeholder analysis. First, strategic managers need to identify the key stakeholders in the organization's business environment worldwide. Second, significant relationships among the stakeholders are charted to make a stakeholder map. The stakeholder map is a tool that strategic managers can use to identify the sources of environmental opportunities and threats and the ways they are transmitted to the organization. Third, managers identify and test assumptions about stakeholders, rank these assumptions, and determine which assumptions are most accurate and advantageous.

Stakeholder analysis is supported by environmental scanning. *Environmental scanning* is a method of identifying the economic, political, social, technological, competitive, and geographic factors that affect the organization and then assessing their potential as opportunities or threats. A stakeholder map can then be used to show how these factors propagate through the environment and where they will have an important impact on the organization. Environmental scanning includes an assessment of the organization's vulnerability to environmental forces, such as price increases in oil by OPEC. Vulnerability analysis helps strategic managers determine whether the firm is in serious danger or is well prepared to cope with these forces. Because the global environment is becoming more uncertain, vulnerability analysis (described in Chapter 5) is becoming more important.

Another important aspect of environmental analysis is predicting global environmental trends and determining how they might affect strategic planning in the future. Qualitative environmental forecasting was described in Chapter 4 as a method for identifying possible future events and determining how they could affect the organization's performance. This method involves developing alternative scenarios and planning possible responses to them. Forecasting is important because the desirability of a strategic plan can easily change in light of events beyond the organization's control, such as actions of competitors or new government regulations.

Assessing the global environment should begin with examining basic forces at work and determining their effects on the organization or industry under consideration. Major global trends occur in the following areas:

1. Global money and capital markets
2. Information technology
3. A symbol-based economy
4. Diminished power of nation-states
5. Deregulation of markets
6. Global trade
7. Collapsing of the raw-materials economy
8. Demographic diversity
9. Transitional ecology

GLOBAL MONEY AND CAPITAL MARKETS

In today's global economy, money flows easily and quickly throughout the world. Generally it seeks the best interest rates or the best investment opportunities. One of the side effects of OPEC's 1973 increase in oil prices was that great amounts of cash (mostly dollars) began to pour into Middle East countries, from which it was deposited in European banks. Because, at the time, neither the U.S. trade position nor its gold stock was adequate to the task of providing a nesting place for these dollars, they were free to float around the world. This meant that there were a lot of dollars available to be invested or used without the control of U.S. banking authorities. These dollars came to be called "Eurodollars." By the late 1980s, Eurodollar deposits exceeded $1 trillion. In other words, for every $2 deposited in a bank or savings and loan inside the United States, there is another $1 deposited outside, beyond the reach of U.S. regulatory bodies.

This has become "stateless money." We can consider the world as having stateless money that has led to a stateless banking system without national boundaries. International business now relies on the stateless banking system. Another crucial event leading to stateless money occurred on August 15, 1971, when President Richard Nixon suspended the convertibility of dollars into gold and imposed a 10% surcharge on all imports to restore some balance to the United States's deteriorating international monetary flows. Before that, dollars had been convertible to gold at $35 per ounce. Now the value of the dollar was allowed to "float" according to market forces. By the end of 1973, all the major currencies in the world had stopped pegging their exchange rates to the dollar; true global floating had begun.

There are two major implications of stateless money. One is that money is free to flow to wherever in the world it is needed or demanded. The second is that floating exchange rates create volatility in the money markets. This means that a company that does business in other countries is directly vulnerable to changes in exchange rates (from which it may either profit or lose, depending on the nature of its investment). It also means that any company doing business in any country is vulnerable to changes in exchange rates in other countries that affect the relative prices of its goods or services compared to those of its actual or potential foreign competitors. And because the costs of international transportation and communication are decreasing, foreign firms have the capacity to invade other countries' markets rather effectively.

Stateless money has led to many profound changes in the U.S. and global economies. Foreign investment in other countries' economies has increased. In 1977, for example, foreign investment equaled about 2% of the total net worth of all non-financial corporations in the United States; by 1988, it exceeded 9%. It is expected to reach about 15% by 1995. In 1989 Americans were investing about 10% of their portfolios in foreign securities. Cross-border equity investments by the Japanese, British, and West Germans (before unification with East Germany) have been increasing at a rapid rate. Table 7.4 summarizes the extent of cross-border equity flows for 1989. This means that one nation's savings can easily be invested in another nation, depending on the rates of return. Consequently, our young real estate developer in Colorado may find his best source of capital in Germany or Japan, and these foreign banks may find attractive investments with him.

TABLE 7.4   **Cross-border Equity Flows (Dollar amounts in billions)**

From / To	United States	Britain	Other European Countries	Japan	Total Equity Imported
United States	X	83	50	84	217
Britain	97	X	110	76	283
Other European Countries	107	29	X	66	202
Japan	61	5	8	X	74
Total Capital Exported	265	117	168	226	$776 Billion

Source: The Economist, July 21, 1990.

The investments described above are equity investments and not the direct foreign investments made by companies abroad. Investments made, for example, by General Electric in its European plants and facilities are not included in Table 7.4. Direct foreign investment is also increasing. In 1987 all foreign countries, led by the British, invested some $35 billion in U.S. businesses and real estate. In the same year, however, U.S. companies invested over $50 billion in their subsidiaries and affiliates abroad, especially those in the European Common Market. At the end of 1987, total U.S. investment abroad was estimated to exceed $310 billion.

Equity investment and direct investment money is long-term money. Short-term money moves even faster globally. Every night, for example, about $1.5 trillion flows through New York's Clearing House Interbank Payment System (CHIPS), which processes all the domestic and foreign payments passing through New York banks. This amounts to about one-third of the United States's *annual* gross national product and, of course, it does not account for all short-term cross-border money flows. Trade payment accounts for only a very small portion of this volume, perhaps less than 1/300th. Advances in information technology have made this enormous change in the world's foreign exchange (FX) markets possible. In *The Borderless World* (1990), Kenichi Ohmae explains.

> At the root of these developments is the recent explosion of superliquidity in the Triad's [the U.S., Japan, and the EEC] financial markets. In Japan, for example, private savings and the corporate sector generate more than $1 billion in surplus capital every day that has to be invested somewhere. . . . The global, interlinked, tradable FX empire allows money literally to travel around the globe in seconds. Even if, for instance, the Bank of Japan decides to tighten up the money supply at home, desired funds are instantaneously available from abroad. During 1988 more funds were raised in Europe than at home for the entire Japanese private sector. (pp. 159–162)

Financial deregulation and technological breakthroughs in computers and telecommunications have created the world of fast-moving, stateless money. With it, many of our concepts about the economic environment of a firm have also changed. Exchange rates are no longer tied to the balances of trade among nations. Interest rates do not necessarily follow economic activities. The effects of national fiscal and monetary policies are no longer predictable. This means that every business—no matter where in the world it is located—is affected by events in the global financial markets. Increasingly, these events happen quickly and without warning. Successful strategic management requires that events taking place in global money and capital markets be monitored, examined, and evaluated for their impact on the business and its plans.

Two significant arenas are emerging as the dominant world markets. The first is a more unified Europe after 1992 and the second is the world's fastest growth area in the Pacific rim (Kraar, 1992). For example, Kraar describes the size and GDP of major Asian countries as follows:

China: GDP of $371.2 billion, 1,139 million people

Japan: GDP of $3,369.7 billion, 123.9 million people

South Korea: GDP of $283.5 billion, 43.3 million people

Taiwan: GDP of $175.7 billion, 20.4 million people

Indonesia: GDP of $107.8 billion, 179.3 million people

Thailand: GDP of $92.0 billion, 56.9 million people

Hong Kong: GDP of $82.7 billion, 5.8 million people

The fastest-growing country is China, which increased its GDP from $100 billion in 1983 to $371.2 billion in 1992. With its huge population, China can be a major outlet for U.S. goods and services, provided that Americans can compete with China's neighbors. The European market represents a key area for U.S. companies because of a longer history of trade and a number of restrictions placed on Japanese products. Tully (1992) claims that despite a recession in Europe, there is a growing drive to unify in order to serve a potential combined market of 340 million people who have funds to spend. The movement in this direction is obvious when one examines the objectives established to date:

Sector	Objectives	Results
Airlines	Open skies	Free international pricing by 1993
Telecommunications	Deregulation	Open competition by 1993
Automobiles	End quotes	National quotas until 2000
Borders	Remove customs	Barriers and free movement by 1993
Social policy	Heavy regulations	Lack of progress

Two important questions arise in any discussion of trade with Europe. First, will Germany lead the pack? Unification may be taking longer than anticipated, but Germany is Europe's largest economy and is on its way to becoming a global superpower (Rapoport, 1992). The GDP in eastern Germany is projected to grow 8% in 1992 and 10% in 1993, compared with growth of 1.5% in the western sector. Germany's trade surplus is expected to reach $33 billion in 1992 and $40 billion in 1993, which is second only to Japan's. (As evidence of Germany's clout, its unwillingness to reduce interest rates has wreaked havoc on all European countries.) It has been suggested that Germany offers a good model for American managers (Wever and Allen, 1992). The German market is based on social concerns and blurs the boundaries between what is good for business and what is needed by society. For example, the union used a government program as a strategy for modernizing industry. Even German banks reformed themselves without government intervention. Can U.S. companies follow Germany's model? The answer is: not "the work ethic." Rather, U.S. firms can compete on the basis of innovation and creativity.

The second question that arises is whether we can meet European standards. This has proved a real challenge for most American companies. The International Standards Organization in Geneva has issued the ISO-9000 guideposts, which can significantly affect the ability of U.S. companies to compete in Europe (Levine, 1992). Examples of the new requirements include design and service specifications, manufacturing process controls, supplier approval controls, after-sale service support, verification of inspection and testing, and record of training requirements.

In order to meet the hundreds and eventually thousands of EC rules, U.S. exporters—especially small ones—will have to make significant changes in the way they do business. Most exporters have not invested in European contacts, nor does the United States have a coordinated policy to deal with the coming standards (Oster, et al., 1992). The result is a major hurdle for U.S. exporters to overcome on many products that have never been regulated. One approach that has been suggested is for business and the government to coordinate their combined R&D expenditures, which can be critical to future competitiveness (Smith, 1992).

INFORMATION TECHNOLOGY

Technological advances in telecommunications and in computers have radically changed the flows of information throughout the world. As a result of the expansive use of fiber-optic cables, satellites, radio, television, and phone lines, it is possible for people and computers—be they large-scale "super" computers or "micro" or personal computers—to communicate with one another in seconds, wherever they are located in the world. Modern computer networks allow data, video, and voice communications to flow among entities and make it possible for organizations to share technological resources such as laser printers and mainframe computers. They also enable organizations to extend the size and scope of their operations by collapsing time and distance.

One of the results of these breakthroughs has been the advent of "interorganizational" systems and globally distributed systems. These are systems that permit direct communication and information exchange across organizational and national boundaries. Electronic data interchange (EDI) among organizations and their customers, suppliers, and other business partners is one result. Electronic mail (E-mail) and electronic funds transfer (EFT) are others. E-mail allows messages to flow quickly between one point and another. EFT makes possible the movement of funds between accounts wherever they are located. The CHIPs system and SWIFT (Society for Worldwide International Funds Transfers) are long-established worldwide electronic utilities that permit fully coupled, shared electronic business transactions to take place throughout the world. EFT has revolutionized the world's banking and financial services industries. Added to these technological tools are telephone systems—domestic and worldwide—and information product delivery services. Dow Jones News Retrieval Service, Reuters, and McGraw-Hill, for example, make news, commodity and financial quotes, and other information electronically available, worldwide, instantaneously. CNN and other television and radio networks also report on events soon after they occur.

The use of these technologies is characterized by both widespread cooperation and competition. Electronic alliances have led to standards such as the U.S. grocery industry's uniform communication standard (which is often bar-coded on products), the SWIFT EFT standard, EDIFACT and X.12 standards for moving business messages, and comparable standards in transportation, warehousing, automobiles, and aerospace. These standards have defined a playing field in which intense competition is taking place. Much of this was set in motion when Judge Harold Greene broke up AT&T into a long-distance carrier and seven regional telephone companies in the United States in 1984. Now, in most countries of the developed world, there is fierce competition for telecommunications business. AT&T has to contend with MCI, U.S. Sprint, and the seven Bell operating companies; British Telecom has Mercury; Nippon Telegraph and Telephone has three long-distance rivals; KDD, Japan's international carrier, has two competitors. Only in continental Western Europe, where telecommunications is centralized in state-owned postal telegraph and telephone companies (PTTs), and in Canada are telephone monopolies intact. Competition has been pushing the industry ahead rapidly, especially in the field of global information services. Most of these services have been deregulated throughout the developed world.

There are several important implications of the widespread use of information technology for strategic managers.

1. Technology can now be used for competitive advantage. Companies such as American Airlines with its SABRE system, Merrill Lynch, Citicorp, Baxter International, and Frito-Lay have developed systems that enable them to provide high-quality services, rapidly, to their customers and suppliers. This has helped them compete effectively in both local and global markets.

2. As we have noted, information technology is being used to move money and information to any place in the world. This has led to "superliquidity" and has permitted available funds to flow rapidly to those places in the world that offer the best financial opportunities. It has also increased the volatility of exchange rates among the world's currencies.

3. Information technology has enabled companies to coordinate and control their activities on a worldwide basis by greatly compressing time and distance. It can be used for collaborative work, electronic meetings, the exchange of knowledge and information products, bilateral communication, and many command and control functions. Texas Instruments, for example, operates manufacturing facilities in 18 countries and has sales and marketing operations in more than 30. In its Avezzano, Italy, facility an international team from the United States, Japan, Italy, Germany, and France worked together (in large part electronically) to build a new, advanced semiconductor facility. Some of its software products are designed in its European facilities, written in other countries, and incorporated in products produced in the United States. All of this and a myriad of other activities are managed electronically by means of a worldwide network operated out of Dallas, Texas. TI and many other companies whose products are information-intensive can move product knowledge and products themselves electronically around the world. This means that companies are able to disburse their value-adding chain and to perform functions wherever in the world it is most economically feasible. This flexibility redefines the comparative advantages of nations.

As the world continues to move toward a symbol-based economy, sometimes called the information society, and away from a material-based, or industrial, society, information technology will play an ever-increasing role in the strategies and management of firms. An environmental assessment should include an examination of global technological trends as they affect the firm and its industry. It should focus especially on the new opportunities and threats that information technology presents.

EMERGENCE OF A SYMBOL-BASED ECONOMY

The increased contribution of knowledge and information to the world's economies has created a symbol-based economy in which the creating and processing of symbols adds more economic value than the processing of raw materials. Drucker explains: ". . . in the world economy of today, the 'real' economy of goods and services and the 'symbol' economy of money, credit, and capital are no longer bound tightly to each other; they are, indeed, moving further and further apart" (Drucker, 1989, p. 12). Until recent times, few jobs required much in the way of knowledge. Today, however, knowledge and education have become the passport to good jobs and careers. Knowledge has become a developed economy's capital, and its knowledge workers and symbol processors are the group that sets the society's values and norms. Political economist Robert Reich (1991) calls the people who engage in this handling and processing of symbols "symbolic-analysts." *Knowledge workers* and *information workers* are other terms commonly used for these kinds of specialists, who include management consultants, architects, research scientists, design engineers, software engineers, civil engineers, biotechnology engineers, sound engineers, public relations executives, investment bankers, lawyers, real estate developers, and accountants.

Reich distinguishes these symbolic jobs from those that provide routine production (blue-collar) services and those that provide in-person services, such as attendants at fast-food outlets. Each of the three job categories plays a different role in the global economy. Routine production workers function in domestic economies and compete in world markets on the basis of their cost for manual labor. Personal service workers primarily serve the residents of their domestic economies and visiting tourists. Their services are not generally traded in global markets. As Rob Kling (1990) put it, "After all, one doesn't fly to Seoul just for a haircut or a cab ride, even if it is cheap! But a publisher may well have a book typeset in Southeast Asia, and thus displace clerical jobs in the United States" (p. 101).

Symbolic-analytic services, on the other hand, become distinctive competencies of firms and of the nations in which they reside. They are traded worldwide. Thus the people who offer these services "must compete with foreign providers even in the American market. But they do not enter world commerce as standardized things. Traded instead are the manipulations of symbols—data, words, oral and visual representations" (Robert Reich, 1991, p. 177).

Economic and social researchers have developed two different but related concepts to describe the global effects of the trend toward knowledge-based and information work. One is the *postindustrial society*. Proposed by Daniel Bell (1973), it highlights the importance of the service sector in modern economies and stresses the central role that credentialed experts such as scientists, engineers, and other knowledge producers play in them. Marc Porat (1977) offered the concept of the *information society*. He focused on the fact that in an increasing number of jobs, the processing of information has become a central and time-consuming activity.

Porat and others have found that information occupations have grown in size from 17% of the U.S. workforce in 1900 to over 50% in 1980. Since then the information sector has continued to provide a majority of jobs in the U.S. workforce and is growing rapidly in Japan, Western Europe, and other developed countries.

This trend has major implications for the management of organizations. In *In the Age of the Smart Machine* (1988), Shoshana Zuboff argues that organizations with highly "informated" jobs require specially skilled workers who can challenge traditional managerial styles and authority and whose skills become a novel resource upon which to base the organization's strategy. These special information skills often provide a comparative advantage in international markets. These forces are creating a new type of capitalism, *informational capitalism* (Luke and White, 1985). In an informational capitalistic society, "data-intensive techniques, cybernetic knowledge, and electronic technologies" are the crucial strategic resources. And, as Reich (1991) reminds us, they have also become the crucial resources in global trade. Reich summarizes: "In the emerging global economy, even the most impressive of positions in the most prestigious of organizations is vulnerable to worldwide competition if it entails easily replicated routines. The only true competitive advantage lies in [the symbolic-analysts'] skill in solving, identifying, and brokering new problems" (p. 184).

DIMINISHED POWER OF NATION–STATES

A trend toward fragmentation within nation–states is also prevalent. In what was formerly the Soviet Union, Eastern Europe, and the Middle East, factions are beginning to break away from the center and form local political economies, often around ethnic lines. Within the United States during the Reagan years, considerable power and responsibility, especially in the social realm, devolved to states and local governments. Consequently, Tennessee can compete directly with Ohio and Texas for a new Japanese auto plant without necessarily involving the federal government. Denver, Miami, Atlanta, Dallas, and Los Angeles can and do compete in the global market for foreign plants, conventions, conferences, international tourism, and special events such as the Olympics. According to *Time* (May 27, 1991), the competition is getting ugly.

> Virtually every state is going after a piece of the $400 billion worth of foreign investment in the U.S. . . . The number of state development offices abroad, which function almost like consulates, has doubled in the past five years, to 160. Illinois has more foreign offices than many small nations; it has outposts in Moscow, Shenyang, Brussels, Warsaw, Budapest, Toronto, Mexico City, Hong Kong and Osaka. No fewer than 38 states—plus San Bernardino, Calif. and Houston—maintain offices in Tokyo. (p. 42)

By engaging in these activities, local governmental units have assumed powers that previously were primarily the federal government's. In doing so they challenge the very core concepts that the country's founders invoked to bind the states (and cities) together.

This means that an assessment of a firm's environment must include an examination of stakeholders and forces in the broad global, transnational economy and political system. It should focus on the power and role of stateless corporations and on trading regions and blocs. The role of domestic regional, state, and local governmental units should also be carefully examined. Nation–states and their agencies and laws remain important, but long-term trends indicate that supranational and subnational entities are becoming even more so.

DEREGULATION OF MARKETS

A market is an idea, an artifact created by humans. No market is entirely open or free. Governments supervise and control many of the activities of private enterprises operating within their jurisdiction in the interest of economic efficiency, fairness, health, and safety. The rules and orders set by the executive authority to achieve these purposes are called regulations. Regulations usually take one of two forms. Either standards are established that must be adhered to, or limitations and controls are imposed on competition. Every nation sets different standards and controls competition in a different way and thus creates its own version of a market. There is a long-term trend, however, for these human-made markets to become similar and to become more open. This tendency fosters increased globalization.

In extreme cases of government regulation, industries are nationalized, such as coal was in the United Kingdom during the 1930s, or private natural monopolies are established, as were many U.S. utility companies. In the United States and other market-based economies, regulations are used to control activities in which normal market forces, operating alone, fail to achieve social objectives. In planned economies, such as the former Soviet Union, regulations are used to control almost all economic activities. In this case, market forces such as prices have little effect.

The origin of government regulations antedates the Industrial Revolution. Problems created by industrialization, however, brought on the need for more regulations. Child labor laws, foreign exchange controls, restrictive trade practices acts, employment protection acts, and licensing controls are among the regulations that governments have seen fit to impose as industry developed. Product standards, restrictions on entry, and trade barriers are among the other areas that have been regulated. Market externalities—consequences for public welfare or costs not fully accounted for in the market system—such as pollution, reclamation, visual impact, and noise have also required environmental and other controls.

In the years following World War II, a large body of regulations was put into effect in most Western, market-oriented nations. During the 1970s concern about the costs of these regulations began to rise, and substantial political pressure was brought to bear on governments to repeal, reform, or abolish some existing regulations. Under the Thatcher government in the United Kingdom, several large government-owned companies such as British Telecom were privatized. In the United States, the financial and airline industries (among others) were substantially deregulated. In Eastern Europe, efforts are being made to move toward a market economy. The People's Republic of China has established free trading zones in order to take advantage of market forces. The EC in 1992, the Pacific Rim "yen bloc," and the North American Free Trade Agreement all serve to lower trade barriers among the countries agreeing to the pact. These alliances are strong indications of a worldwide trend to liberalize markets both within and among nations. Such "deregulation" might better be referred to as "reregulation," because governments are still responsible for controlling for socially undesirable results.

As we have noted, global financial markets were among the first to become deregulated. During the last two decades, many restrictions on financial flows across national borders have been dropped. Several countries have deregulated their internal financial markets, and financial firms have developed innovations that separate the choice of currency and other aspects of contracts from the jurisdiction of the nation in which they originate. This has led to the increased integration of international financial markets. Originally, American securities firms benefited from this global integration, because the financial deregulation movement began in America, and many U.S. firms learned to deal with it first. A freer flow of funds across borders, permitted by deregulation, encourages a freer flow of other economic activities and serves as a stimulus to increased globalization.

GLOBAL TRADE

World trade has grown steadily since the end of World War II. In 1991 world trade reached almost two and three-quarters trillion dollars, of which about 73% was accounted for by OECD countries. *Since 1980 world trade has increased at a faster rate than has world output.* This means that the countries of the world have developed a greater propensity to trade goods and services among one another. As countries develop economically, they become more efficient at producing goods and services, frequently specializing in particular products for which they have a comparative advantage. At the same time, their populations tend to demand more complex, luxurious, and specialized goods and services. Together these factors provide a stimulus for imports and an opportunity for exports. Thus they encourage nation–states to trade with one another globally. This trend is facilitated by advances in transportation and communication technology. It also means that these trading nations become more dependent on each other and that their economies become more "exposed" to events that happen throughout the world. The companies that are directly involved in foreign trade and those that are indirectly dependent on it are also vulnerable to changes in world conditions.

In world statistics, trade is classified as either visible or invisible. *Visible trade* involves the exchange of physical goods and products. *Invisible trade* involves the exchange of services—such as financial, accounting, consulting, and advertising services—and includes financial transactions, profits, and interest payments. Invisible trade accounts for about 25% of the total world trade and is increasing at a faster rate than visible trade. (This confirms the fact that the world is being transformed from a material-based economy to a symbol- or information-based economy.) The United States is the world leader in invisible exports. When both visible and invisible exports are taken into account, the United States is found to have led all countries in world trade in 1988, with about 14.9% of the world total. (West Germany had 11.1%, Japan 10.4%, the United Kingdom 8.2%, and France 7.0%.) West Germany had a slight lead over the United States with respect to visible exports (11.9%) and Japan, France, and the United Kingdom followed in that order.

General Electric has nearly always been an international company. Formed in 1892 from Thomas Edison's old company, it soon began to work with Westinghouse, Siemens, and AEG in Europe to form a global oligopoly. After World War I, under the leadership of Gerard Swope, GE began to take an active role in Britain, Germany, France, Mexico, South Africa, Australia, and Japan. Following World War II, in 1953 GE was among the first companies to sell patents to the Japanese and help them build new factories. Since then the company has been an unchallenged leader in a large number of markets in the United States, including industrial machinery, medical electronics, and consumer electronics. As the global business environment began to change during the 1980s, however, CEO Jack Welsh and his management team crafted a new global strategy. They decided to get out of any business, anywhere (including the United States), in which GE could not attain a major position *worldwide*, even if the business was profitable. GE was restructured. It even sold off profitable U.S. businesses such as those marketing small appliances and semiconductors, because it was not a strong global competitor in those industries. About $10 billion of business was jettisoned. At the same time, the company acquired several new businesses abroad, especially in Europe, in which management believed GE could become a global leader. The total acquisition cost was about $19 billion; acquisitions were as diverse as the securities firm of Kidder, Peabody and the Tungsram lighting company of Hungary. Today the GE label goes on microwave ovens designed, fabricated, and assembled by Sansung in South Korea, and GE has become the largest private employer in Singapore and a major contributor to the Asian trading city's spectacular economic development.

As an editor at Kiplinger's (August, 1991, p. 22) put it, "Chief among GE's strategies is Welch's notion of a 'boundaryless' company that can do business in Cairo, Egypt, as easily as in Cairo, Ill." Welch's vision is to blend the company with its suppliers, customers, and other stakeholders into a global "seamless mass." The strategy seems to be working. GE's worldwide revenues topped $58 billion in 1990. The company has had 15 straight years of growth in earnings per share and expects earnings to continue to grow in 1991 and 1992. On May 31, 1991, GE had a total market value of over $67 billion, making it the fourth largest company in *Business Week*'s Global 1000 (behind Nippon Telegraph & Telephone, Royal Dutch/Shell, and Exxon).

COLLAPSING OF THE RAW-MATERIALS ECONOMY

There is a long-term trend in production to substitute knowledge and information for primary raw materials and for manual labor. This has changed the nature of industry in developed countries and placed additional stress on Third World countries. Most of the Third World labor force is engaged in agriculture, forest products, metals, minerals, and other primary materials. During the last 10 years, worldwide production of these primary materials has risen between 20% and 35%. Since about 1950, however, the prices of these products have been erratic and have generally trended downward. Demand has weakened. As the World Bank (1987) reported, the economic situation of those countries most heavily involved in exporting traditional primary raw materials deteriorated during the last 40 years, as prices declined relative to the prices of industrial goods.

Management theorist Peter Drucker (1986) sees major implications in this trend:

> The raw materials economy has thus come uncoupled from the industrial economy. This is a major structural change in the world economy, with tremendous implications for economic and social policy . . . in developed and developing countries alike. (p. 4)

He goes on.

> Why this decline in demand [for primary materials]? It is not that industrial production is fading in importance as the service sector grows—a common myth for which there is not the slightest evidence. What is happening is much more significant. Industrial production is steadily switching away from heavily material-intensive products and processes. One of the reasons for this is the now high-technology industries. In a semiconductor microchip the raw materials account for 1 to 3 percent of total production cost; in an automobile their share is 40 percent, and in pots and pans 60 percent. But also in older industries the same scaling down of raw materials needs goes on, with respect to old products as well as new ones. Fifty to 100 pounds of fiberglass cable transmit as many telephone messages as does one ton of copper wire. (p. 6)

The semiconductor industry is a good illustration of Drucker's point. It was born with the invention of the transistor at Bell telephone laboratories in 1947. Since that time its basic raw material, silicon (sand), has not changed. During the same period, however, the information that can be stored on a single wafer has expanded from about 1,000 bits to 64 million bits. The power of chip-based microprocessors has increased several thousand times. This has come as the result of research and development that has resulted in denser integrated circuits in which simple cells are replicated hundreds of thousands or millions of times. With each new infusion of knowledge, the relative role of raw materials has decreased. While the semiconductor industry has experienced exceptionally high technological velocity and innovation—as have the pharmaceutical, telecommunications, analytical instrument, and computer industries—the same trend is occurring less dramatically in many other industries. Since 1972 the number of beer and soft drink cans produced from a pound of aluminum has increased from less than 22 to almost 30. In the automotive industry, the cumulative value of quality improvements made in safety, fuel economy, emissions controls, and other intellectual inputs during the last 15 years has added about $3,500 to the retail value of cars. During World War II, bombs had to be deployed within about 3 miles of their target and were expected to land within a radius of about a mile of it. In the Gulf War of 1991, laser-guided bombs were released about 50 miles from their target and landed within 20 feet of it (*Fortune,* June 3, 1991). These are but a few indications of the fact that knowledge and information inputs into products are becoming ever more important. As a consequence, the economic forces affecting global raw-materials markets have become substantially uncoupled from those affecting global industrial markets.

DEMOGRAPHIC DIVERSITY AND THE WORLD DIVISION OF LABOR

Lewis Galoob Toys, headquartered in San Francisco, recorded sales of about $127 million on assets of approximately $75 million in 1990. Micro Machines®, mini-vehicles, dolls, games, and Game Genie™, are among the products it sells worldwide and the majority of its revenues come from North America and Europe. In addition to its own designers and engineers, the company engages independent designers and engineers from all over the world. It produces substantially all of its products under proprietary and character licenses obtained from toy inventors and designers also located around the globe. Some 40 "partner" factories in Hong Kong, Thailand, and the People's Republic of China manufacture Galoob's products. In order to reduce the risk of political or economic disruptions in its countries of manufacture, the firm has a $40 million insurance policy with Lloyds of London. For this global capability, Galoob relies on only about 100 employees of its own and about 199 in its wholly owned Hong Kong subsidiary.

A world market for labor is emerging as individuals and countries seek comparative advantage in the global division of labor. This means that most managers will be managing a more diverse workforce. As Jamieson and O'Mara (1991) have described it, in most countries today, and especially in the United States,

> the contemporary workforce doesn't look like, think like, act like, or have the same desires as the workforce of the past. Workforce 2000—and the workforce of today—is significantly different in its age distribution, increasing equality of men and women, cultural diversity, range of educational levels, inclusion of persons with disabilities, and mix of values and attitudes. These translate into portraits of diversity—a workforce of individuals who bring different resources and perspectives to the workplace and who have distinctive needs, preferences, expectations and lifestyles. (p. 14)

As a result, managers are confronted daily with new, complex challenges.

In the past, in most developed countries there was a dominant majority in the workforce (for example, white males in the United States). Often there was also a dominated minority, such as the black slaves in the antebellum South, who were imported to do hard, manual labor. William Johnson (1991) describes this as part of a long-term trend.

> The movement of people from one country to another is, of course, not new. In previous centuries, Irish stonemasons helped build U.S. canals, and Chinese laborers constructed North America's transcontinental railroads. In the 1970s and 1980s, it was common to find Indian engineers writing software in Silicon Valley, Turks cleaning hotel rooms in Berlin, and Algerians assembling cars in France.

> During the 1990s, the world's workforce will become even more mobile, and employers will increasingly reach across borders to find the skills they need. These movements of workers will be driven by the growing gap between the world's supplies of labor and the demands for it.

As a consequence, world economies are moving from an era in which large portions of the workforce are similar—and in which those who are different are expected to adapt or follow orders—to an era in which the workforce is composed of many different individuals. Johnson (1991) has identified several key trends in the global workforce:

1. The world workforce is growing rapidly. From 1985 to 2000, the workforce is expected to grow by some 600 million people, an increase of about 27%.

2. The vast majority of these new workers, about 95%, will come from developing countries such as Mexico and Pakistan.
3. Women will enter the workforce in great numbers, especially in the developing countries, where relatively few women have been absorbed to date.
4. The average age of the world's workforce will rise, especially in the developed countries.
5. People worldwide will be increasingly well educated. The developing countries will produce a growing share of the world's high school and college graduates.
6. Developed countries will send a higher percentage of their young to school.
7. Developing countries will supply a growing share of the world's educated people.

These trends will bring about pressures for workers, especially educated ones in developing countries, to emigrate to find better job opportunities. As Reich observed, the demand for these services will depend on levels and type of education and on class of job—routine production, in-person, or symbolic-analytic activities.

> Not all workers are equally likely to emigrate—or equally likely to be welcome elsewhere. . . . Typically, unskilled workers—janitors, dishwashers, or laborers—are recruited locally. At higher skill levels, companies often search across states or regions. Among college graduates, national labor markets are more common: New York banks interview MBA's from San Francisco; Midwestern manufacturers hire engineers from both coasts. At the highest skill levels, the labor market has been international for many years. Bell Laboratories physicists, for example, come from universities in England or India as well as from Princeton or M.I.T. At Schering-Plough's research labs, the first language of bio-chemists is as likely to be Hindi, Japanese, or German as it is English. (Johnson, 1987, p. 123)

This trend toward global demographic diversity in the workforce poses many opportunities and threats for strategic managers. First, firms will have to be prepared to compete in the global market place for the capabilities and skills they need. They may find these skills in a country other than the one(s) they operate in. Then they will be faced with deciding whether to import the labor from the other country or export the relevant business functions to it. If the required labor is physical—routine production, then the work should be transported to the other country. If the required labor is symbolic, however, it may be possible to "import" it electronically.

Second, managers will continually have to manage a workforce that is more diverse ethnically and in other major characteristics. They can no longer use management practices that are focused on the "average" worker. They must be able to treat people from different cultures and backgrounds equitably and effectively if they are to draw on the broad range of power that diversity provides and to compete effectively in global markets.

TRANSNATIONAL ECOLOGY

Nature does not adhere to the artificial boundaries that humans draw. Winds and waters flow according to the laws of the planet, not those made by governments. Humankind can, however, destroy the natural environment. If this lesson was not learned before, it was brought home forcefully during World War II with the dropping of atomic bombs on Japan. And the lesson has continued in the effects of modern technology. The nuclear catastrophe at Chernobyl, for example, reminded us that incompetent and sloppy control of local technologies can cause significant harm across national borders. The winds blew damaging doses of radioactive particles as far north as Scotland, Norway, and Sweden, and clouds still circulating the earth may affect other parts of the world. The effect of the use of chemicals on the ozone layer is another example. River pollution, acid rain, and smog easily cross borders. There is no longer any doubt that all human beings are united in their dependence on a natural environment that transcends national boundaries.

Nature is ordered in a different way from nation–states and other governmental units. The historian of cultures Thomas Berry (1988) refers to this ordering as dividing the earth into "bioregions," which he describes as follows:

> The planet presents itself to us, not as a uniform global reality, but as a complex of highly differentiated regions caught up in the comprehensive unit of the planet itself. There are arctic and tropical, coastal and inland regions, mountains and plains, river valleys and deserts. Each of these regions has its distinctive geological formation, climatic conditions, and living forms. . . . Each is coherent within itself and intimately related to the others. Together they express the wonder and splendor of this garden planet of the universe. (pp. 163–164)

Managing the world as a set of interrelated bio-regions requires a global set of institutions and a *transnational* point of view. Peter Drucker (1989) relates:

> The destruction of the ecology on which humankind's survival depends is thus a common task. To tackle it as a national (or local) task is futile—though obviously a good deal of national, and even local, implementation will be needed. It is futile too to try to tackle it adversarially, with one country accusing its neighbor of befouling the environment. . . . Inevitably the accused country will proclaim its innocence and deny that there is a problem. No effective action can be taken until we accept that serious environmental damage anywhere is everybody's problem and threatens all of us. (pp. 134–135)

As the leaders of cities, states, nations, and regions have sought to deal with the problems of pollution and mutual destruction and, more important, as concerned citizens in all nations of the world have sought better solutions, a global awareness has emerged. This too is serving to globalize our economic and political activities.

THE NEW GLOBAL ECONOMY RECAPITULATED

The nine major global trends that we have noted, taken together, paint a picture of a new global economy. The "global village" originally envisioned by McLuhan (1964) is becoming a reality, and its emergence has major consequences for strategic management and planning. The United States is no longer the preeminent political and economic power in the world. Together with the recovered economies of Japan, Germany, and the other EC countries, the United States now is part of an economic "triad" that collectively controls a large part of economic activity. For this reason, Ohmae (1985) has argued that corporations that hope to compete in the global arena must become "insiders" in the triad. Although it is possible for a few institutions, such as the ill-fated Bank of Credit and Commerce International (it conducted illegal transactions with other countries), to develop effective "outsider" strategies based on cornering business in Third World countries and the Middle East, insider strategies are likely to be the most effective overall. Even BCCI, operating out of Luxembourg, had its main offices in London, and surreptitiously tried to acquire several U.S. banks.

The U.S. multinational corporation also no longer dominates. Companies operating out of other countries, especially those from within the triad, are strong—sometimes dominant—global competitors. Equally important is the emergence of the stateless, global corporation that conducts activities and moves resources around the world without particular reference to national borders. These companies, and the nations in which they operate, now compete with each other on the basis of the overall value they add to their inputs during production.

The major contributor to value in production is knowledge, brain power, and intellectual capital. This fact has become the basis of competition among high-wage nations. Thus the knowledge workers whom Reich calls "symbolic-analysts" are pivotal to the long-term economic success of global corporations and of the developed nations of the world.

Newly industrialized countries (NICs) such as Korea, Taiwan, Hong Kong, Singapore, and Spain are seeking to move up toward a higher-value adding economy and will eventually become a threat to the economic competitiveness of developed nations. They also represent an opportunity for global corporations. The NICs, and Third World and developing nations as well, compete in producing low-cost, high-quality commodities and also such primary materials as agricultural produce, forest products, metals, and minerals. But as the world has become an information society and increased emphasis has been placed on high-value-adding, knowledge-intensive products and services, the industrial economy has been uncoupled from the raw-materials economy. Many manufactured goods and information products now react to forces different from those that influence materials markets.

A global division of labor is emerging as a result of nations capitalizing on their comparative economic advantages. Consequently, world trade continues to grow at about 4% per annum. World trade is growing faster than the rate of growth of world output. This means that the propensity to trade among nations of the world is increasing, as each seeks to exploit its national comparative advantage. Few nations or businesses can escape the effects of this trend.

There is also a global trend toward liberalization and deregulation of economies. Eastern Europe, Russia, and China are all shifting toward more market-oriented economies. The United Kingdom, especially under Margaret Thatcher, has made major strides in privatization of its industries and liberalization of its financial markets. In the United States, airlines, financial institutions, and other industries have been deregulated. Adding to this is a trend for nations to band together in regional trading blocs. The EC 1992, the informal Pacific Rim or "yen bloc," and the United States, Canada, and Mexico Free Trade Agreement are illustrations. The European Community will drop most trade barriers among its 12 nations, and perhaps other countries from the European Free Trade Association will join as well. This will create the largest single pool of freely flowing goods, ser-vices, capital, and people in the world. All these arrangements will promote greater competition among nations and among companies and will further fuel national and corporate attempts to draw on comparative economic advantages.

A greater political freedom has come at the same time during which markets have been liberalized, heralded most prominently by Gorbachev's policy of *glasnost*. This has encouraged the fragmentation of nations (most spectacularly that of the former Soviet Union) into smaller political (often ethnic) groupings and has spawned a new politics of secession.

As a consequence of all these forces, the 300-year-old political conception of the nation–state is losing sway. Global and regional economic and political forces are usurping and undermining, from above, many of most nation–states' former powers. At the same time, internal political fragmentation and pressures from state and local governments are tugging away from below. This means that although national sovereignty remains an important factor in strategic planning, it must be supplemented substantially with a deeper understanding of both global and local political and economic forces. Nation–states acting alone have also proved ineffec-tive in dealing with ecological forces, the problems of pollution, and the threat of mutual destruction. The search for transnational institutions and solutions has fur-ther accelerated the trend toward globalization.

These trends have led to an absence of cohesive global economic leadership, as nations and stateless corporations jockey for preferential positions of comparative economic advantage. Political leaders no longer carry the global clout they once enjoyed. Multinational corporations may wield more power than they formerly did, but most are counterbalanced by strong competitors in many locations in which they operate. These global competitors serve to restrain the excessive use of political power. "Engine Charlie" Wilson's contention that what was good for General Motors was good for the United States, and vice versa, may have had an element of truth in 1953. It is not true today. It is probably not true of any corpo-ration in any country today, and it is certainly not true of any global corporation with respect to the world. Yet in the overall balance of things, multinational corpo-rations have gained power at the expense of nation–states.

The effects of increased competition are complicated by the emergence of new industries based on technological innovations and services and by the massive restructuring of old industries through leveraged buyouts, mergers, acquisitions, divestitures, and internal reorganizations. Global corporations such as General Electric and ASEA Brown Boveri are far different today from the organizations they were 10 years ago.

One of the consequences of these changes has been greater economic volatility. The rapid fluctuations in foreign exchange rates over the last decade or so have had substantial effects on businesses of all types and in all locations. Commodities have become pawns in bigger economic and political games. These games are seri-ous because many nations have become dependent on foreign sources for basic supplies, as the growth in trade demonstrates. Nominal crude oil prices, for exam-ple, have varied from under $3 a barrel to nearly $40 since the mid-1970s when the OPEC countries began to control oil supply and prices. The United States, like many industrialized nations, depends on foreign sources for some 30 critical or "strategic" minerals such as stontium, beryllium, chromium, columbium, cobalt, graphite, natural rubber, tin, bauxite, and zinc. These minerals are essential inputs for such products as jet engines, TV screens, computer memories, home insulation, and automobile starter switches. Most of them come from Third World countries that are politically unstable. Trading patterns among nations and national balances of payments are also subject to wide fluctuations. The result of these forces is a higher level of global economic volatility that adds increased uncertainty to the strategic-planning environment.

Global competition and global trade are also affecting the global movement of labor. Knowledge workers (symbolic-analysts) move, compete, and contribute fluidly in the global markets as they are attracted to areas where they can add the most value. Manual labor and routine production work are being performed primarily by people who accept low wages and offer their employers the advantage of low overall cost. Thus, either these jobs are exported to low-cost locations or the workers themselves immigrate to places where jobs are available. These employment-related movements, coupled with the differential population increases among ethnic groups within countries and between countries (Third World countries in Africa, Asia, and Latin America tend to have higher population increases), mean that managers can expect greater demographic diversity within their workforces. This potential source of the benefits that diversity offers will at the same time complicate the planning of human resources management.

Two global developments mutually support and contribute to the globalization of the economy. One is the presence of global money and superliquidity. Short-term and intermediate funds and long-term investments now flow rapidly and easily across national borders in pursuit of the best opportunities. The other "globalizing" development is the considerable innovations in transportation and information technologies that allow information, people, and goods (as well as money) to go quickly anywhere in the world they are demanded. This has put a premium on speed. As George Stalk and Thomas Hout (1990) argue, the effective management of time has become the most powerful new source of corporate competitive advantage. And time-based competition is reshaping global markets. Among the corporations that have effective global, time-based strategies are Federal Express, Ford, Milliken, Honda, Toyota, Citicorp, and Mitsubishi. The activities of these companies and other global organizations have changed the economics of production, distribution, and marketing. Large scale and scope no longer necessarily lead to economies or lower costs. Micro-markets have become economically attractive in many areas. Products now grow obsolete or are redefined quickly. As a consequence, virtually all relationships between stakeholders are redefined. In short, global superliquidity and rapid information flow offer many new opportunities to organizations, but they can also pose considerable threat if they are not monitored and taken advantage of.

The new global environment of business is characterized by great uncertainty in its economic, political, social, technological, and competitive factors. The role of time and distance and geography are being redefined. This severely complicates the task of strategic management. It also invites—and can richly reward—entrepreneurship and innovative business practices.

COMPETITIVE BUSINESS STRATEGIES FOR GLOBAL MARKETS

To compete effectively in the global environment, the United States may have to change the rules by which it plays (Tumulty, 1992). Japan and Germany have such radially different approaches between business and government that the United States is finding it difficult to compete effectively in the markets in which those two countries compete. For example, the United States frowns on unwarranted collaboration among competing firms and has sent people to prison for it. In Japan and Germany, such collaboration is not only legal but also abetted by the government. For example, MITI, the Ministry of International Trade and Industry, helps formulate Japan's business policy on a global level. Recently, Mitsubishi and Daimler-Benz had their top strategic planners meet for two days of private talks in Singapore. Can the United States continue to compete when it ignores these kinds of pressures? In addition, the United States tends not to provide the support that small, growth-oriented corporations need. Without adequate financial support, such as SBA loans, these companies find it increasingly difficult to compete in a global marketplace where, for example, a number of smaller German companies have captured nearly 80% of their respective world market shares (Simon, 1992).

To be truly global, a company must have products that can be sold in the growing overseas markets. Differences in electrical requirements often make American products unsaleable in Europe and/or Asia. The potential economies of scale are needed in a growing global market. Companies will have to focus on outstanding, creative products rather than compromising by reducing cost. Manufacturing may provide the basis for sidestepping the economies of scale traditionally needed to compete effectively (McGrath and Hoole, 1992). For example, when Xerox in 1981 began to restructure its company in order to go global, it considered five basic changes:

1. Products would be designed only once in a way that fit the global marketplace.
2. Purchasing would consolidate sources of raw materials.
3. Economies in production would be achieved by larger capacity and geographic diversity.
4. Marketing and sales forecasts would become the basis for establishing production schedules.
5. Closer coordination would be sought between customer orders and distribution for the global market.

The key is matching manufacturing strategy to the business strategy to achieve well-integrated management practices and measurement systems. With this approach, manufacturing can coordinate its global resources to become a more responsive company.

GLOBAL BUSINESS DRIVERS

The emergence of the global economy and the fact that national and regional economies no longer exist as independent structures offer several new opportunities and threats for businesses. Among the responses that companies and their competitors are marshaling to cope with the changing environment are the following global business drivers.

1. Produce global or semiglobal products. Coca-Cola and Pepsi-Cola are globally standardized products sold almost everywhere. McDonald's hamburgers and french fries are becoming global products. Gucci bags are too. Some successful "semiglobal" products establish primary markets in selected countries and bolster these sales with lucrative secondary markets in other countries.
2. Supply the needs of global customers. For example, it is possible to design a car for select, perhaps top-of-the-line, customers around the globe. Ohmae (1990) cites the Rolls-Royce and the Mercedes-Benz as examples.
3. Serve global corporate customers. General Electric, General Motors, Royal Dutch/Shell, Toyota, British Petroleum, Daimler-Benz, Fiat, and Samsung are among the large corporations that have global operations. They answer a worldwide need for many products and services.
4. Buy from global suppliers. A domestic firm serving domestic customers may well find that its best source of raw materials and components or of financing lies outside its home nation. As more nations strive to trade on their comparative economic advantages, global sources of inputs will become more attractive.
5. Defend against global competitors. A global competitor can use cash flow, profits, and economies of scale secured in one country or business intelligence gained from operating in that country to improve its competitive position in another country. A company may have to go global to mitigate this advantage.
6. Disperse the firm's value-added chain globally. Companies such as Lewis Galoob Toys act like global strategic brokers and place their operations wherever in the world it is best to execute any business function in their value-adding chain. As more countries specialize for comparative economic advantage, and as the workforces of the world compete for jobs, this driver will become more attractive. It is important to note that quality considerations as well as cost considerations can influence the decision to disperse a firm's value-adding chain globally. Some spots in the world are "world-class" performers or "best of class" performers in executing certain aspects of the value-adding chain.
7. Disperse globally to minimize risk. Because of the increased uncertainty in the global environment, it may be necessary for a firm to spread its activities over several countries in order to reduce its exposure to political, economic, and social changes in any one country or location.

ASSUMPTIONS ABOUT DOING BUSINESS ABROAD

Some time ago, the government of Brazil decided to buy buses for interurban transportation. Rolls-Royce expressed interest in submitting a bid and asked the

Brazilians to send representatives to London to help work out the details. Rolls' communiqué, in typical British style, defined responsibilities: the Brazilians would have to manufacture their own spare parts and be responsible for all maintenance. Meanwhile, Mercedes-Benz sent a team of executives to Brazil. Before negotiations began, Mercedes executives announced that the company would build a spare-parts plant in São Paolo and train nationals for jobs in the plant and for maintenance positions in the field.

Mercedes got the deal, although its price was no lower than Rolls'. Why? Mercedes was chosen primarily because of its approach and style, which met the needs of the Brazilians better. Mercedes offered services that accommodated the community with which it sought to do business.

As the world becomes smaller and more intertwined culturally and economically, people in business must reconsider assumptions about how they do business. Domestic companies have significant opportunities to expand into foreign markets if they go about it in a manner compatible with the new cultures they enter. It is equally important to recognize that dangerous economic threats are mounting for firms that ignore foreign competition and fail to devise a strategy to deal with it.

In the following sections, we examine multinational competition and factors to consider in developing global strategies. Competing in international markets requires a different perspective than competing in domestic markets. How to enter a foreign market, how best to interact with customers, how to manage foreign joint ventures or subsidiaries effectively, and how to determine vulnerability and risk are examples of considerations pertinent to global competition.

International operations cannot be undertaken by every business. For some, it may be a matter of survival to enter the global arena. For others, it may be a question of how to protect an existing domestic market from foreign competition. Few businesses, however, can afford to ignore the potential impact of foreign products or the growth potential that foreign markets offer.

The reason is simple, yet powerful: the world has become a single marketplace. National economics is being replaced by "globeconomics." Companies that ignore this fact find themselves in jeopardy. Today, well over 70% of U.S.-made products face foreign competition.

TYPES OF INTERNATIONAL STRATEGIES

To compete effectively in a global environment requires an entirely different strategic thrust than that used in domestic markets. The multinational company usually does not have the luxury of allowing its units to compete as individual subsidiaries. Rather, successful multinational companies organize in ways that position their system of products, marketing, and fabrication so as to obtain the maximum leverage possible from economies of scale, lower prices, barriers to entry, standardization of components, and joint ventures or other actions deemed necessary to compete effectively. This view of global strategy is equivalent to creating a portfolio of markets that are highly interdependent and need to be balanced to achieve optimal performance.

The values outlined by Peters and Waterman in *In Search of Excellence* (1982) form a solid basis for determining what organizations are required to do in order to maintain a competitive strategic posture. The eight premises that these authors espoused (see Chapter 1) are equally applicable in domestic and international markets. Global strategies extend these premises into a more complex arena and require their augmentation. Exchange rates, stability of local governments, and culture are, for example, factors not normally taken into account in a domestic market.

To formulate global strategies, managers normally view the world as a group of interacting markets that have the potential of being mutually supportive. Four approaches to international strategy are shown in Figure 7.2. The axes represent two critical aspects of doing business in a foreign environment. One is the company's marketing orientation. The other is the company's approach to control of foreign operations. The four international strategies are defined below.

1. *Ethnocentric strategy.* The ethnocentric strategy is based on the presumption that one country's products or services are superior to those of another country. Consequently, the strategy is narrowly focused on that product. Under centralized control the product is sold in other countries wherever a market exists for it. Americans, for example, long felt that their automobiles were superior because they were made in the United States and attempted to sell them abroad with few changes in design or features. As has become painfully obvious, this is no longer a widely held view.

FIGURE 7.2 | **Four International Strategies**

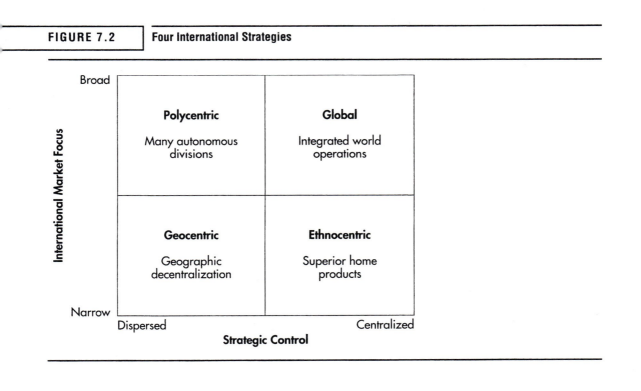

Although a multinational company pursuing an ethnocentric strategy would market its home products, it would have to be customized or modified to satisfy the tastes and desires of the host country. If the home product is clearly superior, the ethnocentric strategy should work well. But industrial nations around the world may develop products that better fit their own needs. In the aircraft industry, for example, where the United States dominated manufacturing for years, a consortium from England, Germany, and France produced the Airbus, which became a formidable competitor and contributed to the demise of two American airframe manufacturers.

2. *Geocentric strategy.* The second strategy is based on geographic decentralization with a narrow product line. This approach reduces risks by establishing markets, finances, and manufacturing in different countries. Therefore, if one country is having difficulty, the remaining divisions can continue to function normally.

   Geographic decentralization has both advantages and disadvantages. On the minus side, managing many different units in multiple locations poses a major management problem. On the plus side, each unit's performance can be evaluated easily by comparing it to the performance of other units. Funds, goods, and personnel can be shifted from one location to another, as needed. This strategy permits adaptation to local requirements and, if done correctly, is more effective than the polycentric strategy, which takes geographic decentralization to an extreme.

3. *Polycentric strategy.* The polycentric strategy is based on reducing risks by having a large number of autonomous units marketing a broad set of products. The many units are less vulnerable than one large subsidiary would be. Risk reduction is accomplished by a number of actions, such as the use of multiple currencies. The disadvantage of this strategy is that diversification and local autonomy limit the exchange of information among units regarding price, products, design, and movement of managers. If the need to reduce risks outweighs the disadvantages caused by lack of coordination among units, the polycentric strategy is a good choice.

4. *Global strategy.* The global strategy is based on an integrated view of foreign markets. Hout, Porter, and Rudden (1982) believe that the world is one market and should be treated as such. They recommend that the strategies of various subsidiaries, divisions, or strategic business units fit into a single comprehensive long-term strategy of the parent company. The countries, then, are considered a portfolio of interdependent entities.

   The global strategy assumes that worldwide distribution of the product can be justified on the basis of economies of scale and that R&D is related to the product rather than to a specific market. Lynn Townsend's attempt at Chrysler to build a world car—a base model that with appropriate modifiers in each country could be used everywhere—is an illustration of this strategy. Potential disadvantages include problems caused by trade barriers and fragmented distribution.

Whichever strategy is chosen—ethnocentric, geocentric, polycentric, or global—the social, political, and economic environment in each country needs to be analyzed carefully, and the firm's approach must be tailored to satisfy local needs.

When Mercedes-Benz offered its standard bus to the Brazilians, the company added other products and services to the package to meet the needs of Brazil.

Marketing theorist Theodore Levitt (1983) observes that because communications and transportation have become "proletarianized" and are available to all, the world is converging on commonality. Consequently, successful global companies will offer globally standardized products that are advanced (they are difficult to copy), functional (so they answer a real need), reliable (they meet quality standards), and low-cost (they are affordable and competitively priced). Only standardized products meet these requirements. Furthermore, this global market is enormous—potentially over 5 billion people. Only global companies with global products will be able to reach this large market. They will do it by "concentrating on what everybody wants rather than worrying about the details of what everyone *thinks* they might like" (p. 92). McDonald's hamburgers and fries, Revlon cosmetics, Levi's jeans, Sony TVs, Coca-Cola, and Pepsi qualify as global products.

If a pure global strategy is not possible, semistandard products can be designed and produced and customized after they cross national boundaries. Having products that are readily modifiable reduces lead time and cost. It still leverages a firm's development and manufacturing capabilities and permits global marketing and brand-name recognition.

Figure 7.3 shows four international strategies that reflect how multinational companies relate strategic thrust to segmentation of their markets. When a company serves a few market segments, it can choose either a global or a country segment as its main focus, depending on its products or services and on the competition. On the other hand, a company that serves many market segments must carefully choose whether to be the cost leader or to use trade barriers to exclude competitors from its local market segment. The strategic thrust that a company chooses depends both on the number of market segments that are being served and on whether its products or services can compete effectively in a global market.

An emerging requirement for ensuring effective marketing in a global environment is the development of strategic alliances (Ohmae, 1989). As we have noted, IBM, Toshiba, and Siemens—all major corporations in their respective countries—have recognized the global logic of strategic alliances. Managers will have to overcome their focus on competitor-oriented strategy and choose alliances that help reduce fixed costs and contribute to product enhancement. When examining ways of entering foreign markets, Bleeke and Ernst (1992) found that two-thirds of the 49 strategic alliances they analyzed had significant managerial or financial problems to overcome in the first two years. In the companies studied, 51% were successful and only 33% failed. These investigators advise that in order to improve their chances of success, managers should remember that

1. Alliances work as well as acquisitions and have the benefit of entering new markets with less capital investment.
2. Where a strong company forms an alliance with a weak company, the alliance rarely succeeds or, at best, turns in a mediocre performance.
3. Successful alliances require that the venture have autonomy and that the two organizations be flexible in their expectations.

FIGURE 7.3 | **Global Strategic Alternatives**

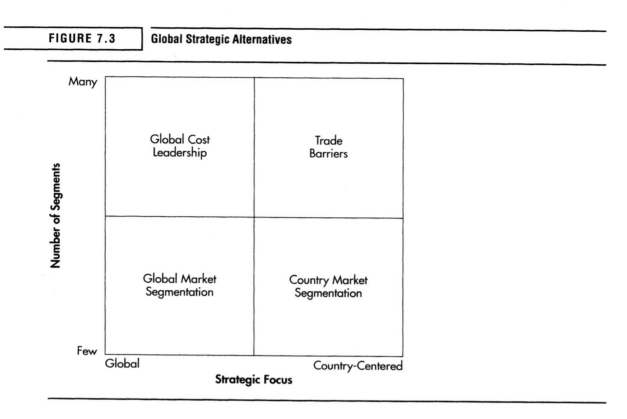

4. The alliance is most likely to succeed when financial ownership is shared equally between two companies.
5. In over 75% of alliances that were terminated, only one of the organizations needed the venture.

Thus, although strategic alliances are very attractive, business organizations must approach them more carefully than joint ventures or outright acquisitions.

Bartlett and Ghoshal (1989) have identified three sets of key thrusts and strategic capabilities that shape the way a firm conducts its international activities.

1. Build strong local presence through sensitivity and responsiveness to national differences. Companies that adopt this approach manage a portfolio of multiple national entities according to the needs of each location and compete on the basis of differentiation of their products and services. The authors call firms that take this approach "multinational." Phillips, ITT, and Unilever are cited as examples.
2. Build cost advantages through centralized global-scale operations. Such companies treat the world as an integrated whole and compete on the basis of cost leadership created by economies of scale. These "global" companies include the Japanese firms Matsushita, NEC, and Kao.

3. Exploit the parent company's knowledge and capabilities through worldwide diffusion and adaptation. Use of the firm's knowledge and skills is controlled but is modified by the local units to form products, processes, and marketing approaches that fit local requirements and to compete on the basis of their ability to leverage their intellectual capital instead of strict economies of scale. General Electric, Ericsson, and Procter & Gamble are examples of these "international" companies.

According to Bartlett and Ghoshal, however, these three thrusts and capabilities are inadequate for competing successfully in the emerging global economy. They argue that in the future, companies must embrace a fourth approach if they are to succeed. This "transnational" company is today an unrealized ideal because no firm yet exhibits all its characteristics. A transnational firm must be effective simultaneously in all of the three strategies summarized above. To achieve global competitive advantage, the transnational firm must manage both its cost and revenues together and must encourage innovations from all parts of the organization. It seeks global economies of scale where feasible, but it makes selective decisions about centralizing or decentralizing its assets primarily on an individual basis, depending on which approach will contribute most to the overall performance of the company. Its organizational form is an "integrated network" in which flows of components, products, resources, people, information, and funds between geographically dispersed units are managed dynamically. Local responsiveness is developed by building multinational flexibility. And, because differentiation is not necessary or desirable in all markets, a transnational varies its product and marketing approaches among different national operations. Above all, the transnational must be a learning organization that gathers knowledge and mines intellectual capital from all of the geographic areas in which it operates. The authors conclude, "In the future, a company's ability to develop a transnational organization capability will be the key factor that separates the winners from the mere survivors in the international competitive environment" (p. 212).

ENTRANCE STRATEGIES FOR SPECIFIC FOREIGN MARKETS

The choice of entrance strategy is as important as the decision to become a multinational company. If a company has had little or no experience in a foreign country, it should consider working with or through a foreign national. There are a number of ways in which an organization can work with a country's nationals. These include

1. *Employing local agents.* Local agents are presumed to know the territory and all the ramifications of doing business in a particular country or region. These individuals may have the connections needed to ensure the smooth entry of a product or subsidiary into the market. But because local agents are independent, they may be difficult to control, and there is no guarantee that they will pursue the product introduction forcefully.
2. *Employing local representatives.* Local representatives may be independent distributors or employees of the company. More than agents, these individuals

have a stake in both the sale of the product and the welfare of the company. Use of local representatives facilitates much better control and communication with the home office. Selecting representatives may, however, be more difficult than selecting local agents or distributors.

3. *Entering into licensing agreements.* The significant advantage of a licensing agreement is that it avoids the necessity of direct investment or involvement in the foreign country. If it is a high-technology product and the research for continued development is done in the United States, a foreign company is likely to want the license. On the negative side, there is no guarantee that the technology or product will be exploited appropriately. Other potential problems include patent infringements and poor execution of the technology locally, which can lower the product's reputation in the foreign market.

4. *Forming a joint venture.* The joint venture, unlike the first three approaches described, generally involves considerable investment and risk. The local requirements for a joint venture can also be prohibitive. For example, in many countries the foreign investor cannot own more than 49% of the joint venture, thus leaving control in the hands of the local company. On the positive side, the local company generally has an established position in the market and knows how to do business in the country. The joint venture is typically difficult to control and often results in a buyout by one of the partners.

5. *Acquiring local companies.* Acquisition ensures entry into the foreign market because the local company already has a market position. The physical facilities, workforce, distributors, and even managers are typically part of the arrangement. If the acquisition and the market potential are properly evaluated, this method of penetrating a foreign market is rapid and generally satisfactory. Risk is high, though, because key local personnel may quit, leaving an inexperienced U.S. company to run the acquisition. In addition, the tax and financial implications and obligations often far exceed those of other methods of market entry.

6. *Forming a foreign subsidiary.* This approach is analogous to the acquisition of a foreign company in that the multinational has complete control of the firm. Unlike acquisition, however, forming a subsidiary takes considerable time and effort. Obtaining the licenses, capital, and personnel necessary for formation of a subsidiary may be worth it if no appropriate company is available for sale. Sometimes the only possible way to enter a market is by investing in a subsidiary that will produce the product in the foreign country.

MARKETING STRATEGIES FOR SPECIFIC FOREIGN MARKETS

Global business not only involves working in a new and often radically different environment under different conditions, but it also poses difficult marketing questions. Most companies that decide to market internationally recognize their lack of expertise and tend to enter foreign markets gradually after careful strategic planning. This is wise because it helps international neophytes to avoid pitfalls. More often than not, a foreign country's way of doing business differs radically from that in the United States. Patents and copyrights, for example, are not equally protected in all countries; contractual or payment customs may differ from American practices; and local duties and restrictions can be formidable barriers to entry.

Having made the decision to market globally, a firm can choose from a number of entry strategies. It might, for example, consider one or more of Porter's four approaches (Porter, 1985).

1. Find a protected niche in which there is a minimum likelihood of interference from the local government.
2. Focus on supplying some particular need that the given country cannot supply locally. Large construction companies, such as Fluor, have pursued this strategy.
3. Choose a product that is unique in terms of cost, performance, or other attribute that can be marketed globally. McDonald's has succeeded with this strategy.
4. Choose an entire product line to market globally. This last approach requires that the company have a well-established product line and some experience in international marketing. The goal is to extend market penetration.

A fifth strategy for entering a foreign market is to customize the product or service to suit the unique demands of each country. Coca-Cola, for example, customizes its syrup and packaging for each country.

Quelch and Hoff (1986) identified four areas that a company should examine before customizing its strategy. Examination of these areas can help the company match its unique capabilities and products to the demands of each foreign market. The four areas are (1) the structure of the company's marketing function, (2) the types of products to be marketed, (3) the market mix in the country, and (4) other data about the country. Perhaps the most important factor is the way the company manages its marketing function. Problems can arise if marketing is controlled too tightly from corporate headquarters or is totally decentralized. To ensure a uniform marketing strategy, multinational companies such as Unilever employ marketing specialists who regularly visit the foreign locations to provide coaching and support. Kodak's approach is to control its worldwide operations from corporate headquarters. The most appropriate approach is to balance local autonomy with guidance and coordination from corporate headquarters. According to Quelch and Hoff, this balance can be achieved by

1. Encouraging field managers to generate ideas and participate in developing marketing strategies
2. Having country managers take on general management functions, such as control of their own budgets
3. Developing a product that permits economies of scale through use of both local and global resources

Porter (1985) stated that the following ten substrategies should be considered by companies seeking advantage in foreign markets.

1. Ascertain how to achieve comparative advantage, such as through the low cost of labor in a given country.
2. Determine how to achieve economies of scale and whether their achievement will involve a large capital investment.

3. Build on foreign experience rather than attempting to export products from a saturated domestic market.
4. Attempt to find economies of distribution so that these can be spread among the products sold.
5. Utilize large-scale purchasing to achieve economies of procurement.
6. Spread marketing costs by applying the same approach in many countries.
7. Differentiate the product whenever possible.
8. Incorporate unique technology into the product.
9. Maintain mobile production and service capability.
10. Avoid global impediments, such as high transportation costs, the need for specialized regional management skills, or restrictive regional government policies.

A number of emerging trends can have a direct impact on strategies for foreign marketing. International marketing practices are becoming less diverse, and distribution channels are reducing impediments to foreign competition. Intense competition among the Asian countries will affect some Western competitors. In particular, Asian countries will further protect their assets, making it more difficult for the United States to exploit cost advantages there. A freer flow of technology and the emergence of large new markets in China, what was formerly the Soviet Union, and developing nations such as Brazil will present new global opportunities and new sources of competition.

Global marketing often results from a desire to grow, especially if domestic markets are saturated. Growth must be managed, however, and entering foreign markets is no guarantee of growth or profitability. Blindly entering an overseas market can be disastrous. Like domestic strategy, global strategy requires research about markets, competitors, customers, and so forth. If research shows that a market exists and that the firm would have a competitive advantage, a well-planned and well-implemented global strategy can reap handsome rewards.

RISK ASSESSMENT

Regardless of a company's strategy for entering and marketing in a foreign market, managers need to consider the risks involved in doing business abroad. To assist in assessing such risks, Haner (1980) identified two major considerations: human and physical variables. The human variables relevant to risk assessment are

1. *Stability of temperament:* tendency toward violence, attitude toward corruption, emotional stability, and level of discipline prevalent in the culture
2. *Level of economic activity:* education and training of the workforce, work ethic, and attitude toward business typical in the country
3. *Social structure:* culture, traditions, elitism, distribution of wealth, languages, and religion of the people
4. *Political stability:* government-run or private enterprise, restrictions on foreign investments, and degree of regional autonomy

The physical variables that can influence the decision to locate in a given country are

1. *Availability of natural resources:* energy sufficiency, raw materials, agriculture, and water
2. *Severity of the climate:* seasons, storms, extreme heat or cold, and sunny days
3. *Geographic considerations:* desirability of location, historic or tourist concerns, and topology
4. *Infrastructure:* ease of access, communications, transportation, airports, roads, storage, support industries, financial support, and living accommodations

Haner also identified other factors that can directly affect the operation of a firm in a foreign market.

1. *Political stability:* attitudes regarding foreign investors, cost of social benefits, possibility of expropriation, preferential treatment of nationals
2. *Monetary considerations:* possibility of inflation and devaluation, balance of payment, currency convertibility, and exchange rate
3. *Infrastructure:* possibility of bureaucratic delays, support available in professional services and construction, communication, and transportation facilities
4. *Managerial considerations:* ability to enforce contracts, labor cost and productivity, sophistication of equipment, quality of local management, availability of skilled labor and of raw materials
5. *Economic and tax considerations:* rate of economic growth in the country, availability of short-term credit, availability of long-term capital and venture capital, tax benefits in that country

When addressing these five key factors, a strategic manager should be careful to identify and evaluate the overall goals and strategies of a country, its reigning ideology, and the policies it has adopted to achieve its goals—fiscal, monetary, income, foreign trade, and investment policies and policies with respect to various sectors such as health, education, welfare, housing, natural resources, telecommunications, transborder data flows, favored industries, and agriculture. Also important are the country's trading relationships with other countries, the global companies that operate in the country, and the country's relationships with international institutions such as the General Agreement on Tariffs and Trade, OPEC, the International Monetary Fund, the World Bank, and regional trading blocs.

An assessment of the riskiness of entering a given market in a country that might otherwise be considered appropriate is shown in Worksheet 7.1. The purpose of the country risk assessment is not to establish a precise mathematical model, but rather to quantify the key factors involved in determining the desirability of doing business in a given country. A simple weighting scheme is used to determine whether there is a high or low likelihood of encountering a risky situation in the country. To perform the risk analysis, the manager reviews the environmental data on the country under consideration and relates them to each of the five factors listed in the worksheet. For each factor, the manager assigns a numerical score from 1 to 100. A score of 50–70 indicates that the company's risks are moderate with respect to that factor. A score of 90–100 indicates a superior business environment. A score of 1–40 indicates unacceptable risks.

By averaging all the scores, the manager can approximate the riskiness of a given country.

WORKSHEET 7.1	Country Risk Assessment

Case   Multinational

Date   1992

Name   John Doe

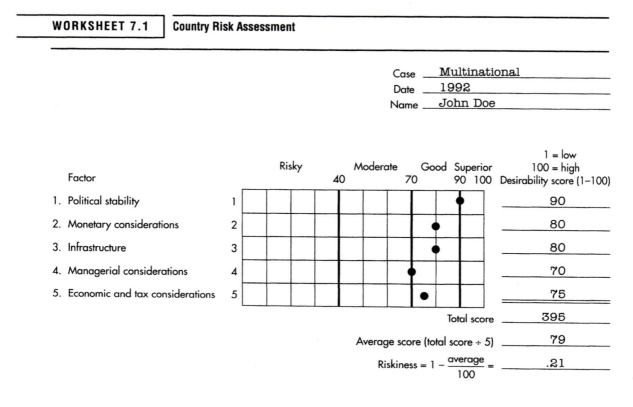

Factor		Desirability score (1–100)
1. Political stability	1	90
2. Monetary considerations	2	80
3. Infrastructure	3	80
4. Managerial considerations	4	70
5. Economic and tax considerations	5	75

Total score   395

Average score (total score ÷ 5)   79

$$\text{Riskiness} = 1 - \frac{\text{average}}{100} = \quad .21$$

Explanation:

The above analysis shows that there is a low risk for a multinational company wanting to enter the Singapore market. Thus the company would find this a potentially attractive environment from the perspective of riskiness.

The outcome of the analysis shown in Worksheet 7.1 would amount to endorsement entry by a multinational company. Singapore would be chosen because the risk of doing business there is low. This analysis does not indicate probability; rather, it is an assessment or subjective evaluation of the conditions that one is likely to find in a given country.

Another type of risk is inherent in the strategy used to enter a foreign market. A high risk of failure is associated with joint ventures, and such failures can be very costly (Killing, 1982).

The three main categories of risk factors can be rated and combined to form a *desirability index* for a given country. This involves rating the desirability of (1) the human and physical variables, (2) Haner's five risk factors (see Worksheet 7.1), and (3) the method used to enter the foreign market and averaging the scores of each. If Singapore's average desirability score were (.79), its human and physical variables averaged .30, and the entry variables averaged .51, then Singapore's combined desirability index would be .79 × .30 × .51, or .121. If another country had an index of .55 × .60 × .50, or .165, it would have a higher desirability index than Singapore.

It is difficult, of course, to anticipate catastrophic events, such as political upheavals or natural disasters, which can seriously disrupt foreign operations. Few companies, for example, anticipated the events in Iran prior to the Shah's leaving or the Persian Gulf operation that involved Iraq and Kuwait. Alternative future scenarios can define but not predict possible futures. As a minimum precaution, the multinational firm must constantly monitor the environment for signs that initial assumptions are no longer valid.

ORGANIZATIONAL ARRANGEMENTS FOR GLOBAL FIRMS

In his book *Scale and Scope: Dynamics of Industrial Capitalism* (1990), the noted business historian Alfred Chandler describes how successful, large industrial corporations developed at the end of the nineteenth century and grew during the first half of the twentieth century by exploiting economies of scale and scope. This required a "three-pronged" approach to innovation. Investments were made (1) in production facilities large enough to secure cost advantages, (2) in international and national marketing and distribution networks, and (3) in organizational structures capable of administrating large and far-flung enterprises. Chandler also discovered first-mover advantages. The first companies to make these three-pronged investments achieved the economies of scale and scope necessary to dominate their industries for decades.

The multidivisional, hierarchic structure (sometimes referred to as "M-form" by economists) proved to be the most effective organizational form for these purposes. DuPont and General Motors were the pioneers. American firms such as General Electric and Borden, British firms such as Lever, and German firms such as Bayer and Siemens also followed suit. Each became a competitive success in its industry. In each country, capitalism as a form of overall economic organization took on its own unique shape. In the United States it was competitive managerial capitalism; Germany fostered cooperative managerial capitalism; and in Great Britain personal capitalism flourished. In counterdistinction to America and Germany, firms in Great Britain were managed by "individuals or by a small number of associates, often members, of founders' families, assisted by only a few salaried managers, or they were federations of firms" (p. 235).

In *Scale and Scope* and elsewhere, Chandler maintains that a successful company's structure supports its strategy, and vice versa. These concepts will be developed in more detail in Chapter 10, where we discuss implementing strategic change. In this chapter we will explore some of the implications of the global environment for the choice of organizational structure and for a firm's ability to compete. We will also see why the M-form has become inadequate and why the network organization seems best suited for the new global environment.

ORGANIZATIONAL STRUCTURES

An organization may be conceived of as a collection of nodes. The nodes are individual units that do the work and add elements of value to the organization's final outputs. Materials, money, and information flow between the nodes. The term *structure* refers to the way the nodes are related to one another. In a multidivisional organization, for example, materials may flow horizontally—say, from sourcing to receiving to processing to distribution—but information and finances generally flow vertically. Information goes up to the central, controlling node, and instructions flow down to the operating nodes. A general organizing principle is that strategy and structure must be mutually supporting. This means that all the nodes must be carefully aligned with each other and well articulated with the global environment. As organizations become more complex, and as they add more diverse nodes dispersed throughout a wider geographic area, new ways of relating nodes to one another must be developed. When firms seek to implement truly global strategies, they typically find that the classical hierarchic M-form organization is wanting and must be modified. What modifications are appropriate depends on the strategies and capabilities of the organization as a whole and on how it adds value to its inputs.

Bartlett and Ghoshal (1989) have found that the particular organizational form that firms operating in several countries tend to employ depends on their individual strategies and capabilities. Specifically,

- Firms building on economies of scale and scope tend to seek cost advantages through centralized, global-scale operations. They employ an M-form organization in which overseas nodes are used to carry out the parent company's strategies. R&D and other knowledge-producing and learning activities are primarily conducted at the center. (Matsushita is an example.)
- Firms building on a strong local presence in various countries via sensitivity and responsiveness to national differences tend to be decentralized, each node being self-sufficient. Overseas nodes are used to sense and exploit local opportunities in each geographic location. For the most part, knowledge is developed and retained within each node. (Unilever is an example.)

■ Firms exploiting the parent company's knowledge and intellectual capital through worldwide diffusion and adaptation tend to rely on core competencies that are centralized, augmented by unique decentralized competencies. Overseas operations adapt and leverage these competencies. Knowledge is usually developed at the center and then transferred to overseas nodes where it may be adapted to local needs. (General Electric is an example.)

The nine emerging global trends described at the beginning of this chapter have caused managers and students of organizations to question the long-term effectiveness of these three organizational forms. Indeed, critical questions can be raised about whether the hierarchic, multidivisional form will continue to be the most effective in the global, postindustrial, information economy. As a rule, the M-form organization does not have the speed and agility necessary to compete in a time-based manner. Stalk and Hout (1990) and Keen (1991, 1986), for instance, argue convincingly that speed and agility are essential to competing effectively in today's global markets and explain why traditional organizational models may be inappropriate. The M-form, for example, emphasizes high-volume economies. It does not stress adding value by applying knowledge dynamically throughout the firm's value-adding chain. Thus it lacks the flexibility and swiftness to respond to a rapidly changing global environment.

Three related concepts have been put forth. As we have seen, Bartlett and Ghoshal (1989) developed the concept of a transnational firm. Miles and Snow (1986) also developed the idea of "network organizations," and Reich (1991) the notion of an enterprise web. All purport to overcome the deficiencies of the M-form. A successful transnational, network, or web organization is more flexible and better capable to learn from its diverse environments. These firms' assets and capabilities are clustered in nodes that have three general characteristics. They are dispersed, interdependent, and specialized. Differential contributions are made by all the overseas and domestic nodes, and these contributions are coordinated and integrated into worldwide operations. Generally speaking, learning is conducted and knowledge is developed jointly by the nodes and shared worldwide. This calls for a flatter organization consisting of many semi-autonomous nodes. There must be considerable horizontal communication among them. Bartlett and Ghoshal describe such a structure as an "integrated network configuration."

Reich (1991) provides imagery for such a network organization. Instead of a pyramid, his "new web of enterprise" resembles a spider's web. Strategic brokers (executives who manage ideas rather than things and who dynamically link problem identifiers with problem solvers) are at the center, but there are all sorts of connections that do not involve them directly, and new connections are being spun all the time. At each point of connection are a relatively small number of people—depending on the task, from a dozen to several hundred. Lewis Galoob Toys is an example of a global firm organized in this manner. The concept, however, is still evolving. As Miles and Snow (1986) explain, "New organizational forms are arising to cope with the new [global] environmental conditions. However, no new means of organizing or managing arrives full-blown; usually it results from a variety of experimental actions taken by innovative companies. . . . A few businesses, in the U.S. are on the verge of a breakthrough in organizational form" (p. 62).

The most thorough description of how this new type of organization works is provided by Miles and Snow. Their "dynamic network" organization has four major features.

1. *Vertical disaggregation.* Business functions such as product design and development, manufacturing, marketing, and distribution are performed by independent organizations within a network.
2. *Brokers.* Because each function is not necessarily part of a single organization, business groups are assembled by or located through brokers. (See the discussion of global brokering in the last section of this chapter.)
3. *Market mechanisms.* The major functions are held together in the main by market mechanisms (such as transfer prices) rather than by plans and controls. Contracts and payment by results are used more frequently than progress reports and personal, hierarchically based supervision.
4. *Full-disclosure information systems.* Broad-access computerized information systems are used as substitutes for lengthy trust-building processes. (Some degree of trust, however, is important to ensure the proper sharing of accurate and former proprietary information.) Each of the participants in the network agrees on a general structure of payment based on the value it adds. They all then hook themselves together in a continuously updated information system so that each others' contributions can be mutually and instantaneously verified. (p. 65)

The dynamic network organization requires a new managerial approach. To be effective it must be balanced.

> In order to understand all its ramifications, the dynamic network must be viewed simultaneously from the perspectives both of its individual components (nodes) and of the network as a whole. For the individual firm (or component, or node), the primary benefit of participation in the network is the opportunity to pursue its particular distinctive competence. A properly constructed network can display the technical specialization of the functional structure, and the balanced orientation characteristic of the matrix. (That is, it can achieve the best features of the other organizational forms.) Therefore, each matrix component can be seen as complementing rather than competing with the other components. (p. 70)

Matrix organizations and other forms are discussed more fully in Chapter 10.

Balance and dynamism are achieved through continual and active organizational learning, so the web that Reich describes is also learning-oriented. Actions are taken, and that experience is reflected on to gain knowledge. Knowledge and information are accumulated at each node and either communicated to other nodes or used as a resource in negotiating contracts and alliances. Nodes that do not learn or whose learning becomes obsolete are eliminated from the network. Learning creates distinctive competencies and skills at each node in the enterprise web. Each node, consequently, represents a unique combination of skills that can be drawn on when required. Exactly how these capabilities are drawn on is not so important as the fact that they are available when needed (or can be discarded if they become irrelevant). Direct ownership and control of each node in the web are not essential, perhaps not even preferred. Contractual and other agreements can serve just as well.

Miles and Snow conclude that in order for the organization to remain balanced, its major nodes must be "assembled and reassembled (frequently) to meet complex and changing competitive conditions." This requires forming strategic alliances with organizations well beyond the organization's boundaries and engaging in global brokering.

STRATEGIC ALLIANCES

Alliances are associations and agreements that define relationships between two independent entities. Frequently this is done by enforceable contract; occasionally it is accomplished by simple verbal agreement. Strategic alliances are coalitions that an organization forms with other organizations in order to achieve one or more of its strategic goals. An assumption of most large-scale, multidivisional corporations is that they must own and carefully control the assets and capabilities at every node in their network. Globalization is challenging this assumption. A corporation need not own every node in its value-adding network (or even most of them) as long as each node delivers its output on time and within cost objectives and meets quality standards. In fact, there are several reasons why, in the global environment, alliances are preferred to ownership. Alliances offer special capabilities that the firm can not acquire otherwise. They can be formed and disbanded quickly in order to respond to changing market conditions. They force a clear pinpointing of responsibility between nodes. And, by forming (or holding open the option to form) multiple alliances, a firm can use competitive pressure to hold down costs and manage risk.

The value of strategic alliances has been questioned by many companies because of the difficulties that can arise. This attitude is reinforced by the problems associated with carrying out agreements, maintaining trade secrets, and keeping the relationship viable for long periods of time. Sherman (1992) has shown that strategic alliances can work when there is considerable flexibility on the part of both partners and where there is an openness in sharing power between the two. In spite of any obstacles, many of the major companies in the United States have formed strategic alliances to improve their competitive position. For example, IBM formed an alliance with Siemens and Toshiba to develop DRAM chips. Other companies that have formed strategic alliances include AT&T, GE, Merck, and Time Warner. Although half of all alliances are failures, they do facilitate entering a new market, preventing a competitor from gaining position in a market, and exploiting new technology or the expertise of a partner. Often a strategic alliance is used as a prelude to an eventual acquisition or merger. Ultimately, successful strategic alliances depend on relationships that are built to persist rather than on those that simply take advantage of an opportunity for short-term gain.

Two terms are commonly used in the current management literature to describe the business decisions that surround forming strategic alliances: sourcing and outsourcing. *Sourcing* usually refers to the process of securing a source of supply for some basic component or product in the firm's product line. Apple Computer, for example, buys its laser printer engines from Canon, a very successful Japan-based global company with a reputation for quality. Laser printer technology is expensive and difficult to manage. Although the availability of quality laser printing is essential to Apple's strategy, it is not a primary basis for the company's competitive advantage. (Apple printers are sold in conjunction with Apple Macintosh microcomputers, and it is the unique software of the Macintosh that is at the core of Apple's strategy. The company owns and controls fiercely the "Mac look and feel.") By forming an alliance to obtain the engines for its printers, however, Apple has assured itself of a quality source of supply for an important complementary product. It also has been able to leverage its product and sales capacity without diluting its technical or financial resources on a secondary technology. Furthermore, laser printing technology changes rapidly, so the company has managed some of its risk of market obsolescence. If Canon does not continue to learn and innovate and keep current, Apple can turn to another supplier.

Outsourcing generally means contracting with an outside party to deliver some corporate service that is usually performed within the organization. Product design services and even janitorial services have been successfully outsourced. Recently the outsourcing of information systems services has become a much-discussed item on the management agenda. Eastman Kodak, the world's largest-selling scientific and photographic equipment manufacturer, formed "partnership alliances" with three companies to provide it with various information services worldwide. IBM will manage its data centers, which are located in various countries, via its global communications network; Digital Equipment will manage its voice and data telecommunications activities, which are also distributed worldwide. Businessland will procure, install, and support its personal computers and microcomputers.

Data entry, a tedious and time-consuming job, has been successfully outsourced by many organizations, including American Airlines. By offering lower labor costs and plenty of qualified workers, Ireland, South Korea, Jamaica, Haiti, Barbados, and even China have successfully bid on contracts to assume many firms' data entry functions. The global outsourcing of software programming is following suit. Countries such as India and the Philippines now have corps of trained programmers. A professional programmer in the United States costs about $100,000 per year on a full-cost basis, whereas an equivalent programmer in India or the Philippines works for about $35,000 a year. These factors have encouraged firms with considerable information systems activities to consider purchasing some of these functions abroad. A few small, information-intensive firms have also found global outsourcing profitable.

The decision to source or outsource by means of global alliances also entails a decision on the best organizational relationships to form. Reich identifies five basic forms of relationships between the organization and the nodes in its global network.

1. In *independent profit centers*, authority for product development and sales is pushed down to each node. In this case, each node is owned but is autonomous in decisions it makes.

2. In *spin-off partnerships*, independent businesses are spawned from the main organization, taking former employees and assets. The node then contributes to the organization on a contractual basis.

3. In *spin-in partnerships*, ideas and unique assets from external groups are acquired and become nodes in the organization itself.

4. In *licensing*, headquarters contracts with independent businesses to use its brand name, sell its special formulas, or otherwise market (that is, find applicable problems for) its technologies.

5. In *pure brokering*, headquarters contracts with independent businesses for identifying and solving problems as well as for production. This highly decentralized and flexible form is used by Lewis Galoob Toys.

All five of these arrangements can be used to construct a global organizational network.

GLOBAL BROKERING

One of the greatest challenges a business faces in establishing a global orientation is to *think globally* to begin with. Old habits of thought, reinforced by years of use and training, have rewarded us for thinking in a more traditional way, constricted by tacit local, national, and regional assumptions. The global environment renders many of these old modes of business thinking obsolete. Today it is possible—in fact, in many industries it may be necessary—to manage as a global broker. A global broker creates and manages a global network organization.

The global broker begins by breaking the business down into individual business functions according to the firm's value-adding chain. Typical functions include raw-materials sourcing, supplies, inbound logistics, production and operations of components and units, distribution, marketing, sales, customer service, finance, human resources, R&D, planning, product design, advertising, administration, government relations, legal services, technology development and evaluation, competitive intelligence, and the like. Then it is assumed that these subfunctions can be performed *anywhere*. The global broker then asks, "Where in the world *should* these tasks be performed?" The globe is scanned to determine where the candidate sites are. Each candidate location is next evaluated on the basis of such location factors as population, natural resources, existing products, trade conditions, markets, availability of labor and requisite skills, financing and capital, political stability, transportation infrastructure, communications, education, research capabilities, presence of allied or competitive businesses, and availability of the arts, entertainment, and hotels. The costs of land, taxes, utilities, and labor are also assessed. Now the subfunctions are matched to the candidate locations. A choice is made on the basis of feasibility, advantages, disadvantages, and the relative distinctive competencies of each location. Each location chosen becomes a node in the global network.

The firm must also decide whether to buy or build its own assets or to enter into an alliance and how much of each subfunction should be sourced or outsourced. The integrative organizational network must be formed, and patterns established for coordinating and controlling among nodes. This having been done, the proposed new business is ready to operate as a global, stateless organization. It could, for example, do its product design in the United States, the United Kingdom, and Italy, do its engineering in Japan, import raw materials from Brazil, produce parts in Taiwan and Malaysia, assemble and ship out of Singapore, finance in Germany and Japan, market primarily in Europe, and be headquartered in Toronto. The role of the headquarters node in this case is to perform the strategic brokering function. In the modern, global environment, more and more organizations will be developing their business strategies along these lines.

UMMARY

All businesses today are affected by the global environment. A global economy is emerging in which local, national, and regional economies no longer exist as independent structures. Business today operates in a worldwide framework of interactions and interdependencies among all of these economies.

One of the most important determinants of an organization's success is its global environment. A business is like an ecological entity. It has mutual relationships with other entities, called stakeholders, in its environment, and it must be effective in managing these external relationships. Some companies have quite effective internal operations and yet fail because their managers overlook unfavorable conditions in the global environment, such as changes in foreign exchange rates. Others are able to generate acceptable—even outstanding—profits, despite a number of internal problems, simply because they positioned themselves in the right place at the right time.

To maintain its competitive edge, an organization must identify and understand its global stakeholders—all of the parties whose actions affect it and whom its plans affect. It also must monitor constantly changes in events, trends, and stakeholder demands in its economic, political, competitive, geographic, social, and technological environments. Nine basic trends toward globalization and their implications for the business must be observed and evaluated. These are (1) global money and capital markets and the trend toward superliquidity, (2) developments in information technology and their implications for worldwide services, (3) the emergence of a symbol-based economy in which symbolic activities such as handling money and information are core processes, and knowledge, know-how, and brain power are crucial resources,

(4) the diminished power of nation–states as institutions and the rise of stateless corporations and supranational institutions, (5) a movement toward the deregularization of markets, (6) the continuous expansion of global trade and an increasing propensity to trade on the part of almost all nations, (7) the uncoupling of the raw-materials economy from industrial, service, and information-intensive economies, (8) increased demographic diversity resulting from population shifts and the emerging world division of labor, with global mobility for workers to migrate to where work is or for work to be exported to where workers are, and (9) the growing awareness of a transnational ecology in which natural phenomena and human-made phenomena such as pollution move around the globe without regard to national or other artificial boundaries.

A comprehensive global environmental analysis is needed to interpret these trends and their effect on a business. Such an analysis would include (1) a detailed examination of the global stakeholders and the underlying assumptions being made about them, (2) an overall scan of the environment, (3) assessment of the organization's vulnerability to global environmental threats, and (4) the writing of scenarios and the use of quantitative and qualitative forecasting methods to predict how the global environment might change in the future.

Effective strategies are based on exploiting differences between a firm and its competitors and seeking competitive advantage based on those differences. Exploiting these differences, or just retaining competitive parity, may require doing business in foreign countries. Most international strategies must be positioned with respect to the developed world's powerful "triad": the United States, Japan, and the EC. International strategies are necessarily more complex than exclusively domestic ones. A business must decide whether its products, processes, and organizational structure are well suited to foreign markets and, if so, must devise strategies that match the company's strengths with the environmental characteristics of each foreign market it seeks to enter. There are several different ways in which a business can enter another country. These include employing local agents, employing local representatives, entering into licensing agreements, forming a joint venture, acquiring local companies, and forming a foreign subsidiary. Every candidate country and the method of entry should be assessed for risk with respect to that country's political stability, social structure, types of existing economic activity, and other factors.

Even in the face of considerable risk, there are forces at work that may still require the development of a global strategy. Among these "global business drivers" are (1) competing against global or semiglobal products, (2) supplying the needs of individual, mobile customers wherever they are located in the world, (3) serving corporations with global operations, (4) sourcing from efficient suppliers located around the globe, (5) defending against a global competitor, (6) dispersing each element of the firm's value-adding chain to that place in the world in which it is best performed, and (7) minimizing overall risk by diversifying globally. The business objectives that respond to these global drivers may help the firm meet these objectives: becoming a financial intermediary, securing geographic diversification, taking advantage of a technological lead, and creating a new or expanded market. This last objective grows important as domestic markets become mature and saturated. These global drivers may indicate a preemptive move. A proactive organization takes responsibility for creating its own environment whenever possible—and adapting to change when necessary—through a continuous process of long-range planning, objective setting, and forecasting of changes in the environment. The changing global environment has made proactive behaviors important for survival.

There are four pure forms of international strategies: (1) ethnocentric, which focuses on the supposed superiority of products made in the firm's own country, (2) geocentric, which focuses on specific regions, (3) polycentric, which treats every

location as a separate and unique entity, and (4) global, which focuses on standardized products and services marketed basically the same in all countries of the world.

Whatever strategy is adopted, the organization's structure must meet that strategy's requirements. Chandler has shown that during the first half of the twentieth century, a hierarchic, multidivisional form—the M-form—proved to be the most competitive for large industrial organizations. Although this may continue to be the most effective form for heavy industry, it is unlikely to be best for knowledge-intensive and other global organizations that require speed, agility, and flexibility. The choice of organizational strategy depends on the capabilities of the firm and the demands of the industry. Some firms should continue to stress economies of scale and scope. There are other alternatives, however. One option is to build on the strengths the firm developed by way of a strong local presence in various countries and to compete via sensitivity and responsiveness. Another is to exploit the parent company's special knowledge and intellectual capital by applying them appropriately in each geographic location. Finally, the solution may be to form a transnational, stateless corporation. A successful transnational firm employs an integrated network configuration, or web of enterprise. It is composed of nodes that are dispersed, interdependent, and specialized, and it communicates more horizontally than vertically. Hence it is more flexible and better able to learn from its diverse global environment than organizations that exhibit any other structure.

Transnational organizations need not own or directly manage all or even most of the nodes in their networks. Instead they can form strategic alliances with other organizations. These alliances may serve almost any function in the organization's value-adding chain and can take on any of several forms. Among these forms are independent profit centers, spin-off partnerships, spin-in partnerships, licensing, and pure brokering. Pure brokering involves contracting with a variety of independent businesses to perform general business processes such as research, product design, advertising, financial management, and information services, as well as to undertake production.

The transnational organization includes global brokering, in which an organization decomposes its value-adding chain into individual units and determines, on the basis of country characteristics, where in the world each function is best performed. Information technology and advanced transportation systems are then used to construct the network organization and to guide and coordinate its activities. Some nodes in the network are owned; others result from strategic alliances. As an archetype, the transnational organization is best suited to coping with the nine major global trends that are reshaping the business environment.

An appendix included in this chapter provides sources of information needed to support strategy development for a global environment.

REFERENCES AND SUGGESTIONS FOR FURTHER READING

Bartlett, Christopher A. and Sumantra Ghoshal. 1989. *Managing across borders: The transnational solution.* Boston: Harvard Business School Press.

Bell, Daniel. 1973. *The coming of postindustrial society: A venture in social forecasting.* New York: Basic Books.

Berry, Thomas. 1988. *The dream of the earth.* San Francisco: Sierra Club Books.

Bleeke, J. and D. Ernst. 1991. The way to win in cross-border alliances. *Harvard Business Review,* November–December, pp. 113–133.

Chandler, Alfred D., Jr. 1990. *Scale and scope: The dynamics of industrial capitalism.* Cambridge, Mass.: Harvard University Press.

Chandler, Alfred D., Jr. 1977. *The visible hand: The managerial revolution in American business.* Cambridge, Mass.: Harvard University Press.

Demaree, Allan T. 1992. What now for the U.S. and Japan? *Fortune,* February 10, pp. 79–95.

Drucker, Peter F. 1989. *The new realities: in government and politics/In economics and business/In society and world view.* New York: Harper & Row.

Drucker, Peter F. 1986. The changed world economy. *Foreign Affairs,* Spring.

Gibney, F. 1992. China's renegade province. *Newsweek,* February 17, pp. 35–38.

Haner, Frederick T. 1980. *Global business strategy for the 1980s.* New York: Praeger.

Holstein, William J. et al. 1990. The stateless corporation. *Business Week,* May 14.

Hout, Thomas et al. 1982. How global companies win out. *Harvard Business Review.* September.

Jamieson, David and Julie O'Mara. 1991. Managing Workforce 2000. San Francisco: Jossey-Bass.

Johnson, William B. 1991. Global Workforce 2000: The new world labor market. *Harvard Business Review,* March–April, pp. 115–127.

Johnson, William B. and A. E. Packer. 1987. *Workforce 2000: Work and workers for the 21st century.* Indianapolis: Hudson Institute.

Jordan, Thomas P. et al. 1992. Global management in the 1990s. *Fortune.* July 27.

Keen, Peter G. W. 1991. *Shaping the future: Business design through information technology.* Boston: Harvard Business School Press.

Keen, Peter G. W. 1986. *Competing in time: Using telecommunications for competitive advantage.* New York: Ballinger.

Kelly, K. 1992. Learning from Japan. *Business Week,* pp. 52–60.

Killing, J. Peter. 1982. How to make a global joint venture work. *Harvard Business Review,* May–June.

Kling, Rob. 1990. More information, better jobs? *The Information Society* 7, no. 2.

Kraar, Louis. 1992. Asia 2000. *Fortune,* October 5, pp. 111–142.

Kupfer, Andrew. 1992. Who's Winning the PC Price Wars? *Fortune,* September 21, pp. 80–82.

Labate, John. 1992. The world economy in charts. *Fortune.* July 27.

Levine, Jonathon. 1992. Want EC business? You have two choices. *Business Week,* October 19, pp. 58–59.

Levitt, Theodore. 1983. The globalization of markets. *Harvard Business Review,* May–June, pp. 92–102.

Luke, Timothy and Stephen K. White. 1985. Critical theory, the information revolution, and an ecological path to modernity. In *Critical Theory and Public Life,* ed. John Foster. Cambridge, Mass.: M.I.T. Press.

McGrath, Michael E. and Richard W. Hoole. 1992. Manufacturing's new economies of scale. *Harvard Business Review,* May–June, pp. 94–102.

McLuhan, Marshal. 1964. *Understanding media: The extensions of man.* New York: McGraw-Hill.

Ohmae, Kenichi. 1990. *The borderless world: Power and strategy in the interlinked economy.* New York: Harper Press.

Ohmae, Kenichi. 1989. The global logic of strategic alliances. *Harvard Business Review,* March–April, pp. 143–154.

Ohmae, Kenichi. 1985. *Triad power: The coming shape of global competition.* New York: The Free Press.

Oster, Patrick et al. 1992. 10,000 new EC rules. *Business Week,* September 7, pp. 48–50.

Pennar, Karen. 1992. One way the U.S. lags behind. *Business Week*, January 27, p. 99.

Peters, T. J. and R. H. Waterman, Jr. 1982. *In search of excellence.* New York: Harper & Row.

Porat, Marc Uri. 1977. *The information economy: Definitions and measurement,* United States Office of Technology Special Publication 77-12(1). Washington D.C.: Department of Commerce, Office of Telecommunications.

Porter, Michael E. 1990. *The competitive advantage of nations,* New York: The Free Press.

Porter, Michael E. ed. 1986. *Competition in global industries.* Boston: Harvard Business School Press.

Powell, B. 1992. Japan's Quality Quandary. *Newsweek,* June 15, p. 48.

Quelch, John A. and Edward J. Hoff. 1986. Customizing global marketing. *Harvard Business Review,* May–June.

Rapoport, Carla. 1992. What Germany will lead Europe? *Fortune,* September 21, pp. 149–158.

Reich, Robert B. 1991. *The work of nations: Preparing ourselves for 21st century capitalism.* New York: Knopf.

Riesenbeck, H. and A. Freeling. 1991. How global are global brands? *The McKinsey Quarterly,* no. 4, pp. 3–18.

Schonfeld, Erick. 1992. The global overview. *Fortune,* July 27, pp. 62–82.

Schrage, M. 1992. What's behind IBM's dutch-treat strategy? *Los Angeles Times,* July 16, p. D3.

Sera, K. 1992. Corporate globalization: A new trend. *Academy of Management Executive* 6, no. 1, pp. 89–96.

Sherman, Stratford. 1992. Are strategic alliances working? *Fortune,* September 21, pp. 77–78.

Simon, H. 1992. Lessons from Germany's midsize giants. *Harvard Business Review,* March–April, pp. 115–123.

Smith, Lee. 1992. What the U.S. can do about R&D. *Fortune,* October 19, pp. 74–76.

Stalk, George Jr. and Thomas M. Hout. 1990. *Competing against time: How time-based competition is reshaping global markets.* New York: The Free Press.

Stewart, Thomas A. 1991. Brain power: How intellectual capital is becoming America's most valuable asset. *Fortune,* June 3, pp. 44–60.

Templeman, J. 1992. Germany takes charge. *Business Weekly,* February, pp. 50–58.

Therrien, L. 1989. The rival Japan respects. *Business Week,* November 13, pp. 108–118.

Tully, Shawn. 1992. Europe 1992: More unity than you think. *Fortune,* August 24, pp. 135–142.

Tumulty, K. 1992. Global competition: Can U.S. still play by its rules? *Los Angeles Times,* June 8, p. A8.

Weber, J. 1992. Chipping away at national boundaries. *Los Angeles Times,* July 14, p. D5.

Wever, Kirsten and Christopher Allen. 1992. Is Germany a model for managers? *Harvard Business Review,* September–October, pp. 36–43.

Woods, Wilton. 1992. It was a bad year everywhere. *Fortune.* July 27.

World Bank. 1987. *World development report.* New York: Oxford University Press.

Zuboff, Shoshana. 1988. *In the age of the smart machine: The future of work and power.* New York: Basic Books.

APPENDIX A

Selected Sources of Information for International Business

Predicasts F&S Index Europe. Predicasts, Inc. (monthly, with quarterly and annual cumulations)

(Prior to the summer of 1978, *Predicasts F&S Index International* covered all countries other than the United States.) This is an excellent index for current information on companies and industries in the Common Market, Scandinavia, what was formerly the U.S.S.R., and other Eastern and Western European countries. It covers about 400 business, industrial, and financial periodicals and is arranged in three parts: (1) by SIC number or product, (2) by region and country, and (3) by company name.

Predicasts F&S Index International. Predicasts, Inc. (monthly, with quarterly and annual cumulations)

A companion to the above-mentioned index, this index covers articles on industries and companies in Canada, Latin America, Africa, the Middle East, Japan, Oceania, and other Asian countries that appear in more than 600 foreign and domestic periodicals. It has the same three-part arrangement as *Predicasts F&S Index Europe.*

INTERNATIONAL BUSINESS TRENDS

Business Asia
Business China
Business Eastern Europe
Business Europe

Business International
Business International Money Report
Business Latin America
China Hand (on reserve)

The reports issued for each series provide current news about companies, recent developments in laws and practices related to such topics as taxes, licensing, capital sources, politics and profitability, worldwide and regional trends, and news about specific countries. It also includes checklists and statistical tables. *Business International Money Report* provides weekly news about the international capital market, currency exchange rates, interest rates, credit controls, and related subjects.

TAX AND TRADE GUIDES

Common Market Reporter. Commerce Clearing House. (Looseleaf service, periodically updated)

   This service provides information on law, regulations, decisions, and rulings relevant to conducting business in, and in competition with, the EEC.

Doing Business in Europe. Commerce Clearing House. (Looseleaf service, periodically updated)

   This two-volume service provides an overall summary designed to help businesspeople and lawyers obtain a general understanding of relevant aspects of the European legal system.

Exporter's Encyclopedia. Dun & Bradstreet. (Annual)

   This is a comprehensive world marketing reference guide in five sections. Section 2, "Export Markets," gives important market information for specific countries (import and exchange regulations, shipping services, communications data, postal information, currency, banks, embassies, and so forth). Other sections contain general export information.

FOREIGN AND INTERNATIONAL COMPANY INFORMATION

Business Week's "The Global 1000." (Issued annually in July)

Forbes's "Forbes International 500 Survey" (issued annually in a July issue) includes the 100 largest foreign investments and the 100 largest U.S. multinationals.

Fortune's "500 Largest Industrial Corporations Outside the U.S." (issued annually in July) includes the 100 largest commercial banking companies outside the U.S. and the world's 100 biggest industrial corporations.

Nomura Company and Industry Research on the Pacific Basin

Country Reports. Economist Intelligence Unit. (Quarterly, with annual summaries)

   This report presents a wide variety of country-specific statistical and narrative information. Countries covered include China and North Korea, Philippines and Taiwan, Indonesia, Singapore, Japan and South Korea, Thailand and Burma, and Hong Kong and Macau.

International Financial Statistics. International Monetary Fund. (Monthly)

   For each country this publication gives statistics on exchange rate, international liquidity, money and bank statistics, interest, prices, production, international transactions, government finance. Daily exchange rates, exchange transactions, international reserves, changes in money, and the like appear in comparative tables.

Marketing in Europe. Euromonitor Publications. (Monthly)

   This is a research journal covering consumer goods markets, marketing, and distribution by country in Western Europe.

Markets of Asia Pacific. Facts on File. (Irregular)

   Market analyses in this series are available on such countries as PRC, Malaysia, Singapore, Thailand, Philippines, and South Korea.

Statistical Yearbook. United Nations. (Annual)

   This is a basic reference work for statistics in all UN countries. The sections cover population, manpower, agriculture, production, mining, manufacturing, construction, energy, foreign trade, transport, communications, consumption, balance of payments, wages and prices, national accounts, finance, public finance, development assistance, health, housing, education, science and technology, and culture. Current figures are in the Monthly *Bulletin of Statistics.*

Worldcasts. Predicasts, Inc. (Quarterly)

This detailed service gives both short- and long-range forecast statistics for basic economic indicators of specific countries and also for industries outside the United States. Its eight volumes are in two parts: *World Regional Casts* and *World Product Casts* (which is arranged by SIC code as in *Predicasts P&S Europe* and *Predicasts F&S International*).

Financing Foreign Operations. Business International Corp. (Looseleaf)

This service is arranged in three parts: Part 1 covers general financial techniques; Part 2 deals with cross-border financing; Part 3 covers domestic financing for each country that lends funds, and it includes information on the monetary system, sources of capital, long-, medium-, and short-term financing techniques, capital incentives, public stock and bond financing, export insurance, and credit. A bimonthly "FFO Updated and Forecasts of Interest Rates" is included.

Foreign Economic Trends and Their Implications for the United States. U.S. Department of Commerce, International Trade Administration. (Annual)

This is a series of reports for over 100 countries, covering current economic situations and trends.

Foreign Tax and Trade Briefs. Matthew Bender. (Looseleaf service, periodically updated)

Basic data on taxation and trading laws are presented for the principal countries of the world where American capital is frequently invested.

Information Guide for Doing Business in (Name of Country). Price Waterhouse & Co. (Updated periodically)

International Trade Reporter: Export Shipping Manual. Bureau of National Affairs. (Weekly service)

This is a compendium of useful shipping facts about 180 countries, including ports and shipping routes, principal imports and exports, tariff system, shipping regulations, postal information and rates, labeling, warehousing, government information offices, major banks, and travel requirements.

International Trade Reporter: U.S. Export Weekly. Bureau of National Affairs. (Weekly)

These reports provide current news about legislation, regulations, international negotiations, court decisions, tariffs, taxes, foreign investment, international monetary developments, etc. Text of legislation and periodic "Special Reports" are also provided. The other part of this service, *Export Shipping Manual,* is described in the above entry.

Investing, Licensing, and Trading Conditions Abroad. Business International Corp. (Looseleaf service with monthly supplements)

For each country, these analyses usually give current information on the state's role in industry, organizing for foreign investments, rules of competition, price controls, licensing, corporate and personal taxes, incentives, capital sources, labor, and foreign trade.

Overseas Business Reports. U.S. Domestic and International Business Administration, Department of Commerce. (Updated periodically)

This is a series of useful reports for about 100 countries, with varying titles such as "Marketing in (name of country)," "Selling in . . . ," and "Doing Business in . . . ."

Separate booklets give concise information about the commercial entities, accounting methods, taxes, labor legislation, and so on in about 60 countries.

Trade Regulation Reporter. Commerce Clearing House. (Looseleaf service, periodically updated)

This service covers laws and rates of antitrust and trade regulation at the federal and state levels.

NTDB.

The NTDB info-base lets you search over 30,000 entries in the *National Trade Data Bank* from a variety of government agencies that deal in international trade. Some of the agencies included are the Central Intelligence Agency; the Departments of Agriculture, Energy, and State; the U.S. Trade Representatives; and many organizations within the Department of Commerce. The NTDB also includes information from periodicals, including the *International Market Research Reports* and data from the *U.S. Industrial Outlook* and *Business America.*

CHAPTER EIGHT

Financial Planning and Competitive-Cost Analysis

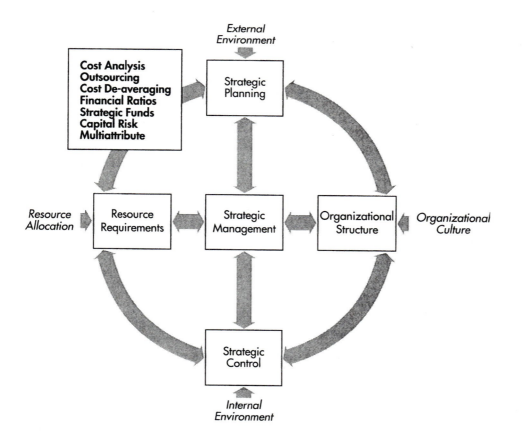

Cost Analysis
Outsourcing
Cost De-averaging
Financial Ratios
Strategic Funds
Capital Risk
Multiattribute

External Environment

Strategic Planning

Resource Allocation

Resource Requirements

Strategic Management

Organizational Structure

Organizational Culture

Strategic Control

Internal Environment

Chapter 1 A Framework for Strategic Management	**Chapter 2** Strategic Analysis	**Chapter 3** Strategic Visioning, Goals, Ethics, and Social Responsibility	**Chapter 4** The Competitive Environment	**Chapter 5** Capability-based Strategy	**Chapter 6** Market Dynamics and Sustainable Competitive Advantage
How to approach strategic management	*Application of strategic analysis*	*Understanding vision, values, ethics*	*Coping with competitive forces, stakeholders*	*Assessing company capability, timeliness, quality*	*Determining trends, gap analysis, and market dynamics*

Chapter 7 Strategy in a Global Environment	**Chapter 8** Financial Planning and Competitive- Cost Analysis	**Chapter 9** Entrepreneurship, Mergers and Acquisitions, Restructuring, and the Service Sector	**Chapter 10** Leadership Factor in Strategy and Implementing Strategic Change	**Chapter 11** Information Technology and Future Directions in Strategy
Assessing global trade, foreign markets, monetary exchange	*Preparing a financial plan and competitive-cost analysis*	*Importance of small business, entrepreneurs, restructuring*	*Strategy implementation, leadership, culture*	*Information technology, trends, new management*

INTRODUCTION

The financial viability of a firm determines its capacity to survive. Without a source of funds, internal or external, an organization cannot continue to exist. It is estimated that 90% of new ventures that file for bankruptcy do so because they lack working capital. Measures such as funds flow and financial indicators provide a basis for examining the performance of an organization and determine the value contribution of products, services, R&D, advertising, and other investments. Assessing the desirability of entering an industry, determining product value, and ascertaining whether the firm can meet competition also require appropriate financial analysis.

To compete effectively in today's global markets, companies must focus their efforts where they can achieve the best possible cost advantages relative to their rivals. To determine where the best cost advantages lie, strategic managers need to analyze the cost structure of their own company and the cost structures of their main competitors. The strategic manager can then develop strategies that reduce costs where possible.

Financial analysis has traditionally focused on an historic explanation of facts. Financial ratio analysis compares a company to its competition with respect to profitability, liquidity, leverage, and activity for the preceding period(s). The DuPont formula in Appendix D uses past data to show how the firm has managed its assets. And the flow-of-funds analysis highlights the past use of discretionary funds. Though all these techniques are widely used in industry, they were not designed for strategic planning. Nonetheless, they provide valuable data that can be used in formulating alternative strategies for the future.

Another important consideration in financial analysis is how to manage the shareholder's value in the company. Outsourcing has been used as a means of eliminating the need for funds for capital investment, which affects stakeholder value.

What has been termed the "miracle mill," Utah's Geneva Steel, has confounded all the experts by turning out profits from what was considered a hopeless plant (Ansberry, 1991). How did Geneva managers accomplish the miracle? They took an "ancient" open-hearth furnace facility and, by holding down costs, were able to outperform the nation's six largest steelmakers, who all were losing money. The payoff came from encouraging workers to find new but simple ways of reducing cost. One example was storing finished coils of steel indoors rather than leaving them outside to rust. Geneva also caters to mid-sized or small users rather than coping with what it calls "Detroit gorillas." The result was earnings of $16 million, or $1.10 per share on a share price of $19, giving Geneva a 17.3 PE ratio.

The costs that competitors incur are inferred via analogy, research, and estimates based on known advantages or disadvantages that each competitor has, such as access to cheap labor or length of shipping distances. Strategic managers can use models to predict a competitor's strategic moves and, in turn, develop strategies to take advantage of the competitor's cost disadvantages. Using knowledge gained through a competitive-cost analysis, a company could, for example, develop strategies to

- Engage in price competition if the company enjoys a cost advantage
- Avoid price competition if the company has a cost disadvantage
- Implement marketing maneuvers that exploit and expand sources of market premiums

Another method that strategic managers can use to identify sources of cost advantage is cost de-averaging. *Cost de-averaging* is an accounting procedure that allocates costs to particular products or business units, rather than averaging and allocating costs equally. This procedure shows which products or businesses actually contribute to the company's competitive advantage. Using cost de-averaging, a company can focus its resources where they will result in the greatest competitive cost advantage and profitability.

Financial analysis and planning are important aspects of strategic management because they help managers to answer the following questions about a proposed strategy:

- Is the strategy appropriate, given the company's current financial position in the industry?
- Does the company have the financial resources to initiate the strategy and carry it out?
- Are financial resources being allocated correctly to achieve the firm's strategy?

Additional issues that need to be addressed include

- When to expand capacity

- Which new products should be developed
- Whether acquisitions should be considered
- How much is needed for advertising
- How must research and development is needed
- How much maintenance and replacement is required
- Whether outsourcing should be considered

Many of these questions are related to assumptions that are made about funds availability, price elasticity, projections of income and expenses, estimate of cash-flow requirements, economic conditions, competitor actions, consumer demand, taxes, and regulatory requirements.

Answers to these questions can be obtained through the application of methods such as financial ratio analysis, strategic funds programming, and financial planning models. *Financial ratio analysis* is particularly useful for (1) determining a company's financial position relative to that of competitors in an industry and (2) projecting the company's probable future financial position. This analysis involves computing various financial ratios that indicate profitability, liquidity, leverage, and activity, and comparing them to averages for the industry, to ratios from periods during the past, or to absolute standards.

Strategic funds programming helps to identify sources of funds that could be used to initiate a strategy and to implement it over the long term. This method involves assessment of (1) cash flow generated by operations, (2) funds generated by total debt, and (3) the company's ability to generate additional funds by increasing long-term debt. Strategic funds programming enables managers to determine not only whether sufficient funds are available for a given strategy but also whether the company is likely to have sufficient funds to sustain its rate of growth throughout the implementation period.

For over a decade, Intel has used its net income and depreciation to bolster its research and development, which has run as high as 80% of its net income (Flannigan, 1984). In 1982 Intel sold 17% of its stock to IBM in order to obtain the capital needed to be a leader in the chip and semiconductor marketplace. Profits are viewed as another source of funds needed to compete in the extremely volatile semiconductor business.

A number of *financial planning models* have been used to determine the company's ability to implement its strategy or to adapt that strategy to changing environmental conditions. Three of these are baseline projections, what-if analysis, and assessing capital risk analysis.

In addition to these methods, a number of other approaches are used in financial planning. They include break-even, payback period, inflation accounting, cash-flow management, return on value added, risk assessment, shareholder value analysis, activity costing, and cost de-averaging. Qualitative forecasting has also been included in this chapter to supplement the financial risk analysis that is covered.

Computerized financial planning systems have contributed to the financial aspects of strategic planning and implementation. The use of financial planning programs can help managers avoid major mistakes and enables them to

- Create and edit their own financial models using a simple language

- Generate reports, such as pro-forma balance sheets, income statements, and cash-flow analyses
- Test the assumptions on which a plan is based by asking "what-if" questions and performing sensitivity analyses
- Examine alternative goals to ensure that the stated corporate goals and objectives are properly incorporated in the plan
- Perform, for each of the alternatives, a risk analysis that takes into account the uncertainty and risk inherent in every major strategic decision

Many of the problems confronting strategic managers include a large number of factors. Each factor can have different levels of importance and priority. To assist the strategic manager in making these decisions, multiattribute decision making analysis is employed. Considerations to take into account in preparing a budget close the chapter.

A number of related types of analyses are shown in the appendices to this chapter. Appendix A covers the learning curve and its implications for cost analysis. Appendix B shows how to prepare a discounted cash flow. Appendix C illustrates a cost/benefit analysis. Appendix D shows how to apply computer analysis to evaluate financial factors. Appendix D includes a number of printouts from the fisCAL computer program, which provides computerized support for strategic financial analysis.

MANAGING SHAREHOLDER VALUE AND OUTSOURCING

An important concern emerging in financial analysis is how to resolve the apparent conflict between competitive advantage and shareholder value. *Shareholder value analysis* attempts to define which strategies improve shareholder value while sustaining a competitive advantage. By focusing on productivity, financial planners can increase the value of products produced and at the same time lay the foundation for a competitive edge in the marketplace (Rappaport, 1992). Obviously, factors such as competitor costs, market share, product life cycle, and product niche all influence a company's competitive position and may not depend on productivity improvement alone. One of the reasons why companies focus on short-term profitability rather than long-term improvements is the former's potential for lowering stock prices. Apple introduced the Macintosh in 1984 and was able to achieve a highly differentiated market position because of its user-friendly language. The result was that from 1986 to 1990, Apple achieved a 30% return on equity and its annual earnings exceeded 30%. This performance increased shareholder value on the basis of product differentiation rather than productivity. It also illustrates that shareholder value can be increased by long-term investment. Difficulty often arises because shareholder value is not the same as sustainable competitive advantage. Unfortunately, shareholder value is often overlooked when a firm is making investments needed to sustain market position (Day and Fahey, 1990). However, a sustainable competitive advantage can lead to a sustainable shareholder value.

Too often shareholder value is viewed from the perspective of stock prices rather than growth potential, which ultimately is the real shareholder value. Wenner and LeBer (1990) describe shareholder value analysis as the process of analyzing the economic value determined by the net present value of expected cash flows, discounted at the cost of capital. They cite four key factors that create shareholder value:

- Performance of the company's product portfolio
- Assumptions underlying its strategy
- Level of potential improvement
- The company's priorities and goals

An illustration of how goals can affect strategy is the restructuring of companies and retention of businesses. Disney owns or has shares in only those businesses that meet its expected return on capital and growth potential. Marriott Corporation sold off its hotels and increased its ROS from 9% to over 20%. The company felt that its core competency was in managing hotels, not owning them (Willigan, 1990). Using other people's financing, Marriott built hotels that it could manage and achieved an annual growth of over 20%.

Shareholder value is measured by the return received from an investment to compensate for the risk involved. A comprehensive framework for determining shareholder value proposed by McLean (1990) includes

- The net present value of future cash flows
- The value of stock options
- The value of restructuring
- Costs of the corporate office
- Outstanding claims based on liabilities or pending litigation

An approach that can be used to determine shareholder value would cover

1. Which strategies increase cash returns
2. A forecast of cash flow by asset and tax base
3. Determination of equitable return for a specified risk

Ultimately, where equity is a critical source of funds, strategies must incorporate shareholder value as a critical aspect of any analysis. One of the approaches being used to reduce a firm's asset base and thereby increase its cash flow is outsourcing. Outsourcing has become critical for computer service, where the cost of computers is high and it is difficult to attract and retain competent employees. One of the more successful companies in outsourcing services is Electronic Data Systems. The industry has grown from sales of $25 billion in 1989 to $38 billion in 1992 and is projected to grow to $49 billion in 1994 (Weber, 1992). Merrill Lynch analyst Stephen McClellan describes outsourcing as a rapidly developing tidal wave. The rapid growth in outsourcing goes along with the financial benefits derived. However, Bettis, Bradley, and Hamel (1992) claim that improperly used outsourcing may account for our declining competitive position in world trade. Outsourcing amounts to giving up the firm's ability to control its manufacturing or other processes needed to deliver a product to market. Akio Morita, CEO of Sony Corporation, describes the effect of outsourcing as the "hollowing of American industry where the U.S. is abandoning its status as an industrial power." The consumer electronics industry has seen the decline in competitiveness of once-prestigious companies such as RCA. For example, in 1960 the United States had a 100% share of the color television market; that share had shrunk to 55% in 1990. This decline resulted from improved economics of scale in the supplier countries, who eventually took over the manufacture of the entire products, not just the portion that was outsourced. U.S. computer manufacturers such as AST and Everex started as suppliers of boards and components to other PC manufacturers, but as they perfected their components, they turned around and manufactured the entire computer. The critical assumptions made by companies who choose outsourcing are

1. Strategy is primarily having a strong market position.
2. A brand name is sufficient even without manufacturing capability.
3. Manufacturing can be separated from engineering design.
4. Manufacturing knowledge is not critical for understanding the marketplace.

The result of these assumptions is that firms that scale back manufacturing in favor of outsourcing find it difficult to introduce new designs that take advantage of the latest technology, often because suppliers are unwilling to make the necessary investment without assurance of its paying off. In short, there are a number of hazards associated with outsourcing.

Another perspective on outsourcing is described by Welch (1992), who claims that the make-or-buy decision is too often based on unit cost without regard for the strategic or technological implications. The advantages claimed for outsourcing have been that it

- Changes fixed costs to variable costs
- Creates a better balance of the workforce
- Reduces capital investment
- Reduces cost where a supplier offers economies of scale
- Encourages a focus on product development rather than manufacturing
- Enables the firm to benefit from suppliers' innovations
- Focuses resources on those activities that have a high added value

Outsourcing is most effective where

- Process technology is unavailable, as in chip manufacturing
- Competitors have superior technology
- The supplier has lower scrap, rework, returns, recalls, or warranty costs
- Capital for investment is limited and there is a need to focus on high-value-adding activities
- There is flexibility in changing suppliers or where outsourcing could readily be discontinued by either acquisition or new investment in strategic capability

COMPETITIVE-COST ANALYSIS

To compete successfully, a company must analyze its cost position relative to that of competitors. The aim of *competitive-cost analysis* is to get an accurate picture of the competitive situation in an industry. If all competitors' costs are known, the company can project future price levels, anticipate competitors' moves, prepare countermoves, and assess the potential of its strategies for success.

Data that reflect what has transpired in the manufacturing and distribution of a company's products are required for cost analysis. What managers need is accurate and timely information that can help them introduce more effective operating procedures. Kaplan (1988) maintains that not one but three cost systems are required for meeting managerial needs. The first is inventory valuation to allocate production costs between goods that are sold and goods in stock. The second system should supply the feedback needed for operational control; it should focus especially on the resources consumed. Third is a basis for measuring product cost. This same theme is echoed by Ohmae (1989), who contends that company-centered accounting does not adequately deal with overcapacity and can lead to the ruin of companies and industries. Ohmae suggests that to deliver value requires adopting a flexible operating outlook, not simply spending more money to gain market share. Companies must change to fit the changing customer, which implies that accounting systems must accommodate these changing requirements rather than relying on "last year's data."

Cooper (1989) has proposed a number of measures for determining when a new cost system is needed. A new system should be designed when

1. Managers want to drop unprofitable lines
2. Profit margins can't be explained
3. Difficult products show the largest profits
4. The company is introducing increased automation
5. Functional areas develop their own cost system
6. Every decision requires a special accounting team

Cooper maintains that a good cost system should last 10 years, although it may need to be redesigned sooner in a highly volatile environment.

STRATEGIC COST-DRIVING FACTORS

Competitive-cost analysis begins with an analysis of *strategic cost-driving factors*: those factors that determine a company's relative long-run position. These include product design, factor costs, productivity, scale, experience, focus, and capacity utilization. Before the company's relative cost position can be determined, its own cost behavior must be known and differentiated by business segments.

The initial question is "Which costs are relevant in a strategic sense?" That is, which can be influenced by a new strategy? Compared to operational cost control, the goal of which is to cut costs in the short run by "doing things right," strategic cost analysis has the goal of positioning the firm for long-term cost advantages by "doing the right things." Managers sometimes confuse their ability to reduce cost in the short run, such as by laying off personnel, with the fundamental need to achieve strategic cost-competitiveness. Massive layoffs and plant closures can be only a short-term measure to adjust capacity. The roots of the long-term cost disadvantage must be addressed differently.

When considering which products should be produced, where, and for what customers, the strategic manager should ask questions about the following cost-driving factors.

1. *Product design.* Does product design influence product cost? How much of an advantage can be gained by designing a lighter-weight product, a product with fewer parts, a product with more functions integrated into individual components, or a more rugged product that results in lower cost to produce a given quality?

2. *Factor costs.* How much do the basic factor costs (labor, capital, and energy) influence the final cost of the product? How much of an advantage could be gained, for example, by moving production to a country with lower labor costs?

3. *Productivity.* How does productivity differ among competitors in this industry (for example, in terms of sales per employee or value added per employee)? What factors determine these differences (for example, level of employee skills or education, level of automation, differences in applied technology)? With productivity factored in, what advantage would production in a country having lower-cost labor really yield?

4. *Scale/sales.* What is the impact of overall sales volume on costs? Which costs can be shared among businesses or functions (such as overhead, sales costs)? Would building a larger production facility have an impact on costs?

5. *Experience.* How much learning—and thus time and cost—does it take for a relative newcomer in this business to reach a competitive level of efficiency? What future cost and price level can be projected?

6. *Focus.* What are the potential advantages of increased focus with respect to production or distribution? Is it better to invest in single-purpose, specialized machines or in multipurpose, flexible machines? Should all potential customers be addressed in order to maximize volume, or should the sales effort be concentrated on one specific customer group?

7. *Capacity utilization.* What are the cost penalties of overinvesting or underinvesting in new capacity? What cost penalties are associated with underuse of a plant? How would the industry react if actual demand were to exceed expectations?

Figure 8.1 shows the impact of these different cost-driving factors on the cost structure of a company's product. The X's indicate which parts of the cost structure a particular factor affects. The cost structure itself gives an indication of the size of each factor's potential impact. This simple evaluation can be a useful check to remind management of the sources of strategic advantage. The analysis illustrated in Figure 8.1 enables managers to see the relative importance of the different cost-driving factors underlying the company's competitive advantage. Management at AMP may conclude that the focus should be on overall volume and product design because these factors have an impact on many parts of the cost structure. (It might be desirable at this point to review the AMP case in Chapter 6.)

Given a set of product and infrastructure decisions, the analysis of cost-driving factors can be used to determine the firm's relative cost position in the future. It can also be used to determine the competitors' positions, once their products and infrastructures are analyzed in detail. Analysis of competitors enables the firm to gauge its competitive-cost position. AMP, for example, has a size and factor cost disadvantage relative to its main competitors. AMP may be able to overcome this disadvantage with better product design, a stronger focus on production and marketing, and better utilization of its resources. Before making any detailed comparisons, however, AMP must thoroughly investigate its own cost situation.

FIGURE 8.1 **Strategic Cost-driving Factors for AMP, Inc.**

Cost Element	Percentage of Total Costs	Cost-Driving Factors							
		Product Design	Factor Costs	Productivity	Scale/ Volume	Volume per Product Group	Volume per Customer	Capacity Utilization	Experience
Material	31	X	X		X				
Parts treatment and manufacturing	9	X	X	X	X	X		X	X
Assembly	18	X	X	X	X	X		X	X
Quality control	4	X			X	X			
Packaging	5	X			X	X	X		X
Warehousing and distribution	8				X		X		
R&D	2	X			X	X			
Applications engineering	3	X				X	X		X
Sales and marketing	12				X		X	X	
General administration	8				X			X	
Total	100								
AMP's relative position		+	–	0	–	+	+	+	+

Note: Volume per product group and volume per customer involve the issue of focus. In bottom line of table, + = better than competitors; 0 = equal to competitors; and – = worse than competitors.

Source: Courtesy of The Boston Consulting Group, Inc. Reprinted with permission.

COST DE-AVERAGING

Normal accounting procedures assign some costs directly to particular products sold to specific customers. All other costs are averaged—that is, divided among all products and customers—on the basis of a specified allocation. The broader the product line and the larger the number and variety of customers, the greater the use of cost averaging. This often leads to a misstatement of real costs. Overhead and other costs can differ greatly from one product to another, but this fact is obscured through existing accounting practices.

Cost averaging can lead to a loss of market share. The leading company in any industry often has the lowest costs, unless some competitor has exclusive use of better technology. Yet, in business after business, new entrants gain on the leader and eventually displace it because they are able to take advantage of the leader's practice of cost averaging. This happens because a specialized factory, for example, can produce a high volume of products much more cheaply than a factory designed for flexibility. Similarly, a focus on the uniform needs of certain customers can reduce costs. It costs less to serve large, sophisticated buyers who care about price and delivery than to serve smaller buyers who require education, service, and support. In a company serving both markets, cost averaging leads to price averaging, which means that some customers are overcharged while others are subsidized. By focusing on a market segment where the leader is either overcharging or undercharging the customer, a new competitor can gain a foothold. The companies that produce clones of the IBM PC are a good example. Using low-cost components made overseas, they are able to underprice IBM.

An even more subtle and often more damaging effect of cost averaging is that, as the leader increases its product offerings in order to gain sales volume, the overhead charges for all products go up as a result of increased complexity. This effect of product proliferation is demonstrated in Figure 8.2, which shows how in one company, overhead charges for all products went up in three years from 235% to more than 310% as the number of product varieties increased from 8 to 20.

The market leader can prevent some of these problems by averaging costs for the basic product configuration and *then* adding market-segment-specific costs related to product complexity, higher quality, and price. To do this, the company's strategic managers practice cost de-averaging. *Cost de-averaging* requires that they

1. Analyze costs by products as well as by customer groups.
2. Intentionally bias cost allocations, where they are necessary, away from rapidly growing, vulnerable market segments.
3. Differentiate the service to each market segment as required, and organize and price accordingly.

Figure 8.3 shows how costs can be separated by market segments. In this case, a manufacturer produced different-quality products that were targeted at different price points in the market. Basic costs, such as for manufacturing, distribution, and selling, were shared among all products, while segment-specific costs, such as for better quality and advertising, were allocated to specific brands (A, B, and C). This way,

FIGURE 8.2 | **Effect of Product Proliferation**

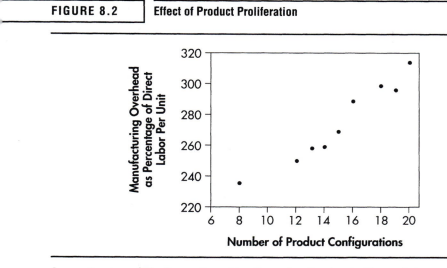

Number of Product Configurations

Source: Courtesy of The Boston Consulting Group, Inc. Reprinted with permission.

the manufacturer was able to reduce its basic or necessary costs by increasing volume overall without overcharging customers in the price-sensitive segment (brand A).

The isolation of market-segment-specific costs is seldom this simple, or more firms would do it on a regular basis. Figure 8.4 is an analysis of costs for a producer of stock forms (continuous computer printout paper) by job size. The company's current accounting data showed that small accounts were most profitable, and management considered investing more in machinery for this segment and increasing its marketing to smaller customers. But a more detailed cost analysis revealed the astonishing fact that small accounts were *not* as profitable as large ones.

First, the cost of waste during startup had not been accounted for regularly. On the average, all jobs had a 7% waste (see Figure 8.4). Yet when managers accounted for the minimum startup waste inherent in all jobs regardless of run length, they saw that the smaller jobs had startup waste factors as high as 57%. Because materials represented a significant percentage of total costs, failure to account for this difference in waste costs led to grave errors in statements of total manufacturing costs.

Second, the cost of selling to small accounts turned out to be higher. When segment-specific sales activities were analyzed, it turned out that sales to small accounts, even over the telephone, involved greater costs per ton than sales to large accounts because of the complex and varying demands of customers in the small-account segment. As Figure 8.4 shows, cost averaging did not reflect actual selling costs to accounts of any size. The average of 18% is way above actual selling costs for large accounts, most of which merely required negotiation of a basic contract for the year and a few visits after that.

When the company de-averaged its job costs per ton of paper sold, it learned that small jobs were twice as expensive as originally reported, medium-sized ones

---

FIGURE 8.3	Basic and Segment-specific Costs

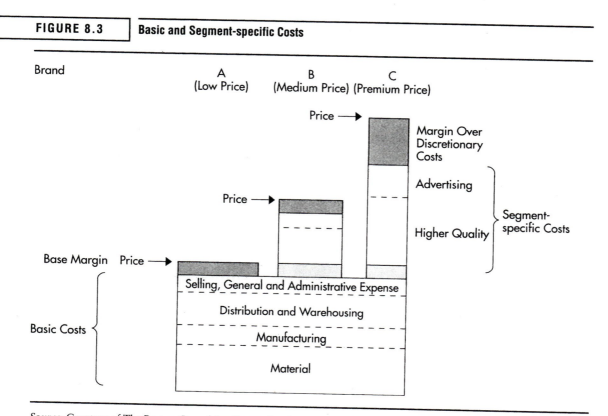

Source: Courtesy of The Boston Consulting Group, Inc. Reprinted with permission.

were 8% more expensive, and large jobs were 14% less expensive. Given the company's pricing policy, it was losing a substantial amount on small jobs while gaining substantial profits on the large ones. As a result of cost de-averaging, management decided to invest in larger machines and automated warehousing. Small jobs were eliminated from the production program, but a separate organization was installed to customize forms produced by other companies.

COMPETITIVE-COST MODELING

Once the firm's costs have been properly allocated, they can be compared to those of competitors in particular market segments. Competitive-cost analysis generally begins by examining the firm's own costs. Competitors' costs are estimated by using an appropriate analogy. To model competitive costs, managers need data covering

- Internal cost behavior
- Competitive microeconomics
- Financial performance of the firm
- Knowledge about competitors

FIGURE 8.4	Cost De-averaging

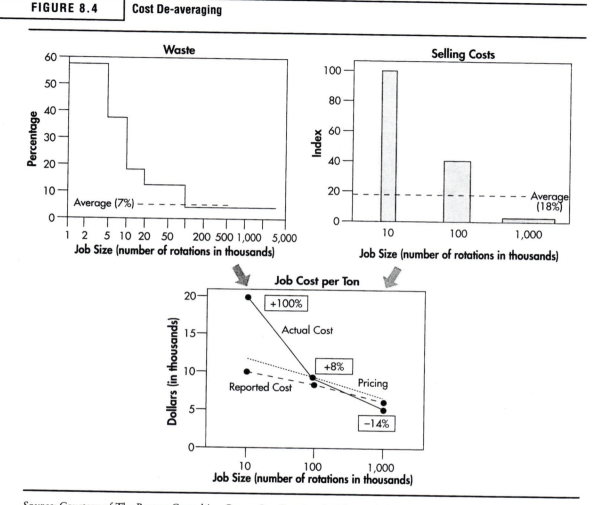

Source: Courtesy of The Boston Consulting Group, Inc. Reprinted with permission.

Figure 8.5 is a competitive-cost model based on these sets of data. Using data about the firm's own costs, managers establish microeconomic relationships to explain how costs behave relative to changes in the cost-driving factors (see Figure 8.1). Next they acquire data on the competitors' infrastructure, such as plant size, location, sales by market segment, number of employees, and technology used. These data can be obtained from public sources such as annual reports, Form 10-Ks, analysts' reports, and other publications. Other important sources include industry specialists, academics, suppliers and customers of the competitors, and sometimes even the competitor itself. The competitor's financial performance is

| FIGURE 8.5 | Competitive-Cost Modeling |

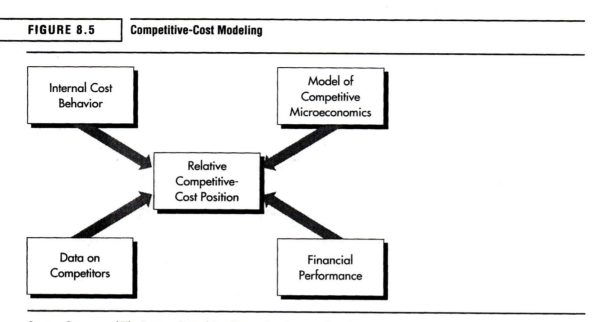

Source: Courtesy of The Boston Consulting Group, Inc. Reprinted with permission.

another important element; it can be used to spot inconsistencies between performance as predicted by the competitive-cost model and the competitor's actual performance. Discrepancies may, for example, reveal important facts about operations or technology use.

The key question to ask in performing a competitive-cost analysis is "Where are the firm's sources of competitive advantage, and can the advantage be defended over time?" The answer to this question depends on those posed in the sections that follow.

Product Design

What would our costs be if we produced our competitor's product (in our existing plant)? In other words, what are the production costs, given the weight, complexity of design, number and quality of parts, and performance of a competitor's product characteristics? This analysis enables managers to draw some immediate conclusions about the material costs of competitive products and to make inferences concerning the competitor's technology and production process. It is important to recognize that the competitive product would often cost more to produce using the firm's machines even if it were, for example, lighter and had fewer parts, because production technology and process are optimized as a product is developed. Either specialized machines are bought to produce a particular design, or the product is designed such that it optimally utilizes existing processes and technology.

Differences in product design and the resulting cost differences can be significant and can also reveal differences in production philosophy among competitors. For example, Japanese electronics manufacturers tend to integrate product components more than Western countries do. Such a practice means higher initial costs for development and production, but its long-term effects on quality overcome the short-term cost disadvantages by far. Similarly, the designs of European cars tend to fulfill expectations about performance and longevity, enabling European car manufacturers to dominate the luxury segment of the market.

Factor Costs

What would our costs be if our plant were in the same location as the competitor's? The purpose of this hypothetical question is to assess the competitor's factor costs. What if, for example, the competitor's plant is in South Korea or Taiwan instead of the United States? The potential savings in labor costs can be substantial, as is shown in Table 8.1. It is important to recognize that these data are average and that regional differences exist within each country. Furthermore, when one isolates those parts of the cost structure that really are comparable, it is often surprising how little total costs are affected by labor costs. Wages paid to sales personnel, for example, typically depend on where the product is marketed, not on where it is manufactured, and

TABLE 8.1	International Comparison of Labor Costs	

Country	Hourly Wages ($)*	Index
High Labor Rates		
United States	14.45	100
Germany	17.45	121
Medium Labor Rates		
Japan	11.90	82
France	12.10	84
Great Britain	10.25	71
Italy	11.15	77
Sweden	12.95	90
Finland	11.80	82
Low Labor Rates		
Taiwan	2.30	16
South Korea	2.00	14

* Average hourly wages in machinery manufacturing, including additional compensation, at currency exchange rates of July 1987.

Source: U.S. Bureau of Labor Statistics, 1987.

tend to be the same whether the plant is in the United States or Taiwan. Low labor costs are beneficial if manufacturing and assembly still dominate the product's value chain and if the upstream activities of sales and marketing are difficult to differentiate.

Productivity

How do differences in productivity affect the costs of competitors? Productivity comparisons can be based on a number of indicators, such as value added per employee, sales per employee, or fixed-asset turnover. These comparisons should be done at the plant level and, if possible, on the machine level. Discussions with machine suppliers can help managers understand a competitor's approach to achieving productivity gains.

Production technology is a major determinant of productivity. In recent years, for example, considerable progress has been made in factory automation and machine flexibility, at little or no additional cost. Many leading Western competitors have recognized the potential of the "factory of the future" and are using production technology to retain their competitive edge, while at the same time maintaining employment in countries with high labor costs. In textile manufacturing, for example, so-called quick-response systems are helping to restore jobs to high-cost countries.

Figure 8.6 shows how the production costs of standard bolts declined as new technologies emerged. Currently, a machine shop with many workers has cost

| FIGURE 8.6 | Technological Evolution in the Production of Standard Bolts |

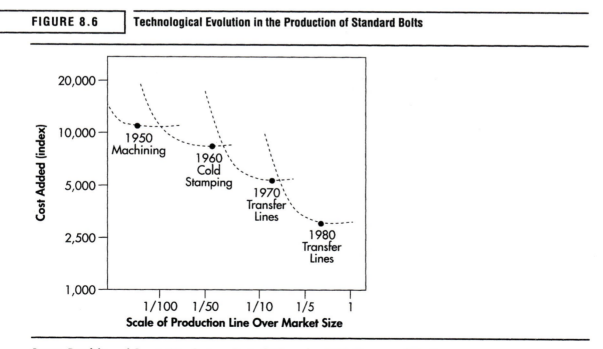

Source: Portfolio and Competitive Systems, Paris, © November 1985. Courtesy of The Boston Consulting Group, Inc. Reprinted with permission.

added that is at least four times the cost added for a competitor employing the most recently developed transfer lines. As can be seen in the figure, the volume supplier needs to retain a significant portion of the total market in order to maintain its productivity advantage in the face of the competition from alternative technologies.

As many Japanese competitors proved in the early 1980s, significant gains in productivity can also be made without massive investments in new technology. Table 8.2 shows the increases in labor and capital productivity of a number of Japanese manufacturing firms. These companies achieved gains by pioneering new concepts, such as Kanban or just-in-time (JIT), on the shop floor. What makes these productivity gains particularly impressive is the fact that they were accomplished while product variety was increasing.

Scale Effects: Total Volume

What would our production costs be if our production facility were the same size as our competitor's? Total volume of production is a cost-driving factor for virtually every element in the cost structure (see Figures 8.7 and 8.8). Other advantages of scale depend on the size of plant or machines (Figure 8.9). Production costs in the paper industry, for example, are strongly influenced by the width of the paper machine used. Paper machines today have sophisticated automation systems, and the employee-hours per ton required to operate a paper machine decrease as the machine size increases. As a result, the labor cost per ton of paper declines as machine size increases. In the machine-tool industry, on the other hand, more volume means more machines and more personnel to operate them. Therefore, increased investment in machines does not reduce production costs. Yet costs at the plant level (such as quality control, warehousing, repair and maintenance, and general administration) do not tend to increase with higher volume.

TABLE 8.2	Productivity Improvements: Japanese Manufacturing Firms, 1976–1982

		Increases		
Company	Product	Labor Productivity	Capital Productivity	Product Variants
Yanmar	Diesel engines	1.9×	2.0×	3.7×
Hitachi	Refrigeration equipment	1.8×	1.7×	1.3×
Komatsu	Industrial equipment	1.8×	1.7×	1.8×
Toyo Kogyo	Automotive components	2.4×	1.9×	1.6×
Isuzu	Automobiles	2.5×	1.5×	NA
Jidosha Kiki	Brakes	1.9×	NA	NA
Average		2.0×	1.8×	2.1×

Source: Introduction to Time-Based Competition and Operational Effectiveness, Vol. 1, p. 10, © August 1987. Courtesy of The Boston Consulting Group, Inc. Reprinted with permission.

FIGURE 8.7	The Leader's Advantage: Advertising Costs of Tire Companies

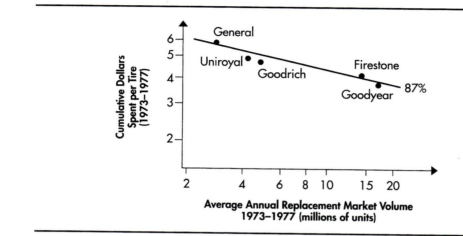

Source: Courtesy of The Boston Consulting Group, Inc. Reprinted with permission.

FIGURE 8.8	Purchasing Scale Economics for Hydraulic Components (Price per unit includes full amortization of tooling costs)

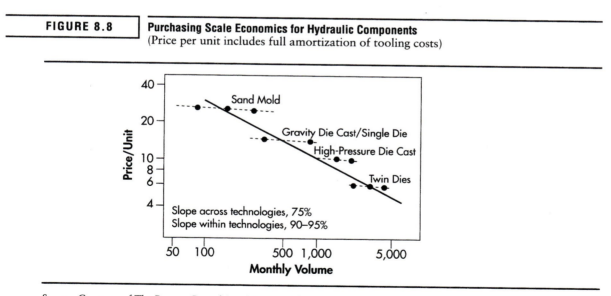

Source: Courtesy of The Boston Consulting Group, Inc. Reprinted with permission.

Figure 8.9 also illustrates how different scale effects are determined. Through discussions with management as well as suppliers, different machine configurations and their labor requirements can be modeled and then plotted. The scale effects can then be calculated or read directly from the chart. When all the scale effects for

| FIGURE 8.9 | Effects of Machine Size and Plant Capacity on Labor Costs |

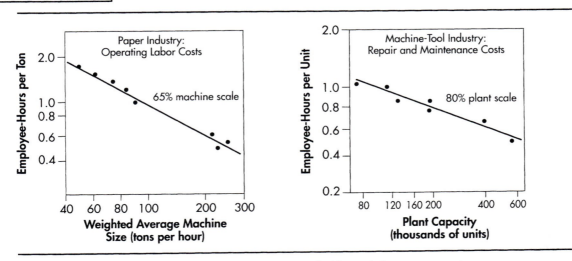

Source: Courtesy of The Boston Consulting Group, Inc. Reprinted with permission.

every part of the cost structure have been derived, the company's total potential cost advantage or disadvantage relative to that of a competitor can be established.

Focus: Volume per Product Group or Customer

How would a change of focus alter our competitive-cost position? In today's competitive environment, few companies can base their success on an overall volume advantage, particularly in a shrinking market. In this kind of environment, the focused competitor beats the broad-line supplier every time. General Motors' massive lead in market share, for instance, today is being eroded by competitors who "build a car like a car" (Ford), make an automobile "engineered like no other car in the world" (Mercedes-Benz), or "sell cars you can afford" (Hyundai). Focus involves better understanding of the business and greater attention to detail. The more focused a company is, the better it can identify and increase the value of its products to customers.

A focused company concentrates on activities that it does best. Focus is usually associated with closing or selling off weak businesses and pruning unprofitable products. Therefore, focus is driven by a thorough understanding of markets and customers, an understanding that can be converted directly to cost advantages and higher profitability.

Figure 8.10 shows the relationship between production lost and the annual volumes of different models of a ceramic product. Clearly, the higher the volume per model, the lower the percentage of production rejects. Small-volume models had rejection rates of up to 30% at the end of the production line, whereas some high-volume models had rejection rates of less than 5%. Yet customers were

---

FIGURE 8.10 | Production Lost versus Volume per Model of a Ceramic Product

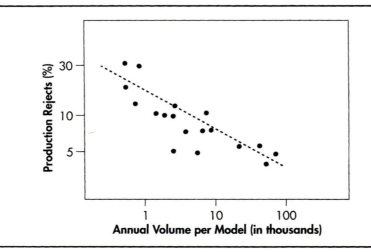

Source: Courtesy of The Boston Consulting Group, Inc. Reprinted with permission.

---

willing to pay a higher price for the unique (low-volume) designs, and this market segment was growing fastest. Therefore, the company decided to focus on the low-volume, unique items, manufacture all of its products in a single factory, and arrange the production process so that the low-volume products would benefit from production economies made possible by their high-volume counterparts. With this system, the company was able to reduce the rejection rate of all products, but particularly that of the low-volume items. Focusing on these items enabled the company to establish itself firmly as the leader in the high-priced, designer market.

Focus can also involve concentrating marketing in particular geographic regions. Figure 8.11 shows how regional focus affected the profitability of seven U.S. supermarket chains. Independent of their size, supermarkets tend to be more profitable if they dominate particular regions. The regional leader has logistical advantages, such as distribution efficiency and collective advertising in local newspapers. Because of its lack of geographic focus, A&P, though about equal in size to the market leader (Safeway), had a significantly lower profitability, even compared to smaller regional competitors such as Winn-Dixie and Stop & Shop. Once A&P recognized this, it closed its unprofitable stores and expanded in areas where it had a strong position. As a result, A&P has recovered from near bankruptcy to become very profitable.

Capacity Utilization

How do we compare with respect to optimal use of product capacity? Capacity utilization is most important for industries with high capital investments and declining markets. Competitors in this situation often enter into intense fights over volume leadership to avoid having to reduce capacity and lay off personnel in response to lower market demands. The ensuing price-cutting wars often lead to vicious circles in which competitors convert any cost reductions into immediate price cuts, thereby pushing all competitors' break-even points further out of reach. Eventually, the industry undergoes a shake-out and consolidation, after which capacities are brought back in line with market demands through competitive restructuring.

Price Realization

What is our relative position with respect to price realization? Pricing is often ignored in comparisons among competitors. Yet, in one industry after another, patterns of differing price realization for almost identical products emerge. Figure 8.12 shows how the prices charged for radial tires vary, even though it would be difficult for the average buyer to distinguish one brand of radials from another if the brand names were removed. Some reasons for greater price realization are based on customers' perceptions of the product. Customers may, for example, associate certain features with the product because of their perception of a supplier's image. A more typical reason is that the leading supplier is in a position to influence price realization through better or more numerous locations, a loyal base of existing customers, better employees and better service, or better availability and shorter delivery times. These advantages combined to allow the market leaders, Goodyear and Firestone, to charge about 5% to 10% more per tire than their smaller competitors. In stalemated industries with little potential for cost differentiation, a difference in price realization can often make the difference between failure and long-term survival.

| FIGURE 8.11 | Regional Focus of U.S. Supermarkets |

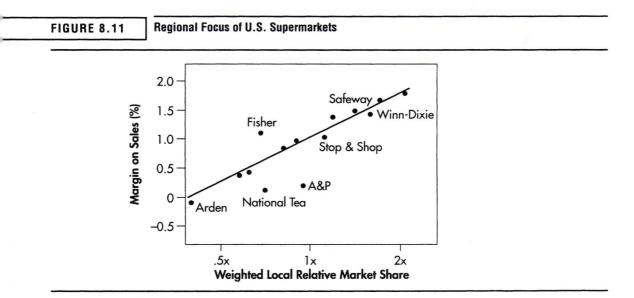

Source: Courtesy of The Boston Consulting Group, Inc. Reprinted with permission.

FIGURE 8.12 | Retail Weighted Average Price Realization of Steel and Economy Radial Tires, 1978

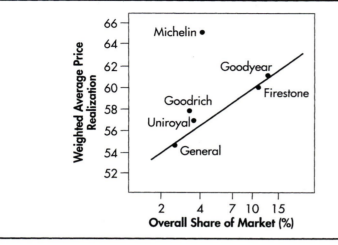

Source: Courtesy of The Boston Consulting Group, Inc. Reprinted with permission.

A COMPLETE COMPETITIVE-COST COMPARISON

The purpose of competitive-cost analysis is to obtain an accurate picture of the supply situation in an industry. A company that knows all its competitors' costs can readily make projections concerning the industry price development, anticipate competitive moves, prepare countermoves, and assess the potential success of strategic moves.

Figure 8.13, for example, shows the result of a competitive-cost analysis for a commodity product in the paper industry. In the graph, the cost of each competitor, as calculated, is plotted along with its supply. The largest competitor (competitor A) has the lowest cost. When the supplies from all competitors are added, the total supply from the industry can be shown relative to market demand. As seen in this example, the total industry supply exceeds the market demand of about 1.25 million tons. In such a situation, the price level typically is reduced to the cash operating cost of the marginal competitor. Competitors with higher cash costs are often forced to leave the market. As new capacity comes on stream, the price level is brought down to the cash operating cost of the new marginal competitor, and those with higher cash costs become noncompetitive. Because it takes at least two years to complete a new paper mill after announcing the investment decision, there is sufficient time for marginal competitors to adjust their strategies and switch to more specialized paper grades.

A recently suggested approach to costing is to link activities with resource usage. Cooper and Kaplan (1991) recommend substituting activity-based costing for traditional cost accounting systems. The key, they contend, is to separate expenses based on the level of activity that consumes resources. Thus expenses would be allocated not by individual products, but by the activity level needed to "produce different products or to serve different customers, independent of how many units are produced or sold." Activities are grouped as follows:

FIGURE 8.13	**Paper Product Supply Curve and Its Effects on Price Realization**

(Full cost equals cash operating cost plus depreciation and capital costs)

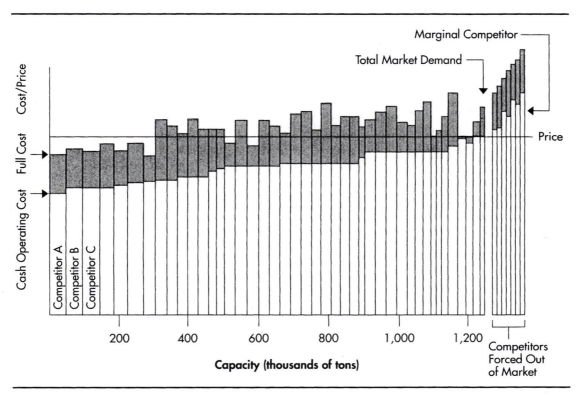

Source: Courtesy of The Boston Consulting Group, Inc. Reprinted with permission.

1. Facilities—expenses of maintenance and operations
2. Products—expenses to design and improve products
3. Batch level—support for producing products
4. Unit level—direct cost of producing products

They conclude by stating, "Bad information on product costs leads to bad competitive strategy."

Understanding the strategic cost drivers in an industry and doing a competitive-cost analysis can be very helpful in defining areas that offer the best potential for future profitability. A carefully done competitive-cost comparison can also yield direct conclusions on how to maintain or improve the company's competitive position, such as by

- Investing in improved product design to match a rival
- Moving a new factory to a lower-cost country
- Raising productivity to projected levels on the experience curve
- Increasing volume in specific segments to gain scale advantage and focus
- Closing plant sites to achieve better capacity utilization

FINANCIAL RATIO ANALYSIS

One widely used technique for evaluating performance and for comparing a business with others in an industry is financial ratio analysis. Financial ratios can provide a quick overview of a company's recent or past profitability, liquidity, leverage, and activity. Key financial ratios are defined in Table 8.3. Financial ratios, which often are employed for merger or acquisition decisions, can be used to show

1. The firm's position in its industry
2. The degree to which strategic objectives are being accomplished
3. The firm's vulnerability to decreases in revenue
4. The future borrowing power and growth potential of the firm
5. The firm's ability to react to unforeseen changes in the environment
6. The risk of corporate failure

Financial ratios have been used for years as indicators of the well-being of a company. Financial ratio analysis is used in assessing a company's internal strengths and weaknesses and, because considerable amounts of financial data are available about competitors, and for making comparisons within an industry. It is important to recognize, however, that these ratios reflect the past; therefore, they are often more useful for evaluating past performance than for planning future strategies.

Each of the four key areas chosen for analysis—profitability, liquidity, leverage, and activity of the firm—comprises a number of ratios. It is usually sufficient to focus on only a few, such as the ones defined in Table 8.3. To evaluate the performance of a company with respect to these ratios, the following three methods are used.

1. *Industry comparisons.* To perform this analysis, managers compare the company's financial ratios to those of similar firms in the same industry. The other firms must be comparable; that is, they should be of about the same size, sell similar products, and serve the same markets. If this is not the case, results of the comparison can be misleading.
2. *Time-series analysis.* This method involves computing the company's financial ratios for several past years and plotting them on a graph to detect changes and trends over time and project future performance.
3. *Comparison to absolute standards.* In many organizations, minimum financial ratios serve as absolute standards for performance. Such absolute standards include
   a. Profitability: net profit, the ratio of profits after taxes to sales: no less than 3%
   b. Liquidity: ratio of current assets to current liabilities: greater than 1
   c. Leverage: ratio of long-term debt to total equity: less than 1
   d. Activity: average collection period: less than 60 days

A complete financial analysis generally includes all three of these methods.

These methods are often supplemented by doing an industry comparison. An example is shown in Appendix D, where the fisCAL program is used. Managers also rely on comparative data from companies such as Dun & Bradstreet to assess their relative profitability, liquidity, leverage, and activity ratios.

1. *Profitability.* Profitability ratios indicate how well a company is allocating its resources in relation to income generated.

TABLE 8.3	Key Financial Ratios

Ratio	Definition	Ratio	Definition
1. Profitability		**3. Leverage**	
a. Gross profit margin $$\frac{\text{Sales} - \text{cost of goods sold}}{\text{sales}}$$	Total margin available to cover operating expenses and yield a profit	a. Debt-to-assets ratio $$\frac{\text{total debt}}{\text{total assets}}$$	The extent to which funds are used to finance the firm's operations
b. Net profit margin $$\frac{\text{profits after taxes}}{\text{sales}}$$	Return on sales	b. Debt-to equity ratio $$\frac{\text{total debt}}{\text{total equity}}$$	Ratio of funds from creditors to funds from stockholders
c. Return on assets $$\frac{\text{earnings before interest and taxes (EBIT)}}{\text{total assets}}$$	Return on the total investment from both stockholders and creditors	c. Long-term debt-to-equity ratio $$\frac{\text{long-term debt}}{\text{total equity}}$$	The balance between debt and equity
d. Return on equity $$\frac{\text{profits after taxes}}{\text{total equity}}$$	Rate of return on stockholders' investment in the firm		
2. Liquidity		**4. Activity**	
a. Current ratio $$\frac{\text{current assets}}{\text{current liabilities}}$$	The extent to which the claims of short-term creditors are covered by short-term assets	a. Inventory turnover $$\frac{\text{sales}}{\text{inventory}}$$	The amount of inventory used by the company to generate its sales
b. Quick ratio $$\frac{\text{current assets} - \text{inventory}}{\text{current liabilities}}$$	Acid-test ratio; the firm's ability to pay off short-term obligations without having to sell its inventory	b. Fixed-asset turnover $$\frac{\text{sales}}{\text{fixed assets}}$$	Sales productivity and plant utilization
c. Inventory to net working capital $$\frac{\text{inventory}}{\text{current assets} - \text{current liabilities}}$$	The extent to which the firm's working capital is tied up in inventory	c. Average collection period $$\frac{\text{accounts receivable}}{\text{average daily sales}}$$	The average length of time required to receive payment

2. *Liquidity.* Liquidity measures are based on the simple notion that a business cannot operate if it is unable to pay its bills. A sufficient amount of cash and other short-term assets must be available when needed. On the other hand, because most short-term assets do not produce any return, a great amount of

liquidity damages profits. The goal is to keep liquidity as low as possible while ensuring that short-term obligations will be met. This means that industries competing in a stable and predictable environment generally require smaller current ratios than more volatile industries.

3. *Leverage.* Leverage ratios show how a company's operations are financed. Too much equity often means that management is not taking advantage of the leverage associated with long-term debt. Outside financing does, however, become more expensive as the debt-to-equity ratio increases. Therefore, managers have to consider leverage in light of the company's profitability and the volatility of the industry.

4. *Activity.* Activity ratios are used to measure the productivity and efficiency of a firm. Comparing the fixed-asset turnover ratio to the industry average, for example, shows how well the company is using its productive capacity. The inventory-turnover ratio indicates whether the company used too much inventory in generating sales and whether the company is carrying obsolete inventory.

Worksheet 8.1 is a complete financial ratio analysis for AMP. The evaluation of the different ratios can be summarized in a financial ratio profile, such as the one shown in Worksheet 8.2. AMP's position is indicated by the shaded areas.

FINANCIAL IMPLICATIONS OF THE PRODUCT LIFE CYCLE

As one traces the changes that take place in the life cycle of a typical product, it becomes obvious that there are significant impacts on the financial performance of a firm as well as on its competitive advantage. As can be seen in Figure 8.14, the expected revenue for any given product reaches a maximum at what is termed maturity and then declines until the product is totally obsolete. One of the major reasons why products become obsolete is the investments made in R&D that lead to new technology, which helps new products surpass mature products in performance, service, reliability, cost, and so on. A consequence of this technology's forcing out the old product is a decline in profit, despite the lower unit cost that results from the learning curve. Figure 8.14 shows that it is necessary to make continuous investment in new products in order to have a sustainable competitive advantage.

Another significant effect of the product life cycle is the change in strategy needed to sustain a competitive advantage. Depending on the firm's market position, the strategy needs to be continuously modified to meet competitive forces and market demands. Table 8.4 shows the changes required as the product moves through its life cycle. This table also shows when investment is required to improve the product's features and when funds are required because of reduced prices or a need to advertise or improve the product. Cash flow thus changes in each phase of the product life cycle.

| WORKSHEET 8.1 | Financial Ratio Analysis |

Case   AMP
Date   1990 Company Data
Name   John Doe

1. Profitability

   a. Gross profit margin

   $$\frac{\text{sales} - \text{cost of goods sold}}{\text{sales}} = \frac{3,043 - 2,092}{3,043} = \underline{33.9\%}$$

   b. Net profit margin

   $$\frac{\text{profit after taxes}}{\text{sales}} = \frac{287}{3,043} = \underline{9.4\%}$$

   c. Return on assets

   $$\frac{\text{EBIT}}{\text{total assets}} = \frac{488}{2,929} = \underline{16.7\%}$$

   d. Return on equity

   $$\frac{\text{profits after taxes}}{\text{total equity}} = \frac{287}{1,793} = \underline{16.0\%}$$

2. Liquidity

   a. Current ratio

   $$\frac{\text{current assets}}{\text{current liabilities}} = \frac{1,618}{953} = \underline{1.70\%}$$

   b. Quick ratio

   $$\frac{\text{current assets} - \text{inventory}}{\text{current liabilities}} = \frac{1,618 - 482}{953} = \underline{1.19\%}$$

   c. Inventory to net working capital

   $$\frac{\text{inventory}}{\text{current assets} - \text{current liabilities}} = \frac{482}{1,618 - 953} = \underline{0.72\%}$$

(continued)

WORKSHEET 8.1	Financial Ratio Analysis (continued)

3. Leverage

   a. Debt-to-assets ratio

   $$\frac{\text{total debt}}{\text{total assets}} = \frac{1,136}{2,929} = \underline{39\%}$$

   b. Debt-to-equity ratio

   $$\frac{\text{total debt}}{\text{total equity}} = \frac{1,136}{1,793} = \underline{63\%}$$

   c. Long-term debt-to-equity ratio

   $$\frac{\text{long-term debt}}{\text{total equity}} = \frac{69}{1,793} = \underline{3\%}$$

4. Activity

   a. Inventory turnover

   $$\frac{\text{sales}}{\text{inventory}} = \frac{3,043}{482} = \underline{5.5}$$

   b. Fixed-asset turnover

   $$\frac{\text{sales}}{\text{fixed assets}} = \frac{3,043}{1,122} = \underline{2.7}$$

   c. Average collection period

   $$\frac{\text{accounts receivable}}{\text{average daily sales}} = \frac{557}{3,043/365} = \underline{67 \text{ days}}$$

WORKSHEET 8.2	Financial Ratio Profile

Case ___AMP___

Date ___1990 Company Data___

Name ___John Doe___

Profitability

Very low   Average   Very high

Liquidity

Very tight   About right   Too much slack

Leverage

Too much debt   Balanced   Too much equity

Activity

Too slow   About right   Too fast

Comments:

Excellent profitability, high liquidity. AMP applies a very conservative financial policy in financing the company. Very little debt is used. The activity ratios indicate potential for improvement, especially in the inventory turnovers.

The product life also has a direct impact on financial ratios. As described in the previous section, financial ratios reflect a static perspective on the performance of a firm. But when we look at them from the point of view of the product life cycle, we obtain a dynamic perspective on the significance of the financial ratios. Table 8.5 shows how the financial ratios change with each of the four principal

| FIGURE 8.14 | **Financial Implications of the Product Life Cycle** |

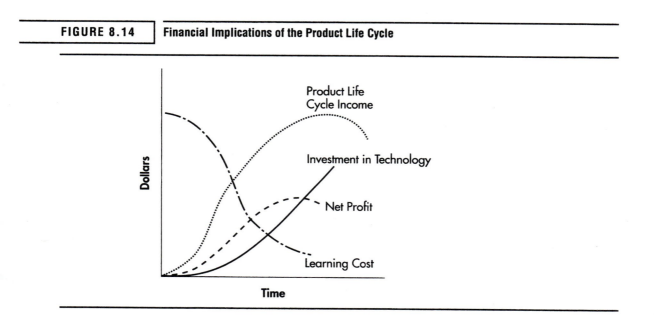

| TABLE 8.4 | **Typical Product/Market Strategies Based on the Experience Curve and Product Life Cycle** |

| | Product Life Stage | | | |
Market Share	Introduction	Growth	Maturity	Decline
High: market leader	Sacrifice current profits in order to gain market share as fast as possible	Reduce prices as costs come down to discourage new competitors	Hold market share by improving quality and increasing sales effort and advertising; utilize capacity fully	Maximize cash flow by reducing investment and advertising; allow market share to decline in order to maximize short-term profits
Low: market follower	Invest to increase market share	Concentrate on a market segment that can be dominated	Withdraw from the market or maintain share by keeping prices and costs below those of market leaders	Withdraw from the market

phases of the product life cycle. Table 8.6 is a summary of the general effects on financial ratios and how they should be interpreted.

As is apparent, industry norms are at best an average over the life cycle for a product or in some cases an SBU, where the business unit concentrates on a specific product line.

Another factor that affects financial ratios is the change that takes place in given industries. For example, Boise-Cascade experienced wide fluctuations in its ratios over a ten-year period, as shown in Table 8.7. The ratio of current assets to current liabilities had almost a threefold variation, from 3.4 to 1.3, during this period. Net profit over net worth was more stable, with a maximum variation of 6.2 to 12.6. Inventory over net working capital ranged from 71.3% to 137.0%, again almost a 2-to-1 variation. Like changes attributable to the product life cycle, financial ratios should be averaged over a number of years.

TABLE 8.5	**Summary of Table 8.4 Strategies**

Market Position	Introduction	Growth	Maturity	Decline
High	Sacrifice current profits	Reduce prices	Improve, quality, advertise	Maximize cash flow
Low	Invest	Concentrate on segment	Withdraw from market	Withdraw

TABLE 8.6	**Relationship of Financial Ratios and Product Life Cycle**

Phase	Introduction	Rapid Growth	Maturity	Decline
Impact on financial ratios	Ratios are lower than industry	Ratios are near or higher than industry	Ratios are higher than industry	Ratios are lower than industry

OTHER ANALYSES USING FINANCIAL RATIOS

As we have seen, much can be learned by examining how ratios change over time. Financial ratios can also be used to assess several other factors.

1. *The degree to which objectives are being accomplished.* For this purpose, any of the ratios discussed so far can be plotted against a projected or targeted rate of change in order to reveal the firm's ability to close performance gaps. Many companies aim for above-average performance, in which case, the company's ratios are compared to those of the industry leaders rather than to averages for the industry.

2. *The firm's vulnerability to decreases in revenue.* This assessment is particularly valuable as the company's products reach the maturity phase of the product life cycle. The *DuPont formula* (see Appendix D) is a method of using financial ratios to determine return on assets (ROA). Here, ratios for earnings as percent of sales (operating margin) and for asset turnover are particularly useful. Because ROA is equal to the product of these two ratios, profitability depends to a large measure on the firm's ability to maintain or improve these ratios over time.

TABLE 8.7	Changes Over 10 Years in 3 Financial Ratios at Boise-Cascade

Ratio	Year									
	1	2	3	4	5	6	7	8	9	10
Current assets / Current liabilities	3.4%	3.1	2.3	2.0	2.6	2.9	2.3	1.6	1.6	1.3
Net profit / Net worth	7.2%	6.2	9.7	11.4	9.0	10.3	8.8	10.7	12.6	9.8
Inventory to net working capital	71.3%	77.3	91.3	100.0	84.3	73.8	90.0	123.4	137.0	100.5

3. *The future borrowing power and growth potential of the firm.* The growth potential of a firm is based on its ROI, the average interest rate on total debt, and on its degree of financial leverage (debt-to-equity ratio). A significant change in one of these indicators suggests a change in the firm's growth pattern. By plotting these ratios over time, strategic managers can often see behind the "window dressing" that a firm may employ to make financial data for a specific period look good.

4. *The firm's ability to react to unforeseen changes in the environment.* Market-oriented ratios, such as the price/earnings (P/E) ratio or the market-to-book-value ratio, can reflect a firm's ability to deal with unforeseen changes. These ratios reflect investors' estimations of how well the company will be able to cope with such environmental changes as a turnaround of the economy, entry of a major new competitor into the market, or development of a new technology.

5. *The chances for company survival in the long run.* In 1968, Edward Altman developed a useful predictor of corporate bankruptcy for manufacturing companies. His predictor of corporate survival is the value of *factor Z,* which is based on a discriminant function with five significant ratios, X_1 through X_5.

$$Z = .012X_1 + .014X_2 + .033X_3 + .006X_4 + .999X_5$$

where

X_1 = Working capital/total assets (%). This ratio measures net liquid assets relative to total capitalization. Ordinarily, a firm experiencing consistent operating losses has shrinking current assets relative to total assets.

X_2 = Total retained earnings/total assets (%). This is a measure of cumulative profitability over time, so the age of a firm is implicitly considered in this ratio. In general, the incidence of failure is much higher among young firms.

X_3 = Earnings before interest and taxes (EBIT)/total assets (%). This ratio, which measures the productivity (or earning power) of the firm's assets, seems to be particularly useful for predicting corporate failure.

X_4 = Market value of equity/book value of total debt (%). This measure shows how much the firm's assets can decline in value before the liabilities exceed the assets and the firm becomes insolvent.

X_5 = Sales/total assets. The asset-turnover ratio measures management's ability to deal with competitive conditions.

In some cases, the Z-factor can be approximated with the simplified equation

$$Z \approx \frac{\text{sales}}{\text{total assets}}$$

Altman found that companies with a Z-factor higher than 2.99 have a minimum risk of corporate failure, whereas companies with a Z-factor less than 1.81 have a significant risk of bankruptcy. Companies with a Z-factor between 1.81 and 2.99 fall into a "zone of ignorance," where it is not possible to predict which way the company will go. A single Z-factor in this zone may not be cause for immediate concern, but Z-factors in this zone over several periods indicate financial and competitive difficulties that could become quite serious. As with other ratios, the Z-factor must be related to companies in a given industry and at a given phase of their organizational life cycle. In the case of AMP, the Z-factor is above 6 which indicates that AMP is in a good financial situation.

STRATEGIC FUNDS PROGRAMMING

Attempting to introduce a new strategy is like trying to rebuild a ship at sea. The current business must be kept operating properly so that it generates enough funds to carry out the new strategic programs. A common error in strategic planning is for managers to become so enamored of the possibilities and opportunities of a new strategy that they fail to provide enough support for the current business.

Strategic funds programming helps managers to avoid this pitfall by identifying the funds required to meet the new conditions. Strategic funds programming is a budget and control system that provides managers with the decision-making information they need to implement strategy. It is designed to balance the financial requirements of maintaining current business with the financial needs of launching a new strategy.

FLOW-OF-FUNDS ANALYSIS

A first step in strategic funds programming is to identify how a company uses its financial resources. Table 8.8 shows how AMP managed its flow of funds during the fiscal year 1989–1990. By examining these numbers, managers can identify additional sources of funds that can be obtained by renegotiating long-term debt and can see where adjustments might be made to free funds for strategic use. As Table 8.8 shows, AMP increased its allocation of funds to inventory and accounts receivable.

Funds can be obtained either by selling off a company's assets or by increasing its liabilities or owners' equity. The funds so obtained are used to increase other assets of the company or to reduce liabilities or equity. If a company pays off some of its long-term debt, for example, its cash position diminishes, thereby keeping the flow of funds in balance.

GENERATING STRATEGIC FUNDS

Organizations can generate new funds from three sources, which constitute the company's resources for strategic growth.

1. Regular operations and other internal sources (examples include profits after taxes, depreciation, and distress sales or auctions to dispose of excess inventory or unused buildings)
2. Expansion of debt consistent with the financial structure of the organization (having banks or suppliers provide extended lines of credit, factoring accounts receivable, leasing rather than buying equipment)
3. The addition of new long-term debt or equity funds through changes in the financial structure of the firm (issuing new stock, negotiating additional long-term loans)

TABLE 8.8	Flow-funds Analysis for AMP
	(Dollar amounts in millions)

Category	1989–1990	Amount
Sources of Funds (Inflow)		
Cash	460 – 334 =	126
Accounts receivable	557 – 520 =	37
Inventories	482 – 495 =	13
Fixed assets	1,122 – 954 =	168
Other investments and receivables		81
Total		399
Uses of Funds (Outflow)		
Accounts payable	245 – 225 =	20
Short-term loans	708 – 501 =	207
Long-term debt	183 – 179 =	4
Common stock and retained earnings	1,793 – 1,625 =	168
Total		399

SUSTAINABLE RATE OF GROWTH

A company's sustainable growth rate is limited by (1) the rate at which it can generate the funds necessary to achieve its growth target and (2) the return it can expect to earn on these funds. The critical variable in generating strategic funds is the growth in shareholders' equity. Shareholders' equity generates internal sources of funds in the form of retained earnings, and it also serves as collateral for raising new debt. In other words, a firm's growth potential is directly linked to its return on equity (ROE).

Sustainable growth rate is computed as follows:

Sustainable growth rate =

$[D/E \times (ROA - i) + ROA] \times k$

$or = f$ (return on equity $\times k$)

where

D/E = total debt-to-equity ratio

ROA = return on assets

i = average interest rate on total debt

k = retention rate = 1 – dividend payout rate

In a strategic context, therefore, leverage, dividend policy, and equity funds exhibit an important interrelationship. By using ROE as a standard performance target, a firm can often improve performance and growth through a careful reevaluation of its different businesses. As long as ROA exceeds the average interest rate on total debt, a firm can achieve a higher growth rate by increasing its financial leverage. This is accomplished without changing the firm's characteristic rate of return on assets. In fact, a firm could accept lower returns on investment than its competitors and still grow at a more rapid rate by assuming a significant amount of debt. This tactic does, however, change the risk characteristics of the business, because creditors normally demand a higher interest rate as the debt-to-equity ratio increases. There is a limit to how much a company can increase its growth rate by taking on more debt.

Dividend policy is another variable that has a critical influence on the growth of a firm. There is a direct tradeoff between current and future dividends, because higher retention rates (or lower payout rates) support higher growth rates. Also, in the majority of cases, it is substantially cheaper to finance growth by reducing the dividend payout than by issuing new stock.

AMP in 1990 has a substantial growth rate of 9.5%.

$$[0.63 \times (16.7\% - 13\%) + 16.7\%] \times 0.50 = 9.5\%$$

In order to grow faster than that—for example, at the rate of 15% that it hopes to achieve—AMP will have to assume more debt, raise its profitability further, gain lower-cost financing, or retain a larger portion of earnings.

ALLOCATION OF STRATEGIC FUNDS

The funds a firm generates are used to

- Support the organization's current business and its ongoing operation. These are called *baseline funds*.
- Invest in the new programs required to meet the organization's strategic objectives and goals. These are called *strategic funds*.

Baseline funds are used to pay current operating expenses, maintain adequate working capital, or maintain current plant and equipment. Depending on product/market dynamics, baseline funds are used to maintain a specified level of production, market share, or growth rate.

Strategic funds are allocated to purchase such new tangible assets as facilities, equipment, and inventory; to increase working capital; and to fund direct expenses for research and development, marketing, advertising, and promotions. They are also used for mergers and acquisitions if these growth alternatives are the most attractive ones for the firm.

Strategic funds programming is conducted in eight basic steps, through which managers seek to

1. Identify the strategic business units (SBUs).
2. Formulate goals and objectives for each SBU.
3. Determine the amount of strategic funds available:
   Strategic funds = total funds available – baseline funds

4. Formulate a strategic program to meet the goals and objectives of each SBU.
5. Estimate the funds needed for each strategic program.
6. Rank the programs according to their contribution to the strategy, taking into account the amounts of strategic funds used and the level of risk involved.
7. Allocate the available strategic funds to each program in order of program priority. Key decision points concerning risk and return are reached when the funds available from internal operating sources are exhausted and when readily available credit sources are used up. Managers evaluate the proposed strategy in terms of the change in financial structure it requires.
8. Establish a management planning and control system to monitor the generation and application of funds and to ensure that the desired results are achieved.

Worksheet 8.3 is an illustration of strategic funds programming for AMP. AMP will require significant investments in fixed assets (about $300 million a year) and in market development (about $100 million a year) if it wants to grow at the projected 15%. Baseline funds are therefore estimated at $400 million.

The calculation of total funds available from internal sources is reasonably straightforward. When calculating the augmented debt, managers should keep in mind that they need to estimate how much additional debt capacity can be obtained in the next period. Using the current total debt-to-equity ratio as a multiplier, they obtain a first estimate (but not necessarily the best estimate) of additional leverage to be gained from retained earnings. AMP's debt-to-equity ratio, for example, is very high, and it is likely that a more conservative estimate for augmented debt will be below $439,000. The newly negotiated long-term debt-to-equity ratio is an estimate of the firm's additional future leverage from long-term debt. This estimate of $536,000 may be viewed as a "ceiling" on additional long-term debt from which management can "borrow" when necessary.

The worksheet shows a sample calculation of the total funds available to AMP under different financing options, and it also shows a strategic funds analysis of the three identical options.

It is important to point out that strategic funds programming only identifies *feasible options* under different financial assumptions. The strategic manager should also make a capital assessment (discussed later in this chapter) before choosing the final strategic option.

FINANCIAL PLANNING MODELS

Executives increasingly are looking for planning tools that enable them to project financial statements, test key assumptions on which a plan is based, explore the impact of possible changes or disruptions in the plan, and factor in the risk or uncertainty associated with different projections. To meet these needs, managers usually turn to commercially available software packages. The first step in using a computer spreadsheet or similar software package is to create a financial planning model that reflects the financial structure of the company. This section will

---

WORKSHEET 8.3	Strategic Funds Programming

Case	AMP (in $ millions)
Date	1992
Name	Mary Doe

Internal Sources

Profit after taxes	287	
Less dividends	145	
Retained earnings	142	
Plus depreciation	207	
Other non-cash expenses	000	
Cash flow from operations		349

Augmented debt

Retained earnings	142	
Times current <u>total</u> debt-to-equity ratio = augmented debt	0.63	90
Funds from within current structure		439

Expanded debt capacity

Newly negotiated <u>long-term</u> debt/equity ratio	0.10	
Minus current long-term debt/equity ratio	0.03	
Equals unused debt factor	0.07	
Times shareholders equity = expanded debt capacity	1,763	126

Total funds available (maximum)   565

(continued)

WORKSHEET 8.3	Strategic Funds Programming (continued)

Analysis of funds use	Source of funds (in $ thousands)		
	Internal sources	Internal plus augmented	Internal, augmented, and expanded
Total funds available	349	439	565
Baseline requirements	400	400	400
Strategic funds	−51	39	165
Option A			
Option B			
Option C			

Comments:

AMP cannot finance its future growth from operational cash flow alone. That debt will have to be increased. Should AMP consider any additional strategic moves, such as an acquisition, the financing with debt would have to be increased substantially.

describe such a model, based on projections of AMP's income statements, cash-flow statements, and balance sheets.

BASELINE PROJECTIONS

What will happen to AMP's profitability and growth if sales trends are as forecast and everything else remains the same? To answer this question, AMP's managers start with a set of plausible assumptions about significant relationships in a spreadsheet, such as the one in Table 8.9. As a starting point, they use a sales forecast as the driving force and project the remaining numbers by linking them to this sales forecast by means of a set of constant financial ratios. After this baseline projection has been completed, it can serve as the vehicle for developing alternative financial scenarios.

AMP used the following step-by-step approach to develop a baseline projection. In Table 8.9, the entries A1, B1, and so on identify individual cells in the spreadsheet. AMP's managers begin by calculating the expected sales revenues for 1991 and 1992. Sales growth is forecast to be 3,043 times A1 for 1991 and times B1 for 1992.

TABLE 8.9	Baseline Projections: Pro-forma Financial Statements for AMP		
	(Dollar amounts in thousands)		

	Pro-Forma Income Statements		
	Actual	Projected	
	1990	1991	1992
Sales revenue	3,043	A1	B1
Cost of goods sold	2,012	A2	B2
Gross profit	1,013	A3	B3
Selling, general and administrative	543	A4	B4
		A	B
EBIT	488	A5	B5
Interest expenses	26	A6	B6
Taxable income	462	A7	B7
Taxes	175	A8	B8
Net income	287	A9	B9
Dividends	145	A10	B10
Retained earnings	142	A11	B11

(continued)

TABLE 8.9	Baseline Projections: Pro-forma Financial Statements for AMP (continued)

(Dollar amounts in thousands)

Pro-Forma Balance Sheets

	Actual	Projected	
	1990	1991	1992
Assets			
Cash	460	A12	B12
Accounts receivable	557	A13	B13
Inventories	482	A14	B14
Other current assets	119	A15	B15
Total current assets	1,618	A16	B16
Property, plant and equipment	2,303	A17	B17
Less accumulated depreciation	1,181	A18	B18
Equals net property, plant, and equipment	1,122	A19	B19
Investment	189	A20	B20
Short-term debt	379		
Accounts payable	254		
Other short-term liabilities	329		
Total assets	2,929	A21	B21
Total current liabilities	953	A22	B22
Long-term debt and deferred liabilities	183	A23	B23
Liabilities			
Beginning equity	1,651	A24	B24
+ Retained earnings	142	A25	B25
= Ending equity	1,793	A26	B26
Total liabilities	2,929	A27	B27

WHAT-IF ANALYSIS

Though baseline projections merely extrapolate current trends, they are quite valuable when it comes to building a financial planning model. The next step is to use this model to ask "what-if" questions in order to test the plausibility of the different assumptions underlying the model and determine their impact on the firm's financial performance. The what-if analysis is carried out as follows.

1. *Review the assumptions that were used to arrive at the baseline projections.* If some of the figures appear to be unreasonable or implausible, make adjustments

to the projections or define a different relationship. This is very important, because all of the numbers in the spreadsheet are interdependent. Consequently, an error in projecting one particular item can easily cause errors in many other numbers.

2. *Incorporate any additional information or forecasts to ensure the relative accuracy of projections.* For example, because of economies of scale, some of the fixed costs and sales revenues may not be related in a strictly linear fashion. On the other hand, some of the expense items may grow faster than the company's sales revenues because of general inflation or growing complexity.

3. *Enter all of the strategic decisions that have already been approved for the planning period.* Although this particular step may appear to be out of sequence, it reflects the fact that many strategic decisions are made without an assessment of their financial impact.

4. *Propose any changes that can improve profitability or lead to a sounder financial structure.* The baseline projection for AMP suggests several improvements. EBIT is expected to decline in 1990, despite an increase in gross profit. Therefore, AMP should make every effort to check increases in operating expenses, particularly administrative expenses. Also, by reducing its inventories and accounts receivable, the company would reduce interest expenses, generate much-needed cash flow, and reduce the debt burden.

5. *Simulate different financial scenarios to test the sensitivity of results to changes in different variables.* One could ask, for example, "What would happen to AMP's financial position if sales unexpectedly grew by only 3%, or even less?" or "What if AMP cuts its R&D budget to improve short-run profitability?" or "How would a 1% rise in interest rates affect AMP's profitability?" or "How would a change in the depreciation method affect cash flows and profits?" These what-if scenarios can help managers to detect and reduce areas of potential vulnerability.

6. *Evaluate strategic alternatives.* Finally, and perhaps most important, different strategic proposals are evaluated. For example, AMP may want to consider different financing options for each of its three strategic alternatives in order to maximize the company's net worth at an acceptable level of risk. For this purpose, the basic model would have to be expanded to incorporate additional variables and relationships, such as might be seen in a discounted cash-flow analysis.

ASSESSING CAPITAL RISK

Assuming too much debt can place a company in jeopardy. The Cloud Tool Company used a worst-case scenario to address the potential risk of a $15 million investment for expansion of capacity. One year after the investment was made, the bottom fell out of the oil business and Cloud Tool was facing bankruptcy. Only then did management realize that what it thought was a worst-case scenario was, in fact, too optimistic (Arnold, 1986). How can managers who are constantly faced with such situations avoid the dire consequences of a miscalculation? To avoid the potential for disaster, they must

1. Define the company's staying power in a hostile environment.
2. Estimate the possible market erosion and the dollar consequences.

3. Project the future cash flow needed for working capital.
4. Determine what options are available if they are needed, such as cost cutting.
5. Determine future source of funds if they are needed. Unfortunately, many estimates tend to be based on assumptions rather than verifiable data. Or they may simply be expressions of opinion, which may or may not reflect the reality of a situation.

An example of how to forecast the potential impact of alternative scenarios is shown in Table 8.10. Factor forecasts provide a base-line projection for key economic indicators. This can be used for the pro-forma projections shown in Table 8.11.

The financial models generally are *deterministic;* that is, the manager can specify a single estimate for each of the input variables. Yet many estimates are based on assumptions made with a great deal of uncertainty. As Hertz (1964) pointed out, behind any precise calculation are data that are not precise. Together, these uncertainties can result in considerable uncertainty.

An assessment of risk can be carried out using the approach shown in Tables 8.10 and 8.11. Each factor that is relevant to an investment can be examined on a risk basis of pessimistic (risky), most likely (average risk) and optimistic (least risky). The strategic manager can examine the results to determine whether or not to proceed.

RISK ANALYSIS

To deal with the risk inherent in strategy, a manager can perform a *risk analysis,* which consists of the following steps:

1. *Identify the key variables that have an impact on the decision.* For instance, in the AMP case, the important variables for determining what strategy the company should follow include
   a. Market growth rate
   b. Company's market share
   c. Investment required
   d. Cost of production
   e. Selling price of product
   f. Useful life of technology
2. *Assign a subjective probability distribution to each variable.* A subjective probability distribution can be estimated, first by determining the range of values that can occur. In Figure 8.15, for example, the range for market growth is −10 to +20%, and the range for the useful life of strategic option A is 2–16 years. Next, the frequency for a reasonable number of intermediate values is estimated. These values are now plotted and a smooth curve drawn through the points to obtain a frequency distribution.
3. *Identify what criterion will be used to determine whether the strategy in question is successful.* The criterion might focus on the financial aspects of the strategy, such as whether the strategy increased the return on investment. Another criterion might be whether the strategy contributed to sustainable growth. Each of these criteria becomes the goal or objective that is related to achieving success for a given strategy.

TABLE 8.10 Factor Forecasts

Factor	Current	1991			1992			1993			1994			1995		
		PE	ML	OPT	PE	ML	OPT	PE	ML	OPT	PE	ML	OPT	PE	ML	OPT
Consumer confidence (growth factor)	0.05	−0.02	0.05	0.08	−0.05	0.07	0.1	−0.07	0.08	0.12	−0.1	0.09	0.14	−0.12	0.1	0.16
Gross National Product (GNP factor)	4.1 TR. −0.03															
Tax level Internal Revenue Service (IRS)	0.34	0.34	0.34	0.34	0.34	0.34	0.34	0.34	0.34	0.34	0.34	0.34	0.34	0.34	0.34	0.34
Interest rate (debt factor)	0.09															
Banking (debt available)																
Oil prices (transportation factor)																
Inflation																
Unemployment (unemployment factor)	0.07															
Economic forecast (combination-growth factor)	0.02															
Market forecast (market growth potential)	0.03															
Productivity (cost of goods sold factor)																
Capital spending (equipment profit factor)																
Durable goods orders (capacity growth)																
Materials prices (raw-materials factor)																

PE = Pessimistic   ML = Most likely   OPT = Optimistic

TABLE 8.11 | **Pro-forma Projections**

Factor	Current*	1991			1992			1993			1994			1995		
		PE	ML	OPT	PE	ML	OPT	PE	ML	OPT	PE	ML	OPT	PE	ML	OPT
Sales/revenue	$100	98	105	108	93	112	119	86	121	133	77	132	152	68	145	176
Cost of goods sold																
Materials	10															
Subcontractors	5															
Freight	2															
Direct labor	12															
Manufacturing overhead	3															
Total	32															
Gross profit	68															
Expenses																
Marketing/selling																
Advertising	5															
Commissions	2															
Promotion/co-op	1															
Other	0															
Total marketing	8															
Administrative expense																
Rent/lease/mortgage	5															
Salaries	7															
Heat/light	1															
Telephone	1															
Office Supplies	1															
Depreciation	2															
Total administrative	17															
Total expense	25															
Operating income	43															
Other charges																
Interest	2															
Sale of assets	0															
Misc.	0															
Total other	2															
Before tax income	41															
Income tax	14															
Loss carry-over	−1															
Investment credit	−1															
Net income	29															
Dividends	2															
Retained/reinvestment	27															

*Dollars × 10,000.

PE = Pessimistic ML = Most likely OPT = Optimistic

FIGURE 8.15	**Risk Analysis: Examples of Subjective Probability Distribution for Two Key Decision Variables, Rate of Market Growth and Useful Life of AMP's Strategic Option A** (Relative frequency stands for the probability with which an event occurs)

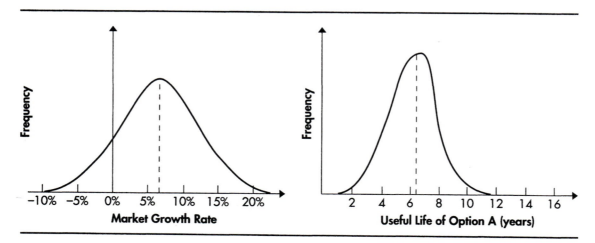

4. *Use a random sampling procedure as the basis for computing whether the criterion for success has been achieved.* To prepare for a random sample, one can use a table of random numbers or a computer program that generates random numbers. The random number is used to select a value from each frequency distribution.

Random sampling is a fairly straightforward statistical procedure that allows the manager to sample from any distribution of values without introducing bias. The steps involved in generating a random number and then using it to select a value from a frequency distribution are described in most books on statistical methods.

Applying the random sampling procedure to AMP, the manager can examine how ROI can be used as a criterion for evaluating which strategic option is most likely to be successful. Using this approach, AMP's management can evaluate the effect of alternative strategic options and see how the financial variables are related. Sounder judgments are possible when random sampling procedures are used to determine which goals are most likely to be achieved.

MULTIATTRIBUTE DECISION MAKING

All strategic decisions are subject to uncertainty and risk. In addition, there inevitably are conflicting values. Thus it is important that strategic managers consider all the factors, or attributes, inherent in each strategic alternative under consideration.

An *attribute* is a characteristic, quality, or desirable aspect of a given situation. It must be measurable in order for managers to determine the relative value or worth of the attribute for each alternative strategy. A criterion is the basis used to choose that combination of attributes, goals, or objectives that is judged relevant to reaching a decision. For example, growth is a criterion that could be used to determine which attributes would best achieve the desired objective. A multiattribute approach to decision making simultaneously considers each of the factors that is likely to sway a decision.

Multiattribute decision making uses a weighting scheme to establish the relative importance or impact of each attribute of a strategy. The weighting scheme enables managers to compute a single, combined score for each strategy. The computation helps to increase the decision makers' confidence in whichever solution or alternative is chosen.

To understand multiattribute decision making, it is helpful to consider single-attribute decision making first. Suppose a building contractor in Southern California wishes to expand his operations. The contractor is considering four possible alternative strategies for growth:

A1. Expand the level and type of advertising.
A2. Hire additional personnel to increase sales.
A3. Subcontract to expand the sales base.
A4. Enter a new market to expand the sales base.

Having stated some strategic alternatives, the contractor needs criteria by which to evaluate them. Suppose he chooses to judge each alternative on the basis of a single criterion, profitability, and that he decides to judge profitability on the basis of a single measurable attribute, growth of net profits. The next task is to rate the profitability of each alternative. Table 8.12 shows how he rated profitability on a scale of 1 to 10. Table 8.13 shows how the contractor rated each alternative. A rating of 7 indicates the contractor's opinion that entering a new market might be

---

TABLE 8.12 | **Profitability Rating: Single-attribute Decision Making**

Level of Profitability	Rating
Marginal	1–2
Below average	3–4
Average	5–6
Above average	7–8
Outstanding	9–10

TABLE 8.13 | **Profitability Ratings of Four Strategic Alternatives**

Alternative	Rating
A1 Expand advertising	5
A2 Hire sales personnel	6
A3 Subcontract	6
A4 Enter new markets	7

the most profitable alternative. Should he choose this alternative? Not necessarily: profitability is not the only important consideration. A more extensive list of criteria is shown in Table 8.14.

At this point, the contractor begins to apply the multiattribute approach. To do this, he must decide which criteria are most important to his strategic goal of expanding his business.

Table 8.15 shows how he rated each criterion on a scale of 1 (least important) to 10 (most important). In employing this scheme, the contractor defined *importance* as his best judgment of the chance of success and relative value in contributing to meeting his personal objectives.

Having assigned values to the criteria, the contractor realized that they would be different for each alternative. Profitability's relative value of 6, for example, would not be appropriate for each alternative. Table 8.16 shows how he felt profitability (C1) would change from alternative to alternative.

Why should the contractor change the relative value of each criterion for each alternative? Why would he give profitability (C1) a value of 5 for the advertising alternative (A1) and a value of 7 for the new-markets alternative (A4)? These ratings reflect the contractor's belief that the profit potential changes with each alternative (see Table 8.16).

Using similar reasoning, the contractor assigned cost (C2) a value of 10 for the advertising alternative (A1). Even though the overall relative value for cost is 8 (Table 8.15) he felt that the advertising strategy would have a better cost/benefit payoff than the personnel strategy (A2), so he assigned (A2) a value of only 4.

Table 8.17 is a decision matrix that shows values for each criterion depending on which alternative is being considered. Once all the values are entered in the matrix, the contractor averages the values for each alternative (see the far-right column of Table 8.17).

TABLE 8.14	**Multiple Criteria and Attributes**

Criterion (C)	Attribute (Basis for Measurement)
C1 Profitability	Net profit (dollars)
C2 Cost	Cost/benefit ratio
C3 Control	Ability to meet requirements
C4 Adaptability	Speed of response to change
C5 Work load	Amount of time spent in executive activities
C6 Organization	Information flow and control
C7 Market potential	Revenue from sales

TABLE 8.15	Judged Importance (Value) of Each Criterion

Values Assigned by the Contractor

Criterion	Values
C1 Profitability	6
C2 Cost	8
C3 Control	5
C4 Adaptability	6
C5 Work load	6
C6 Organization	5
C7 Market potential	7

Weighting Scheme Used to Assign Values

Ranking	Value Range
Very important	9–10
Important	7–8
Moderately important	4–6
Unimportant	1–3

TABLE 8.16	Values for the Profitability Criterion by Strategic Alternative

Alternative	Profitability Value
A1 Expand advertising	5
A2 Hire sales personnel	6
A3 Subcontract	6
A4 Enter new markets	7

The averages shown in Table 8.17 do not differ significantly. It is dangerous to choose the alternative with the highest average (in this case A3), because averages do not consider intangible factors, such as risk propensity, prior experience, and personal values. What the contractor needs, therefore, is to apply the 10-point weighting scheme that accounts for the judged importance of each criterion (Table 8.15). Next, the contractor takes the values shown in Table 8.15 and multiplies them by the values for each alternative strategy (Table 8.17) to obtain a weighted

TABLE 8.17	Decision Matrix 1: Values for Each Criterion by Strategic Alternative

Alternative	C1	C2	C3	C4	C5	C6	C7	Average
A1	5	10	8	4	4	9	3	6.1
A2	6	4	4	6	8	4	8	5.7
A3	6	6	5	6	9	5	7	6.3
A4	7	6	4	7	3	5	9	5.8

value for each alternative. This is shown in Worksheet 8.4 where he obtained a total for each alternative by adding its seven weighted scores. Alternative 3(A3)—subcontract to expand the sales base—has the highest weighted total. But the contractor chooses alternative 1 (A1), to expand advertising. Why? A1's weighted total is almost as high as that of A3; therefore, it is legitimate to choose either one if other considerations are important. The subjective aspects of choice and uncertainties associated with criteria or goals can influence decisions, as can interdependence among the criteria. Profitability and market potential may, for example, be interdependent. Rather than incorporating all such considerations in the formal method, it is preferable to start with a few simplifying assumptions that can be removed, one by one, after the weighted scores are obtained (see Worksheet 8.4). Ultimately, the choice of an alternative depends on the objective results of multiattribute decision making and subjective factors, which often have to do with acceptance of the choice.

The multiattribute approach can be summarized as follows.

1. Specify the strategic goal (such as to expand the business).
2. State the available strategic alternatives.
3. Identify criteria to be used in evaluating the degree to which the strategic goal is achieved.
4. Determine how each criterion will be measured on the basis of attributes.
5. Rank the criteria to establish their overall value or importance.
6. Establish the value of each criterion with respect to each alternative.
7. Examine the sensitivity of each alternative to changes in each criterion's value.
8. Determine the weighted score of each alternative with respect to each criterion. This yields relative importance.
9. Compute the weighted total score for each alternative.
10. Rank the alternatives according to their weighted totals.
11. Choose an alternative, taking into account the objective and subjective benefits of each.

WORKSHEET 8.4	Multiattribute Decision Making

Case __Contractor Example__
Date __1989__
Name __Southern California Building Contractor__

Decision Matrix

Alternative	C1 (6)	C2 (8)	C3 (5)	C4 (6)	C5 (6)	C6 (5)	C7 (7)	Other ( )	Weighted Total
A1	×5 = 30	×10 = 80	×8 = 40	×4 = 24	×4 = 24	×9 = 45	×3 = 21		264
A2	×6 = 36	×4 = 32	×4 = 20	×6 = 36	×8 = 48	×4 = 20	×8 = 56		248
A3	×6 = 36	×6 = 48	×5 = 25	×6 = 36	×9 = 54	×5 = 25	×7 = 49		273
A4	×7 = 42	×6 = 48	×4 = 20	×7 = 42	×3 = 18	×5 = 25	×9 = 63		258
Other									

Criterion / Weight

Justification of the alternative chosen:

The contractor feels that he has limited time available to manage the business. He is also reluctant to risk the money required either to expand his staff or to advertise to increase sales. He feels that earnings, ease of operation, and low risk justify adopting alternative A1, which will change the way the business is being run because he would have less direct marketing effort. If he selected A3, subcontract, this would require additional involvement on the contractor's part, which he did not want.

An example of how the ABC Entertainment Company used multiattribute decision making appears in Table 8.18, which shows how it rated the benefit that could accrue from an attribute. Criteria C1 through C11 are listed in the first column. The next column identifies the criteria and gives the attributes used for measurement. For example, criterion C1, profitability, is measured in terms of the attribute internal rate of return (IRR), or the net profit for the project. The weights for benefits and importance are shown in the next two columns. The alternatives are shown along the top of the figure, and the computed values are shown for each criterion and each alternative. When the computed values are added for each alternative, Primetime TV (with a value of 85) emerges as best, and Video Rentals (with a value of 78) is second best. Through weighting, the results clearly reflect the preference and judgment of the strategic manager who must choose one of the alternatives to pursue.

THE STRATEGIC BUDGET

Budget preparation is usually the final step in strategic planning. Money and other resources must be allocated to translate a strategic plan into programs of action. A budget is the principal place where current decisions are made in accordance with longer-range plans. Therefore, operating plans and capital investment plans are the financial base of the strategic plan.

Although preparing a strategic budget is generally the last stage of resource allocation, it can be made an integral part of long-range financial planning. For example, financial information (such as an income forecast) depends on strategic decisions and

| TABLE 8.18 | Multiattribute Decision Making for the ABC Entertainment Co. |

Benefit-of-Attribute Rating		Weighting for Criteria		Alternatives
	0		0	A1 Primetime TV
Marginal	1	Unimportant	1	A2 Commuter Talk Radio
	2		2	A3 Movie Channel
Below Average	3	Low Importance	3	A4 Video Rentals
	4		4	
Average	5	Moderately Important	5	
	6		6	
Above Average	7	Important	7	
	8		8	
Outstanding	9	Very Important	9	
	10		10	

(continued)

TABLE 8.18   Multiattribute Decision Making for the ABC Entertainment Co. (continued)

Criterion	Attribute Basis for Measurement	Benefit Importance	A1	A1 Importance	A2	A2 Importance	A3	A3 Importance	A4	A4 Importance
C1	Profitability (IRR, or net profit on the project)	7	49		28		7		42	
C2	Low cost/investment (resource requirement)	5	5		5		5		5	
C3	Capability/control (ability to carry out)	8	8		8		8		8	
C4	Contingency demands (speed of response)	3	3		3		3		3	
C5	Management demands (executive time needs)	3	3		3		3		3	
C6	Organizational demands (information flow and control)	5	3		3		3		3	
C7	Growth potential (market potential)	7	5		5		5		5	
C8	Product life cycle (long-lived)	2	7		7		7		7	
C9	Risk level (favorable risk)	3	2		2		2		2	
C10	Ease of exit (if worst case)	1	3		3		3		3	
C11	Other	1	0		0		0		0	
			0		0		0		0	
			A1		A2		A3		A4	
			85		64		43		78	

	A1	A2	A3	A4
	Primetime TV	Commuter Talk Radio	Movie Channel	Video Rentals
	85	64	43	78

assumptions, including pricing policy, product life cycle, and so on. The following outline summarizes some of the strategic factors that affect the budget process.

1. Income estimate using sales forecast
   a. Basis for the forecast
   b. Market dynamics (impact on sales)
2. Depreciation
   a. Adequacy of reserves for capital replacement
   b. Length of time for depreciation
   c. Technological forecast and obsolescence of investments
3. Research and development expenditures
   a. Requirements to meet competition or technological changes
   b. New products or product mix required
   c. Relation to profitability (PIMS approach)
4. Acquisitions and mergers
   a. Impact on cash flow or growth
   b. Ability to obtain funds
   c. Consolidated financial statements
5. Employee benefits
   a. Incentives, bonuses, training
   b. Management development programs and career planning
6. Production requirements
   a. Inventory: amount, variety, safety stock, vendors
   b. Delivery and production cycles
   c. Required capacity
7. Pricing policy
   a. Tradeoff between quality and cost
   b. Experience curve effect
8. Marketing requirements
   a. Product-life-cycle effects
   b. Advertising cost and effectiveness
   c. Funds for market research
9. Cost
   a. Basis for estimating (history or formulas)
   b. Standards and variances to be used in budget
10. Profit desired
    a. Basis for allocating general, administrative, and overhead expenses
    b. Use of profit centers
    c. Joint profits

Each of the factors listed requires analysis of financial data relevant to the firm. The budget for strategy implementation is based on decisions about the source, use, and allocation of funds.

UMMARY

Traditionally, financial analysis has focused on an historic explanation of facts. Financial ratio analysis compares a company to its competition with respect to profitability, liquidity, leverage, and activity for the *preceding* period(s); the DuPont formula uses past data to show how the firm has managed its assets; and the flow-of-funds analysis shows the past use of discretionary funds. Though all these techniques are widely used in industry, they were not designed for strategic planning. Nonetheless, they provide valuable data that can be used in formulating alternative strategies for the future.

Financial ratio analysis provides the strategic manger with a direct analysis of the company's financial well-being. It is a widely used approach in industry and provides an easy way of comparing one company with another.

Strategic funds programming is a future-oriented financial planning approach. It helps strategic managers to identify potential sources of discretionary funds and to plan their allocation on the basis of the concept of sustainable rate of growth.

Competitive-cost analysis can be a very useful tool in defining the right strategy and focus for a company. Competitive-cost analysis identifies the strategic cost-driving factors and de-averages costs prepared for the company's accounting system. Once strategic managers understand the firm's own costs in detail, they can model competitors' costs through microeconomic analysis of the cost structure. Managers who model competitors' costs gain an understanding of each competitor's situation in great detail, which helps them to anticipate their competitors' strategic moves.

Computerized financial planning systems have revolutionized the financial aspects of strategic planning and implementation. The use of financial planning programs can help managers to avoid major mistakes and enables them to create and edit their own financial models, generate reports, test the assumptions on which a plan is based, examine alternative goals, and perform a risk analysis for each of the alternatives.

The strategic budget is the final output of a financial analysis. It reflects the decisions made regarding allocation of funds and which strategies can be pursued.

REFERENCES AND SUGGESTIONS FOR FURTHER READING

A matter of opinion. 1992. *The Economist*, April 4, p. 106.

Altman, Edward J. 1968. Financial ratios, discriminant analysis and the prediction of corporate bankruptcy. *Journal of Finance* 23, no. 4.

Ansberry, Clare. 1991. Utah's Geneva Steel, once called hopeless, is racking up profits. *The Wall Street Journal*, November 10, pp. A-1 and A-5.

Arnold, Jasper. 1986. Assessing capital risk: You can't be too conservative. *Harvard Business Review*, September–October, pp. 113–120.

Bettis, Richard, Stephen Bradley, and Gary Hamel. 1992. Outsourcing and industrial decline. *Academy of Management Executive* 6, no. 1, pp. 7–22.

Boston Consulting Group. 1974. *Segmentation and strategy*. BCG Perspective No. 156. Boston, Mass.

Boulden, James B. 1976. *Computer-assisted planning systems*. New York: McGraw-Hill.

Chen, Kung H. and Thomas A. Shimerda. 1980. An empirical analysis of useful financial ratios. *Financial Management* 10 (Spring), pp. 51–60.

Cooper, Robin. 1989. You need a new cost system when.... *Harvard Business Review*, January–February, pp. 77–82.

Cooper, Robin and Robert Kaplan. 1991. Profit priorities from activity-based costing. *Harvard Business Review*, May–June, pp. 130–135.

Cooper, Robin and Robert Kaplan. 1988. Measure costs right: Make the right decisions. *Harvard Business Review*, September–October, pp. 96–103.

Day, George and Liam Fahey. 1990. Putting strategy into shareholder value analysis. *Harvard Business Review*, March–April, pp. 156–162.

Donaldson, Gordon. 1985. Financial goals and strategic consequences. *Harvard Business Review*, May–June, pp. 57–66.

Dun & Bradstreet. 1981. *Key Business Ratios.* New York.

Flanigan, James. 1984. The formula that makes a business succeed: Invest, invest, and reinvest. *Los Angeles Times,* February 1.

Hamilton, William F. and Michael A. Moses. 1974. A computer-based corporate planning system. *Management Science,* October.

Hedge, Gary W. 1987. Designing modern accounting software. *Byte,* Summer, pp. 47–52.

Hertz, David B. 1964. Risk analysis in capital investment. *Harvard Business Review* 42, no. 1 (January–February), and 1979, 57, no. 6 (November–December).

Kaplan, Robert. 1988. One cost system isn't enough. *Harvard Business Review,* January–February, pp. 61–66.

Mason, Richard O. and E. Burton Swanson. 1981. *Measurement for management decision.* Reading, Mass.: Addison-Wesley.

McLean, Robert. 1990. Planning for value. *Managing Value,* Spring, pp. 75–82.

Ohmae, Kenichi. 1989. Companyism and do more better. *Harvard Business Review,* January–February, pp. 125–132.

Porter, Michael E. 1985. *Competitive advantage: Creating and sustaining superior performance.* New York: The Free Press.

Rappaport, Alfred. 1992. CFOs and strategists: Forging. *Harvard Business Review,* May–June, pp. 84–91.

Rappaport, Alfred. 1981. Selecting strategies that create shareholder value. *Harvard Business Review,* May–June, pp. 139–149.

Rock, Milton L. 1987. *The mergers and acquisitions handbook.* New York: McGraw-Hill.

Rudden, Ellen M. 1982. Why DCF doesn't work. *The Wall Street Journal.* November 1.

Troy, Leo. 1980. *Almanac of business and industrial financial ratios.* Englewood Cliffs, N.J.: Prentice-Hall.

Wang, Penelope. 1987. What-if accounting. *Forbes,* May 30, pp. 112.

Warren, F. M. and F. P. Shelton. 1971. A simultaneous equation approach to financial planning. *Journal of Finance* 26, no. 5.

Weber, Jonathon. 1992. Computer services for hire: Outsourcing thrives as firms shed data processing chores. *Los Angeles Times,* August 2, pp. D-1 and D-2.

Welch, James and P. Ranganath Nayak. 1992. Strategic sourcing: A progressive approach to the make-or-buy decision. *Academy of Management Executive* 6, no. 1, pp. 23–41.

Wenner, David and Richard LeBer. 1990. Managing for shareholder value—from top to bottom. *Managing Value,* Spring, pp. 95–109.

Willigan, Geraldine. 1990. The value-adding CFO: An interview with Disney's Gary Wilson. *Harvard Business Review,* January–February, pp. 85–93.

Worthy, Ford S. 1987. Accounting bores you? Wake up. *Fortune,* October 12, pp. 43–52.

APPENDIX A

Learning Curve

How much of an impact on cost does learning have? Competitors accumulate know-how over time. This accumulated experience can be measured, and it has been shown for many industries that the total cost per unit can decline between 20% and 30% every time total accumulated production is doubled. This assumption is portrayed graphically by what is known as a *learning curve* or *experience curve* (Figure 8A.1).

The experience curve results from four basic effects:

1. *Learning effects.* Efficiency increases as operators, supervisors, and staff personnel become familiar with the required tasks. As these individuals gain experience, planning, tooling, and coordination become more cost-effective.
2. *Economies of scale.* These occur as the total fixed cost of productive capacity is allocated among a larger number of products. In addition, materials can be more economically purchased, handled, and processed as production volume increases.
3. *Substitution.* The substitution of less expensive materials helps to reduce costs.
4. *Innovation and value engineering.* Cost benefits are realized as improved methods, procedures, and technologies emerge.

A simple way of demonstrating this relationship between the cost per unit and the cumulative volume is to plot it on a log–log scale (Figure 8A.2) Obviously, as costs come down, profit opportunities go up. Prices, however, generally do not parallel the cost curve; rather, they follow a pattern similar to the one shown in Figure 8A.2. During phase A, the new product struggles to establish a position in the market, and price is frequently lower than cost. At the end of this phase, the experience effect takes over and the price remains relatively constant. During phase B, supply is relatively low compared to demand. Price cuts, therefore, are very moderate. Toward the end of the growth phase, the competitive situation becomes very unstable as new competitors are attracted by high profit margins. As a result, prices drop dramatically, and marginal producers are forced out of the market. At the end of this shakeout, the competitive situation usually stabilizes as the product matures and market growth slows (phase C). Profits also tend to stabilize, while the costs of production and marketing (the cash

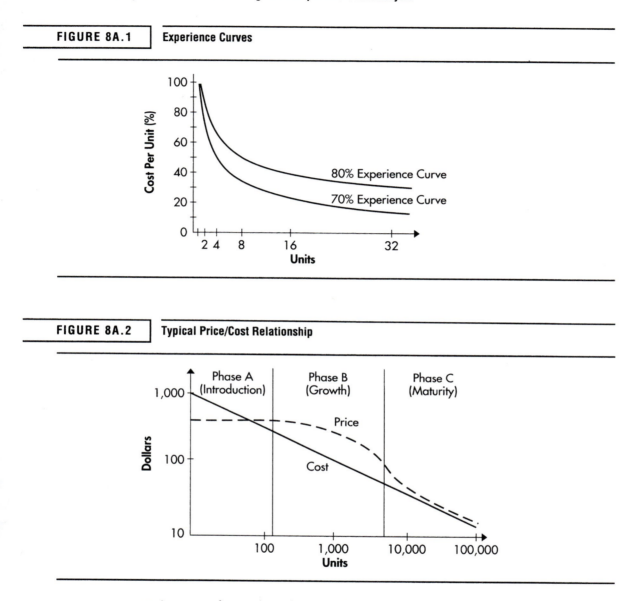

FIGURE 8A.1 | **Experience Curves**

FIGURE 8A.2 | **Typical Price/Cost Relationship**

requirements of a product) decrease. Products with high market shares tend to generate increasing amounts of cash during this phase. Finally, profit margins become smaller and smaller as the demand for the product starts to decline, and the majority of competitors phase out the product. The product/market effects of the experience curve are very similar to those of the product life cycle.

From its analysis of experience curves and cost–price relationships, The Boston Consulting Group concluded that the best strategy is one in which the price of a product is closely related to cost (BCG, 1974). The BCG argued that this pricing strategy would discourage competition while allowing market share to build and would result in larger profit margins in the long run.

APPENDIX B

Discounted Cash Flow

The discounted cash flow (DCF) method is an important factor in all cash generation by a business. To arrive at the DCF, managers use

1. A financial pro-forma statement projecting AMP's future free cash flow as shown (see Table 8B.1). Free cash flow is defined as *net income* plus *depreciation* minus *capital expenditures* minus *change in net working capital*. Because only a limited number of years can be projected with fair accuracy, managers establish a terminal value in the form of an annuity for the last year.
2. The discount factor. The discount factor is based on the weighted average cost of capital (WACC), which is derived as follows:

$$WACC = k_c \times e + i \times (1 - t) \times d$$

where

k_c = cost of equity capital
e = share of equity in total capitalization
i = average interest rate on debt
t = tax ratio
d = debt share of total capitalization

If, for AMP, $k = 15\%$, $i = 8\%$, and $t = 40\%$, then

$$WACC = .15 \times 1,793/2,929 + .08 \times (1 - .4) \times 1,136/2,929 = 11.04\%$$

AMP sales revenues projected for 1991 are $1.15 \times 3,043 = 3,499$, for 1992 they are $1.15 \times 3,499 = 3,989$, and so on. The assumptions for the entries in the pro-forma statements are contained in Table 8B.1.

TABLE 8B.1	Assumptions Used for AMP Projections

Item	Assumption
Sales revenue	Grows at 15% per year
Cost of goods sold	66% of sales
Selling, general and administrative	18% of sales
Interest	13% interest paid on short- and long-term debt in previous year; 9% interest earned on investments
Taxes	40% of taxable income
Dividends	50% payout rate
Accounts receivable	19% of sales
Inventories	Inventory turnover of 6
Other current assets	Grow at 15% per year
Property, plant, and equipment	Grows at 10% per year
Depreciation	11% of property, plant, and equipment from previous year
Investments	Grow at 30% per year
Current liabilities	30% of sales
Long-term debt and deferred liabilities	Constant
Beginning equity	Equals ending equity from previous year
Ending equity	Equals beginning equity plus retained earnings
Cash	A plug-in to balance total liabilities and total assets

The results of these assumptions and calculations are given in Table 8B.2.

The DCF value can now be calculated as shown in Table 8B.3. If managers at AMP can realize their ambitious growth plans of 15% per year, the value of equity will be $7.275 billion. Compared to a current market capitalization of about $6 billion, this would add a substantial value to shareholders.

Unfortunately, discounted cash flow is often misunderstood. Critics claim that it has led to a decline in the competitive advantage of U.S. companies by discouraging them from making investments that could have improved productivity. *Discounted cash flow (DCF)* is, in fact, a sound financial model that evaluates financial health on the basis of cash flow rather than accounting profits, which may prove elusive because they are not always based on operations. Evaluations based on earnings may not take into account (1) the importance of the flow of funds needed to conduct the business or (2) the cost of funds so employed. DCF explicitly takes into account the interest that a comparable investment could have earned by discounting future cash flows and showing what cash the business would have now if it had made the alternative investment.

TABLE 8B.2	Completed Baseline Pro-forma Projections for AMP*

(Dollar amounts in millions)

Income Statements	1990	1991	1992	1993	1994	1995	1996	1997	1998	1999	2000
Sales revenue	3,043	3,499	3,989	4,508	5,049	5,604	6,165	6,720	7,257	7,765	8,231
Cost of goods sold	2,012	2,310	2,633	2,975	3,332	3,699	4,069	4,435	4,790	5,125	5,433
Gross profit	1,031	1,190	1,356	1,533	1,717	1,905	2,096	2,285	2,467	2,640	2,799
Selling, general and administrative	543	630	718	811	909	1,009	1,110	1,210	1,306	1,398	1,482
EBIT	488	560	638	721	808	897	986	1,075	1,161	1,242	1,317
Interest	−26	−40	14	21	29	41	55	74	99	131	172
Taxable income	462	520	652	742	837	937	1,042	1,149	1,260	1,373	1,489
Taxes	175	208	261	297	335	375	417	460	504	549	596
Net income	287	312	391	445	502	562	625	690	756	824	894
Dividends	145	156	195	222	251	281	313	345	378	412	447
Retained earnings	142	156	196	223	251	281	312	345	378	412	447

Balance Sheets	1990	1991	1992	1993	1994	1995	1996	1997	1998	1999	2000
Cash	460	452	551	653	725	848	914	953	942	858	668
Receivables	557	665	758	857	959	1,065	1,171	1,277	1,379	1,475	1,564
Inventories	482	583	665	751	841	934	1,027	1,120	1,210	1,294	1,372
Other current assets	119	137	157	181	208	239	275	317	364	419	481
Total current assets	1,618	1,837	2,131	2,442	2,761	3,081	3,388	3,666	3,895	4,046	4,086
Property, plant, and equipment	2,303	2,533	2,787	3,065	3,372	3,709	4,080	4,488	4,937	5,430	5,973
Less accumulated depreciation	1,181	1,434	1713	2020	2,357	2,728	3,136	3,584	4,078	4,621	5,218
Net property, plant, and equipment	1,122	1,099	1,074	1,046	1015	981	944	904	859	809	755
Investments	189	246	319	415	540	702	912	1,186	1,542	2,004	2,606
Total assets	2,929	3,182	3,524	3,903	4,316	4,764	5,245	5,756	6,295	6,859	7,446
Total current liabilities	953	1,050	1,197	1,352	1,515	1,681	1,849	2,016	2,177	2,330	2,469
Long-term debt	183	183	183	183	183	183	183	183	183	183	183
Beginning equity	1,651	1,793	1,949	2,145	2,367	2,618	2,900	3,212	3,557	3,935	4,347
Retained earnings	142	156	196	223	251	281	312	345	378	412	447
Ending equity	1,793	1,949	2,145	2,367	2,618	2,900	3,212	3,557	3,935	4,347	4,794
Total liabilities	2,929	3,182	3,524	3,903	4,316	4,764	5,245	5,756	6,295	6,859	7,446
Return on equity	17.3%	16.0%	16.0%	18.8%	19.2%	19.4%	19.5%	19.4%	19.2%	19.0%	18.6%

*(See Chapter 6, p. 230.)

Perhaps more important than earnings is a company's value to shareholders. In an article about strategies that create shareholder value, Alfred Rappaport (1981) pointed out that conventional five-year pro-forma accounting statements do not accurately reflect a company's value to management or shareholders. He claimed that the ultimate test of a strategic plan is whether it creates shareholder value. Rappaport posed three questions:

TABLE 8B.3	**Discounted Cash Flow (DCF) for AMP**
	(Dollar amounts in millions)

	1990	1991	1992	1993	1994	1995	1996	1997	1998	1999	2000
Net income	287	312	391	445	502	562	625	690	756	824	894
Plus depreciation	207	253	279	307	337	371	408	449	494	543	597
Minus capital expenditures	−375	−230	−253	−279	−307	−337	−371	−408	−449	−494	−543
Minus net working capital change[1]	46	−122	−147	−155	−157	−153	−139	−112	−67	1	100
Free cash flow[2]	165	213	269	318	376	443	523	618	734	874	1,048
Discount factor	1.110	1.233	1.369	1.520	1.688	1.874	2.081	2.311	2.566	2.850	
Present value	191	219	233	247	263	279	297	317	341	368	
Sum of present values	2,754										
+ Terminal value[3]	4,704										
− Long-term debt	183										
Total company DCF	7,275										

[1] Capital expenditures equal to increase in fixed assets
[2] Net working capital = current assets minus current liabilities; change from previous year
[3] Terminal value = discounted market value from final period
= net income times P/E-ratio divided by discount factor
= $894 \times 15/2.850 = 4{,}704$

1. Does the strategic plan create shareholder value, and how much?
2. Are some of the company's SBUs more profitable than others?
3. Would an alternative strategic plan increase shareholder value more than the one in use or under consideration?

Rappaport believes that earnings per share (EPS) can, in fact, be misleading. Of 400 industrial companies rated by Standard and Poor's, only 172 had EPS of 15% or better. More than 50% of the 172 companies had EPS that were negative or inadequate to cover inflation. In part, this is due to the fact that EPS do not reflect the unique status of each SBU. The SBUs usually differ with respect to the risk taking inherent in their strategies, their use of working capital, their need for fixed investments, and their dividend payouts.

Rappaport recommended the use of DCF to determine shareholder value. This approach involves anticipating cash flow discounted by the cost of capital. DCF is analyzed as follows:

1. Estimate the pretax operating return on incremental sales that is needed to create shareholder value.
2. Compare the rate of return on incremental sales realized during the previous five-year period to that for the projected five-year period.
3. Estimate the contribution that alternative strategies would make to shareholder value.
4. Determine whether the proposed growth strategy is financially feasible, taking into account return on sales, investments required, capital structure, and dividend policy.

5. Determine whether the financial evaluation shows that the company is a potential takeover target. If the aggregate value of the individual components of the company is greater than the present equity of the shareholders, then the company may become a takeover target.

A major advantage of the shareholder-value approach is that the data are already available in most companies.

DCF has some disadvantages. It is often difficult to apply for evaluating single investments. It also relies on assumptions about the future sales of products, price levels, competitor actions, government tax policies, and interest rates. For strategic managers, the real value of DCF is its use in determining what would happen to market share, cost of production, or similar considerations, given the returns expected on an investment.

DCF is most readily applied to assessment of labor-saving or cost-reducing investments. But even these kinds of investments require assumptions regarding the learning curve, quality, supplier prices, and overhead costs. Assumptions become increasingly problematic in times of widely fluctuating interest rates or inflation. Again, the question is what alternative investments, such as government bonds, would yield.

Another important consideration that is often overlooked is the fact that running a successful business requires expenditures for such items as advertising and warehouse facilities, without which the business could not function effectively. Toys-R-Us, a major sales outlet for children's toys, maintains a large inventory of toys year-round. This chain of stores would not be competitive without a large inventory and a huge display area. If Toys-R-Us completed a discounted cash flow on the investment in warehouse and display space, Toys-R-Us might find that the return was not justified; its liquidated values might exceed the discounted cash flow from operations. For another example, the cash flow in many high-tech companies in the Los Angeles area is quite low, yet the replacement value of their facilities and land has risen dramatically, leading to handsome potential returns on the sale or exchange of those assets. Discounted cash flow might have suggested divesting assets, whereas the real value, because of appreciation, exceeded the discounted value. Because of these considerations, many financial planners now take into account a number of factors, in addition to discounted cash flow, when recommending an investment. They look at what contributes to maintaining a sustainable competitive advantage, because decisions that rely solely on discounted cash flow can create an unfavorable competitive position. Relying on a single approach can adversely affect pricing, market share, customer service, or other factors needed for a competitive advantage.

APPENDIX C

Cost/Benefit Analysis

A company that plans to invest large sums of money in a new strategy cannot ignore the costs and benefits associated with each strategic alternative. An alternative can be considered efficient when it meets objectives at the lowest possible cost, and yet it can still be a poor choice. Efficiency alone is not a sufficient measure. The desirability of any given strategic alternative depends on both cost and value. Factors that need to be considered include efficiency, ability to implement, urgency of the strategy, and politics that often play a major role in strategic decision making.

A cost/benefit analysis helps managers to determine whether the benefits of a strategic alternative exceed its cost and to choose the alternative that provides the maximum net benefit. The analysis includes both tangible and intangible costs and benefits. Potential tangible benefits might include

Lower administrative costs	Effective work-load balancing
Reduced inventory	Reduced communication costs
Faster delivery to customers	Reduced scrap and rework
Reduced workforce	Reduced transportation
Reduced overtime	Improved utilization of workforce
Reduced cost of new-plant start-up	

The tangible benefits can usually be related directly to their costs, so that each strategic alternative can be ranked according to its net monetary benefit. The net value of a strategy's intangible benefits is much more difficult to assess. This does not mean, however, that intangible benefits cannot be quantified. In fact, under some circumstances, the analysis of intangible benefits is fairly straightforward, and the choice of an alternative can often be justified on the basis of intangible benefits alone. Benefits that fall into the intangible category include

Improved customer service	Improved product decisions
Better control	Competitive product advantage
Earlier information	Improved cost control and performance measurement
Industry leadership	Organizational flexibility
Decentralized management	Improved forecasting and business planning
Improved employee morale	Improved resource utilization
Improved planning for long-range capacity	

Once managers have determined the net benefit of each strategic alternative, they compare the alternatives that have positive net benefits to determine which one can best meet the goals and objectives of the main strategic thrust. To do this, they first assign each alternative a score of 0 to 1 for the three main success factors shown in Table 8C.1.

Table 8C.2 shows how the scores might be weighted.

TABLE 8C.1	Factors That Determine Strategic Success

Main Success Factors	Contributing Factors
1. Impact	Long-run profitability (ROI)
	Number of strategic business units and people affected
	Number of needs served
	Ability to accomplish overall objectives
2. Implementation	Ability to estimate implementation cost
	Degree of acceptance
	Ability to plan implementation
	Degree of certainty of implementation
	Resources available
3. Urgency	Desirability of proposed strategy
	Political support expected
	Urgency of need for solution

TABLE 8C.2	Scores Indicating Level of Support for a Strategy

Potential for Success	Score
Strong	0.8–1.0
Moderate	0.5–0.79
Weak	0–0.49

The maximum potential of each alternative is obtained by multiplying the alternative's scores for the three main factors. If, for example, an alternative's scores were 0.7 for impact, 0.8 for implementation, and 0.3 for urgency, its maximum potential would be

$$0.7 \times 0.8 \times 0.3 = 0.168$$

which represents the likelihood that the alternative under consideration will succeed. In this example, the low score for urgency (0.3) lowers the strategy's chance of success.

Cost/benefit analysis, then, involves

1. Determining the net benefits of each alternative and eliminating alternatives with low net benefits.
2. Rating the maximum potential of each remaining alternative with respect to impact, implementation, and urgency.
3. Applying judgment to ensure that some obvious critical factor (such as meeting the needs of a key customer) is not overlooked.

An application of the cost/benefit analysis is shown in Worksheet 8.5.

WORKSHEET 8.5	Cost/Benefit Analysis

Case ___AMP – example___
Date ___1993___
Name ___Mary Doe___

	Alternatives			
	A Related	B Advanced	C High Technology	D
Incremental benefit				
Tangible	$430,000[1]	$570,000[2]	$710,000[3]	
Intangible	50,000[4]	100,000[5]	500,000[6]	
Incremental cost	50,000[7]	190,000[8]	940,000[9]	
Net incremental value				
Tangible alone	380,000	380,000	–230,000	
Total	430,000	480,000	270,000	

Footnotes:

[1]Assuming 3% increase in growth; [2]4% increase; [3]5% increase; [4]additional benefits from new technology; [5]additional benefits from new markets and new technology; [6]benefits from improved market position; [7]initial outlays distributed over four periods; [8]same as note 7, [9]same as note 7, plus yearly operating expenses of $840,000.

Analysis:

Options A and B have roughly the same tangible value. The investment in related technology is lower, but benefits from advanced technology appear to be higher. The total value of option B seems to be highest, but the final decision has to consider available funds for investment. Costs for high technology (option C) exceed tangible benefits, and the total net incremental value is the lowest of all three options.

(continued)

| WORKSHEET 8.5 | Cost/Benefit Analysis (continued) |

| Alternative | Criterion | | | | | |
	Impact ×	Implemen-tation ×	Urgency =	Belief in success ×	Investment level =	Potential
A. Related	0.85	0.95	0.9	0.73	430	312.5
B. Advanced	0.9	0.8	0.95	0.68	480	328.3
C. High tech.	0.99	0.5	0.85	0.42	270	113.6
D. _____						

Interpretation and Recommendations:

Option B is the most attractive alternative for AMP. It has a high impact on long-run profitability as well as on overall objectives. It is, however, riskier than option A and uses more resources. Therefore, an overbearing reason (such as timing, availability of funds, high interest rates, or similar factors) could make option A the best choice because there is little difference in the potential between options B and A.

APPENDIX D

The fisCAL Computer Program

A number of computer programs are available for preparing detailed financial analyses. One that is especially helpful for analyzing cases or for strategic evaluations is fisCAL. This computer program is available from the Halcyon Group at 447 Fleming Road, Charleston, SC 29412. This appendix shows a sample set of printouts, which simplify many of the calculations needed for a financial analysis. Included are programs for

- Comparison of financial statement and ratio analysis with industry norms
- Balance sheet—operating capital requirements
- DuPont formula for return on assets
- Trend analysis
- Net worth diagram

Comparison with industry standards provides an important base for evaluation. The program also does pro-forma statements and strategic evaluation.

INTRODUCTION TO fisCAL

Before using fisCAL, one needs to read the basic diagnostic reports described in Chapters 1–5 of the *fisCAL Key Disk & Manual*.

The videotape that comes with the fisCAL package can be particularly useful as an introduction.

To better understand fisCAL, use it for reports for which the same data were analyzed by hand. To prepare the fisCAL reports, follow these steps:

1. Read Chapters 1–5 and 8 of the *fisCAL Key Disk & Manual*.
   Chapter 8 of this manual provides a step-by-step description of how to enter data into fisCAL and how to print reports. The earlier chapters explain the specific reports to be run and provide information on how to interpret the output.
2. Read the tips handout provided with the teaching guide.

3. Go over the company's financial statements and insert three years of data into *copies* of the data entry sheets provided in the manual.

At the end of the teaching note in the *fisCAL Key Disk & Manual,* you will find copies of fisCAL's data entry screens. We have found that transcribing the correct figures onto these copies prior to starting a fisCAL computer session saves a great deal of time, because it takes new fisCAL users extra time to translate company data to correspond with pre-set categories. Examples of computer printouts follow.

TABLE 8D.1	Industry Standard Data for Company Comparisons

INDUSTRY STANDARDS DATA

NAME - OFFICE SUPPLIES AND EQUIPMENT

SIC # - 59431

ASSETS

Cash and Equivalents	7.2
Accounts Receivable - Trade (net)	31.0
A/R Progress Billing	0.0
A/R Current Retention	0.0
Inventory	37.5
Cost & Est Earnings in Excess of Billings	0.0
All Other Current	1.3
TOTAL CURRENT	77.1
Fixed Assets (Net)	16.8
Joint Ventures & Invest	0.0
Intangibles (net)	1.7
All Other Non-Current	4.5
TOTAL ASSETS	100.0

LIABILITIES

Notes Payable - Short Term	9.7
Current Matured Long Term Debt	4.5
Accounts Payable - Trade	23.9
Accounts Payable - Retention	0.0
Billings in Excess of Costs & Est Earnings	0.0
Income Taxes Payable	0.0
All Other Current	7.7

(continued)

TABLE 8D.1	Industry Standard Data for Company Comparisons (continued)

TOTAL CURRENT	46.5		
Long Term Debt	18.2		
Deferred Taxes	0.1		
All Other Non-Current	2.7		
Net Worth	32.5		
TOTAL LIABILITIES & NET WORTH	100.0		

INCOME DATA

Net Sales	100.0
Gross Profit	37.1
Operating Expenses	34.3
Operating Profit	2.8
All Other Expenses (net)	0.7
Profit Before Taxes	2.1

RATIOS	L	M	U
Current	1.3	1.7	2.4
Quick	0.6	0.8	1.1
Receivables/Payables	0.0	0.0	0.0
Sales/Receivables	8.3	10.8	15.2
Cost of Sales/Inventory	3.3	5.1	9.0
Cost of Sales/Payables	6.0	9.0	13.5
Sales/Working Capital	22.1	10.1	6.0
EBIT/Interest	1.1	2.4	5.2
Cash Flow/Cur Mat LTD	0.5	1.3	3.7
Fixed/Worth	1.4	0.5	0.2
Debt/Worth	5.7	2.1	1.1
% Profit Bef Taxes/Networth	3.5	16.4	44.3
% Profit Bef Taxes/Total Assets	0.7	6.1	13.6
Sales/Net Fixed Assets	13.7	26.1	48.1
Sales/Total Assets	2.1	3.2	4.1

Source: Reprinted from fisCAL Analysis Software with permission of The HALCYON Group, Inc.

TABLE 8D.2	Balance Sheet

FINANCIAL STATEMENT COMPARISONS
BY DOLLARS
STUDY FOR GENERIC RETAIL, INC. STUDY CASE

ANALYSIS PROCESSED ON 4/25/1989 FOR INCOME/BALANCE ON 12/31/00

	STUDY CASE ($)	SIC# 9999 ($)	VARIANCE ($)
ASSETS			
Cash and Equivalents	1,000	1,825	−825
A/R - Trade (net)	9,500	7,325	2,175
A/R Progress Billings	0	0	0
A/R Current Retention	0	0	0
Inventory	10,500	10,025	475
Cost & Est Earnings in Excess of Billings	0	0	0
All Other Current	900	275	625
TOTAL CURRENT	21,900	19,450	2,450
Fixed Assets (Net)	3,100	4,275	−1,175
Joint Ventures & Invest	0	0	0
Intangibles (net)	0	150	−150
All Other Non-Current	0	1,150	−1,150
TOTAL ASSETS	25,000	25,000	
LIABILITIES			
Notes Payable - Short Term	1,950	3,050	−1,100
Current Matured Long Term Debt	1,050	1,325	−275
Accounts Payable - Trade	950	5,400	−4,450
Accounts Payable - Retention	0	0	0
Billings in Excess of Costs & Est Earnings	0	0	0
Income Taxes Payable	0	300	−300
All Other Current	1,150	2,350	−1,200
TOTAL CURRENT	5,100	12,425	−7,325
Long Term Debt	2,000	3,750	−1,750
Deferred Taxes	0	125	−125
All Other Non-Current	0	575	−575
Net Worth	17,900	8,100	9,800
TOTAL LIABILITIES & NET WORTH	25,000	25,000	
INCOME DATA			
Net Sales	100,000	100,000	
Gross Profit	49,000	37,100	11,900
Operating Expenses	36,200	33,800	2,400
Operating Profit	12,800	3,300	9,500
All Other Expenses (net)	3,700	800	2,900
Profit Before Taxes	9,100	2,500	6,600

Source: Reprinted from fisCAL Analysis Software with the permission of The HALCYON Group, Inc.

TABLE 8D.3	DuPont Formula for Return on Assets

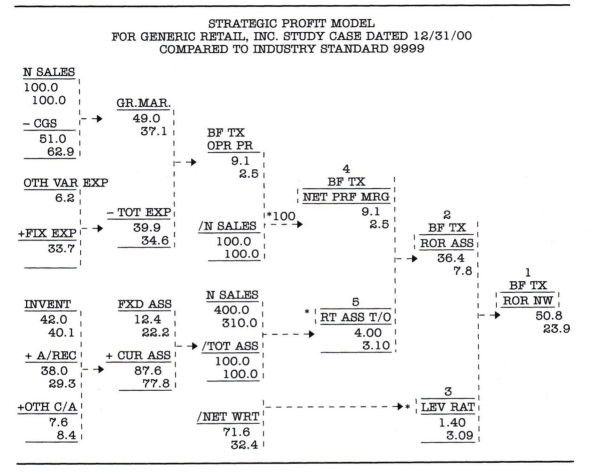

STRATEGIC PROFIT MODEL
FOR GENERIC RETAIL, INC. STUDY CASE DATED 12/31/00
COMPARED TO INDUSTRY STANDARD 9999

Source: Reprinted from fisCAL Analysis Software with the permission of The HALCYON Group, Inc.

TABLE 8D.4	Trend Analysis

fisCAL TREND ANALYSIS FOR GENERAL RETAIL, INC.   RUN DATE: 4/25/1989

	STUDY CASE 12/31/00 $000	STY CS +01 12/31/01 $000	STY CS +02 12/31/02 $000	SIC # 9999 $000	VARIANCE $000
BALANCE SHEET DATA					
Cash and Equivalents	1.0	7.0	10.9	2.2	8.7
Accounts Receivable	9.5	7.5	6.5	8.8	−2.3
Inventory	10.5	10.0	11.0	12.0	−1.0
All Other Current	0.9	0.9	0.9	0.3	0.6
TOTAL CURRENT ASSETS	21.9	25.4	29.3	23.3	6.0
Fixed Assets (Net)	3.1	1.9	0.7	5.1	−4.4
Intangibles (Net)	0.0	0.0	0.0	0.2	−0.2
All Oth. Non-Current	0.0	0.0	0.0	1.4	−1.4
TOTAL ASSETS	25.0	27.3	30.0	30.0	
Notes Pay-Short Term	2.0	0.9	0.5	3.7	−3.2
Cur Mat Lng Term Dbt	1.1	1.1	0.0	1.6	−1.6
Accounts Payable	1.0	3.0	3.1	6.5	−3.4
Income Taxes Payable	0.0	0.0	0.0	0.4	−0.4
All Other Current	1.2	1.1	1.3	2.8	−1.5
TOTAL CURRENT LIAB	5.1	6.1	4.9	14.9	−10.0
Long Term Debt	2.0	0.9	0.0	4.5	−4.5
Deferred Taxes	0.0	0.0	0.0	0.2	−0.2
All Oth. Non-Current	0.0	0.0	0.0	0.7	−0.7
NET WORTH	17.9	20.3	25.1	9.7	15.4
TTL LIAB & NET WORTH	25.0	27.3	30.0	30.0	
INCOME STATEMENT DATA					
Net Sales	100.0	99.0	120.0	120.0	
Gross Profit	49.0	45.0	60.0	44.5	15.5
Operating Expenses	36.2	36.7	47.1	40.6	6.5
Operating Profit	12.8	8.3	12.9	4.0	8.9
All Other Exp (Net)	3.7	4.6	5.2	1.0	4.2
Profit Before Taxes	9.1	3.7	7.7	3.0	4.7
Profit After Taxes	7.6	3.7	7.7		
CASH FLOW-OPERATIONS		8.3	9.0		
CASH MARKET VALUE	56.0	30.2	55.0	21.4	33.6
BREAKEVEN POINT	78.7	89.6	101.6		
OPERTNG CAPITAL RQRD	20.1	21.5	25.3	16.5	8.8
RATIOS					**VAR %**
CURRENT RATIO	4.3	4.2	6.0	1.6	273.7
QUICK RATIO	2.1	2.4	3.6	0.7	407.3

(continued)

TABLE 8D.4	Trend Analysis (continued)

SALES/RECEIVABLES	10.5	13.2	18.5	10.7	72.5
COST OF SALES/INVTRY	4.9	5.4	5.5	5.0	9.1
COST OF SALES/PAYBLS	53.7	18.0	19.4	10.7	80.9*
SALES/WORKING CAPTIAL	6.0	5.1	4.9	10.5	−53.2*
EBIT/INTEREST	14.0	6.3	39.5	3.1	1174.2
CASH FLOW/CUR MAT LTD	9.8	4.5	inf	1.9	inf
FIXED/WORTH	0.2	0.1	0.0	0.5	−94.4
DEBT/WORTH	0.4	0.3	0.2	2.1	−90.7
%PFT BF TX/NET WORTH	50.8	18.2	30.7	21.9	40.1
%PTF BF TX/TTL ASSETS	36.4	13.6	25.7	6.9	272.0
SALES/NET FIXED ASSETS	32.3	52.1	171.4	25.0	585.7
SALES/TOTAL ASSETS	4.0	3.6	4.0	3.1	29.0
DEG OF OPER LEVERAGE	5.26	5.66	4.82		
BANKRUPTCY PREDICTOR	8.50	7.79	10.09		

NET WORTH DIAGRAM

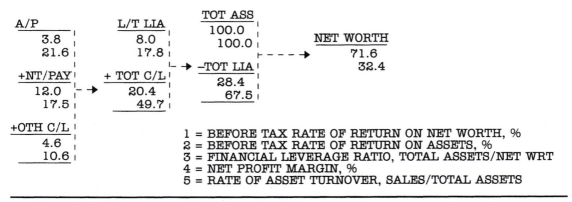

1 = BEFORE TAX RATE OF RETURN ON NET WORTH, %
2 = BEFORE TAX RATE OF RETURN ON ASSETS, %
3 = FINANCIAL LEVERAGE RATIO, TOTAL ASSETS/NET WRT
4 = NET PROFIT MARGIN, %
5 = RATE OF ASSET TURNOVER, SALES/TOTAL ASSETS

Source: Reprinted from fisCAL Analysis Software with the permission of The HALCYON Group, Inc.

CHAPTER NINE

Entrepreneurship, Mergers and Acquisitions, Restructuring, and the Service Sector

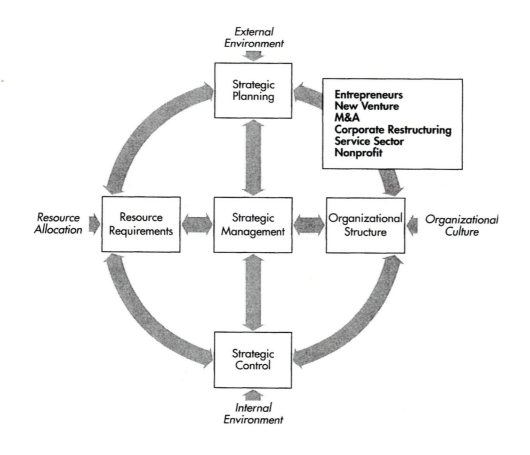

Chapter 1 A Framework for Strategic Management	**Chapter 2** Strategic Analysis	**Chapter 3** Strategic Visioning, Goals, Ethics, and Social Responsibility	**Chapter 4** The Competitive Environment	**Chapter 5** Capability-based Strategy	**Chapter 6** Market Dynamics and Sustainable Competitive Advantage
How to approach strategic management	*Application of strategic analysis*	*Understanding vision, values, ethics*	*Coping with competitive forces, stakeholders*	*Assessing company capability, timeliness, quality*	*Determining trends, gap analysis, and market dynamics*

Chapter 7 Strategy in a Global Environment	**Chapter 8** Financial Planning and Competitive- Cost Analysis	**Chapter 9** Entrepreneurship, Mergers and Acquisitions, Restructuring, and the Service Sector	**Chapter 10** Leadership Factor in Strategy and Implementing Strategic Change	**Chapter 11** Information Technology and Future Directions in Strategy
Assessing global trade, foreign markets, monetary exchange	*Preparing a financial plan and competitive-cost analysis*	*Importance of small business, entrepreneurs, restructuring*	*Strategy implementation, leadership, culture*	*Information technology, trends, new management*

INTRODUCTION

Smaller, entrepreneurial businesses are a driving force in the nation's economy, and small business management is taught to business majors in over 400 colleges. Even so, the entrepreneurial or small business sector is often not considered a candidate for strategic management. The service and public sectors also are often neglected. Nevertheless, now more than ever, strategic management methods can be utilized by the small business, service, and public sectors to achieve more effective performance. Although these sectors may look different on the surface, there are many similarities and strategic management approaches could be used more widely by both the small business and the service sectors.

M&A (merger and acquisition) activity is another area where strategic analysis is important. Recently, those involved with mergers and acquisitions have become concerned with strategic fit. The majority of deal makers in the past focused on short-run financial considerations. Strategic fit needs to be analyzed in relation to the long-term impact of merger. Because mergers and acquisitions often result in corporate restructuring, this also is included in this chapter.

Although many small business owners may not choose to develop a strategic plan, every business that seeks capital funding must provide a business plan. No bank or venture capitalist would consider providing funds to a business that does not have up-to-date information. The strategic plan for a small business is usually an abbreviated one containing only enough information to satisfy a bank or venture-capital group. Though it may be more operationally oriented than a strategic plan for a large corporation, it is a document that can determine the long-term survivability of the business. The action plan, or tactical plan for carrying out a strategy, ultimately determines how well strategic management functions.

Problems confronting service businesses and businesses that manufacture, distribute, market, and/or sell a product are often similar. A product is a tangible item that can be seen, felt, weighed, or measured, whereas a service is generally intangible. A service business, such as a law practice, has no visible results or impact other than a decision handed down by a judge. A service can be highly subjective, as is the case with food service; here the value is determined by the person who receives the service. The personality or attitude of the person providing the service can also directly affect the value perceived. Thus the exact same service may be perceived by one person as valuable and by another as worthless. In many cases, a service can be considered equivalent to a product. Tangible products also can have psychological value, such as that inherent in the prestige they confer. Although the majority of service providers are small businesses, large entities such as government agencies, hospitals, and schools also provide services. Many of these may be not-for-profit, but strategic analysis is still critical to their performance.

With a high of almost 4,000 acquisitions in 1986, merger mania has subsided to approximately 2,000. The highest dollar amount, almost $240 billion in 1989, dropped to approximately $80 billion in 1991 (Woolley, 1992). Serious questions have been raised concerning the efficacy of acquisitions. Some claim that acquisitions threaten the basis of the capitalist system because of the exploding corporate debt. By 1988 there was almost $1.8 trillion of debt outstanding, propelled largely by the cost of acquisitions. As an example of the outcome of an acquisition, the RJR Nabisco deal had the following results (Greenwald, 1988):

1. Shareholders: $8–14 billion in profit
2. New owners: $2 billion or more
3. LBO investors: a 40% annual yield
4. Investment bankers received: $170 million
5. Commercial bankers received: $170 million
6. Lawyers were paid: $100–200 million
7. Junk bond holders: 14.5% annual return
8. Corporate bond holders: loss of $1 billion
9. Taxpayers: loss of $2–5 billion

The fear is that greed, debt, and buyout are spiraling out of control. Furthermore, of the 25 best-performing U.S. companies, twelve made acquisitions in 1988 but only three of these acquisitions showed significant value for the companies' shareholders (Coley and Reinton, 1988).

The divestiture of a strategic business unit (SBU) or division of a company is different from the selling of an entire company. In many respects, a strategic business unit can be considered a "small business" within a larger company. Many small businesses are acquired and become SBUs in larger companies. When these small companies are acquired, the small business ceases to exist. This does not mean that these small companies fail, even though statistics show them as "no longer in business."

Finally, a merger and acquisition deal may actually determine whether a company survives or grows. The deal itself is a strategic decision but it may or may not involve a strategic analysis or a strategic plan. And although in many cases there is no impact, research has shown that the majority of mergers fail. For example, W. T. Grimm and Company reported that in 1985 there were 1,237 divestitures and 1,764 acquisitions, reflecting a 70% failure rate for acquisitions. By comparison, in 1985 approximately 700,000 new businesses were started. In that year the failure rate for new businesses was lower than that for M&As.

Most businesses do not suddenly appear as large corporate entities, fully functioning and mature. Most businesses start relatively small. They usually start as entrepreneurial activity in a garage, basement, or some small rented area. There is a "natural" organizational life cycle from birth through growth and maturity to decline and death. This is much like the product life-cycle metaphor. As businesses grow, they may decide to speed growth through merger, or they may be acquired and merged with larger organizations as a business unit or even as a separate division or company. Some businesses, however, tend to stay small. Most service businesses remain small because of their labor-intensive nature. All the topics addressed in this chapter—entrepreneurship, mergers and acquisitions, restructuring, and the service sector—reflect aspects of the development and evolution of growing businesses. That is why they are grouped together in this chapter. And, because they all start with entrepreneurial activity, the first main area we shall discuss is entrepreneurship and small business.

ENTREPRENEURSHIP AND THE SMALL BUSINESS SECTOR

In the business press, small business is said to account for 80% to 90% of all new jobs created. If businesses employing fewer than 100 people are considered small businesses, then over 87% of all businesses are small. If 500 employees is taken as the cut-off point, 99% fall in the small business category! These figures are from the U.S. Small Business Administration and the National Federation of Independent Business. The U.S. Chamber of Commerce (1988) stated that small businesses represent 98% of the 14 million non-farm businesses and that they employ 48% of the total workforce. They also provide two-thirds of all first jobs and initial training.

The economic welfare of the United States is closely linked to a favorable environment for small business. When national and local laws have favored small business, the economy has been strong. When these laws have hurt small businesses, the economy has suffered. Recent laws in many states, such as those that require small businesses to provide a comprehensive medical plan and those that mandate the taxing of service businesses at 5 to 6%, have seriously threatened the existence of many small businesses.

Small business is widely considered "the American way." From the beginning, many Americans have wanted to be in control of their own lives, to be independent. Such "rugged individualists" believe the entrepreneurial spirit is what made this country strong. Today, many national, state, and municipal officials encourage the development of small business and recognize its contribution to the economy. A survey of law makers by the National Conference of State Legislatures, reported in the *Wall Street Journal* in 1992, showed that 29 states favor measures to spur economic development in hard-hit communities. Even in the face of severe budget crises, these states are expected to pass laws aiding new and small businesses and promoting development in rural areas.

Unfortunately, the weakened banking industry, the numerous leveraged buy-outs that created highly unbalanced corporate debt, and the federal deficit that demands unreasonably high debt service have all eaten away at the pool of capital available for small business. Without this capital, the potential for small business is very poor. It is highly desirable for new state programs to come to the rescue.

Definitions of the term *small business* are numerous and varied. Some definitions are based on how a business is taxed or pays for services. In some organizations the fee structure is based on size and/or number of employees. Most definitions are based on a combination of the number of employees, the volume of sales, and the size of the capital structure. In manufacturing, capitalization is more important than the number of employees. In a retail business, sales volume is more important, and for service firms, the number of employees is given more weight.

Often, 100 employees is considered the magic number. These definitions tend to change from time to time, making it necessary to keep up with specific legislation affecting the business and the industry. Many books on small business give different measures. Megginson et al. (1988) give the following guidelines for classifying a company as a small business.

Manufacturing—maximum employee range between 500 and 1,500, depending on the industry

Construction—average annual receipts less than $17 million for the past three years

Wholesale—maximum of 500 employees

Retail—annual sales not over $3.5 to $13.5 million

Service—annual sales not over $3.5 to $14.5 million

Between being a small business and a large business, a company may go through several stages, which include being a "mid-sized" firm. In time, a special discipline for mid-sized companies may emerge. A classic measure of growth stages is Greiner's (1972) "Evolution/Revolution" stages or "crises." From startup to the *crisis of control* is the first stage. When a business grows to a size where the entrepreneur can no longer stay on top of all business activities, the business has reached a crisis of control. The delegation of authority and the division of activities into functional areas with independent managers are required. This is often a wrenching experience for the entrepreneur, who may find it hard to let go. At this point, the entrepreneur must become a small business manager who can delegate and plan strategically if he or she is to survive. Many entrepreneurs are unable to make the transition to being a strategic manager. One of the most important reasons for the failure of so many small businesses and mergers is a lack of strategic analysis, strategic fit, and strategic management.

The small business sector is often a special focus of the national media. Magazines such as *Inc.* and *Entrepreneur* have become successful by concentrating on small business concerns. For several years the *Wall Street Journal* has published a special section that takes an in-depth look at small business, and it has a column called "Enterprise" that focuses on small business and entrepreneurial issues.

ENTREPRENEURS

Entrepreneurship is more than starting a new business—it is a style of managing. Consider Digital Equipment Corporation (DEC), for example, which by being entrepreneurial outfoxed IBM in the mini-computer market. Another strategy used by DEC was to introduce XCON, an expert-systems approach to manufacturing and distribution that is said to have saved the company $80 million. DEC was expected to post a loss for 1992, but its entrepreneurial spirit has resurfaced with the introduction of the Alpha chip that is reputed to operate at 150 million calculations per second. This is twice the speed of any current computer. Even industries can have an entrepreneurial spirit. Consider biotechnology (Hamilton et al., 1992), which looks like it will be the dominant growth industry of the 1990s. Its range of products is mind boggling: recombinant DNA, gene therapy, chemical synthesis, and many others.

Most often, however, entrepreneurship is associated with individuals who have the vision, drive, and courage of their convictions, such as Land at Polaroid and, more recently, Steven Jobs, who helped start Apple Computer, and William Gates, who started Microsoft. In a study of why some new businesses succeed while others fail, Brokaw (1991) found that although cash is indispensable, flexibility in responding to the unpredictable was a key requirement for a startup business. Furthermore, she found that "nobody likes your product as much as you do," that ignoring competitors can be deadly, and that upper management's ability to delegate is vital to the company's survival.

Three major reasons why small businesses fail are a lack of planning, severe competition, and a lack of working capital. Successful entrepreneurs, however, are creative individuals who have vision (conceptual style); have little patience, and want to control everything (directive style); are able to motivate others (behavioral style), and finally are willing to take risks (analytic style).

A study by Rowe (1987), based on the initial validation of a test instrument called the Decision Style Inventory (DSI) with members of the Young Presidents Organization (YPO), revealed these four styles. That study showed that YPO members are extremely flexible and can use all four decision styles. In a second study, of 57 company presidents identified as "up-and-comers" by *Forbes* magazine, Rowe found that 17 exhibited the entrepreneurial style (a combination of the conceptual and the directive styles). Twenty of the young presidents had a planning or executive style (analytical and conceptual decision styles). These findings help explain why startup companies need the entrepreneurial style but growth companies need to emphasize strategic management.

Barbara Bird's 1989 research on entrepreneurs explodes some of the old myths. In general, however, research supports the view that most entrepreneurs had difficult childhoods and tended to be misfits in "normal" society. They were impatient with rules and formal education. Once they had an idea, they became fanatical about it and would not give up. Failure was not a crushing defeat; rather, it spurred them on to try harder. If they failed, they did not give up or get depressed. Instead, they persisted until they succeeded or found a new idea to pursue.

Although entrepreneurs tend to see the big picture, they often jump to conclusions. The Rowe (1989) profile of the entrepreneur reveals that he or she has a conceptual and directive style, which is consistent with the studies by Bird. Hodgetts and Kuratko (1986) list five characteristics that are crucial to entrepreneurial success:

1. *Technical competency*—Entrepreneurs must have technical know-how and know what they are doing.
2. *Mental ability*—Primary is the ability to view operations in broad terms and see how everything fits together.
3. *Human relations skills*—The entrepreneur must get along with others and must communicate, motivate, and influence.
4. *High achievement drive*—The entrepreneur must be action-oriented and should gauge success according to results through feedback. (David McClelland's seminal work on the achieving society equated the achievement orientation of most Americans with the success of America as a land of opportunity.)
5. *Creativity*—It is important to process information in a way that results in new, original, and meaningful ideas, concepts, processes, and products.

The research by Jeff Hansen (1985) shows the importance of relating decision style to the conditions confronting the entrepreneur. For example, we can describe the development of a new venture as shown in Figure 9.1. Table 9.1 shows what style(s) of decision making Hansen found to be most effective in each stage of development.

FIGURE 9.1 | **New-Venture Development**

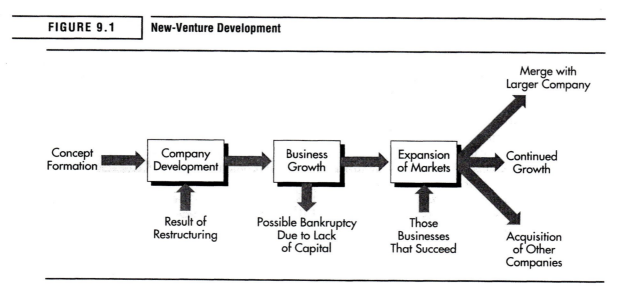

TABLE 9.1	The Decision Style That Tends to Be Most Effective at Each Stage of the Company Life Cycle

Life Cycle Stage	Number of Employees	Most Effective Decision Style
1. Concept development	1 to 9	High conceptual Low analytic
2. Company development	10 to 25	High analytic High behavioral Low conceptual Low directive
3. Company positioning	26 to 75	High conceptual Low behavioral
4. Process operation	75 or more	High directive

Hansen studied entrepreneurs who were funded by venture capitalists. He found that decision style could assist venture capitalists in the funding decision. Of the 59 individuals studied, 41% had a decision style pattern that was consistent with the data shown for entrepreneurs in Table 9.2.

As can be seen in Table 9.2, entrepreneurs were higher in the directive and conceptual styles than either typical managers or the population at large. The high conceptual is typically creative and has the vision needed to create new endeavors. When such an individual is also a high directive (energetic and results-oriented), she or he is clearly an appropriate person to start a new venture. Interestingly, the shortcoming of typical entrepreneurs is the low analytical score, which may account for their lack of planning, low use of data, and tendency to have financial difficulties. Rowe's (1983) study of CEOs and chairmen of the board also showed a pattern similar to that of entrepreneurs. They have high conceptual scores and average directive scores. Thus they have the vision for creating change but tend to rely on subordinates to carry it out. The entrepreneurs, however, not only had the vision but also were able to carry the vision out.

TABLE 9.2	Decision Style Scores for Entrepreneurs, Managers, and the General Population

	Entrepreneurs (score)	Managers (score)	Population (average score)
Directive style	83	71	75
Analytical style	76	88	90
Conceptual style	97	84	80
Behavioral style	44	57	55

Brokaw (1991) pointed out that there are a number of lessons that have been learned which can help new ventures.

1. If cash is considered king, then flexibility must be god.
2. What has broken many startups is their inability to respond to the unpredictable.
3. New ventures often overlook the fact that nobody likes their products as much as they do.
4. New ventures may ignore the fact that competitors who are ensconced have a viable business, which the startup does not have.
5. Experience is generally needed to run a successful business, and startups are often reluctant to buy it.
6. Underestimating competitors can lead to disastrous results.
7. Founders who are able to delegate responsibility are best able to survive.
8. Few founders correctly estimate the time or money needed to penetrate a market.
9. Founders do not realize how much time it will take to start and run their own business.
10. Entrepreneurs may not be aware of the risk and the emotional drain that running their own business entails.

The Barnett tape of Mo Siegel, who started Celestial Seasonings teas, also supports the entrepreneurial profile. According to Siegel, "niche picking" is the key to success in a small business. Siegel was a formal-education dropout who was a fanatic about his herb teas, especially Red Zinger. He says he has an "M.B.A." based on experience gained from the streets and a "Ph.D." in "marginality." "Being on the streets" consisted of 15 years of listening to Peter Drucker tapes while bicycling to work. The "marginality" was his fanatical scrutiny of expenses and cost of goods sold. However, he believes in a good business education, because a person needs to have the knowledge to succeed. He said he became autodidactic, reading and studying everything he could. Every morning he would tell himself and his employees to take care of the "customer's needs" not one's own "greed." He added that if this is done in an intelligent, businesslike way and if basic rules of good business are followed, a lot of money will be made. (Many business leaders and professors of business agree that management is a "people business." If one can develop and maintain good relationships with customers and employees, one will be successful. Making lots of money is only a "side benefit" of being able to deal effectively with people.)

In describing growth, Siegel says the problem is first not having enough product, then distribution, and finally too much inventory. Different problems arise at each level of growth. Because people tend to disappear, new people have to be hired for the next level. Picking the right people for each job, position, and project is extremely important. Siegel says he always hires people smarter than himself for the job that needs to be done. Managers who are afraid to hire people who are smarter than they are make a big mistake.

Siegel identifies three stages of corporate development by sales level. Sales of up to about $9 million characterize the *entrepreneurial stage*. Strategic planning starts at about $5 million. At this stage, Siegel brought in an expert in planning who stayed for three years and whose efforts led to the growth that became the core of a crisis. Many of the people who were initially with the business did not like to plan, so they left. Between $5 and $10 million in sales, there was a complete house cleaning. People who did not grow were out.

Siegel's experience reflects the fact that the levels of financial activity and analysis are quite different at the various stages of growth. When comparing small business with large corporations, one must interpret ratio analysis differently. For large corporations, industry averages are useful benchmarks, although that has changed for firms saddled with huge debt as the result of LBO or junk-bond activity. These firms are more like small businesses in that a deteriorating economy may threaten their existence. Small businesses focus on avoiding large debt in the event that the economy turns down. Entrepreneurs typically have a low equity position at the start and make maximum use of an accounts payable "float." They also contribute many hours of "sweat equity" that does not show up on a financial statement.

The next stage of growth for Mo Siegel was between $10 and $25 million in sales. He describes this as the *corpreneurial stage.* Most of the people hired at this stage were mavericks who left large companies so that they could get experience and later start their own businesses. One of these was Keith Brenner, who later started Wishbisquetts. Most of the people at this stage did not like planning.

The last stage of growth was from $25 million up. At this level, personnel changed to those who were comfortable with planning and wanted the certainty of knowing what the policies were. In this traditional *corporate stage,* planning dominates and is the focus of strategic management. People who are comfortable at the corporate level are easier to manage. They prefer structure and want policy guidelines. They like to fit in. They dislike uncertainty and ambiguity. Therefore, it is easier to devise planning systems, to formulate strategy, and to implement policies, procedures, and rules.

The entrepreneur dislikes all this. The transitional stage from entrepreneurial to small business management has talent that is quite "mavericky" and resists structure. If the business passes this transition and becomes a large successful company, the mavericks tend to be replaced by "corporate types" who like structure.

According to Kuratko and Hodgetts (1989), the reasons why most small businesses do not plan are

1. Time scarcity: many owners work 14–16-hour days, seven days per week with continual day-to-day operating problems.
2. Lack of knowledge of the processes, components, or sequence of factors involved.
3. Lack of expertise: owners tend to be generalists with no specialized expertise in planning.
4. Lack of trust and openness: owners may be guarded about their business and decisions and may refuse to share information with employees or outside consultants.

APPLICATION OF ANALYTICAL METHODS TO SUPPORT ENTREPRENEURS

The National Federation of Independent Business (NFIB), the largest small business trade group, collects data on small business members, but, as NFIB concedes, there are no averages that apply to all small businesses. Smaller "industry" trade groups may have data more useful to that specific industry. Nevertheless, ratios for a startup are very different from those of a well-established and well-run business. Furthermore, the success of a small business is much more dependent on the drive and dedication of the entrepreneur than on financial ratios.

According to Baruch Lev (1974) only two ratios are good predictors of corporate failure. These are cash flow to total debt and net income to total assets. These tend to give a five-year lead time. Two others give a lead time of about three years: total debt to total assets and working capital to total assets. All others give a warning of only a year or less. For small business, these important ratios are less favorable in general (lower cash flow and net income in the early years). Of course, total debt and total assets are also lower. And the so-called unfavorable ratios can be more than compensated for with drive, hard work, and long hours. These rules of thumb vary somewhat according to the author or source, but one example is the suggestion of a 30% debt-to-equity ratio for a corporation and a 50% ratio for a small business.

Looking at the bright side, however, the methods and analytical models described in this book are useful at any stage of growth. Furthermore, the use of these tools will change the odds for success in favor of the entrepreneur. Entrepreneurial managers with conceptual/directive profiles resist analytical rigor, and it is a real challenge for them to apply these approaches. One way to gain acceptance of a methodological approach is to keep it simple and amenable to "guestimates" rather than insisting on rigorous data. The models and tools set forth here can be used in a variety of ways and are helpful even if data are weak. The methodologies in this book can be used with subjective data as well as with well-analyzed, objective input. The degree of risk a manager is willing to live with determines the level of uncertainty in data that he or she is willing to tolerate. Because entrepreneurs are moderate-to-high risk takers, they tend to use intuition and hunches rather than careful analysis.

"Corporate types," on the other hand, tend to be risk-averse and prefer hard, objective data. However, this data can also lead to fatal errors.

The advantage of a systematic approach is that it reduces the likelihood of overlooking important factors or of not understanding basic principles such as product life cycle, balanced portfolios, or strategic funds programming. But because many entrepreneurs are intuitive thinkers, they make spur-of-the-moment decisions on the basis of minimal information. They also avoid analysis paralysis (defined as immobility caused by substituting data analysis for courage). Steven Greenberg, Anametrics chairman, says, "Don't dillydally. Make decisions in a hurry" (Rowan, 1986).

It is difficult to convince entrepreneurs to use a structured analysis, but they do realize that there is a need for planning when they must raise money from a bank or venture capitalist. This effort requires the use of careful analysis, which can help the entrepreneur make the transition to the small business stage and then to the large corporation stage. However, the desire for growth is dependent on the psychological makeup and decision style of the entrepreneur. He or she may not want to grow and many bail out before reaching the small business stage. Those who leave tend to be the rugged individualists who cannot stand structure. Rather than succumb to structure, they strike out in a new direction with a new idea and start another new business. They seem to be driven to do this. Some entrepreneurs "fail" many times before they finally succeed; and often they fail and start right over again in the same business.

Henry Ford failed twice before he produced a car that captured the imagination of a mass market and became the most successful automobile manufacturer in the twenties. Ford started small but did not stay small. In the beginning, entrepreneurs focus all their energies on market forces and economic impacts. They do not have the time, personnel, or energy to deal with government regulations, taxes, and other considerations. To a large company, such impediments to doing business may be no more than minor annoyances, but to the small company, these "interferences" can be fatal. (As William F. Buckley said in a television debate on April 3, 1992, the best thing the government could do for small businesses is just get out of the way.)

Do founders learn from these sobering experiences? Brokaw's 1991 studies suggest that most do not and in turn, most do not survive.

NEW-VENTURE DEVELOPMENT

To better understand the new-venture development process, let's consider the wide range of conditions found in the new-venture arena.

1. *New products.* The list of new ventures built on products is legion. Successes include billion-dollar Sun Microsystems, Apple Computer, and Lotus Development Corporation. The first product of The Games Gang, called Pictionary (a way to play Charades on paper), went from zero in 1986 to more than $125 million annual sales in just two years (Deutsch, 1989).

2. *A new technology.* In December 1982, three young Harvard MBAs started Orbital Science Corporation (OSC). The product introduced by this space transportation company was a winged rocket booster, called Pegasus, that is launched from an airplane rather than from the ground. This innovation makes it possible to carry heavier payloads into space, and at much lower cost. The unusual aspect of this venture, one of the largest private ventures ever undertaken in space technology, is that the three founders functioned as "project managers." They neither invested their own money nor manufactured the rocket (Martin Marietta did that). They put the deal together with NASA and raised money from private investors (Perry, 1989). The first successful Pegasus was launched in April 1990 ("Petite Payloads," 1990).

3. *A new approach to retailing by mail.* A number of mail-order firms thrived in the 1980s by selling sportswear to baby boomers who had little time to shop: J. Crew started in the early 1980s and had sales close to $150 million in 1989; Tweeds started in 1987 and had an estimated revenue of $37 million in 1989; Lands' End started in 1963 and had sales close to $500 million in 1989 (Rudolph, 1989).

4. *New retailing services.* These ranged from fingernail decorating and polishing to high-priced barber shops, 24-hour mailbox and mailing services, and video-game parlors. Various segments of this wide range of services have flourished

at one time or another in the past decade. When carefully planned, they have all been fairly effective in generating good cash flow.

5. *A new entrant into an existing area.* It is generally agreed that in order to succeed, a new venture has to have something different. The difference, however, does not have to be an innovative product or service. For example, in real estate during the mid-1970s and early 1980s, it was possible to conservatively buy property in metropolitan areas such as New York and be able to make a substantial amount of money simply by doing well what was already being done. Converting apartment buildings into cooperatives required little more than following well-established legal patterns and dealing effectively with a variety of complex operational and regulatory problems. Many of these ventures resulted in returns of over 500% in less than three years.

6. *A new approach to pet care.* Pet sitting in an owner's home is an example of smaller new ventures. Patti Moran's service called "Crazy 'bout Critters," in Winston-Salem, N.C., for example, employs 39 part-time pet sitters, She wrote a book, *Pet Sitting for Profit,* and in 1989 started the National Association for Pet Sitters. Membership was expected to be over 300 by the end of 1990.

7. *A new airline service.* More than 50 applications are filed each year for new airline services. North American found out that before starting its one-plane operation, it had to file more than 10,000 pages of manuals. In addition, it had to pass a battery of inspections by federal regulatory agencies, buy $500 million of insurance, spend $300,000 on training and $250,000 on FAA testing, arrange financing to lease a new Boeing 757, and enter into a cooperative arrangement with El Al Israel Airlines, which own 2.9% of the company. All this had to be done in the ten-month period preceding North American's first commercial flight (Dahl, 1990).

The accelerating pace of entrepreneurial activity experienced during the 1980s, which is expected to continue throughout the 1990s, seems to be an international phenomenon. For example, during the 1980s Italy experienced an entrepreneurial boom that rivaled and in some cases exceeded that in the United States and in other European countries (Haberman, 1980). Entrepreneurial activity is also beginning to show up in Eastern Europe, especially in Hungary (Greenhouse, 1990).

Contrary to popular belief, many new ventures are well planned and well managed. Often, what is needed by new ventures is help in managing the business more effectively. As in any business, the strategic-planning processes described in this book include tools and approaches that can help the new venture be more successful.

TASKS INVOLVED IN STARTING NEW VENTURES

Starting a new venture takes a special kind of mentality and strategic approach. The major tasks involved in planning and management include

1. Identifying an opportunity
2. Deciding to explore and proceed with the venture
3. Formulating the business concept and plans
4. Acquiring resources and determining future source of funds

5. Managing the venture within an appropriate organizational structure
6. Controlling cost, quality, and value (important after the venture has been started)
7. "Growing" the venture (important after a successful start)

IDENTIFYING AN OPPORTUNITY

An in-depth survey of the general economic social system and marketplace will turn up any number of needs and wants not being met or will suggest where needs and wants could be satisfied more efficiently and effectively. For example, Rupert Murdoch's publishing organization identified a market niche, a magazine for women aged 38 to 50. Those who make up this market niche are much older than readers of *Glamour* and *Mademoiselle,* a little older than those of *Harper's Bazaar* and *Vogue,* and younger than those of *Lear.* This niche is growing with the aging of baby boomers and looks promising because of the high incomes in the target market. The new magazine Murdoch produced is called *Mirabella* (Kleinfield, 1989).

DECIDING TO EXPLORE AND PROCEED

After opportunities are identified, the decision to explore further depends on a number of other factors. In most cases, the first considerations are whether the opportunity is something you want to do, whether it fits your style or personality, and whether it fits your budget or provides the lifestyle you want. At this point there are no "right" answers, but asking the right questions is absolutely essential. The kind of person who could work well with a group of high-tech professionals, as at Orbital Science Corporation, may not be the kind who would succeed at running a retail health food store or chain of stores. A high-powered developer of innovative financial packages, such as mortgage-backed bonds, may be a very different entrepreneurial type from the person who can succeed at developing a fashion magazine, a toy company, a mail-order clothing company, a real estate venture, or a retail store. Decision style and/or personality may or may not be a major consideration. In many entrepreneurial ventures, drive, commitment, hard work, and persistence often overcome many so-called "personality handicaps."

FORMULATING THE BUSINESS CONCEPT

The formulation of a viable strategic approach often is the key to the success of the business. Von Clausewitz, one of the early writers on military strategy, is now widely quoted as saying that a war is won or lost before the first shot is fired, depending on what strategic decisions were made beforehand. The same can be said for a new venture. The success of a business depends on the strategic decisions made before the doors are opened for business. The strategic plan must establish an effective working relationship between the opportunities and threats in the external environment and the internal strengths and weaknesses organized for implementation of the plan.

The Games Gang, which developed Pictionary, followed "fad-product strategy" and did not sink a lot of money into building a manufacturing plant. Companies that *did* incur that cost include Atari (home video games) and Caleco (Cabbage Patch dolls). Both of these companies suffered when the fad died. The Games Gang farmed out productions, owned no distribution units, and avoided building a plush corporate headquarters. Its strategy was focused on keeping costs low and was based on finding a game that was already selling well in a local market, testing it for "playability," setting up a royalty arrangement, subcontracting manufacturing, and letting publicity and word of mouth build sales (Deutsch, 1989).

Strategy formulation is an iterative process that cycles continually from beginning to end. The best one can do is relax between cycles and then jump back into the race.

ACQUIRING RESOURCES

Once a plan has been developed, it is a relatively straightforward matter to determine the cost. Typically, cost is more than was planned, which gives rise to the need to raise capital. Orbital Science Corporation did not have to invest its own money because it had an arrangement with Martin Marietta and NASA. It also raised several million from private sources, including $50 million from selling R&D limited partnership units. Orbital's situation illustrates that capital can be raised from many sources. The primary sources of capital for new ventures include

1. The entrepreneur's personal savings
2. Friends and relatives
3. Banks, insurance companies, and so on
4. Private investors
5. Venture-capital firms
6. Mortgage financiers
7. Potential suppliers and customers
8. SBA loans

Each source of capital has its own special requirements. Some require a substantial equity position and/or control or insist on final authority in decision making. There are always tradeoffs, but without sufficient capital, there is no business. As Harvey Mackay says in *Swim with the Sharks,* 1% of something is worth more than 100% of nothing.

MANAGING THE VENTURE

After an initial success raises the prospects for continued survival, attention shifts to managing an on-going business. This sometimes requires a change in both approach and personnel. As Mo Siegel (of Celestial Seasonings) indicated, managers eventually replace the entrepreneurs, who go on to start other new ventures.

Within seven years, Sun Microsystems grew to over $2 billion in sales, but earnings dropped and resulted in a loss in 1989. The crisis was due to their lack of capable management for that stage of growth. Sun needed to abandon the seat-of-the-pants style for a more structured and disciplined approach. Failure to train managers or change management style has derailed many new ventures. Sun managed to recover and make the necessary transition successfully and more quickly than anyone expected (Fisher, 1990).

Some entrepreneurs have successfully undergone the necessary metamorphoses and have stayed with the business for years. Digital Equipment and Hewlett-Packard offer good examples. Here the owners developed and grew with the business. Scott McNealy has likewise expressed his determination to stay with Sun Microsystems and grow with the company. Thus far, prospects look good (Pollack, 1989). At DEC, Ken Olsen finally departed in July 1992. For a long time he had refused to go, but things had gotten so bad that he had to face reality and leave.

Probably a more interesting example of how new ventures can lose their way is found in the experience of *Venture* magazine. In mid-1989 *Venture* suspended publication for two months and laid off much of its staff. This was done after a deal to sell the magazine fell through. As a result, Arthur Lipper, the founder, lost a substantial amount of money because the magazine had failed to keep pace with the market (Scardino, 1989). Unfortunately, when strategy is poorly planned and not continuously updated, it is easy to lose sight of what's happening in the marketplace and of the needs and wants of customers.

ACHIEVING A COMPETITIVE EDGE

Clearly, small and entrepreneurial businesses have much to contribute to the overall economy. In a number of cases, these companies have produced significant exports and actually have reduced the trade deficit. As Table 9.3 shows, the potential for global exports is enticing (Holstein and Kelly, 1992).

TABLE 9.3	Global Exports in Billions of Dollars	
	1986	1991
Canada	55	85
Japan	27	48
Mexico	12	33
Germany	10	21
Britain	11	22
Korea	6	15
France	7	15
Taiwan	5	13
Other (including capital goods)		153
Total		415

For example, Vita-Mix now exports 20% of its $15 million a year in sales. The key is serving a niche market that is too small or too difficult for competitors to penetrate. Relying on the toll-free 800 number, faxes, and translators offered by phone companies, small businesses are increasingly able to compete in the global marketplace. With a stagnant U.S. market, the global marketplace is increasingly inviting.

Franchises are beginning to "teach the corporate elephants to dance" (Matusky, 1990). For example, Union Carbide is recruiting personnel for a new "intrapreneurial" program within specialty chemicals. To change Union Carbide from a production-driven company to a service-oriented business, franchising may be the answer. Within nine weeks, Union Carbide started a national network for Mobile Care. A radical change in culture may be impossible in an established entity, but a new organizational division can create its own culture.

Who are the "hottest growth companies" in the United States, and what makes them run? While the big three auto makers lost $7.5 billion in 1991, Spartan Motors, an auto parts manufacturing firm, doubled its sales to $51 million. What accounted for this difference was the highly innovative chassis that Spartan made. *Business Week*'s 100 best small companies represent those where sales grew 48.3%, compared with 6.2% for Standard and Poor's industrial-stock index. The same companies' earnings grew 100.9%, compared with a decline of 14.3% for the industrials (Touby, 1992). What contributed most to the growth of these companies was focusing on a niche market, reacting rapidly to change, being highly innovative, and—most important—serving a customer need.

One of America's fastest growing companies is Connor Peripherals. Using nonstop innovation, Connor has been able to fend off the competition, including the Japanese. In addition, Connor listens to its customers, has smart manufacturing, and utilizes rapid product development. Connor improves its products incrementally, thus ensuring quality and reliability (Kupfer, 1990).

In spite of the many success stories, simply being a nimble entrepreneurial company is not enough to survive in an environment that has stable, concentrated, and well-protected industrial alliances (Ferguson, 1988). To illustrate this, in 1981 the United States exported $27 billion in high-technology products. For high-technology industries to succeed, they require increased investment in wide marketing and customer support. Since 1980 the U.S. semiconductor world market share has slipped from 60% to 40%. Japan has twice as many integrated-circuit patents as the United States. Table 9.4 illustrates some of the differences between U.S. and Japanese semiconductor companies.

Considering the relative size of the workforce in the two countries and their relative gross domestic product (GDP), the Japanese have significantly outperformed the United States. Interestingly, U.S. GDP grew by 2% in the first quarter of 1992 and is projected to grow by as much as 4% by the second quarter of 1993 (Liscio, 1992).

Fragmentation, instability, and entrepreneurism have contributed to the structural problems in the U.S. semiconductor industry. It is projected that without a coordinated development process in semiconductor technology, the U.S. industry will doom itself. Evidence of this prophecy can be seen in the once-successful Wang

TABLE 9.4	Comparison of Capital and R&D Spending Between U.S. and Japanese Semiconductor Companies (Dollar amounts in millions)			

	U.S. Companies		Japanese Companies	
Year	Capital	R&D	Capital	R&D
1976	306	228	237	165
1977	179	300	413	200
1978	453	384	650	376
1979	656	470	887	428
1980	956	624	1,300	484
1981	1,047	776	1,424	621
1982	1,301	875	1,188	725
1983	2,234	944	1,323	941
1984	3,508	1,414	3,010	1,078
1985	2,961	1,596	1,789	1,314
1986	2,585	1,582	990	NA

Laboratories, Inc., which filed for protection under Chapter 11 of the Bankruptcy Code after it fell $550 million in debt. The reason given was Wang's inability to keep pace with change. In the absence of a more cohesive policy of support for the small business segment, Wang may be only one of many future failures.

One bright spot is the number of recent joint venture deals for developing and manufacturing microchips. On July 13, 1992, Toshiba, IBM, and Siemens announced that they would collaborate in developing advanced memory chips. Shortly thereafter, the Pentagon proposed a cut in the funds to support Sematech, a consortium designed to boost U.S. semiconductor competitiveness. Congress, however, restored the amount to the $100 million level previously authorized. Shortly afterward, a National Science Foundation study revealed that the United States is losing its technology edge (Bloomberg, 1992). In their article on industrial policy, Christopher and Mandel (1992) clearly point up the problem caused by not having a national policy that supports technology growth. They cite the R&D gap, productivity lag, investment drops, erosion of high-tech trade, and the decline in factory jobs as evidence of the need for a national strategy to spur growth. Their recommendations include the following:

1. Increase federal spending above $20 billion per year for R&D, and reduce defense spending below its current $43 billion per year.
2. Increase federal spending for technical assistance to industry.
3. Improve data collection on R&D.
4. Rebuild the U.S. infrastructure to encourage high-tech industries.
5. Expand the Export-Import Bank to make export financing easier.

6. Increase funds for scientific education.
7. Provide tax incentives for R&D investment.

The new-growth agenda will not come cheaply, but to fail to implement it could adversely affect the quality of life in the U.S. for years to come.

MERGERS AND ACQUISITIONS

Because many new ventures are acquired, the merger–acquisition process is a natural part of the business life cycle. One of the differences between U.S. and Japanese industry is that the businesses in the United States focus on short-term acquisitions, whereas in Japan the emphasis is on growth. Furthermore, the sales of smaller U.S. companies have increased from approximately 30% of all mergers and acquisitions to over 50% in 1990. Mergers and acquisitions will undoubtedly continue for many years.

A January 1992 business news program on CNN stated that in 1991 mergers were down 32% from 1990. Other reports had mergers down 34%. In 1992, Colgate-Palmolive raised $446 million in a public offering in order to restructure debt and committed $900 million to acquisitions, including the Mennen takeover. *Fortune,* discussing the "Deals of the Year," stated that companies are turning to equity financing and that leverage-laden companies are paying down debt. In the eighties over $640 billion of equity disappeared from corporate books. A little is creeping back. Of the 50 biggest deals in 1991, 16 were stock transactions, compared to only 2 in 1990. Former junk-bond gurus are now claiming to be "restructuring experts." In the *Fortune* article, Fisher (1992) says this is like a fire department made up of reformed pyromaniacs.

Mergers effected for strategic reasons can be beneficial to both the acquiring company and the company acquired. Strategic fit implies that the merger is synergistic and that the new, combined firm produces more benefits to the stakeholders than the two did separately before the merger. Most mergers based on strategic fit perform well and are enduring. Those that were formed to reap financial gain or to raid corporate assets have caused more harm than good. The use of the LBO (leveraged buyout) saddled so many firms with so much debt that they could not survive when the economy turned down. These over-leveraged companies just could not service their enormous debt.

As in all strategic analysis, it is important to examine each SBU and evaluate the fit among all those affected by a proposed merger. The methods described here can be used to evaluate the strategic fit between an SBU and the acquiring company. As we noted earlier, each SBU is similar to a small business entity. This suggests that a similar culture may prevail. Whether cultural differences can be accommodated and clashes minimized can make or break a merger.

CULTURAL ISSUES IN A MERGER

To effectively implement a strategy designed to achieve specific goals and objectives, it is imperative to put appropriate rewards in place. Rewards either reinforce or inhibit certain activities, depending on how the reward system operates.

A merger or acquisition attempt tends to drive up the stock price of the target company, and if a company is acquired by issuing junk bonds, the capital structure is changed. In these cases, although stock prices may rise in the short run, shareholder value can suffer in the long run.

Another serious consideration is that after an acquisition, many so-called "non-essential" positions are cut; some of these may be in research and development. Because R&D typically is a critical "life force" to many companies, cutting research and development can lead to the eventual demise of the company.

Conflicting corporate cultures account for much of the criticism of acquisitions and explain why so many fail. One large national consulting group (Selkirk) insists that culture must be considered because people often cling to ingrained values and beliefs about what they are willing to do, even when logical analysis should convince them otherwise. The mores, values, norms, roles, and relationships that define a particular culture determine the organization's ability to introduce or adapt to change. The ability to adapt is a key determinant of the success of a merger. Organizational culture questionnaires can be very helpful in analyzing the fit between two companies contemplating a merger.

The large-company mentality and structure can destroy the enthusiasm that makes high-tech and entrepreneurial companies so successful. The large-company culture demands management discipline, but the imposition of tight controls and red tape is anathema to the undisciplined flow of the creative genius. When the Ford team that designed the successful Taurus was interviewed on CNN (December 1991), various members of the team complained that the "corporate types," who have authority over their R&D activities, are constantly looking over their shoulder and interfering with their creativity. Members of the team said their enthusiasm, creativity, and morale are down and that they had recently been unable to come up with any new ideas. Under these conditions, morale declines and the dedication to be the best often disappears. In some cases, the affected managers just depart from such intolerable situations.

The introduction of *any* change creates anxiety and fear. When a major change is in the offing due to a proposed merger, fear and anxiety may cause high levels of fight, flight, or "freeze" (those who are paralyzed because they just don't know what to do). The result is that the change flounders in a morass of opposition, sabotage, neglect, and inaction. The company taking over promises that no one will be fired. Whether or not this is the acquiring company's intention, those in the acquired company who don't fit the new corporate culture soon take "flight," even when the company taking over wants them to stay.

The USAir takeover of PSA and Piedmont teetered on the verge of disaster for several years but is now beginning to stabilize. This takeover was plagued by a really bitter cultural war between USAir and Piedmont, which ended in USAir's firing 3,800 employees and closing the Dayton hub. USAir also closed out service to many smaller cities previously served by PSA. Piedmont had a relaxed culture, and the employees balked at the rigid and bureaucratic rules imposed by PSA. The result was chaos, canceled flights, missed connections, misplaced baggage, and hostile or nonexistent service. The outlook is considered favorable, but USAir has high fuel costs because of short hops with many takeoffs and landings. This makes

USAir one of the highest-cost airlines in business. If the economy does not improve, cash flow could cause serious problems and USAir's life might be short.

Smart managers generally jump ship before the merger or acquisition talks reach a serious stage. That is what happened at Celestial Seasonings when it reached $25 million in sales, and the departure of key executives put the company in a precarious position after it was acquired by Kraft. Celestial's managers were knowledgeable about the other company as well as their own, and they knew whether the deal would actually take place and whether the "fit" would work. They also knew whether they would be able to work in the new cultural environment. These managers had an early-warning "radar" that gave them the edge in finding the best relocation alternatives. Unfortunately, such managers are often the better managers, and when those at Celestial left, the company was without the managers who understood how the company ran and how to protect its vital resources.

Because of a cultural mismatch, six months after a merger, the exodus of managers heats up with 20–25% leaving; it peaks in the second year at about 35–40%, and then declines to barely a trickle after three years. On average, some 52% of top management personnel are gone in less than three years after a merger. Eventually, two-thirds to three-quarters of the managers find greener pastures elsewhere.

MAKING A MERGER WORK

To make a merger work, the decision makers must deal with more than the desirability of the merger (in strategic or financial terms) to the acquired organization. It may be more critical to the success of a merger to consider the acceptability of the change, in terms of cultural expectations, to those individuals who must carry out the activities involved.

Whether a merger is successful involves the following four considerations:

1. The executive who becomes the change agent
2. The culture, which reflects the change environment
3. The values of individuals whose activities affect the change process
4. The match between pre-merger values and culture and those of the new entity

The change agent is the key executive (often the founder of the company) whose values dominate the culture of the company. Such key executives determine the company's strategy in accordance with their own preferences. They expect others to support them. When the change agent is ready to make a change, the "team" needs to be to be ready to follow and support him or her. (See Chapter 10 for a further discussion of organizational change.)

The change environment is a second factor to be considered. The internal change environment reflects the corporate culture. It is largely created by the key change agent but must be responsive to the external environment. The "corporate culture" is immediately affected by actions taken at top levels of management. If the internal environment does not fit the needs and demands of the external market environment, the corporate culture can inhibit performance. And if it ignores the realities of the marketplace, there will be conflicts.

Rothchild (1991) has detailed one of the biggest financial disasters of the 1980s and described how Robert Campeau's decision style (he charmed, cajoled, and bullied with audacity and ego) was both an asset and a fatal flaw. Campeau was the change agent. He also determined the culture and the values of the company. The conflict between Campeau's values and culture and those of the acquired companies eventually spelled financial disaster.

The values and beliefs of those whose activities are needed to implement the strategic change constitute the third ingredient of the change process. Some values are so ingrained and may be so irrational that they seriously inhibit or prevent the implementation of strategic change. Another factor is the mind set of the managers charged with the implementation process. Managers who are not supportive of change often continue to carry out an inappropriate strategy even in the face of obvious problems and changed market conditions.

The concept of fit is also a vital concern. Gaining acceptance of a merger plan is critical, and it is often where a deal breaks down. It is not until the proposed changes are accepted, internalized, and made a part of the values of those involved that the merger has any chance of success.

For companies to operate effectively in a particular market environment, the internal corporate culture must blend with the external cultural imperatives. Over years of successful operations, a company tends to evolve into an appropriate fit. However, when the external environment changes enough to affect the way business is done, the internal corporate environment must adapt or suffer failure.

The sale of Microflat Corporation to Esterline Inc. turned into a problem for the founder of the small company because there was conflict with management of the acquiring company. The initial offer was fair, and the final offer included a five-year contract to the seller. However, after the sale the corporate office started interfering in management, countermanding orders and making life difficult for the former owner. There was a conflict that made managing almost impossible. After three years of valiant effort, the former owner of Microflat resigned his position because he was not allowed to perform in the entrepreneurial mode that made him successful in his own company.

Making an acquisition is often only the tip of the iceberg. Making the merged company a cohesive, compatible company can become a nightmare. Anthony D'Amato, CEO of Borden, is finding that acquiring good companies is not enough. Borden has recently acquired Creamette and Prince Pastas, Classico and Aunt Millie's pasta sauce, Eagle condensed milk, ReaLemon lemon juice, Wise potato chips, Cheez Doodles, Cracker Jack, Cremora, and Elmer's glue, which add up to $7.2 billion in revenue. The outcome in 1991 was a $72 million loss due to layoffs. Between 1986 and 1991, Borden spent $1.9 billion making 90 acquisitions, and it has the leading market position in six major product lines. But having made these acquisitions so rapidly, management was unable to integrate them and to take advantage of economies of scale. The result was a "patchwork of loosely related fiefdoms." D'Amato, as a consequence, has instituted a crash integration process that is beginning to pay off. D'Amato, who is considered outspoken and pugnacious, is spending 80% of his time visiting and grilling managers to avoid complacency. He says he won't hesitate to "make changes that will get the job done" (Lubove, 1992).

In many mergers, changes are too rapid, and in any merger it is impossible to make changes "by decree." Some people have a need for stability and tend to resist any change. They must be able to see and understand the value of the change. Trying to convince someone with very strong contrary beliefs is difficult. Recognizing that many entrepreneurial ventures will eventually be acquired, it is doubly important to develop strategies for growth and for making the new venture attractive to a potential buyer. Most of the approaches described in this text can provide the kind of support needed to ensure growth and to make possible an eventual merger or acquisition that is successful.

CORPORATE RESTRUCTURING

Mergers and acquisitions during the 1980s often were a result of "restructuring" organizations to focus on core competency. In many companies, divestitures become available for another company's acquisition. Figure 9.2 shows the changing emphasis in mergers from conglomerate to leveraged reorganization, which typically leads to corporate restructuring.

| FIGURE 9.2 | Waves of Mergers and Acquisitions |

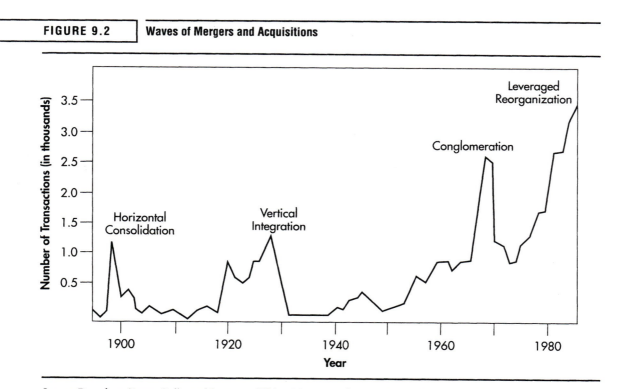

Source: Data from Devra Golbe and Lawrence White, *Mergers and Acquisitions*, University of Chicago Press. Courtesy of The Boston Consulting Group, Inc. Reprinted with permission.

Leveraged reorganization is beginning to pay off for companies that have used the process to become "leaner and meaner." Among other things, leveraged reorganization inspires strategies that cut costs, increase productivity, and boost profit margins. In numerous instances, poorly performing operations are sold or eliminated, and assets are redeployed to those with better promise of returns. This process has led to a boom in divestitures, mergers, and acquisitions. If management is not ready to make adjustments, an outside raider will come in to break up a company's assets and reduce the bloated corporate staff, usually to the benefit of the company's shareholders. The results of such moves are significantly lower break-even points for a number of companies and significant gains in earnings.

This kind of restructuring occurs in five partly overlapping phases:

1. Formulation of a corporate vision
2. Divestment or closure of underperformers
3. Acquisition search
4. Strategic valuation
5. Postmerger integration

These phases are addressed in the sections that follow.

CORPORATE VISION FORMULATION

The first step in corporate restructuring is to develop a clear understanding of the new direction the company wants to take. The key strategic question is, "Where can the firm gain a long-term competitive advantage?" In other words, in which strategic and market segments can the firm (1) maintain or create a competitive cost advantage, and (2) generate new customer values?

Figure 9.3 is a competitive-advantage matrix for the strategic business units (SBUs) of a large, diversified company. As the shaded circles show, several businesses had entered into decline and were losing money. Competitive-cost analysis quickly showed that the company had only four leading businesses. Some had irreversibly lost their ability to compete.

Through its competitive analysis, top management came up with a new vision of the company's position for the 1990s. This vision was based on the two types of successful businesses the company had:

1. A core of specialized businesses in the company's main fields of operation. These had good potential for becoming international and dominating the industry.
2. A range of fragmented and stalemated domestic businesses that could be sold as opportunities arose and the proceeds used to fund new businesses in the future.

DIVESTMENT OR CLOSURE OF UNDERPERFORMERS

Once the strategic direction was clear, the company's top management was ready for some fairly major changes. Within a single year, more strategic decisions were made and implemented than within the previous 10. Among other things, three major businesses were sold, despite strong resistance from certain stakeholders.

FIGURE 9.3	**Competitive-Advantage Matrix Showing Strategic Business Units of a Large, Diversified Company** (Circle size indicates size of business)

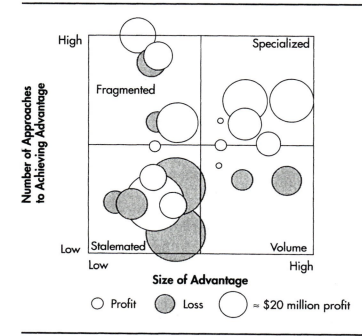

Source: Courtesy of The Boston Consulting Group, Inc. Reprinted with permission.

The result of divestment is shown in Figure 9.4. Now the business portfolio consisted mainly of profitable businesses with good potential for development. Two of the money losers were retained for their technology and growth potential.

The projection of sales and return on investments for the remaining business signaled a significant turnaround in earnings (Table 9.5). Sales growth, however, was severely cut by divestment. Therefore, the next step was to explore possible areas for growth in the new business structure.

ACQUISITION SEARCH

Having reduced the company to a few businesses with long-term profitability, management sought to acquire similarly focused businesses that had the same potential for sustained advantage. The most attractive targets were quickly identified and screened on the basis of

1. Their inherent, stand-alone capabilities
2. The synergistic effects they were likely to have if merged with the company
3. The risks of the merger

FIGURE 9.4	**Competitive-Advantage Matrix After Divestment: Same Company as in Figure 9.3**

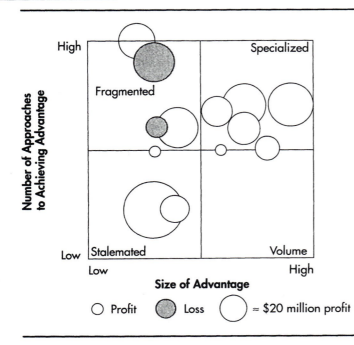

Source: Courtesy of The Boston Consulting Group, Inc. Reprinted with permission.

TABLE 9.5	**Results of Focused Portfolio Structure** (Dollar amounts in millions)

Indicators	Before Restructuring	Projections 3 Years After Restructuring	Difference
Sales	9,300	7,600	−1,700
Capital invested in operations	6,500	3,800	−2,700
Operating profit	−250	+430	+680
Return on investment	−3.8%	+11.3%	

This preliminary phase of acquisition is often termed the *strategic logic phase.* Its purpose is to help managers determine whether an acquisition makes sense strategically.

During the strategic logic phase, the company analyzed each candidate based on available data. Then each firm was ranked with respect to a number of criteria, including

Size	Efficiency of operations
Growth	International network
Brand awareness	Quality of management
Market share	Information and reporting systems
Profitability	Proprietary technologies and patents
Asset utilization	Availability of the firm
Leverage	

The next part of the strategic logic phase included identifying the synergistic interfaces for the combined businesses. These were broken down as follows:

1. Cost synergies
   a. Joint R&D
   b. Joint manufacturing locations and greater capacity utilization
   c. Joint marketing and distribution
   d. Joint administrative management
   e. Combined (greater) buying power
   f. Financing options/bond ratings
2. Price synergies
   a. Combined market shares; increased selling power
   b. Influence on the industry's pricing structure
   c. Segment dominance
   d. International roll-out potential
3. Other synergies
   a. Access to larger customer base
   b. Attractiveness to its own personnel

Finally, the risks of merging the two business operations were evaluated. These risks included

- Potential for loss of key personnel
- Potential for loss of market share
- Threat of competitive retaliation
- Legal issues
- Potential loss of image in the marketplace

The company decided to concentrate further research on the three best candidates in each business.

STRATEGIC VALUATION

During the next phase of acquisition, the *financial logic phase,* managers established what the company stood to gain financially. Each of the remaining candidates was evaluated with respect to its

1. Book value
2. Replacement value
3. Market-to-book value

4. Price–earnings value
5. Discounted cash flow (DCF) value

Because these methods are covered in detail in finance textbooks, only a simple application will be described here. Suppose that MPS was one of the candidates being evaluated and that the acquiring company was AMP.

AMP's 1988 book value, or shareholders' equity, is $2.8 million. To determine AMP's replacement value, its balance sheet would have to be audited and estimates made for particular assets. This usually is not possible until after an agreement has been reached—that is, during the due diligence period of acquisition. A first estimate should be attempted, however, because it helps managers to determine possible proceeds from sales of assets that will not be needed after the merger—particularly hidden assets, such as prime office locations or proprietary technologies.

Table 9.6 shows how a first estimate of MPS's replacement value was made by obtaining basic information about the company and its assets, especially its real estate holdings. This approach yields a value of the assets closer to $9 million than to the $7.8 million shown in the books.

The market-to-book value can be derived from similar transactions in the industry. If the average market-to-book value ratio in the industry is 3.5, then the market value of MPS based on this analysis is 9.8 (2.8 × 3.5).

Another method of valuation is to use price–earnings ratios typical for the industry. If the price–earnings ratio for companies comparable to MPS is 18, and

TABLE 9.6	Book Value and Replacement Estimates for AMP

(Dollar amounts in millions)

	Book Value	Replacement-to-Book Multiple (%)	Replacement Value
Assets			
Cash	0.5	100	0.50
Accounts receivable	3.4	95	3.23
Inventories	2.8	90	2.52
Property, plant, and equipment	1.1	250	2.75
Total	7.8		9.00
Liabilities			
Accounts payable	2.3	100	2.30
Short-term loans	1.2	100	1.20
Long-term debt	1.5	100	1.50
Total	5.0		5.00
Valuation	2.8		4.00

MPS's net profit for 1988 was $550,000, then the company is worth $9.9 million ($18 \times 550,000 = 9.9$ million).

Perhaps the best method of valuation is the discounted cash flow (DCF) method, because DCF "factors in" all future cash generation by the business. (DCF is explained in Chapter 8.) To arrive at the DCF, managers at AMP used

1. A financial pro-forma statement projecting MPS's future free cash flow. Free cash flow is defined as *net income* plus *depreciation* minus *capital expenditures* minus *net working capital change*. Because only a limited number of years can be projected with fair accuracy, managers establish a terminal value in the form of an annuity for the last year.
2. The discount factor. The discount factor is based on the weighted average cost of capital (WACC), which is derived as follows:

$$WACC = k_e \times e + i \times (1 - t) \times d,$$

where

k_e = cost of equity capital

e = share of equity in total capitalization

i = average interest rate on debt

t = tax ratio

d = debt share of total capitalization

Based on financial projections, MPS's cash flow stream can be projected as shown in Table 9.7.

If, for MPS, k_e = 14%, i = 12%, and t = 40%, then

$$WACC = .14 \times 2,800/7,800 + .12 \times (1 - .4) \times 5,000/7,800 = 9.64\%$$

Now the DCF value can be calculated as shown in Table 9.8. MPS's most probable worth is $9.975 million based on DCF valuation. Estimates of MPS's worth were fairly consistent—between $9.8 and $10 million—whether market-to-book value, price earnings ratio, or DCF value was computed.

TABLE 9.7 | **Free Cash Flow Projection for MPS**
(Dollar amounts in millions)

Computation	1988	1989	1990	1991	1992	1993	1994	1995
Net income	0.6	0.5	0.6	0.8	1.2	1.4	1.5	1.6
Plus depreciation	0.2	0.3	0.2	0.2	0.3	0.3	0.3	0.4
Minus capital expenditures	−0.3	−0.3	−0.3	−0.4	−0.4	−0.4	−0.4	−0.4
Minus net working capital change	−0.3	−0.4	−0.4	0.0	−0.2	−0.3	−0.2	−0.3
Free cash flow	0.2	0.1	0.1	0.6	0.9	1.0	1.2	1.3

TABLE 9.8	Calculation of MPS's Discounted-Cash-Flow Value

(Dollar amounts in millions)

Year	Free Cash Flow	Discount Factor	Present Value
1988	.2	1.0000	.200
1989	.1	0.9036	.090
1990	.1	0.8165	.082
1991	.6	0.7378	.443
1992	.9	0.6666	.600
1993	1.0	0.6024	.602
1994	1.2	0.5443	.653
1995	1.3	0.4919	.639
Terminal value	16.6	0.4919	8.166
Total NPV			11.475
Long-term debt			−1.500
Total company DCF			9.975

Note: Terminal value = net profit 1995/WACC = 1.6/.0964 = 16.6   NPV = net present value

Once the stand-alone value of a potential acquisition is known, managers also estimate the candidate's potential for restructuring and synergy. First, they need to estimate the cash-flow impact of the synergistic interfaces listed earlier. If, for example, AMP can absorb all MPS's administrative functions within its existing management structure, it will save about $1 million per year. The after-tax impact of eliminating the administrative functions on the free cash flow will result in an increase of over $7 million in MPS's present net value. If the cost of eliminating MPS's administrative functions were $3 million, the net effect of this synergy alone would be $4 million. Once all the synergies have been estimated and added, the acquirer can set an upper limit on any premium paid to the seller and establish a negotiating strategy accordingly.

According to Drexel Burnham Lambert (1988) to restructure or not to restructure is not the question. Nine out of ten executives are looking at restructuring as a way to concentrate energies and resources, increase efficiency of operation, and become more cost-competitive, thereby increasing the value of their companies. A number of qualifications are necessary to carry out restructuring successfully, including knowledge about mergers and acquisitions, leveraged buyouts, securities, and public and private fundraising. Restructuring is not for the amateur. It has to be carefully thought out, skillfully executed, and effectively managed.

Some companies have difficulties with restructuring. When in 1987, the word came out that Western Union would be out of cash in 10 days, Robert Laventhal, the president, threatened to file for Chapter 11 bankruptcy if Wall Street security holders called for a restructuring vote. For the previous three years, Western Union had survived a strike, losses of $1 billion, junk bonds, and then the October 1987 stock crash. Unfortunately, Western Union had few growth businesses and had sustained massive losses. A restructuring plan presented in 1986 was badly flawed, and the outlook for Western Union was dim. In 1986 Western Union reported a loss of $531 million. For the first nine months of 1987, the company reported a $17.2 million loss. Finally, the company had to attempt a major refinancing of $500 million to purchase and merge with ITT's Worldcom. The merger took place in 1987. The 136-year-old company's salvation came on the very last day of 1987, when debt holders voted to exchange their debentures for stock in the restructured company. This step rescued Western Union from the brink of bankruptcy.

Other companies have fared better. A successful restructuring was accomplished by TRW, which sold off $800 million worth of low-growth and low-return subsidiaries so that it could concentrate on its core business: automotive accessories and parts, electronics, and defense. TRW sold a money-losing foundry that made aircraft castings to Precision Castparts, which proceeded to turn it into a winner, with half the scrap rate and increased sales.

Although the cutbacks, spin-offs, and buyouts may bring pain to some employees, restructuring really does work (Magnet, 1987). Restructured companies are more competitive in the world market. In fact, restructuring is imperative precisely because of global competition. The theory that greater size leads to economies of scale and therefore to competitive advantage does not hold true if low performance and inefficiency creep in, as has happened in American industry since World War II.

POSTMERGER INTEGRATION

Actions taken immediately after contracts have been signed are critical to the success of a merger. In too many cases, the managers who prepared the acquisition move on to new positions or tasks, and promises that were made are not kept. Consequently, the synergistic potential of the merger is only partially realized. The following proven guidelines can often prevent these negative effects and ensure the success of a merger.

1. *Keep your promises.* The new relationship will sour if employment and other guarantees are not honored. The resulting decline in morale will damage the new business.
2. *Convey a clear vision.* The new management team needs immediate information about the firm's philosophy and about changes that are to be implemented during the first months after the merger.
3. *Demonstrate competence in the new business.* Displaying knowledge about and interest in the acquired business shows the new employees the advantages of the merger and builds their confidence in the success of the new venture.
4. *Provide sufficient resources for success.* Adequate resources include both funds and technical resources.
5. *Implement a new organization rapidly.* Integration of another business invariably leads to management changes. It is important to clarify the new structure and relationships between managers of the two firms quickly.
6. *Change the rules of the game gradually.* Integration should not result in loss of identity for individuals or the acquired corporation. The corporate culture of the acquired firm should not abruptly be renounced.

7. *Improve compensation.* Reductions in personnel usually mean more responsibility for those who remain. Better pay and more incentives can go a long way toward ensuring the success of the new company.

These dos and don'ts of postmerger integration demonstrate how critical it is to prepare well for this phase even before entering into acquisition negotiations.

Restructuring and downsizing are often viewed as a means of bringing new life to troubled companies. By abandoning declining products and focusing on innovation and new lines of business, many companies have gained a second life. Williams Company of Tulsa, for example, exchanged a pipeline business for fiber optics and landed MCI Communications as its major west coast customer. Goodyear had been the number-3 tire maker in the United States but gave it up to produce polyvinyl chloride, specialty chemicals, and aircraft parts. Although Goodyear lost $53 million in 1991, its managers agreed this was better than staying in the tire business. Chesapeake Corporation, known for production of wood pulp, gave it up to become the leading producer of customized cartons, store displays, and paper products. Conversion is not easy, but it's better than remaining in a declining business or in one where the competition prevents growth or profitability (Hage and Geier, 1992).

The problem with downsizing is the potential loss of qualified personnel and the resulting frustration, resentment, and possible disloyalty. Recognizing these problems, management needs to take appropriate action to minimize the damage. An approach called transformational leadership that was developed by Noel Tichy (1986) emphasizes people's response to change and loss. Losing middle managers along with widespread layoffs creates in the "survivors" a feeling comparable to the loss due to death or divorce. A period of mourning is normal and should be considered legitimate. Employees should be encouraged to bring their grief out into the open where it can be dealt with (Fisher, 1988). When contemplating a change, management should consider the following guidelines:

1. Make sure employees understand the new strategy, how it affects them, and why it is needed.
2. Those who must be let go should be given an opportunity to transfer, should be treated with kindness and respect, and should be assisted in any way possible.
3. Those whom management wants to stay need to be given reinforcement, a clear description of their new role, and an idea of what they might expect in the future.
4. Build a new culture that is responsive to the needs of employees and promotes the organization's ability to cope with the changing external environment.

THE SERVICE SECTOR

When one examines the relationship between gross national product (GNP) and the number of new businesses started, it is apparent that enterprise formation is alive and well (see Table 9.9). Even so, according to the SBA (Small Business Administration), one in every five new ventures fails within two years, and only 5% really take off (Pouschine and Kripalani, 1992).

	TABLE 9.9		Growth of New Enterprises

Year	GNP (in $ trillions)	New Enterprises
1970	2.8	22,000
1975	3.0	28,000
1980	4.0	49,000
1985	4.3	59,500
1990	4.7	50,000
1991	4.75	55,000

Why does U.S. enterprise formation continue to grow? In part it's the entrepreneurial spirit, and in part it's the individual's desire for independence. As one individual put it, "I got tired of forcing myself to go to the office." What is not obvious is that approximately 75% of the U.S. workforce will soon be in the service industry. This sector of the economy is often overlooked but in health care, for example, gross income is approaching 20% of the GNP (approximately $900 billion for 1992). Because manufacturing has been the focus of study over the years, the special needs of the service industry have tended to be ignored.

Linda Grant's recipe for the survival of the service sector is to slim down and work "smarter" (Grant, 1992). Although the service sector is approaching 75% of private employment in the United States, and manufacturing accounts for less than 20%, productivity in the service sector is a little over 105% (1982 = 100), whereas that in manufacturing is almost 130%. This condition exists despite the high investment in computers that was supposed to "slim down" information workers and provide support so they could work smarter. Unfortunately, the service industry allowed white-collar employees to grow without a comparable payback in productivity. Although it is clear that banks, phone companies, the credit card industry, and other aspects of the service industry could not exist without computers, more needs to be done to utilize fully the mammoth capability that computers offer.

A number of companies have risen to the challenge of helping to shape up the service sector. The need is overwhelming, as Connecticut Mutual Life found out. It was taking this company 2 weeks and as many as 30 people just to process a claim. Using specialized equipment, the same job now takes two people 4 days and is expected to repay the $6 million invested in just 2 years (Pomice, 1991). Among the companies providing support to the service sector are

- Octel: high-tech communications
- FileNet: systems to reduce paperwork
- Kelly Services: temporary work support to reduce overhead
- Telxon: portable computers for inventory control
- Medco Containment: mail-order pharmaceuticals that help reduce health care costs

These are a small sample of the "service" companies that can help the service industry become more efficient.

Without a strategy, service companies are likely to falter because they don't know their customers, competitors, and funding sources or how to use technology to reduce cost. What may be even more bothersome are the low wages and dead-end jobs. The percentage of the workforce that is stuck in dead-end jobs has been approximately 70% since 1983 (Schlesinger and Haskett, 1991). Most of the failures in the service industry are a result of the way the system has been designed. For example, Sears experimented with reducing cost by shifting to 70% part-time salespeople; the result was a significant drop in customer satisfaction. Attracting skilled employees is difficult because of limited opportunities for growth and low pay, which leads to a "cycle of failure." For example, Merck & Co. found that the total cost of turnover equaled 150% of employees' annual salary. In spite of massive investment in technology, the service industry has as many employees as before. Compounding the problem are foreign competition, deregulation (in the phone and airline industry, for instance), and the fact that the United States spends more than twice what Japan does for services and 20 times what Canada does (Roach, 1991).

For service companies to be successful, they need to focus on "serving" customers' needs while making the services more affordable. Shouldice Hospital near Toronto, Canada, has reduced the stay for surgery (5 to 8 days for the typical hospital) to 3½ days. Doctors perform more surgeries than at other hospitals at a salary less than what they could charge in private practice. Allowing patients to care for themselves whenever possible reduces the nurses' work load. To cap it all, Shouldice is 10 times more effective in eliminating the need for repeat treatment for the same problem, and patients rate them very high. Shouldice accomplished all this by segmenting the market so that it could focus its efforts (Davidow and Uttal, 1989).

There is considerably more psychology involved in selling a service than in selling a product. But computer programs and consulting service often can be considered as much a tangible output as a service. Developing a computer program or designing a system is merely a different way of providing a product. Some states include software development under "manufacturing" in their planning for improving the state's economy.

A service that is highly intangible is the "900" telephone number services that sell information only. There is no product; nevertheless, even this service is amenable to the strategic management approach. Market research is needed to determine how many people in various geographic areas would use a given service. There are laws and government regulation controlling this business, and there are opportunities and threats even in this environment.

NOT-FOR-PROFITS

Not-for-profit organizations often have the same problems as profit-making organizations. The differences are shown in Table 9.10 (adapted from Cornwall and Perlman, 1990, Table 13-1).

Although not-for-profit organizations may appear to be more ambiguous and less focused than profit-oriented businesses, Peter Drucker (1989) maintains that "the best management practices and the most innovative methods come from the

TABLE 9.10	Profit-Making Versus Not-for-Profit

Function	Profit-Making	Not-for-Profit
Mission	CEO or board of directors	Legislation or committees
Goals	Provide products and services for a profit	Serve community or constituents
Measures of performance	Return on investment, return on assets, equity or sales growth, market share, competitive position	Improvement in quality of life, improvements in community services provided
Need for change	Needed for adaptation in a competitive marketplace and customer needs	Population requirements, demographics, taxation
Control systems	Managerial and budget-based	Constituencies
Life cycle	Changes in organization	Reacts to societal needs
Government regulation	Responds to regulatory agencies and laws	Reports directly to political bodies

Girl Scouts and the Salvation Army." For businesses to become more effective, they will have to learn more about the way not-for-profit organizations motivate knowledge workers, achieve productivity, and work out policies and practices. The average American volunteer spends 5 hours a week at a not-for-profit. Thus these 80 million volunteers are equivalent to 10 million full-time people. Another way of describing this is to say that it amounts to $150 billion a year. For example, using a strict work program, the Salvation Army is able to rehabilitate 20,000 young criminals each year for less than it would have cost to keep them in jail.

The not-for-profits have to be more concerned about funding because of the difficulty in raising money. They also are less able to exercise tight control. Rather, the CEO of a nonprofit has to rely on convincing others by a clear mission statement with which they can identify. Making a board operate as an effective unit requires carefully organizing the work to be done and defining the board members' role in helping to carry out the organization's functions. The lesson for businesses that manage knowledge workers is that such workers need clear communications, role definition, challenging assignments, empowerment to perform their jobs, and accountability for results.

An interesting approach to introducing efficiency into the public sector has been proposed by de Conink-Smith (1991). With increasing pressure on budgets and slowing growth, ways are being sought to provide more value for the available dollars. The implication is that public-sector activities need to find ways to deliver products that better satisfy the needs of constituents (customers), especially in a competitive environment. A classic example is the post office, which is using technology to improve efficiency and is also being innovative to fend off competitors such as UPS and Federal Express. Smith estimates that a 15% to 20% saving is possible without reducing the level of service provided. Restructuring and better management will be the critical challenge of the 1990s. This can be achieved by a program that introduces "competition" into activities that have been "protected." Unfortunately, the indiscriminate introduction of efficiency or privatization can create serious dislocations and unemployment, which means it must be planned carefully.

Privatization has become increasingly popular around the world because it provides a source of income to the public coffers at the same time as it introduces deregulation and competition. This typically is not possible for natural monopolies such as the TVA authority. However, such public enterprises often outsource subcontract work to private companies that specialize in a given area, such as computers. Another approach is to make public entities more businesslike by

1. Separating the purchasing decisions from the political arena
2. Introducing business approaches such as strategic management, organizational change, and so on
3. Separating administration from operating roles
4. Introducing incentives and recognition for achievement
5. Introducing empowerment and creative problem solving

Introducing change of this magnitude is formidable, but the payoff can be astounding.

AN EXAMPLE OF STRATEGIC MANAGEMENT IN A SMALL BUSINESS

Strategic fit is a key priority in a merger, for growth, and in other kinds of change. Strategic analysis that evaluates opportunities, threats, strengths, and weaknesses and the way they "fit" is the first step. There are a number of methodologies that are useful in accomplishing this task. What follows is an example of their application for a small business.

The company, TTS (a real company, disguised), was in a very competitive niche in the textile industry and was losing customers, market share, and money. TTS had fewer than 100 employees, under $5 million in plant and equipment, and under $1 million in sales. In addition to standard financial analysis, the methodologies applied included a company capability profile, industry analysis, strategic positioning and action evaluation (SPACE), organizational culture evaluation, and decision style analysis. A modified Delphi approach and an in-depth questioning of each executive on the basis of the ten managerial roles defined by Mintzberg (1971) was undertaken. These roles were then compared to the roles expected of executives in their positions. (As is true for any case analysis, the methodologies used for TTS were the ones deemed most appropriate. Rarely are all the methodologies covered in this book applied for a given situation.)

INDUSTRY AND SPACE ANALYSIS

The annual industry rate of growth was estimated to be 3% to 4% and slipping. This parallels the general economic growth of the U.S. economy. There are few barriers to entry for new firms, and there is a high intensity of competition among firms in the industry. An increasing number of substitutes are being developed for various products, and there is a high dependency on complementary, or supporting, products and services. In most cases, the buyers seem to be able to dictate terms as well as prices. The degree of bargaining power of suppliers and vendors varies with the product but is not generally a problem. The degree of technological sophistication in the industry is moderately low. There has been very little (if any) innovation in the industry for a number of years. In addition, there are few capable managers available with experience in this industry. New management talent is not being trained, and young potential managers are not being attracted to the industry. Many managers in the industry who currently hold top positions are approaching retirement age.

The SPACE analysis indicated either a defensive or a competitive posture, depending on the general economic outlook.

- The *defensive* position would be suggested by a lack of strong competitive products and/or a lack of financial strength in an unattractive industry. The critical factor is the level of competitiveness. Indicated alternatives are
  - Prepare to retreat from the market.
  - Discontinue marginally profitable products.
  - Reduce costs aggressively.
  - Reduce capital investments.
  - Defer or minimize investments.

- The *competitive* position for TTS would be suggested by a moderate competitive advantage in a somewhat unstable environment. The critical factor is low financial strength. The indicated alternatives are
  - Acquire resources to increase market penetration.
  - Increase the sales force.
  - Extend or improve product lines.
  - Invest in productivity.
  - Reduce cost.
  - Protect advantages in declining markets.
  - Increase prices for products that are relatively "inelastic."
  - Attempt to merge with a cash-rich firm.

Which actions are recommended depends on what the company is able to implement satisfactorily. As an example, the ability to merge with a cash-rich firm depends on whether there is an actual firm available that satisfies the company's needs. Adding to the sales force would require hiring salespeople and training them at reasonable cost within a reasonable time. The expected increase in sales volume would have to justify the cost of implementing this alternative.

DECISION STYLES AND FIT WITH CORPORATE CULTURE

The strategic alternatives to be chosen also depend on the fit among the strategic needs of the company, the decision styles of the executives who will implement the strategy, and the constraints of the culture. At the first meeting with TTS, decision styles and corporate culture were discussed. Then the general profiles for the positions involved were drawn up and used to develop requirements for the positions. The ten managerial roles described by Mintzberg (1973) were discussed to determine whether the actual jobs of the executives conformed to the profiles commonly accepted. All the positions studied were very close to generally accepted profiles. In addition, the decision styles of the executives were very close to what was considered appropriate. Let's look at the specifics for several positions.

General Manager

The typical profile for this position emphasizes the analytical and conceptual characteristics. Top managers generally need more conceptual strength, whereas line managers generally need more directive strength with strong analytical ability. According to the decision style inventory, the profile of the general manager at TTS was a combination of directive and conceptual, with an analytical backup. The corporate culture profile showed that the incumbent had an appropriate fit. The following decision style analyses for individuals currently employed at TTS were performed to determine whether they were suited to their jobs based on how their style matched the job characteristics.

Operations Manager

The decision style profile of the operations/manufacturing manager was directive and analytical. The position requirements at TTS are almost identical to the general norm. The incumbent has a higher than average analytical decision style and a strong emphasis on the directive style. The culture in the manufacturing department emphasizes productivity. However, the overall fit indicates that it is flexible and able to adapt to what the conditions require. The incumbent needs to make difficult decisions related to conflicts among people and the financial requirements.

Sales Manager

The sales manager's position requires someone who is able both to understand customers and to close the sale. This typically requires a combination of drive and empathy and is reflected in a combination of the directive and behavioral styles. The job as described at TTS was a combination of directive and conceptual, with a low behavioral score. These results suggest that this job may need to be re-engineered. The decision style of the incumbent was consistent with what is required of the sales management position, where both directive and behavioral styles are present. On the other hand, a marketing manager's job would require a combination of conceptual and directive styles. This distinction is reasonable because the sales manager had been involved with marketing. There is currently some confusion about the distinctions between marketing management and sales management.

Marketing Manager

As we have noted, the ideal marketing manager profile is conceptual/directive. The marketing manager's job as described at TTS was highly analytical with a directive backup. This is due to the fact that the marketing manager was heavily involved in marketing research rather than marketing management. Marketing research requires a strong analytical component. The incumbent had an analytical/behavioral/conceptual profile and was low in directive. This may be the result of wearing two hats and of the emphasis on marketing research. The incumbent might have trouble exercising control and making the hard decisions necessary of the marketing manager. It is suggested that the functions be realigned.

Financial Manager

The typical profile for a financial manager is one that is both analytical and directive, with analytical being the dominant factor. The job description at TTS is identical to this requirement. The incumbent, however, has a very strong behavioral profile but is low in both directive and analytical styles. There is a backup in the directive style, but the analytical portion is very low. This presents a problem for matching the incumbent to this position. Immediate attention to this position is required. One solution would be to have the incumbent attend a quantitatively oriented program. This person desires to succeed in the position and has a very strong wish to please his superiors as well as his fellow workers. It is questionable whether this person is capable, at present, of doing the sophisticated analysis and making the hard decisions required in future allocation.

RESULTS

The company struggled to find a buyer, a company to merge with, or a source of cash. This effort was not successful. Two salespersons were hired on a commission basis, and reorganization of the financial and marketing functions was undertaken. Informal training is starting to show minor but encouraging results. The financial manager enrolled in an MBA program on his own time. Things are still tenuous, but the company has stopped losing money, and a small profit was achieved in the face of very poor and deteriorating economic conditions. Had it not undertaken this analysis and implemented the actions suggested by the analysis, TTS would have had to file under Chapter 11 over two years ago.

 UMMARY

This chapter addressed an important and growing concern in United States: entrepreneurship, which is one of our major competitive weapons in a global environment. The relationship of entrepreneurship to small business was discussed, as were the characteristics of the entrepreneur. Entrepreneurism is not only the style of an executive but can also be a company's spirit or that of a whole industry.

Growth often involves mergers and acquisitions, which in turn have a profound influence on the culture of an organization. Because mergers appear to be a normal part of the business environment, how to introduce organizational change was covered. Along with change, we discussed the corporate restructuring whereby many companies are divesting parts of their business portfolios, which often wind up as the small businesses of employees who want to be entrepreneurs.

Other sectors of the economy were covered, including the service sector and not-for-profits. Often a service business is a small or entrepreneurial business. And not-for-profit organizations have a similar need for strategic planning as other industries, a fact that is becoming increasingly important for HMOs and other health care providers.

REFERENCES AND SUGGESTIONS FOR FURTHER READING

Barnett, John H. and William D. Wilsted. 1988. *Strategic management concepts and cases.* Boston: PWS-Kent.

Bianco, Anthony and John J. Keller. 1987. The sad saga of Western Union's decline. *Business Week,* December 14, pp. 108–114.

Bird, Barbara J. 1989. *Entrepreneurial behavior.* Glenview, Ill.: Scott, Foresman.

Bloomberg Business News. 1992. U.S. losing technology edge, panel says. *Los Angeles Times,* August 13, p. D-1.

Boroughs, Don. 1992. Amputating assets. *U.S. News & World Report,* May 4, pp. 50–52.

Boston Consulting Group. 1987. Growth: The vital imperative. Paper presented at the Conference for Chief Executives, Phoenix, AZ. Summary of Discussion. Boston: The Boston Consulting Group.

Brokaw, Leslie. 1991. The truth about start-ups. *Inc.,* April, pp. 52–67.

Changing a corporate culture. 1984. *Business Week,* May 14, pp. 130–138.

Chip diplomacy. 1992. *The Economist,* July 18, pp. 65–66.

Coley, Stephen and Sigurd Reinton. 1988. The hunt for value. *The McKinsey Quarterly,* Spring, pp. 29–34.

Cornwall, Jeffrey R. and Baron Perlman. 1990. *Organizational entrepreneurship.* Homewood, Ill.: Irwin.

Cornwall, Jeffrey R. and Baron Perlman. 1980. Corporate culture: The hard-to-change values that spell success or failure. *Business Week,* October 27, p. 148.

Curtis, David A. 1983. *Strategic planning for smaller businesses.* Lexington, Mass.: D.C. Heath.

Dahl, Jonathan. 1990. Starting up an airline is not an easy process, even a one-jet outfit. *Wall Street Journal,* January 22, pp. A1 and A8.

Davidow, William and Bro Uttal. 1989. Service companies: Focus or falter. *Harvard Business Review,* July–August, pp. 77–85.

Davis, Bob. 1990. Space gamble: Start-up firm faces big risks in launching rocket from plane. *Wall Street Journal,* March 23, pp. A1 and A4.

Debono, E. 1969. Virtues of zig-zag thinking. *Think,* June.

De Conink-Smith, Niels. 1991. Restructuring for efficiency in the public sector. *The McKinsey Quarterly,* no. 4, pp. 133–150.

Deutsch, Claudia. 1989. A toy company finds life after Pictionary. *New York Times,* Business Section, July 9, pp. 6 and 7.

Diebold, John. 1990. *The Innovators.* New York: Dutton.

Drexel Burnham Lambert. 1988. To restructure or not to restructure. That isn't the question. *Business Week* advertisement.

Drucker, Peter. 1989. What business can learn from nonprofits. *Harvard Business Review,* July–August, pp. 88–93.

Farrell, Christopher, Michael Mandel, Karen Pennar, John Carey, Robert Hof, Zachary Schiller, and bureau reports. 1992. Industry policy. *Business Week,* April 6, pp. 70–75.

Ferguson, Charles. 1988. From the people who brought you voodoo economics. *Harvard Business Review,* May–June, pp. 55–62.

Fisher, Anne B. 1992. Deals of the year. *Fortune,* January 27, pp. 104–111.

Fisher, Anne. 1988. The downside of downsizing. *Fortune,* May 23, pp. 42–52.

Fisher, Lawrence M. 1990. Sun's rebound in work stations. *New York Times,* March 5, p. D6.

Flanigan, James. 1986. As U.S. firms merge, Japan's keep growing. *Los Angeles Times,* Tuesday, August 19.

Grant, Linda. 1992. Recipe for survival: Service sector forced to slim down, work smarter. *Los Angeles Times,* May 31, pp. D-1 and D-3.

Greenhouse, Steven. 1990. "A new formula in Hungary: Speed service and grow rich." *New York Times,* June 5, pp. A1 and D20.

Greenwald, John. 1988. Where's the limit? *Time,* December 5, pp. 66–70.

Greiner, Larry E. 1972. Evolution and revolution as organizations grow. *Harvard Business Review,* July–August.

Haberman, Clyde. 1989. For Italy's entrepreneurs, the figures are bella. *New York Times Magazine,* July 16, pp. 32–34 and 62–63.

Hage, David and Thom Geier. 1992. Corporate reincarnation. *U.S. News and World Report,* June 15, pp. 43–50.

Hamilton, Joan, Emily Smith, Larry Armstrong, Geoffrey Smith, and Joseph Weber. 1992. Biotech: America's dream machine. *Business Week,* March 2, pp. 66–74.

Hanson, Jeff. 1985. Meeting the challenge of entrepreneurial growth—CEO management style. Atkinson Graduate School of Management, Willamette University.

Harris, Roy J. 1990. After entrepreneurial studies, the real learning begins. *Wall Street Journal,* June 27, p. B2.

Holstein, William, Kevin Kelly, and bureau reports. 1992. Little companies, big exports. *Business Week,* April 13, pp. 70–72.

Jespersen, Fred. 1992. The top 100 deals. *The 1992 Business Week 1000,* pp. 65–72.

Kleinfield, N. R. 1989. Grace Mirabella, at 59, starts over again. *New York Times,* Business Section, April 30, p. 13.

Koff, Richard M. 1984. *Using small computers to make your business strategy work.* New York: Wiley.

Kupfer, Andrew. 1990. America's fastest-growing company. *Fortune,* August 13, pp. 48–51.

Kuratko, Donald and Richard Hodgetts. 1989. *Entrepreneurship.* New York: Dryden Press.

Lawrence, John F. 1985. A company's culture shapes performance. *Los Angeles Times,* January 27.

Liscio, John. 1992. The ABCs of GDP. *U.S. News & World Report,* May 4, p. 55.

Loss at Sun Microsystems. 1989. *New York Times,* July 29, p. 34.

Lubove, Seth. 1992. Pulling it all together. *Forbes,* March 2, pp. 94–95.

Magnet, Myron. 1987. Restructuring really works. *Fortune,* March 2, pp. 38–46.

Main, Jeremy. 1987. Wanted: Managers who can make a difference. *Fortune,* September 28.

Mann, Richard. 1982. *Relationship between the decision-making styles of corporate planners and other planning executives.* Dissertation, University of Southern California, p. 55.

Matusky, Gregory. 1990. The competitive edge: How franchises are teaching the corporate elephants to dance. *Success,* September, pp. 58–70.

McClelland, David C. 1961. *The achieving society.* New York: Wiley.

Megginson, Leon C. 1988. *Successful small business management.* Homewood, Ill.: Irwin.

Mergers and Acquisitions. 1987. *The elements of restructuring.* Philadelphia: MLP Publishing Company.

Merwin, John. 1987. Not the next 30 days. *Forbes,* July 13, pp. 72–80.

Mintzberg, Henry. 1971. Managerial work: Analysis from observation. *Management Science,* October, pp. B97–B110.

Mockler, Robert J. 1991. *Strategic management: An integrated situational decision making orientation.* New York: D&R Publishing Company.

Mockler, Robert J. 1989. *Knowledge-based systems for strategic planning.* Englewood Cliffs, N.J.: Prentice-Hall.

Nasar, Sylvia. 1987. Competitiveness: Getting it back. *Fortune,* April 27.

Outrageous! Master the art of everyday showmanship. 1992. *Success,* March, pp. 40–42.

Pentagon to cut funds to chip consortium. 1992. *Los Angeles Times,* August 18, p. D-3.

Perry, Nancy D. 1989. Shooting for the stars. *Harvard Business School Bulletin,* June, pp. 47–55.

Petite payloads: Pegasus puts into orbit the first of a new class of small satellites. 1990. *Time,* April 16, p. 62.

Petruno, Tom. 1992. Simple plan makes Sunrise Medical a Wall Street star. *Los Angeles Times,* February 27, pp. D-1 and D-5.

Pollack, Andrew. 1989. For Sun, a difficult world. *New York Times,* July 20, pp. D1 and D7.

Pomice, Eva. 1991. Shaping up services. *U.S. News & World Report,* July 22, pp. 42–44.

Porter, Michael E. 1985. *Competitive advantage: Creating and sustaining superior performance.* New York: The Free Press.

Pound, John. 1992. Beyond takeovers: Politics comes to corporate control. *Harvard Business Review.* March–April, pp. 83–93.

Pouschine, Tatiana and Manjeet Kripalani. 1992. I got tired of forcing myself to go to the office. *Forbes,* May 25, pp. 104–114.

Prokesch, Steve E. and William J. Howell, Jr. 1985. Do mergers really work? *Business Week,* June 3, p. 89.

Quinlan, Michael. 1991. How does service drive the service company? *Harvard Business Review,* November–December, pp. 146–158.

Rappaport, Alfred P. 1981. Selecting strategies that create shareholder value. *Harvard Business Review,* May–June.

Reston, James Jr. 1982. Genius hunting. *Omni,* November, pp. 78–86.

Roach, Stephen. 1991. Services under siege—the restructuring imperative. *Harvard Business Review,* September–October, pp. 82–91.

Rock, Milton L. 1987. *The mergers and acquisitions handbook.* New York: McGraw-Hill.

Rothchild, John. 1991. Betting the store. *Esquire*, November, pp. 104–113.

Rowe, Alan J. and Richard O. Mason. 1987. *Managing with style*. San Francisco: Jossey-Bass, pp. 189–205.

Rudden, Ellen M. 1982. Why DCF doesn't work. *Wall Street Journal*, November 1.

Rudolph, Barbara. 1989. The chic is in the mail. *Time*, July 17, pp. 74–75.

Sathe, Vijay. 1983. Implications of corporate culture: A manager's guide to action. *Organizational Dynamics*, Autumn.

Sauriders, Laura. 1988. How the government subsidizes leveraged takeovers. *Forbes*, November 28, pp. 192–196.

Scardino, Albert. 1989. The magazine that lost its way. *New York Times*, Business Section, June 18, pp. 1 and 10.

Schlesinger, Leonard and James Heskett. 1991. The service-driven service company. *Harvard Business Review*, September–October, pp. 71–81.

Schumpeter, Josef. 1962. *Capitalism, socialism, and democracy*. New York: Harper & Row.

Stevenson, Howard H., Michael J. Roberts, and H. Irving Grossbeck. *New business ventures and the entrepreneur*, 2nd ed. Homewood, Ill.: Irwin.

Tannenbaum, Jeffrey A. Entrepreneurs and second acts. *Wall Street Journal*, May 17, p. B1.

Tichy, Noel M. and Marv A. Devanna. 1986. *The transformational leader*. New York: Wiley.

Timmons, Jeffrey A. 1985. *New venture creation*, 2nd ed. Homewood, Ill.: Irwin.

Touby, Laurel. 1992. Hot growth companies. *Business Week*, May 25, pp. 89–90.

Toy, Stewart. 1985. Splitting up. *Business Week*, July 1, pp. 50–55.

Troubled Wang decides to file for Chapter 11. 1992. *Los Angeles Times*, August 18, pp. D-1 and D-4.

Tunstall, W. Brooke. 1983. Cultural transition at AT&T. *Sloan Management Review*, Fall (Vol. 25, no. 1), pp. 1–12.

Utall, Bro. 1983. Corporate culture vultures. *Fortune*, October 17, p. 66.

Western Union clears last hurdle for reorganization. 1987. *Los Angeles Times*. December 31, Part IV, p. 3.

Woolley, Suzanne. 1992. The top 100 deals. *Business Week*, April 13, pp. 65–73.

Worthy, Ford S. 1987. Accounting bores you? Wake up. *Fortune*, October 12, pp. 35–38.

CHAPTER TEN

The Leadership Factor in Strategy and Implementing Strategic Change

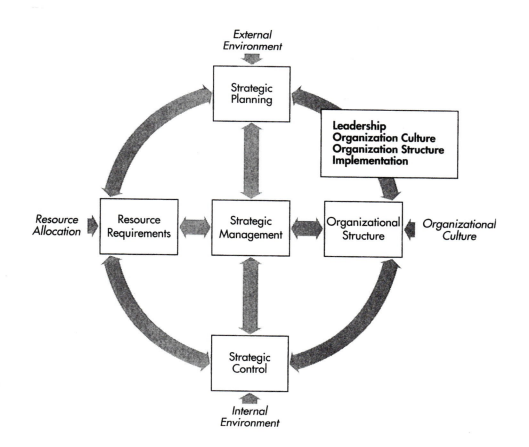

Chapter 1 A Framework for Strategic Management	**Chapter 2** Strategic Analysis	**Chapter 3** Strategic Visioning, Goals, Ethics, and Social Responsibility	**Chapter 4** The Competitive Environment	**Chapter 5** Capability-based Strategy	**Chapter 6** Market Dynamics and Sustainable Competitive Advantage
How to approach strategic management	*Application of strategic analysis*	*Understanding vision, values, ethics*	*Coping with competitive forces, stakeholders*	*Assessing company capability, timeliness, quality*	*Determining trends, gap analysis, and market dynamics*

Chapter 7 Strategy in a Global Environment	**Chapter 8** Financial Planning and Competitive-Cost Analysis	**Chapter 9** Entrepreneurship, Mergers and Acquisitions, Restructuring, and the Service Sector	**Chapter 10** Leadership Factor in Strategy and Implementing Strategic Change	**Chapter 11** Information Technology and Future Directions in Strategy
Assessing global trade, foreign markets, monetary exchange	*Preparing a financial plan and competitive-cost analysis*	*Importance of small business, entrepreneurs, restructuring*	*Strategy implementation, leadership, culture*	*Information technology, trends, new management*

INTRODUCTION

To remain successful, organizations must change with changing conditions. In many cases, the alternative is simply to fade away. Why is it imperative that organizations be capable of change? And how should the change be carried out? The answers to these questions are found in the material covered in this chapter.

Creating the kind of "learning organization" that can change successfully is a challenge and opportunity that confronts management. Global demands increase the importance of strategic learning in an organization, even though it involves doing things differently than in the past. Meen and Keough (1992) make the following points about achieving a "learning organization."

1. Large organizations have difficulty with learning that crosses functional lines.
2. The impetus for change should come from the people in the organization rather than change being imposed from outside.
3. The central task of management is the continuous building of a knowledge base that contributes to the learning process.

Supporting the concept of a "knowledge-creating company," Nonaka (1991) points out that Japanese companies have in place the organizational roles, structures, and practices needed to guide continuous innovation. Knowledge is typically generated by individuals who have gained insight into a problem area. The ability to develop new knowledge depends on the culture and values of an organization. Managing a knowledge-creating organization requires

1. Understanding the creation of knowledge and how it affects managerial roles and responsibilities
2. Continuously challenging employees to re-examine things they have always taken for granted
3. Responding quickly to customer needs by modifying existing products or developing new products
4. Dominating emerging technology by being able to create new knowledge

Creating technology is described as

1. Sharing specific knowledge with others
2. Combining specific knowledge about a problem into a pattern that leads to new knowledge
3. Converting this new knowledge into a usable form
4. Applying the new knowledge to previously unknown problems

Although creating knowledge can be understood, unless it is shared in an organization, it has limited value. Using teams or other organizational forms to work together on creating new knowledge that is shared freely helps lead to the knowledge-creating organization.

Creative organizations require a culture that helps to link a company's values and norms with its performance. Dumaine (1992) describes research suggesting that "the single most visible factor that distinguishes major cultural changes that succeed from those that fail is competent leadership at the top." This chapter describes the strategic change models that show the relationship of leadership style, organizational culture, and individual values (willingness to change) to the organization's ability to implement change.

In discussing basic truisms about leadership, Warren Bennis (1991) describes leaders as people who know the right thing to do. Individuals follow a leader who is consistent, even if they have different viewpoints. Bennis describes the role of leadership as empowering the collective effort of the organization toward meaningful goals. This becomes evident when

1. People feel important
2. Learning and competence are reinforced
3. People feel they are part of the organization
4. Work is viewed as exciting, stimulating, and enjoyable

Phillips (1991) describes Abraham Lincoln's approach to leadership as

1. Communicating your vision clearly
2. Being accessible at all times
3. Being discreet and never losing your temper
4. Building a team that can achieve results
5. Not compromising, but rather searching until you find the right person for the job
6. Creating a culture in which high achievers flock together

These ideas and others are covered in the section on leadership.

It is usually easier to think about things than to do them. As Vince Lombardi, the great football coach of the Green Bay Packers, once said, "The best game plan in the world never blocked or tackled anybody." It is for this reason that the implementation of strategies, policies, and plans is a crucial and very challenging part of strategic management. Consider, for example, the implementation problems that President Kennedy encountered in 1962. During the Cuban missile crisis he assured Khrushchev that the U.S. missiles located in Turkey would be removed, and several times he issued very clear orders to the military to do so. Nevertheless, as Kennedy learned later, the missiles were never removed (Allison, 1971).

The Ford Motor Company faced a slightly different implementation problem. In the early 1970s, Ford embarked on its "European car" strategy. Ford sought to unify its diverse product lines, to manufacture spare parts in the country with the lowest cost, and to focus its sales efforts on the most promising growth markets. Among the countries involved were England, Germany, Belgium, France, Ireland, the Netherlands, and Portugal. Ford undertook this strategy in hopes of obtaining the economy-of-scale advantages of the "experience curve," focusing its advertising and marketing efforts in a more efficient and effective manner, and eliminating the cost of duplicate facilities.

After the first several years of the strategy, almost *none* of these advantages had materialized. Instead, Ford ran into problems in integrating the differing levels of precision that existed in manufacturing, in standardizing on the metric system, and in dealing with currency fluctuations and exchange rates. Additional difficulties resulted from its effort to centralize paperwork and management systems in order to encourage cooperation rather than "back-biting" and price wars, as well as from its attempt to integrate the different cultural outlooks and views of the many diverse workers and managers in the countries involved. In short, a strategy that was grand in conception was thwarted in implementation. Even so, the European design now provides Ford with all its new models in the United States. Nonetheless, Ford has recently sustained a $2.3 billion loss, the worst it has had in its 89-year history (Woutat, 1992).

Why is introducing strategic change such a difficult problem? According to *Fortune* (Utall, 1983), only one in ten big-league companies successfully implements a complex new strategy. Is one of the problems that planners concentrate on the technical or financial requirements of change without due regard for organizational considerations?

What are the social dimensions of strategic change? For a strategic change to succeed, it must be accepted and supported by the people who are involved in the change. The style of the change agent, the values of individuals, the corporate culture as a whole, the structure of the organization, and the organization's position in its life cycle all affect the implementation of a change—and, in turn, all are affected by the change.

Strategic decision making involves a continued assessment of the current situation confronting an organization in light of the leader's vision for the future. One of the best illustrations of effective decision making is that of Jack Welch, CEO of General Electric Company. His leadership style encouraged teamwork and transformed General Electric from a ponderous organization into one that is profitable and growth-oriented. How executives like Welch make strategic decisions and demonstrate leadership styles is another important subject of this chapter.

Strategic decision making can be best understood by examining the factors that influence the decision and the individual who makes it. Here we will use a decision style inventory that examines how individuals think and process information as the basis for determining how choices among strategic alternatives are made. Both the mode of processing information in the brain (whether the decision maker relies more on left- or right-hemisphere processing) and the cognitive complexity of that individual influence the style of decision making. For example, managers who are planning-oriented in their decisions tend to rely on their "left brain," whereas those who are leader-oriented in their thinking tend to rely on their "right brain."

LEADERSHIP—THE FORCE THAT MAKES THINGS HAPPEN

In her provocative article "Will George Bush Really Change?", Dowd (1992) raises a critical issue in leadership. The American public is concerned about a lingering recession, the "Iran-gate" scandal, race riots, abortion rights, health care, unemployment, and the incomplete Iraq affair. George Bush claimed that the Democratic Congress was to blame for the lack of progress. President Clinton likewise has been confronted with a Republican Senate that has refused to go along with his stimulus package in what is called "porklock" instead of "gridlock." Clinton is faced with resolving the Bosnian crisis, job stimulus program, gays in the military, and lack of a definitive plan to reinvigorate the U.S. His ability to lead America out of its current miasma will determine whether he really is an effective leader.

SEVERAL EFFECTIVE LEADERS

By contrast, others who have a grand vision have been able to create an environment where change can and does take place. For example, there are "masters of the impossible" who break down barriers, recognize opportunity, exploit change, build teams, and turn problems into opportunities (Maren and Wallace, 1992). Examples of such leaders include Rene Anselano, who managed to break a global monopoly that was controlled by Intelsat for all international communications. He formed Alpha Lyracom/Pan American Satellite against all odds, including country regulations on communications. His break came when the Intelsat monopoly charged exorbitant rates during the Persian Gulf War.

Another example of a trend setter is Jack Welch. The CEO of General Electric is a villain or a hero, a rejuvenator or a destroyer. There is little question that Welch has a dynamic style and has made a flexible, lean machine of the once-ponderous GE. There is also little doubt that he has raised considerable controversy since taking office in 1981. He is noted for having made GE less bureaucratic. He has pushed authority down to the lowest level possible, while still fostering teamwork and expecting candor and trust. The results of Welch's leadership are unmistakable: in five short years, GE's revenues increased from $28 billion to $40 billion and its operating profits increased from $3 billion to $5 billion.

On his tenth anniversary, Jack Welch is again reinventing General Electric (*The Economist*, 1991). Now he intends to create an organization that is "boundaryless" by transforming its culture in such a way as to blur the distinctions among internal divisions and encourage everybody to work as a team. GE is a partner with its customers, and there is no distinction between domestic and foreign operations. The results in 1990 showed an annual growth of 8%, profits of 11% per year for a total of $4.3 billion in 1990, a workforce reduced from 410,000 to 300,000, and return on equity of approximately 19% per year. He fixed, closed, or sold businesses that were not number one or two in their industry. Over the 10-year period, he sold $10 billion worth of GE companies and bought others worth $25 billion. "Neutron Jack" has the reputation of being arrogant and ruthless, but he claims he is "hard-headed but warm-hearted." His leadership style would be described as inspirational and directive.

In an interview with Tichy and Charan (1989), Welch commented that insecure managers use complexity and clutter to distract others. Self-confident leaders, however, use speed and simplicity to achieve a transformation of attitudes that releases "emotional energy, encourages creativity and creates a feeling of ownership and self worth." This is consistent with what a directive/inspirational leader would say and do. Having a leadership style paradigm makes us better able to understand different leaders and to predict how they would behave in transforming their organization in terms of the vision they propose.

A very different style of leadership is that of James Dutt, the controversial boss of Beatrice Companies. At one time Dutt was considered easygoing and amiable, but he has become short-tempered and autocratic. At management meetings he shouts and demoralizes his executives. He is a driven man, who expects his management to work incredibly hard and to be absolutely loyal. Dutt's goal for Beatrice is to make it attractive to investors. In pursuit of this vision, he sold off profit centers that did not meet his standards. Yet he then acquired Esmark for $2.7 billion—23 times the price–earnings ratio. In an effort to make Beatrice the world's premier marketeer, he has so far made it bigger but not better or more profitable. Profits are down, top executives have quit or have been fired, and some describe Dutt's vision as a mirage.

Dutt's tight-fisted style of leadership eventually led to a leveraged buyout through Drexel Burnham Lambert for $8.4 billion. In 1986 the deal was called Drexel's greediest. Frederick B. Reutschler, the new president and chief executive officer, is attempting to reduce Beatrice's debt by using various recapitalization alternatives, including redeeming outstanding debenture bonds. Beatrice was initially hailed as the deal of the century but now is proving very disappointing because of its inability to obtain sufficient funds from the sale of a number of divisions.

Lee Iacocca is a person many people think of when asked to name a strong leader. He was able to turn the nearly defunct Chrysler Corporation into a viable entity. He claims that he was not looking for a challenge when he took over Chrysler Corporation and that the people who made the turnaround happen were not looking for challenges either. They did have the desire to accept new leadership that had the potential to help the company survive and grow. His lessons for success include the following (Iacocca, 1984).

1. Don't look for easy answers neatly tucked away in some ideology, because you won't find them.
2. Don't let the people with pat answers take over—they will always mess things up if they are put in charge.
3. Don't be afraid to compromise when you can't win, but also don't be afraid to dig in your heels when you think that you are right.
4. Don't be overly idealistic and miss the world around you; don't be so overly pragmatic that you take no strong stands.
5. Don't be afraid to make mistakes, but don't make the same big mistake twice.
6. Finally, don't let anyone tell you that you can't go up the mountain—you can if you really want to.

WHAT IS LEADERSHIP?

Leadership has often been characterized as the ability of management to create an environment that fosters commitment on the part of workers and that evokes performance beyond normal expectations. This has been called "transformational leadership." True leadership involves a complex transaction between leaders and followers. Zaleznick (1977) describes managers and leaders as having fundamentally different world views. *Leaders* think about goals in a way that creates images and expectations about the direction a business should take. Leaders influence changes in the way people think about what is desirable, possible, or necessary. *Managers*, on the other hand, tend to view work as a means of achieving goals based on the actions taken by workers. Thus leaders make decisions that are systematic and pragmatic in marshalling resources, designing organizations, motivating workers, solving problems, and controlling activities.

In his book *Mind of a Manager, Soul of a Leader* (1990), Hickman describes how managers and leaders differ. The manager is a person who typically is analytical, who prefers structure and control, and who is deliberate and orderly. At the other end of the spectrum, the leader (who is conceptual) typically is a visionary who is willing to experiment and be flexible, uncontrolled, and creative. Managers and leaders deal with organizational problems in a different manner because of their differences in style and perspective. Hickman claimed it is important that both be respected and work for the benefit of the organization. A leader tends to make a poor manager, however, and vice versa.

Zaleznick (1990) characterized the leader as the one who induces change and often is a disruptive force in an organization. Leadership inevitably requires using power to influence the thoughts and actions of other people and to develop fresh approaches and open new options. To be effective, the leader must be able to project her or his ideas into images that excite people in their work. Leaders who are concerned with ideas relate in intuitive and empathetic ways and arouse strong feelings of identity, difference, love, or hate. Warren Bennis (1976) warned that leaders may be a beleaguered species. He felt that to lead others, the leader must first know himself or herself. Further, he stated that "the leader must be a social architect who studies and shapes what is called the culture of work—those intangibles that are so hard to discern but are so terribly important in governing the way people act, the values and norms that are subtly transmitted to individuals and the group and that tend to create binding and bonding." Warren Bennis further describes leaders as people who have a passion for the promise of life. Leaders transform vision into action by harnessing diffused power to empower others who can then translate the vision into reality. "Leaders have to lead under uncertain, risky conditions where it is virtually impossible to get ready for something when you have to be ready for anything." Bennis identified the following dictums as characterizing the strategies of the 90 exceptional CEOs he studied (Bennis, 1985).

1. *Vision.* Create a compelling vision.
2. *Communication and alignment.* Communicate that vision to gain the support of constituencies.
3. *Persistence, consistency, and focus.* Maintain the organization's direction under all conditions.
4. *Empowerment.* Create environments—the social architecture—that can harness the energies of those in the organization to bring about the desired results.
5. *Organizational learning.* Find ways and means for the organization to monitor its performance and to compare its results with objectives. Access an evolving database on which to review past actions and base future ones. Determine how to restructure the organization and key personnel when faced with new conditions.

Bennis elaborated on these five dictums by identifying the ways in which they can be made operational:

- Make your intentions simple, complete, and easily communicable.
- Transform the organization into an integral unit by using symbols, such as ceremonies, that demonstrate leadership.
- Provide creative space for leaders to make their intentions aesthetically attractive and compelling.

James Zumberge, president of the University of Southern California, singled out three fundamental abilities of leaders, which are highly consistent with Bennis's observations. Zumberge says that leaders (1) see opportunities for change that are consistent with their concept of what the organization should be, (2) possess qualities that enable them to share their vision with others, and (3) know how to mobilize the power base needed to bring about changes in the behavior of others (Zumberge, 1988).

The headline in a *Fortune* magazine article (1987) read, "Wanted: Leaders Who Can Make a Difference." The thesis was that good management is no longer sufficient to tackle the tough problems confronting American industry in the face of new economic realities and foreign competition. In particular, the writers disclaimed the value of the rational decision maker who coolly prepares plans for growth and competitive advantage. Rather, the executive of the future will have to have a vision and the ability to inspire others to join him or her in making that vision a reality. The most important difference between the old-style decision maker and the new-style leader is that the new leader recognizes the need for change and then makes it happen.

Although the natural tendency of an organization is to preserve the status quo, the new leader is not content with things as they are. Whereas an old-style decision maker might say, "We've been doing it this way for the last twenty years and it works," thus adhering to the old adage "If it ain't broke, don't fix it," the new leader would look at the organization and see not what it is, but what it could be. In today's dynamic environment, anything that is more than a year or two old is probably in some sense obsolete. The skills needed to create and carry out a vision are different from those needed to keep an organization going. A leader is not afraid to change the structure of the company in order to carry out the new vision.

In examining what leaders really do, Kotter (1990) found that whereas managers are good at "controlling" complex situations, leaders are effective change agents who produce useful results. He describes leaders as people who

1. Set direction vs. planning or budgeting
2. Align individuals with organizational goals vs. developing organizational structures
3. Motivate employees by satisfying basic human needs vs. using controls to enforce performance
4. Create exciting opportunities for young employees
5. Develop a culture that encourages participation
6. Create a sense of belonging that values strong leadership

Others have commented on the question of vision. Langeler (1992), for example, describes the vision trap. He maintains that abstract visions can be too grand and inspirational and can wind up weakening a company because it lacks focus. Ultimately, a vision must satisfy customers as well as employees. Kiechel (1989) warns that executive vision can sometimes ignore the realities of experience and the demands of customers and stockholders. He questions the value of such lofty aspirations as being the best in the industry or making the highest-quality products. Unless it is possible to deliver on these visions, they may turn out to be no more than sources of frustration.

If the new-style leader is in fact unique, what are the ways in which he or she is different? Is it possible to determine ahead of time which people are most likely to be successful leaders? Decision-style analysis shows that leaders combine elements of the conceptual style, which gives them vision and creativity; the behavioral style, which helps them understand people; and the directive style, which focuses on getting results. Note that the only style missing (see Chapter 9) is the analytical style— the one most characteristic of the rational decision maker. What we can conclude is that leadership ability is related to the executive's personality and cognitive skills. In a study of senior executives, the decision style that stood out was the conceptual style (Rowe and Mason, 1987). Although conceptual-style executives have been successful so far, the question is whether they will continue to be successful in dealing with an increasingly complex environment characterized by the ongoing electronic revolution; very sophisticated and vocal pressure groups of employees, customers, and stakeholders; changing economic and monetary systems; and foreign competition. Their future success will depend on their ability to bring to bear other styles of leadership as warranted by the situation.

Fortunately, the decision style inventory is ideally suited to measuring the attributes identified above as leadership qualities. The fact that this instrument has been validated with a large number of senior executives creates confidence that it can be used to determine who has these qualities. To support this approach, a leadership style model has been developed that is shown in Figure 10.1. This model identifies the leadership styles associated with different change emphasis and goal orientation. As with decision styles, we have found that leaders exhibit various combinations of leadership styles.

Jeff Hansen's study of successful entrepreneurs clearly showed that leadership style, in conjunction with the phase of the organization life cycle, can be used to predict the likelihood that a particular individual will succeed (Hansen, 1984). The truly effective leader is the one whose style best matches the requirements of the situation. For example, Lee Iacocca needed both a strong authoritarian style (directive) and a creative style (inspirational) to undertake the radical transformation that was needed at Chrysler. President Zumberge, on the other hand, needed a more creative

---

FIGURE 10.1 | **Leadership Styles**

	Logical	**Inspirational**
Broad Goals	Analyzes New Directions Solves Complex Problems Formulates Plans Persuades by Reasoning Prefers Incremental Change	Envisions New Opportunities Introduces Radical Ideas Empowers Others Persuades by Creating Trust Relies on Radical Change
Specific Goals	**Directive** Focuses on Controls Achieves Results Takes Charge Persuades by Directing Expects Rapid Change	**Supportive** Tries for Consensus Facilitates Work Encourages Openness Persuades by Involving Reacts to Change

Goal Orientation

Performance   Transformation

Emphasis of Change

Source: ©Alan J. Rowe and Kathleen K. Reardon, Rev. August 1, 1992.

(inspirational) and considerate (supportive) style of leadership, because a highly authoritarian style would conflict with the cultural values of a university.

Using an approach such as that shown in Figure 10.1, strategic managers can match individuals' leadership styles to the situation confronting the organization to determine who is most likely to succeed.

STRATEGIC CHANGE

INTRODUCING STRATEGIC CHANGE

Before strategic change can take place, there must be trust in management on the part of employees. Farnham (1989) maintains that there is a "trust gap" wherein corporate America is split between top management and employees and that it is crucial to regain employee confidence. In part, the gap exists because management does not know what employees really want. A Harris poll done for Steelcase Corporation revealed that employees value respect, management ethics, recognition for contributions and closer, honest communications above even high pay, better working conditions, and benefits. Unfortunately, many differences separate employees and top management. When top managers do not hear about products, markets, competitors, operating problems, or creative opportunities, they are in danger of losing touch with reality. Managers need to earn people's confidence if they expect acceptance of and commitment to strategic change.

Could American workers themselves be at fault for the gulf that exists between them and top management? Not according to Magnet (1992), who claims that those who accuse American workers of being lazy haven't examined the facts. For example, the real gross domestic product (GDP) grew at an annual rate of 1.3% for the past decade and remains the highest in the industrial world. Thus the men and women who are employed in the United States hold their own against global competition. The culprits are managers who fail to channel the pent-up energy and creativity that many employees are willing to contribute to their organization.

There are two approaches that have been used for strategic change. The first is working with the people in the organization to achieve mutual understanding. This is largely an informal approach. The second is making formal changes in the organizational structure, culture, or relationships. Effective implementation generally requires that both approaches be used in order for the change to be appropriate and to be accepted by participants.

Globe Metallurgical, the first small company to win the Malcolm Baldrige Award, believes that to achieve strategic change, managers must be tenacious and must be willing to get some dirt under their fingernails (Rayner, 1992). The company has achieved strategic change through

1. A management-led leveraged buyout
2. Flexible work teams
3. A strong focus on R&D, leading to high quality and low cost
4. Following a high-value niche strategy
5. Tight control of quality

6. Continuous improvement of operations
7. Insisting on obtaining agreement from all employees

The transformation from an old-line metallurgical company to the new vision was a traumatic experience described as "trial-by-fire transformation." The change was led by Arden Sims, the slow-speaking CEO who used total quality management and flexible work teams to bring about the strategic change he wanted.

In order for a strategic plan to be successful, the organization and many of its stakeholders need to accept the plan. There are, however, individuals whose behavior is especially crucial to the success of strategic change. Most successful implementation requires active participation from the CEO and other senior executives in an organization. Top executives provide the power, authority, and resources necessary to carry out the strategic plan. Next, someone has to champion the change. This could be the CEO (as was the case with Jack Welch at General Electric), or it could be a junior executive who has the vision and inspiration and is given an opportunity to move the organization in a new direction. Finally, there are all the other members of the organization—production workers, sales personnel, office workers and the like—who must change how they work in accordance with the new strategic plan. Of particular importance are the middle managers whose expertise is often rooted in the old ways of doing things and who are in a position to control the flow of information and activities. Middle managers are often the principal source of resistance to change. The new strategy's champion must play the role of change agent and influence the behavior of senior management, middle management, and all other members of the organization. Participation and the effective use of authority are the change agent's key tools. These and other tools are used to obtain commitment on the part of all involved parties. As Drucker (1974) observed, "The best plan is only a plan; that is, it shows good intentions. Unless there is a commitment made, there are only promises and hopes, but no plan." Thus effective strategic change absolutely requires acceptance and commitment on the part of the organization's members.

CREATING CHANGE

In an era when people are often suspicious that they are being manipulated (in contrast to being motivated), workers face a battle of beliefs. Most people concentrate on a small percentage of what they are exposed to and exclude all the competing stimuli. Marshall McLuhan dubbed those elements in the environment with which one chooses to interact the "environmental surround." Unfortunately, most workers do not experience the "revolution in ideas, concepts, values, traditions, ideologies or human relations" (Ledford, 1991). Recognizing this lost opportunity, management needs to find ways to release the potential that exists in most employees. Rod Canion, Compaq's CEO and president, understood the need to achieve consensus in his organization (Webber, 1990). He created a culture where teamwork and consensus management contributed to Compaq's phenomenal growth. Compaq believes in a careful and methodical approach to making new-product decisions, even though it also believes in bringing new products to market rapidly. With a low labor cost and well-designed products, Compaq has enjoyed remarkable financial results. It has been flexible enough to respond to a market where new products often show up in six to twelve months. Considering the high-tech nature of Compaq's business, Rod Canion has a culture that fits the needs of his industry.

Four key elements are needed to bring about strategic change. They are

1. The *style* of the executive who is the change agent.
2. The *corporate culture,* which reflects the change environment.
3. The *values* and *beliefs* of the individual performers who affect the change process.
4. The *match,* or *fit,* between the values of the individual performers and the corporate culture. This match determines whether the change is acceptable and whether change will take place or will become distorted or blocked.

These four factors are shown in Figure 10.2.

THE STYLE OF THE CHANGE AGENT

The *change agent* is generally a key executive whose values are strong and dominate the culture. This person may be a founder of the company, the strategic planner, or any other key executive.

FIGURE 10.2 | **Elements of Strategic Change**

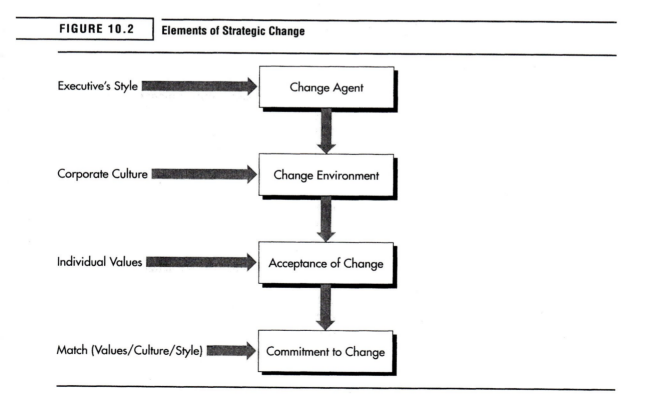

The founders' vision is generally so strong and powerful that others "buy into" it. This vision is built on a recognition of opportunities, needs, and requirements. The founders determine the company's strategy based on their preferences about the means of implementing what they believe to be in the best interests of the company. The classic example of such a founder is Thomas J. Watson of IBM. Watson created an enduring culture that had made IBM a world leader in computers. Watson's vision and support of people still permeate the organization. In his son's book *A Business and Its Beliefs* (1963), Watson is quoted as saying, "I believe the real difference between success and failure in a corporation can very often be traced to the question of how well the organization brings out the great energies and talents of its people." He also expressed the opinion that the single most important factor in success is adherence to "a sound set of beliefs."

Howard Schwartz, a vice president of Management Analysis Corporation, is actively involved with organizations that are dealing with changing culture (Sethia, 1984). He believes that if the chief executive is to be an effective change agent, he or she must place any new strategy in the context of the organization's core values and guiding beliefs.

When implementing a new strategy, the change agent should

1. Communicate the need for changes that will enable the organization to meet competitive forces in the environment
2. Develop a vision that can be shared by members of the organization
3. Determine what beliefs, values, norms, structures, and protocol must be changed for the new strategy to succeed
4. Make the CEO's office the focal point of support for the proposed changes
5. Ensure that the changed culture is reinforced and supports the new strategy

The success of the social change process often depends on the decision style of the change agent. An overly analytical manager will often focus on current problems without regard to the need to employ an appropriate change process. On the other hand, a broadly conceptual manager may be overly concerned with examining many options and involving other employees in the organization in the decision-making process and thus may miss opportunities or diffuse the means of bringing about a change. Once again, a combination of styles provides the best balance.

THE CORPORATE CULTURE

Why is it that intelligent, well-thought-out strategies are so often thwarted in the implementation phase? Often it is the organizational culture that prevents the strategic change from taking place. Indeed, one large international consulting group insists that a strategy cannot be executed without first considering corporate culture, because people often cling to well-established beliefs about what they are willing to do, even when logical analysis should convince them otherwise.

Heirs and Pehrson (1982) described stakeholders' collective and collaborative thinking on behalf of the organization as the "organization's mind." However, because the thinking process is different for each individual, figuring out how all these diverse perspectives can be brought together to produce a harmonious whole that will bring about the desired activities is difficult.

Corporate culture is the sum total of shared values, attitudes, beliefs, norms, rituals, expectations, and assumptions of the people in the organization (see Chapter 3). The culture is affected by the organization's structure, power centers, and climate (the degree of openness and level of trust and consensus in the organization). In his bestselling book on corporate cultures, Terrence Deal (1984) observed that culture meets social needs by defining relationships, specifying roles and duties, and establishing standards to be followed. Corporate rituals provide a means of demonstrating the values and beliefs of the organization and thus define the culture, the social interaction, the priorities, and the way individuals deal with one another.

Culture depends on key decision makers as well as on the history of the organization. Just as civilizations grow and develop their own cultures, organizations mature and incorporate the culture of the founders and their key executives.

Defining corporate culture is one thing—making it work is another. Companies whose cultural values have worked in the past include

- Hughes Aircraft, which had pursued Howard Hughes's vision of dedication to science and innovation
- IBM, where Thomas Watson's dedication to customer service was paramount
- ITT, where financial discipline demanded total dedication
- Digital Equipment, which focused on freedom with responsibility by emphasizing innovation
- Delta, which still promotes teamwork and customer service
- ARCO, which encourages action by fostering intrapreneurship
- J. C. Penney, which considers long-term employee and customer loyalty more important than being an aggressive competitor
- Wal-Mart, which follows a modern version of Penney's ideals

These companies have produced significant results in different fields, all by adhering faithfully to a corporate culture that fit the organization and helped it to meet competitive challenges.

When a change agent introduces a new strategy, it is critical that the culture be ready to lend support. The fact that the corporate culture at the top level is supportive does not necessarily mean that the entire organization is ready to pursue the same goals. Members of the organization who must implement the change are often insulated from the dynamics of the corporate culture at the top. Thus the corporate culture may be very different at different levels. The prevailing viewpoint at some levels may even be antithetical to that of top management. For example, union workers on the production lines may believe management is out to exploit them.

When two organizations are merged, cultures often conflict because their underlying values, norms, and beliefs differ. Drucker (1982) reported that from one-half to two-thirds of mergers turn out to be counterproductive or fall far short of expectations. In the face of such findings, why does merger mania still have a strong hold on so many corporate executives? The answer appears to be that the potential financial gains overshadow consideration of the factors that are needed to make a merger work.

As the following examples show, the sad reality is that many mergers should never have taken place.

- Reports indicate that Exxon spent over $600 million for an office systems company it acquired. What started as a great concept wound up as an implementation fiasco. Exxon's purchase of Reliance Electric, which cost some $1.2 billion, produced elusive benefits.

- When Honeywell bought Synertek, some managers of Synertek grumbled that rather than concentrate on the job, they had to spend their time haggling over resources. Finding the haggling culturally unacceptable, many of the managers left.

- North American's merger with Rockwell is an example of an attempt to marry the science and technology of one company with the commercial prowess of the other. The effort to combine North American's high technology with the cost-conscious market orientation of Rockwell has met with only limited success.

- After Wells Fargo paid $1.07 billion to buy Crocker National Bank from the British Midland Bank, the *Los Angeles Times* business headline read, "Wells Fargo Is Ready to Crack Whip at Crocker" (Broder, 1986). Given Wells Fargo chairman Carl Reichardt's relentless drive to cut costs, an estimated 19% of the Crocker workforce was eliminated over a two-year period. Ten out of the top 50 Crocker officers remained after the takeover, and as many as 100 of the combined 626 offices were closed.

A strategic change that is incompatible with corporate culture often flounders in a morass of opposition, sabotage, neglect, and inaction. Even if a takeover company promises that no one will be fired, those in the acquired company who do not fit in with the new corporate culture will soon take flight or else try to sabotage the change.

In evaluating or planning for a strategic change such as a merger, it is important to consider both how the corporate culture will affect the proposed change and how the change will affect the culture. Corporate culture provides clues to appropriate change strategies. There are many examples of cases in which the culture's norms, values, beliefs, and assumptions determined what actions were taken and how they were carried out. By studying the elements of the corporate culture and their potential effect on proposed strategies, a change agent can greatly increase the likelihood of successfully implementing a strategic change.

The various combinations of organizational values and orientations produce four types of cultural environments within which organizations function (Figure 10.3). *Organizational values* range from performance in a controlled system to achievement in an open system. The *organization's orientation* can be technical, and hence differentiated, or social, with high levels of integration and coordination.

An organization's values and orientation combine to bring about a particular cultural environment. For example, valuing the achievement of individuals leads to the development of a quality culture if there is a strong technical orientation or to a creative culture if there is a more social focus. When organizational values and norms stress performance, a technical orientation leads to a productive culture, whereas a focus on interpersonal competency brings about a supportive or cooperative culture.

| FIGURE 10.3 | Organizational Cultural Model |

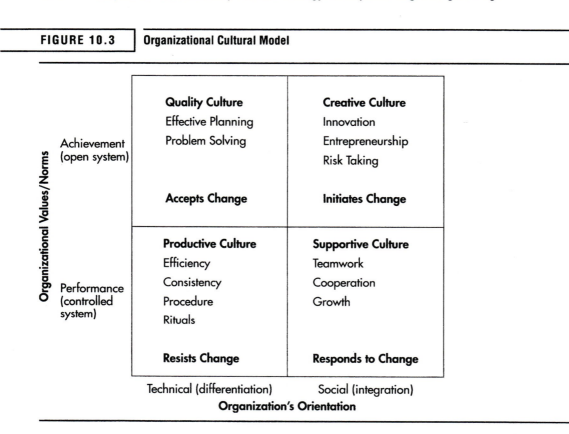

These four cultures have different characteristics. The productive culture concentrates on efficiency and consistency, whereas the quality culture focuses on the growth of employees within the organization through effective planning and problem solving. In practice, the productivity-oriented organization tends to employ many rigid procedures and rules, whereas the quality-oriented organization is more flexible in its approaches. The creative culture tends to be innovative and entrepreneurial, inclined toward risk taking. Change is most easily made in this type of culture. Most organizations would like—or think they would like—to have a creative culture. They may even go about trying to make change as though they did have one. But more often than not, they have some other type of culture, and the change fails. The supportive culture produces an environment characterized by teamwork, cooperation, and reinforcement.

Worksheet 10.1 is an example of cultural elements that are likely to affect the success of a strategic change at General Electric. The scores reflect the culture of GE in 1992. The first column of blanks is used to rate the culture in each of these categories. The importance of the various cultural elements depends on their pervasiveness, strength, and relation of a specific element to acceptance of change.

The second column is used to evaluate the compatibility of the proposed strategy with each of the elements as they exist in the present culture. A high score means that the strategy is likely to go in a direction that is consistent with that of the existing culture. This approach was proposed by Snyder (1984).

The four ways in which culture and strategic change can be related are shown in Figure 10.4. If the scores in the two columns in Worksheet 10.1 are high, the fit is supportive: elements that are important in the culture are strongly compatible with the strategic change. A low score in the first column and a high score in the second indicate that the culture is related to the strategy, so little attention to cultural elements is required. Low scores in both columns suggest that the change is inconsistent with the culture and that factors other than culture should be considered. A high score in the first column and a low score in the second signify a seriously constrained relationship between the culture and the strategy. The stronger the elements in the culture and the more incompatible the proposed strategy, the more difficult it is for the strategy to succeed. Thus Worksheet 10.1 provides a way of focusing on the elements of culture that must be changed if the proposed strategy is to succeed.

INDIVIDUAL VALUES AND BELIEFS

The values and beliefs held by those who are expected to implement the change are the third factor in the effectiveness of strategic change.

Values are the fundamental premises that we all use to determine what is important and what we believe in. They are intrinsic, deep-seated beliefs so pervasive that they influence every major decision one makes, moral judgments, reactions to others, willingness to make commitments, and support for organizational goals. Values determine what "really counts." Values can be so ingrained and strongly held that they can seriously inhibit or prevent change, even when the connection between the change and the values is irrational. Thus values must be

---

FIGURE 10.4 | **Importance of Cultural Fit to Strategic Change**

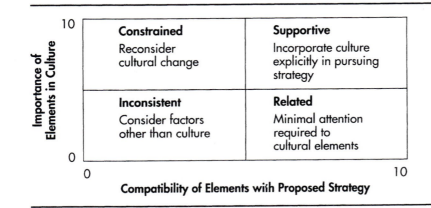

WORKSHEET 10.1	Assessment of Cultural Elements

Case   General Electric

Date   1992

Name   John Doe

Score (0–9) for each

	Importance of culture	Compatibility with strategic change
1. Founder's beliefs and values	5	3
2. Key executive's style	9	9
3. Maturity of organization	8	3
4. Cohesiveness and collaboration	7	5
5. Openness and trust	7	5
6. Climate of organization	8	6
7. Recognition of individual	8	7
8. Rewards for performance	9	8
9. Support of individual	6	5
10. Participation in decisions	6	6
11. Consistent communication	8	7
12. Enforcement of policies	9	6
13. Degree of social interaction	7	5
14. Opportunity for growth	8	6
15. Level of job security	7	5
16. Level of technology	9	9
17. Degree of innovation	8	9
18. Sense of belonging	8	8
19. Latitude in job execution	8	8
20. Sense of urgency	7	8

understood and dealt with to ensure commitment to a proposed change. Examples abound of cases in which strategies ran into serious conflicts with values. Ross Perot's shock troops ran into flak at GM when proposing change (Mason and Brandt, 1985), and in the end the company chose to buy Perot out for about $1 billion rather than change GM's culture. Culture shock also shook up the Bell system when it was deregulated. In short, recognition of potential differences can help smooth transitions and forestall confrontation.

When strategies and individual values mesh, the results can be impressive. Recognizing the importance of the social values of employee security, welfare, and happiness, the president of National Duplicating chose to emphasize slow but steady growth of a high-quality product rather than compete on price (Guth and Taguiri, 1965). Although he was aware of the economic risks, the president chose a strategy that fit the personal values of his employees. Unlike the chairman of People Express (see page 478), the president of National chose not to let changing market conditions affect basic values.

Acoustic Research has maintained a policy of providing high quality at the lowest possible cost to the consumer (Guth and Taguiri, 1965), in spite of pressure and unfounded claims by competitors. For many years Hewlett-Packard has emphasized concern, trust, and respect for employees. During a downturn in business, the company opted to reduce the work week by 10% rather than lay off employees. The result has been employees' unflinching loyalty and dedication, which has helped Hewlett-Packard maintain a technological lead. Tandem Computers is another company that has upheld values such as loyalty, hard work, self-esteem, and respect for co-workers. These values are reinforced by rites, rituals, and extras such as parties and jogging trails. Tandem still has a unique niche in the "non-stop" computing system arena. Sales have continued to increase rapidly; however, profit growth has not kept pace.

The importance of values cannot be underestimated. They go way beyond normal incentives or rewards in creating a hidden source of strength, commitment, and dedication. In a study involving nearly 1,500 managers across the United States, Posner and Schmidt (1984) found that those who felt that their values were consistent with the goals of the organization were more committed to realizing those goals. The strength of commitment leads to a sense of success and fulfillment, a healthy attitude toward work, and an understanding of the values and ethics of colleagues, subordinates, and management, along with a more positive attitude toward organizational objectives and organizational stakeholders. Obviously, values alone do not make the difference. But if the values of individuals match the strategy of the organization, a synergy is created that transcends almost any other relationship in an organization.

THE FIT OF VALUES TO CULTURE

Behavior within organizations and between organizations ultimately depends on the match, or fit, between individual values and the corporate culture. Management often must alter the corporate culture in order to introduce a strategic change. If the new culture conflicts with individual values, however, it might not be accepted. It is at the acceptance stage, called "the third level" by Sathe (1983), that the change process often breaks down. Not until the proposed change has been accepted, internalized, and made a part of the values of those involved can the change be successfully implemented.

If an organization focuses on conformity and emphasizes production and control, and if the individual worker is very self-oriented and internally focused, the result is likely to be avoidance on the part of the worker. This individual shows up for work but, at best, does as little as possible or, at worst, sabotages the strategy at every opportunity. If an organization demands conformity and the individual is externally focused, the result is generally a compromise. The person meets demands, but that is all. Internalization of goals and performance demands does not occur. Acceptance takes place only when the corporate culture is characterized by values consistent with individual values. When workers who are externally oriented are exposed to such a culture, the result is accommodation: they become committed, and there is goal congruence and support for the organization. The more internally focused employee working in a corporate culture of openness relates closely with the organization, and the result is identification with the goals of the organization and collaboration. This is the "secret" of Japanese management style. It works particularly well in Japan because of Japan's relatively monolithic culture.

Acceptance and internalization of cultural change is by no means easy to come by (see Figure 10.4). Even when individuals have shown unswerving loyalty in the past, growth, competition, or dramatic changes in the environment can bring about changes in the corporate culture that are hard to accept. Take, for example, the case of People Express. Donald Burr, founder and chairman, started the airline with his humanistic vision of a company where every employee would be an owner–manager. His most important goal was developing people. As revenues grew from zero in 1980 to an estimated $1 billion in 1985, Burr's goal changed. Mounting competition made it imperative that he acquire Frontier Airlines to meet the demand for a broader geographic system. His decision to install a layer of managers in what had been a lean organization disturbed the match between the corporate culture and the values and beliefs of the individual performers. Unable to accept the new culture, in which employees were prevented from asking questions and a humane style was replaced by a more autocratic one, employees substituted fear for commitment. People Express was acquired by Texas Air, Inc. in September of 1986 because the airline was facing bankruptcy (*Business Week,* 1989).

The final effects of the change in culture at AT&T have yet to be determined. Before the process of divestiture began at AT&T, Chairman Charles L. Brown started the process of culture change with a speech in which he emphasized that the telephone company had to satisfy customer requirements by utilizing high technology and applying advanced marketing strategies. The new strategy included starting a joint venture with a Dutch firm, Phillips, and reorganizing Western Electric and Bell Labs. The reorganization involved reassigning 13,000 corporate staff employees (Tunstall, 1983). The result was described in *Fortune:* "Waking Up at AT&T: There's Life After Culture Shock" (Mendes, 1984). After 103 years, suddenly AT&T's culture, with its focus on lifetime employment, promoting from within, consensus decision making, and high-quality service, was obsolete. The new culture emphasized the marketplace, lower costs, and a streamlined organization. AT&T employees are learning, and time will tell whether the culture will be internalized or will be replaced. The evidence appears to favor bringing in new personnel, such as Archie McGill, a former IBM vice president, to establish a new AT&T marketing department.

How did AT&T go about shifting to a new culture? It started by changing the managerial mind-set and then followed up by creating a new environment. First a new system of management was developed that was carefully related to the change in corporate values. Training was then used to create a new cultural environment consistent with the new strategy. Ultimately, however, the success of implementation will depend on acceptance of the new culture by the employees who will be needed to carry out the plans.

Today, AT&T is still forging ahead with the culture it changed in 1983. Having acquired NCR, their CEO, Bob Allen, is now pursuing the seemingly impossible dream of uniting computers and telecommunications (Verity and Coy, 1992). He had to battle a culture that was known for its turf battles, yes-men, and internal bickering. Building on a culture of teamwork, Allen considers this the driving force that will help AT&T achieve its goals. He empowers people by giving all employees a role in the organization and the opportunity to do their best.

Other companies have used a similar approach to introduce a new culture. In one organization, the decision to change from a low- to a high-technology company was made by the CEO and his executive committee, at the urging of outside consultants. The executive's decision style was clearly entrepreneurial—a combination of the conceptual and directive styles. The culture of the company was primarily production-oriented, with cost, delivery, and availability being dominant objectives. To change the cultural environment, a combination of approaches was used. Training was provided to help personnel understand the strategic change and the management systems that would be needed to support it. In addition, a major reorganization was undertaken, which involved shifting individuals to new responsibilities, hiring technically qualified personnel, and establishing an R&D lab. The development of new, higher-technology products required putting the company's resources on the line. The payoff was a new strategic direction and a changed cultural environment in which the focus had shifted from daily shipments to new-product development.

Changing culture is tantamount to asking a person who is mean to become friendly. More often than not, changing a culture requires bringing in a new team that does not have entrenched habits that are hard to break. What a leader does is develop a sense of loyalty based on three factors (Sashkin, 1990): compliance (where reward and punishment are used), identification (where employees psychologically find that they identify with the leader's characteristics), and internalization (where employees endorse the leader's values and accept them as their own). The outcome is a sense of loyalty that is a natural consequence of transformational leadership, an "unwritten contract" in which employees and management share common goals.

The survival of U.S. companies depends on their ability to change strategy to meet the new challenges as markets and competition become more global in nature. In making changes, however, management must take into account the fit between the values and beliefs of the individuals affected and the new cultural environment. Learning about and adapting to all types of individuals on a global scale will help managers deal more effectively with the diversity that exists in America. Only if a match can be made between individual values and the culture of the organization will proposed changes work smoothly.

In addition to working directly with people to change their behavior, implementing strategic change also requires designing and managing *systems* to achieve effective integration of people, structures, processes, and resources. As Miesing (1984) has found, successful implementation of strategies requires the right organizational structure, resource allocation, and compensation programs. These formal methods include policies, programs, budgets, procedures, and information systems.

Policies are broad guidelines for the behavior of the organization's members and are intended to ensure that the organization achieves its stated objectives. They include guides to decision making and rules to follow in various situations. A discount store, for example, may have the policy "We are never undersold." Policies about hours, advertising, and reporting may also be established for the purpose of securing the desired change within the organization.

Programs are specifications of activities or steps needed to accomplish some aspect of the overall plan. Frito-Lay, for example, embarked on a multi-product-line strategy during the early 1980s. It changed its investment policy so that a new product needed to have an annual market potential of only about $10 million instead of $100–$500 million. Consistent with these strategies and policies, Frito's management developed advertising and promotion programs for each of its product lines, such as the new sour-cream-flavored Lay's potato chips. Among the most important policies are those that specify how people will be rewarded and paid for their contributions. These compensation and incentive policies must be consistent with the demands of the strategy.

Budgets detail the allocation of the organization's resources to particular activities and programs. They are statements of the organization's operational plans and programs, expressed in dollars or sometimes in terms of the assignment of people and assets to tasks. Every Frito-Lay product has an advertising budget.

Procedures consist of a detailed, usually step-by-step, set of actions required to carry out a day-to-day task. They are sometimes called standard operating procedures, or SOPs. Frito has very precise steps that each of its 10,000 route sales representatives are to follow in displaying individual bags of chips in a retail customer's store so that sales potential is maximized. These procedures are coordinated with the advertising programs.

Information is the glue that holds a strategy together. *Information systems* are required to inform members of the strategies, policies, programs, and plans to be followed; to provide the data that members need to make decisions and take appropriate actions; and to track and measure performance. If a strategy is to be implemented successfully, the organization's information system must be designed and operated in such a way as to get the right information to the right people at the right time. Policies, programs, budgets, procedures, and information systems are all executed within the context and constraints of the organization's structure.

LOGICAL INCREMENTALISM AND INTRAPRENEURSHIP

Logical incrementalism and intrapreneurship are two alternative approaches that have been proposed for introducing strategic change. *Logical incrementalism* is an alternative to the rational-analytical process that is often suggested by formal planning systems. In real life, the strategic planning process is typically fragmented and evolutionary and is often based on intuition or dearly held beliefs. Quinn (1978) claimed that the support for an evolving strategy that generates widely shared consensus among key top executives is so strong that logical incrementalism provides a more realistic description of the planning process than does the step-by-step approach generally proposed.

Logical incrementalism incorporates crucial organizational and behavioral factors into the process of strategy formulation. Multiple goal structures, politics, bargaining, negotiation, and coalitions all enter into the choice of particular substrategies for dealing with specific issues. Decisions on each issue, such as acquisitions, reorganization, or new-product development, blend incrementally and opportunistically to create a cohesive pattern that ultimately becomes the organization's strategy. The overall strategy thus is developed after, not before, the substrategies. Because the organization has only a limited ability to link all of the major considerations and factors that need to be taken into account when a strategy is developed, logical incrementalism facilitates the integration of both formal analytical and behavioral aspects of strategy.

Clearly, assessment of internal capabilities or strengths, forecasts of future conditions, analysis of competitors' actions, and identification of performance gaps are at best tenuous. Communicating assumptions, integrating divisional and corporate plans, taking politics into account, and providing the means for implementing strategy and measuring performance are equally difficult. It is small wonder, therefore, that effective strategies tend to *emerge* rather than springing full-blown from the mind of the executive. Logical incrementalism allows the organization to respond continuously to changing environmental conditions and to do so in a way that builds cohesion and commitment. At the same time, it in no way precludes the use of the relevant information or appropriate analyses necessary to determine which strategy to pursue.

Change also can be brought about by fostering what is presently called *intrapreneurship*—that is, entrepreneurial behavior "inside" the organization. A focus on intrapreneurship shifts the emphasis from planning to fostering innovation and productivity. The actual changes are introduced by the people responsible for carrying out specific strategic decisions.

IBM's move into the personal computer market is a case in point. The company broke with all previous traditions by establishing a separate development group that was allowed to function like a startup company. The IBM parent organization acted as a venture capitalist, providing guidance, money, and a building in Boca Raton, Florida. The building was not swank—it was a converted warehouse with few windows, a leaky roof, and malfunctioning air conditioning. Don Estridge, a go-getting entrepreneurial type, was put in charge. Under his direction, design team members were allowed to work on their own, with only quarterly corporate reviews. With this freedom and under these spartan conditions, working 80 to 100 hours a week, they were able to bring out their product, the IBM PC, on time. They opted not to use proprietary electronic circuitry—a move hitherto unheard of at IBM—and settled on the Intel microprocessor as the heart of the system. They also went to outside vendors for the software programs and used over 800 retailers, such as Computerland and Sears, to market the PC. A highly automated factory kept costs low, enabling them to pursue an aggressive pricing policy. Because IBM allowed Don Estridge and his PC team to operate in an entrepreneurial mode, without having to worry about corporate policy or the fit with other IBM product lines, IBM became a dominant factor in the PC market in less than a year.

The tried and true ways of pursuing new developments are not always the best. By giving employees the freedom to pursue their own ideas, management can achieve the desired innovation and at the same time provide opportunity and challenge to valued employees.

IMPLEMENTATION OF STRATEGY

Implementation is one of the most critical components of strategic management. A strategy that is not implemented is no strategy at all. In fact, as Thomas Bonoma has observed, good execution may save a poor strategy, whereas poor implementation ensures trouble or failure regardless of how appropriately the strategy has been formulated (Bonoma, 1984). Although implementation is covered here among the last steps in the strategic management process, the astute manager starts thinking about implementation at the very outset of strategy development. Each step in strategy formulation, evaluation, and choice should be undertaken with the implementation requirements clearly in mind.

Judson (1966), in *Manager's Guide to Making Changes,* delineated five phases of managerial action necessary to implement change:

1. Analyzing and planning the change
2. Communicating about the change
3. Gaining acceptance of the required changes in behavior
4. Making the initial transition from the status quo to the new situation
5. Consolidating the new conditions and continuing to follow up

Gibson, Ivancevich, and Donnelly (1988) elaborate on these phases as follows:

1. Examine the internal and external forces that require a change.
2. Diagnose the reasons for change.
3. Determine an appropriate intervention to introduce the change.
4. Examine the constraints and limitations that may inhibit change.
5. Identify the performance objectives and outcomes.
6. Apply methods (such as those suggested by Judson) to implement the change.
7. Provide means for evaluating the effectiveness of implementation and feedback mechanisms to correct the implementation if required.

The ideal in strategic implementation is to reach a state in which everyone in the organization understands what she or he is to do and why. This is the state of mutual understanding. Although it is the only state in which implementation can be secured for an extended period of time, few organizations fully achieve it. Generally speaking, there are four possible relationships that can exist between strategic managers and those they plan for (see Figure 10.5). These relationships depend on how well the managers understand the needs, wants, and capabilities of the organization's members and on how well the members understand the goals, objectives, tasks, and assumptions of the plan.

Managers can either make an effort to understand the members or not. Members can either be encouraged to understand the plan or not. This results in four possible outcomes. If the managers do not understand the members and the members do not understand the plan, then they are acting at cross purposes. Managers can attempt to implement the plan by fiat, drawing on their authority, but this approach is unlikely to succeed. (It is, in large measure, what happened to Ford's European car plan.) If, on the other hand, the managers understand the members but the members do not understand the plan, the managers must sell the plan to the members and motivate them by means of rewards and incentives. Because the members do not understand the reasons for the plan, however, it is

---

FIGURE 10.5 | **Understanding Strategic Change**

	Members do not understand the plan.	Members do understand the plan.
Managers do not understand the members' needs, wants, and abilities.	**Failed Implementation** Power and authority are the only available approaches.	**Partial Implementation** Participation and education are possible approaches.
Managers do understand the members' needs, wants, and abilities.	**Partial Implementation** Motivation and selling are possible approaches.	**Full Implementation** Requires full use of the social change process.

unlikely that the plan will be fully implemented or that the organization will achieve its maximum potential. If the managers do not understand the members but the members are educated to understand the plan and its underlying assumptions—a condition reached because of the participation and education activities that the organization has engaged in—some of the plan will be implemented and some of the organization's potential may be realized. The U.S. military officers who let Kennedy's orders get "stalled" in red tape understood the directive perfectly. They just didn't believe in its assumptions and objectives. At the time, Kennedy did not understand how to get orders carried out effectively within the military establishment. The only way to ensure full realization of an organization's potential is for its managers to understand its members well and for the organization's members to understand and believe in the plan fully. This involves the coordinated use of research, education, participation, motivation, and authority. One of the reasons why Wal-Mart has been so successful is that all its members understand the reasons behind the company's creed, its policies, and its plans. Reaching this level of mutual understanding requires the use of a social change process.

Social change is a key element of implementation. There are very few instances where introducing a strategy does not involve changing the social system. Yet managers become so concerned with the economic aspects of strategy that they fail to see that it requires changes in the social system as well. Organizations are composed of people, and unless the manager can introduce a strategy in a way that leads people to accept and support it, the strategy may be doomed to failure.

Thus social change must be considered part of any strategic change. The phases in implementing a strategy should include

- Determining what social change is required for a proposed strategy and then introducing that change.
- Obtaining commitment to the change.
- Carrying out the implementation, utilizing managerial controls that balance behavioral and technical requirements to achieve specified objectives. This phase often requires re-evaluation of the original strategy or its adaptation to new environmental demands. Management may have to engage in many "unfreezing, changing, and refreezing" cycles over several years. How is the strategic manager to make these choices? The social change model has been designed to help in this difficult but exceedingly important undertaking.

A method for carrying out the social change process is presented in Appendix A.

ORGANIZATIONAL STRUCTURE AND STRATEGY

Present-day approaches to relating strategy and organizational structure evolved from two important efforts. The first was Chandler's (1962) study on strategy and structure, based on an analysis of four of the largest U.S. corporations: Sears Roebuck, General Motors, Standard Oil, and DuPont. He found that strategy determines structure and that environmental changes result in strategic options, which may, in turn, necessitate changes in organizational structure.

Later, Lawrence and Lorsch (1967), in their empirical work on organization and environment, examined differentiation and integration in three different types of industries. *Differentiation* implies breaking organizational units and functions apart and distributing them throughout the organization. *Integration* brings them back together again so that they are coordinated and unified. The amount of differentiation in an organization influences the way people are oriented toward goals and time, the role of interpersonal relationships, and the degree of formality of the organizational structure. The extent of integration affects the degree of collaboration and the mode of communication among departments with respect to common projects.

Lawrence and Lorsch found that the appropriate degrees of differentiation and integration were contingent on the organization's environment. In turbulent environments, successful companies tended to be both highly differentiated and highly integrated (a finding also reflected in Peters and Waterman's simultaneous "loose–tight" properties).

In stable environments, however, far less differentiation was needed and lower levels of integration were utilized.

In general, four factors determine the amount of differentiation needed. These are

1. The degree of certainty of the information used. Manufacturing would typically have well-defined information, whereas a market research department would be likely to utilize rather uncertain information.
2. The importance of rapid response.
3. The functions of the unit and the stakeholders with whom it interacts. Units with broad goals or objectives typically require less specialization than do those that focus on specific areas of the organization's environment.
4. The decision style of key executives. Decision styles determine the type of response to the manner in which the organization is structured.

Integration coordinates diverse groups within an organization. The factors that determine the amount of integration needed are similar to those that determine the appropriate degree of differentiation: the level of certainty, the response required, the goals that need to be met, and the orientation of the managers.

In many organizations it is necessary to differentiate activities and at the same time to provide for integration. Both processes have to be considered in dealing with the inevitable conflicts that arise in the process of formulating a strategy and designing a structure to carry it out.

Mintzberg (1979) developed a taxonomy of organizational structures, which include

1. Entrepreneurial structures
2. Bureaucratic structures
3. Divisional structures
4. Matrix structures

In addition to the four categories developed by Mintzberg, an intermediate structure, the strategic business unit (SBU), is often used as the basis for developing strategic plans. We will review all five organizational forms here to determine their strategic requirements.

ENTREPRENEURIAL STRUCTURE

A formal organizational chart or structure is typically nonexistent or of little consequence in an entrepreneurial firm.

The principal advantages of such an organization are that

- It permits maximum opportunity for flexibility and innovation.
- It allows rapid response to a startup situation.
- It permits initiative and informality.

The principal disadvantages are that

- The organization is critically dependent on the president.
- Employees must be very flexible and willing to assume multiple responsibilities.
- Nonspecialization may lead to inefficiencies in operation and lack of responsibility.

BUREAUCRATIC STRUCTURE

As a company evolves from the introductory stages of its life cycle to the growth stage, the organization is often formalized into a centralized structure. This type of structure is referred to as a bureaucratic, or *functional*, form of organization.

The principal advantages of the bureaucratic form of organization are that

- It provides centralized control of policies and procedures.
- It requires specialized knowledge on the part of each functional manager.
- If each functional area is staffed and managed effectively, product opportunities receive more thorough analysis.

The principal disadvantages are that

- Problems of functional coordination often occur.
- Overspecialization may result.
- Tight control may stifle creativity.
- An overload is often forced on the chief executive.

The functional form of organization requires effective leadership and integration by the chief executive. Coordination at the strategic level is needed to offset a tendency for one or more functional areas to dominate the company. The chief executive must provide the long-term focus, because the individual managers of functional areas are not likely to possess an integrated view of the firm.

DIVISIONAL STRUCTURE

In *decentralized,* or divisional, organizational structure, each division manager is typically in charge of a specific product. An alternative form of divisional structure is based on geographic areas, with a division manager for each region.

The advantages of a divisional structure are that

- It permits shared authority and responsibility.
- It allows more rapid response to changing environmental and market conditions.
- It allows direct measurement of product or geographic performance.

- Shared authority and responsibility help develop future management.

The principal disadvantages are that

- A duplication of effort often results.
- A large staff is needed.
- Divisions may become too independent.

This structure requires a long-range planning process based on shared authority and responsibility. The planning process must enable division managers to retain responsibility for product market decisions and must enable top management to coordinate allocation of resources.

STRATEGIC BUSINESS UNITS

As a company moves through the mature stages of its life cycle, the focus often shifts to consolidation of effort and efficiency of operations. In a large multi-product company, there may be many divisions or product managers. To manage the diverse products effectively, management may seek ways to group products logically. The basis for logical groupings may be production processes, marketing methods, demand for the product, or channels of distribution. The logical grouping of products into strategic business units (SBUs) permits management to take advantage of synergy. For example, because of leverage, the divisions' combined market potential may be greater than that of individual divisions.

When a company is organized into strategic business units, resource allocation can more easily be evaluated in terms of each product group.

Each strategic business unit can be systematically examined as though it had its own product portfolio. Of course, effective and forward-looking strategic management of a firm made up of SBUs requires considerable skill. A comprehensive plan for an SBU entails the same analytical steps that are required for the overall strategic plan of an enterprise, and consolidation of all SBU plans can be a formidable task. In the case of General Electric, for example, resource allocation among approximately 40 identifiable SBUs represents a significant undertaking. It is an easier task, however, than integrating the more than 170 product departments that existed at GE prior to reorganization or attempting to group the departments on some functional basis.

The advantages of the SBU approach are that

- Synergistic effects are obtained from product groupings.
- Coordination of functional activities within each SBU is improved.
- It fosters a broad and long-range management viewpoint at the SBU level.

The disadvantages of this structure are that

- Rivalries and competition over resource allocation may develop among product groups.
- A proliferation of staff functions may result.
- Empire building may occur at the SBU level.

In 1989, GE restructured into 14 business segments, which are an aggregation of SBUs based on major industries.

MATRIX STRUCTURE

In recent years, another form of organizational structure called the *matrix* organization has evolved. The matrix form of organization combines the product form with the functional form.

The matrix structure operates by vesting authority in a particular project manager (such as the interest-bearing checking accounts manager) so that he or she can use functional experts (marketing, systems design, administration) to carry out the project. The performing individual at any given point in the matrix has dual authority and responsibility relationships with his or her functional superior and project manager.

The matrix organization is not a panacea for a poorly designed or ineffective functional or divisional organizational structure. The shared responsibility, the different reporting channels, and the different superiors for each subordinate present potential difficulties for a firm that operates as a matrix organization. A complex set of relationships is required to utilize a matrix structure. Among the many corporations that have adopted this approach are Citibank, Dow Chemical, Shell Oil, and Texas Instruments.

The principal advantages of the matrix structure are that

- It permits major projects to be worked on within the functional structure.
- It focuses on specific requirements of a given market, product, or project.
- Decisions can be made by project managers with the input and perspective of top management.
- Management of new projects that do not fit into a current product or functional structure is facilitated.

Disadvantages of this structure are that

- Problems may develop from dual command and multiple responsibilities.
- Authority relationships are constantly changing.
- Problems of organizational continuity and conflict of authority may arise.
- It is difficult to reward adequately individuals who perform well.

In the past, a hierarchic or structured form of organization dominated industry. But in today's complex environment, structured relationships are often an impediment to effective strategy formulation and implementation. The matrix form was one of the first to deviate from the simple linear relationship among units of an organization. The matrix form of organization required the crossing of classic organizational boundaries and necessitated multiple reporting relationships. To have an effective matrix, one focuses on building an organization whose concern is strategic innovation rather than structural complexity. The characteristics of a successful transition to the matrix form include

1. A clear and consistent vision, carefully communicated
2. Emphasis on the individual's identification with company goals

3. Integration of the thinking and activities of the individual with the broad agenda of the company, which builds a shared vision

GE failed to achieve these three conditions in their Brazilian subsidiary, where they shifted from TV manufacturing to large appliances and finally to housewares. After the RCA acquisition, GE sold off its Brazilian subsidiary because it really was engaged in international outsourcing rather than building a responsive and self-sufficient subsidiary (Bartlett and Ghoshal, 1990).

The matrix form of organization was the first major break with conventional hierarchic forms of organization. The matrix is a transitional step toward the evolving concept of a "boundaryless," or open, organization wherein relationships are what is important, not the rigid lines of authority. In this organizational form, the emphasis is on coordination, involvement, shared vision, and individual empowerment. In the boundaryless organization, employees question activities and it is incumbent on managers to listen. Hirschhorn and Gilmore (1992) consider four key elements that need to be addressed in the new organizational form.

1. *Authority boundary*: defining who is in charge of what
2. *Task boundary*: defining who is responsible for doing which tasks
3. *Political boundary*: defining who gets what in return for organizational support
4. *Identity boundary*: finding the feelings of individuals and how they relate to the organization

Teams often replace departments or divisions in the boundaryless organization and erase group labels. To be effective, however, teams require a leader who can balance the four elements of authority, task, politics, and identity. In one example of team failure, the leader did not specify a clear authority boundary, and the team reacted by emphasizing an identity boundary. The overly strong identity boundary kept the team members from developing the task and political boundaries needed to do the job. Authority boundaries, then, are needed, but they are designed to define limits rather than control the effort.

STRATEGY/STRUCTURE LINKAGES

Organizations ideally function as coordinating mechanisms that facilitate coping with strategic problems. As a result, organizational structures vary from simple hierarchies to complex divisional arrangements.

The structured relationships shown on organizational charts, however, are static. They identify titles of incumbent managers and the roles and formal authority associated with the structure. Although these relationships have a pervasive influence on how strategies are determined and executed, they do not reflect the continuous adjustment that is made to accommodate environmental demands. The link between strategy and structure will now be examined from three perspectives: the organizational life cycle, integrative mechanisms, and the contingency approach to determinants of structure.

ORGANIZATIONAL LIFE CYCLE

The dynamics of organizational change are often referred to as the *organizational life cycle*. On the basis of his research on organization life cycles, Kimberly (1976) argued that a dynamic perspective on organizations is badly needed. An understanding of organizational cycles, which include creation, transformation, and decline, can help change agents to determine what intervention strategies are appropriate for organizational change and at what stage in the organization's development they should be introduced.

In another work about organizational change, Child (1972) described growth as a means of fulfilling the aspirations of organizational members, enhancing the chance of survival, and improving the organization's performance. Growth can contribute to economies of scale, reduce vulnerability, and improve the firm's ability to bargain with other constituents. However, growth also leads to organizational complexity, which in turn requires more staff and support to sustain growth. The unpredictability of environmental demands further complicates the task of the organization. Thus the benefits of increased size often give way to problems, in the classic biological pattern of birth, maturation, and decline. Small companies particularly tend to follow this pattern because of an inability to cope with externally imposed requirements and lack of adequate resources.

Pfeffer and Salancik (1978) distinguished between growth based on internal decisions to achieve organizational or individual goals and growth based on a biological model, which is limited by resources and constraints. In their view, growth represents an "intentional" response to problems of interdependence such as uncertainty or external control. For example, mergers are seen as a means to control interdependence by domination or avoidance of exchanges. Although increased size does not necessarily lead to the economies of scale often attributed to large companies, growth often does stabilize profits, reduce uncertainty, and enhance the organization's ability to apply leverage in the environment—benefits that increase the organization's survival potential. Thus firms merge and grow in an attempt to manage environmental dependence.

Filley, House, and Kerr (1976) suggested that regular growth patterns are predicted fairly well by a biological model that reflects the strategic adaptive behavior (provided no overt departures, such as mergers, affect the organization's product and structural base). Because of the interdependence between the firm and its environment, strategic adaptation leads to cyclical patterns of change.

Mintzberg (1979) maintained that there is strong evidence that organizations undergo structural change as they grow. The four basic stages of growth parallel the types of organizational structure described previously.

The nature of the transition from stage to stage depends on whether the firm starts in a simple or a complex environment. In any case, structural change is difficult to accomplish because of resistance by individuals in the firm.

Another perspective on organizational growth and the crisis of transition was described by Greiner (1972). He identified five phases in the growth cycle and characterized each as leading to a crisis that is resolved by a change in the form of management or organizational structure.

A typical organizational growth curve is shown in Figure 10.6. The first phase is characterized by an entrepreneurial management style. The organizational structure is informal, and the main emphasis is on creating a product and a market. As the company grows, however, the founders find themselves burdened with unwanted management responsibilities. This situation leads to a crisis, because the firm needs a manager who has the skills to introduce more effective control. In many cases, the founders lack such skills but still do not want to step aside.

The next phase of growth is characterized by increased efficiency in operations and centralized and directive management. At some time, however, these methods in turn become inappropriate. As the organization becomes larger and more complex, lower-level executives find themselves restricted by a centralized hierarchy. When these managers possess more knowledge about their operations and markets than does top management, they begin to demand greater freedom in their decision making. Thus the critical choice for top management is whether to give up some of its responsibility or lose creative middle management.

| **FIGURE 10.6** | **Organizational Life Cycle: The Curve Identifies Crises That Lead to Changes at Different Stages of Growth** |

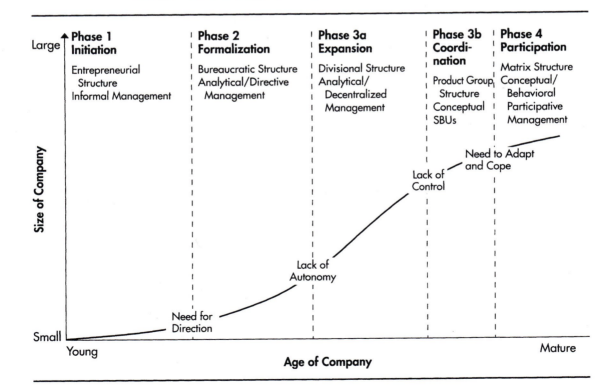

The third phase of the organizational life cycle evolves from the successful application of a decentralized organizational structure. Much greater responsibility is given to managers of company divisions and market territories, which tends to lead to strong market expansion for the firm. Serious problems eventually result from this new structure, however. When top executives sense that they are losing control over an operation that is becoming more and more diversified, they attempt to regain total control over the company.

An extension of the decentralized, or divisional, organizational structure is the strategic business unit, or product group, structure. It ensures that autonomous field managers do not run their own shows without coordinating plans, money, technology, and personnel with the rest of the organization. The product group approach offers the potential for increased efficiency and effectiveness because it does not lead to the creation of more and more staff positions, the way a strictly divisional structure often does. As we have noted, the SBU is an organizational structure that allows a high degree of centralized control yet retains the advantages of decentralized decision making.

The fourth, but not necessarily final, phase may be characterized as participative and/or matrix management. Environmental factors such as rapid technological innovation or increased demand for democratization in the firm make adaptability to change the most important single determinant of survival. Future organizations will need to be "adaptive, rapidly changing temporary systems. These will be organized around problems-to-be-solved. The problems will be solved by groups of relative strangers who represent a set of diverse professional skills" (Bennis, 1966, p. 12).

Different leadership styles are needed at various stages in the life cycle. In a study of successful entrepreneurs, Hansen (1985) found that there was a high correlation between the style of the executive and his or her success at a particular stage. Figure 10.7 relates style to the life cycle of the organization.

In phase 1 of the organizational life cycle, the successful executive has a creative style, with a vision and the drive to make things happen. The organizational structure is flexible and informal. The market environment tends to be uncertain but limited in scope.

For phase 2, the successful executive is one who focuses on growth and on building an appropriate infrastructure. This structure tends to be fragmented, as a result of the transition from an informal to a more formal organization. The successful executive's style is a combination of highly analytical and behavioral. An analytical style is needed to develop the necessary transition plans, and a behavioral style is needed to influence people to stay with the organization. In the second phase, the environment begins to shift, as a more complex relationship develops between the organization and the customer.

At the start of phase 3, the successful executive is one who is forceful, can achieve results, and can select appropriate strategies. For this executive, the directive style is dominant, and the analytical style is backup. Executives with this combination of styles prefer a flat structure, where control is tight. Their focus is on maintaining the growth begun in the second phase, on achieving a sustainable competitive advantage, and on increasing the customer base. The competitive environment is typically relatively stable. In the latter part of phase 3, the best executive is

FIGURE 10.7 | **Match of Style with Life Cycle**

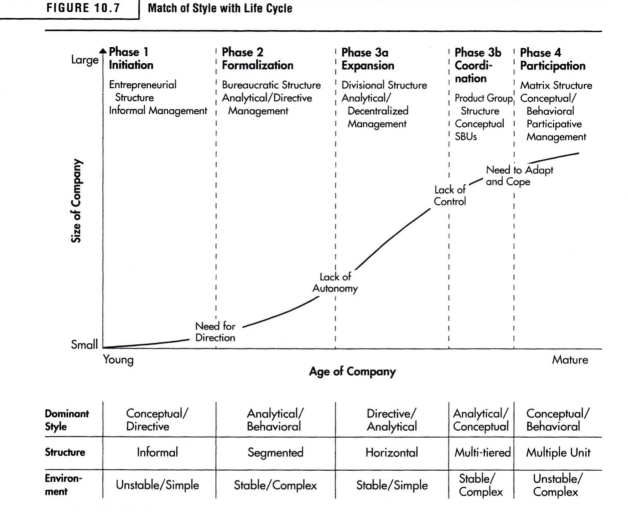

Dominant Style	Conceptual/ Directive	Analytical/ Behavioral	Directive/ Analytical	Analytical/ Conceptual	Conceptual/ Behavioral
Structure	Informal	Segmented	Horizontal	Multi-tiered	Multiple Unit
Environ-ment	Unstable/Simple	Stable/Complex	Stable/Simple	Stable/ Complex	Unstable/ Complex

the one who exhibits a combination of the analytical and conceptual styles. This manager has a broad outlook and is able to deal with highly complex situations. The organizational structure shifts to a multi-tiered one, involving coordination and grouping of products and divisions. At this point, the overall environment is complex but manageable.

In the last phase, the best style is a combination of analytical, conceptual, and behavioral. This combination forms the strongest leadership style of all. Leaders with this style are able to deal with uncertain and complex situations—including increased competition, changing technology, and more demanding customers—and still maintain the confidence of employees. They use a multiple-unit or matrix structure to permit more delegation. At this stage, a leader who does not have an analytical/conceptual/behavioral style often cannot sustain the organization's competitive position.

Hansen's findings shed light on how to choose an entrepreneur whose style best matches the requirements of the situation. Venture capitalists, for example, find that his ideas are useful in determining which enterprises they are willing to fund.

INTEGRATIVE MECHANISMS

An important question that needs to be resolved is "What specific conditions, processes, and structural mechanisms will be required to implement a given strategy?" Galbraith and Nathanson (1978) suggested that various integrative mechanisms may be used to coordinate implementation. They include

- Structural hierarchy
- Rules or policy guidelines
- Goal setting and strategic planning
- Direct contact among individuals
- Interdepartmental liaison roles
- Temporary task forces for problem solving
- Permanent teams to handle continuing problems
- Integrating roles to facilitate communication and change
- Integrating departments that provide required support

The particular integrative mechanisms that should be used depend on several variables. The variables that have been suggested include

- Level of environmental uncertainty or turbulence
- Type of technology predominantly employed
- Degree of task interdependency and uncertainty
- Stage of the organizational life cycle
- Decision style of key executives
- Information and coordination systems
- Primary purpose or goals
- Competitive market structure
- Numbers of products and customers

Using the integrative mechanisms and the situational variables, one can construct the organizational structure matrix shown in Figure 10.8. Although the matrix may appear to suggest a normative approach to structure, it is intended merely to be descriptive of changes that are likely to take place as organizations confront changing situations.

The organizational structures shown in Figure 10.8 correspond to the four categories described by Mintzberg and to the life cycle stages. As an organization grows, it encounters increasing environmental uncertainty. Growth is a means of coping with uncertainty, but it gives rise to the need for integrative mechanisms. What integrative mechanisms are appropriate depends on the size of the organization, the

| FIGURE 10.8 | Organizational Structure Matrix |

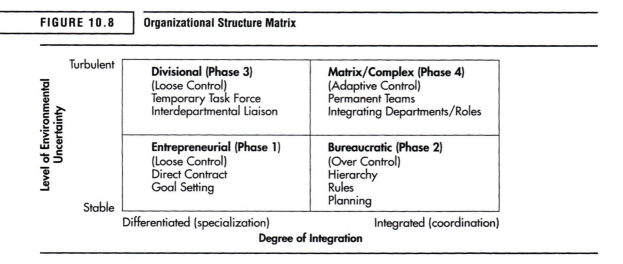

level of environmental uncertainty, the degree of interdependency in task or environmental linkage, the type of technology, the product characteristics, the competitor analysis, and the market structure. The matrix structure associates particular integrative mechanisms with given levels of uncertainty and need for integration. It suggests that structural changes often correspond to both environmental demands and internal requirements.

THE CONTINGENCY APPROACH

Tosi and Hamner (1974) relied on a contingency approach to structure. They asserted that the organizational structure is affected by (is contingent on) the organizational design, the external environment, individual and group factors, and the internal work system. Figure 10.9 shows how these situational forces affect the organization's structure.

Organizations with a mechanistic design are relatively routine-oriented, with high task specialization, clear job definitions, and strong pressures for compliance. The work requires a moderate amount of skill, and authority is based on position. Organic systems, on the other hand, are open systems in which individuals have greater control because authority is based on individual competency. Work is less structured and changes take place constantly, requiring greater flexibility and integration. Performance is evaluated on the basis of output.

The environmental determinants that directly influence the long-term survival and structure of the organization include external turbulence, social change, competition, and technological advances. All affect the adaptive response required by the organization. Because of the need for the organization to adapt to continuous changes in the external environment, internal restructuring occurs constantly. This

FIGURE 10.9	Determinants of Structure

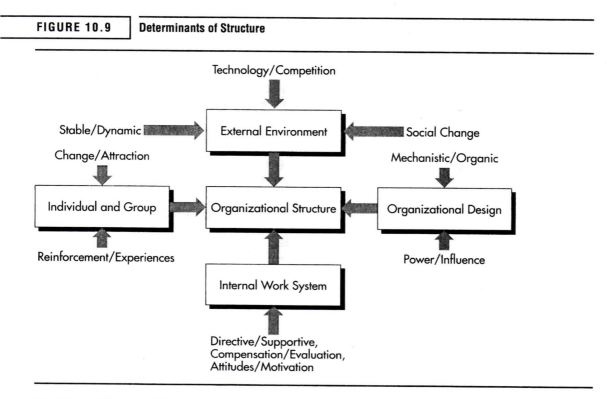

After Tosi and Hamner, 1974, p. 2.

restructuring, of course, leads to power struggles, changes in individual roles, and work redesign. Some of the reasons for change when the environment is turbulent are

- Inability to respond to environmental demands
- Increases in product line uncertainty and competition
- Shifts in market structure and relationships
- Product obsolescence and changes in technology
- Increases in interdependencies in the task and with the environment
- Changes in resource requirements
- Shifts in personnel and products
- Requirements of stakeholders, government regulations, or social response

Although it cannot provide a prescription for achieving organizational change, the contingency approach lends insight into possible alternative structures that might be considered during each phase of growth and illustrates the complex interactions of factors that influence the organization's structure.

Miles (1982) saw the analysis of external contingencies as one of the main tasks confronting the strategic manager. He believed that a strategic manager has two primary responsibilities. The first is to develop the internal competencies that allow the firm to compete effectively. The second is to develop an understanding of the constraints and opportunities posed by the external environment. Because organizations are never really independent of society and its values, a significant aspect of adaptation to the external contingencies is establishing the organization's legitimacy so that it gains acceptance and can perform effectively. Adaptations, therefore, must incorporate external as well as internal structural requirements.

THE TEAM APPROACH

Because formal organizational structures inhibit communication and interaction among personnel, subcultures tend to evolve that protect their own turf and are less than effective when implementing decisions. The recently developed team approach (Rowe and Boulgarides, 1992) removes artificial organizational barriers and encourages a sense of openness. Teams share a common goal and help to focus energy by emphasizing "self-control" on the part of participants. Companies such as Nabisco have solved their labor problems when factory workers and management joined forces to solve high-tech problems (Lord, 1991). Another instance of teamwork producing meaningful results occurred at Gould, where the total quality management approach was adopted. This approach is based on cooperation and scraps traditional methods and management-labor roles. The plant's manager, Kevin Harris, said, "I had to give up my ego and understand how to share decisions." The results have shown up in Gould's improved performance (Sanchez, 1991).

There are many problems that are best solved by a team effort, but some teams work better than others. What characteristics of teams facilitate effective problem solving? In general, teams that are cohesive, that interact cooperatively with members possessing compatible personality characteristics, and that are operating under mild to moderate (but not extreme) pressure appear to be most effective. In addition, patterns of communication and the leadership available significantly affect performance. A feeling of cohesiveness among members is the most influential determinant of behavior. Cohesive groups experience a high degree of attraction to the group, feel good about their membership, and tend to want to "stick together." Highly cohesive groups work harder than those with low cohesiveness. The fact that they are likely to do so regardless of outside supervision is of particular significance. In addition to feeling a sense of cohesiveness, the members must also be identified with, or feel enthusiastic about, the goals of the group—that is, the problem to be solved. A highly cohesive group is well launched on a successful problem-solving venture if the members feel enthusiastic about the assigned problem, provided that the solution is reasonably within reach of the group's capabilities.

Membership in cohesive groups increases the likelihood of member responses that are helpful in problem solving. Cohesiveness generally increases

1. When the members feel they are highly valued by the group
2. When the members are in a cooperative rather than a competitive relationship with each other
3. When they have full opportunity for social interactions
4. When the group is small

Group cohesiveness is reduced

1. When false expectations are raised about the group
2. When a few members dominate group activities and decision making
3. When disagreement or failure is experienced too often

The administrator reading this list may feel overwhelmed by the many things to keep in mind when forming a problem-solving group. Yet each factor, considered by itself, can readily be controlled by relatively simple effort on the part of the group leader or the administrator responsible for the group.

It is not a simple matter, however, to assess individual personality traits and thus to assemble groups whose members are compatible. Such groups should be more productive than groups with incompatible members. Generally, the assessment of personality is a complex process and raises questions about the feasibility of selecting compatible group members in any precise fashion in an organizational setting.

Successful groups appear to follow similar patterns. In a series of studies of airplane crews that had to solve the problem of surviving after bailing out over enemy territory, three principal procedures were followed by successful crews. These crews were able

1. To make sense of an initially unstructured, unclear situation (a necessary first step in many problem situations)
2. To resume communication among members
3. To establish a goal to work toward

The problems of business groups are rarely so critical, and are rarely presented in such a challenging setting, yet the procedures for solving problems are presumably the same.

Margerison and McCann (1985) have developed a team approach that is used for training, development, and more effective problem solving. They have an index called the TMI (team management index) that has been used by a number of companies, including Hewlett-Packard, DuPont, Mobil, and Shell. The index covers four basic behaviors that have been observed when people work together in teams: exploring, advising, controlling, and organizing. The key aspects of work behavior that the TMI measures are

1. *Advising:* These individuals obtain and disseminate information to others who can use it.
2. *Innovating:* These individuals are very creative and willing to experiment with new ideas and to pass these ideas along.
3. *Promoting:* These individuals search for new opportunities and are constantly looking for ways to persuade others to pursue what they have found.
4. *Developing:* These individuals are very good at assessing and testing how well new approaches apply to the particular problems the team is addressing.
5. *Organizing:* These individuals are very good at establishing and implementing the means for making things work, including relationships, assignments, and organizational structure.

6. *Producing:* These individuals focus on establishing procedures and practice so that the performance can be done on a more systematic basis and the desired results achieved.

7. *Inspecting:* These individuals are the ones who check and audit the performance of the system to ensure that it is meeting its targets and goals.

8. *Maintaining:* These are the people who ensure that processes continue and that standards are met.

There is considerable similarity between the team approach and the use of the TMI in management control systems. The team approach involves planning effectively and facilitates performance appraisal as well as career planning. The TMI is very helpful in training for team building as well as individual development. It is a tool that makes managers more effective in carrying out their functions.

Teamwork is a means for developing creative collaboration. In an open organization, team members communicate across divisions and can even report to a manager who may not be the team leader. In some respects, a team operates in a manner similar to projects in a matrix organization. The key is flexibility in the assignment of team members and an increase in information flow among individuals and among groups, which contributes to consensus decision making (Nunamaker, 1992). Because teams often consist of peer experts, it is critical to have a sensitive team leader who understands the need for communication and coordination.

Many new computer tools that can enhance the effectiveness of teams are becoming available for use in the strategy arena. They include

1. Brainstorming software
2. Idea organizers using IBM's TeamFocus tool kit
3. Electronic voting using Option Finder
4. Group support systems, including electronic mail
5. Expert choice for issue exploration
6. Mathematical decision support programs
7. Stakeholder analysis using the Strategic Models program

(The above section, The Team Approach, is reprinted with the permission of Macmillian Publishing Company from *Managerial Decision Making* by Alan J. Rowe and James D. Boulgarides. Copyright © 1992 by Macmillian Publishing Company.)

IMPLEMENTING STRATEGY: CONTROL

Strategies are, after all, only a means toward an end. Thus determining how best to implement a strategy requires an analysis of what controls are needed to achieve the desired results.

If one takes a broad view of achieving productivity and performance, control must be viewed from an organizational rather than a purely technical perspective. The following considerations need to be taken into account prior to establishing strategic control.

1. Identification of critical factors using decision criteria as the basis for analysis or comparison between actual and desired performance. In many respects, this is comparable to problem formulation, because before controls can be put to work, one must identify what needs correction.

2. Operating on symptoms is an inappropriate control approach. Rather, what is needed is a way of identifying the underlying causes of any problems and of using the symptoms as flags or indicators that there may be a serious situation that needs correction.

3. Before corrective action is taken, the costs and benefits should be examined. Then the appropriate corrective action can be determined. In many respects, this is comparable to problem solving, because the decision maker must understand the constraints limiting what can be done to correct a system.

4. The decision environment is an important concern, and the manager must take this into account when attempting to change or correct any aspect of performance.

5. Corrective action is needed when performance is poor or decisions are wrong. Corrective action should lead to improved performance.

6. A management control system must relate the needs of the organization to the needs of the individual. The functions of an organization must be consistent with the task demands, technology, external environmental forces, and members' personal needs.

Management controls in organizations are different from controls used in technical systems, such as quality control and inventory control. Drucker (1954) has stated this succinctly:

> Controls in a social institution are goal setting and value setting, they are not objective, they are of necessity moral. The only way to avoid this is to flood the executive with so many controls that the entire system becomes meaningless, becomes mere noise, and this means that the basic question is not how do we control but what do we measure in our control system. That we can quantify something is no reason at all for measuring it. The questions that should be asked: Is this what the manager should consider important? Is this what a manager's attention should be focused on? Is this a true statement of the basic realities of the enterprise? And is this the proper focus for control, i.e. effective direction with maximum economy of effort?

Some work environments require strict and demanding management control systems that ensure quality output, as in mass-production manufacturing. In the United States, quality control is often separated from manufacturing and is carried out by sampling methods. Thus problems are identified after the fact. Parts are scrapped and new parts made, which results in additional costs and time delays. In Japan, the manufacturing and quality control functions are combined in the worker responsible for producing quality parts. This simultaneity yields savings in both cost and time. When a worker is held responsible for the quality of work produced, responsibility is taken more seriously. The worker—not a checker—examines the product. Making the worker responsible for the quality of the work produced is "control at the point of action."

As the organizational structure evolves, so must the control process. We shall examine the following six types of control:

■ *Management control*, which is based on past performance, historical data, or performance measurement.

- *Management by objectives*, which emphasizes the setting of objectives and frequent evaluation to be sure that those objectives are being met. MBO has been widely used to achieve personal commitment and motivation and to improve both performance and job satisfaction. Typically, if individuals participate in setting their own goals and objectives, they tend to be committed to achieving them.

- *Performance management*, which is concerned with goal congruence and organizational effectiveness. The performance management system (PMS) is an extension of MBO; it also attempts to ensure that subordinates receive constructive feedback on their performance. This feedback is provided by using a profile to evaluate the individual's strengths and developmental needs with respect to performance goals.

- *Adaptive control*, which focuses on responding to required changes rapidly and in an effective manner.

- *Strategic control*, which involves anticipating and minimizing potential deviations from the desired outcome.

- *Real-time control*, which uses computers to provide information as current as possible.

This list reveals that control is multidimensional and that it affects many aspects of strategic management. All six types of control are involved in ensuring implementation of strategic decisions.

In the following discussion of control, the measurement aspects of management control and performance management are combined. Likewise, adaptive, strategic, and real-time control are covered together. For other purposes, each of these approaches could be considered separately.

MANAGEMENT CONTROL

An important question in control is "How frequently and in what form should performance be measured?" Frequent interaction and multidimensional measures are needed to assess performance. Evaluation of such factors as cohesiveness, responsiveness, adaptability, and effectiveness provides additional insight into the organization's performance.

The identification and measurement of deviations in performance—a crucial aspect of implementation—cannot be accomplished simply by adopting a set of standards. Dependencies and interactions, along with change, give rise to a variety of problems in implementing any strategy; thus it is almost impossible to predict precisely the course that should be followed or the standard of performance that is appropriate.

The estimates that form the basis for standards are typically determined from historical data, which, by definition, are "after the fact." Furthermore, estimates rarely include any provision for variability. Absolute standards such as the following are often used: "keep equipment busy 100% of the time" or "meet 100% of quotas." However, 100% utilization of capacity can rarely be achieved. The use of averages is equally problematic; they tend to hide variability in performance.

Arbitrary allocations, such as for overhead, also create difficulties, because there is little relationship between performance and the standard.

It is almost axiomatic that because of the problems inherent in establishing standards, goals, and objectives and in defining the basis on which measurement is made, measuring performance is difficult.

Unfortunately, the manner in which control is imposed often has unintended consequences, such as widespread antagonism, successful resistance, noncompliance, unreliable performance, need for close surveillance, and high administrative costs. Ridgway (1956) showed that there are many dysfunctional consequences of performance measurement and that using a single criterion of performance or a single standard generally leads to undesirable or suboptimal results.

MANAGEMENT BY OBJECTIVES

Management by objectives (MBO) is an approach in which individuals are involved in determining milestones for improving performance. Table 10.1 shows how MBO was applied in a large aerospace company. Five vice presidents, each in charge of a major function, first identified key milestones they hoped to achieve in their specific areas of responsibility. The milestones were specific targets to be reached in pursuit of the company's overall strategy. For example, in the financial area, the milestones included a 5% reduction in overhead costs, a profit objective of 15%, and the hiring of two additional controllers for the decentralized operations. The marketing vice president's objectives included analyzing 13 new products and increasing sales per employee to $90,500 per year. In the personnel area, the targets included hiring 16 new key personnel and reducing the ratio of indirect to direct costs to 10%. In the area of engineering, not only did managers plan to recruit 25 additional senior engineers, but they also agreed to start a minimum of 5 research and development projects related to advanced technology. The operations vice president wanted to increase capacity by 150% and also had other targets, such as increasing interdivisional sales by $200,000 per year and installing 15 new computer systems.

Each month the president held a performance review meeting to compare the current status with the plan. At the time MBO was instituted, a reduction of 2% in overhead had already been achieved, and the forecast was that 3% would be possible by the end of the year. Thus a deficit of 2% is shown in the column labeled Projected Deviation. Because all aspects of the milestones are defined, including the target, current status, future forecast, and what has to be achieved, management is in a position to examine alternative actions that might be taken in order to meet the objectives.

In some instances, the target underestimated the vice president's ability to meet objectives. For example, in marketing, the plan for increasing sales effort called for a 20% increase, but 30% was actually achieved. Because this value overshot the target, a reduction to a 25% increase was planned, for a residual net 5% increase. In the case of product mix, the plan was for a 50% shift in product mix, but an 80% shift was achieved; the revised forecast of a 75% change for the year exceeded the initial target by 25%. Some of the targets did not exhibit the degree of precision that one might think was desirable, such as those for personnel development.

TABLE 10.1	Management by Objectives: Key Milestone Plan

Key Milestones for Each Major Functional Area	Plan/Objective	Current Performance	Forecast Performance	Projected Deviation
Financial				
Reduction in overhead cost	5%	2%	3%	–2%
Profit on sales	15%	12%	13%	–2%
Hiring of new controllers	2	1	2	0
Marketing				
Analysis of new products	13	2	10	–3
Increase in sales effort	20%	30%	25%	+5%
Shift of product mix (civilian/military)	50%	80%	75%	+25%
Sales per employee	$90,500	$90,000	$90,000	–$500
Personnel				
Number of key personnel needed	16	10	13	–3
Standard of labor efficiency	88%	80%	82%	–6
Personnel development	400	418	418	+18
Ratio of indirect to direct cost	10%	17%	15%	+5
Engineering				
Recruitment of senior engineers	25	16	18	–7
Application of project control systems	3	0	1	–2
Increase percentage of R&D per sales	5%	6%	6%	+1
New technological programs	15	10	12	–3
Operations				
Increase in production capacity	150%	110%	150%	0
Reduction in labor variance	10%	0	2%	–8
Increase in interdivisional sales	$200,000	$20,000	$50,000	–$150,000
Application of new computer systems	15	3	4	–11

It was estimated that 400 managers would be sent to various training courses. As it turned out, 418 actually went to courses, a difference of 18. This difference, however, should not be construed as indicating a lack of control or bad estimating. Obviously, 400 was only an estimate. An allowable variation should have been specified so that the variance of +18 would not be considered as reflecting poor performance. One of the most difficult targets for the company to achieve was increased interdivisional sales. The results showed only a $20,000 increase in sales, whereas the target was $200,000. The difference of $150,000 between the latest forecast and the target indicated that new strategies must be selected if performance is to match the desired objectives.

The MBO approach shown here illustrates how information, properly utilized and properly displayed, can provide management with a tool for achieving more effective performance. However, it is important to recognize that both the measurement aspects and the behavioral aspects of control must be considered jointly. These vice presidents set their own targets or objectives and were held accountable for their own estimates. Typically, if individuals determine their targets, they will be committed to achieving them. And the data they report will give management the information needed to assess performance and evaluate the basis for the targets. What has made MBO so popular is that it both provides meaningful measures and takes behavior into account.

PERFORMANCE MANAGEMENT

Performance management is concerned with a multidimensional way of measuring output, including

1. Behavioral measures, which relate to the actions required and rely on observable, behaviorally anchored rating scales
2. Objective measures, which directly focus on the outcomes rather than on the process of achieving them
3. Evaluation techniques, which rely on the judgment and experience of the individual conducting the performance appraisal

Performance management is often equated with performance appraisal that has had mixed success in implementation. Successful programs, however, tend to have the following three elements in common.

1. Objectives are specific and are set jointly with management.
2. Feedback is concrete and periodic.
3. Top management is involved in the program and supports it.

Because it is a system-oriented approach, performance management takes into account the degree of specificity with which work can be defined and the reaction or expectation of the individual who will perform the task. Objective measures, such as those used in MBO, can create problems merely because of the way in which the objectives are established or the way measurement is conducted.

On the other hand, where the task can be defined in specific terms, such as by objectives, direct measurement of output may be the most appropriate approach.

Behavioral measures are most useful where the work is well defined and the individual's expectations can be taken into account. Finally, subjective evaluation is generally required where the task cannot easily be defined or where no direct measurement is possible.

An approach to performance appraisal that builds on MBO is called the *performance management system (PMS)*. Developed by Beer and Ruh (1976), it was applied at Corning Glass Works with 3,800 managerial and professional employees. The PMS approach provides subordinates with constructive feedback about their performance. It emphasizes the manager's role in meeting organizational goals and in developing and evaluating subordinates. A profile is used to determine the individual's strengths and development needs. The results are then used to identify goals and means for achieving them.

Some of the factors considered in a performance profile include initiative, priorities, accomplishment, accuracy, communication, cooperation, decisiveness, and flexibility. With the profile as a starting point, a development program is designed to improve the employee's attitude, abilities, or interpersonal skills. Given this base, evaluation interviews are held covering the subordinate's current performance, promotion potential, and salary increase. At Corning, merely identifying performance dimensions helped improve organizational effectiveness.

The principal difference between PMS and MBO is in the process of arriving at performance standards. MBO starts with agreed-upon objectives and then allows individuals to establish their own criteria and plans for achieving these objectives. PMS starts with a description of the subordinate's behavior, showing his or her strengths and weaknesses. Using a sequence of interviews, the manager and subordinate jointly identify areas where improvement is required. Plans are then established for developing the abilities the individual needs to perform effectively.

In the past, the emphasis in performance management has been on a closed-loop feedback approach. In such a system, however, objectives are often unclear, missing, or changing; accomplishment is difficult to measure with unambiguous, quantitative output standards; and feedback information is often not relevant or usable. Because of the complexity of control, the emphasis is increasingly being placed on behaviorally oriented systems, such as a combination of MBO and PMS.

More recent approaches emphasize a relaxation of the rigid control systems that have been applied in the past. For example, Chaparral Steel, which operates in an extremely competitive environment, has been able to produce steel at a record low of 1.6 hours per ton, compared with 2.4 hours for mini-mills and 4.9 hours for integrated steel mills. This was accomplished by relaxing controls and emphasizing the contributions that workers can make. Gordon Forward, CEO of Chaparral, has developed a "classless" organization. Workers receive a salary and a bonus based on individual performance, the company's profits, and the skills they have learned. There are no time clocks; lunch hours and breaks are set by the workers themselves. There is an open parking lot and executive offices are also open. Forward was seeking the commitment of employees by providing extraordinary freedom, and they, in turn, were expected to show initiative in their work. The result has been significant improvements in equipment design, inventions, and overall performance. Chaparral has emerged as a quality, low-cost producer that is highly profitable in an industry most would shun (Dumaine, 1992).

The opposite was the case at TopChem, where CEO Sam Verde based employee compensation on incremental improvements (Ehrenfeld, 1992). The following were specified targets:

1. Base pay would be 75% of former pay
2. Flexible pay would be 25% of former pay based on
   a. The team's ability to show a 5% annual improvement defined as follows: achieving a 30% improvement in quality, keeping unit cost to market at 25%, improving speed to market by 20%, and increasing safety and environmental compliance by 10%
   b. Improving divisional financial performance by 15%

The feeling at TopChem was that teamwork was a motivational kick that did not reflect the way people worked. The pay plan proposed at TopChem provided a negative rather than positive incentive. It set arbitrary targets in difficult-to-define areas that simply "justified" the salary with no bonus or incentive attached. It failed.

ADAPTIVE, STRATEGIC, AND REAL-TIME CONTROL

Because the basic strategy of a firm undergoes continuous modification, so must its implementation. Although adaptive controls have been used principally at the operating level, modifying *all* aspects of the internal environment to match the changing external requirements is critical for achieving desired strategies. An obvious approach is to anticipate possible deviations, just as is done in statistical quality control. For example, if an expenditure is proposed, the possibility that it might exceed the budget should be considered ahead of time rather than after the fact.

Dell Computers offers an example of control that is done on a timely basis. Increasingly, customers are demanding on-time delivery from their suppliers. When the product cannot be delivered promptly, customers go elsewhere. Dell managers meet at 7:30 A.M. every Friday to review the week's performance from the point of view of customer satisfaction. Dell has set as a target to be number one in customer satisfaction. To achieve this objective, Dell simplifies products and components and transmits customer order information to the factory, where a "made-to-order" operation ensures delivery within three or four days. Just as was the case with AHSC (see Chapter 1), when this system was launched, sales increased by 70% in less than two years (Kumar and Sharman, 1992).

A strategic control system permits management to change both the desired objectives and the methods of control. Organizations with many products, or with large and complex projects, may need a computer-based system to achieve strategic control. Evaluating a complex system generally requires large amounts of data, and the system must be continuously monitored if appropriate corrective action is to be taken "in time" to achieve desired objectives. Thus an adaptive computer-based approach often depends on a system that utilizes large-scale databases and simulation models to forecast the future states of the system. Such systems are closely tied to decision support systems as shown in Figure 10.10.

The operation of a realtime, adaptive computer-based system is shown in Figure 10.10. The data gathered by the computer are used to update the database and to produce management reports or other displays for real-time inquiries. Appropriate simulation models supply the strategic information that is an essential part of a decision support system. Expert support systems are beginning to emerge as another tool for adaptive controls, because they can answer "what if" questions and provide useful advice (Mockler, 1989).

An important question is "When has the system changed sufficiently to warrant a modification?" Because performance involves randomness and uncertainty, deviations from a narrow target, objective, or budget do not necessarily indicate a need for correction; most deviations will be due to chance. To deal with this problem, management can use appropriate control limits. Furthermore, because objectives are often based on estimates derived from experience, comparable work, or some arbitrarily determined standard, considerable uncertainty exists about the validity of the objective itself. Therefore, it is inappropriate to use the estimate as a "rigid" base for measuring performance or to adapt the system. It is precisely because of rapid and often unpredictable change that a strategic control system is needed to pinpoint the need for corrective action.

Managerial and strategic control are so intimately intertwined with behavioral and analytical considerations it is small wonder that no simple, straightforward solution has emerged to the problem of strategy implementation. Rather, there are

FIGURE 10.10 | **Adaptive Computer-based Control System**

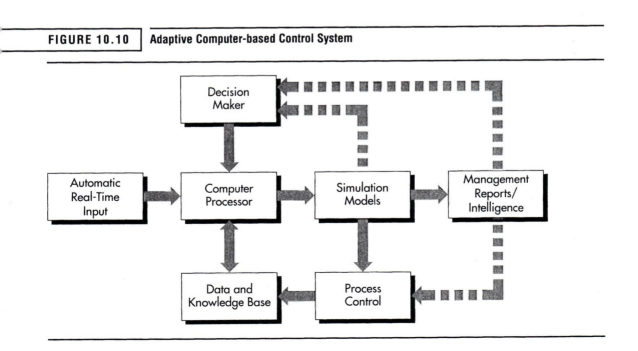

multiple perspectives. Managers with behavioral styles contend that quantitative controls are dysfunctional. The analytic school claims that without numbers, suboptimization is inevitable. Computer specialists tout the need for decision support systems that can provide adaptive, real-time control. Where does the answer lie? Obviously, the answer is with none of the above taken singularly. The approach must be an integrative one that recognizes the strengths, pitfalls, and problems of each individual approach and attempts to reconcile them into a single effective method. For a strategy to be implemented, it is necessary to create a supportive organizational culture and to bring consensus and commitment to the control process so that organizational goals and objectives are achieved. This task is an essential one for strategic management.

S UMMARY

As soon as a strategic repositioning of the company is proposed, a plan of action is needed. A well-conceived strategy is one that has been planned with the company's capability to carry out the proposed change in mind.

A strategy that is not implemented is no strategy at all. Therefore, the astute manager incorporates implementation into the plan from the very beginning. After the strategic change has been instituted, continuous and systematic follow-up is necessary to ensure that resistance is minimized, that the strategy is executed, and that its full potential is realized. Thus both formal and informal methods are needed to ensure stakeholder acceptance of proposed changes, to maximize motivation and commitment on the part of those who have to carry out the plan, and to evaluate completely and objectively the results achieved.

Four factors affect the implementation of any strategy:

1. The style of the executive who is the change agent
2. The corporate culture—the norms, values, and beliefs that guide the organization
3. The values held by individuals in the organization
4. The fit, or match, of corporate and individual values

Using the implementation model presented, the decision maker can determine how compatible a particular culture is with a proposed change.

The executive's decision style and leadership style affect the strategic alternatives and direction an organization will pursue. Few decisions have as significant an impact on the organization as the choice of an overall strategy. Therefore, it is not surprising that the decision styles of those in charge play a major role in determining the overall success of an organization.

The decision style model provides insights into both how and why decisions are made. Decision style analysis shows how much information and what approach a manager generally uses in solving strategic problems. It also helps to identify the focus of the manager in terms of technical versus organizational problems. Given this perspective, one can determine the approach most likely to be taken by the decision maker, provided no extraneous factors influence the decision.

Not only is a knowledge of decision styles helpful in determining how someone will respond to a situation, it also lends insight into who has leadership qualities. Most leaders today have the conceptual style as their dominant style. They have a vision and are more idea-oriented than those who are predominantly concerned with operational management activities. Visions are turned into reality when the leader has a supportive, directive style that focuses on results. The increasing number of factors affecting business decisions may make the rational or analytical decision maker unable to cope with the social and political requirements of an organization. Furthermore, those with leadership qualities may not succeed if they do not have the power or authority to carry out their ideas. The way in which power is exercised within an organization depends on the kinds of uses of power that a particular manager prefers, as well as on his or her level of authority.

The structure of an organization is a function both of its size and of its complexity. Mintzberg's (1979) four basic categories of organizational form provide a means for examining the relationship of organizational structure to strategy. The traditional view of the structure of an organization as a response to a given strategy is no longer adequate, given the rapid change in environmental forces and in the contextual variables internal to the organization. A structure is not simply a rigid artifact that reflects the manner in which strategies are carried out. Rather, organizations are constantly changing and adapting to external exigencies and to internal political coalitions and technology requirements.

Organizations exhibit a cyclical pattern that often follows the familiar biological growth curve. This pattern, called the organizational life cycle, provides useful insights into how the size of the organization and the rate of change influence both strategies and controls. The most appropriate leadership style also changes with the organization life cycle. The start-up phase requires an entrepreneurial style, whereas a mature organization needs the vision and direction that an analytical or conceptual style can provide. Although the exact pattern an organization follows depends on competition, product life cycle, technology, general economic conditions, and managerial career life cycle, the general pattern can be used to guide strategic decisions.

The organizational structure matrix relates the level of environmental uncertainty to the degree of integration needed; that is, it shows the strategy/structure linkages. The amount of integration and coordination required is in turn related to the stage in the organizational life cycle.

The contingency approach relates the organizational structure to the external environment, individual and group factors, and the internal work system. The model proposed by Tosi and Hamner shows the factors that contribute to the constant realignment of the organization.

When all three approaches are combined—the life cycle, the uncertainty/integration matrix, and the contingency model—it is readily apparent that no one structure is most appropriate nor will any structure remain best for a long period of time. The structure must be tailored to the external constraints as well as the internal culture of the firm, and it must be fine-tuned and adjusted regularly.

Logical incrementalism and intrapreneurship are two alternative means of gaining acceptance of strategic change. These approaches rely on motivational and political bases for influencing behavior. However, they do not eliminate the need for an analytical basis for determining which alternatives are viable and consistent with the overall mission of the organization.

REFERENCES AND SUGGESTIONS FOR FURTHER READING

Allison, Graham T. 1971. *Essence of decision: Explaining the Cuban missile crisis.* Boston: Little, Brown.

Anderson, Carl R. and Frank T. Paine. 1975. Managerial perceptions and strategic behavior. *Academy of Management Journal,* December.

Barnes, Louis B. and Mark P. Kriger. 1987. The hidden side of organizational leadership. *The McKinsey Quarterly,* Winter, pp. 15–35.

Bartlett, Christopher and Sumantra Ghoshal. 1990. Matrix management: Not a structure, a frame of mind. *Harvard Business Review,* July–August, pp. 138–145.

Beer, Michael and Robert A. Ruh. 1976. Employee growth through performance management. *Harvard Business Review,* August.

Bennis, Warren G. 1991. Learning some basic truisms about leadership. *Phi Kappa Phi Journal,* Winter, pp. 12–15.

Bennis, Warren G. 1976. Leadership a beleagured species. *Organizational Dynamics,* Vol. 5, no. 1, pp. 3–16.

Bennis, Warren and Burt Nanus. 1985. *Leaders.* New York: Harper & Row.

Bonoma, Thomas V. 1984. Making your marketing strategy work. *Harvard Business Review,* March–April.

Broder, John M. 1986. Wells Fargo is ready to crack whip at Crocker. *Los Angeles Times,* February 16, pp. IV 1–2.

Bryon, Christopher. 1981. How Japan does it. *Time,* March 30, p. 54.

Byrne, John A. 1989. Donald Burr may be ready to take to the skies again. *Business Week,* January 16, pp. 74–75.

Byrne, John A. 1985. Up, up and away? *Business Week,* November 25, pp. 80–94.

Chandler, Alfred D. 1962. *Strategy and structure.* Cambridge, Mass.: M.I.T. Press.

Changing a corporate culture. 1984. *Business Week*, May 14, pp. 130–138.

Child, J. 1972. Organizational structure, environment and performance. *Sociology*.

Clark, Rolf. 1992. TQM from the trenches: The role of the individual. *Program Manager*, March–April, pp. 28–32.

Corporate culture: The hard-to-change values that spell success or failure. 1980. *Business Week*, October 27, pp. 148–160.

Deal, Terrence. 1984. *Corporate cultures: The rite and rituals of corporate life.* Reading, Mass.: Addison-Wesley.

Deshpande, Rohit and A. Parasuraman. 1986. Linking corporate culture to strategic planning. *Business Horizon*, May–June, pp. 28–37.

Diesing, Paul. 1962. *Reason in society.* Westport, Conn.: Greenwood Press.

Dowd, Ann Reilly. 1992. Will George Bush really change? *Fortune*, June 29, pp. 61–64.

Driver, Michael and Alan J. Rowe. 1979. Decision-making styles: A new approach to management decision making. In *Behavior problems in organizations*, ed. Cary Cooper. Englewood Cliffs, N.J.: Prentice-Hall.

Drucker, Peter. 1982. Why some mergers work and many more don't. *Forbes*, January 18, p. 34.

Drucker, Peter. 1974. *Management: Tasks, responsibilities, and practices.* New York: Harper & Row.

Dumaine, Brian. 1992a. The corporate culture connection. *Fortune*, May 4, p. 119.

Dumaine, Brian. 1992b. Unleash workers and cut costs. *Fortune*, May 18, p. 88.

Ehrenfeld, Tom. 1992. The case of the unpopular pay plan. *Harvard Business Review*, January–February, pp. 14–18.

Epstin, Edwin M. 1974. Dimensions of corporate power, part 2. *California Management Review*, Summer.

Epstin, Edwin M. 1973. Dimensions of corporate power, part 1. *California Management Review*, Winter.

Farnham, Alan. 1989. The trust gap. *Fortune*, December 4, pp. 56–78.

Fiedler, Fred E. 1958. *Leadership attitudes and group effectiveness.* Urbana: University of Illinois Press.

Filley, Alan C., Robert J. House, and Steven Kerr. 1976. *Managerial processes and organizational behavior.* Glenview, Ill.: Scott, Foresman.

Galbraith, Jay R. 1973. *Designing complex organizations.* Reading, Mass.: Addison-Wesley.

Galbraith, Jay R. and Robert K. Kazanjian. 1986. *Strategy implementation.* Los Angeles: West Publishing Company.

Galbraith, Jay R. and Daniel A. Nathanson. 1978. *Strategic implementation: The role of structure and process.* St. Paul: West.

Gibson, John L., John M. Ivancevich, and James H. Donnelly, Jr. 1988. *Organizations.* Plano, Texas: Business Publications Inc.

Greiner, Larry E. 1972. Evolution and revolution as organizations grow. *Harvard Business Review*, August.

Guth, William D. and Renato Taguiri. 1965. Personal values and corporate strategy. *Harvard Business Review,* September–October, pp. 123–132.

Hampton, William. 1984. Why Honeywell and Synertek couldn't make a go of it. *Business Week*, December 17, p. 39.

Hampton, William J. 1980. Corporate culture: The hard-to-change values that spell success or failure. *Business Week*, October 27, p. 148.

Hansen, Jeffrey A. 1985. CEO management style and the stages of development in new ventures. Unpublished paper. Salem, Oregon: Atkinson Graduate School of Management.

Hansen, Jeffrey A. 1984. Decision and management styles in emerging companies. Unpublished paper, Atkinson Graduate School of Management, Willamette University, Oregon.

Heiko, Lance. 1989. Some relationships between Japanese culture and just-in-time. *The Academy of Management Executive* III, no. 4, pp. 319–321.

Heirs, Ben and Gordon Pehrson. 1982. *The mind of the organization.* New York: Harper & Row.

Heller, Frank A. and Bernard Wilper. 1981. *Competence and power.* New York: Wiley.

Here comes the intrapreneur. 1983. *Business Week*, July.

Hickman, Craig R. 1990. *Mind of a manager, soul of a leader.* New York: Wiley.

Hillkirk, John. 1991. AT&T chief makes teamwork a driving force. *USA Today*, March 12, pp. 12–13.

Hinings, Christopher R. et al. 1974. Structural conditions of intraorganizational power. *Administrative Science Quarterly* 19.

Hirschhorn, Larry and Thomas Gilmore. 1992. The new boundaries of the "boundaryless company." *Harvard Business Review*, May–June, pp. 104–115.

Iacocca, Lee and William Novak. 1984. *Iacocca.* New York: Bantam Books.

Jack Welch reinvents General Electric—again. 1991. *The Economist*, March 30, pp. 59–62.

A Japanese boss whose "consensus" is an iron fist. 1984. *Business Week*, November, pp. 176–178.

Judson, Arnold S. 1966. *A manager's guide to making changes.* London: Wiley.

Kiechel, Walter, III. 1989. A hard look at executive vision. *Fortune*, October 23, pp. 207–210.

Kilman, Ralph H. and Mary J. Saxton. 1983. *Kilman-Saxton culture gap survey.* Pittsburgh: Organizational Design Consultants.

Kimberly, J. R. 1976. Organizational size and the structuralist perspective. *Administrative Science Quarterly*.

Kimberly, John R. and Robert H. Miles. 1980. *The organizational life cycle*. San Francisco: Jossey-Bass.

Kotter, John. 1990. What leaders really do. *Harvard Business Review*, May–June, pp. 103–111.

Kotter, John P. 1988. The leadership factor. *The McKinsey Quarterly*, Spring, pp. 71–78.

Kouzes, James M. and Barry Z. Posner. 1988. From manager to leader. *Newsweek—Management Digest Quarterly*, Fall.

Kumar, Anil and Graham Sharman. 1992. We love your product, but where is it? *The McKinsey Quarterly*, no. 1, pp. 24–44.

Langeler, Gerard. 1992. The vision trap. *Harvard Business Review*, March–April, pp. 46–55.

Lawrence, John F. 1985. A company's culture shapes performance. *Los Angeles Times*, January 27.

Lawrence, Paul R. and J. W. Lorsch. 1967. *Organization and environment*. Homewood, Ill.: Irwin.

Ledford, Bruce. 1991. The battle of beliefs: In the age of manipulation. *Phi Kappa Phi Journal*, Winter, pp. 33–35.

Levinson, Harry. 1973. Asinine attitudes toward motivation. *Harvard Business Review*, February.

Lewin, Kurt. 1951. *Field theory and social science*. New York: Harper & Brothers.

Lindblom, Charles E. 1965. *The intelligence of democracy*. New York: The Free Press.

Lord, Mary. 1991. How Nabisco solved its labor problem. *U.S. News & World Report*, May 20, p. 60.

Lundberg, Olof and Max D. Richards. 1972. A relationship between cognitive style and complex decision making: Implications for business policy. *Proceedings of the Academy of Management*, August.

Magnet, Myron. 1992. The truth about the American worker. *Fortune*, May 4, pp. 48–65.

Main, Jeremy. 1987. Wanted: Managers who can make a difference. *Fortune*, September 28, pp. 92–98.

Mann, Richard B. 1982. Relationship between the decision-making styles of corporate planners and other planners. Unpublished dissertation. Los Angeles: University of Southern California.

Maren, Michael and Don Wallace. 1992. Masters of the impossible. *Success*, January–February, pp. 22–32.

Margerison, C. J. and D. J. McCann. 1985. *The team management index*. New Berlin, Wis.: National Consulting and Training Institute.

Maruyama, Magoroh. 1991. Policy for international talent utilization. *Technology Analysis & Strategic Management* III, no. 4, pp. 323–331.

Maruyama, Magoroh. 1991. Contracts in cultures. *Human Systems Management*, 10, pp. 33–46.

Maslow, Abraham H. 1954. *Motivation and personality*. New York: Harper & Row.

Mason, Todd and Richard Brandt. 1985. How Ross Perot's shock troops ran into flak at GM. *Business Week*, February 11, p. 118.

McClelland, D. C. 1971. *Assessing human motivation*. New York: General Learning Press.

McConkey, Dale D. 1973. MBO—Twenty years later, where do we stand? *Business Horizons*, August.

Meen, David and Mark Keough. 1992. Creating the learning organization. *The McKinsey Quarterly*, 1, pp. 58–86.

Mendes, Joshua. 1984. Waking up AT&T: There's life after culture shock. *Fortune*, December 24, pp. 66–74.

Miesing, P. 1984. Integrating planning with management. *Long-Range Planning*, October, pp. 118–124.

Miles, Robert H. 1982. *Coffin nails and corporate strategies*. Englewood Cliffs, N.J.: Prentice-Hall.

Miller, Danny. 1983. The correlates of entrepreneurship in three types of firms. *Management Sciences* 29, no. 7 (July).

Mintzberg, Henry. 1979. *The structuring of organizations*. Englewood Cliffs, N.J.: Prentice-Hall.

Mockler, Robert J. 1989. *Knowledge-based systems for strategic planning*. Englewood Cliffs, N.J.: Prentice-Hall.

Morse, John J. and Jay W. Lorsch. 1970. Beyond theory Y. *Harvard Business Review*, June.

Nonaka, Ikujiro. 1991. The knowledge-creating company. *Harvard Business Review*, November–December, pp. 96–104.

Nunamaker, Jay. 1992. Teamwork tools lead the way to creative collaboration. *Corporate Computing*, August, pp. 196–198.

Patz, Alan L. and Alan J. Rowe. 1977. *Management control and decision systems*. New York: Wiley.

Perot, Ross. 1988. How I would turn around GM. *Fortune*, February 15, pp. 44–50.

Pfeffer, Jeffrey and Gerald R. Salancik. 1978. *The external control of organizations*. New York: Harper & Row.

Phillips, Donald. 1992. *Lincoln on leadership: Executive strategies for tough times*. New York: Warner Books.

Platt, John R. 1966. *The step to man*. New York: Wiley.

Posner, Barry Z. and Warren H. Schmidt. 1984. *The significance of values compatibility between managers and their organization*. Unpublished paper, Academy of Management, Western Regional Meeting, Vancouver, Canada, April, pp. 1–16.

Prokesch, Steve E. and William J. Howell, Jr. 1985. Do mergers really work? *Business Week*, June 3, p. 89.

Quinn, James B. 1978. Strategic change: Logical incrementalism. *Sloan Management Review*, Fall.

Raia, Anthony P. 1974. *Managing by objectives*. Glenview, Ill.: Scott, Foresman.

Rayner, Bruce. 1992. Trial-by-fire transformation: An interview with Globe Metallurgical's Arden C. Sims. *Harvard Business Review*, May–June, pp. 117–129.

Reddin, William J. 1970. *Managerial effectiveness.* New York: McGraw-Hill.

Ridgway, V. P. 1956. Dysfunctional consequences of performance measurements. *Administrative Science Quarterly.*

Rowe, Alan J. 1981. Decision making in the 80's. *Los Angeles Journal of Business and Economics*, Winter.

Rowe, Alan J. and James D. Boulgarides. 1992. *Managerial decision making.* New York: Macmillan.

Rowe, Alan J. and James D. Boulgarides. 1983. Decision styles—A perspective. *Learning and Organizational Development Journal* 4,4.

Rowe, Alan J. and John Carlson. 1974. Adaptive control systems for operating management. *Logistics Spectrum Journal*, September.

Rowe, Alan J. and Richard O. Mason. 1988b. Are you in the right job? *Newsweek—Management Digest Quarterly*, Winter.

Rowe, Alan J. and Richard O. Mason. 1988a. The impact of style, values, and culture on strategic change. Paper presented at the International Planning Conference, Boston.

Rowe, Alan J. and Richard O. Mason. 1987. *Managing with style.* San Francisco: Jossey-Bass.

Sanchez, Jesus. 1991. Cooperation forges a success story. *Los Angeles Times*, April 26, P. D1.

Sashkin, Marshall. 1990. What causes loyalty? Unpublished paper, pp. 1–16.

Sathe, Vijay. 1983. Implications of corporate culture: A manager's guide to action. *Organizational Dynamics*, Autumn.

Schein, Edgar H. 1985. *Organizational culture and leadership.* San Francisco: Jossey-Bass.

Schumacher, Ernst F. 1973. *Small is beautiful.* New York: Harper & Row.

Sethia, Nirmal. 1984. Observations on *Shaping the Culture of the Firm: The Role of Management.* Unpublished review of the conference at Pepperdine University, Los Angeles, April 10.

Shaw, Russell. 1990. Robert E. Allen: Chairman & CEO, AT&T. *Sky Magazine.* October, p. 50.

Sherman, Straford P. 1989. The mind of Jack Welch. *Fortune*, March 27, pp. 39–50.

Sirota, David and Alan D. Wolfson. 1972. Job enrichment: Surmounting the obstacles. *Personnel*, July.

Smith, Lee. 1985. Japan's autocratic managers. *Fortune*, January 7, pp. 56–64.

Snyder, Richard C. 1984. To enhance innovation, manage corporate culture. Unpublished paper, University of Southern California.

Springer, Sally P. and Georg Deutsch. 1981. *Left brain, right brain.* San Francisco: W. H. Freeman.

Starbuck, William H. and Paul C. Nystrom. 1981. Designing and understanding organizations, in *Handbook of organizational design*, Vol. 1. Ed. Paul C. Nystrom and William Starbuck. New York: Oxford University Press.

Steers, Richard M. 1977. *Organizational effectiveness.* Santa Monica, Calif.: Goodyear.

Tandem computers. 1988. *Value Line*, Vol. 1110, November 4.

Tichy, Noel and Ram Charan. 1989. Speed, simplicity, self-confidence: An interview with Jack Welch. *Harvard Business Review*, September–October, pp. 112–120.

Tosi, Henry L. and W. Clay Hamner. 1974. *Organizational behavior and management.* Chicago: St. Clair Press.

Toy, Stewart. 1985. Splitting up: The other side of merger mania. *Business Week*, July 1, pp. 50–55.

Tunstall, W. Brooke. 1986. The breakup of the Bell System: A case study in cultural transformation. *California Management Review*, Winter, pp. 110–125.

Tunstall, W. Brooke. 1983. Cultural transition at AT&T. *Sloan Management Review*, Fall, pp. 1–12.

Utall, Bro. 1983. Corporate culture vultures. *Fortune*, October 17, p. 66.

Verity, John and Peter Coy. 1992. Twin engines: Can Bob Allen blend computers and telecommunications at AT&T? *Business Week*, January 20, pp. 56–61.

Vroom, Victor H. and Philip W. Yetton. 1973. *Leadership and decision-making.* Pittsburgh: University of Pittsburgh Press.

Watson, Thomas J., Jr. 1963. *A business and its beliefs: The ideas that helped build IBM.* New York: McGraw-Hill.

Webber, Alan. 1990. Consensus, continuity, and common sense: An interview with Compaq's Rod Canion. *Harvard Business Review*, July–August, pp. 115–123.

Weber, Max. 1969. *Bureaucracy.* New York: Wiley.

Weber, Max. 1947. *Theory of social and economic organization.* New York: Oxford University Press.

White, F. B. and L. B. Barnes. 1971. Power networks in the appraisal process. *Harvard Business Review*, May–June.

Woutat, Donald. 1992. Ford loses $2.3 billion; Diahatsu quits U.S. market. *Los Angeles Times*, February 14, pp. D-1 and D-2.

Zaleznick, Abraham. 1977. Managers and leaders: Are they different? *Harvard Business Review.* May–June.

Zumberge, James. 1988. Presidential address, University of Southern California.

APPENDIX A

The Social Change Model

The *social change model* can help a manager determine how a new strategic plan will be perceived by the stakeholders and how management can cope with possible resistance. The purpose of the model is to identify the target area for introducing strategic change and the best means of communicating the plan. Management must make clear to those involved why the proposed change is necessary and how it can be accomplished.

PRELIMINARY ANALYSIS

The first step in the preliminary analysis is to prepare a description of the social system required to carry out the new strategy. In other words, identify the stakeholders and their primary motivating interests. This involves identifying the role of each stakeholder in the system, discovering how that role is related to other roles, and investigating the sentiments, norms, values, and ideals that operate in the interactions between each pair of roles. This description enables strategic managers to analyze the attitudes and probable reactions of individual stakeholders and the organization as a whole.

The following method can be used to gauge stakeholders' support for a strategic plan. First, each stakeholder is identified and assigned a weight from 1 to 10, indicating the importance of that stakeholder in implementing the strategy. If a strategy plan cannot be carried out without the involvement of a given stakeholder, this stakeholder should be assigned an importance weight of 10. A weight of 1 indicates that the plan can be implemented without this stakeholder's support.

Next, the attitude of each stakeholder toward the expected results of a strategy should be evaluated. There obviously is a wide spectrum of sentiments concerning change, ranging from active resistance at one extreme to enthusiastic support at the other. Possible behaviors in between these two extremes include cooperation, acceptance, protests, and simply doing what is ordered. The introduction of change often creates anxiety and fear. When a major change is in the offing as the result of some newly proposed strategy, anxiety may cause undesirable reaction that needs to be countered. Table 10A.1 can be used to score the attitude of each stakeholder.

By multiplying the importance weights by the attitude scores, one can determine the approximate effect that each stakeholder will have on implementation of a new strategy. Often the best one can do with important stakeholders who actively resist the implementation of a strategy is to attempt to neutralize their effect. If they are less resistant, managers may try to convert them. Stakeholders with little importance can usually be ignored, whereas strong supporters should be reinforced. The weighted total of all the scores will indicate the overall disposition of a system toward translating a strategic plan into action. Table 10A.2 lists some potential causes of resistance and suggests ways of dealing with them.

The second step in the preliminary analysis is to assess the level of social resources the manager has available for implementing the strategy. Social resources, as distinct from economic resources, are particular and unique to each stakeholder. Friendships, loyalties, habits, perceptions, psychological style, anxieties, prejudices, shared beliefs, identification

---

TABLE 10A.1	**Attitude Scales for Stakeholders**

Behavior	Score
Active resistance	1
Passive resistance	3
Indifference	5
Cooperation	7
Enthusiastic support	10

TABLE 10A.2	**Resistance to Change**

Typical Problems Causing Resistance	Technique for Overcoming Resistance	Expected Outcome
1. Those affected lack knowledge about the proposed change	Communicate in meetings, encourage involvement	Achieve understanding and acceptance
2. Groups are exerting power to maintain the status quo	Encourage participation and power sharing or cooperation	Integrate group members into change strategy
3. Change is having dysfunctional consequences	Negotiate or provide inducements to obtain consensus	Avoid major confrontation
4. Timing of the change is critical	Facilitate change and provide support	Help to accelerate change
5. The change is so radical as to be mistrusted	Provide open climate, accept ideas, create respect	Gain acceptance by including others in the decision

with purpose, will power, and dedication are examples of social resources. They are very specialized, and generally they cannot be allocated or used for other purposes.

The third step is to form a general opinion of the social change problem. The problem statement describing the current situation is critical. The social dimension of a strategy generally involves righting some current misalignment, disorganization, or conflict that is serving as a barrier to executing the strategy. A method is needed for achieving a new pattern of integration and organizational equilibrium.

PRINCIPLES OF NONECONOMIC DECISION MAKING

Once these three preliminary steps have been accomplished, the three *principles of noneconomic decision making* can be employed (Diesing, 1962). As the application of the principles unfolds, the information obtained during the three preliminary steps can be augmented and reorganized. All three of Diesing's principles should be applied. If required, the process should be repeated until a final social change solution emerges. Here is the first principle of noneconomic decision making:

Principle of changeability: *Select the easiest possible relevant changes within the organization.*

The easiest changes are most likely to be successful. They will generate less conflict and resistance. The ease of change is based on two variables: introducibility and acceptability.

Introducibility, in turn, depends on two factors. First, roles must exist in the social system that permit one to put new changes in place. Second, people must have sufficient skill to execute these roles effectively. The first requirement for introducibility is evaluated by examining the activities and interactions inherent in each role, the second by assessing the social resources available in the system and available to those who might occupy the role of change agent. Ideally, the role of those who introduce a new strategy is to win over people who play roles that must be changed if the strategy is to be effective. Thus the change agent should be a credible source for the change. For example, a county agricultural agent is a credible and presumably skillful source for initiating changes in agricultural practice but might not be a credible or skillful source for introducing changes in, say, a computer system.

The success of a new strategy may lie with a single individual and the social resources he or she can bring to bear. For example, John Platt (1966) credits the scientist Leo Szilard with playing a crucial role in formulating and implementing U.S. atomic energy policy during the early years of World War II. Szilard used his status in the scientific community to persuade British and American atomic scientists to keep their activities secret during the prewar years. Later he drew on his friendship with Einstein to encourage Einstein to write the letter to President Roosevelt that started the U.S. Atomic energy project in 1940. From the standpoint of introducibility, Szilard was the right man, in the right place, at the right time.

Acceptability depends on something more than just acquiring the conscious approval of the stakeholders. The new strategy must be capable of being integrated into the existing organizational system with a minimum of disruption, incompatibility, and conflict. A new strategy is more likely to be accepted if it is functionally similar to the one it replaces. For example, a school district policy that requires teachers to employ a new text that embodies the same educational philosophy as previous texts is more likely to be accepted than is a policy that calls for a major redesign in texts, teaching style, facilities, grading systems, and administrative support. Educational innovations such as team teaching, open classrooms, and curricular revision often have not been accepted because they require changing many social relationships.

A similar point is made by E.F. Schumacher (1973) with respect to the field of economic development. He argues that smaller innovations are more likely to be accepted than major changes. For example, new agricultural implements that fit into the existing Indian peasant culture—tightly organized communities, small land holdings, traditional furrowing methods—are more likely to be accepted by the community than large-scale agricultural equipment. Intermediate technology—such as a scientifically designed steel plow or a small, one wheel, hand-held motorized plow—is more appropriate than, say, a large tractor or combine. Many businesses that have tried to export U.S. manufacturing and sales methods into foreign countries have learned the very same lesson, often at a great expense.

Acceptability, then, is greater if *functional similarity*—the pattern of activities and interactions among the stakeholders—remains substantially the same and only the content changes. A new strategy is less acceptable if it destroys old activities and interactions and institutes completely new ones. The stronger the sentiments for an old activity or interaction and the more deeply ingrained the norms and habits related to participating in it, the less likely it is that a new strategy will be acceptable. Exceptions occur if subordinates feel a strong need for change in the system or if an intense conflict has been held in check. At that point the system is ready (occasionally too ready) to accept changes.

In applying the principle of changeability, the strategic manager should ask the following questions:

- What change is possible? Can it be introduced? Is it acceptable?
- Which is the easiest change to effect with the social resources available?

The second principle of noneconomic decision making is as follows:

Principle of separability: *Select a target area that is sufficiently independent from its context to be susceptible to separate implementation while protected from outside pressures.*

Implementation of strategies takes time—often several years and sometimes decades. Consequently an entire strategy can seldom be implemented all at once. Instead, a workable target area or substrategy must be identified and a change proposed that can be implemented in that limited area. For any given strategy many target areas can typically be identified. Separation is needed because large, highly interconnected target areas are too massive for full implementation at once. The likelihood of success is improved if the strategy can be focused on manageable, smaller target areas or substrategies.

This task is often a difficult one for the strategic manager because problems are generally highly interconnected, complex, uncertain, ambiguous, and political in nature. Yet this complexity is also to some extent organized. *Organized complexity* implies that some parts of the strategy are relatively separable from the others and that the relevant relationships can be changed to a limited extent without simultaneous change in the entire system. Identifying a relatively independent target area in the organization may involve observing social relationships within a single group or class of stakeholders, such as a work group, a kinship group, an age group, a particular organization, a geographic region, or an occupational class. Alternatively, it may involve changing a cluster of roles, beliefs, drives, values, rituals, or symbols.

The principle that is being applied here differs from Lindblom's (1965) concept of incrementalism, or "muddling through." Although both concepts recommend a small, manageable increment of change, the principle of separability requires that the choice of a target area be guided by a concept of the strategy as a whole. This point will take on more force in light of the next principle.

Principle of growth: *Begin a change in such a way that extension of the change is possible.*

This principle is equivalent to initiating a *social chain reaction*. Organizations are typically conservative and foster mechanisms that reject innovation. When properly triggered, however, the same mechanisms can be used to encourage the change, expand it, and facilitate its diffusion.

When a positive feedback loop is activated, a change escalates. The positive feedback loop acts as a multiplier, amplifying the output for every cycle that occurs. It is this phenomenon that causes a child's quarrel to escalate into a brawl, each step louder and noisier than the previous one. The snowball effect comes into play, each cycle adding exponentially to the mass of the underlying problem.

John Platt (1966) has argued that it is possible to select points of entry into a social system where the multiplier is greater than 1, and thus a chain reaction is released. He calls the initial, narrowly defined implementation the *seed operation*. Usually changes in a few activities and interactions lead to changes in sentiments and norms, thus reinforcing the changes and permitting new activities and interactions to be started. Then the process is repeated. During each iteration, the target area gradually increases in size and in complexity. More social resources become available to deal with the problem because each iteration leads to a decrease in conflict and tension in the original target area, freeing the psychic and physical energy that was tied up in these conflicts. The new energy is now available to deal with the new, larger, and more difficult strategic target area.

Examples of this effect can be found in virtually every field. The invention of metal coins eliminated barter and permitted modern commerce to take off. The advent of the horse collar, according to one theory, increased the productivity of the farmer, leading to enlarged medieval farms, which, in turn, created a surplus of production, releasing people so that they could move into the cities and thereby making the Renaissance possible.

Ideally, the chain reaction ends when the entire strategy has been fully implemented and relationships in the organization have all been modified according to the prescriptions of the strategy. The chain reaction can stop prematurely, however, if it encounters a barrier somewhere in the process—that is, if an iteration of the cycle exposes too large and difficult a strategic target for the energy accumulated thus far. Anticipation of these barriers permits seed operations to be begun in places with relatively low positive feedback at first, but with a growth pattern that will permit the accumulation of enough energy to overcome the barriers when they are encountered. For this reason, successful social change often takes a long time.

In applying the principle of growth, the strategic manager should ask where the seed operation should be begun. That is, what social relationships can be changed so that a chain reaction is triggered in the direction specified by the policy?

Targets for change that satisfy one of the three basic principles may not fulfill the requirements of the other two. If this is the case, the strategic manager must re-examine the options until a strategy is found that begins with a relatively separable strategic target area, introduces an acceptable change rather easily, and then triggers a social chain reaction.

APPLYING THE SOCIAL CHANGE MODEL

Once the overall strategy has been identified, the social change model can be applied by means of the following steps.

1. Identify a series of possible change tactics, such as starting a new advertising program, installing new equipment, implementing a new compensation package, or instituting a new information system. *Summarize each change tactic as an action to be taken in a target area.*

2. Evaluate each change tactic in relation to its changeability, separability, and growth characteristics. Use a scale ranging from 1 to 10, with 10 the highest score possible.
3. Multiply the changeability, separability, and growth scores ($C \times S \times G$) to obtain a total score. The change tactic with the highest total score is the most effective change tactic.

An application of the social change model applied to the AMP company is shown in Worksheet 10A.1. This example illustrates how the process can be applied to determine an appropriate strategic action. Three strategic options have been identified. (Refer to Chapter 6 for details on the AMP company.)

■ Option A: New design involving improved, but not advanced, technology, promising savings of between 2% and 3% in direct cost. This option would require a minimum investment of $200,000 for new equipment and engineering design.
■ Option B: Advanced technology requiring an investment of up to $750,000 for special-purpose equipment and assembly devices. This technology could save up to 5% in direct cost.
■ Option C: High technology involving new approaches that have not been fully tested. If successful, this technology would give AMP a clear edge in the connector field for many years to come. Some experimentation is required, however, and its cost could run as high as $70,000 per month for an extended period, although the investment in equipment would not exceed $400,000.

The principles of social change have been applied to these three options in Worksheet 10A.1. With respect to an evaluation of the social change possibilities, option B rates the highest. The evaluation points out the following features of option B:

■ Option B is rather easy to introduce, and because of the technical and professional nature of AMP's personnel, it should be acceptable. Moreover, its potential cost savings makes it attractive to management.
■ Because it is based on advanced technology, option B is undoubtedly easier to protect from outside interference than is option A.
■ Option B also provides growth opportunities through advanced research. This should give AMP a sound foundation for moving toward the high-technology capability required by option C.

In making a final choice, the strategic manager must balance the social change evaluation against the economic and other evaluations covered earlier in this book. The correct approach is the one that best incorporates the advantages offered by all the evaluation methods utilized.

WORKSHEET 10A.1	Social Change Model

Case __AMP__
Date __1992__
Name __Mary Doe__

Change Option	Comment	Evaluation	Score C × S × G
A	*Changeability:* Easy to change from a technological and cost point of view.	8	
	Separability: Not very separable.	2	
	Growth: Provides minimum growth because it is focused on current technology.	4	64
B	*Changeability:* Relatively easy to introduce and get accepted. Economical if investment can be made advantageous.	6	
	Separability: Reasonably separable.	5	
	Growth: Provides relatively high growth potential because it builds on an advanced technological base.	5	150
C	*Changeability:* Because of uncertainty and heavy investment required, very difficult to introduce and get accepted.	2	
	Separability: Very separable.	9	
	Growth: Would provide maximum growth if successful, but is very uncertain now.	6	108

APPENDIX B

Decision Styles

McDonnell Douglas, at one point, was described as the Pentagon's most proficient and lowest-cost producer. What contributed most to this reputation was "Mr. Mac's" style. He was an engineer and aircraft designer who developed a company with thrift and paternalism. Because of Mac's style, an infatuation with engineering permeates every aspect of the company's activities and decision making. It was the basis of Mac's power in the organization, and it was reflected in the organization's structure.

An important conclusion is that the manager's style has a direct effect on strategy. The entrepreneurial risk taker who is highly innovative, for example, may not do well supervising the cost cutting that must be emphasized during the second and third phases of an organization's life cycle.

It takes a hard-driving spirit to lift a company out of the doldrums. Joe Alibrandi, the wiry, fast-talking, energetic president of Whittaker Corporation, dumped almost 100 operating units in order to launch the company into a new phase of the life cycle. As a result, Whittaker has enjoyed a startling turnaround. Lee Iacocca transformed Chrysler from a company plagued by a loss of $1.7 billion into a profitable enterprise with a whole new outlook. In both of these cases, the style of management matched the requirements of the organization's life cycle. As organizations mature and change, so must management if it is to ensure continued and profitable growth. Thus a key element of meeting strategic objectives is to find the right manager to fit the situation. Knowing the decision styles of potential managers can help one determine who would be most likely to succeed in a particular situation.

Table 10B.1 lists characteristics that distinguish flexible decision styles from focused, or rigid, ones. Style flexibility affects the manager's ability to deal with highly ambiguous or changing conditions. Although the flexible manager is better at handling complex problems, the focused manager is better able to deal with problems that require quick decisions or rapid action.

TABLE 10B.1	Style Flexibility		
Factor		**Rigid Style**	**Flexible Style**
Tolerance for ambiguity		Low	High
Need for structure		High	Low
Use of power		Authoritarian	Sensitive
Need for control		High	Low
Values that are important		Rules	Honesty
Dealings with others		Expects results	Supportive
Personal orientation		Self	Others

COGNITIVE ASPECTS OF DECISION STYLE

Cognitive processes help to explain the differences that individuals exhibit in thinking and perceiving. These processes determine the way information is used and conceptual ability applied in formulating and evaluating strategies.

Information Processing. Springer and Deutsch's (1981) research on the left and right hemispheres of the brain has shown that each hemisphere has specific functions. The left hemisphere deals with logical thought, is analytical, processes information serially, and is used for processing language. It handles speaking, pointing, and smiling, as well as the abstract logical reasoning needed for mathematics. Individuals whose left hemisphere is dominant tend to be able to readily differentiate diverse elements in a set of data. The right hemisphere specializes in intuition and creativity. Individuals whose right hemisphere is dominant tend to perceive things as a whole, have a comprehensive sense of timing, and consider many ideas at the same time (parallel processing of information). They appreciate space, imagery, fantasy, and music. These individuals tend to integrate data into a broad or cohesive perspective leading to more general constructs. Dreams seem to be predominantly right-brain functions. Many right-brain thinkers are artistic.

Cognitive Complexity. *Cognitive complexity* refers to a person's ability to consider a number of interdependent variables at once. One element of cognitive complexity is the ability to differentiate a number of dimensions in perceived data or to discriminate among bits of data (a left-hemisphere function). Another element of cognitive complexity is the ability to combine data in such a way as to find new constructs or complex rules (a right-hemisphere function). This ability is called *integration*. Because strategy involves many complex, interdependent variables, the manager's ability to comprehend and deal with a given situation depends on his or her cognitive complexity. Individuals with a high level of cognitive complexity have little difficulty in perceiving patterns of interrelatedness among data. Individuals with low cognitive complexity tend to rely on a few specific rules as the basis for interpreting the data in a given strategic situation.

MODELS OF DECISION STYLE

The decision style model shown in Figure 10B.1 applies the concept of cognitive complexity to strategy. This model relates decision style to cognitive complexity and to values orientation, which in turn reflects a propensity toward left- or right-hemisphere dominance. The degree of cognitive complexity is high at the top of the model and low at the bottom. The values orientation is toward technical or task-oriented matters on the left, reflecting left-hemisphere processing, and toward organizational or people-oriented matters on the right, suggesting right-hemisphere processing.

The four basic decision styles are as follows:

1. *Directive style.* Directive managers have a low tolerance for ambiguity and tend to be oriented toward technical matters. Often, people with this style are autocratic and have a high need for power. Because they use little information and consider few alternatives, they are typically known for speed and results. Directive managers tend to prefer structure in their environment and to want detailed information given orally. They also tend to follow procedures and to be aggressive. Although they are often effective at getting results, their focus is internal to the organization and short-range, with tight controls. They generally have the drive required to control and dominate others, but they need security and status.

2. *Analytical style.* Analytical managers have a much higher tolerance for ambiguity than directive managers; they also have more cognitively complex personalities. They desire considerable amounts of information, preferably in written form, and consider many more alternatives than does someone with a directive style. Like directive managers, however, they have a technical orientation and an autocratic bent. Individuals with this style are oriented to problem solving; they strive for the best that can be achieved in a given situation. They enjoy variety and challenge but emphasize control. Analytical individuals tend to be innovative and good at abstract or logical, deductive reasoning.

FIGURE 10B.1	**Cognitive Decision Style Model**

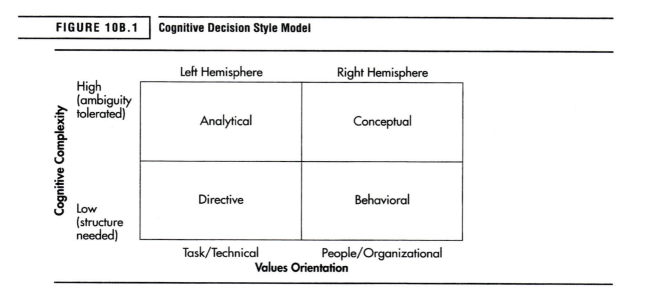

3. *Conceptual style.* Having both high cognitive complexity and a focus on people, conceptual managers tend to be achievement-oriented and yet to believe in trust and openness in relations with subordinates. In making decisions, they look at considerable data and explore many alternatives. Conceptual managers are often creative in their solutions and can visualize complex relationships. Their main concern is with long-range problems, and they have high organizational commitment. Conceptual managers are often perfectionists, emphasizing quality. Preferring loose control over the more directive use of power, they frequently invite subordinates to participate in decision making and goal setting. They value praise, recognition, and independence.

4. *Behavioral style.* Although low on the cognitive complexity scale, behavioral managers have a deep concern for the organization and for the development of people. Behavioral-style managers have a high need for acceptance and tend to be supportive of others, showing them warmth and empathy. They enjoy counseling others. Preferring persuasion to direction, they provide loose control. Behavioral managers are receptive to suggestions and communicate easily. They require relatively little data and prefer verbal communication to written reports. They tend to focus on short- or medium-range problems.

Although the preceding discussion makes the styles appear to be distinct, in reality a manager's style rarely falls neatly into one category. Most managers have multiple styles; the style adopted in a particular situation depends on the context in which the decision is made. Typically, however, even the most flexible managers have a dominant style and use the others as backup styles. Thus, style categories describe general ways of thinking.

Even though it is never possible to gauge another's decision styles exactly, having an idea of an individual's dominant style can be useful information. The manager who can identify another's dominant cognitive style and orientation to values can better predict that person's decision-making behavior. An application of decision styles was illustrated in the section on entrepreneurship in Chapter 9.

The decision style inventory (DSI) in Worksheet 10B.1 can be used to determine how frequently an individual uses each decision style. Answers to the questions in the inventory, when scored, provide a valid indicator of a person's style. The worksheet has been left blank so that readers can fill it in to determine their own style.

The total score for the appropriate column of the inventory is used to determine the level of dominance of each style. A standard deviation of 15 has been found for each of the four style categories. Given that scores follow a normal probability distribution, 49% of the scores will fall within the following ranges: directive, 68–82; analytical, 83–97; conceptual, 73–87; and behavioral, 48–62. If a person's score for a style is 7 or more points (approximately ½ standard deviation) above the mean (average) for that style, the style is considered to be dominant. If it is more than 1 standard deviation (15 points) over the mean, that style is considered to be very dominant. A score within 7 points (plus or minus) of the mean indicates that the style is a backup style. A score more than 7 points below the mean indicates that the style is a least-preferred style; the style either is latent and used only when needed or is seldom used.

A decision style graph can be generated from the results of the decision style inventory. Each bar indicates how much the individual's score deviates from the mean for that score. Bars for scores that are greater than the mean extend to the right of the average score line; bars for scores that are lower than the mean extend to the left. Worksheet 10B.2 displays scores for Pfeffer and Palma, two managers at Lift Inc.

The first graph shows that Pfeffer uses the directive style as his dominant style and the analytical style as a backup. The second graph shows that Palma uses the conceptual style as

| WORKSHEET 10B.1 | Decision Style Inventory |

Case _____
Date _____
Name _____

The following decision style inventory is used to determine the manager's self-perception in terms of the cognitive-contingency model. Each question is answered by assigning an 8 to the answer that is most like them, a 4 to the next answer most like them, then a 2, and finally a 1 for the answer least like them. For example, in the first question an individual may want to assign an 8 to "be recognized for my work," a 4 to "have a position with status," a 2 to "feel secure," and a 1 to "be outstanding in my field." Remember that each score can be assigned only once to each question. In other words, all four numbers, 8, 4, 2, and 1, must be used for each question. Do not repeat any of these four numbers for any one question. Thus using two 8s would not be a correct response to any given question. An interpretation of the scores follows the inventory.

One should relax when filling in the inventory and recognize that it reflects one's self-image. There are *no* right or wrong answers. Each person is different and will, therefore, score the questions differently. Generally the first answer that comes to mind is the best to put down.

Decision Style Inventory III*

Please score the following questions based on the instructions given. Your score reflects how you see yourself, not what you believe is correct or desirable, as related to your work situation. It covers typical decisions that you make in your work environment.

1. My prime objective is to:	Have a position with status	Be the best in my field	Achieve recognition for my work	Feel secure in my job
2. I enjoy jobs that:	Are technical and well defined	Have considerable variety	Allow independent action	Involve people
3. I expect people working for me to be:	Productive and fast	Highly capable	Committed and responsive	Receptive to suggestions
4. In my job, I look for:	Practical results	The best solutions	New approaches or ideas	Good working environment
5. I communicate best with others:	In a direct one to one basis	In writing	By having a group discussion	In a formal meeting
6. In my planning I emphasize:	Current problems	Meeting objectives	Future goals	Developing people's careers
7. When faced with solving a problem, I:	Rely on proven approaches	Apply careful analysis	Look for creative approaches	Rely on my feelings
8. When using information I prefer:	Specific facts	Accurate and complete data	Broad coverage of many options	Limited data that is easily understood
9. When I am not sure about what to do, I:	Rely on intuition	Search for facts	Look for a possible compromise	Wait before making a decision
10. Whenever possible, I avoid:	Long debates	Incomplete work	Using numbers or formulas	Conflict with others
11. I am especially good at:	Remembering dates and facts	Solving difficult problems	Seeing many possibilities	Interacting with others
12. When time is important, I:	Decide and act quickly	Follow plans and priorities	Refuse to be pressured	Seek guidance or support
13. In social settings I generally:	Speak with others	Think about what is being said	Observe what is going on	Listen to the conversation
14. I am good at remembering:	People's names	Places we met	People's faces	People's personality
15. The work I do provides me:	The power to influence others	Challenging assignments	Achieving my personal goals	Acceptance by the group
16. I work well with those who are:	Energetic and ambitious	Self confident	Open minded	Polite and trusting
17. When under stress, I:	Become anxious	Concentrate on the problem	Become frustrated	Am forgetful
18. Others consider me:	Aggressive	Disciplined	Imaginative	Supportive
19. My decisions typically are:	Realistic and direct	Systematic or abstract	Broad and flexible	Sensitive to the needs of others
20. I dislike:	Losing control	Boring work	Following rules	Being rejected

© A.J. Rowe, revised 3/3/83. Reprinted with permission of the author.

Interpretation of Scores
To score the decision style inventory, simply total each of the four columns. The first column total score is associated with the *directive* style, the second column total is the *analytical* style, the third column total is the *conceptual* style, and the fourth column total is the *behavioral* style. Enter each of these totals into the four respective boxes of the decision style diagram. The combined score should total 300 points.

WORKSHEET 10B.2 | **Decision Style Graph**

Case LIFT Inc.
Date 1992
Name Pfeffer (top); Palma (bottom)

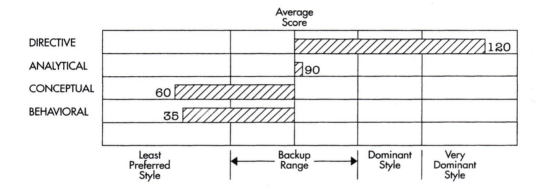

		Average Score		
DIRECTIVE				120
ANALYTICAL		90		
CONCEPTUAL	60			
BEHAVIORAL	35			

Least Preferred Style | ← Backup Range → | Dominant Style | Very Dominant Style

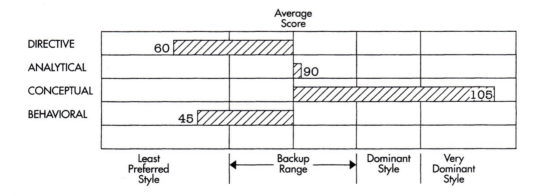

		Average Score		
DIRECTIVE	60			
ANALYTICAL		90		
CONCEPTUAL				105
BEHAVIORAL	45			

Least Preferred Style | ← Backup Range → | Dominant Style | Very Dominant Style

TABLE 10B.2	Style Scores of General Population

Style	Average Score
Directive	75
Analytical	90
Conceptual	80
Behavioral	55

his dominant style, again with the analytical style as a backup. These findings are consistent with the descriptions of these individuals. Pfeffer's left hemisphere is dominant, and he is task-oriented. Palma delegates authority, prefers long-range planning to day-to-day operations, is innovative, and wants independence.

DECISION STYLES AND LEADERSHIP ABILITIES

Are some decision styles used more by those who concentrate on managing, and others by those who lead? Zaleznick (1977) considered tasks requiring little cognitive complexity to be the maintenance functions of *management*; in those areas, the focus is on obtaining results and motivating employees. The *leadership* functions are the tasks that deal with ideas and therefore require a higher level of cognitive complexity. A leader is a person who is more concerned with the direction or outlook of the firm than with accomplishing detail assignments.

Figure 10B.2 focuses on the differences among the decision styles in terms of thinking versus action and leader qualities versus manager qualities. This table suggests that leaders, who are proactive and change-oriented, would be more likely than managers to have as a dominant style one of the styles in the upper half of the model—either the analytical style or the conceptual style.

FIGURE 10B.2	Cognitive Decision Style Model

This hypothesis has been supported by studies of scores shown for managers and leaders on the decision style inventory. Over 20,000 managers and professionals have taken the decision style inventory since 1977. The average scores for the population at large are shown in Table 10B.2. Managers, on the whole, have been found to have scores similar to the population norms. For example, in a study of 194 managers in the southern California area (Mann, 1982), the average scores were as follows: directive, 74; analytical, 89; conceptual, 83; and behavioral, 54.

The scores of 26 young presidents who took the decision style inventory were also nearly the same as those of the overall population in all four categories.

Specific groups, however, have been found to have characteristic patterns of style that reflect the demands of their positions and the selection processes that brought them there. In a research study based on interviews with 80 senior executives (including chief executive officers, chairpersons, presidents, executive vice presidents, and directors of major industrial corporations, financial institutions, foundations, and consulting firms), Rowe found distinct style patterns (Rowe and Mason, 1987). The results clearly showed the central role that conceptual thinking plays in high-level management. For 90% of these executives, the conceptual style was either dominant or backup. For 76%, the analytical style was dominant or backup, and for 70%, the directive style was dominant or backup. The executives' mean scores for each style are graphed in Figure 10B.3.

An especially revealing insight into differences in style is contained in Mann's study of financial and strategic planners (1982). The scores of the two groups are shown in Table 10B.3. Note that among financial planners the dominant style is the analytical style needed to collect and analyze large amounts of financial data. Among strategic planners, on the other hand, the very dominant style is the conceptual style needed to think of the business as a whole and to create new options for it to pursue. Strategic planners have profiles similar to those of executives, reflecting the importance of intuition and creative thinking.

Table 10B.4 summarizes the differences in style patterns of various demographic and occupational groups. The exhibit reveals that female managers have higher directive and behavioral scores than do female architects, who are more analytical and conceptual. One

---

FIGURE 10B.3 | **Decision Styles of 80 Senior Executives**

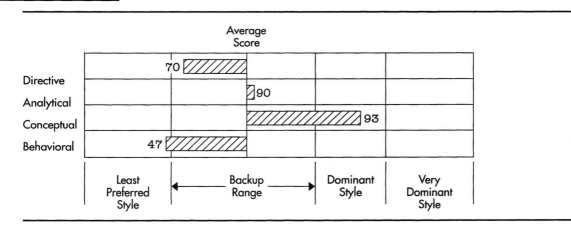

would expect these results, considering that the manager's job involves directing others and the architect's job involves analysis and visualization of structures to be built.

In one study, police chiefs were compared with engineering executives. This study showed that, typically, police chiefs are more analytical and behavioral than engineering executives, who are more directive. The conceptual scores of both groups were comparable. On the surface, this finding seems surprising inasmuch as it is often assumed that police are highly directive.

Table 10B.4 shows that U.S. managers, in general, have high analytical scores. One group of male engineering executives, however, had an analytical score of only 83.0, which is below the typical male score. The same group had a directive score of 82.9, which means that these engineering executives were focusing more on results than does the typical manager.

The comparison of U.S. and Japanese managers is very revealing. Japanese managers had an average score of 84 for the conceptual style and 68 for the behavioral style, which would make them predominantly right-brain-oriented, in contrast to male managers in the United States.

TABLE 10B.3	Style Scores of Financial and Strategic Planners

		Decision Style			
Planning Function	Number	Directive	Analytical	Conceptual	Behavioral
Financial	19	75	100*	74	51
Strategic	11	62	81	100*	57

* Dominant style

Source: Richard B. Mann, 1982.

TABLE 10B.4	Comparison of Decision Styles

	Number	Directive	Analytical	Conceptual	Behavioral
Female managers	93	74	88	74	64
Female architects	224	65	95	85	55
Police chiefs	151	71	90	81	58
Ph.D. psychologists	5	62	75	103	60
Male architects	141	65	95	86	54
Male U.S. managers	54	72	94	81	53
Male engineers	39	78	96	73	53
Japanese managers	21	69	79	84	68

CHAPTER ELEVEN

Information Technology and Future Directions in Strategy

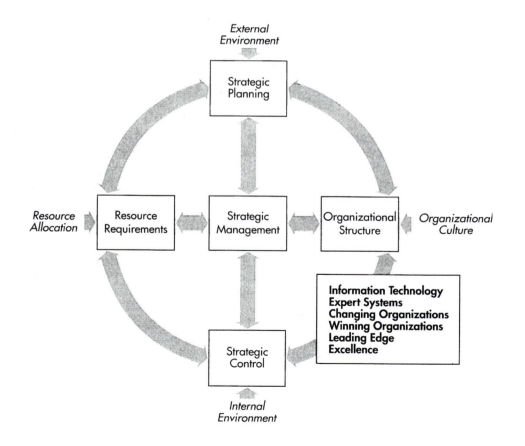

Chapter 1	**Chapter 2**	**Chapter 3**	**Chapter 4**	**Chapter 5**	**Chapter 6**
A Framework for Strategic Management	Strategic Analysis	Strategic Visioning, Goals, Ethics, and Social Responsibility	The Competitive Environment	Capability-based Strategy	Market Dynamics and Sustainable Competitive Advantage
How to approach strategic management	*Application of strategic analysis*	*Understanding vision, values, ethics*	*Coping with competitive forces, stakeholders*	*Assessing company capability, timeliness, quality*	*Determining trends, gap analysis, and market dynamics*

Chapter 7	**Chapter 8**	**Chapter 9**	**Chapter 10**	**Chapter 11**
Strategy in a Global Environment	Financial Planning and Competitive-Cost Analysis	Entrepreneurship, Mergers and Acquisitions, Restructuring, and the Service Sector	Leadership Factor in Strategy and Implementing Strategic Change	Information Technology and Future Directions in Strategy
Assessing global trade, foreign markets, monetary exchange	*Preparing a financial plan and competitive-cost analysis*	*Importance of small business, entrepreneurs, restructuring*	*Strategy implementation, leadership, culture*	*Information technology, trends, new management*

INTRODUCTION

Today's strategic managers must be prepared to invoke new and flexible approaches to strategic management in order to ensure their companies' survival in the turbulent and uncertain business environment. This chapter covers several important areas that are likely to affect whether an organization will succeed or fail in the years ahead.

One of the principal changes on the horizon is the role of information as a strategic imperative. The rate of increase in the application of information technology is nothing short of astounding. A mere ten years ago, the personal computer was just beginning to come on the horizon. Today, not only are personal computers more powerful than some of the mainframe computers of the 1970s, but their cost has been reduced to the point where "information power" is available to any executive who is willing to utilize it.

This chapter will explore the role of information technology in sustaining competitive advantage as well as supporting decisions that managers make within the organization. For example, telemarketing today is used by over 80,000 companies, IBM is banking on super-fast RISC computers to help sustain its competitive advantage, and Digital Equipment Corporation has just introduced, at a competitive price, the Alpha computer, which boasts the awesome performance of 150 million instructions per second—double that of any computer available at this time.

How is all this powerful technology utilized to enhance strategic management? The applications explored in this chapter include decision support systems, expert systems for strategic management that include knowledge-based systems.

Technology by itself no more changes an organization than a written score creates a symphony. The organization must implement strategies for coping with massive technological innovations, extreme uncertainties, and a rapidly changing world environment. Thus the counterpoint to more sophisticated applications of information technology is the role of the organization in the future. Previous chapters have covered organizational structure, organizational change, strategy implementation, and leadership. This chapter takes a broader perspective: how managers will have to deal with problems in the 1990s. A reading on "Sustaining Competitive Advantage from IT," by John Cecil and Michael Goldstein, concludes the chapter.

THE CHANGING OUTLOOK

Tomorrow's companies will have to think strategically about new products, new markets, and new competition (Peters, 1989). By adapting their core expertise to a new view, large companies that can move toward a flatter structure, that continuously innovate, and that cope with chaotic conditions can survive. As markets become increasingly fractured, products become more customized. Timely response, quality design, high value, and customer focus will be the key to meeting these challenges.

But how does a company reinvent itself? It is not sufficient to create new products in the absence of an organizational structure that emphasizes continuous innovation. In 1970, Xerox created the Palo Alto Research Center (PARC) to pursue advanced research in the areas of computers, electronics, and materials. This center contributed

1. Fundamental innovations in computer technology
2. Bit map computer screens
3. Local area networks
4. Mouse editing
5. Object-oriented language
6. The first prototype laser printer

In 1991 the Center was focusing on the relationship of technology to work and on how information technology can support group collaboration.

The continuously innovating company improves operating practices as well as products, innovates at all levels in the organization, and innovates with the customer. GE is an example of a company that is trying to tap employee brainpower. Welch's vision for GE's success is "speed, simplicity, and self-confidence." He feels that removing the domination of the boss is tantamount to eliminating whips and chains. This helps to release the innovative power of workers, which, in turn, leads to greater satisfaction and improved performance. Over the past ten years, GE has improved its productivity by a total of 4% going from an improvement of 2% to 6%. U.S. manufacturers, on the other hand, have witnessed a decline of 2% over the same time period, going from a 1% productivity improvement to a 1% loss (Stewart, 1991).

Because of the importance of environmental factors in the determination of strategy, future manufacturers will need a better understanding of market structures and market dynamics. Porter (1980) clearly pointed out the need to take marketing forces into account in determination of strategy. The profit impact of market strategy (PIMS), which was discussed in Chapter 6, is used to maintain a current database of information for determining what strategies are most effective in a given industrial sector.

As the influence of stakeholders in the conduct of the organization becomes greater, the importance of such methods as stakeholder analysis will become apparent. Both consumers and the government are increasingly demanding that organizations be more socially responsible. Companies are responsible for not polluting the environment, making safe and durable products, being concerned with the well-being of their employees, not discriminating in hiring practices, and contributing to the good of society while meeting investor expectations. No longer does an organization choose to be socially responsible purely for altruistic reasons; rather, management recognizes that the external environment now plays a key role in determining the ultimate success or failure of the enterprise.

Certainly resources, investments, and technology still play key roles in determining both the effectiveness of operations and the ability to penetrate or defend a market. These three factors, however, are no longer considered synonymous with strategy. Although it would be foolhardy to ignore the importance of resources, investments, or technology in formulating strategic alternatives, coping with the market and with the formulation and implementation of strategy are equally important. In the microcomputer field, for instance, the first company to market a portable model, Osborn Inc., went bankrupt despite its technology, whereas IBM, which had no technological advantage in the personal computer area, came to dominate the field because of its reputation, resources, and marketing expertise.

Poor profitability or inadequate funding typically necessitates a defensive strategy. The innovative leader, however, can turn a defensive position into a positive approach, as occurred at Chrysler under Lee Iacocca. Strategic funds programming (see Chapter 8) permits planners to determine what resources are required for strategic alternatives. The resources available can have a significant impact on the level of expenditures for products in the firm.

The strategic managers need better methods to assist in allocating the available resources. Improved means to allocate limited resources and alternative strategies for accomplishing goals can substitute for technology or other capabilities that are not available in the firm. The strategic manager ensures that requirements of the strategic plan are met, while at the same time meeting external requirements and satisfying stakeholder demands.

After technological, marketing, and other problems are overcome, there still remain the human problems of implementing change and ensuring desired performance. We have discussed the importance of commitment on the part of the individual as a basis for ensuring performance. The performance management system (PMS) approach, combined with management by objectives (MBO), is widely used to match jobs to behavioral as well as skill requirements. (PMS and MBO are described in Chapter 10.)

In an article entitled "Meeting the Challenge of Global Competition," Gluck (1982) pointed out that a company's skill at responding rapidly to change is no guarantee of eventual competitive success. Rather, he maintained, managers will have to radically alter their thinking and behavior to cope effectively with the new environment. Planners will have to become change agents, and top management will have to shift from reactive to proactive leadership and achieve a quantum leap in corporate performance. (The next section examines in more detail the characteristics needed for excellent management in the future.) Gluck stated that strategic approaches based purely on analyses and forecasting will be inadequate to deal with the turbulence and instability that most companies will be encountering in the 1990s. It appears that he accurately predicted future requirements.

Strategic managers will have to "create the future" and at the same time integrate it with operational performance. Management will shift from a prescriptive approach to a more creative approach based on insights and tolerance for ambiguity. External conditions will be viewed as opportunities rather than problems, and planning will be concerned as much with understanding requirements as with involving those who must carry out the strategy. Thus the planner will become a change agent, matching the internal and external requirements with the motivational and structural needs of the organization.

Whereas the structure of an organization was at one time considered a key factor in carrying out strategy, the current trend is to consider more flexible structures, or "adhocracies," as preferable to bureaucracies. The typical life cycle of an organization illustrates the need to change the organizational structure to meet the demands of the environment. As the level of uncertainty and the size of an organization increases, there is a need for greater levels of differentiation to meet the new requirements. (The organizational life cycle is discussed in Chapter 10.)

The change models discussed in Chapter 10 show that there are effective means for bringing about change in an organization. With the many rapid changes now taking place, conventional approaches to strategy and structure do not suffice. Thus managers are increasingly turning to temporary structures or to the team approach. In addition, the consensus approach advocated by Japanese management is receiving increased attention as a means of improving communication and dedication to performance.

EXCELLENCE IN MANAGEMENT

A company's success is measured not solely by financial indicators but also by factors such as growth, competitiveness, ability to attract and retain excellent individuals, innovation, quality, responsiveness, adaptability, and social responsibility. Thus the "bottom line," although important, does not by itself ensure excellence in management. Rather, it is the combination of a leader's vision, plans, and action that contribute to effective organizational performance.

Japanese managers have demonstrated what many consider to be excellence in management. What makes their management excellent? Studies indicate that it is the great natural talent of the founder or chief executive who grasps intuitively the basic elements of strategy. These executives have a way of looking at the company, customers, and competition that enables them to merge the three in a comprehensive set of plans and objectives. The process is both creative and intuitive, and it often disrupts the status quo in the marketplace. It is the drive, the will, and the mind of the chief executive that gives these strategies their extraordinary competitive impact.

In a three-year study of vanguard management, O'Toole (1985) asked over 200 managers the simple question "If you could work in any large American corporation, which would it be?" Having identified the eight top companies, O'Toole then went about determining what made them "vanguard companies." He found that they were concerned about stakeholders, consumers, and the future; had visible leaders; planned for employee stability; gave every worker a sense of ownership; and were linked to small entrepreneurial businesses. They also were dedicated to a high purpose, committed to adapting to new conditions, and determined to be the best at what they did. Thus these vanguard companies employed a combination of two decision-making styles: the conceptual and the behavioral. (See Chapter 10 for a description of decision styles.) These findings are consistent with the results of a well-known study by Peters and Waterman (1982) of the causes of organizational malaise. The study showed that the successful companies were those that had a sharp sense of the changes taking place in the environment and that were especially good at responding to those changes.

Organizations that were not considered vanguard were also found by O'Toole to have a lot in common. They were insensitive to the external environment, lost sight of the basics, emphasized action rather than planning, and ignored the need for change. They single-mindedly pursued short-term goals, especially if they were run by left-brain–oriented engineers. The most serious limitation of a purely directive executive is the tendency to focus too much on the end results; insufficient attention is paid to the broad issues confronting the firm and even less to the needs of the workers.

Among the eight companies originally identified as vanguard, several have since had difficulties, including Levi Strauss, Weyerhaeuser, Polaroid, Xerox, and Cummins Engine. Perhaps leaders of vanguard companies also need a directive or analytical component to ensure that the companies' goals are successfully carried out.

Another perspective on the issue of excellence in management is described in the book *Decision Making at the Top*. Authors Donaldson and Lorsch (1983) conducted in-depth interviews with 12 chief executive officers to find out what executives consider the major factors leading to success. The executives all felt a commitment to do well for the shareholders in the company. None of the executives was concerned about the current market value of the company's stock. What was important to most of them was the "drive to excel"—to do better than others. Because the executives interviewed were at the top of their respective companies, their competitiveness seemed to be focused more on how well their companies were doing relative to other companies than on how they were doing relative to peers inside the company. As one executive put it, "My personal goals are to do a good job, to be profitable, to have high-calibre people around me, and to be concerned about how I am viewed by customers, stockholders, and the community. My objective is to be number one, to do as well as or better than anyone else."

The underlying themes revealed by the executives were pride in their work, desire to compete, and commitment to excellence in performance. People, ideas, and products were all part of the key objective: perpetuating the firm.

The effectiveness of the individual leader will become an increasingly important factor in making and carrying out strategy in the future. Research on decision styles indicates that there is a clear relationship between the demands of the position and the effectiveness of a particular decision style (Rowe and Mason, 1987). Furthermore, the climate of the organization depends on the style of leadership. Strategic decision styles can be categorized as follows:

1. *Entrepreneurial style:* combination of the conceptual and directive styles.
2. *Executive style:* combination of the analytical and conceptual styles.
3. *Planner style:* combination of the analytical and directive styles.
4. *Leader style:* combination of the conceptual and behavioral styles.

The most effective style of management shifts with different phases of the organizational life cycle (discussed in Chapter 10). The entrepreneurial-style manager does best where conceptual creativity must be combined with a directive, results-oriented approach.

The executive-style manager, who is a highly cognitive, complex individual, is most effective in running a large, well-established organization. An analytical style is needed to understand extremely complex phenomena and translate them into meaningful data. A conceptual style is needed to handle ambiguity and comprehend future possibilities.

The planner is typically very analytical and thus is ideally suited to working on advanced technology, computer-based decision support models, forecasting models, and so on. Often, however, this individual is not as creative as the conceptual manager. The planner tends to be a good problem solver, who understands complex environments.

The leader, basically a right-brain-oriented individual with an interest in people, is able to focus the strength of the organization on problem areas and to be creative in finding solutions. Unlike the other three strategic styles, the leader style is likely to succeed where organizational or motivational requirements are critical.

Let's take a closer look at two of these strategic decision styles.

THE ENTREPRENEURIAL STYLE

As we have noted, the entrepreneurial style is most appropriate in the startup phase of an organization. Ohmae (1982), in *The Mind of the Strategist,* describes how Japanese management has achieved results that are considered outstanding. Japanese managers were observed to have a high conceptual style with a backup directive style that has many of the attributes of an entrepreneur, the vision and creativity of the conceptual style, and, when needed, the "results" focus of the directive style. Ohmae goes on to describe how the Japanese utilized four basic strategic thrusts to accomplish their goals. Japanese managers dissect the market, build on relative superiority, exploit strategic degrees of freedom, and apply strategic vision. The Japanese strategist is creative, intuitive, and committed and has the drive and the energy to carry out difficult decisions.

Entrepreneurs can also operate within well-established companies. Many organizations are recognizing that one means of encouraging commitment and talent is to provide an organizational climate that fosters innovation and entrepreneurship. Minnesota Mining and Manufacturing prides itself on offering such an environment to its employees. IBM, when it introduced the personal computer, recognized the need to form an entrepreneurial group in order to enter a market more quickly than usual.

Toffler (1985), in *The Adaptive Corporation,* describes many U.S. companies as organizational dinosaurs. These companies are not able to adapt to new environmental pressures, and many will disappear. T. Boone Pickens is among a growing group who feel that U.S. managers are more concerned with rigid administrative procedures and their own perks, including outrageous salaries, than with accommodating the requirements of social and competitive pressure and the interests of their stockholders. The implication is clear: adapt or die. Furthermore, an emphasis on entrepreneurship can help overcome being an organizational dinosaur by focusing on flexibility and innovation that take advantage of emerging opportunities.

Rosabeth Ross Kanter (1987) claims that a new breed of U.S. manager is starting to replace those who stubbornly cling to formulas, products, and marketing strategies that long ago lost their appeal. These managers are called *innovators.* They combine innovative management with discipline, focusing initiative on common goals and rewarding employees for collaborative efforts. This upbeat message is being parroted by a number of management gurus who argue that the intrapreneur—the innovator and risk taker *inside* the organization—is what will make the organization of the future competitive. Intrapreneurs are the mavericks who do not seem to fit in traditional company roles yet are able to exploit opportunities and bring about major changes in how organizations are managed and strategies carried out.

THE LEADER STYLE

A leader style that focuses on freedom of expression and fosters achievement is the one most likely to enable executives to deal successfully with a complex future. Can a leader be both strong and understanding of the needs and aspirations of others? Bennis and Nanus (1985) use the term *transformative leadership* to describe the ability to create a vision and generate the energy needed to initiate and sustain actions that will make the vision a reality. Leaders with a combination of conceptual and behavioral styles can move organizations to new heights by recognizing potential opportunities and instilling in others the commitment and energy needed to carry out strategies. The conceptual style provides the vision, and the behavioral style provides the empathy and skill to make people feel involved. As a backup style, the directive style provides energy and the skillful exercise of power.

Tandem Computers is an example of a highly successful company that has a very informal management style. The company's philosophy is to treat people as the most important ingredient and then give them the support and the incentives they need to achieve outstanding performance. The control is self-control; individual workers are not constantly monitored. At Tandem, employees carry out the company's strategy while at the same time they are able to meet their own needs.

There are many examples of effective leadership that produces results. Consider the remodeling of Chrysler's Ontario plant for production of the Minivan. Normally it takes 18 months to rebuild a facility and install new robotic devices. Under the leadership of Lee Iacocca, the retooling was completed in 17 weeks!

Even the military is beginning to recognize the value of conceptual/behavioral leadership. Admiral Crowe, who chaired the Joint Chiefs of Staff, was described by his friends as looking like an unmade bed, but he had the ability to build rapport and exercise finesse in difficult situations. His congenial outlook, along with his ability as a strategic thinker, gave him a head start in one of the toughest jobs in the military.

Given the wave of mergers and acquisitions—a trend that is likely to continue well into the future unless regulations curtail it—it is important to consider what style of management is most effective at keeping the organization on track during the traumatic period that follows takeover. In one large aerospace company, a division director who had a conceptual/behavioral style was able to retain the loyalty of his staff despite successive cuts and transfers of personnel. In a Ciba-Geigy subsidiary that had been for sale for over a year, a manager with a conceptual/behavioral style was able to hold the key executives together because of his understanding of their needs and his ability to exude confidence about the outcome of the sale. The chairman of a department at a large metropolitan university was able to change the structure and the responsibilities of the faculty so that what had been considered an onerous task became a desired and sought-after responsibility.

In the past, dogmatic, directive management may have been the most effective means of dealing with recalcitrant workers. Today, however, with a better educated, more mobile, and more achievement-oriented workforce, management can no longer rely on what worked in the past. Politics, power, and dogmatic approaches will not disappear overnight, but eventually they will be overtaken by the entrepreneurial spirit, energy, and vision that have allowed companies such as Honda to challenge the most prestigious automakers.

Adherence to outmoded managerial concepts and approaches has already left a number of companies in the lurch. In his book on management mistakes, Hartley (1983) showed that many well-known, large organizations have made serious strategic errors. As he pointed out, past success does not guarantee continued success. He also noted that there is a significant difference between adapting to changing requirements and innovating in the very way change itself is made.

The vanguard organization, the entrepreneurial organization, and the innovative organization all require a conceptual style, combined with a directive or analytical style or a behavioral style, depending on organizational requirements. Such managers are most likely to lead organizations to new levels of competitive effectiveness and thus to characterize the excellent executives of the future.

No matter what strategic decision style is used, balance is crucial. An approach based on dealing with the future can easily overlook the present. Creativity must be balanced with pragmaticism. Use of sophisticated tools must be combined with a better understanding of the needs of individuals in the organization. New approaches, such as dealing with personal values and organizational culture, have to be integrated with more awareness of the individual differences in management decision styles. These differences often account for how performance is achieved.

THE LEADING-EDGE STRATEGIST

A leading-edge strategist is one who uses the latest approaches to cope with the onslaught of unforgiving global competition. For companies to succeed in tomorrow's turbulent environment, the approach to strategy formulation will have to change, and there will have to be a new paradigm for business that ensures that the strategy will be implemented effectively. Not only will the way business is being conducted change, but many of the old rules that worked in the past will have to be thrown out. But what is this new direction? And is it achievable? Hewlett-Packard threw out the old rules when it set out to develop a desk-top laser printer. Today it is the leader in the field. Huey (1991) states that "nothing is impossible" but that incrementally changing the old bureaucratic structure and rules will no longer suffice. What is needed is a quantum leap in ideas, products, services, and organizational structures so that business can give customers what they want. Unfortunately, these major paradigm shifts rarely take place in today's organizations.

If we examine the crisis that faced General Motors, we see just how difficult it can be to make a major paradigm shift. Introducing teamwork and a new-product design, General Motors had hoped that the Saturn car would bring about the change it sought. Over the last twenty years GM had built many new plants, hired many new workers, and introduced the J car, the L car, and the A car, but it did not reduce the overlap among its divisions. This led to a day of reckoning, when Stemple (the CEO) announced that he would eliminate 74,000 jobs and close a score of plants. In short, teamwork and new products were not enough. The old bureaucratic order itself had to be replaced, and that need eventually spelled the replacement of Stemple himself and of several other senior executives.

What is needed are businesses that focus on problem solving, opportunity identification, anticipation, and a new leadership that can achieve responsive change. For example, Ann Morrison, in her book *The New Leaders* (1992), shows what is needed for companies to achieve broader market share, improved employee satisfaction, and increased productivity. Her focus is on the management of diverse employees who include women, foreign workers, and minority groups. The successful manager will have to know how to invoke rotational assignments, mentoring programs, and internal networking to ensure high performance and equitable pay. One approach to achieving a competitive edge is to introduce information technology to support human resource management (Broderick and Boudreau, 1992). Because managers must control labor cost, motivate employees, and encourage customer-oriented performance that produces high-quality products and seeks new and better ways of doing work, they will need computer support from transactional reporting systems, expert systems, and decision support systems. A distribution revolution that is based on computer technology may also be in the works.

Because the time in which goods must be delivered is constantly shrinking, distribution may be the key to meeting customer expectations (Koselka, 1992).

To enhance strategies, one must first overcome common failings in corporate strategy (Bleeke, 1989). These include

1. A tendency to place too much emphasis on where to compete instead of how
2. Insufficient consideration of how to introduce uniqueness and adaptability
3. Lack of consideration of networking
4. Failure to recognize what contributes to success

What these failings point up is the need for a new or revised basis for formulating and evaluating competitive strategies. Instead of applying conventional measures (such as financial yardsticks, which only indirectly indicate what went wrong, rather than what to do to correct a situation), managers should evaluate strategy in terms of its ability to achieve objectives.

Over the next several decades, opportunities for growth are likely to be associated with

1. Information as a resource
2. The aging of the population
3. The collaborative and integrated regional economic grouping of countries
4. Emerging new technologies

Companies that can determine when to jump aboard these major trends will have a chance to achieve enormous growth and profitability (Fromson, 1988). Creation of wealth requires the vision to organize and dominate emerging industries where growth potential is the strongest. A first mover in new technologies can provide the basis for competing globally with "mold-breaking" ideas. This strategic thrust requires constant innovation. Although the United States is still the leader in generating patents, other nations are closing the gap. The competitive global battles will be won by those companies that escape shrinking markets by finding and dominating markets that did not exist before. Examples include Federal Express, Microsoft, and Hewlett-Packard. Not merely responding to current needs, a creative company finds products that lead the customer. Japan spends 3% of its GNP for nondefense R&D, compared with less than 2% for the United States. The result is that Japan receives 44% increased revenues from new products, compared with 28% for the United States. However, it is not enough to put more money into R&D. The prevailing culture must also change for innovation to pay off (Dumaine, 1991). A look at some emerging technologies shows the magnitude of change. Scientists are beginning to develop machines that have microscopic dimensions, such as tiny sensors (Allman, 1992); portable, pocket-sized telephones that can go anywhere (Cook, 1992); and a plasma chamber wherein ionized gases etch circuits on monolithic integrated gallium oxide chips.

The need to devise creative strategies mounts a challenge that is not met by conventional wisdom. Economics is important in the final analysis, but the full range of economic opportunities needs to be considered. If a company examines the total *distribution chain,* it may be able to turn what looked like a lackluster industry into a winner by exploiting the surplus potential at some given point along the chain. A *complements chain* also helps firms identify where in the total distribution cycle an opportunity exists to add to, or complement, a product. For example, TV manufacturers offer an insurance policy for repairs of their sets. A *substitutes chain* may reveal opportunities to expand beyond the product (an example is a hotel being in the recreation business). Putting these various analyses together can provide new and creative insights into what might otherwise appear to be a stalled strategic response (Hanna and Lundquist, 1990).

Harold Poling, CEO of the Ford Motor Company, says, "You not only have to meet the needs and expectations of customers, you have to exceed them" (Kahalas and Suchon, 1992). By focusing on quality, Ford has developed an enviable reputation that affects both its operating and its marketing strategies. Ford is credited with being the first domestic automaker that implemented a comprehensive quality program. Rosabeth Moss Kanter (1989) throws out the challenge to large bureaucratic organizations in her book *When Giants Learn to Dance*. After an extensive study of many companies, Kanter found what she terms a "post-entrepreneurial" revolution in business. One of the important themes is her focus on human resources and the requirement to develop skills needed to be responsive to changing external demands.

The Bureau of Labor Statistics (1992) projects what it expects to be the fastest-growing occupations for 1990–2005 for persons who have a bachelor's degree. A summary is shown in Table 11.1.

What is most striking about these data is the growth in the computer and medical professions. This growth clearly reflects the needs of an information society and problems of an aging one.

TABLE 11.1	Projection of Fastest-growing Occupations (1990–2005)

Occupation	Percent Growth
1. System analysts and computer scientists	79
2. Physical therapists	76
3. Operations research analysts	73
4. Medical scientists	66
5. Psychologists	64
6. Computer programmers	56
7. Occupational therapists	55
8. Management analysts	52
9. Marketing, advertising	47
11. Preschool teachers	41
13. Securities and financial analysts	40
16. Accountants	34
19. Engineering, mathematics	34

Other areas that leading-edge strategists will have to consider include radical change in global trade and the changing boundaries of business. On August 13, 1992, the United States, Mexico, and Canada agreed to form a huge common market that would eliminate barriers to the flow of goods and services. U.S. firms are mapping ways to take advantage of this accord (Brooks and Sanchez, 1992).

A world leadership survey published in the *Harvard Business Review* (1991) describes the changing boundaries that will be confronting business in the next decade.

1. The world will see changing relationships between government and business, whereby a company that pays taxes and does business in a country is considered a corporate citizen of that country.
2. Human resources will become the principal source of wealth and power for individuals, corporations, and nations.
3. Shortages of technology, capital, and skilled people will continue in developing nations.
4. Degradation of the environment will accelerate in developing nations because of the emphasis on building an industrial base.
5. Managers will continue to find it difficult to break with old practices and theories, especially concerning authority, control, and use of information.

Although we may not see radical change in business as a whole, the leading-edge strategists will learn how to cope with the strange new world that business will inhabit in the 21st century.

Environmental issues affect how countries deal with each other and how advanced countries deal with developing countries. The changes in Eastern Europe have shown how disregard of pollution can contaminate our environment, and the cutting down of rain forests in Brazil and Malaysia has affected the whole world's climate. The greenhouse effect may radically alter conditions around the globe. Nations must learn to share the responsibility for maintaining a "livable environment." For example, the largest emissions of carbon dioxide, relative to GNP, occur in China and India, whereas the United States still spews out the largest overall emission of carbon dioxide from fossil fuel (*The Economist*, 1992).

To meet the challenge of sustainable development, a number of U.S. businesses are taking action. Chrysler Corporation is producing vehicles powered by ethanol and natural gas. The American Gas Association is focusing on natural-gas-fired combined-turbine generating systems. Atlantic Richfield has introduced a new emission-control gasoline. Xerox has concentrated on producing products that are energy-efficient and that reduce waste. And Southern California Edison is committed to reducing carbon dioxide emissions by 10% and helping to introduce the electric car (*Forbes*, 1992). Many other companies are contributing to the effort of cleaning up the environment so that all can live in a quality world.

The year 2000 marks the end of the century and the beginning of a new era, the twenty-first century. The past hundred years have witnessed unparalleled material and social progress, but human nature with all its frailties has not kept up (Grunwald, 1992). We are still plagued by gangs, killings, drugs, starvation, nationalism, fundamentalism, and a deteriorating environment. For humanity to survive on the planet in a harmonious manner, simple profit-driven goals can no longer be the prime objective of strategy. Rather, being a good corporate citizen may go a long way toward curing the ills of the twentieth century. Leading-edge strategists can contribute to this effort, but a new government-industry paradigm is needed to ensure progress in the twenty-first century.

What is being recommended to propel the United States back into a dominant position for the year 2000 and beyond? First, if one examines U.S. productivity closely, the findings are very interesting (Stewart, 1992). At present, for example,

1. The average U.S. worker produces $40,000 worth of goods and services.
2. The average German worker produces $37,850 worth.
3. The average Japanese worker (who has the longest work week) produces $34,500.

Even so, the United States cannot be complacent. Although it is ahead in productivity, the rate of improvement has declined. Only substantial investments in new technology and worker innovation will stop the downward trend. Recommendations include the following:

1. Redesign work and the reward system.
2. Emphasize total quality management.
3. Re-engineer manufacturing processes to allow for teamwork and concurrent design.
4. Eliminate low-value-adding components.
5. Upgrade the skill of the workforce by more training.

The "new gurus" of management (Byrne, 1992) extend this list to include

1. Create a learning organization that can change as requirements change.
2. Re-engineer the organization to focus on outcomes rather than on functional departments.
3. Focus on core competencies rather than on products or markets.
4. Re-examine organizational architecture to incorporate new thinking on leadership, autonomous work groups, empowerment, job ownership, entrepreneurial spirit, and a flexible structure that includes strategic alliances.
5. Employ time-based management and emphasize quality, value, service, and energizing innovation.

Other suggestions for repositioning the United States in a more competitive environment include

1. Develop a more effective global communication approach that enhances customer perceptions of the product (Makovsky, 1992).
2. Build the infrastructure by dealing effectively with the environment, telecommunications, technology, transportation, energy, education, and services (Jacobson, 1992).

Business Week's special 1992 edition on "Reinventing America" also emphasized a broad range of issues from managing change to creating a government for the people.

Changing organizational requirements

Why is concern so often expressed about the future of U.S. management? In part, this concern is a result of the impressive advances that have been made by Japan and other advanced countries. The literature on what constitutes excellent management illustrates the need for a redefinition of what we must look for in developing strategies that will carry U.S. industry successfully into the next century. The major changes in store for future businesses have been identified by Naisbitt and Aburdene (1985). They include a greater emphasis on information, high technology, a world economy, and use of participation as an organizational style. Organizations are clearly entering an era of increased ambiguity, complexity, and turbulence and will need to draw on all their resources to compete effectively in a world market.

The search for an ideal organization continues unabated because structure alone does not determine effectiveness. Recognition of the "adaptive" organization merely points to the need for a new or different perspective on how organizations are viewed and on how to achieve effective performance in a diverse workforce that expects to satisfy ever more complex needs.

Consider Table 11.2 where the corporate environments of Japanese and American firms are compared (Tsurumi, 1991). The obvious difference between the U.S. and Japanese corporate environments is the U.S. focus on the "bottom line" compared with the Japanese recognition of the importance of employee contributions. The employee-centered environment fosters strong group norms, a paternalistic culture, job rotation for flexibility, and job security for commitment and trust.

Can American managers manage as well as the Japanese? When dealing with American workers, who are a very heterogeneous group (compared to Japanese workers) with a low sense of company loyalty, can American managers achieve the same level of output in terms of quality and cost as their Japanese counterparts?

Consider two General Motors plants: one in Fremont, California, and the other in Van Nuys, California. The Fremont plant is a joint venture between Toyota and GM. The Fremont plant had been closed by GM in 1982. There had

TABLE 11.2	Comparison of Corporate Environments	
Environmental Factors	**Japanese Firms**	**American Firms**
Strategic orientation	Long-term growth	Short-term profitability
Strategic goals	Global market share	Primarily domestic
Job security	Ensure long-term commitment and innovation	Considered costly and not attainable
Executive staffing	Promote from within	Fill positions both from within and from outside
Organizational control	Use of implicit rules and shared goals	Explicit rules, MBO, and cost control

been a high level of unrest in that plant, and there were 800 unresolved grievances at the time of the plant closing. In 1983 Toyota, GM, and the United Auto Workers embarked on a historic effort to fuse the dramatically different American and Japanese labor-management traditions. A form of Japanese management that applied quality circles was introduced as a way of improving performance.

During the same period, the GM plant in Van Nuys was having difficulties and faced the threat of being closed. While the Fremont plant was managed by the Japanese, the Van Nuys plant was managed by Americans. In 1990 the Fremont plant was highly successful, whereas the Van Nuys plant was still experiencing major problems (Stavro, 1990).

Some new employees of the New United Motor Manufacturing, Inc., The GM-Toyota joint venture, were flown to Japan for training. One American commented that "while there is more work per man, they make it easier for the worker. They listen to suggestions from the worker on how to improve his job" (Jameson, 1984). In 1992 workers at the GM Van Nuys plant suffered the traumatic experience of being laid off when the plant was finally closed.

WINNING ORGANIZATIONS

The top 100 of America's fastest-growing companies are exploiters of change and exemplify the entrepreneurial spirit that still pervades the United States. Deutschman (1991) admonishes that "old-line giants had better learn from them." Table 11.3 profiles ten of the top 100 growth firms and suggests that the effect covers most industries, especially those that are not so capital-intensive as the industries in which GE and GM operate. Note further that a number of the top 100 growth

TABLE 11.3	Ten of the Top 100 Growth Companies			
Rank in Growth	Company	Sales Growth (%)	Growth in Earnings/Share (%)	Price-Earnings Ratio
1.	Zeos International	256	—	17
4.	Synoptics Communications	209	129	16
8.	American Waste Services	180	116	21
12.	Columbia Hospital	153	81	14
14.	California Energy	151	—	31
17.	Ivax Pharmaceuticals	139	—	367
29.	Symantec	97	—	55
31.	First Financial Management	89	41	15
46.	Amgen	76	—	125
59.	Centex Telemanagement	69	72	27

companies were startup organizations. This reflects the power and advantage enjoyed by a cohesive and nimble organization that has a good product or service.

Reinforcing the requirement for speed and for satisfying a more demanding workforce, the winning organization is able to outperform the larger, more sluggish organization by being responsive to customer needs, providing individual service, making decisions quickly, and adapting products and organizations to fit changing requirements. The 1990s will have even more stringent requirements in fast and extraordinary global competition (Main, 1988). Speed is not limited to small, nimble companies. IBM, for example, uses computer simulations to skip two to three generations of prototypes in developing new integrated circuits. And Limited Inc. tracks daily sales of clothing by using point-of-sale computers that provide the base for orders sent by satellite around the globe.

It is predicted that corporate staffs will virtually disappear, as will dozens of layers of management. The horizontal organization described by Ostroff and Smith (1992) will replace the traditional vertical/hierarchic structure that impedes information flow, restricts empowerment, and limits worker satisfaction. A horizontal organization leverages capability by allowing greater cross-functional work flow that adopts and responds to customers and suppliers. The primary defect of vertical organizations is their inability to be responsive. The horizontal form of organization is built around a small number of business processes or the flow of work that links employer with customers and suppliers. The result is reduced cycle time, reduced cost, and greater throughput. Performance evaluation and resource allocation focus on continuous improvements. In effect, this structure is organized around processes, not specific tasks. To create a horizontal structure, the company needs to identify a limited number of core processes (three to five), which include activity flows, information flow, and material flow.

Motorola has shifted from a fragmented vertical organization to an integrated horizontal organization in its Government Electronics Group. The results have been a reduction in the workforce, linked flows, and the elimination of non-value-adding activities. Team leaders and technical experts provide overall guidance, and there are only two levels between the group head and the teams. "Ownership" of processes and performance is at the team level, as is evaluation of the extent to which the team has met objectives and satisfied customers. Teams become the building block for performance and design and combine managerial with non-managerial activities whenever possible. Self-management builds on intrinsic motivation rather than on control that imposes constraints and frustration. Flexibility is achieved because team members assume multiple competencies. Finally, team performance and skill development are emphasized over individual performance. Of course, this requires that team members hold themselves mutually accountable and that they be rewarded on the basis of joint performance. It is true that changing to a horizontal form of organization can be frustrating, but Motorola achieved a significant reduction in cycle time, a 30% reduction in workforce, and an astounding tenfold improvement in supplied quality. Others, including IDS, GE, and Knight-Ridder, have had similar results (Ostroff and Smith, 1992).

This same theme is echoed by Stewart (1992), who describes the organization of tomorrow as one with a bold new look that is flat and lean. High-performance teams use redesigned work and unbridled information to achieve their goals. Lawrence Bossidy, CEO of Allied Signal, predicts a corporate revolution in the way organizations will be structured to cope with the dramatically new environment. The consensus is that the hierarchic structure of the past will wither away and will be replaced by an organization that fosters high involvement, self-managing teams, and the use of business processes to replace functional departments and to bring information technology to the point where accountability depends on knowledge. The key is an integrated activity flow that can enhance performance.

Byrne (1989) poses an intriguing question when he asks, "Is your company too big?" Perhaps he is alluding to the dinosaurs of the past that could not survive in the rapidly changing environment of the Ice Age. Are our monster organizations of today facing extinction because of their inability to adapt? Table 11.4 compares large companies with small ones. Large companies and small, agile, entrepreneurial companies also differ in other ways. These include the ability to obtain funding, to develop capital-intensive products, and to compete effectively in the global market place. Largeness does not guarantee competitiveness, and we must not forget that large corporations have to satisfy stockholders. Finally, responsiveness depends primarily on information flow, which is horribly sluggish in large organizations.

Can large organizations act the same as small ones? Some evidence suggests that they can. AT&T has split into 6 major businesses and 19 smaller groups to encourage individual risk taking. At GE, Jack Welch wants to avoid encumbering the divisions. He has reduced the number of levels of management from 9 to 4 and uses staff only for advice. GM's Roger Smith vowed to eliminate entrenched layers of management. Hewlett-Packard emphasizes self-direction by individuals, which leads to ownership. It also subdivided the business into 50 units, each with responsibility for its own performance. McDonald's relies on incentives, awards, and autonomous operation.

TABLE 11.4 | **Comparison of Large and Small Companies**

Factor	Large Companies	Small Companies
Size	Sprawling plants	Unitized factories
Integration	Vertical	Subcontracting
Cost-effectiveness	Economies of scale	Flexibility
Organization	Hierarchic	Flat
Orientation	Organization	Innovation
Market share	Large	Create new markets
Distribution	Mass marketing	Niche markets
Manufacturing focus	Quantity	Quality

M.I.T.'s Ferguson claims that a small company can succeed in a niche market but that to compete effectively with Japanese giants, a small company must either grow or join in the coordinated efforts of a number of small companies. Only a large, strong company such as IBM or GE is in a position to compete effectively in the global marketplace. Although size confers some important advantages, it does not effectively confer job ownership or worker commitment, the lack of which can lead to difficulty when dealing with complex organizational problems. The answer may well be that to compete effectively, the United States needs a combination of small entrepreneurial companies and large ones that organize for agility, creativity, and commitment from employees.

A final consideration in redesigning the corporation is how to accelerate change at the middle-management level, which appears to be the major obstacle to the flattening of organizations. Organizational change can be a wrenching, challenging, and time-consuming process. Redesigning structures in such a way that critical skills are retained means changing the mass of middle and front-line managers who currently are responsible for performance. One reason why Japan has found change and adaptability easier is its relatively homogeneous population that believes in harmony in the workplace. As pressures mount and the need for redesigning U.S. businesses becomes acute, a new approach to the management of change will be required. It will be necessary to utilize information technology and careful planning to fit the varied organizational pieces back together again in a new pattern. Heygate (1992) cites the case of a major bank that had a maximum of only three years to cut costs by 30%, increase profit by 100%, restructure the branch network, and teach new skills to 20,000 members of the staff. The redesigned positions meant a reduction of 50% in the workforce, and 80% of the remaining jobs were changed. Also required was information technology support that could easily have been sabotaged.

To achieve its objective, the bank had to overcome several obstacles, including middle-management resistance, the need for training in new skills, inflexible information systems, and an inflexible program for implementing changes in strategy.

To overcome these barriers to accelerated front-line change, the bank took the following steps:

1. Used precise redefinition of tasks and roles.
2. Used computer workstations to support training.
3. Sidestepped inflexible approaches to redesign of the computer system by using incremental improvements.
4. Used logical modules to proceed in parallel with the design process.
5. Applied program management techniques to avoid the traditional sequential approach to design.
6. Kept improvements flowing via communications and empowerment.
7. Remained current by using a disciplined release of new updates.
8. Kept key team leaders and senior management involved at every stage.
9. Maintained a central logistics unit to ensure appropriate delegation of the line and functional units.
10. Relied on active participation of team leaders to ensure effective communications.

Clearly, implementing an accelerated massively parallel change requires new approaches and new support tools, because conventional approaches are much too slow and do not ensure meeting the overall design objective.

To be competitive in the 1990s, organizational structure will need to embrace a new model that is more entrepreneurial and that focuses on increasing value and customer satisfaction (Dichter, 1991). The GE Salisbury plant had five levels of management and separate design and manufacturing departments. After restructuring, the plant has only three levels of management, and the workforce consists of self-managing teams. Cross-functional committees meet weekly and performance reports are available from computers, which facilitate being flexible. This resulted in a 10% cost reduction, an average delivery time of 3 days instead of 3 weeks, and only one-tenth as many complaints as there were before. Since the early 1980s, over 400 companies or divisions have created similar organizational structures.

To be successful, organizations of the 1990s will need to

1. Provide superior value to customers
2. Continuously improve performance
3. Operate as self-leading teams
4. Have an organizational structure that is flat and flexible
5. Empower workers and share values
6. Exhibit leadership that has value-driven vision
7. Create fundamental changes in culture
8. Involve workers in the redesign process
9. Provide guidelines for redesign that are based on
    a. A new corporate vision
    b. A challenge to improve performance
    c. Simpler structures and systems
    d. A new change process
    e. The provision of intensive training and support
10. Accelerate change by
    a. Loosening control
    b. Providing clearly defined performance standards, training, rewards, shared values, and motivation
    c. Making teams accountable for performance
    d. Making individual performance the responsibility of the team
    e. Reducing the influence of the remaining hierarchy
    f. Making all decisions participatively and by consensus

Does this model apply to all organizations equally well? Certainly, some organizations are more amenable than others to introducing the changes described here. But those that do not change will be in jeopardy of losing their competitive position and may even risk failing to survive.

One of the key elements of organizational change is the CEO, who becomes an "organizational architect" (Howard, 1992). Some companies achieve the creativity that small units nourish while preserving the strength and vision of a large organization. The structure that makes this possible has been referred to as the C^2D^2 of organization design, where C^2 stands for centralized coordination and D^2 for decentralized decision making. Restructuring is not merely redesigning an organization. Rather, it calls for a major paradigm shift that leads to new thinking, culture, and flexibility. A redesign will not by itself lead to improved performance. Implementing a change requires a new set of relationships, such as the teamwork or cluster groups that were used for GM's Saturn car. It requires empowerment, ownership, rewards that match effort and commitment, and a changed set of values that contribute to a new work ethic.

INFORMATION TECHNOLOGY

Redefining the role of information is perhaps the most critical aspect of using computers as a competitive tool. Information can play three key roles in a firm's strategy.

1. *Information can be used to report the transactions of the business.* In this role it performs the stewardship function. It keeps track of "what things are where" and "who owes what to whom." The ability to scan local and global markets rapidly has fundamentally altered the processes of planning and distribution. Retail stores such as Wal-Mart can now determine when a particular item is selling well in one store and not moving well at all in another. Rather than let the merchandise remain dormant, they can move it around as needed. American Hospital Supply Corporation (see Chapter 1) used its computer system to deal directly with the needs of hospitals and thereby gained a competitive advantage.

2. *Information can be used to guide business decision making.* In this role it informs the decision maker how well the business is functioning, what problems need attention, and what alternatives should be considered. Management science, management information, and decision support systems all address this role of information in business. (The next section will describe some decision support systems in use today.)

3. *Information can be an integral part of the product or service the business offers to its customers.* In this special role, information becomes—in the customer's eyes, at least—indistinguishable from facilities, people, and commodities. Hence it becomes part of the business's product/market planning. This role is perhaps the most crucial one that information plays—the one that has the tightest link to strategic planning, as well as the most potential.

It is the third function of information that opens opportunities to businesses to make information systems the vanguard of their strategy. Being close to the customer is one of the keys to excellence in business. A strategy that emphasizes closeness focuses on revenue generation as opposed to cost reduction and requires that a business be obsessed with providing service and quality as distinctive competencies.

Among the many companies that have used information services to achieve a competitive advantage are American Airlines, with its Sabre reservation system; Avis, with the "Wizard"; Merrill Lynch, with its cash management system; and Citibank, with its international telecommunications system. Sears is using videodiscs and personal computers to automate its customer catalogs and provide information to customers in their homes. Mobil Oil is using point-of-sale terminals to link the gasoline pumps to automated tellers of local banks. The list of applications is growing exponentially; the possibilities seem to be limited only by the creativity of planners and strategists. What all this portends is radical change, not only in the way information is viewed and used but also in the impact of information processing as a competitive weapon.

The formula for successfully using information systems as a part of the product is straightforward:

1. Identify an unfulfilled customer need or want.
2. Create a means by which information services can fill that need in a manner that enhances the level of service, improves the quality and reliability of the product, and distinguishes both from the offerings of all competitors.
3. Bring the information systems and services to the marketplace as an integral part of the corporate product and marketing strategy.

DECISION SUPPORT INFORMATION SYSTEMS

Information systems can play an important supporting role in developing and carrying out business strategies. There are several approaches to using information systems in strategy formation.

Warren McFarlan and Gregory Parsons developed a technique for applying Porter's concepts (Porter's concepts are described in Chapter 4, beginning on page 123) to information technology. They initially assess the threat (low to high) of each of the five competitive forces affecting the firm and then determine how information technology can influence each threat. They use a two-dimensional matrix to show the firm's competitive position and the role of information systems. This matrix becomes a planning tool for determining new strategies and forecasting changes.

The MAIN Information System

Kodak focuses its information system, the MAIN system, on answering managers' strategic questions. J. Phillip Samper, group vice president and general manager of Kodak's Photographic Marketing Group, summarized the intent of Kodak's information system as follows:

> Our job is to insure, on a worldwide basis, that the information about the marketplace, about technology, about competition, about our performance—that all these are joined together to develop a scenario that allows us to properly position ourselves in the marketplace.
>
> I am convinced that the Kodak *MArket INtelligence System* (the MAIN system) can enhance these functions greatly with the availability of a worldwide data bank—retrievable on demand—that ties business objectives to critical issues.

A basic premise of the MAIN system is that there is no limit to the amount of information that can be obtained about markets and customers. A basic pitfall, unfortunately, is that there is no limit to the amount of money that can be spent on acquiring marketing information. Spending too much money to acquire information is the common error that Russell Ackoff (1967) considered in his classic paper,

"Management Misinformation Systems." The solution is to focus the firm's information systems and services on a few high-payoff areas. The MAIN system does so by translating important yet uncertain strategic-planning assumptions into critical market research questions (CMRQs). The CMRQs cover technical issues (hardware and software), environmental forces, and interpersonal considerations within the organization, as well as design criteria for decision support information systems. After the CMRQs have been prioritized and budgets allocated accordingly, a search is made for data that will answer the questions they pose.

A second basic premise of the MAIN system is that information is not just a "thing in itself," but rather part of a complex relationship among four key entities:

1. The marketplace, which provides signals as to what customers need or say they need
2. The firm's market research department, which collects information, assesses its reliability and validity, analyzes it, and reports it to decision makers
3. The organizational decision makers, who determine what products and services the business is able and willing to present to the marketplace and what the economic results will be
4. The strategic managers, who are responsible and accountable for the performance of the other three

The MAIN system is an information utility that coordinates the activities of these four entities. It contains market data, a library of past studies, a system bibliography, analytical software, graphic and portrayal software, communications software, user help (both automated and interpersonal), a support organization, and, of course, the requisite hardware. All of these information resources are focused on the prioritized CMRQs and the planning process.

Thus the MAIN system has four functions:

1. It helps strategic management to determine what information about the marketplace is needed.
2. It is used, in conjunction with the market research function, to collect data from the marketplace.
3. It provides an interface between the market research department and the organizational decision makers—largely product planners, market managers, brand managers, and so forth—so that information can be summarized, stored, retrieved, and disseminated as needed.
4. It analyzes and interprets the organizational decision-making process so that strategic management can evaluate it.

Critical Success Factors

Jack Rockart and Christine Bullen developed an approach for helping businesses identify what information is required for strategic planning (Rockart, 1979). Their approach uses critical success factors (CSFs) to define strategic objectives and meaningful action steps. (Critical success factors are described in Chapter 5.) Arthur Young and other consulting firms have used CSFs for three related purposes:

1. To clarify managerial focus by highlighting similarities and differences among executives' CSFs

2. To develop top management's information needs by relating CSFs to specific items of decision support information
3. To set information systems priorities by defining the gap between available and required information as it is related to the importance of the CSF

Used in these ways, CSFs help managers to establish a businesswide perspective and define initial requirements.

The CSF approach focuses on critical high-payoff factors, it is relatively fast and inexpensive to administer, and it frequently reveals new insights to the executives involved. Its major disadvantages are that it is not comprehensive and that it results in a snapshot of the business, which can quickly become obsolete if any major change occurs.

Information Needs and the Product Life Cycle

Analysts at Nolan Norton and Company have developed a methodology for linking corporate strategic planning with information systems planning. The primary support needs of a product are determined by considering its stage in the product life cycle (see Chapter 6) and its relative market share. The Nolan and Gibson (1974) model distinguishes four stages:

- *Initiation*, in which technological specification, systems creation, and original investment are crucial
- *Expansion*, in which learning and adaptation are crucial
- *Control*, in which rationalization and elaboration are crucial
- *Maturity*, in which a careful review of projects for continued viability and the need for integration is crucial

In general, early-life-cycle/low-market-share products tend to need strategic information support, early-life-cycle/high-market-share products tend to need operational support, later-life-cycle/high-market-share products tend to need management control support, and later-life-cycle/low-market-share products tend to need strategic support. The market needs for each product can then be identified and placed into one of three categories—cost reduction, improved productivity, and product differentiation. Finally, existing and proposed applications of information systems are reviewed via a functional portfolio model. The functional portfolio model represents all the key activities in the business, shown in a portfolio similar to the product portfolio.

The results of these analyses can then be used to answer broad questions:

- How are the product needs related to market needs?
- How are the stages of the information system related to the product needs?
- How are the product needs related to the functional portfolio?
- How are the stages of the information system related to market needs?
- How are the market needs related to the functional portfolio?
- How are the stages related to the functional portfolio?

Each of these questions can be answered in terms of costs, coverage, and systems support. The result is an overall evaluation of the application and information systems. Guidelines emerge for budgets, improvements in existing systems, and opportunities for new systems.

ASSESSMENT OF INFORMATION-SYSTEMS NEEDS

Mark Porat, Alvin Toffler, and others have asserted that society has entered an information age (Porat, 1977; Toffler, 1990). A large number of people are involved in the production and dissemination of information. Many firms spend 1% to 3% of total revenues on information systems. They draw heavily on the more than 500 databases and other commercial information services available. How can managers determine whether a company is using information systems appropriately? One method is to compare the company's usage of information (and the return received therefrom) to that of its competitors. Another approach is to consider the value added by the systems.

Industry Comparisons

Information services can contribute to the total value added by every business. Moreover, the percentage of value added by information has been increasing over the past two decades. This percentage is, however, greater in information-processing and financial services industries than in manufacturing industries. Robert Hayes, dean of the UCLA Graduate School of Library and Information Science, has produced econometric evidence suggesting that manufacturing industries in the United States are *underinvesting* in information (Hayes, 1982). His results, based on data from 51 industries, indicate that the manufacturing segment is utilizing less information than is needed to maintain a competitive position in a global economy. As the potential for information systems to contribute to total value added increases (2–3% per year has not been unusual), alert managers must maintain their company's ability to obtain information services at the optimal level.

One way to determine whether a business is making optimal use of information is to

1. Make a list of the business's major information and communication functions.
2. Rate the company and its competitors on each of these functions in terms of (a) their dependence on information technology and (b) the effectiveness of the technology in use.
3. Combine the two ratings to yield an information-systems "absorption" rate.
4. Compare the results. A firm whose absorption rate is below the industry average may have some catching up to do. A firm whose rate is above the average may be a technological innovator or may have assumed too much risk.

Value-Added Approaches

Another approach is to consider the total value-adding chain within the business and ask how improved information services might result in improved performance. The value chain, which was discussed in Chapter 5, helps to determine those activities in which a company performs better in terms of technology and cost (Porter and Millar, 1985). Although a product's value is whatever the buyer is willing to pay, its ultimate cost depends on the interdependent activities linked together by the value chain.

Along with capital and labor, information adds value during production. Information is used in raw-materials acquisition, materials processing, manufacturing, distribution, and customer service. Value chain analysis reveals not only promising business opportunities but also opportunities to improve profits.

In determining whether information systems will add value, strategic managers should ask

- What major decisions are made?
- What are the constraints and problems?
- What role does information play?
- How can improved use of information lead to improved performance of the business?
- Could better information lead to better profits?

Value is added through the transformation of inputs into outputs. Thus the key to understanding a business is to identify the dominant features of the transformation. Information can play two key roles in the transformation process. First, it can be used to coordinate and smooth the flow of activity from one stage to another. Second, it can be used in production. For example, by using information systems technology in the design process, a firm can improve performance and thereby secure a competitive edge. Long-linked technology is likely to uncover some strategic opportunities for the application of information technology to a business. A long-linked technology accomplishes its task by sequential interdependence between tasks and relies on effectiveness through planning and control. An example of a long-linked technology is an assembly line that mass-produces a standard product at a constant rate and is dependent on feeder lines supplying material to the right place at the right time.

James Thompson first identified the basic technological cores that underlie the transformation of inputs into outputs (Thompson, 1967). He labeled these cores long-linked technology, extensive technologies, intensive technologies, and mediating technologies. Long-linked technology is described above.

1. *Extensive technologies* convert one input into two or more distinct outputs. Examples of this type of input/output process are the conversion of timber into lumber and paper; of grapes into raisins, table grapes, and wine; and of sheep into mutton and wool. In the cases of timber and grapes, a firm can decide how much input to allocate to each output. In the case of sheep raising, the conversion ratios are relatively fixed; one cannot change the proportions of input used to produce mutton and wool. Many industries (notably oil) fall somewhere between these two extremes. In the petroleum industry, the chemistry of hydrocarbon bonding constrains the range of alternative outputs that can be produced. Within these constraints, however, the chemistry is flexible enough to offer a considerable number of options.

Information systems can have several important functions in these highly technological industries. First, the demand and price characteristics of each of the potential output areas can be closely monitored so that the business can shift its emphasis to the most profitable products. Anticipating changes in demand and price is part of strategic product-portfolio management. Second, the technological environment can be scanned in order to find ways of increasing the range of outputs and the flexibility to shift among them. Third, information can be used to allocate the cost of inputs used to produce each output. Only with a logical system for allocating joint costs can a company establish profitability and determine whether to shift its emphasis from one product output to another.

2. *Intensive technologies* are the mirror image of extensive technologies. Intensive technologies combine a variety of inputs into a single output. Construction projects and one-time events, such as rock concerts, are generally intensive in nature. Information must be used to guide the application of inputs to output so that time/cost objectives can be met.

Case-management systems are archetypical intensive technologies. A *case* in this context is a business transaction with an individual that is opened, processed, and closed. Examples of case-management systems include transactions with patients in a hospital, claimants in an insurance firm, and clients for a professional's services. Stephen Rosenthal (1982) pointed out that case-management systems have four principal phases:

- *Identification,* in which new cases are sought, received, screened, and either rejected or accepted for further processing
- *Analysis,* in which data about each case are collected and interpreted and the case is diagnosed, prioritized, and scheduled
- *Response,* in which the resources are actually applied to the case and an output (such as a finding, verdict, or cure for a patient) is reached
- *Resolution,* in which the case is closed, although it may be monitored for performance and possible chronic relapse.

Each of these phases requires information and thus is a good target for the application of information-services technology.

3. *Mediating technologies* add value by matching diverse inputs with diverse outputs. They constitute a combination of intensive and extensive technologies. An example is a real estate brokerage system, in which an input case is opened for each property listing and an output case is opened for each prospective buyer. Then the firm seeks to match properties with buyers.

Reservation systems, such as American Airlines' Sabre system and Avis's Wizard, fall into this category. Wizard permits an Avis customer anywhere in the United States to order a particular style of car to be available in another city at a specified time. A complex telecommunications and computer system does the matching, informs Avis decision makers, and keeps track of accounting transactions once the entry is made. Both American Airlines and Avis gained strategic advantages over their competitors by designing systems that facilitated their mediating activities. By improving their mediating function, they were able to provide better services to their customers and reduce their cost of performance.

As financial intermediaries, banks and other financial institutions are classic users of mediating technologies. They can separate the two technologies, however. Operations dealing with deposits and sources of funds are intensive technologies, whereas those dealing with loans and investments are extensive technologies. This separation is possible because money can be used to transfer a debt, and because bank management uses indicators such as the loan-to-deposit ratio to balance the flows of inputs and outputs. Today, more financial institutions are trying to manage a diverse customer base by matching customers to the combination of deposit, loan, and investment services they want. This practice also gives bankers an opportunity to estimate the profit (loss) contribution of a customer—information that has eluded them in the past.

Information is central to mediating technologies. It is used to identify and service suppliers (input) and customers (output) and to match them in an effective and profitable manner.

INFORMATION TECHNOLOGY AND STRATEGY

There is a new meaning of power in today's economic and political world. As Alvin Toffler (1990) observes, a new system of wealth creation has emerged. Information and knowledge—including facts, art, science, moral values, intelligence, and even misinformation—provide the raw material for creating wealth. But information was not always a principal source of power. To the ancient Athenians, Thucydides tells us in his account of the Peloponnesian war, "might made right." For the ensuing nearly 2,500 years, the capability to do violence and to inflict harm on others has been a major source of power. Starting in the sixteenth century, however, as market economies began to form, money began to be used more pervasively in all political and economic relationships. In the process, money emerged as a second, and in a sense a more flexible, source of power (Braudel, 1981). Then, as the Industrial Revolution unfolded in England and the United States, and especially as the modern corporation came into being, money became a dominant source of power. With money one could buy goods, services, influence, and if necessary, war-making capacity.

Yet the sheer complexity of bigger businesses and governments themselves (as expressed in the form of railroads, steamship companies, automobile makers, nationwide mail order houses, steel makers, chemical companies, and agencies) created a massive problem of managerial control. In response, new information-based technologies such as the telegraph, the telephone, the adding machine, the typewriter, and the punched-card accounting machine were invented. These new technologies were used to provide the information needed to cope with the increased distance, speed, volume, and complexity involved in doing business. Sociologist James Beniger (1986) calls this phenomenon the "control revolution." These events, he argues, form the technological and economic origins of the information society. After World War II, major advances in computers and telecommunications technology and an expanding global economy worked together to change the fundamental nature of the economy and of society. Western capitalist societies became information-based. And this occurrence, Toffler states, brought about another shift in the basis of power. Knowledge and information replaced money as the fundamental source of power.

Information, it turns out, is a higher-quality source of power. Toffler continues:

> High-quality power is not simply clout. Not merely the ability to get one's way, to make others do what you want, though they might prefer otherwise. High quality implies much more. It implies efficiency—using up the fewest power resources to achieve a goal. Knowledge can often be used to make the other party *like* your agenda for action. It can even persuade the person that she or he originated it.

Knowledge also serves as a wealth and force multiplier. It can be used to augment the available force of wealth or, alternatively, to reduce the amount needed to achieve any given purpose. In either case, it increases efficiency, permitting one to spend fewer power "chips" in any showdown. (p. 16)

The shift to information and knowledge as a basis of power has profound effects for corporate strategy. For many years, information played an auxiliary role in business affairs. It was used primarily for stewardship purposes—for record keeping and to keep track of labor, capital, and other resources. As time passed, the potential role of information as an input to decision making and as a fundamental element in the delivery of goods and services was discovered, and strategies for the effective linking of information with operations and decision making were developed. Businesses embarking on these strategies changed the concept of information itself. Information ceased being merely a way of accounting for other resources and *became a resource in its own right*. Information, it was soon learned, could be acquired, manipulated, and allocated just as any other economic resource could. Thus information became a major source of corporate power, and information technology became the instrument for harnessing this power.

Information technology (IT) is the means used to gather, process, store, and transmit data, text, sound, graphics, and other symbolic images. It has strategic significance. In an information-rich economy, a company can use information technology to "reduce costs, upgrade product quality, improve customer service, or even integrate a customer's operations with its own, thus assuring repeat business." Insofar as it achieves these goals, information technology is a tool for increasing the economic power of a firm.

The potential sources of this power are expanding almost daily as new technologies are developed and made available. Parallel computers, optical networks, massive data storage, and a whole host of new information processing and handling technologies are being released, and several decades more of new technologies are currently moving through the research and development pipeline. As a consequence, the information networks of the 1990s and well beyond will dwarf those of today in size, level of sophistication, and efficiency. They will link hundreds of suppliers (that offer thousands of products) with who knows how many millions of customers.

A prototype firm of the future is Rosenbluth Travel. Rosenbluth, which operates out of Philadelphia, is one of the five largest travel agencies in the United States. Since 1980 it has grown from a regional agency with annual sales of $40 million into a "global virtual corporation" with annual sales well over $1.3 billion. The company formed Rosenbluth International Alliance (RIA) by entering into partnerships with some 34 local travel agents spanning over 37 countries. Information technology was the tool for linking them. According to Rosenbluth executive David Miller,

> Information technology enables the company to coordinate travel services throughout the world. Through IT, specific information concerning clients and travelers is available anywhere in the world to provide superior travel support. A U.S. executive traveling in the U.K. will find that the local RIA representative is aware of her itinerary and travel preferences as well as her company's travel policies and special rate programs. And through IT, information can be consolidated across the world to coordinate decision making and leverage global purchasing power. (Personal interview, January 1992)

We need not travel around the globe, however, to see IT being used as an effective strategic tool. Just visit the local Wal-Mart or Sam's. During the first quarter of 1991, Wal-Mart Stores, the brainchild of pioneering discounter Sam Walton, surpassed Sears and became America's largest retailer. Sears' annual sales reached $32 billion; Wal-Mart's were in excess of $32.6 billion and still growing. Wal-Mart was also considerably more efficient. Its expenses were only 16% of sales, and its employees generated an average of $95,000 in sales per employee. Sears' costs, on the other hand, were a lofty 29% of sales, and its employees averaged only about $85,000 each in sales. IT played a crucial role in this remarkably successful strategy. As *Time* magazine reported,

> Walton—Mr. Sam to his 350,000 employees—invested in a state-of-the-art corporate satellite system that has enabled the company to perfect round-the-clock inventory control so that the products customers want are nearly always in stock. In Bentonville (Arkansas), a computer center the size of a football field controls the widespread operations, tracking inventory, credit, and sales via a Hughes satellite. (Castro, 1991)

Wal-Mart's network provides real-time data and voice and video links to about 1,600 stores. In addition to making possible just-in-time inventory replenishment to the stores from distribution centers, the network is linked to suppliers. In early 1992 over 2,200 suppliers were on line to Wal-Mart; about 2,000 more were slated to join. The satellite network is also used for direct television broadcasting of messages to the stores and for training employees. Buyers use the network to tell stores what new items are available in a particular department and how those items should be displayed. Executives use the network to share ideas about what is selling well and what merchandising ideas work for particular products (Booker, 1990).

Telemarketing has become another IT-based tool of strategy. It is already being used by over 80,000 companies large and small, and the list is growing every day. Although applications such as telemarketing have succeeded in increasing direct sales, the greatest potential of IT still lies in adding a new capability to the company's competitive arsenal. IT allows companies to enter new markets rapidly, differentiate their products through better service and response, dramatically improve sales performance, and gather the intelligence needed to compete in a dynamic marketplace.

Warren McFarlan (1984) has shown that companies can use IT to build barriers to entry, to increase customer switching costs, or to change the basis for competing, thereby throwing the competition off balance. A notable example of such a strategy is that of Digital Equipment Corporation (DEC). Severely hurt by its failure to compete in the personal computer field, DEC needed a new strategic thrust. A computer-based expert system proved to be a key part of the answer.

DEC found that it could outperform IBM, Apple, and other competitors when it used an artificial-intelligence-based system called XCON (Expert Configurator) to communicate directly with customers. When customers place orders, XCON provides them with complete specifications and delivery dates and at the same time sends the information to the factory so that work on orders can commence. This competitive advantage saved the ailing giant, making DEC a formidable competitor once again.

Another example is a new expert system, Business Insight, that is being employed to help determine the best strategies for introducing new products

(Lewis, 1991). Business Insight is the most comprehensive of a number of available computerized strategic-planning programs. The business development manager for the Dynatel Systems Division of 3M claims that this program provides the broadest perspective of any. The program operates in an interactive mode and starts by asking questions such as "How likely is it that a competitor will retaliate?" The value of the program is that it forces a systematic evaluation of the factors that a company must consider when introducing a new product.

At Rockwell International, engineers use an object-oriented expert system to design payloads on the computer screen. This allows them to see how well the payload fits into a space shuttle's cargo bay. Engineers have been enthusiastic about using the program and say that it saves them considerable time and effort (Callahan, 1992). Numerous accounts of the successful application of expert systems have been published in recent years. The expanding use of expert system technology to support more effective design and strategic analysis paints a bright picture for its future use.

Professor Eric Clemons has summarized some of the ways in which information technology can empower a firm:

1. *Increased efficiency.* "Use information technology to address fundamental requirements of the business or its customers and suppliers, thereby gaining competitive advantage." (p. 23)
2. *First-mover advantage.* "Hustle and continuously improve your uses of information technology; or rely on switching costs to keep customers tied to you and thus defend your gains in the face of competitors' response." (p. 24)
3. *Leverage resource advantages.* "Use information technology to add value to resources you already enjoy and that your competitors lack and cannot readily acquire." (p. 24)
4. *Achieve parity.* Once a competitor has innovated in an industry, the use of information technology can become a strategic necessity. This has happened, for example, in the airline and banking industries. In these industries, applications involving computers and communications have become an unavoidable part of the cost of doing business.
5. *Interorganizational cooperation.* Companies are increasingly crafting strategies that are based on strategic alliances with other companies, often located in other countries.

Rosenbluth Travel is a case in point, and there are many others that use electronic data interchange (EDI). For example, Levi Strauss has formed cooperative electronic arrangements with its suppliers of denim and other textiles so that orders are placed and goods arrive just in time for manufacture (in retailing this is called "quick response"). Similarly, Levi's has links to its retail customers, such as J.C. Penney, for automatic replenishment of apparel inventory at retail stores.

There are several strategic objectives that can be achieved by employing information technology as an integral part of a corporate strategic plan. They include

1. Improved economies of scale
2. Improved economies of scope

3. Creation of proprietary information
4. Enhanced organizational learning and skills development
5. Compression of time to market

Are open systems the wave of the future in information technology? An open system relates more to information than hardware. It can be understood by users who readily can apply information in their work. Knowledge workers—persons who are primarily responsible for managing information systems—will soon represent the single largest occupational group. The real advantage that open systems confer from a strategic perspective is that they enable companies to compete with the benefit of a sounder technological base. Open systems allow companies to run computer programs on more than one computer system and thus make programs portable (White, 1991). The competitive advantage of using information technology derives from its being almost universally available, which facilitates the electronic transmission of all kinds of records, forms, and raw data. This allows a company to readily expand services, products, distribution, and timeliness. For example, American Express can respond to a credit card inquiry from any of its millions of subscribers in a matter of seconds. The question is not whether to use information technology but how to use it to achieve a significant competitive edge.

EXPERT SYSTEMS IN STRATEGIC MANAGEMENT

The magnitude of the problems confronting strategic managers is such that they often appear overwhelming. The ability to evaluate all available information and to maintain a knowledge base is beyond most managers. More effective means than are now used are required to cope with the avalanche of data that confronts strategic decision makers and to advise them regarding strategic options. Much more is involved than industry and competitor analysis. Factors to be considered include

1. Interdependencies among organizational functions
2. Interactions in the network of manufacturing activities
3. Timing and concurrency of product manufacturing
4. Periodicity and life cycles of products
5. Trends and discontinuities in customer demand, growth, and so on
6. Uncertainty and vulnerability in the external environment
7. Technology advances and their impact on products, growth, and position
8. Leadership and culture requirements to provide an environment conducive to change
9. Balance in product and business portfolios
10. Requirements for a sustainable competitive advantage

DEVELOPING A KNOWLEDGE BASE FOR STRATEGY

Mockler (1989) views the development of an expert system for strategy as built on a knowledge base. He examines strategy by using a frame hierarchy, as shown in Figure 11.1. The frame provides a basis for determining what factors make up the

FIGURE 11.1 | Frame Hierarchy

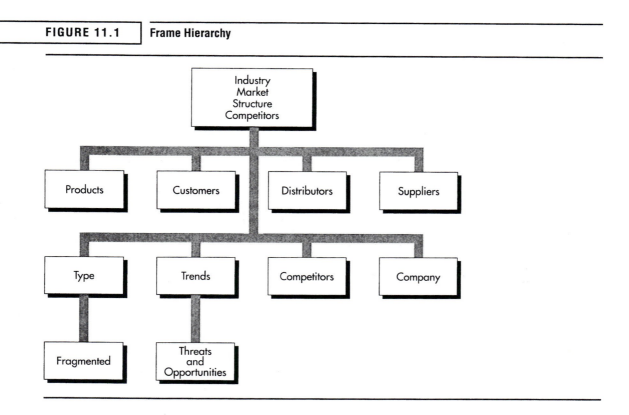

knowledge base when one is assessing the desirability of strategic alternatives. For example, he considers whether the industry is fragmented, declining, mature, or emerging when determining a strategy recommendation.

In developing a marketing strategy, he examines the recommendations that the expert system could make:

1. Introduce an existing product without alterations but change the brand name.
2. Introduce the product as an extension to an existing product line.
3. Introduce the product as a replacement of an existing product.
4. Change the product and introduce it with a new brand name.
5. Change some elements of the product and then introduce it as a new brand.
6. Change some elements of the product and then introduce it as a replacement for an existing product.
7. Reject the proposed product and do not introduce it.

The expert system chooses from among these recommendations using appropriate heuristic decision rules. Industry data such as rate of growth, financial ratios, fragmentation, concentration, and elasticity can also be included in a knowledge base. For example, a high debt-to-equity ratio might be perfectly acceptable for certain industries but not for others. The knowledge base is thus used to support which strategic options will be recommended. In addition, an explanation of why a specified option was chosen can be included. Table 11.5 lists possible strategic options that are stored in the knowledge base. They illustrate the advice such a program can provide.

The four basic strategies that Mockler identifies are

1. *Aggressive:* this recommendation suggests that the firm exploit its strong position by concentric diversification, vertical integration, overall cost leadership, and the like.
2. *Competitive:* this strategy includes concentric mergers, conglomerate mergers, turnaround, product uniqueness, differentiation, and value added.
3. *Conservative:* this recommendation focuses on niche or market segment, global diversification, conglomerate diversification, or protecting the status quo.
4. *Defensive:* this is essentially a survival strategy that focuses on harvesting products, divestitures, retrenchment, cost reduction, liquidation, or merger.

These four basic strategies can be considered generic strategies. A generic strategy matrix is shown in Figure 11.2.

These strategic alternatives are consistent with Porter's generic strategies.

1. *Overall cost leadership* requires the aggressive construction of efficient facilities, vigorous pursuit of cost reduction, tight cost control, reduction of marginal customers, and reduction of expenses for R&D, sales, and advertising. It is analogous to the *aggressive* strategy.
2. *Differentiation* requires creating something that is unique, such as design, brand image, special features, or outstanding quality. It is comparable to the *competitive* strategy.

TABLE 11.5	Strategic Options

Pricing level	New market penetration
De-averaging cost	Joint venture
Quality required	When to buy competitors
Guarantee level	Level of R&D expenditure
Service level	Product innovations required
Timing of delivery	Advertising level
Uniqueness of products	Comparative productivity
Value-added level	Customer information
Market niche to pursue	Competitor information
Opportunities and product gaps to pursue	Portfolio balance
Barriers needed	Strategic restructuring required
Market potential	Competitive posture
Location	Vertical integration
Technology required	Resource allocation

FIGURE 11.2	Generic Strategies

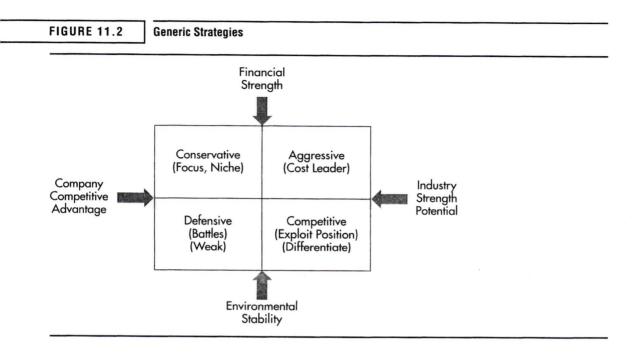

3. *Focus* deals with a specific buyer group, market segment, product line, or geographic market. This strategy is based on the premise that the firm can do something specific better than other firms and thus is able to capture a limited market share. It is comparable to the *conservative* strategy.
4. *"Stuck in the middle"* is what Porter calls a company that has an extremely weak strategic position and finds it difficult to extricate itself. This is analogous to the *defensive* strategy.

Mockler (1989) also describes the use of a strategic decision rule matrix for making strategic decisions. An example is shown in Figure 11.3. The rule matrix displays the "if" conditions (sometimes called premises) and the "and" conditions (sometimes referred to as rules) and relates them to the "then" decisions (or recommendations or classifications, depending on the problem being considered). The matrix format has the advantage of ease of construction and ease of reading. Note that different combinations of conditions may lead to the same decision or action. For example, *consider* occurs twice, as does *pursue*.

A SPACE output is shown in Figure 11.4. The company is low on all four factors, and as a result, the defensive strategy is indicated. This survival strategy is consistent with the fact that the company is weak competitively and financially. It is operating in an industry that is not attractive and in an environment that is not very stable.

Expert systems have provided important support in many areas of managerial decision making. And the use of such systems for strategy formulation is sure to become one of the critical aspects of operating in a complex, sometimes hostile, and always highly competitive global environment.

FIGURE 11.3	Strategic Decision Rule Matrix

If-Conditions	And-Conditions				
	1	2	3	4	5
1. Competitors	Many	Few			
2. Elasticity	Yes	No			
3. Differentiation	Yes	No			
4. Market Share			Small	Medium	Large
5. Growth Potential			Low	Moderate	High
6. Technology			Not Critical	May Be Critical	Critical
7. Barriers			Low	Increasing	High
8. Substitutes			Many	Increasing	Few
9. Change in Customer Base			No	Some	Yes
10. Change in Distribution			No	Some	Yes
Then-Decision	Avoid	Consider	Consider	Pursue	Pursue

FIGURE 11.4	SPACE Analysis

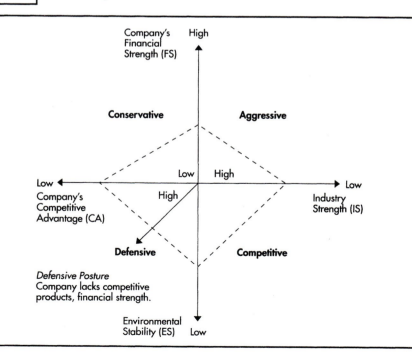

Company's Financial Strength (FS) — High

Conservative   Aggressive

Low — Company's Competitive Advantage (CA)

Low   High

High

Low — Industry Strength (IS)

Defensive   Competitive

Defensive Posture
Company lacks competitive products, financial strength.

Environmental Stability (ES)   Low

INTELLIGENT DECISION SUPPORT SYSTEMS

The CEO of Information Technology, Richard Heygate (1990) believes that the key role of decision support systems is to leverage information in order to provide analytical support, control current activities, enhance performance, and make trans-organizational information available. His emphasis is on the use of information, not on the methodologies used to obtain or store data. Given this perspective, how should one go about the design and use of knowledge bases so that they can serve as an intelligent decision support system?

A number of approaches can be employed to add intelligence when using a knowledge or database. For example, the Pareto law can be used to partition knowledge into "currently significant" information versus "archival information" that is needed only for reference or audit (Rowe and Watkins, 1992). Research by Kandelin (1990) suggests that in order to have intelligence added to data, one has to form an "events database." As economic events occur, they are recorded as such in the database. The intelligence component is based on the automatic updating of reports as new data, information, or knowledge, in the form of events, is recorded. This automated updating serves to "signal" the users of changes in activities that may be of interest and concern. Thus relevant data are quickly and efficiently put to use, whereas data that are not relevant are ignored or not stored at all.

Current technology permits images to be stored in large-scale databases. Thus, image data that were not needed for current operations could be kept in permanent archival storage devices such as optical discs. If such data were ever needed to support an audit or provide backup, they would be available. American Express, for example, processes all credit card transactions by image processing and also stores all the scanned images. What should be stored, and for how long, are the critical issues for a large-volume transaction processor; clearly, an economic solution is required.

From their inception, the objective of computer-based systems has been to provide decision makers with information in a more meaningful and useful form. Unfortunately, most current systems do not really "support" decision making (Dickinson, 1991). There are efforts underway to ameliorate this situation. Lotus Development introduced the personal information manager ("AI + database," 1988) that allows users to enter information into an "Agenda" database in natural, free-form units called "items" without the normal structure required in the typical database system. Lotus Agenda assists the user by applying intelligence to an expert's knowledge using contextual cues and historic information to perform logical inferences. Storey and Goldstein (1990) suggest that what is needed to improve the design of a database is an expert system to elicit user views in order to determine storage requirements. This approach avoids inconsistencies, ambiguities, and redundancies because they can be detected and resolved ahead of time.

To overcome the sheer magnitude of the task of handling data more efficiently, one needs to utilize data more intelligently. For example, what is the value of increased information? When would aggregate data be more appropriate for decision making than all the elemental or detail data? When inundated with mountains of details, most decision makers go into "information overload." What is needed is a process whereby decision making leads to appropriate actions that accomplish specified strategies. However, strategic decisions involve actions that take place in the future, and the outcome is uncertain. In order to reach an acceptable level of risk, data and knowledge are needed. Adding intelligence to data in accordance with the following formula can reduce the risk to a level that is acceptable.

Acceptable risk = Uncertainty + Intelligent use of data and knowledge

The following guidelines are suggested for adding intelligence to data and knowledge.

1. Define the data requirements for critical issues.
2. Structure problems so that the intelligent use of data and knowledge is possible.
3. Devise intelligent methods of storing and retrieving data and knowledge.
4. Use expert systems and heuristics to explore ways of storing data efficiently.
5. Determine what is an acceptable level of risk for given strategic decisions.

THE GROWING IMPORTANCE OF KNOWLEDGE-BASED SYSTEMS (KBS) IN BUSINESS

The importance of knowledge-based systems in business is increasingly being recognized, judging by the number of companies involved in developing them, the amount of money spent on them, and the number of systems already developed and in operation.

The importance of these systems is likely to increase in the future, especially systems designed to support and replicate lower- and middle-level management tasks. This is the level at which shortages of managerial personnel arising from the "baby bust" will be occurring over the next twenty years. These shortages are already showing up in the retail and service areas today. A wide range of knowledge-based systems can be useful in helping fill this management gap.

Their importance is also likely to increase as KBS become more and more integrated with conventional computer systems. KBS are ultimately just another technology information tool among the many available, which can be used to help managers make more effective decisions.

PROBLEMS INHIBITING THE GROWTH OF KBS

Enormous problems have been encountered in introducing KBS technology into business. One study (Cullen, 1988) found that half the systems failed. Rose (1988) describes another somewhat typical project, in which two years and $300,000 were spent in developing an 80-rule system that is not being used. Such stories can be discouraging to those thinking about entering this area.

In addition to technological limitations, a key problem inhibiting rapid growth of these systems is that considerable work still needs to be done in defining in precise detail how the thousands of management and operational decisions occurring daily in business are made. Solving this problem is difficult, largely because not enough business managers and experts have the time or financial incentive to do this work. Yet, as with other types of decision support systems, input from these managers about the thinking processes (heuristics) involved in their decision making is an extremely important ingredient in creating effective KBS (Mockler, 1991,

1992). These kinds of difficulties and failures are not unexpected at this stage of a newly emerging technology such as knowledge-based systems.

Introducing any computer technology into an organization requires integrating technological and user requirements. The job is especially difficult when introducing knowledge-based system technology, because

- The technology (hardware and software) is relatively new and still developing rapidly, so that neither the technology nor its benefits and applications are yet widely understood.
- Many advocates of the technology have promised more than the technology can deliver, given the present state of the art (Bulkeley, 1990), causing many to become disenchanted with the technology.
- Developing these systems requires skills that are substantially different from those required for conventional computer system development, creating major problems for computer systems personnel.

Although the development and use of knowledge-based systems continue to grow, they have not been implemented to any significant degree in strategic management. This is due in part to lack of experience in their use, but to a larger extent, the problem involves the issues discussed in Chapter 10: leadership and bringing about organizational change. A bright light on the horizon is the growing use of large-scale networks that can interact more readily than before. New programs are being developed to handle what are called large-scale distributed heterogeneous databases. Simply stated, this refers to the large number of computer systems scattered around the country that have to interact in an "open system" format so that divisions of companies, no matter how widely dispersed, can interact in real time and utilize the latest technological approaches available. The future is bright, but only for those with the foresight and courage to make the vision a reality which requires

- Expert/user involvement in the development process much greater than that found in conventional computer system development, creating substantial management and organization problems in efforts to develop knowledge-based systems.
- There are few readily available, detailed accounts of (1) how these expert systems affect an existing company organization situation and the people in it or (2) what type of organization and management style is best for developing and deriving maximum benefit from these systems.
- There is resistance to KBS because the need for such systems is not as apparent to managers as is the need for conventional computer systems, such as those found in the financial and accounting areas.

Planning and carrying out KBS development efforts involves integrating technical, human, and organization factors. This process can be complicated by the fact that development situations vary so widely.

At one extreme, a company situation may involve smaller systems and a single or small group of users/operating managers who are computer-literate or have access to expert systems development shells and who perceive expert systems as being potentially useful in their jobs. At the other extreme, application development situations may involve a large, diversified group of users who are in sales or other primarily nontechnical jobs, who have varying degrees of computer literacy, who are not aware of the potential benefits of expert systems, who vary widely in ages and work experience, and who work in widely dispersed geographic locations for a large, diversified company.

The range of system technology and complexity can also vary, from small user-developed systems employing personal computers (PCs) and PC expert system shells, to very large systems developed by computer scientists using mainframe or dedicated computer hardware technology.

UMMARY

In describing information and decision technology in the 1990s, Forgionne (1990) indicated that new information systems will be required to support all phases of decision making. Included are problem recognition, formulation, analysis, solution, interpretation, and implementation. These new systems will be required to provide all the technology needed by management and to provide an integrated system so that individuals or group decision makers will have the best possible information to support their decisions. This complete technology for management will include all the various approaches and decision tools (such as simulation models, expert systems, forecasting, and various kinds of economic and accounting models), as well as the system hardware needed to network computers. Everybody will have access to the same data and will receive the kinds of displays that will make information more meaningful.

The application of expert knowledge in expert systems will introduce an important consideration into such future systems. Using the decision maker's knowledge makes him or her a part of the system. Such "ownership" is an important aspect of introducing motivation, and managers who are unfamiliar with systems tend to disregard them. On the other hand, if such information systems provide data, trends, analysis, forecasts, tables, graphs, or whatever the decision maker wants, then he or she is more likely to use that system. The computer will become interactive and will enable managers to incorporate many more insights and judgments into evaluating problems, so the technology that involves a computer

will change from decision support to augmenting the manager's ability to make better decisions. This will also tap into the creativity and intelligence that managers have and will allow them to enhance that creativity through their ability to use available information in databases or knowledge bases.

A look far into the future suggests some startling possibilities in the application of information to support decision making. Neural networks provide a frontier that may change the way managers look at decision making and at support systems. Neural networks are crude but powerful simulations of the nervous system that try to mimic the way the brain works. Neural networks are hybrid analog/digital computers with speeds about 1,000 times faster than current systems. They are able to process information 1 billion times faster than current conventional digital computers. Applications include a variety of tasks from machine vision and robotics to speech recognition, tests, and handwriting recognition. They have been able to solve very complex problems that involve patterns, such as interpretation or evaluation of military vehicles and analysis of integrated computer circuitry. In banking, neural networks have helped Chase Manhattan detect credit card fraud. Security Pacific Bank uses such a system to analyze commercial and automobile loan risks. In addition to such applications, neural networks have been applied in medicine to detect abnormal heart sounds and interpret electrocardiograms. At Roarck University in England, an electronic nose that recognizes smells has been developed. A similar system is used in Japan to test the freshness of sushi. Ford Motor Company is developing a computer, which is actually on the automobile, that simultaneously monitors all aspects of the automotive operation—the engine, power train, suspension, electronic steering, brakes, climate control, and so forth (Moore, 1990).

In addition to the capabilities mentioned, neural networks have been used in Japan for a variety of applications that try to simulate human behavior. They incorporate a concept of "fuzzy logic." This logic does not deal with precise values but with concepts, such as a very bright finish. *Bright* can have a range of values, which is why this logic is called fuzzy. On the other hand, the Japanese have applied it to washing machines, where the water can be determined as being dirty or not dirty. Again, a fuzzy concept. We will also see a drastic change in the way computers are built and in the kinds of software they use. In particular, parallel architecture that allows the program to process over a large number of electronic routes provides the ability to do things that we cannot do very efficiently with digital computers. This will enhance the processing speed but will also introduce some interesting new, and yet untested, capabilities.

The future presents untold opportunities for those who have the appropriate tools and approaches to deal with the requirements of the long-term growth and survival of the organization. Changing markets, changing expectations, and changing stakeholders all portend a change in the approach managers will need for successful organizations in the future. The emphasis on the entrepreneurial and leadership styles of management will contribute to greater use of newer methodologies, complex scenarios, and interactive computer-based systems.

With more and more data becoming readily available as the information age progresses, managers are asking, "How can any given information become a strategic resource?" Information has evolved from being merely a tool for tracking the use of labor, capital, and other resources to being a resource and a product itself. By using information systems, companies can gain a strategic edge over competitors. Here again, balance is crucial. Simply having the relevant data does not ensure that decisions will be made correctly or carried out properly. Although decision makers may avoid serious errors because they have the data needed to evaluate alternative futures, data are only a means to an end. Effective performance in a highly turbulent environment requires leaders with the ability to integrate the individual performer into the formulation and implementation of strategy.

In the coming years, leaders, managers, researchers, and educators will continue to grapple with the question of how best to utilize information systems for strategy. Those who find answers will benefit most.

Changes in organizational structure and managerial approaches to improving performance are the key to success. The evidence suggests that flatter organizations with fewer layers of management exhibit improved communication and enhanced worker responsibility. De facto reliance on teams has been adopted by many companies. Team leaders assume responsibility for performance, design, motivation, innovation, and commitment on the part of team members. Teams become self-monitoring and can reduce the need for traditional management control approaches such as MBO. Most important, teams in flatter organizations seem to achieve significant performance and to improve the company's competitive position.

Innovation and technology are key determinants of competitive advantage. Companies such as Lincoln Electric, GE, Xerox, and Hewlett-Packard are shining examples of how effective innovation leads to breakthrough new products and helps fend off competition while creating customer needs that did not previously exist.

This book has been directed toward helping managers determine strategies for success. The methods and approaches presented here can help ensure that an appropriate analysis has been done so that the creative manager knows where to start and what is needed. To bring these ideas to fruition requires an appropriate way of thinking and a managerial process that recognizes the role and the needs of the individual as a key element in implementing strategic change.

REFERENCES AND SUGGESTIONS FOR FURTHER READING

Ackoff, Russel E. 1967. Management misinformation systems. *Management Science,* December, pp. 147–156.

AI + database = personal information manager. 1988. *AI Week,* September 1, p. 9.

Allman, William. 1992. Shrinking the future. *U.S. News & World Report,* March 9, pp. 52–53.

Anderson, Howard. 1991. The open corporation. *Forbes,* October 28, advertisement.

Bender, Paul S., William D. Northrup, and Jeremy F. Shapiro. 1981. Practical modeling for resource management. *Harvard Business Review,* January–February, pp. 163–173.

Beniger, James R. 1986. *The control revolution.* Cambridge, Mass.: Harvard University Press.

Bennis, Warren and Burt Nanus. 1985. *Leaders.* New York: Harper & Row.

Bleeke, Joel. 1989. Peak strategies. *The McKinsey Quarterly,* Spring, pp. 19–27.

Booker, Ellis. 1990. IS trailblazing puts retailer on top. *Computerworld,* February 12, pp. 69–73.

Braudel, Fernand. 1981. *Civilization and capitalism, 15th–18th century,* vol. 1. New York: Harper & Row.

Broderick, Renae and John Boudreau. 1992. Human resource management, information technology, and the competitive edge. *Academy of Management Executive* 6, no. 2, pp. 7–17.

Brooks, Nancy and Jesus Sanchez. 1992. U.S. firms map ways to profit from the accord. *Los Angeles Times,* August 13, pp. D-1 and D-2.

Brown, John Seely. 1991. Research that reinvents the corporation. *Harvard Business Review,* January–February, pp. 102–111.

Bulkeley, William M. 1990. Bright outlook for artificial intelligence yields to slow growth and big cutbacks. *Wall Street Journal,* July 5, pp. B1 and B3.

Byrne, John. 1992. Management's new gurus. *Business Week,* August 31, pp. 44–52.

Byrne, John. 1989. Is your company too big? *Business Week,* March 27, pp. 84–94.

Callahan, Tom. 1992. The changing strategist. *Beyond Computing,* Premier Issue, pp. 12–14.

Castro, Janice. 1991. Mr. Sam stuns Goliath. *Time,* February 25, pp. 62–63.

Clemons, Eric. 1991. Corporate strategies for information technology. *IEEE Computers,* November, p. 23.

Clemons, E. K., M. C. Row, and D. B. Miller. 1992. Rosenbluth International alliance: Information technology and the global virtual corporation. *Proceedings of the Hawaii International Conference on Systems Science.* IV, pp. 678–686.

Cook, William. 1992. Dialing the future. *U.S. News & World Report,* February 3, pp. 49–51.

Cullen, J. and A. Bryman. 1988. The knowledge acquisition bottleneck. *Expert Systems,* August, pp. 216–250.

Day, George S. 1986. *Analysis for strategic market decisions.* St. Paul, Minn.: West.

Deutschman, Alan. America's fastest. *Fortune,* October 7, pp. 46–68.

Dichter, Steven. 1991. The organization of the 90's. *The McKinsey Quarterly,* no. 1, pp. 145–155.

Dickinson, John. 1991. An intelligent user interface should possess business smarts. *PC Computing,* May, p. 52.

Drucker, Peter. 1988. The coming of the new organization. *Harvard Business Review,* January–February, p. 45.

Dumaine, Brian. 1991. Closing the innovation gap. *Fortune,* December 2, pp. 56–62.

The fastest-growing occupations (1990–2005) for careers requiring a bachelor's degree. *Florida Leader* 9, no. 4.

Ferguson, Charles H. 1990. Computers and the coming of the U.S. keiretsu. *Harvard Business Review,* July–August, pp. 55–71.

Flint, Jerry. 1992. Platform madness. *Fortune,* January 20, pp. 40–42.

Forgionne, Guisseppi A. 1990. OR/MS and decision technology in the 1990s. *OR/MS Today* June, pp. 20–21.

Fromson, Brett. 1988. Where the next fortunes will be made. *Fortune,* December 5, pp. 185–196.

Gittelson, Steven. 1992. Future edge: Find tomorrow's opportunity now—or else! *Success,* April.

Grunwald, Henry. 1992. The year 2000: Is it the end or just the beginning? *Time,* March 30, pp. 73–76.

Gwynne, S. C. 1990. The right stuff. *Time,* October 29, pp. 74–84.

Hanna, Alistair and Jerold Lundquist. 1990. Creative strategies. *The McKinsey Quarterly,* no. 3, pp. 56–79.

Heygate, Richard. 1992. Accelerating front-line change: Cross-border alliances. *The McKinsey Quarterly,* Winter, pp. 134–147.

Howard, Robert. 1992. The CEO as organizational architect. *Harvard Business Review,* September–October, pp. 107–121.

Huey, John. 1991. Nothing is impossible. *Fortune,* September 23, pp. 135–140.

Jacob, Rahul. 1992. The search for the organization of tomorrow. *Fortune,* May 18, pp. 93–98.

Jacobson, George. 1992. Are we producing a future work force of Bart Simpsons? *Business Forum,* Winter, pp. 18–21.

Jamison, Sam. 1984. U.S. trainees praise Toyota system. *Los Angeles Times,* June 19, p. 1.

Kahalas, Harvey and Kathleen Suchon. 1992. Interview with Harold A. Poling, chairman, CEO, Ford Motor Company. *Academy of Management Executive* 6, no. 2, pp. 71–82.

Kanter, Rosabeth Moss. 1989. *When giants learn to dance: Mastering the challenge of strategy, management, and careers in the 1990s.* New York: Simon and Schuster.

Kanter, Rosabeth Moss. 1987. Increasing competitiveness without restructuring. *Management Review*, 76 (June), p. 21.

Kiechel, Walter III. 1988. Corporate strategy for the 1990's. *Fortune*, February 29, pp. 34–42.

Koselka, Rita. 1992. Distribution revolution. *Forbes*, May 25, pp. 54–61.

Lewis, Peter. 1991. Software to help introduce products. *New York Times*, October 6, pp. F-8N and F-8L.

Main, Jeremy. 1988. The winning organization. *Fortune*, September 26, pp. 50–60.

Makovsky, Kenneth. 1992. How to make your company a powerhouse in the 21st century. *Business Forum*, Winter, pp. 9–12.

Mason, Richard O. and Ian I. Mitroff. 1981. *Challenging strategic planning assumptions.* New York: Wiley.

McFarlan, F. Warren. 1984. Information technology changes the way you compete. *Harvard Business Review*, May–June, pp. 98–104.

McFarlan, F. Warren. 1981. Portfolio approach to information systems. *Harvard Business Review*, September–October, pp. 142–150.

McFarlan, F. Warren, Richard L. Nolan, and David P. Norton. 1973. *Information systems administration.* New York: Holt, Rinehart and Winston.

McNamee, Patrick B. 1985. *Tools and techniques for strategic management.* New York: Pergamon.

Meeting the challenge of sustainable development. 1992. *Forbes* advertising supplement, May 25.

Mockler, Robert J. 1992. *Developing knowledge-based systems: A managerial decision-making approach.* Columbus, Ohio: Merrill.

Mockler, Robert J. 1991. *Computing software to support strategy formulation decision making.* Columbus, Ohio: Merrill.

Mockler, Robert J. 1989. *Knowledge-based systems for strategic planning.* Englewood Cliffs, N.J.: Prentice-Hall.

Moore, John L. 1990. Transportation: Planning the future. *Governing*, December, pp. 43–55.

Morrison, Ann. 1992. *The new leaders: Guidelines on leadership diversity in America.* San Francisco: Jossey-Bass.

Naisbitt, John and Patricia Aburdene. 1985. *Re-inventory the corporation: Transforming your job and your company for the new information society.* New York: Warner.

New products, new markets, new competition, new thinking. 1989. *The Economist*, March 4, pp. 19–22.

Nolan, Richard L. and C. F. Gibson. 1974. Managing the four stages of EDP growth. *Harvard Business Review*, January–February, pp. 76–88.

Nulty, Peter. 1987. How managers will manage. *Fortune*, February 2, pp. 47–50.

O'Toole, James. 1985. *Vanguard management.* New York: Doubleday.

Ohmae, Kenichi. 1991. The boundaries of business: Commentaries from the experts. *Harvard Business Review*, July–August, pp. 127–140.

Ohmae, Kenichi. 1982. *The mind of the strategist.* New York: McGraw-Hill.

Ostroff, Frank and Douglas Smith. 1992. The horizontal organization. *The McKinsey Quarterly*, no. 1, pp. 148–167.

Parsons, Gregory L. 1983. Information technology: A new competitive weapon. *Sloan Management Review*, Fall, pp. 3–14.

Peters, Tom. 1989. Tomorrow's companies: Thriving on chaos. *The Economist*, March 4, pp. 19–22.

Peters, Tom. 1988. *Thriving on chaos: Handbook for a management revolution.* New York: Knopf.

Peters, Thomas J. and Robert H. Waterman, Jr. 1982. *In search of excellence: Lessons from America's best-run companies.* New York: Harper & Row.

Porat, Marc. 1977. *The information economy.* Washington, D.C.: U.S. Department of Commerce.

Porter, Michael E. 1980. *Competitive strategy.* New York: The Free Press.

Porter, Michael E. and Victor E. Millar. 1985. How information gives you competitive advantages. *Harvard Business Review*, July–August, pp. 149–160.

Rockart, John F. 1979. Chief executives define their own data needs. *Harvard Business Review*, March–April, pp. 81–92.

Rose, Frederick. 1988. An electronic clone of a skilled engineer is very hard to create. *Wall Street Journal*, August 12, pp. 1 and 14.

Rosenthal, Stephen R. 1982. *Managing government operations.* Glenview, Ill.: Scott, Foresman.

Rowe, Alan J. and Paul R. Watkins. 1992. Intelligent use of knowledge and data. *Proceedings*, Symposium on Expert Systems in Finance and Business, Pasadena, California.

Saporito, Bill. 1989. Companies that compete best. *Fortune*, May 22, pp. 36–44.

Sharing the environment. 1992. *The Economist*, May 30, pp. 1–14.

Skrzycki, Cindy. 1989. Corporate America learns to listen to workers. *Los Angeles Times*, August 10.

Stavro, Barry. State's two car plants—Study in sharp contrasts. *Los Angeles Times,* January 28, p. D1.

Stewart, Thomas. 1992. U.S. productivity: First but fading. *Fortune,* October 19, pp. 53–64.

Stewart, Thomas. 1991. GE keeps those ideas coming. *Fortune,* August 12, pp. 41–49.

Storey, Veda C. and Robert C. Goldstein. 1990. An expert view creation system for database design. *USC Expert System Review,* pp. 19–45.

Sustainable development. 1992. *Forbes—Special Supplement,* May 25.

Taylor, Alex, III. 1992. The road ahead at General Motors. *Fortune,* May 4, pp. 94–95.

Thompson, James D. 1967. *Organizations in action.* New York: McGraw-Hill.

Toffler, Alvin. 1990. *Powershift.* New York: Bantam.

Toffler, Alvin. 1985. *The adaptive corporation.* New York: Bantam Books.

Tsurumi, Yoshi. 1991. Adaptive corporations for the global age. *Pacific Basin Quarterly,* Summer–Fall, pp. 5–18.

Turban, Efraim. 1988. *Decision support and expert systems.* New York: Macmillan.

Turban, Efraim and Paul Watkins. 1988. *Applied expert systems.* New York: Elsevier.

Vincent, Barbara and Gerald Zaltman. 1991. *Hearing the voice of the market: Competitive advantage through creative use of market information.* Boston: Harvard Business School Press.

Vogel, Todd. 1989. Where 1990s style management is already hard at work. *Business Week,* October 23, pp. 92–100.

White, John. 1991. Open systems: The puzzle and the payoffs. *Optiv,* I, no. 1, Fall, pp. 6–15.

Willenz, Nicole V. 1988. Electronic data interchange. *Price Waterhouse Review* 32, no. 3, pp. 33–45.

Woutat, Donald. 1992. Two top GM executives demoted. *Los Angeles Times,* April 7, pp. D-1 and D-15.

APPENDIX A

Sustaining Competitive Advantage from IT

John Cecil and Michael Goldstein

It's common to hear about yet another successful installation of IT. Then why is it that most CEOs can't point to one in their companies? The authors argue that it is because managers have focused their attention primarily on the technology of IT and not enough on gaining sustainable advantage from IT. Gaining advantage from IT depends on how you use it to change what you do; technical advances aren't enough.

The most commonly cited examples of companies using information technology (IT) to achieve competitive advantage go back 10 years or more. Both American Airlines' SABRE system and McKesson's Economost system for pharmacies were introduced in the 1970s. But CEOs of most companies are hard put to cite even a single example of having achieved more than a short-lived advantage from their investments in information technology.

CEOs frequently complain that the famous examples don't offer much practical guidance about managing their businesses. Most of the famous examples exploit "first-mover" advantage. This sounds great but often bears no relation to the IT investments being funded. Moreover, whenever one company today does get to the market first, competitors seem to catch up before the investment starts to pay back.

Thus, today, after a decade of "strategic" systems investments, few CEOs invest in IT to achieve sustainable advantage. Most view IT only as a necessity to remain competitive. Is this the best that can be achieved? We don't think it is.

IT Benefits "Old Games"

The notion that IT works only for companies that radically redefine their business is wrong. IT can be extremely valuable to companies pursuing established business or "old-game" strategies.

We'll describe how you can use IT to leverage (or drive) one or more existing sources of sustainable advantage (the "Extend" strategy). We'll also look at how companies that trail on some basis of competition can use IT to reduce their disadvantage (the "Reduce" strategy). Both the Extend and Reduce strategies are available to virtually any company, not just overall industry leaders and followers.

Helps "New Games" Too

Companies that are prepared to pursue a "new-game" strategy have more than one way to achieve sustainable competitive advantage. One way is the "First-Mover" strategy, which was followed by such classic IT implementers as McKesson. However, being first is only the initial stage of the strategy and additional actions are necessary if that advantage is to be sustained. In addition, we'll describe a second valid way to achieve advantage, called "Focused Hustle," which is not so well known as the First-Mover model.

The balance of this article will explore the importance of and impediments to achieving competitive advantage using IT. It will discuss the Extend strategy as a model of IT investment and the First-Mover and the Focused-Hustle models as alternatives.

WHY ACHIEVING SUSTAINABLE ADVANTAGE FROM IT IS SO HARD

Despite the attention to and investments in IT over the past decade, it seems more difficult, not less, to achieve sustainable competitive advantage from IT. A sustainable advantage is a capability of one competitor that cannot be duplicated by another. It is a standard that is difficult to achieve or maintain. As more companies invest in IT capabilities, it becomes even harder for someone to carve out a unique, defensible position.

Indeed, we believe that it is virtually impossible for major IT users (excluding vendors) to gain advantage based on IT technology alone. Two issues demand attention:

1. Information technologies (except for application systems) are almost universally supplied by vendors to user companies, and are freely available to all competitors in an industry.
2. Application systems, while custom developed by large user-companies, rarely confer advantage in themselves.

IT Alone Doesn't Deliver

There are several reasons why IT by itself fails to deliver a sustainable competitive edge:

- *Peer competitors generally start with equivalent application knowledge.* There may be differences after an application has been developed, but it's usually difficult to protect. Competitors can hire away key employees or use the same vendors and system integrators to take advantage of the leader's experience.
- *Differences in IT development capabilities among competitors can usually be evened out by vendors.* For many applications, followers can purchase packages or hire systems integrators and end up with equivalent functionality at lower cost than the leaders.
- *Larger scale rarely translates into a cost advantage.* Larger companies generally have more complex requirements, increasing development costs. They are more likely to need (or think they need) customized systems instead of vendor-supplied packages.

A couple of examples illustrate these points. In the early 1970s Procter & Gamble and General Electric led other major consumer companies in developing integrated marketing decision–support systems. These were mainframe systems that allowed users to track and analyze market share and promotion effectiveness, and perform demand analysis, combining both internal and vendor-supplied market research data. At the time this was a leading-edge technical application, and presented the pioneers with technical challenges they couldn't meet without vendor support. While the vendors helped make the original implementations successful, they soon turned around and sold packaged systems to competitors. For example, by 1975 both Kraft and General Foods had installed equivalent functionality.

Involving vendors in new application development continues today. Indeed, it is often the only way—given the endemic shortage of IT skills and the increasing complexity of integrated IT technologies—that companies can hope to develop new, leading-edge applications. Monsanto, for example, is today developing a state-of-the-art flexible manufacturing system for a major fiber plant. Its development strategy is keyed to working with a limited number of "technology partners," including IBM, DEC, and H-P. Monsanto managers acknowledge that competitors will learn from their experience, but feel that it is better to co-develop the system with vendors than to go it alone.

WHY SUSTAINABLE ADVANTAGE IS IMPORTANT

Does it matter if many businesses take advantage of IT at roughly the same rate?

We think it does. *Without competitive advantage, heavy IT investors tend to lose.* Industries that adopt IT uniformly are likely to suffer eroding profitability because IT destroys conventional forms of differentiation and forces businesses to compete head-on. As a result, competitors can't hold on to the benefits of their own investment. They pass them on as lower prices to customers.

How IT Restructured Merchant Credit-Card Banking

The merchant-servicing side of the bank credit-card business, conducted by more than 10,000 institutions in the United States, consists of processing the sales drafts from Visa and Mastercard transactions, and depositing the collected funds, less a discount, to the merchant's account.

Traditionally, this was a paper-intensive business in which the merchant's local bank held a significant advantage. The issue was convenience: the sales drafts needed to be physically deposited with the processor. Since the merchant already needed to travel to a bank branch to deposit cash, it made sense to deposit the Visa and Mastercard sales drafts at the same time.

In the mid-1980s, the industry made a concerted effort to eliminate the paper sales draft, and to replace it with electronic draft capture (EDC) at the point of sale. As the cost of all computer technology fell rapidly, it became economically feasible for even the smallest merchants to submit electronically.

It also seemed to make a lot of sense for the industry. EDC totally eliminated keying in of the sales draft information, as well as the errors which keyboarding introduced. The terminals ensured that end-of-day balances were correct and matched the sales draft totals. And the electronic transmission eliminated several days of unproductive float. In order to encourage widespread adoption, and to pay back the necessary investment in point-of-sale terminals, Visa and Mastercard both lowered their key "interchange" rate for EDC transactions.

By one measure, the incentives were an enormous success. Between 1987 and mid-1990, the share of electronic draft capture transactions grew from roughly 25 percent to 75 percent. However, for most participants in the industry, the transition has been a profitability disaster.

The problem for the many small banks in the business is that their local branch networks no longer conferred advantage. Merchants could dial up the host computer of an out-of-state bank or a non-bank processor as easily as a local bank's host. In any case, funds could be cleared electronically to the merchant's local bank account, if necessary on the next day. Out-of-state banks and low-cost, nonbank processors cut price in order to capture market share from existing players.

For example, in the mid-1980s, a small retailer might have expected to pay a 3 percent discount rate to his local bank. By 1990, the same retailer might pay only 1.5 percent (although he would probably have to lease his EDC terminal). The promised savings to the industry ended up being passed on to consumers. Overall, the industry now operates at a significant deficit, and many players, large and small, have sold their portfolios and exited the business.

Low Cost and High Quality

Paradoxically, as the EDC example shows, the competitive problem with IT that is often both the lowest-cost and highest-quality way to do something. In many service businesses, for example, consumers would rather interact with a well-designed system than face-to-face. In manufacturing business, flexible automation often provides both low cost and high quality. Once an application is automated, therefore, the ability to differentiate can diminish. If an average customer never experiences an error or defect, the ability of one competitor to lower defect rates even further will no longer increase differentiation.

The bottom line is that businesses employing IT should do so in a way that gives them a sustainable advantage. If they don't, they risk competing away the benefits created.

But is it possible to achieve sustainable advantage from IT, given the use of vendor-supplied technology and the difficulty in keeping experience proprietary? We would argue that it can only happen if the underlying strategy is robust enough to survive duplication by competitors. Specifically, gaining advantage with IT depends on how you use IT to change what you do in your business; attaining technical proficiency in IT isn't good enough.

HOW THE "EXTEND" STRATEGY ENSURES SUSTAINABLE ADVANTAGE

We mentioned earlier that companies can use IT to achieve sustainable advantage while pursuing an established business or "Extend" strategy, the key to which is that it leverages or extends existing forms of sustainable advantage in a business.

Take a consumer packaged goods manufacturer, for example, that holds the largest share in a product segment and, as a result, enjoys scale advantage in purchasing, manufacturing, and logistics over its smaller competitors. In this segment, because of the high cost of transportation relative to price, all major competitors manufacture and compete regionally.

Improves Scale Advantage

An Extend strategy here would be to focus IT investments on applications that improve scale advantages: for example, a centralized purchasing system that minimizes raw materials costs across multiple manufacturing plants, trading off volume discounts and shipping costs.

This application could be duplicated by any competitor, but it doesn't help them much. Regional competitors do not benefit at all (since they purchase for only a single plant), and smaller national competitors benefit little because their smaller scale limits their savings.

What makes the advantage sustainable is not the system itself, but the scale advantage the leader originally held, and the way the business reorganized purchasing to leverage that scale. IT is essential to achieving the advantage, however, because without IT the cost of coordination and the impact of lowered flexibility would have offset the savings it might have achieved.

An Extend strategy, on the other hand, would make us less inclined to invest in, say, an IT-based process improvement that simply lowered cost independent of scale—a capability that is bound to be matched by all competitors. Such investments though are a strategic necessity since we can't afford to fall behind our competitors in process improvements, However, leadership in such IT investments shouldn't be the priority.

Other Advantages Too

Extend strategies don't have to leverage scale; they can leverage any structural advantage enjoyed by a business. Moreover, companies don't need to be industry leaders to take advantage of Extend. Most companies enjoy some advantage over competitors on some factor of competition. Any such advantage is a candidate for Extend. Common structural advantages, in addition to scale, which can be leveraged include:

- *Economies of scope*—enjoyed by sharing costs across two or more distinct product/market segments such as in banking, where leading banks have been developing integrated systems to shift from a product to a customer focus. In the credit-card business, for example, a bank which cross-sells credit cards to its mortgage customers enjoys roughly 50 percent higher profitability than banks selling credit cards to the general market. Here, although the IT-based systems enable cross-selling, the *advantage* is created not by the systems, but by the fact that some competitors do not participate in both markets.
- *Proprietary information*—which can be of any form, but the most common and powerful is usually customer information. American Airlines, for example, identifies its best customers through its frequent flyer program, and offers special benefits to the top 2–3 percent of flyers (who make up over half of American's total seat miles). These benefits—allowing customers to book flights that are "full" to others or offering free upgrades to first class—differentiate American's service to its top customers. Again, other airlines can develop and, to some extent, have developed similar systems. But these work only with their own customer bases, while American's works with the strongest franchise among its frequent business travellers. (Delta won't know who the frequent American flyer is when he takes an occasional Delta flight. Thus, the passenger will experience standard Delta service, which will be inferior to the enhanced American service, preserving American's franchise.)
- *Institutional skills or experience*—which are impossible for competitors to duplicate, can be effectively leveraged by IT. One international consulting firm, for example, has achieved in several industries a broader range of consulting experience, spread across a large number of offices, than its competitors. By capturing non-confidential aspects of this experience in written form, and creating a bibliographic database of this information, the firm is able to leverage this experience even in offices that have not worked first-hand in these industries. Again, the IT application is straightforward, and could be duplicated by any major competitor, but, without the extensive experience base, duplication will be less effective.

REDUCING DISADVANTAGE

A flip-side to the Extend strategy, which we call "Reduce," exploits the leveling tendencies of IT, hitherto presented as a problem.

Here, the objective is to use IT to play competitive catch-up: a competitor that suffers a disadvantage on some basis of competition uses IT to improve its abilities in this area. We would expect the current leader to match the application. Nevertheless, a company that today is at a disadvantage would be better off at parity. Analogous to Extend, Reduce is available to most companies, even industry leaders, which may suffer a disadvantage on some factors of competition.

Compressed Time to Market

A shoe company, for example, that possesses no design skills may compete by producing low-cost knock-offs. However, it realizes low prices because it can't deliver the hottest designs at the peak of a fashion trend. By installing a CAD/CAM system, the company compresses the product development cycle and is able to provide timely deliveries. The design leaders can also install the same system, but it helps them less, because the design-to-manufacture interval is less critical if a company originates a design.

In principle, Reduce can apply to virtually any form of competitive disadvantage suffered by a company.

- *Scale disadvantage.* For example, a small-scale industrial products company may suffer a disadvantage because it cannot keep extensive inventories of spare parts in regional warehouses. However, moving to a centralized spare-parts inventory, and using an overnight delivery service and systems that permit same-day shipment of orders, the small-scale company provides equivalent service as large-scale competitors, at equivalent or lower cost.
- *Skill disadvantage,* which includes competitors that may suffer an institutional skill deficiency as compared with industry leaders. A systems company, for example, that lags in providing on-line technical support can install an expert system to catch-up. The technical support leader can also install a similar system, but its distinctive advantage has already been eroded.

Old Game Versus New Game

Both Extend and Reduce are really "old-game" strategies: they reinforce the existing business strategies of a company. Management doesn't need to redefine the product or business. Basically, Extend and Reduce focus attention on what should be the highest leverageable, sustainable opportunities in their current strategy.

These strengths of Extend and Reduce, which make them widely useful and relatively straightforward to execute, are also, in some sense, the strategies' weakness. They ignore the possibility of a "new game" that might obsolete the "old game" entirely.

The "new game" most often described is what we call a "First-Mover" strategy. We'll also argue that there's a second "generic" new-game strategy as well, which we call "Focused Hustle."

How "First-Mover" Strategies Create Sustainable Advantage

Classic outcomes of "First-Mover" strategies, such as McKesson's Economost or Merrill Lynch's CMA account, work not because these companies achieve sustainably better IT capabilities, but because they are able to convert a temporary IT advantage into sustainable forms of conventional advantage such as scale, customer loyalty, and brand image.

A fully executed First-Mover strategy has three stages, requiring companies to:

1. Develop a vision of how to change the business using IT to deliver improved value to customers or to achieve better operating capability.
2. Be the first to use the enhanced operational capability to achieve one or more "first-mover advantages," including the opportunity to grow rapidly, to penetrate distribution networks, or to build a unique reputation.
3. Exploit these first-mover advantages to achieve other sustainable advantages, such as scale, customer loyalty, and brand franchises, which will survive even after competitors duplicate the systems capabilities.

How IT Revolutionized Drug Distribution

The classic example of how McKesson Drugs revolutionized the drug distribution business illustrates the point. In the mid-1970s drug distribution was under attack from two sides. From the bottom, chains were rapidly displacing independent drugstores and were beginning to supplant the traditional independent distributor with captive distribution. From the top, drug manufacturers were finding it cheaper to sell direct to the central purchasing departments of chains than through distributors. McKesson, the only national drug distributor at the time, faced the dilemma of either fixing the business or selling it.

Three-Step Process

Management's vision (step 1 of our three-step process) focused on electronic order-entry as a way to differentiate the company. McKesson sold portable electronic devices to the drugstores that could connect via modem to its computers. Instead of ordering through a telephone clerk, the druggist could walk through the aisles of his store, key in the stock numbers of items that needed to be reordered, and then automatically send the complete order in to McKesson. The company in turn would process the order overnight and deliver it the next day. The value to the druggist was significant. The new process reduced clerical effort and shipping errors. Overnight delivery made it feasible to cost shelf stock. In addition, McKesson was able to provide useful management reports for controlling inventory and profitability.

McKesson, by launching it nationally in 1975, did, in fact, offer this kind of system before any other drug distributor and achieved several first-mover advantages (step 2 of our three-step process). The primary first-mover advantage was rapid acceleration of sales volumes. Druggists who had previously spread orders among two or three different distributors now concentrated all orders with McKesson. The system also differentiated McKesson with new customers. From 15 percent of orders entered electronically in 1975, it grew to handle 50 percent by 1982, and total volume more than doubled from $0.9 billion to $1.9 billion.

However, by 1982, several competitors had matched the order-entry functionality that McKesson offered. What distinguished McKesson is that it pursued step 3 of our three-part process to leverage its first-mover opportunities into a sustainable advantage as the scale-based cost leader. During the early 1980s McKesson changed from an organization where each warehouse acted as an autonomous business, responsible for order entry, billing, and purchasing as well as fulfillment, to one where all functions, except fulfillment, were centralized to maximize scale economies. The savings were significant: order-entry staff was cut from 700 in 1975 to 15 in 1985 (when electronic orders reached 97 percent); purchasing staff from 140 to 12. Subscale warehouses were replaced by fewer, highly automated distribution centers that captured scale benefits in logistics.

WHY FIRST-MOVER SUCCESS STORIES AREN'T MORE COMMON

As we noted earlier, the First-Mover strategy is potentially powerful, but there are only a handful of documented examples. The key problem is that a First-Mover strategy requires not only a powerful vision of how to use IT in a business, but also the ability to implement it quickly.

These conditions are difficult to meet. Worse, in many ways, they are significantly more difficult today than they were 10 years ago because:

- *There are a lot more companies in the game today and basic IT skills are more widely available.* Today, when a company is experimenting with a promising technology, it's likely that its competitors are, too. That wasn't as true in the 1970s. McKesson piloted its order-entry system for close to five years in one region before rolling it out nationally in 1975. It would be much harder today for an industry leader to experiment with a new technology and expect competitors to take 5 to 7 years to match it.
- *Today's more complex installed base slows the roll-out of new systems.* Gradual implementation may also alert competitors before the first mover can capture any real advantage. McKesson, on the other hand, was able to roll out its new system relatively quickly. It was running only simple batch accounting applications on standalone IBM 360/20s in each warehouse. It could install its new order-entry applications without worrying about how it would interact with other applications, or how to preserve data integrity of a mix of on-line and batch applications, or any of the other concerns that systems developers have today in integrating a new application with the existing portfolio.

Another problem with the First-Mover strategy is that it's a very high-risk strategy. By the time you make sure your applications deliver value you may already have alerted competitors and reduced lead-time as a first mover.

Nevertheless, the rapid evolution of information technology is probably increasing the number of opportunities for attempting a First-Mover strategy, particularly in industries that may not have been able to exploit IT in the past—though, given the risks involved, we think many more opportunities are squandered than realized.

Whenever new IT capabilities allow businesses to deliver fundamentally better value to customers, top management needs to consider whether the opportunities for first-mover advantage might not outweigh the risk. If the changes needed to the business can be feasibly implemented in a relatively short period of time, First Mover may be the strategy of choice.

However, there are many businesses in which IT can have a powerful transforming effect, but where the complexity of the business system and the information architectures that support it don't permit rapid roll-out. For such companies, an alternative model is needed.

HOW A "FOCUSED-HUSTLE" STRATEGY CREATES ADVANTAGE

How can you create fundamentally new advantages based on IT, if you can't keep your information technology investment proprietary, if your business is too complex to permit radical changes all-at-once, and if you can't achieve a significant lead-time advantage over your competitors? We think the answer is, in some sense, a synthesis of the Extend model and the First-Mover model of how to achieve advantage:

- *Figure out the most powerful changes you can make in your business.* Consider not simply business changes, and not simply IT changes, but both together.
- *Focus resources*—initially on achieving a breakthrough level of performance in the most important of the IT and business changes identified.

- *Apply development resources* to extend advantage across the entire business system once the basic breakthrough is achieved.
- *Repeat the whole cycle as quickly as possible.* The key is to have a vision guiding the process that is setting a consistent direction and guiding the choice of what is the most important thing to do next.

Restructuring Machine Tool Building

One company that has successfully executed a Focused-Hustle strategy is Yamazaki Mazak, the world's largest manufacturer of machine tools and flexible manufacturing systems. In the mid-1960s, Yamazaki was a small manufacturer of conventionally controlled lathes. It pursued a low-cost manufacturing strategy, and was more aggressive than most Japanese manufacturers at the time in pursuing export markets. A major opportunity occurred a few years later when Yamazaki was one of the Japanese companies selected by MITI to manufacture computer numerically controlled (CNC) machine tools based on the standard Fanuc controller.

Helped by rapid growth in the low-cost CNC segment of the market, Yamazaki continued to grow and expand its product line throughout the 1970s. However, by the end of the 1970s, despite extensive use of CNCs in its own facilities, Yamazaki faced a real bottleneck to further growth: adding new products was forcing Yamazaki to extend shipping intervals. Machine tools took, on average, 90 days to build.

Cutting Throughput Time

Yamazaki's management developed a vision based on cutting throughput time. The idea was not to cut just physical manufacturing time, but total throughput time from product design to shipment of finished product. The first major breakthrough involved developing a basic flexible manufacturing concept* and implementing it in the most bottlenecked parts of the manufacturing process.

Initial implementation of the concept was modest and focused. Between 1979 and 1981, Yamazaki developed two new production lines at its main factory at Oguchi. The effort required significant skill-building and organization change: production management, the key function in Yamazaki's conventional operations, had to be placed under the control of the central engineering department developing the new technology.

Results were spectacular. The most bottlenecked operations fell from 90 days using conventional production to three days with flexible manufacturing. Other operations that were not automated now became the bottlenecks, so that overall throughput averaged 30 days.

Between 1981 and 1983, Yamazaki extended the design concepts proven at Oguchi to a "greenfield" plant at Minokamo. The new plant had five lines (not two as at Oguchi),

---

*Throughput lengthens as product line complexity increases in conventional manufacturing systems, because of a tradeoff between run-length and set-up time. To keep average costs down, manufacturers need to amortize set-up costs over a long production run. As the product line increases, different set-ups are required. Given the thousands of parts needed to make a machine tool, it becomes impossible to schedule production of all parts without experiencing bottlenecks. Flexible manufacturing attacks this tradeoff by driving the set-up times close to zero. The machinery is also built to perform multiple manufacturing operations at a single station. This simplifies scheduling, eliminates time lost in physical movement of work-in-process, and allows operations to be performed in parallel instead of sequentially.

extending the system to include automatic rotational operations. Tool changes and materials movements were performed by robots and the precision of the machinery was improved to handle operations that were previously performed off-line.

Integrating Design and Manufacturing

The second major breakthrough in developing Yamazaki's flexible manufacturing vision was to integrate its CAD with its CAM system. Yamazaki engineers developed software that could evaluate a design specification and decide whether it could be manufactured with the flexible manufacturing system at Minokamo. Designs that could were accepted; those that couldn't were sent back for redesign; in effect, they were standardizing designs to speed throughput. They weren't standardizing parts—which is how you do it in a conventional manufacturing environment; they were standardizing around flexible manufacturing capabilities.

The skills needed to create the Minokamo breakthrough didn't come without organizational change, however. Whereas the emphasis at Oguchi had been on developing individual machines, at Minokamo it was on the system and on the interactions across machines. Software was as important as hardware, and developers organized into multidisciplinary teams combining engineering, production management, and software designers.

Yamazaki extended the Minokamo breakthroughs both by building a greenfield plant in Worcester, England (exploiting even more advanced concepts) and by installing additional flexible manufacturing lines in its conventional plants around the world. This required still another reorganization: Yamazaki's engineering and technical function, historically centralized at the company's headquarters in Japan, was now distributed to the individual plants.

Today, Yamazaki is the largest machine tool builder in the world, enjoying dominant market share in low-cost lathes and several segments of flexible manufacturing systems. Its advantage lies not in the individual pieces of technology it has developed, but in the scope of its manufacturing concepts and in the skills it has developed over the years. Another machine tool builder could attempt to leapfrog from a conventional manufacturing system to the current Yamazaki system, but the odds of it succeeding are remote, and Yamazaki itself would render it obsolete by the time the competitor was finished.

Importance of Vision

This example offers a number of lessons about how Focused Hustle creates sustainable advantage. Initially, competitors that don't share the strategy implementer's vision won't match it step-for-step. The circumstances that motivated Yamazaki to start the small-scale plant at Oguchi were unique to its competitive positioning. Competitors had different agendas. As Yamazaki changed, its manufacturing system and those of its competitors diverged even further. Ultimately, competitors couldn't copy Yamazaki without adopting an entirely new philosophy and system of production.

At the root of the advantage is a difference in skills; not simply IT skills, but in *all* of the skills necessary to manage a transformed business system. It's no longer simply a problem of copying a set of applications. It's a problem of fundamentally changing the business and developing a new set of skills—from the shop floor to the executive suite—that are needed to be successful in the new business. Few competitors are capable of such extensive transformation.

Long-Term Strategy

The Focused-Hustle strategy is not without risks and problems. It's a long-term strategy requiring leadership and patience. Top management's vision has to be farsighted and meaningfully better than that of the competitors. And finally, it is difficult to execute. People in the business need to accept rapid and significant change, which, by definition, will stretch their capabilities.

FOUR MODELS, NOT ONE, FOR SUSTAINABLE ADVANTAGE FROM IT

The four models offer top management a much broader range of options for using IT than they may have considered.

For the CEO pursuing an established, successful strategy, Extend provides a new tool for focusing his, and his organization's, thinking on how IT can help. Extend can either be used proactively by top management to trigger new IT projects or simply as a tool for project evaluation. Similarly, Reduce provides a way to make up for a weakness in an existing strategy.

Most companies can take advantage of both strategies at any given time, since they both apply to specific sources of competition, not to overall positioning. Industry leaders and followers can both leverage Extend and Reduce against different mixes of advantages and disadvantages.

For other businesses the biggest opportunity comes from trying to establish a "new game." Here the choice between a First-Mover strategy and Focused Hustle increases the range of companies that might attempt them.

For companies where the increased value can be realized quickly, a First-Mover strategy may offer the highest potential reward. However, for companies where full realization of the potential is measured in years and decades, Focused Hustle offers a new model for gaining maximum advantage from IT investments.

NAME INDEX

Subject Index